FIFTH CANADIAN EDITION

HRM

FIFTH CANADIAN EDITION

Sandra L. Steen
University of Regina

Raymond A. Noe
Ohio State University

John R. Hollenbeck
Michigan State University

Barry Gerhart
University of Wisconsin—Madison

Patrick M. Wright
Cornell University

McGraw Hill Education

HUMAN RESOURCE MANAGEMENT
Fifth Canadian Edition

ISBN-13: 978-1-25-965493-0
ISBN-10: 1-25-965493-1

2 3 4 5 6 7 TCP 22 21 20

Printed and bound in Canada.

Director of Product Management: *Rhondda McNabb*
Portfolio Manager: *Amy Clarke-Spencely*
Marketing Manager: *Emily Park*
Content Developer: *Veronica Saroli*
Portfolio Associate: *Stephanie Giles*
Supervising Editor: *Jessica Barnoski*
Production Coordinator: *Sarah Strynatka*
Copy Editor: *Karen Rolfe*
Manufacturing Production Coordinator: *Jason Stubner*
Cover Design: *David Montle*
Digital Interior Design: *Dianne Reynolds*
Print Interior Design: *Michelle Losier*
Cover Image: *Creative-Touch/Digital Vision Vectors*
Composition: *SPi Global*
Printer: *Transcontinental Printing Group*

Dedication

In tribute to the lives of Walter and Alice Yung, and to my husband, Aaron, and our children, Matt and Jess

—S.L.S.

In tribute to the lives of Raymond and Mildred Noe

—R.A.N.

To my parents, Harold and Elizabeth, my wife, Patty, and my children, Jennifer, Marie, Timothy, and Jeffrey

—J.R.H.

To my parents, Robert and Shirley, my wife, Heather, and my children, Chris and Annie

—B.G.

To my parents, Patricia and Paul, my wife, Mary, and my sons, Michael and Matthew

—P.M.W.

About the Authors

Sandra L. Steen teaches in the Paul J. Hill School of Business and the Kenneth Levene Graduate School of Business at the University of Regina. Sandra also facilitates executive education and professional development sessions. Sandra has an integrated education and background in both Human Resource Management and Organizational Behaviour. She received her MBA from the University of Regina and has more than 25 years of leading, managing, teaching, and consulting across a wide range of organizations in the private, public, and not-for-profit sectors. Sandra teaches organizational behaviour and human resource management for undergraduate as well as MBA and MHRM students. Along with serving as lead co-author of *Human Resource Management,* Fifth Canadian Edition, Sandra is also co-author with Steven McShane (University of Western Australia) and Kevin Tasa (York University) of *Canadian Organizational Behaviour,* Tenth Edition (2018). Sandra holds the designation of Chartered Human Resources Professional (CPHR) and she is a member of CPHR Saskatchewan. She is a former Commissioner of the Saskatchewan Public Service Commission, the central human resource agency for the provincial government. Sandra has received recognition for her teaching accomplishments including "Inspiring Teacher Award—Business Administration." In her leisure time, Sandra enjoys spending time at the lake with her husband Aaron, and their children, Matt and Jess.

Raymond A. Noe is the Robert and Anne Hoyt Designated Professor of Management at The Ohio State University. He has taught for more than twenty-five years at Big Ten Universities. Before joining the faculty at Ohio State, he was a professor in the Department of Management at Michigan State University and the Industrial Relations Center of the Carlson School of Management, University of Minnesota. He received his BS in psychology from The Ohio State University and his MA and PhD in psychology from Michigan State University. Professor Noe conducts research and teaches all levels of students—from undergraduates to executives—in human resource management, training and development, performance management, and talent management. He has published articles in the *Academy of Management Annals, Academy of Management Journal, Academy of Management Review, Journal of Applied Psychology, Journal of Vocational Behavior,* and *Personnel Psychology.* Professor Noe is currently on the editorial boards of several journals including *Personnel Psychology, Journal of Applied Psychology, Journal of Management, and Human Resources Management Review.* Professor Noe has received awards for his teaching and research excellence, including the Ernest J. McCormick Award for Distinguished Early Career Contribution from the Society for Industrial and Organizational Psychology. He is also a fellow of the Society of Industrial and Organizational Psychology.

John R. Hollenbeck holds the positions of University Distinguished Professor at Michigan State University and Eli Broad Professor of Management at the Eli Broad Graduate School of Business Administration. Dr. Hollenbeck received his PhD in Management from New York University in 1984. He served as the acting editor at *Organizational Behavior and Human Decision Processes* in 1995, the associate editor of *Decision Sciences* from 1999 to 2004, and the editor of *Personnel Psychology* from 1996 to 2002. He has published over 90 articles and book chapters on the topics of team decision making and work motivation. According to the Institute for Scientific Information, this body of work has been cited over 4,000 times by other researchers. Dr. Hollenbeck has been awarded fellowship status in both the Academy of Management and the American Psychological Association, and was recognized with the Career Achievement Award by the HR Division of the Academy of Management (2011), The Distinguished Service Contributions Award (2014), and the Early Career Award by the Society of Industrial and Organizational Psychology (1992). At Michigan State, Dr. Hollenbeck has won several teaching awards including the Michigan State Distinguished Faculty Award, the Michigan State Teacher-Scholar Award, and the Broad MBA Most Outstanding Faculty Member.

Barry Gerhart is Professor of Management and Human Resources and the Bruce R. Ellig Distinguished Chair in Pay and Organizational Effectiveness, School of Business, University of Wisconsin–Madison. He has also served as department chair or area coordinator at Cornell, Vanderbilt, and Wisconsin. His research interests include compensation, human resource strategy, international human resources, and employee retention. Professor Gerhart received his BS in psychology from Bowling Green State University and his PhD in industrial relations from the University of Wisconsin–Madison. His research has been published in a variety of outlets, including the *Academy of Management Annals, Academy of Management Journal, Annual Review of Psychology, International Journal of Human Resource Management, Journal of Applied Psychology, Management and Organization Review,* and *Personnel Psychology.* He has co-authored two books in the area of compensation. He serves on the editorial boards of journals such as the *Academy of Management Journal, Industrial and Labor Relations Review, International Journal of Human Resource Management, Journal of Applied Psychology, Journal of World Business, Management &*

Organization Review, and *Personnel Psychology.* Professor Gerhart is a past recipient of the Heneman Career Achievement Award, the Scholarly Achievement Award, and (twice) the International Human Resource Management Scholarly Research Award, all from the Human Resources Division, Academy of Management. He is a Fellow of the Academy of Management, the American Psychological Association, and the Society for Industrial and Organizational Psychology.

Patrick M. Wright is Professor of Human Resource Studies and Director of the Center for Advanced Human Resource Studies in the School of Industrial and Labor Relations, Cornell University. He holds a B.A. in Psychology from Wheaton College, and an MBA and Ph.D. in Organizational Behavior/Human Resource Management from Michigan State University. Professor Wright teaches, conducts research, and consults in the area of Strategic Human Resource Management (SHRM), particularly focusing on how firms use people as a source of competitive advantage. He has published over 50 articles in journals such as *Academy of Management Journal, Academy of Management Review, Strategic Management Journal, Organizational Behavior and Human Decision Processes, Journal of Applied Psychology, Personnel Psychology,* and *Journal of Management,* as well as over 20 chapters in books and edited volumes such as *Research in P/HRM* and *Handbook of I/O Psychology.* He currently serves on the editorial boards of *Personnel Psychology, Human Resource Management Journal, Human Resource Management Review, Journal of Management, Human Resource Planning, Management and Organization Review, Journal of Management Studies,* and *Journal of Managerial Issues.* He has co-authored two textbooks, and has co-edited a number of special issues of journals dealing with the future of Strategic HRM as well as Corporate Social Responsibility. He has taught in Executive Development programs, and conducted programs and/or consulted for a number of large public- and private-sector organizations. Dr. Wright served as Chair of the HR Division of the Academy of Management, and on the Board of Directors for SHRM Foundation, World at Work, and Human Resource Planning Society.

Brief Contents

Contents

Preface

Welcome to the Fifth Canadian edition of *Human Resource Management.* This book was created to provide you with a focused introduction to HRM in Canada that is rich in content and relevant in its strategic application. The 11 chapters balance theory and practical application, and present the material in a manner that is intended to be engaging as well as thought provoking.

Whether you are a current or future employee, supervisor, manager, entrepreneur, executive, or HR professional, this Fifth edition is even more focused on supporting your need for foundational Human Resource Management thought leadership and applied insight necessary to perform and thrive in organizations today.

New to this edition are additional resources designed to bring real-world relevance to the study of human resource management. New **Evidence-based HRM** and **HRM Social Case Studies** in each chapter encourage students to explore real-world HR applications in both individual and group settings. Most chapters also provide specific **Indigenous content** intended to open important and elevating conversations. Additionally, this edition was crafted to be necessarily inclusive with respect to the stories told and images shared.

Engaging, Focused, and Applied

Managing human resources is a critical component of any organization's overall mission to provide value to customers, shareholders, employees, and the communities in which it operates. Value includes not only profits but also a positive employee experience, creation of new jobs, protection of the environment, and contributions to community programs. All aspects of human resource management including preparing for, acquiring, developing, and rewarding employees enable organizations to address possibilities and challenges, create value, and provide competitive advantages. In addition, effective human resource management requires being mindful of broader contextual issues including economic conditions, legal issues, globalization, as well as technological and social changes. Effective human resource management practices create value for stakeholders, including employees. For example, in this edition, you will find many features that highlight successful and high-performing organizations throughout Canada that are leading the way in effective people management practices.

An important feature of this book is that it is rich with organizational examples and stories that provide practical applications. Regardless of the focus of your career aspirations, and whether or not you directly manage other employees now or will in the future, effective human resource management has never been more critical to achieving organizational success including individual and team accomplishment and providing a positive employee experience. As described in detail in the guided tour of the book, each chapter contains several features that encourage analysis and evaluation of human resource–related situations and applies the chapter concepts.

The author team believes that the engaging, focused, and applied approach distinguishes this book from others that have similar coverage of HR topics. The book has timely coverage of important HR issues, is easy to read, and provides the content, tools, and resources to illustrate the relevance of HR from the perspective of future and current employees, managers, entrepreneurs, executives, and HR professionals.

Organization of the Fifth Edition

- **Part 1, The Human Resource Environment,** (Chapters 1–2) discusses several aspects of the human resource environment. To be effective, human resource management must begin with an awareness of the trends and opportunities shaping this field, including changes in the workforce, technology, and society as well as the profession of HR itself. Such trends and issues are the topic of Chapter 1. On a more detailed level, human resource management must also ensure that the organization's actions comply with and exceed legal requirements in the effort to meet goals including diversity and inclusion, protecting employees' human rights, privacy, and providing for health and safety at work—the focus of Chapter 2.
- **Part 2, Preparing for and Acquiring Human Resources** (Chapters 3–5) explores the responsibilities involved in preparing for and acquiring human resources. Chapter 3 covers the topics of analyzing work and designing jobs. Chapter 4 explains how to plan for human resource needs and recruit candidates to meet those needs. Chapter 5 discusses the selection of employees and their placement into jobs or teams.
- In **Part 3, Talent Management** (Chapters 6–7), the discussion turns to managing the organization's talent. Chapter 6 addresses various ways organizations stimulate learning by training and developing employees to perform

their jobs, prepare for future jobs, and help establish career paths that take into account work interests, goals, values, and other career considerations. Chapter 7 describes the various requirements associated with managing performance, including establishing performance expectations, coaching, and providing feedback.

- An important element of attracting, retaining, and engaging human resources is rewarding employees for the work performed and accomplishments achieved. **Part 4, Compensating and Rewarding Human Resources** (Chapter 8) addresses several topics related to compensation and rewards. Chapter 8 explores decisions related to the organization's overall pay structure, discusses ways organizations can use pay to recognize individual and group contributions to the organization's performance, considers benefits and services—forms of total compensation other than pay—and looks at how to create a total rewards culture.
- **Part 5, Meeting Other HR Goals** (Chapters 9–11) addresses a number of important HR topics. Chapter 9 discusses human resource management in organizations where employees have or are seeking union representation. Chapter 10 focuses on HR activities in global contexts. And Chapter 11, the last chapter, addresses HR's role in creating and maintaining high-performance organizations.

MARKET LEADING TECHNOLOGY

Mc Graw Hill Education connect®

Learn without Limits

McGraw-Hill Connect® is an award-winning digital teaching and learning platform that gives students the means to better connect with their coursework, with their instructors, and with the important concepts that they will need to know for success now and in the future. With Connect, instructors can take advantage of McGraw-Hill's trusted content to seamlessly deliver assignments, quizzes and tests online. McGraw-Hill Connect is a learning platform that continually adapts to each student, delivering precisely what they need, when they need it, so class time is more engaging and effective. Connect makes teaching and learning personal, easy, and proven.

Connect Key Features

SmartBook®

As the first and only adaptive reading experience, SmartBook is changing the way students read and learn. SmartBook creates a personalized reading experience by highlighting the most important concepts a student needs to learn at that moment in time. As a student engages with SmartBook, the reading experience continuously adapts by highlighting content based on what each student knows and doesn't know. This ensures that they are focused on the content needed to close specific knowledge gaps, while SmartBook simultaneously promotes long-term learning.

Connect Insight®

Connect Insight is Connect's one-of-a-kind visual analytics dashboard—now available for instructors—that provides at-a-glance information regarding student performance, which is immediately actionable. By presenting assignment, assessment, and topical performance results together with a time metric that is easily visible for aggregate or individual results, Connect Insight gives instructors the ability to take a just-in-time approach to teaching and learning, which was never before available. Connect Insight presents data that helps instructors improve class performance in a way that is efficient and effective.

Simple Assignment Management

With Connect, creating assignments is easier than ever, so instructors can spend more time teaching and less time managing.

- Assign SmartBook learning modules.
- Instructors can edit existing questions and create their own questions.
- Draw from a variety of text-specific questions, resources, and test bank material to assign online.
- Streamline lesson planning, student progress reporting, and assignment grading to make classroom management more efficient than ever.

Smart Grading

When it comes to studying, time is precious. Connect helps students learn more efficiently by providing feedback and practice material when they need it, where they need it.

- Automatically score assignments, giving students immediate feedback on their work and comparisons with correct answers.
- Access and review each response; manually change grades or leave comments for students to review.
- Track individual student performance—by question, assignment, or in relation to the class overall—with detailed grade reports.
- Reinforce classroom concepts with practice tests and instant quizzes.
- Integrate grade reports easily with Learning Management Systems including Blackboard, D2L, and Moodle.

Mobile Access

Connect makes it easy for students to read and learn using their smartphones and tablets. With the mobile app, students can study on the go—including reading and listening using the audio functionality—without constant need for Internet access.

Instructor Library

The Connect Instructor Library is a repository for additional resources to improve student engagement in and out of the class. It provides all the critical resources instructors need to build their course.

- Access Instructor resources.
- View assignments and resources created for past sections.
- Post your own resources for students to use.

Instructors' Resources

To ensure maximum consistency with the text material, all of the instructor resources have been prepared by the lead text author, Sandra Steen, making Connect a one-stop shop for quality instructor resources, including:

- **Instructor's Manual:** The Instructor's Manual accurately represents the text's content and supports instructors' needs. Each chapter includes the learning objectives, glossary of key terms, a chapter synopsis, complete lecture outline, and solutions to the end-of-chapter critical thinking questions, cases, and other exercises.
- **Computerized Test Bank:** This flexible and easy-to-use electronic testing program allows instructors to create tests from book-specific items. The Test Bank contains a broad selection of multiple-choice, true/false, and essay questions, and instructors may add their own questions as well. Each question identifies the relevant page reference and difficulty level. Multiple versions of the test can be created and printed.
- **Microsoft PowerPoint® Presentations:** These robust presentations offer high-quality visuals from the text and highlight key concepts from each chapter to bring key HR concepts to life.
- **Videos:** This video package contains exclusive videos from *Canadian HR Reporter.* It is an excellent supplement to lectures and useful for generating in-class discussion. Video summary information and teaching notes have been prepared to accompany the video package and that can be integrated with course planning using the Instructor's Manual.

OPTIONAL SUPPLEMENTS

THE MANAGER'S HOTSEAT VIDEOS

The Manager's HotSeat is a resource that allows students to watch real managers apply their years of experience to confronting certain management and organizational behaviour issues. Students assume the role of the manager as they watch the video and answer multiple-choice questions that pop up during the segment, forcing them to make decisions on the spot. Students learn from the managers' unscripted mistakes and successes, and then create a report critiquing the managers' approach by defending their reasoning. The Manager's HotSeat is ideal for group or classroom discussions.

APPLICATION-BASED ACTIVITIES

The Connect Application-based Activities are highly interactive and automatically graded application- and analysis-based exercises wherein students immerse themselves in a business environment, analyze the situation, and apply their knowledge of management strategies to real-world situations. Students progress from understanding basic concepts to using their own knowledge to analyze complex scenarios and solve problems.

The Connect **Application-based Activities** provide students valuable practise using problem-solving skills to apply their knowledge to realistic real-world situations. Students progress from understanding basic concepts to using their knowledge to analyze complex scenarios and solve problems.

SUPERIOR LEARNING SOLUTIONS AND SUPPORT

The McGraw-Hill Education team is ready to help instructors assess and integrate any of our products, technology, and services into your course for optimal teaching and learning performance. Whether it's helping your students improve their grades, or putting your entire course online, the McGraw-Hill Education team is here to help you do it. Contact your Learning Solutions Consultant today to learn how to maximize all of McGraw-Hill Education's resources.

For more information, please visit us online: www.mheducation.ca/he/solutions

Acknowledgments

The Fifth Canadian edition of *Human Resource Management* represents the efforts of an extraordinary publishing team at McGraw-Hill Ryerson. Amy Clarke-Spencley and Kevin O'Hearn, our group portfolio managers, guided the vision for the book, put the team and resources in place, and navigated all the strategic considerations in concert with Veronica Saroli and Lindsay Macdonald, content developers. We also appreciate the expertise and collaboration with Indu Arora throughout the photo research and permissions process. We would also like to thank Karen Rolfe, copy editor, for her excellent work. Thank you to Dianne Reynolds for composing a compelling and crisp design for the book. Thank you to Emily Park, marketing manager, for all of her great work to keep us current and connected to the higher education and learning community. For this edition, we are also very grateful for the contributions of Jack Whelan and Jessica Barnoski, supervising editors, who guided the production process.

We would also like to extend our sincere appreciation to all of the professors and students who shared their experiences and perspectives. Through focus groups, informal reviews, and conversations, their suggestions, insights, and comments helped us develop and shape this new edition.

Features

Each of these features has been designed to take human resource management into the real world—with either a practical exercise, a visit to a website or publication, a connection to quantitative data, an application of ethical insight, innovation, or even an awkward situation in the workplace.

WHAT DO I NEED TO KNOW?

Assurance of learning:

- Learning objectives open each chapter.
- Learning objectives are referenced in the text where the relevant discussion begins.
- The chapter summary is written around the same learning objectives.
- Quizzes and exercises in Connect are tagged to the learning objectives they cover.

WHAT DO I NEED TO KNOW?

After reading this chapter, you should be able to:

LO1	Define human resource management and explain how HRM contributes to and supports an organization's strategies and performance.
LO2	Summarize competencies, careers, professional accreditation, and ethics in human resource management.
LO3	Explain the role of supervisors and managers in human resource management.
LO4	Describe trends in the composition and expectations of the labour force.
LO5	Discuss how technology is impacting human resource management.

HR OOPS!

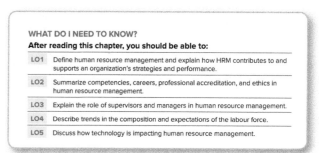

Engages conversations about HR missteps. Discussion questions encourage analysis of the situation. Examples include "Can Job Ads Perpetuate Gender Bias?," "Neglecting Remote Workers," and "Red Flags During Hiring Interviews."

HR Oops!

Neglecting Remote Workers?

Although more people are working remotely, Gallup research identifies three areas where managers fall short in engaging their fully remote workers—not recognizing or praising their good work as frequently; being less likely to have a conversation about career goals and personal growth; and not providing opportunities to connect with co-workers. And, according to a recent survey of 1,153 employees conducted by VitalSmarts, remote workers say that colleagues leave them out and even mistreat them. For example, 84 percent of remote workers report that when they experience routine workplace challenges "the concern dragged on for a few days or more." Remote workers are also more likely to report that "their colleagues don't fight for my priorities, say bad things behind my back, and make changes to a project without warning me," than on-site employees.

Questions

1. What can managers do to build trust and keep remote workers focused and high-performing?
2. What can remote workers do to maintain strong connections to their organizations?

Source: Michael Ferguson, "Stop Neglecting Remote Workers," *Harvard Business Review*, January 17, 2018, https://hbr.org; John Dujay, "Remote workers feeling excluded: Study," *Canadian HR Reporter*, 30 (21), December 11, 2017, p. 3, 10; Joseph Grenny and David Maxfield, "A Study of 1,100 Employees Found That Remote Workers Feel Shunned and Left Out," *Harvard Business Review*, November 2, 2017, https://hbr.org; Annamarie Mann, "3 Ways You Are Failing Your Remote Workers," *Gallup News*, August 1, 2017, http://news.gallup.com, accessed February 1, 2018.

DID YOU KNOW?

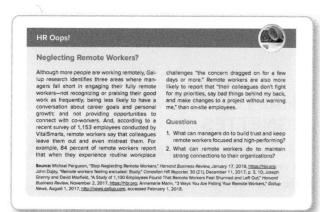

Shares thought-provoking data and stats related to chapter topics. Examples include "Four in Ten Positions are Filled with Insiders," "Mental Illness in the Employed is Increasing in All Age Groups," and Millennials and Gen X Prefer Praise to Corrective Feedback."

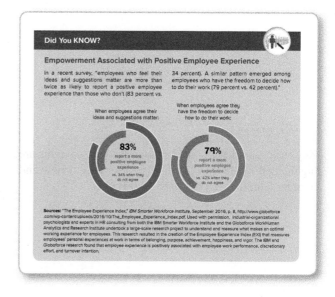

Did You KNOW?

Empowerment Associated with Positive Employee Experience

In a recent survey, "employees who feel their ideas and suggestions matter are more than twice as likely to report a positive employee experience than those who don't (83 percent vs. 34 percent). A similar pattern emerged among employees who have the freedom to decide how to do their work (79 percent vs. 42 percent)."

When employees agree their ideas and suggestions matter:
83%
report a more positive employee experience
vs. 34% when they do not agree
When employees agree they have the freedom to decide how to do their work:
79%
report a more positive employee experience
vs. 42% when they do not agree

Sources: "The Employee Experience Index," *IBM Smarter Workforce Institute*, September 2016, p. 8, http://www.globoforce.com/wp-content/uploads/2016/10/The_Employee_Experience_Index.pdf. Used with permission. Industrial-organizational psychologists and experts in HR consulting from both the IBM Smarter Workforce Institute and the Globoforce WorkHuman Analytics and Research Institute undertook a large-scale research project to understand and measure what makes an optimal working experience for employees. This research resulted in the creation of the Employee Experience Index (EXI) that measures employees' personal experiences at work in terms of belonging, purpose, achievement, happiness, and vigor. The IBM and Globoforce research found that employee experience is positively associated with employee work performance, discretionary effort, and turnover intention.

THINKING ETHICALLY

Focused on ethics. The "Thinking Ethically" feature at the end of each chapter offers intriguing ethical issues that require making and validating decisions about people. Examples include "Should Companies Tell Employees They Have 'High-Potential'?," "Is the Seniority System Fair?," and "Mindsets Shift on Boomerang Employees."

Thinking Ethically

Using Data Analytics Responsibly

"There are certain things that, mathematically, may sound right but, ethically, [do] not," says Arun Chidambaram, global head of talent analytics at Pfizer. In these instances, the talent analytics team defers to legal, HR and other business analysts. "Sometimes data science takes a back step when it comes to sensitive topics such as employment law and data privacy rights."

Pfizer is not the only company advocating for taking a balanced approach to the use of data and analytics. At General Motors, the Talent Analytics team is integrating human capital analytics into organizational decision making and HR practices to drive performance. However, GM is mindful that success is dependent upon the trust that GM employees have about how the data is being used. With a global workforce of 212,000 employees who work in 23 time zones and speak more than 50 languages, integrating data collection technologies to optimize workplace operations is accomplished through a balanced approach.

Chief Talent Officer Michael Arena explains that "at GM, there are no electronic badges, the company does not track email and calendars; it it does not fit employees with odometers, heart monitors, and calorie counters." Data collection is "mostly limited to the tried-and-true," and qualitative approaches are integrated with survey and existing data to use analytics to answer questions. For example, employee engagement is a priority at GM and every 24 months a comprehensive survey is conducted. Kelly Kuras, GM's senior manager of engagement, explains how the data is supplemented with observational insights, conducted by trained HR professionals, to look for patterns in the context of the work environments that would account for high vs. moderate employee engagement results. Insights gained from these observations are used along with the data for action planning. According to Arena, "observations can unmask subtleties that statistics miss." "Second, there is a contract around data collection. Organizations have to manage employees' trust that the data are accurate and used responsibly. . . . We don't take the statistical data as being 100 percent absolute."

Questions

1. Do you think it is appropriate for organizations to monitor employee behaviour with sensors and surveillance that monitor how they work and collaborate? Would you trust an employer that collected this type of information?
2. Why is it important to not rely exclusively on quantitative data when making decisions about people?

Sources: Rachel Ramosa, "Confused by analytics? Take Pfizer's prescription," *HR Tech News*, May 18, 2018, www.hrtechnologynews.com, accessed June 20, 2018, "25 Truths about Talent Management: Insights from The 2018 Talent Management Strategies Conference," *The Conference Board*, (2017), pp. 1-21; Patti P. Phillips, and Rebecca L. Ray, "Human Capital Analytics @ Work Volume 2, *The Conference Board*,. (2017), pp. 1-56.

Carlos Osorio/Toronto Star via Getty Images.

"We're Shopify. Our mission is to make commerce better for everyone—but we're not the workplace for everyone. We thrive on change, operate on trust, and leverage the diverse perspectives of people on our team in everything we do. We solve problems at a rapid pace. In short, we get shit done." In 2004, Shopify consisted of two people working from a coffee shop; today, Shopify has more than 3,000 employees serving 600,000 merchants around the world and has been rated as Canada's Best Place to Work.[1]

CHAPTER-OPENING VIGNETTES

Each chapter opens with a look at events and people in real organizations to encourage reflection and application to the chapter content.

KEY TERMS

Key terms and definitions appear in the text, so terms are highlighted where they are discussed for easy review and in order to introduce the language of HRM.

The structure and responsibilities of HR departments are likely to continue to change in the future to ensure that they remain strategic. Many companies, including Airbnb, are beginning to recognize that providing a positive **employee experience** is critical for keeping employees engaged and committed

employee experience
Set of perceptions that employees have about their experiences at work in response to their interactions with the organization.

HR HOW-TO

Specific steps and methods to implement HRM initiatives. This feature provides the context for understanding typical responsibilities of managers and/or human resources professionals. Examples include "The Process of Developing a Succession Plan," Making Analytics Useful and Relevant," and "HR Services Go Mobile."

HR How-To

Using Wearable Technology to Support Training

As soon as wearable technologies like fitness trackers and smart watches and eyeglasses became available, businesses envisioned ways to use them. More recent developments include electronic sensing badges, which can track employees' interaction patterns in the workplace, and sensor-equipped desks that measure employee keystrokes and mouse-clicks, so it's not surprising that some employers are experimenting with ways to use these technologies to help their employees learn to work more efficiently and safely. Here are some guidelines for using these technologies in support of training goals:

- Keep the focus on how to support business and employee objectives, not on how cool a new device is. For example, employees on the move might benefit from hands-free, instant access to an online guide. At Ericsson, workers' locations are tracked using an app and this information is used to facilitate connections to the closest subject-matter expert "on duty" when needed. Similarly, motion sensors can offer helpful feedback for learning to perform a job that involves physical motions.
- Monitor technology trends, such as augmented reality. With augmented reality delivered by a device such as smart eyeglasses, information is projected in the user's line of sight. Imagine, for example, that trainees learning to service a type of equipment can use augmented-reality displays labelling the parts of the machine they are looking at.
- Respect privacy concerns. Wearables that track an employee's steps, hand motions, or even interactions with others might provide valuable information for improving performance. They also might feel like an intrusion into the learner's privacy. Employers should prepare for these concerns by ensuring that employees know what data is being collected and consent to having their data analyzed. Policies for how the data will be used (for example, looking only at patterns at the departmental level, rather than individuals' actions), how to keep private data from becoming public, and why use of the data could help employees (say, protecting their safety or helping them meet goals by integrating multiple sources of data to gain insight about what high-performing employees do differently from their colleagues)—are also essential.
- Protect the company's data. A company that equips its employees with easily portable technology that gathers data might open itself up to the employee recording meetings or saving other information that might be private. Therefore, employers need measures in place to guard against the information falling into the wrong hands.

Questions

1. Identify two possible risks and two possible advantages of collecting and analyzing employee data collected by wearable technologies.
2. How might data collected by wearable technologies be used to determine employee learning needs?

Sources: Patty Gaul, "Big Data: Using People Analytics to Improve Leadership Development," *TD*, March 2018, pp. 29-33; Alex Moore, "Learning Meets the Internet of Things," *TD*, December 2017, pp. 18-20; Lorri Freifeld, "Wearables at Work," *Training*, September/October 2015, pp. 18–21; Christopher Pappas, "Seven Ways Wearable Technology Could Be Used in Corporate Training," *eLearning Industry*, August 25, 2015, http://elearningindustry.com; Kate Everson, "Learning Is All in the Wrist," *Chief Learning Officer*, April 2015, pp. 18–21; Bill Barlow, "Wear It Well," *Training*, November 14, 2014, https://trainingmag.com.

CHAPTER SUMMARIES

Recap the "What Do I Need to Know?" objectives from the beginning of each chapter with brief summary discussions.

SUMMARY

LO1 Define human resource management and explain how HRM contributes to and supports an organization's strategies and performance.

Human resource management consists of an organization's "people practices"—the policies, practices, and systems that influence employees' behaviours, attitudes, and performance. HRM influences who works for the organization and the experience employees have at work. The organization's human resources have the potential to be a source of sustainable competitive advantage. As part of its strategic role, HR can demonstrate the impact of human resource practices on company results by engaging in evidence-based HRM. Sustainability, organizational agility, and diversity characterize successful organizations. The organizational context is increasingly globalized and rapidly changing, requiring relevant and agile approaches to all HR functions and processes.

LO2 Summarize competencies, careers, professional accreditation, and ethics in human resource management.

Human resources professionals require substantial and varied competencies. Careers in HRM may involve specialized work in fields such as talent acquisition, total rewards, or labour relations—or work as generalists, performing a full range of HR accountabilities. Provincial/territorial associations manage the certification process and award professional designations. Work is underway throughout Canada to move HR from an unregulated to a self-regulated profession. Human resources professionals are required to uphold high ethical standards including duties to the public, profession, clients and employers, and individuals in the workplace.

LO3 Explain the role of supervisors and managers in human resource management.

Supervisors and managers must be familiar with their own important role in managing human resources and implementing HR processes. Supervisors and managers are likely to analyze work, interview job candidates, participate in selection decisions, provide training, set goals, provide coaching and feedback, provide performance feedback, and recommend pay increases. On a day-to-day basis, supervisors and managers represent the company to their employees, so they also play an important role in employee and labour relations.

EXPERIENCING HR

These experiential exercises encourage students to explore real-world HR topics individually or in teams.

EXPERIENCING HR—HOW TO ASSESS ROI OF A WELLNESS PROGRAM

Form groups of four or five. (Alternatively, your instructor may ask students to complete the research independently and discuss their findings in class.) You have been asked by your manager to be part of a workplace task force that will examine how to assess the return on investment (ROI) of a corporate wellness program.

Conduct research using recent academic (e.g., *ACSM's Health & Fitness Journal*) *and* HR practitioner publications (e.g., *Benefits Canada*) *and* credible websites (e.g., the website for the Canadian Centre for Occupational Health and Safety. Discuss your findings about how to determine the ROI of a corporate wellness program. Write a one-page report or make a brief class presentation summarizing your findings.

CRITICAL THINKING QUESTIONS

Serve to open conversations and dialogue about chapter concepts.

CRITICAL THINKING QUESTIONS

1. Why do employees join unions? Have you ever belonged to a union? If you did, do you think union membership benefited you? If you did not, do you think a union would have benefited you? Why or why not?
2. Why do managers at most companies prefer that unions not represent their employees? Can unions provide benefits to an employer? Explain.
3. Can highly effective human resource management practices make unions unnecessary? Explain.

CASES (NEW)

Evidence-based HRM and HRM Social Case Studies have been introduced in each chapter to apply the concepts by looking at organizations and how their practices illustrate chapter content. The Cases provide external examples to bring into the classroom, along with questions for assignment or discussion.

CASE STUDY: EVIDENCE-BASED HRM

Sodexo Examines the Impact of Gender-balanced Leadership on Performance

Rohini Anand, global chief diversity officer at Sodexo, a global food services and facilities management company, collected, analyzed, and shared data showing the value of gender diversity. She conducted a study of the company's 50,000 managers in 80 countries from executive to site management levels to quantify the impact of gender balance in management.

Anand's findings revealed that gender balance in management significantly related to improved financial performance, employee engagement, and client retention. She found that teams with a management male–female ratio of between 40 and 60 percent delivered the consistently best results on both financial and non-financial performance indicators. Specific results of Sodexo's internal study found that gender-balanced management entities had:

- better employee engagement: +4 points
- higher gross profits: +23 percent
- stronger brand image: +5 points

Anand's study also determined that globally, 56 percent of Sodexo's employees currently work in a team with gender-balanced leadership. In Canada, Sodexo reports that 87 percent of its management teams are gender-balanced.

One of the action items moving forward, is the creation of gender-balance targets for leaders. For example, Sodexo's global CEO, Michel Landel, has set a goal that by 2025 at least 40 percent of Sodexo's 1,400 global senior leaders will be women (a total of 560 women leaders). To ensure that goal is reached, 10 percent of senior leaders' bonuses are based on their yearly progress toward that goal.

Sodexo Canada recently announced the appointment of its first female President—Suzanne Bergeron. Bergeron had been the vice-president of human resources and is based in Montreal. Sodexo Canada has more than 10,000 employees and has been recognized for five consecutive years as one of Canada's Best Diversity Employers.

Questions

1. What is your reaction to Sodexo's goal that by 2025 at least 40 of senior global leaders will be women? What could go wrong? What must go right?
2. Why do you think Sodexo teams with gender-balanced leadership have achieve higher levels of performance than teams that do not have gender-balanced leadership?

Sources: Based on J. Simons, "Workplace Diversity Efforts Get a Reboot," *Wall Street Journal*, February 15, 2017, p. B5; Sodexo Canada website, "Sodexo Canada announces the appointment of Suzanne Bergeron as new Country President," May 28, 2018, www.sodexo.com, accessed July 10, 2018, "Sodexo named Top Diversity Employer Five Years Running," *CNW Newswire*, March 2, 2018, www.newswire ca, accessed July 10, 2018; "Case Study: Sodexo Analyzes the Impact of Gender Balance on Performance," *Gender Balance Business News*, https://ca.sodexo.com/files/live/sites/sdxcom-global/files/020_Global_Content_Master/Building_Blocks/GLOBAL/Multimedia/PDF/Diversity_and_Inclusion/SODEXO_GBBN2015_GB_WEB.pdf, accessed July 10, 2018.

CASE STUDY: HRM SOCIAL

Apps Make Giving and Receiving Feedback Quick and Easy

IBM's Checkpoint performance management app allows employees to set short-term performance goals and managers to provide feedback on their progress. Employees and managers at Mozilla can use an app to send each other colourful "badges" to recognize good performance. The badges include slogans such as "you rock" or "kicking butt." Also, employees can receive feedback and coaching from peers and managers by posting short questions about their performance, such as "What did you think about my speech?"

The availability of apps used to ask for and give feedback may not always be positive. Amazon's Anytime Feedback Tool can be used secretly by office workers to praise or critique their colleagues. The peer evaluations can be submitted to members of the management team at any time, using the company's internal directory. Many workers used the app in a dysfunctional way. They described making agreements with colleagues to comment negatively on the same co-worker or to heap high praise on each other. Some employees felt sabotaged by the negative comments from unidentified colleagues. In some cases, the negative comments were copied directly into employees' performance reviews (known as "the full paste.").

Questions

1. Does the use of apps for feedback help or hinder performance management? Explain.
2. Can a performance management app replace the need for a regularly scheduled performance evaluation? Why or why not?

Sources: Based on H. Clancy, "How Am I Doing?" *Fortune*, March 1, 2017, p. 34; D. MacMillan, "Uber to Monitor Actions by Drivers in Safety Push," *Wall Street Journal*, June 30, 2016; M. Weinstein, "Annual Review under Review," *Training*, July/August 2016, pp. 22–29; C. Zillman, "IBM Is Blowing Up Its Annual Performance Review," *Fortune*, February 1, 2016; B. Hassell, "IBM's New Checkpoint Reflects Employee Preferences," *Workforce*, April 2016, p. 12; J. Kantor and D. Streitfeld, "Inside Amazon: Wrestling Big Ideas in a Bruising Workplace," *New York Times*, August 16, 2015, p. A1; E. Goldberg, "Performance Management Gets Social," *HR* Magazine, August 2014, pp. 35–38.

PART 1

The Human *Resource Environment*

CHAPTER 1

Strategies, Trends, and Opportunities for Human Resource Management

CHAPTER 2

The Legal Context for HRM and Creating Safe and Healthy Workplaces

Blend Images/Getty Images

CHAPTER 1

Strategies, Trends, and Opportunities for Human Resource Management

WHAT DO I NEED TO KNOW?

After reading this chapter, you should be able to:

LO1	Define human resource management and explain how HRM contributes to and supports an organization's strategies and performance.
LO2	Summarize competencies, careers, professional accreditation, and ethics in human resource management.
LO3	Explain the role of supervisors and managers in human resource management.
LO4	Describe trends in the composition and expectations of the labour force.
LO5	Discuss how technology is impacting human resource management.

Carlos Osorio/Toronto Star via Getty Images.

"We're Shopify. Our mission is to make commerce better for everyone—but we're not the workplace for everyone. We thrive on change, operate on trust, and leverage the diverse perspectives of people on our team in everything we do. We solve problems at a rapid pace. In short, we get shit done." In 2004, Shopify consisted of two people working from a coffee shop; today, Shopify has more than 3,000 employees serving 600,000 merchants around the world and has been rated as Canada's Best Place to Work.[1]

Earning a Reputation as a Great Employer

What do Shopify, Simon Fraser University, Aboriginal Peoples Television Network Inc. (APTN), PCL Construction, Government of Yukon, Labatt Breweries of Canada, and Google have in common? They have all been recently recognized as excellent employers with progressive human resource management practices.[2]

The list of employment awards is growing, raising the bar on what it takes to attract, retain, and engage top talent. As labour markets become increasingly competitive, human resources professionals are being called upon to provide people management practices that not only support the organization's priorities but also provide for competitive success in a global marketplace. Organizations strive to create an employment brand that attracts top talent and earns a reputation as a great place to work.

Headquartered in Ottawa, e-commerce software solutions and web builder Shopify has been rated as the best place to work in Canada by Glassdoor and was recently ranked third of global tech employers by Hired.com—just behind SpaceX and Google, but ahead of Tesla, Netflix, and Facebook. Setting Shopify apart, according to Hired.com, were company culture, opportunities to learn new skills, and compensation and benefits. Anna Lambert, Shopify's director of talent acquisition, describes Shopify's focus on culture: "We're purposeful and intentional in everything we do, from the physical spaces we design, to our focus on continuous learning and development, to our 'default to open' approach to information sharing. The 'trust battery' is central to our culture." Trust battery is a metaphor critical to understanding the high-performance culture and employee experience at Shopify. CEO Tobi Lütke explains, "It's charged at 50 percent when people are first hired. And then every time you work with someone at the company, the trust battery between the two of you is either charged or discharged, based on things like whether you deliver on what you promise." "We trust our people and we give them the space to make their own decisions, champion their own work, and challenge the status quo. We're building an environment where employees can do their life's work," Lambert adds.[3]

LO1 Introduction

Organizations of all sizes and in all industries are increasingly recognizing the importance of people. "This is a time of rapid change in the market—a time when Canadian organizations are constantly trying to keep pace and remain competitive. In today's knowledge-based economy, we rely on people to generate, develop, and implement ideas"[4] and the "human resource function has an important role in ensuring that organizations have the people capacity to execute strategic objectives."[5]

Human resource management (HRM) centres on the practices, policies, and systems that influence employees' behaviours, attitudes, and performance. Many companies refer to HRM as "people practices." Figure 1.1 emphasizes there are several important HRM practices that should support the organization's business strategy: analyzing work and designing jobs, determining how many employees with specific knowledge and skills are needed (workforce planning), attracting potential employees (recruiting), choosing employees (selection), preparing employees to perform their jobs now and for the future (training, learning, and development), supporting performance (performance management), compensating and rewarding employees (total rewards), and creating a positive work environment (employee and labour relations). An organization performs best when all of these

human resource management (HRM) The practices, policies, and systems that influence employees' behaviours, attitudes, and performance.

FIGURE 1.1

Human Resource Management Practices

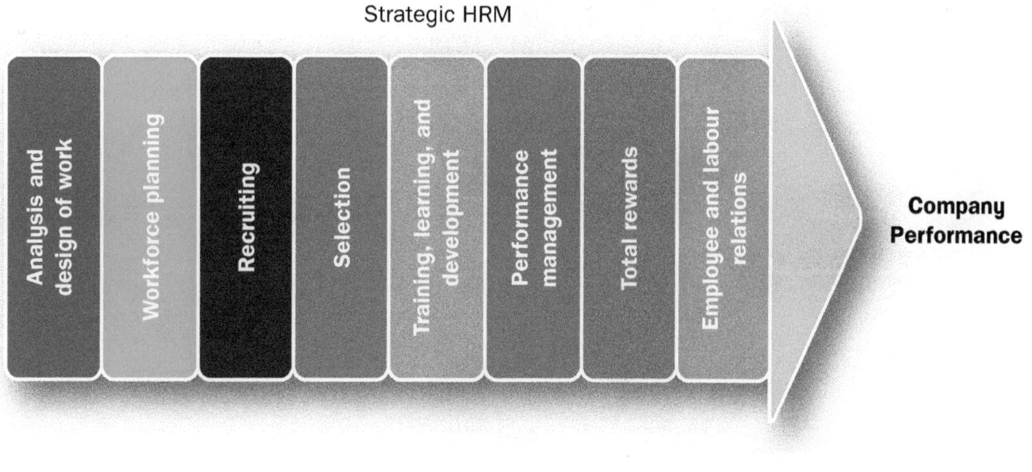

practices are managed well. At companies with effective HRM, employees and customers tend to be more satisfied, and the companies tend to be more innovative, have greater productivity, and develop a more favourable reputation in the community.[6]

In this chapter, we introduce the scope of human resource management, including the ways HRM facilitates and supports organizational strategy. We begin by discussing why human resource management is an essential element of an organization's success. We then turn to the elements of managing human resources and the roles and capabilities needed for effective human resource management. Next, the chapter describes how all supervisors and managers, not just human resources professionals, participate in the functions and processes of human resource management. We then provide an overview of careers in human resource management and the highlights of practices covered in the remainder of the book. The chapter concludes by discussing a variety of trends and developments that impact organizations and HRM.

Human Resources and Organizational Performance

Managers and economists traditionally have seen human resource management as a necessary expense, rather than as a source of value to their organizations. Economic value is usually associated with *capital*—cash, equipment, technology, and facilities. However, "in the changing corporate environment, more and more organizations are awakening to the importance of human capital as the next competitive advantage."[7] A barrier to business expansion is not only availability of financial capital but also access to talent—that is, human capital. In summary, people are crucial to organizational success and the human and intellectual capital of an organization's workforce provides an opportunity for substantial competitive advantage. "As the 'resident people experts,' HR leaders are ideally suited to advise their organization on the best means for realizing their objectives."[8] Decisions such as whom to hire, what to pay, what training to offer, and how to evaluate employee performance directly affect employees' motivation, engagement, and ability to provide goods and services that customers value. Companies that attempt to increase their competitiveness by investing in technology and promoting quality throughout the organization also invest in state-of-the-art staffing, training, and compensation practices.[9] These types of practices indicate that employees are viewed as valuable investments.[10]

The concept of "human resource management" implies that employees are *resources* of the employer. As a type of resource, **human capital** means the organization's employees, described in terms of their training, experience, judgment, intelligence, relationships, and insight—the employee characteristics that can add economic value to the organization. In other words, whether it assembles vehicles or forecasts the weather, for an organization to succeed at what it does, it needs employees with certain qualities, such as particular kinds of skills and experience. This view means employees in today's organizations are not interchangeable, easily replaced parts of a system, but the source of the company's success or failure. By influencing *who* works for the organization and *how* people work, human resource management contributes to fundamental measures of an organization's success such as quality, profitability, and customer experience. Figure 1.2 shows this relationship.

human capital
An organization's employees, described in terms of their training, experience, judgment, intelligence, relationships, and insight.

FIGURE 1.2

Impact of Human Resource Management

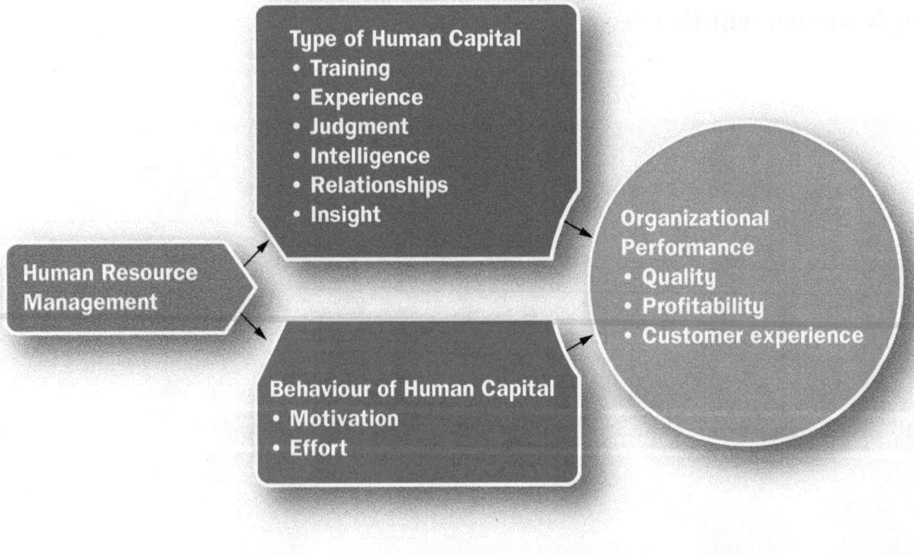

Did You Know?

Engaged and Enabled Employees Deliver Organizational Results

Comparing companies where employees are highly engaged (commitment and discretionary effort) and highly enabled (optimized roles and supportive environment) with low-engagement, low-enablement companies, the HayGroup found significant performance differences.

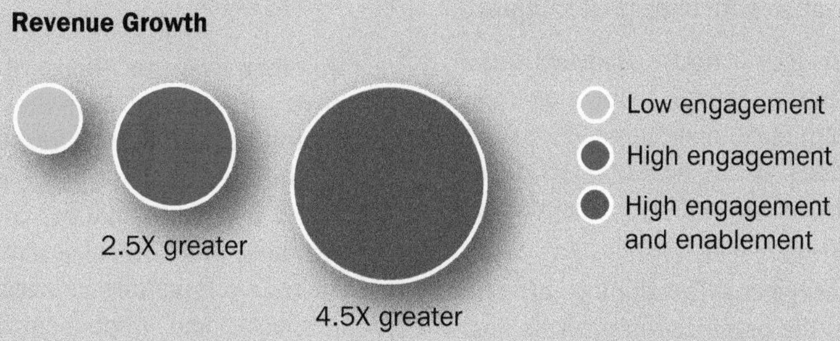

Source: HayGroup (www.haygroup.com), "Are You Missing Something? Engaging and Enabling Employees for Success," www.haygroup.com/downloads/ca/hay_group_employee_engagement_are_you_missing_something.pdf, retrieved January 5, 2015.

Human resource management is critical to the success of organizations, because human capital has certain qualities that make it valuable. In terms of business strategy, an organization can succeed if it has a *sustainable competitive advantage* (is better than competitors at something, and can hold that advantage over a sustained period of time). Therefore, we can conclude that organizations need the kind of resources that will give them such an advantage. Human resources have these necessary qualities:

- Human resources are *valuable.* High-quality employees provide a needed service as they perform many critical functions.
- Human resources are *rare* in the sense that a person with high levels of the needed skills and knowledge is not common. An organization might spend months looking for a talented and experienced manager or technician.
- Human resources *cannot be imitated.* To imitate human resources at a high-performing competitor, you would have to figure out which employees are providing the advantage and how. Then you would have to recruit people who can do precisely the same thing and set up the systems that enable those people to imitate your competitor.
- Human resources have *no good substitutes.* When people are well trained and highly motivated, they learn, develop their abilities, and care about customers. It is difficult to imagine another resource that can match committed and talented employees.

These qualities imply that human resources have enormous potential. As demonstrated in the Did You Know? box, an organization realizes this potential through the ways it practises human resource management.

To benefit from the full capacity and potential of an organization's human resources, an organization should support a culture and management style that focuses on enhancing employee engagement. **Employee engagement** refers to the degree to which employees are fully involved in their work and the strength of their commitment to their job and the organization.[11] How do we know if an employee is engaged? Engaged employees are passionate about their work, are committed to the company and its mission, and work hard to contribute. Employees' engagement is influenced by *how* managers treat employees as well as HR practices. Aon's 2018 Trends in Global Employee Engagement report reveals that, in Canada, engagement is 69 percent for all employees, which is 5 percent higher than the United States (64 percent), but significantly trails Latin America (75 percent). Globally, 27 percent of employees are highly engaged, 38 percent are moderately engaged, 21 percent are passive, and 14 percent are actively disengaged. Additional perspectives about employee engagement and its employee experience drivers will be explored in this chapter and in Chapter 11.[12]

employee engagement
Degree to which employees are fully involved in their work and the strength of their commitment to their job and the organization

What Are the Responsibilities of HR Departments?

In all but the smallest organizations, a human resource department is responsible for the functions of human resource management. On average, an organization has approximately one full-time HR position for every 100 employees on the payroll.[13] One way to define the responsibilities of HR departments is to think of HR as a business within the organization with three product lines:[14]

1. **Administrative services and transactions**—Handling administrative tasks (for example, processing tuition reimbursement applications and responding to questions about benefits) efficiently and with a commitment to quality. This requires expertise in the particular tasks.
2. **Business partner services**—Developing effective HR systems that help the organization meet its goals for attracting, keeping, and developing people with the skills it needs. For the systems to be effective, HR professionals must understand the business so they can understand what the business needs.
3. **Strategic partner**—Contributing to the company's strategy through an understanding of its existing and needed human resources and ways HR practices can give the company a competitive advantage. For strategic ideas to be effective, HR professionals must understand the business, its industry, and its competitors.

Another way to think of HR responsibilities is in terms of specific activities. Table 1.1 details the responsibilities of human resource departments. These responsibilities include the practices introduced in Figure 1.1 plus additional two areas of accountability that support those practices: (1) establishing and administering human resource policies, ensuring compliance with legal requirements, and implementing and maintaining HR technology, and (2) support for strategy.

TABLE 1.1

Responsibilities of HR Departments

Function	Responsibilities
Analysis and design of work	Workflow analysis; job analysis; job design; job descriptions; job specifications
Workforce planning	Labour demand and supply forecasts; labour surplus and shortage projections; succession planning
Recruitment and selection	Recruiting; testing; screening; interviewing; background checking
Training, learning, and development	Needs assessment; learning methodologies; program design, delivery, and evaluation; career management systems; onboarding
Performance management	Organizational framework and criteria; goal setting, appraisal, feedback, and performance improvement tools and processes
Total rewards	Compensation plans; incentive programs; employee benefits and services; retirement plans; payroll
Employee and labour relations	Satisfaction and engagement surveys; communications; employee handbooks; labour relations
HR policies	Policy development and implementation
Employee data and information systems	HR information systems, people (human capital) analytics, record keeping
Compliance with laws	Policies and practices to ensure appropriate behaviour; reporting
Strategy	Advisor to senior management/board; change management

Sources: Bureau of Labor Statistics, "Human Resources Managers," Occupational Outlook Handbook 2016–2017, March 9, 2016, http://www.bls.gov/ooh; Canadian Council of Human Resources Associations National Standards for Human Resources Professionals, www.cchra-caarh.ca/en/phaselreport/, retrieved March 22, 2004; SHRM-BNA Survey No. 66, "Policy and Practice Forum: Human Resource Activities, Budgets, and Staffs, 2000-2001," Bulletin to Management, Bureau of National Affairs Policy and Practice Series (Washington, DC: Bureau of National Affairs, June 28, 2001).

Although the human resource department has responsibility for these areas, many of the requirements are performed by supervisors or others inside or outside the organization. No two human resource departments have precisely the same roles, because of differences in organization size and characteristics of the workforce, the industry, and management's values. In some organizations, the HR department handles all the activities listed in Table 1.1. In others, it may share the roles and duties with managers and supervisors of other departments such as finance, operations, or information technology. In some companies, the HR department actively advises top management. In others, the department responds to top-level management decisions and implements staffing, training, and rewards activities in light of company strategy and policies. And, in a recent trend, some companies are doing away with their HR departments altogether, preferring to flatten their organizational structure and to encourage departmental managers and other employees to handle HR issues as they arise.[15]

The structure and responsibilities of HR departments are likely to continue to change in the future to ensure that they remain strategic. Many companies, including Airbnb, are beginning to recognize that providing a positive **employee experience** is critical for keeping employees engaged and committed to the company. Employee experience refers to the "set of perceptions that employees have about their experiences at work in response to their interactions with the organization."[16] This encompasses all of the elements that influence an employee's perception of the work environment and becomes an important focus for the employee's entire "journey"—from the person's very first contact with a potential employer through retirement and even beyond. Organizational culture is a vital part of the employee experience that is evidenced through HR functions and how they are carried out.[17]

employee experience
Set of perceptions that employees have about their experiences at work in response to their interactions with the organization.

To enhance the employee experience, Airbnb combined three separate HR groups (Talent, Recruiting, and Ground Control) into one group. Airbnb's top HR officer's title is chief employee experience officer (CEEO). At Airbnb, HR involves marketing, communications, real estate, and social responsibility, in addition to traditional functions. The CEEO's responsibilities go beyond more traditional HR functions such as talent management and compensation to include workplace design and facilities, global citizenship, and the network of community managers who interact daily with Airbnb employees. For example, Airbnb's airy, open workplace includes small lockers for employees to charge their devices, which provides more room for a conference room, couches, nap spaces, communal tables, and small spaces for employees to have conversations with their peers. Numerous cafés are available where employees can eat or collaborate on projects. HR also encourages employees to give back to the communities where Airbnb operates by encouraging four hours a month of individual volunteering as well as by participating in larger events such as painting an outreach centre or cooking meals for hospital patients' families.[18]

Let's take an overview of the HR functions and some of the options available for carrying them out. Human resource management involves both the selection of which options to use and the activities related to implementation. Later chapters will explore each function in greater detail.

Analyzing and Designing Jobs

To produce their given product or service (or set of products or services), companies require that a number of tasks be performed. The tasks are grouped in various combinations to form jobs. Ideally, the tasks should be grouped in ways that help the organization to operate efficiently and to obtain people with the right qualifications to do the jobs well. This function involves the activities of job analysis and job design. **Job analysis** is the process of getting detailed information about jobs. **Job design** is the process of defining the way work will be performed and the tasks that a given job requires.

job analysis
The process of getting detailed information about jobs.

job design
The process of defining the way work will be performed and the tasks that a given job requires.

Workforce Planning

Workforce planning, identifying the numbers and types of employees the organization will require in order to meet its objectives, is an "important tool for Canadian organizations seeking to stay competitive in an environment dominated by rapid and unprecedented change."[19] The human resource department helps the organization forecast its needs for hiring, training, and reassigning employees. Workforce planning also may show that the organization will need fewer employees to meet anticipated needs. In that situation, workforce planning includes how to handle or avoid layoffs. At the most basic level, workforce planning takes an immediate ad hoc focus of "hiring as needed"; however, a strategic approach includes developing alternative plans for multiple business scenarios.[20]

workforce planning
Identifying the numbers and types of employees the organization will require to meet its objectives.

Recruiting and Hiring Employees

Recruitment is the process through which the organization seeks applicants for potential employment. **Selection** refers to the process by which the organization attempts to identify applicants with the necessary knowledge, skills, abilities, and other characteristics that will help the organization achieve its goals. An organization makes selection decisions in order to add employees to its workforce, as well as to transfer existing employees to new positions.

recruitment
The process through which the organization seeks applicants for potential employment.

selection
The process by which the organization attempts to identify applicants with the necessary knowledge, skills, abilities, and other characteristics that will help the organization achieve its goals.

Approaches to recruiting and selection involve a variety of alternatives. Some organizations may actively recruit from many external sources using job postings on their corporate websites, social media, and campus recruiting events. Other organizations may rely heavily on internal job postings, counting on the availability of current employees with the necessary skills.

At some organizations, the selection process may focus on specific skills, such as experience with a particular technology or type of equipment. At others, selection may focus on general abilities, such as the ability to work as part of a team or find creative solutions. The focus an organization favours will affect many choices, from the way the organization assesses skills, to the questions it asks in interviews, to the sources it uses to attract candidates. Table 1.2 lists the top five skills/qualities that employers say they are looking for in job candidates.

TABLE 1.2

Top Skills/Qualities Employers Look for in Employees

1. Verbal communication skills
2. Teamwork skills
3. Decision making, problem solving
4. Planning, prioritizing tasks
5. Gathering/processing information

Source: Based on National Association of Colleges and Employers, "Employers Say Verbal Communication Most Important Candidate Skill," news release, March 1, 2016, http://www.naceweb.org.

Training, Learning, and Development

Although organizations base hiring decisions on candidates' existing qualifications, most organizations provide ways for their employees to engage in learning to reinforce, broaden, or deepen their knowledge, skills, and abilities. To do this, organizations provide for employee training, learning, and development. **Training** is a planned effort to enable employees to learn job-related knowledge, skills, and behaviours. For example, many organizations offer safety training to teach employees safe work habits. **Development** involves acquiring knowledge, skills, and behaviour that improve employees' ability to meet the challenges of a variety of new or existing jobs, including preparing employees to work in diverse work teams. Development programs often focus on preparing employees for leadership responsibilities.

training
A planned effort to enable employees to learn job-related knowledge, skills, and behaviours.

development
The acquisition of knowledge, skills, and behaviours that improve an employee's ability to meet the challenges of a variety of new or existing jobs.

Performance Management

Managing human resources includes assessing how well employees are performing relative to objectives such as job descriptions and goals for a particular position. The process of ensuring that employees' activities and outputs match the organization's goals is called **performance management**. The activities of performance management include specifying the tasks and outcomes of a job that contribute to the organization's success; providing timely feedback and coaching; and comparing the employee's actual performance and behaviours over some time period with the desired performance and behaviours. Often, rewards—the topic of the next section—are developed to encourage good performance.

performance management
The process of ensuring that employees' activities and outputs match the organization's goals.

Total Rewards

The pay and benefits that employees earn play an important role in motivation. This is especially true when rewards such as bonuses are linked to the individual's or team's performance. Decisions about pay and benefits can also support other aspects of an organization's strategy. For example, a company that wants to provide an exceptional level of service or be exceptionally innovative might pay significantly more than competitors in order to attract and keep the best employees. At other companies, a low-cost strategy requires knowledge of industry norms, so that the company does not spend more than market rates of pay for similar positions. Planning pay and benefits involves many decisions, often complex and based on knowledge of a multitude of legal requirements. An important decision is how much to offer in salary or wages, as opposed to bonuses, commissions, and other performance-related pay. Other decisions involve which benefits to offer, from retirement plans to various kinds of insurance to other more intangible rewards such as opportunities for learning and personal growth. All such decisions have implications for the organization's bottom line, as well as for employee motivation.

Administering pay and benefits is another big responsibility. Organizations need systems for keeping track of each employee's earnings and benefits. Employees need information about their health plans, retirement plan, and other benefits. Keeping track of this involves extensive record keeping and reporting to management, employees, and others, while ensuring compliance with all applicable legislation.

Maintaining Positive Employee and Labour Relations

Organizations often depend on human resources professionals to help them identify and perform many of the responsibilities related to providing satisfying and engaging work environments and maintaining positive relations with employees. This function often includes providing for communications to employees including maintaining a website on the organization's intranet. The human resource department can also expect to handle certain kinds of communications from individual employees. Employees turn to the HR department for answers to questions about benefits and company policy. If employees feel they have been treated unfairly, see safety hazards, or have other issues and are dissatisfied with their supervisor's response, they may turn to the HR department for help. Members of the department should be prepared to address such issues.

In organizations where employees belong to a union, labour relations entails additional responsibilities. The organization periodically conducts collective bargaining to negotiate an employment contract with union members. The HR department also maintains communication with union representatives to ensure that issues are resolved as they arise.

Establishing and Administering Human Resource Policies

All the human resource activities described so far require fair and consistent decisions, and most require substantial record keeping. Organizations depend on their HR department to help establish policies related to hiring, discipline, promotions, benefits, and the other activities of human resource management. For example, with a policy in place about acceptable use of company-provided vehicles, the company can handle inappropriate vehicle use more fairly and consistently than if it addressed such incidents on a case-by-case basis. The company depends on its HR professionals to help develop and then communicate the policy to every employee, so that everyone knows its importance. Developing fair and effective policies requires strong decision-making skills, the ability to think ethically, and a broad understanding of business activities that will be covered by the policies. Therefore, human resource management requires the ability to communicate through a variety of channels; for example, presentations and social media.

Managing and Using Human Resource Data

All aspects of human resource management require careful and discreet record keeping, from screening job applications, to performance appraisals, benefits enrolment, and government-mandated reports. Handling records about employees requires accuracy as well as sensitivity to employee privacy. Whether the organization keeps records in file cabinets or on a sophisticated information system, it must have methods for ensuring accuracy and for balancing privacy concerns with easy accesses for those who need information and are authorized to see it.

The role of HRM in administration is decreasing as technology is used for many administrative purposes, such as managing employee records and allowing employees to get information about and enrol in training, benefits, and other programs. The availability of the Internet has decreased the HRM role in maintaining records and providing self-service to employees.[21] **Self-service** refers to providing employees online access to, or apps that provide, information about HRM such as training, benefits, compensation, and contracts; enrolling online in programs and services; and completing online surveys. The shift to self-service means that HR can focus more time on consulting with managers on important employee issues and less time on day-to-day transactional tasks.

self-service
Providing employees with online access to, or apps that provide, information about HR issues such as training, benefits, compensation, and contracts; enrolling online in programs and services; and completing online surveys.

Thanks to technology, employee-related information is not just an administrative responsibility; it also can be the basis for knowledge that gives organizations an edge over their competitors. Data about employees can show, for example, which of the company's talent has the most promise for future leadership, what kinds of employees tend to perform best in particular

HR How-To

Making Analytics Useful and Relevant

HR professionals skilled in analyzing data are in demand today. But sophisticated analysis is not of much value if the results don't point to actions that will improve an organization's performance. Therefore, HR professionals also must recognize which analytics will be useful and relevant. The following guidelines can help:

- Find out what performance measures the organization's managers care about. Learn what questions they are asking. Gather data related to those metrics, and explain how the analysis is relevant to managers' priorities.
- Express a performance metric as an equation showing the steps or variables that determine the metric. Then express each step or variable as its own equation. Keep breaking down the process or relationship until you have a set of simple equations showing what the organization must focus on in order to improve the original metric.
- Keep up with the research in business and human behaviour. It can provide insights for making realistic interpretations of how variables might be related. It can also suggest what kinds of data to *stop* collecting because they don't really predict anything or if there is risk that individuals' data privacy rights may be violated.
- Be open to working with service providers that specialize in analyzing data about human resources. They can help ensure that methods are rigorous.
- Make sure to "tell a story" when sharing the results. Providing a strategic summary in the form of a narrative that builds a story and includes visual data increases the likelihood that leaders can use the results for decision making and create value for the organization.

Sources: Rachel Ramosa, "Confused by analytics? Take Pfizer's prescription," *HRD HRTech News,* May 18, 2018, www.hrtechnologynews.com; Jane Cooper and Shannon Jackson, "Scaling the Wall: From HR Metrics to Evidence-Based Analytics," Ottawa: The Conference Board of Canada, 2018, p. 13; Mark Berry, "How to Fail at HR Analytics in Seven Easy Steps," *HR Magazine,* December 2015, https://www.shrm.org; Jeanne G. Harris, "Critical Evaluation: Put Your Analytics into Action," *HR Magazine,* December 2015, https://www.shrm.org; Tomas Chamorro-Premuzic, "Wise Words: Think Again—HR versus the 'Leadership BS' Movement," *Management Today,* November 1, 2015, Business Insights: Global, http://bi.galegroup.com; Martin Berman-Gorvine, "HR Metrics Should Be Relevant, Broken into Manageable Pieces," *HR Focus,* August 2015, pp. 1–2; John Scorza, "Business as Unusual," *HR Magazine,* June 2015, https://www.shrm.org.

positions, and which high-performing employees are most at risk to leave the organization. To use the data for answering questions such as these, many organizations have set up human resource information systems, including predictive capabilities. They may engage in **people (human capital) analytics**, which is the use of quantitative tools and scientific methods to analyze data from human resource databases and other sources to make evidence-based decisions that support business goals. For ideas on how to make analytics relevant to business goals, see the HR How-To box. Later in the chapter, we will also explore evidence-based HRM in more detail.

people (human capital) analytics The use of quantitative tools and scientific methods to analyze data from human resource databases and other sources to make evidence-based decisions that support business goals.

Ensuring Compliance with Federal and Provincial/Territorial Legislation

As we will discuss in later chapters, especially in Chapter 2, governments have many laws and regulations concerning the treatment of employees. These laws govern matters such as human rights, employment equity, employee safety and health, employee compensation and benefits, and employee privacy. Most managers depend on human resources professionals to help them keep up to date and on track with these requirements. Ensuring compliance with laws requires that human resources professionals keep watch over a rapidly changing legal landscape. For example, the increased use of and access to electronic databases by employees and employers suggest that legislation may be needed to protect employee privacy rights and the recent legalization of cannabis for recreational use has far-reaching implications for Canadian workplaces. And, as the age of the workforce increases, as described later in this chapter, the number of cases dealing with age discrimination in layoffs, promotions, and benefits will likely rise. Employers will need to review recruitment practices and performance evaluation systems, revising them if necessary to ensure that they do not discriminate on the basis of age.

Focus on Strategy

Traditional management thinking treated human resource management primarily as an administrative function, but managers today are beginning to see a more central role for HRM. They are looking at HRM as a means to support and shape the organization's strategy—its plan for meeting broad goals such as profitability, quality, market share, and innovation. This strategic role for HRM has evolved gradually. At many organizations, managers still treat HR professionals primarily as experts in designing and delivering HR processes (see the HR Oops! box). But at a growing number of organizations, HR professionals are strategic partners with other managers.

As a result, today's HR professionals need to have a well-internalized comprehension of the organization's business operations, project how business trends might affect the business, reinforce positive aspects of the organization's culture, develop talent for present and future needs, craft effective HR strategies, and make a case for them to top management. Evidence for greater involvement in strategy comes from interviews with finance and HR executives who say they are more interested than ever in collaborating to strengthen their companies.[22] Finance leaders can see that employees are a major budget item, so they want to make sure they are getting the best value for that expense. HR leaders, for their part, are learning to appreciate the importance of using quantitative tools to measure performance.

HR Oops!

Out-of-Focus HRM

In an international survey by Deloitte, only 4 percent of mid- and top-level managers outside the HR department rated their company's human resource programs as excellent. Another 24 percent say the performance is good. That leaves more than 7 out of 10 who consider the performance just adequate or worse. Their colleagues in the HR department tend to agree, with just 5 percent rating their department's performance as excellent and 34 percent calling it good.

What is going wrong? The analysts at Deloitte see the problem as a failure to align HR work with the company's strategy. Many managers and employees in these departments are sticking to their old, familiar roles as specialists in particular functions. Departments are spending more on technology but underinvesting in improvements to their people (through hiring, training, and development) and processes.

For this situation to improve, HR managers and employees need to educate themselves about the business, so they understand how they can contribute to solving business problems. HR professionals who want to take a leadership role may even plan career paths in which they take a turn in line management, responsible for sales or production, so they have a fuller picture of what makes the company tick.

Questions

1. Imagine that you work for a manufacturing company where the HR department's performance on providing the necessary talent is just "adequate." From a business standpoint, what might be the consequences of this less-than-excellent performance?
2. Imagine you lead the HR department in that same manufacturing company. What is one step you could take to improve your department's performance?

Sources: David J. DeFilippo, "HR Will Seat You Now," *Chief Learning Officer*, February 2016, pp. 41–43; Martin Berman-Gorvine, "Less than Half of HR Leaders Rate Their Programs as 'Good' or 'Excellent,'" *HR Focus*, April 2015, pp. 1–3; Josh Bersin, Dimple Agarwal, Bill Pelster, and Jeff Schwartz, introduction to Global Human Capital Trends 2015: Leading in the New World of Work (Westlake, TX: Deloitte University Press, 2015), http://www2.deloitte.com.

Workforce planning provides important information for **talent management**—a systematic, planned effort to train, develop, and engage the performance of highly skilled employees and managers. Approaching these accountabilities in terms of talent management is one way HR professionals are making the link to organizational strategy.

talent management A systematic, planned effort to train, develop, and engage the performance of highly skilled employees and managers.

Organizations do this, for example, when they integrate all the activities involved in talent management with each other and with the organization's other processes to provide the skills the organization needs to pursue its strategy. An integrated approach to talent management includes acquiring talent (recruiting and selection); providing the right opportunities for training, learning, and development; measuring performance; and creating the compensation plans that reward the needed behaviours. To choose the right talent, provide the right training, and so on, HR professionals need to be in ongoing close contact with the members of the organization who need the talent. And when the organization modifies its strategy, HR professionals are part of the planning process so they can modify talent management efforts to support the revised strategy.

HR professionals can support such efforts even in small companies, which often have a human resource department of one. In these situations, the company depends on that one person to understand both HRM principles and the ways they can help the business perform better. Consultant Lori Kleiman urges the one-person HR department to make a point of showing up at business meetings with business-focused data and ideas.[23]

Evidence-based HRM

As part of its strategic role, one of the key contributions HR can make is to engage in evidence-based HRM. **Evidence-based HRM** refers to demonstrating that human resource practices have a positive influence on the company's profits or key stakeholders (employees, customers, community, shareholders). This practice helps show that the resources invested in HR programs are justified and that HR is contributing to the company's goals and objectives. For example, data collected on the relationship between HR practices and productivity, turnover, workplace injuries, and employee engagement may show that HR functions are as important to the business as finance, accounting, and marketing.

evidence-based HRM Collecting and using data to show that human resource practices have a positive influence on the company's bottom line or key stakeholders.

As discussed earlier in the chapter, evidence-based HRM increasingly relies upon people (human capital) analytics. **Big data** refers to information merged from HR databases, corporate financial statements, employee surveys, and other data sources to make evidence-based HR decisions and show that HR practices have an impact on business strategy.[24] Companies are increasingly becoming "data-enabled" by using people (human capital) analytics to analyze data to drive organizational effectiveness and improve HR practices.[25] Google was one of the first companies to use analytics to make people decisions by creating algorithms to predict which job candidates were most likely to succeed. It also produced algorithms to review applications that were rejected. This helped Google hire engineers who its normal application screening process would have missed. A food and beverage company uses analytics to link HR data and organizational data to explore the causes of front-line employee turnover; it turned out it was shift scheduling, not the physical demands as assumed. This company also uses data to determine which universities provide the top candidates.[26]

big data Information merged from HR databases, corporate financial statements, employee surveys, and other data sources to make evidence-based HR decisions.

Change and Sustainability Requires Agility

Often, an organization's strategy requires some type of change—for example, adding, moving, or closing facilities, applying new technology, or entering markets in other regions or countries. Common reactions to change include fear, anger, and confusion. The organization may turn to its human resource department for help in managing the change process. Skilled human resources professionals can apply knowledge of human behaviour, along with performance management tools, to help the organization manage change constructively.

Another strategic challenge tackled by a growing number of companies is how to seek profits in ways that communities, customers, and suppliers will support over the long run. This concern is called **sustainability**—broadly defined as an organization's ability to profit without depleting its resources, including employees, natural resources, and the support of the surrounding community. Success at sustainability comes from meeting the needs of the organization's **stakeholders**, all the parties that have an interest in the company's success.

sustainability An organization's ability to profit without depleting its resources, including employees, natural resources, and the support of the surrounding community.

stakeholders The parties with an interest in the company's success (typically, shareholders, the community, customers, and employees).

Typically, an organization's stakeholders include shareholders, the community, customers, and employees. Sustainable organizations meet their needs by minimizing their environmental impact, providing high-quality products and services, ensuring workplace health and safety, offering fair compensation, and delivering an adequate return to investors. Sustainability delivers a strategic advantage when it boosts the organization's image with customers, opens access to new markets, and helps attract and retain talented employees. In an organization with a sustainable strategy, HR departments focus on employee development and empowerment rather than short-term costs; on long-term planning rather than smooth turnover and outsourcing; and on justice and fairness over short-term profits.[27]

Organizational agility is the "ability of a firm to sense and respond to the environment by intentionally changing."[28] Today's turbulent business environment includes conditions such as rapidly changing customer preferences and options and complex problems with unknown solutions. These conditions necessitate creativity and collaboration. Organizations such as Amazon, Spotify, Google, and Netflix have distinguished themselves as particularly successful in being "born agile" and or with the ability to "agile at scale" by balancing organizational strategy and structure to achieve innovation and high-performance.[29] At the Bank of Montreal (BMO), the shift to "agile" started with cross-functional product-development teams working to enhance customer experience. "Speed is the new business currency," states Lynn Roger, BMO's chief transformation officer.[30]

organizational agility Ability of a firm to sense and respond to the environment by intentionally changing.

The specific ways in which human resources professionals support the organization's strategy vary according to their level of involvement and the nature of the strategy. Strategic issues include emphasis on innovation and decisions about growth. Human resource management can support these strategies, including efforts such as attracting and retaining critical talent, productivity improvement, mergers and acquisitions, and restructuring. For example, a decision to use outsourcing can make an organization more efficient but can also give rise to many human resource challenges. Global expansion similarly presents a wide variety of HRM challenges and opportunities. In an agile organization, HR needs to provide the same services it's always provided—attracting and hiring, training and development, performance management, compensation and rewards—but in ways that are responsive to the ongoing changes in the culture and work style of the organization. For example, at BMO, performance management has shifted to include a focus on teams, rather than just individuals. And at ING, the HR team played a major role in understanding both the skills and mindset needed by a software-based company building agility to renew new processes. HR at ING led a process that required its almost 3,500 head office employees to re-interview for their own jobs. The impact was staggering—40 percent of these employees moved to new positions or left the company.[31]

Productivity Improvement

To compete in today's global economy, companies need to enhance productivity. The relationship between an organization's outputs (products, information, or services) and its inputs (e.g., people, facilities, equipment, data, and materials) is referred to as **productivity**. Canada's record of productivity growth has chronically underperformed the United States over the past two decades. The Conference Board of Canada reported results of a productivity model simulation to establish how much better off Canada would be if its labour productivity growth had kept up with the United States during the past 20 years. The simulation revealed that if Canada's productivity had kept pace with the United States, per capita personal disposable income would have been $7,500 higher, corporate profits would have been 40 percent higher, and federal government revenues would have been more than 30 percent higher.[32]

productivity The relationship between an organization's outputs (products, information, or services) and its inputs (e.g., people, facilities, equipment, data, and materials).

The Business Development Bank of Canada (BDC) explains the gap in productivity between Canada and the United States is mainly attributable to two factors:[33]

- Canada's GDP (Gross Domestic Product) is more heavily weighted to small and medium-sized businesses than the United States. Fifty-three percent of Canada's GDP comes from small and medium-sized businesses vs. 46 percent in the United States.
- Canada's small and medium-sized businesses are less productive than their U.S. counterparts. U.S. small and medium-sized businesses are 67 percent as productive as large businesses; however, Canadian small and medium-sized businesses are only 47 percent as productive as large businesses.

The main strategy for improving productivity, as identified in a recent survey of private Canadian companies, was to provide better training for employees. Additional HR contributions to productivity improvement include supporting an organization's managers in measuring and benchmarking productivity as well as playing a necessary role in assessing applications and investments in information and communications technology.[34]

Mergers and Acquisitions

Often, organizations join forces through mergers (two companies becoming one) and acquisitions (one company buying another). Some mergers and acquisitions result in consolidation within an industry, meaning that two firms in one industry join to hold a greater share of the industry. Other mergers and acquisitions cross industry lines, disrupting traditional organizations and industries. For example, when Amazon acquired Whole Foods in 2017, it was estimated that $22 billion of share value was lost from grocery industry stocks overnight.[35]

HR should have a significant role in carrying out a merger or acquisition. Differences between the businesses involved in the deal make conflict inevitable. Training efforts should therefore include development of skills in collaboration and conflict resolution. Also, HR professionals have to sort out differences in the two companies' practices with regard to total rewards, performance management, and other HR systems. Establishing a consistent structure to meet the combined organization's goals may help to bring employees together.

Non-traditional Employment and the Gig Economy

More companies are moving away from the traditional employment model based on full-time workers to increasingly rely on non-traditional employment. **Non-traditional employment** includes the use of independent contractors, freelancers, on-call workers, temporary workers, and contract company workers. According to a recent study from Randstad Canada, non-traditional workers currently make up 20 to 30 percent of the workforce and this number is expected to rise in the next decade.[36] Companies that rely primarily on non-traditional employment to meet service and product demands are competing in the *gig* economy.[37]

non-traditional employment
Includes the use of independent contractors, freelancers, on-call workers, temporary workers, and contract company workers.

What does non-traditional employment look like? Often, a website or mobile app is used to assign work, and the worker sets their own schedule. Because these workers do not work for a company, they do not have income taxes or other employment deductions such as employment insurance withheld from their earnings, they do not have to receive minimum wage or overtime pay, and they are not eligible for employer-provided benefits. Uber and Lyft are examples of companies that rely on the gig economy. Non-traditional employment has benefits and disadvantages for both individuals and employers.[38]

Non-traditional employment can benefit both individuals and employers. More and more individuals don't want to be attached to any one company. They want the flexibility to work when and where they choose or they may already be working full or part-time and want or need a "side hustle" for extra income or to pursue a passion. Others may want to work fewer hours to better balance work and family responsibilities. From the company perspective, flexibility is provided through the ability to add and release talent as needed; however, the organization's leaders and managers are likely to require additional development and executive coaching to develop skills to work effectively work with on-demand workers who may be highly skilled, experienced, and educated, and have many options in the job market.[39]

Outsourcing

Many organizations are increasingly outsourcing and offshoring business activities. **Outsourcing** refers to the practice of having another company (a vendor, third-party provider, or consultant) provide services. For instance, a manufacturing company might outsource its accounting and transportation functions to businesses that specialize in these activities. Outsourcing gives the company access to in-depth expertise and is often more economical as well. In addition to manufacturing, software development and support, as well as call centre operations, are other functions typically considered for outsourcing.

outsourcing
The practice of having another company (a vendor, third-party provider, or consultant) provide services.

Not only do HR departments help with a transition to outsourcing, but many HR functions are being outsourced. Outsourcing initially focused on routine transactions such as payroll processing and on complex technical specialties such as managing retirement accounts and global relocation. Today's outsourcing is moving more into areas that automate processes and support decision making. For example, outsourcing the recruitment process could allow HR professionals to use data to figure out how to build a pipeline for the right kinds of talent. Providers of benefits administration help companies set up enrolment and training via online platforms that employees—especially younger ones—have come to expect. Small companies sometimes outsource most of their HR work. Benefits Canada reports that 59 percent of Canadian employers outsourced some or all HR services and another 10 percent plan to do so within two years.[40]

Expanding into Global Markets

Companies are finding that to survive and prosper they must compete in international markets as well as fend off foreign competitors' attempts to gain ground in Canada. To meet these challenges, Canadian businesses must develop global markets, keep up with global competition, hire from an international labour pool, and prepare employees for global assignments. This global expansion can pose some challenges for human resource management as HR employees learn about the cultural differences that shape the expectations and behaviours of employees in other parts of the world.

Companies that are successful and widely admired not only operate on a multinational scale, but also have workforces and corporate cultures that reflect their global markets. Yum Brands was quick to seize on the potential of China's massive population: in 1987, its KFC restaurants became the first fast-food chain to enter China, and in 1990 its Pizza Hut brand became the first pizza chain there. Today the company has more than 6,000 restaurants in the country with plans to open hundreds more. More than half the company's sales are made in China. Behind the success of this overseas expansion is a willingness to adapt menus to local tastes and develop local management talent.[41]

The Global Workforce

Talent comes from a global workforce. Organizations with international operations hire at least some of their employees in the countries where they operate. In fact, regardless of where their customers are located, organizations are looking globally to hire talented people (who may be willing to work for less pay than the Canadian labour market requires). The efforts to hire workers in other countries are common enough that they have spurred the creation of a popular term for the practice: **offshoring**. Just a few years ago, most offshoring involved big manufacturers building factories in countries with lower labour costs. But it has become so easy to send information and software around the world that even start-ups have joined the offshoring movement.

offshoring
Moving operations from the country where a company is headquartered to a company where pay rates are lower but the necessary skills are available.

Hiring in developing nations such as India, Mexico, and Brazil gives employers access to people with educational achievements and potential who are eager to work yet who will accept lower wages than elsewhere in the world. Challenges, however, may include employees' lack of familiarity with corporate practices, as well as political and economic instability in the areas. Important issues that HR experts can help companies weigh include whether workers in the offshore locations can provide the same or better skills, how offshoring will affect motivation and recruitment of employees needed in Canada, and whether managers are well prepared to manage and lead offshore employees.

Even hiring at home may involve selection of employees from other countries. The 21st century, like the beginning of the previous century, has seen significant immigration. Figure 1.3 shows the distribution of immigration by continent of origin. Canada's foreign-born population accounts for one in five of Canada's total population—the highest proportion in almost a century.[42] The impact of immigration is especially significant in some regions of Canada. The vast majority of the foreign-born population lives in Ontario, British Columbia, Quebec, and Alberta—particularly in Toronto, Montreal, and Vancouver.[43] Statistics Canada projects that by 2031, nearly one-half (46 percent) of Canadians aged 15 and over will be foreign-born or have at least one foreign-born parent.[44]

International Assignments

Besides hiring an international workforce, organizations must be prepared to send employees to other countries. This requires HR expertise in selecting employees for international assignments and preparing them for those assignments. Employees who take assignments in other countries are called **expatriates**.

expatriates
Employees who take assignments in other countries.

FIGURE 1.3

Where Do Immigrants (Permanent Residents) to Canada Come From?

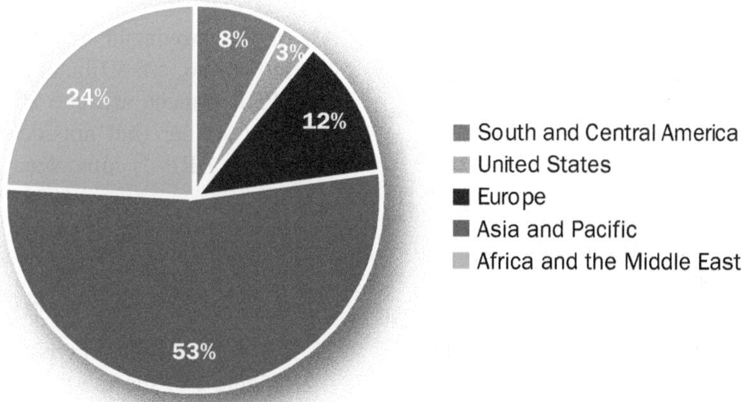

Source: Facts and Figures 2015, Immigration Overview, Permanent Residents Annual IRCC Updates, Government of Canada, Canada Permanent Residents by Age and Source Area, 2015, https://open.canada.ca/data/en/dataset/2fbb56bd-eae7-4582-af7d-a197d185fc93, retrieved June 19, 2018.

Canadian companies must prepare employees to work in other countries. Canadian companies must carefully select employees to work globally on the basis of their ability to understand and respect the cultural and business norms of the host country. Qualified candidates also need language skills and technical ability. In Chapter 10, we discuss cross-cultural training practices.

LO2 What Competencies Do HR Professionals Need?

With such varied responsibilities, human resources professionals need to bring together a large pool of competencies. The Human Resources Professionals Association's (HRPA) *Professional Competency Framework* consists of nine functional areas, groupings, and underlying competencies as shown in Figure 1.4.

1. **Strategy**—a cluster of competencies related to the ability to think and act strategically in regards to organizations, business, and the HR function.
2. **Professional Practices**—a cluster of competencies related to the ability to conduct oneself in a professional manner and to exhibit high levels of professionalism in all contexts and situations.
3. **Organizational Effectiveness**—a cluster of competencies related to using the levers available to HR professionals to maximize the performance of organizations, teams, and individuals within the context of executing the organization's strategy.
4. **Workforce Planning and Talent Management**—a cluster of competencies related to the recruitment and deployment of human resources within an organization.
5. **Labour and Employee Relations**—a cluster of competencies related to managing the relationships between employer and employees.
6. **Total Rewards**—a cluster of competencies related to the management of rewards within an organization in a manner that maximally supports the execution of organizational strategy.
7. **Learning and Development**—a cluster of competencies related to the optimization of the ability of the organization, teams, and individuals to acquire and put to use new competencies.
8. **Health, Wellness, and Safe Workplace**—a cluster of competencies related to the creation and maintenance of healthy and safe workplaces.
9. **HR Metrics, Reporting, and Financial Management**—a cluster of competencies related to the ability to collect, manage, and synthesize information relevant to the management of human resources and the ability to incorporate financial analysis in the making of decisions about HR investments.

FIGURE 1.4

HR Competency Framework—Functional Competencies (HRPA)

Source: "Human Resources Professionals Competency Framework," Human Resources Professionals Association (HRPA), 2014, https://www.hrpa.ca, accessed June 19, 2018.

HRPA's HR Competency Framework provides definitions and specifics and is further supported by identification of *enabling competencies* organized into individual, team, and organizational categories. For example, individual skills include[45]:

- critical thinking and analysis
- technological savvy
- research skills
- quantitative skills
- critical legal thinking.

All of the provincial and territorial HR Associations, except Ontario, are affiliated with CPHR Canada. All of the CPHR Canada affiliate HR associations have a substantially similar (but not identical) competency framework to the HRPA's competency framework.

Careers in Human Resource Management

There are many different types of jobs in the HRM profession. Figure 1.5. shows selected HRM positions and their median salaries and bonuses. The salaries vary according to education and experience, as well as the type of industry in which the person works.

FIGURE 1.5

Median Salary and Median Salary + Bonus for HRM Positions (Toronto, Ontario)

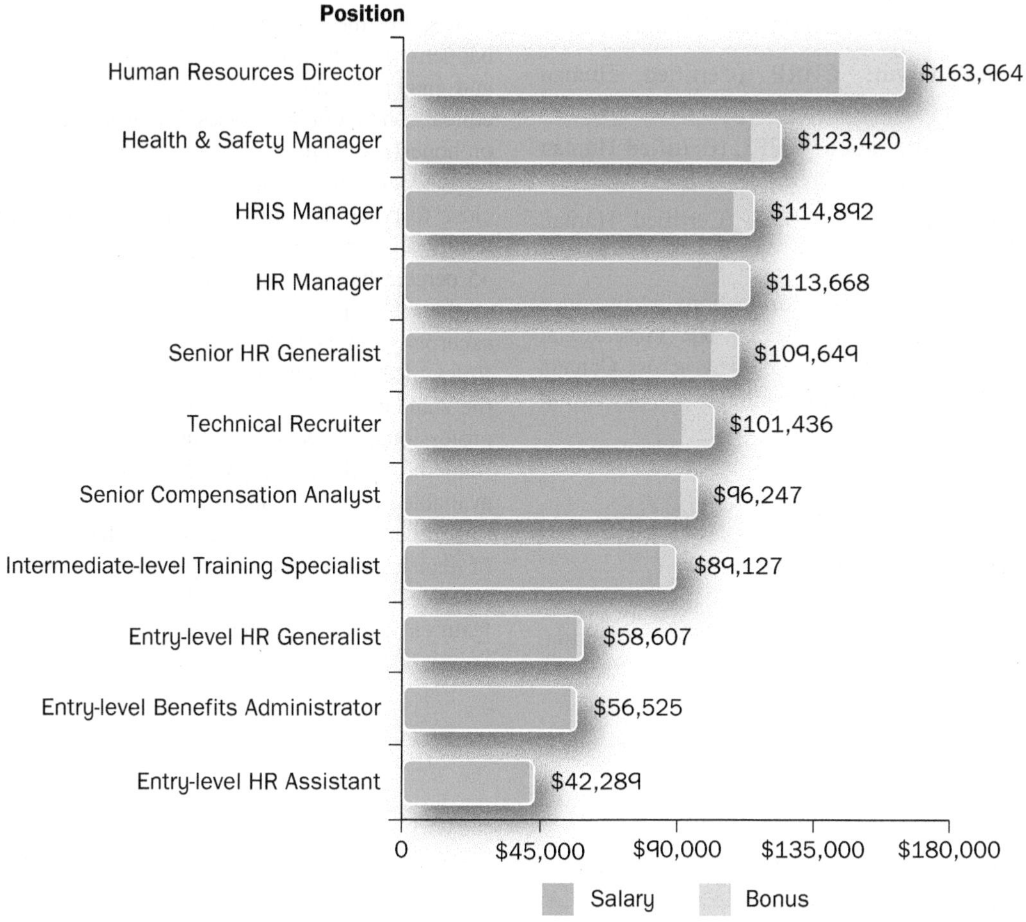

Source: Data from Salary Wizard Canada, Salary.com, http://swz.salary.com/CanadaSalaryWizard/layoutscripts/cswzl_newsearch.aspx, accessed January 7, 2015.

As you can see from Figure 1.5, some positions involve work in specialized areas of HRM such as benefits administration, training, or compensation. Other positions call for generalists to perform a full range of HRM activities, including recruiting, training, compensation, and employee relations. The vast majority of HRM professionals have a university or college degree, and many also have completed postgraduate work. The typical field of study is business (especially human resources or industrial relations), but some HRM professionals have degrees in the social sciences (economics or psychology), the humanities, and law programs. Those who have completed graduate work have master's degrees in HR management, business management, or a similar field. This is important because to be successful in HR you need to speak the same language as people in the other business functions. You have to have credibility as a business leader, so you must be able to understand finance and to build a business case for HR activities.

HR Professional Designations

The CPHR (Chartered Professional in Human Resources) designation is the designation that recognizes achievement and capability for HR professionals in all provinces and territories, except Ontario. Note: In Quebec and in New Brunswick this designation is translated as CRHA. CPHR Canada represents 27,000 members across nine provinces and three territories in Canada. CPHR certification requirements include educational requirements (a minimum of a bachelor's degree in any discipline), assessed proficiency in human resources knowledge—National Knowledge Exam® (NKE), professional experience, and membership in a provincial/territorial HR Association. In Ontario, the Human Resources Professionals Association (HRPA) has a tiered certification framework with three designations and associated requirements:[46]

- **Entry designation:** CHRP (Certified Human Resources Professional)
- **Professional designation:** CHRL (Certified Human Resources Leader)
- **Executive designation:** CHRE (Certified Human Resources Executive).

Table 1.3 summarizes the HR designations by province and territory including their relevant HR Professional Association. Developments are underway across Canada to move the HR profession from an unregulated profession to a self-regulated profession.

Ethics in Human Resource Management

Whenever people's actions affect one another, ethical issues arise, and business decisions are no exception. **Ethics** refers to fundamental principles of right and wrong; ethical behaviour is behaviour that is consistent with those principles.

ethics The fundamental principles of right and wrong.

Business decisions, including HRM decisions, should be ethical, but the evidence suggests that is not always what happens. Recent surveys indicate that the general public and managers do not have positive perceptions of the ethical conduct of businesses. For example, in a Gallup poll on honesty and ethics in 21 professions, only 17 percent of respondents rated business executives high or very high; close to twice as many rated them low or very low. And within organizations, a recent survey of workers found that 45 percent had witnessed some form of unethical conduct at their workplace.[47] Table 1.4 provides brief overview excerpts from CPHR Canada's "Code of Ethics and Rules of Professional Conduct" to provide a glimpse into the standards for professional and ethical conduct of HR professionals.[48] Detailed requirements for each of the four fundamental duties are provided in the complete document available on CPHR Canada's website.

To explore how ethical principles apply to a variety of decisions, we will highlight ethical dilemmas in HRM practices throughout the book in the "Thinking Ethically" features positioned at the end of each chapter.

TABLE 1.3

HR Associations and Designations

Province/Territory	HR Association	Designation(s)	
British Columbia and Yukon	CPHR BC & Yukon	CPHR	https://cphrbc.ca
Alberta, Nunavut, and Northwest Territories	CPHR Alberta	CPHR	www.cphrab.ca
Saskatchewan	CPHR Saskatchewan	CPHR	www.cphrsk.ca
Manitoba	CPHR Manitoba	CPHR	www.cphrmb.ca
Ontario	Human Resources Professionals Association (HRPA)	CHRP, CHRL, CHRE	www.hrpa.ca
Québec	CRHA Ordre des conseilliers en ressources humaines agréés	CRHA	www.portailrh.org
New Brunswick/Nouveaux-Brunswick	CPHR New Brunswick	CPHR/CRHA	www.cphrnb.ca
Nova Scotia	CPHR Nova Scotia	CPHR	https://cphrns.site-ym.com
Prince Edward Island	CPHR Prince Edward Island	CPHR	www.cphrpei.ca
Newfoundland and Labrador	CPHR Newfoundland & Labrador	CPHR	https://cphrnl.ca

TABLE 1.4

CPHR Canada's Code of Ethics and Rules of Professional Conduct (Overview)

Duties to the Public
• Members have a duty to discharge all of their Professional responsibilities honourably, competently and with integrity.
Duties to the Profession
• Members have a duty to protect and promote the Profession and to cooperate with the Association.
Duties to Clients and Employers
• Members have a duty to act in the best interest of their clients and employers.
Duties to Individuals
• Members must at all times act in a manner that advances the principles of health and safety, human rights, equity, dignity, and overall well-being in the workplace.

Source: "Code of Ethics and Rules of Professional Conduct," Chartered Professionals in Human Resources in Canada, 2016, https://cphr.ca/wp-content/uploads/2017/01/2016-Code-of-Ethics-CPHR-2.pdf, accessed June 19, 2018.

LO3 What Are the HR Responsibilities of Supervisors and Managers?

Although many organizations have human resource departments with specialists responsible for developing effective HR practices, *implementation* of these practices ultimately resides with the organization's supervisors and managers. HR practices will have little impact on performance if managers and supervisors are unable—or unwilling—to implement them. When an organization's culture, norms, and attitudes are supportive of HR practices, supervisors and managers are more likely to make efforts to effectively implement HR practices.[49]

Figure 1.6 shows some HR responsibilities that supervisors and managers are likely to have. Organizations depend on supervisors and managers to help them determine what kinds of work need to be done (job analysis and design) and in what quantities (workforce planning). Supervisors and managers typically interview job candidates and participate in the decisions about which candidates to hire. Many organizations expect supervisors to play a key role in onboarding and to train employees in some or all aspects of the employees' jobs. Supervisors work with employees to set goals, provide performance feedback and coaching, and appraise performance, and may recommend pay increases. And, of course, supervisors and managers play a key role in employee relations, because they are most often the voice of management for their employees, representing the company on a day-to-day basis. In all of these activities, supervisors and managers can participate in HRM by taking into consideration how decisions and policies will affect their employees. Understanding the principles of communication, motivation, and other elements of human behaviour can help supervisors and managers engage and inspire the best from the organization's human resources.

FIGURE 1.6

Typical Areas of Involvement of Supervisors and Managers in HRM

Source: Based on National Association of Colleges and Employers, "Employers Say Verbal Communication Most Important Candidate Skill," news release, March 1, 2016, http://www.naceweb.org.

LO4 How Is the Labour Force Changing?

The *labour force* is a general way to refer to all the people willing and able to work. For an organization, the **internal labour force** consists of the organization's workers—its employees and the people who work at the organization. This internal labour force is drawn from the organization's **external labour market**, that is, individuals who are actively seeking employment. The number and kinds of people in the external labour market determine the kinds of human resources available to an organization (and their cost). Human resources

internal labour force
An organization's workers (its employees and the people who work at the organization).

external labour market
Individuals who are actively seeking employment.

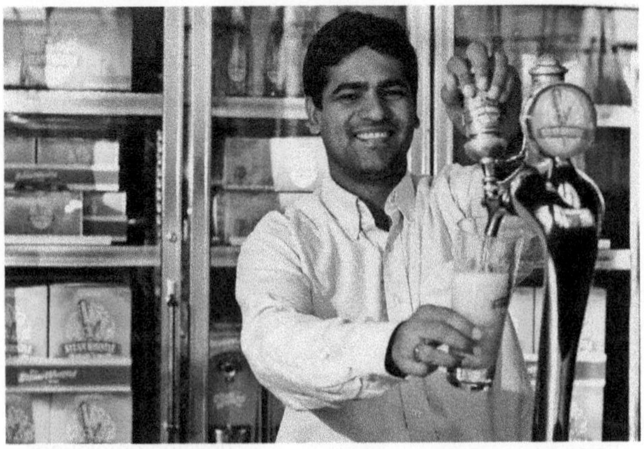

Sean Zaffino, Steam Whistle Brewing

Adrian Joseph (in photo), a Sri Lankan immigrant with a strong financial and accounting background, lacked Canadian work experience but was hired as CFO (chief financial officer) by Toronto's Steam Whistle Brewing only three weeks after his arrival in Canada.

professionals need to be aware of trends in the composition of the external labour market, because these trends affect the organization's options for creating a well-skilled, motivated internal labour force.

Aging of the Workforce

Canada's labour force is aging—quickly. From 2016 to 2026, the only growing age group in the labour force is expected to be workers 55 years and older. The 15–24 and 25–54-year-old groups' share of the total workforce are expected to decrease between 2016 and 2026. By 2026, 4 in 10 working-age Canadians could be aged 55+, representing a steep increase from 30 percent in 2007 and an average of 25 percent during the 1990s. There are fewer people entering the labour force than are exiting it—in 2016, there were 4.4 million people aged 15 to 24 in the Canadian population and 4.9 million people aged 55 to 64. This means there is a widening gap between the number of younger people entering the labour force and the number of people preparing to exit the labour market. The ratio of people aged 15–24 years to people 55–64 was 0.9 in 2016—below replacement. In contrast, in 1976 there were 2.4 people aged 15–24 years for each person aged 55 to 64. This ratio has trended downward for several decades, but actually dipped below 1.0 for the first time in 2013. This trend is expected to continue over the next two decades.[50]

Figure 1.7 shows the change in age labour force representation from 2016 (Actual) to 2026 (Projected).

Today's older generations include many people who are in no hurry to retire. They may enjoy making a contribution at work, have ambitious plans for which they want to earn money, have good health, and/or be among the many who have mortgage debt, family responsibilities, or inadequate savings for full retirement. Gallup recently reported that almost three-quarters of people plan to keep working in some capacity past the age of 65—a significant increase from 1995 when only 14 percent of people said they planned to keep working past the age of 65.[51]

Despite myths to the contrary, worker performance and learning are not adversely affected by aging.[52] Older employees are willing and able to learn new technology. An emerging trend is for qualified older workers to ask to work part time or for only a few months at a time as a means to transition to retirement. Employees and companies are redefining the meaning of retirement to include second careers as well as part-time and temporary work assignments. An aging workforce means that employers will increasingly face HRM issues such as

FIGURE 1.7

Age Distribution of the Canadian Labour Force 2016 (Actual) and 2026 (Projected)

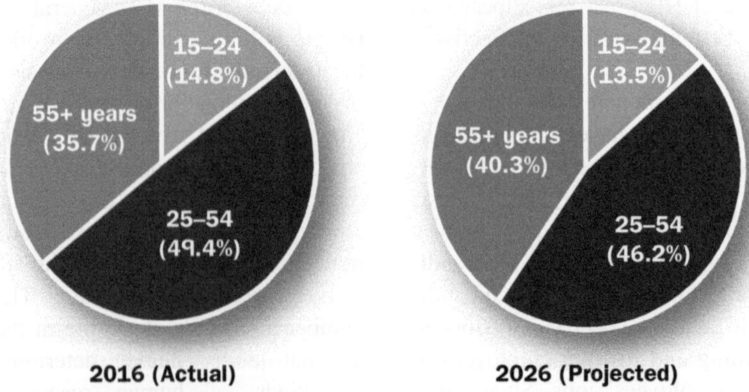

Note: Percentages may not add up to 100 due to rounding

Source: Andrew Fields, Sharanjit Uppal, and Sébastien LaRochelle-Côté, "The impact of aging on labour market participation rates: Chart 1 - Distribution of working-age population, by age group, 1976-2016," *Statistics Canada*, June 14, 2017, https://www150.statcan.gc.ca/n1/pub/75-006-x/2017001/article/14826-eng.htm, accessed June 21, 2018.

career plateauing, retirement planning, and retraining older workers to avoid skill obsolescence. Companies will struggle with how to control the rising costs of benefits and health care. Companies face competing challenges with older workers. Companies will have to ensure that older workers are not discriminated against in hiring, training, and workforce reduction decisions. At the same time, companies will want to encourage retirement and make it financially and psychologically acceptable.

A Multi-generational Workforce

Because employees are working longer, the workforce now has five generations, each one with unique characteristics as well as similarities. Table 1.5 shows the year born and the familiar name(s) for each generation. Consider some of the attributes that are believed to characterize each generation.[53] Generation Z, born after 1995, have started to graduate from university and college and are becoming the newest "faces" in organizations. This generation doesn't know a time before the Internet or smartphones and are even more attached to their devices for learning and connecting with others than are Millennials. Generation Z may be more entrepreneurial than other generations and more interested in meaningful work than money. With Baby Boomers retiring, this generation will have many job and career opportunities. Generation Z wants a work environment that provides in-the-moment communications and access to answers.

Millennials grew up with diversity in their schools and were coached, praised, and encouraged for participation rather than accomplishment by their Baby Boomer parents. Millennials are characterized as being optimistic, willing to work and learn, eager to please, self-reliant, globally aware, and valuing of diversity and teamwork. They are also believed to have high levels of self-esteem. Millennials are a highly educated and technologically connected group who approach the workplace with the mentality, "What's in it for me?" They are the generation most likely to switch jobs and be on the lookout for new opportunities. Millennials want to understand how they fit in with their jobs, teams, and companies. They look for work that fuels their sense of purpose and makes them feel important.

Generation X grew up during a time when the divorce rate doubled, the number of women working outside the home increased, and the personal computer was invented. They were often left on their own after school (latchkey kids). They value skepticism, informality, and practicality; seek work/life balance; and dislike close supervision. They tend to be impatient and cynical. Baby Boomers tend to value social conscientiousness and independence. They are competitive, hard working, and concerned with the fair treatment of all employees. They are often considered to be workaholics and rigid in conforming to rules. Traditionalists grew up during the Great Depression and lived during World War II. They tend to value frugality, are patriotic and loyal, adhere to rules, are loyal to employers, and take responsibility and sacrifice for the good of the company.

Members of each generation may have misperceptions of each other, causing tensions and misunderstanding in the workplace.[54] For example, Generation X leaders may become irritated by having to answer Generation Z employees' questions about why they are expected to perform a job a certain way, and by their employees' preference for instant feedback and praise when they complete work. Consequently, Millennials may think Generation X leaders are uninterested in them or are poor delegators. Millennials might believe that Baby Boomers are too rigid and follow company rules too closely. Employees in the older generations may be perceived to be too slow in adopting social media tools and overvalue tenure rather than knowledge and performance. Traditionalists and Baby Boomers may conclude that Millennials don't have a strong work ethic because they are too concerned with work/life balance. Also, members of the younger generations may resent Baby Boomers and Traditionalists who are working longer before retiring, blocking promotions and career moves. Although generational differences likely exist, members of the same generation are no more alike than members of the same gender or race. This means that we need to be very cautious in attributing differences in employee behaviours and attitudes to generational differences or expecting all employees of a generation to have similar values. Research suggests that the generations of employees have similarities as well as differences.[55] For example, most employees view work as a means to more fully use their skills and abilities, meet their interests, and allow them to live a desirable lifestyle.

TABLE 1.5

Generations in the Workforce

Year Born	Generation
1925–1945	Traditionalists Silent Generation
1946–1964	Baby Boomers
1965–1980	Generation X
1981–1995	Millennials Generation Y
1996–2014	Generation Z

A Diverse Workforce

In addition to age, the Canadian population and labour force is also growing more diverse in other ways. Immigration is an important force in population and labour force growth and diversity. For example, Statistics Canada recently stated that more than 250 ethnic origins were reported for the 2016 Census of Population question.[56] Statistics Canada also reported there are almost 1.7 million Indigenous people (Statistics Canada terminology is "Aboriginal") in Canada (4.9 percent of the total Canadian population). Since 2006, the Indigenous population has grown by 42.5 percent—more than 4 times the growth rate of the non-Indigenous population over the same period. The Indigenous population is young—29.2 percent of First Nations and one-third (33 percent) of the Inuit population in 2016 were 14 years of age or younger in contrast to only 16.4 percent of the non-Indigenous population,[57] thus providing opportunities for a significant source of talent for the future.

According to a study by the Association for Canadian Studies, 80 percent of Canadians aged 18 to 24 describe their school or workplace as ethnically diverse. Jack Jedwab, the association's executive director, says this diversity is helping to make Canadians among the world's most tolerant people. The four-country survey also reveals that "the more diverse your workplace or school, the more accepting you will be of diversity in other areas of life, like the friends you choose and the neighbourhood you live in."[58]

"I think the main difference between us and some other Canadian companies is that when we look at a résumé, first of all we don't put Canadian experience as a criteria," says Cam Heaps, Steam Whistle co-founder. "We don't discredit or put a lower value on a new Canadian's résumé because their experience might have been outside of the country. Actually, we might put a bit of a premium on it because if anything it brings a fresh perspective. You're tapping into a whole other strategy experience when you bring people in from different regions."[59]

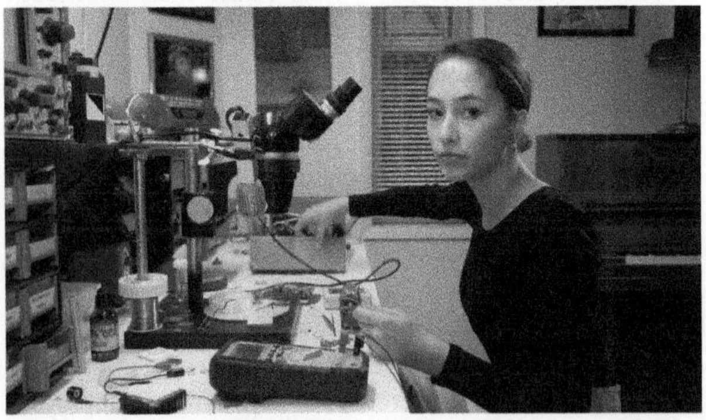

Photo: Don Chaput

It has been reported that Generation Z have a strong work ethic and want jobs with social impact. Ann Makosinski from Victoria, British Columbia, has achieved international fame for these characteristics. At the age of 15, Ann was the winner of Google's Global Science Fair (open to students aged 13–18) for inventing a flashlight powered by the heat of the human hand. The invention was inspired by a friend from the Philippines who failed a grade because she was unable to study at night due to not having electricity. Makosinski has also been recognized in *Forbes, Time* magazine, and *BC Business* magazine's "30 Under 30" and founded Makotronics Enterprises with her father. Ann is a student at the University of British Columbia (UBC), in Vancouver.[60]

Business leaders increasingly recognize diversity as a competitive advantage that drives innovation, creativity, and creates conditions where employees' potential can be fully utilized. However, the benefits of diversity are fully realized only when organizations intentionally engage all employees in a way that is authentically *inclusive.*[61] Diversity and inclusion as well as the composition of Canada's workforce in the context of the employment equity–designated groups—women, Aboriginal peoples, members of visible minorities, and persons with disabilities—will be explored in more detail in Chapter 2.

Throughout this book, we will show how diversity affects HRM practices. For example, from a talent acquisition perspective, it is important to ensure that methods used to attract and select employees are objective and unbiased. With regard to total rewards, organizations are providing benefits to accommodate the needs of a diverse workforce; for example, providing time off without loss of pay and benefits to deal with personal emergencies and to Indigenous employees for cultural events such as wakes or public duties such as Band Elections.[62]

Shift to Knowledge Workers

The increasing use of computers to do routine tasks has shifted the kinds of skills needed. Qualities such as physical strength and mastery of a particular piece of machinery are no longer important for many jobs. More employers are looking for mathematical, verbal, and interpersonal skills, such as the ability to solve math or other problems or reach decisions as part of a team. Often, when organizations are looking for technical skills, they are looking for skills related to using technology. When employees lack advanced literacy and thinking skills, they may be unable to perform their jobs competently and will experience difficulty adjusting to changes in the workplace.[63] Today's employees must be able to handle a variety of responsibilities, interact with customers, and think creatively.

These types of employees, **knowledge workers**, are employees whose main contribution to the company is specialized knowledge such as knowledge of customers, a process, or a profession. Employees cannot simply be ordered to perform tasks; they must share knowledge and collaborate on solutions. Knowledge workers contribute specialized knowledge that their managers may not have, such as information about customers. Managers depend on them to share information. Knowledge workers have many job opportunities. If they choose, they can leave a company and take their knowledge to a competitor. Knowledge workers are in demand because companies need their skills and jobs requiring them are growing.

knowledge workers
Employees whose main contribution to the company is specialized knowledge such as knowledge of customers, a process, or a profession.

To find such employees, many organizations are looking for educational achievements. A college diploma, university degree, or skilled trades certificate is a basic requirement for many jobs today. Competition for qualified college, university, and skilled trades graduates in many fields is intense. At the other extreme, workers with less education often have to settle for low-paying jobs. Some companies are unable to find qualified employees and instead rely on training and re-skilling to address skill gaps.[64]

Increasing Levels of Education

The educational attainment of Canada's labour force is increasing—almost 1 in 3 people in Canada's labour force had a university degree or higher in 2018, up from approximately 1 in 4 people in 2008 and less than 1 in 5 in 1998. See Figure 1.8.

In a survey conducted for a TD Bank Financial Group paper, economists Craig Alexander and Eric Lascalles examined the work of a dozen researchers to discover the rate of return of postsecondary education. The rate of return was calculated using the present-value difference between the lifetime earnings of a postsecondary graduate and those of a high-school graduate, factoring in the cost of tuition, academic fees, and lost earnings while students were in school. Annual rates of return for a university degree ranged from 12 percent to 17 percent for men and 16 percent to 20 percent for women.[65]

LO5 Competing through Technology

Technology has reshaped the way we play, shop, communicate, and live and work. According to Chandran Fernando, managing director of Matrix360, "We need to realize that, at the end of the day, technology is not at the centre of the universe—people are."[66] Bill Morrow, with Deloitte's Human Capital Trends, describes the opportunity as, "How do we augment human abilities with technology? If we have technology augmenting what a person is doing, you're actually making that person superhuman."[67] Head of Research at Bersin by Deloitte, David Mallon describes a recent HR tech conference where there were many competing companies promoting their talent acquisition chat bots to an HR audience wanting to improve the real-time quality of their candidate experience. According to Mallon, the next step for HR is to find additional ways to use technology to augment HR professionals' skills—"How do we use bots, for example, to track down people that fit a certain profile and connect them back to us so we can begin to build long-term relationships with them?"[68]

Social Networking, Artificial Intelligence (AI), and Robotics

Advances in sophisticated technology, along with reduced costs for the technology, are changing many aspects of

FIGURE 1.8

Educational Attainment of Canada's Labour Force (Percentage)

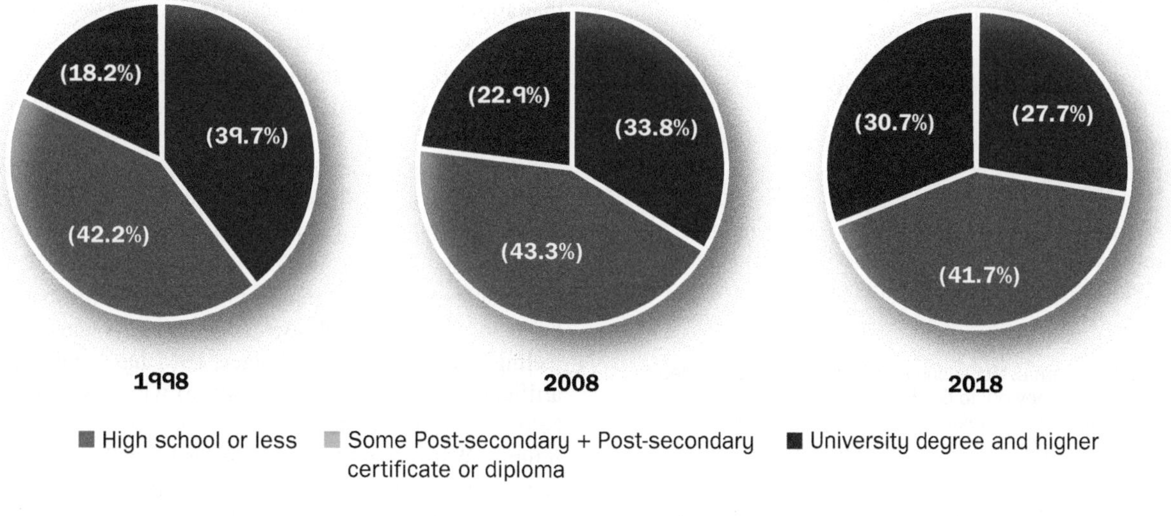

Note: Percentages may not add to 100 due to rounding. January data is provided for each of the indicated years.

Source: Statistics Canada. Table 14-10-0019-01 Labour force characteristics by educational attainment, monthly, unadjusted for seasonality (x 1,000) https://www150.statcan.gc.ca/t1/tbl1/en/cv.action, accessed June 23, 2018

human resource management. Specifically, companies are using or considering using social networking, artificial intelligence, and robotics.

Social Networking

Technological advances in electronics and communications software have made possible mobile devices such as smartphones and tablets which enhance capability for social networking. *Social networking* refers to use of platforms such as Facebook, Twitter, Instagram, LinkedIn, and wikis and blogs that facilitate interactions between people, usually around shared interests. Table 1.6 shows some of the potential issues that can be addressed by using social networking. In general, social networking facilitates communication, decentralized decision making, and collaboration. Social networking can be useful for connecting to customers and valuable for busy employees to share knowledge and ideas with their peers and managers with whom they may not have much time to interact face-to-face on a daily basis. Employees, especially Millennials and Generation Z, have used social networking tools for much of their lives and see them as valuable tools for both their work and nonwork lives.

Despite the potential advantages of social networking, many companies are uncertain whether they should embrace it.[69] They fear that social networking will result in employees wasting time or offending or harassing their co-workers. Other companies believe that the benefits of using social networking for HR practices and allowing employees to access social networks at work outweigh the risks. They trust employees to use social networking productively and are proactive in developing policies about personal use and training employees about privacy settings and social network etiquette. They realize that employees will likely check their Instagram, Twitter, Facebook, or LinkedIn accounts but accept it unless it is interfering with completing their work. In some ways, social networking has become the electronic substitute for daydreaming at one's desk or walking to the break room to socialize with co-workers.

TABLE 1.6

Potential Uses of Social Networking

Issues	Use
Loss of expert knowledge due to retirement	Knowledge sharing, capturing, and storing
Employee engagement	Collect employees' opinions, chat with employees
Identify and promote employee expertise	Create online expert communities
Promote innovation and creativity	Encourage participation in online discussions
Reinforce learning	Share best practices, applications, learning points, links to articles and webinars
Employees need coaching and mentoring	Interact with mentors and coaching peers
Need to identify and connect with promising job candidates	Share job openings, respond to candidates' questions, cultivate a pool of potential employees

Sources: Based on L. McFarland and R. Ployhart, "Social Media: A Contextual Framework to Guide Research and Practice," *Journal of Applied Psychology* 100 (2015), pp. 1653–77; D. Robb, "Cultivating Connections," *HR Magazine*, September 2014, pp. 65–66; M. McGraw, "Managing the Message," *Human Resource Executive*, December 2014, pp. 16–18; P. Brotherson, "Social Networks Enhance Employee Learning," T + D, April 2011, pp. 18–19; M. Derven, "Social Networking: A Frame for Development," *T + D*, July 2009, pp. 58–63; M. Weinstein, "Are You Linked In?" *Training*, September/October, 2010, pp. 30–33.

Artificial Intelligence (AI) and Robotics

Artificial intelligence, robotics, tracking systems, radio frequency identification, and nanotechnology are transforming work.[70] Technology has also made it easier to monitor environmental conditions and employees and operate equipment. Driverless cars, self-driving trucks at iron ore mines that need no human operators, and computers that perform legal research are recent advances in automation.

artificial intelligence (AI)
Technology that can think like a human.

Artificial intelligence (AI) is a technology that simulates human thinking. It works through queries that allow it to learn from data over time so that it can identify trends and patterns that influence future searches and suggestions. Artificial intelligence is in use at home and in the workplace.[71]

For example, artificial intelligence has provided us with personal assistants such as Apple's Siri and Amazon's Alexa that we can give orders to, such as to make a purchase or play our favourite music. AI assistant Google Duplex adds pauses, "ums," "mmm-hmmms" and is able to pick up on nuance and small phrases so well that is leaving some feeling uneasy. In the workplace, IBM has teamed up its artificial intelligence (called Watson) with H&R Block to help clients prepare their tax returns and maximize their tax refunds. Watson has also been used in health care to provide cancer diagnoses and in service industries to answer customers' questions. AI can be used to streamline routine parts of HR functions such as recruitment and onboarding so HR professionals can allocate time to more strategic aspects.

AI's predictive capabilities can also be used to supplement human decision making to reduce bias in hiring, assess potential, and make promotion decisions as well as support a variety of other HR functions; for example, workforce planning and compensation and benefits planning.

Robots are being used in manufacturing.[72] Heasy, a robot with eyes, can help you find your way through a hotel or resort. Airport Guide Robot can answer airline passengers' questions in English, Chinese, Japanese, and Korean; scan a ticket; and give directions. Robots at Whirlpool's dryer factory snap pictures to scan defects. At BMW's auto plants, robots work alongside employees, freeing them from having to perform repetitive, physically demanding tasks so that they can perform more important and knowledge-intensive work. Robots can help companies save money because they can work more efficiently and lower labour costs, but they still can't perform many important tasks.

According to the director of talent at the innovation hub MaRSDD, Daneal Charney, who recently served as moderator of the AI and ethics panel at a recent HR Tech Summit in Toronto, "It's not us vs. the machine. Put yourself back in the driver's seat. We decide why and how to adopt AI at work. We decide the ethical guidelines. We decide what to do with the predictive outcomes AI serves up."[73] The Thinking Ethically feature at the end of this chapter provides additional perspectives about a balanced and ethical approach to the use of data for making decisions about people.

Wearables are being developed and used for training and performance support solutions. Wearable Intelligence provides smart eyewear technology and camera technology that gives employees hands-free, voice-activated access to procedures and checklists and live access to experts using mobile devices. These technologies allow data and live video sharing, the opportunity to review best-practice videos before or during the performance of complex procedures and operations, and real-time notifications and alerts.[75] For example, an operator who might be working on a remote oil rig or a surgeon in a sterile operating room can share live video with experts and get their advice to fix a broken valve or complete a medical procedure, while remaining focused on the equipment or patient.

Photo courtesy of BMW Group

In BMW's Dingolfing factory in southern Germany, a lightweight robot works alongside workers to lift and install a gear that weighs up to 5.5 kg. This collaboration allows the workers to focus on other tasks better suited to their capabilities, while the robot is able to consistently apply the exact force needed.[74]

HRIS, Mobile Devices, Cloud Computing, and HR Dashboards

Companies continue to use human resource information systems to store large quantities of employee data including personal information, training records, skills, compensation rates, absence records, and benefits usages and costs. A *human resource information system (HRIS)* is a computer system used to acquire, store, retrieve, and distribute information related to a company's human resources.[76] An HRIS can support strategic decision making, help the company provide data for evaluating policies and programs, and support day-to-day HR decisions. Hilton Worldwide Inc. is giving managers access to talent data so that they can integrate it with business data to make more effective and strategic decisions about talent and performance.[77] This allows managers to perform workforce planning by seeing the gaps between workforce projections and available supply of staff or projected turnover, and modelling different scenarios.

Mobile devices refer to smartphones and tablet computers. Mobile devices are increasingly being used to provide employees with anytime and anywhere access to HR processes and other work-related information as well as collaborative tools. For example, employees can use their devices to enter time card information, check their pay stubs, share knowledge, participate in a learning event, check for career opportunities, and receive coaching and feedback. For example, Best Buy uses an app-based training tool known as Gravity. Gravity allows employees to scan products from their mobile devices to instantly educate themselves about a product and get information. Gravity provides the employee with product details, warranty information, video demonstrations, selling tools, and FAQs.[78]

Cloud computing allows companies to lease software and hardware and employees don't even know the location of the computers, databases, and applications they are using (they are in the "cloud"). Cloud computing refers to a computing system that provides information technology infrastructure over a network in a self-service, modifiable, and on-demand model.[79] Many companies have moved their HRIS to the cloud or are considering doing so in the next few years.[80] Clouds can be delivered on-demand via the Internet (public cloud)

cloud computing
A computing system that provides information technology infrastructure over a network in a self-service, modifiable, and on-demand model

or restricted to use by a single company (private cloud). Cloud computing gives companies and their employees access to applications and information from mobile devices rather than relying solely on personal computers. It also allows groups to work together in new ways, provide greater access to large company databases, and can make employees more productive by allowing them to more easily share documents and information. This means that tools for conducting people analytics using metrics on turnover, absenteeism, and performance, as well as social media and collaboration tools such as Twitter, blogs, Google documents, and YouTube videos, will be more easily accessible and available for use. Cloud computing also can make it easier for employees to access training programs from a variety of vendors and educational institutions. Siemens has a cloud computing system for its more than 400,000 employees who work in 190 countries. This allowed Siemens to standardize its global recruitment and development processes into a single system using the cloud.[81]

One of the most important uses of Internet technology is the development of HR dashboards. An **HR dashboard** is a series of indicators or metrics that managers and employees have access to on the company intranet or HRIS. The HR dashboard provides access to important HR metrics for people analytics inputs. HR dashboards are important for determining the value of HR practices and how they contribute to business goals. As a result, the use of dashboards is critical for evidence-based HR discussed earlier in the chapter. For example, Cisco Systems views building talent as a priority, so it has added to its dashboard of people measures a metric to track how many people move and why.[82] This allows Cisco to identify divisions that are developing new talent.

HR dashboard
HR metrics such as productivity and absenteeism that are accessible by employers and managers through the company intranet or human resource information system

High-Performance Work Systems and Virtual Teams

Effective management of human resources can form the foundation of a **high-performance work system**—an organization in which technology, organizational structure, people, and processes all work together seamlessly to give an organization an advantage in the competitive environment. As technology changes the ways organizations manufacture, transport, communicate, predict, and keep track of information, human resource management must ensure that the organization has the right people to meet the new challenges. New technology causes changes in skill requirements and work roles and often results in redesigning work structures (e.g., using work teams).[83]

high-performance work system
An organization in which technology, organizational structure, people, and processes all work together seamlessly to give an organization an advantage in the competitive environment.

High-performance work systems maximize the fit between the company's social system (employees) and its technical system.[84] For example, computer-integrated manufacturing uses robots and computers to automate the manufacturing process. The computer allows the production of different products simply through reprogramming. As a result, labourer, material handler, operator/assembler, and maintenance jobs may be merged into one position. Computer-integrated manufacturing requires employees to monitor equipment and troubleshoot problems with sophisticated equipment, share information with other employees, and understand the relationships between all components of the manufacturing process.[85] Maintaining a high-performance work system might also include development of training programs, recruitment of people with new skill sets, and establishment of rewards for behaviours such as teamwork, flexibility, and learning. Chapter 11 examines high-performance work systems in greater detail.

Besides changing the way that products are built or services are provided within companies, technology has allowed companies to form partnerships with one or more other companies. **Virtual teams** refer to teams that are separated by time, geographic distance, culture, and/or organizational boundaries and that rely almost exclusively on technology (e.g. messaging, apps, Internet, videoconferencing) to interact and complete their projects. Virtual teams can be formed within one company whose facilities are scattered throughout the country or the world. A company may also use virtual teams in partnerships with suppliers or competitors to pull together the necessary talent to complete a project or speed the delivery of a product to the marketplace. For example, Art & Logic software developers all work remotely from across Canada and the United States from home offices, rented office space, or at a co-working facility.[86] Their clients represent a diverse set of industries, including education, aerospace, music technology, consumer electronics, entertainment, and financial services. The project teams work on the most unusual and difficult problems, which developers at other companies have failed to solve. Art & Logic tries to accommodate the unique schedule and work-style requirements of its developers, but its work is highly collaborative within project teams. Every project consists of at least a project manager/developer and has a maximum of five to seven developers. Teams use Google's apps for sharing documents and communicating (both within the team and with clients).

virtual teams
Teams that are separated by time, geographic distance, culture, and/or organizational boundaries and that rely almost exclusively on technology to interact and complete their projects.

Thinking Ethically

Using Data Analytics Responsibly

"There are certain things that, mathematically, may sound right but, ethically, [do] not," says Arun Chidambaram, global head of talent analytics at Pfizer. In these instances, the talent analytics team defers to legal, HR and other business analysts. "Sometimes data science takes a back step when it comes to sensitive topics such as employment law and data privacy rights."

Pfizer is not the only company advocating for taking a balanced approach to the use of data and analytics. At General Motors, the Talent Analytics team is integrating human capital analytics into organizational decision making and HR practices to drive performance. However, GM is mindful that success is dependent upon the trust that GM employees have about how the data is being used. With a global workforce of 212,000 employees who work in 23 time zones and speak more than 50 languages, integrating data collection technologies to optimize workplace operations is accomplished through a balanced approach.

Chief Talent Officer Michael Arena explains that "at GM, there are no electronic badges, the company does not track email and calendars; it it does not fit employees with odometers, heart monitors, and calorie counters." Data collection is "mostly limited to the tried-and-true," and qualitative approaches are integrated with survey and existing data to use analytics to answer questions. For example, employee engagement is a priority at GM and every 24 months a comprehensive survey is conducted. Kelly Kuras, GM's senior manager of engagement, explains how the data is supplemented with observational insights, conducted by trained HR professionals, to look for patterns in the context of the work environments that would account for high vs. moderate employee engagement results. Insights gained from these observations are used along with the data for action planning. According to Arena, "observations can unmask subtleties that statistics miss." "Second, there is a contract around data collection. Organizations have to manage employees' trust that the data are accurate and used responsibly. . . . We don't take the statistical data as being 100 percent absolute."

Questions

1. Do you think it is appropriate for organizations to monitor employee behaviour with sensors and surveillance that monitor how they work and collaborate? Would you trust an employer that collected this type of information?
2. Why is it important to not rely exclusively on quantitative data when making decisions about people?

Sources: Rachel Ramosa, "Confused by analytics? Take Pfizer's prescription," *HR Tech News,* May 18, 2018, www.hrtechnologynews.com, accessed June 20, 2018, "25 Truths about Talent Management: Insights from The 2018 Talent Management Strategies Conference," *The Conference Board,* (2017), pp. 1-21; Patti P. Phillips, and Rebecca L. Ray, "Human Capital Analytics @ Work Volume 2, *The Conference Board,*. (2017), pp. 1-56.

How Is This Book Organized?

This chapter has provided an overview of human resource management as well as a summary of trends and opportunities impacting employees, managers and supervisors, HR professionals, and organizations. In this book, the topics are organized according to the broad areas of human resource management shown in Table 1.7. The numbers in the table refer to the part and chapter numbers.

Along with examples highlighting how HRM helps a company maintain high performance, the chapters offer various other features to help you connect the principles to real-world situations. "HR Oops!" boxes identify situations gone wrong and invite you to find better alternatives. "HR How-To" boxes provide details about how to carry out a practice in each HR area. "Did You Know?" boxes are snapshots of interesting statistics related to chapter topics. "Thinking Ethically" at the end of each chapter demonstrates ethical issues in managing human resources. "Experiencing HR" are experiential exercises that encourage exploration of real-word HR topics and situations in both individual and group settings. New to this edition are Evidence-based HRM and HRM Social chapter-ending case studies. These case studies provide stories that illustrate how evidence-based HRM and social media is integrated in the context of human resource management.

TABLE 1.7

Topics Covered in This Book

Part 1: The Human Resource Environment
1. Strategies, Trends, and Opportunities for Human Resource Management 2. The Legal Context for HRM and Creating Safe and Healthy Workplaces
Part 2: Preparing for and Acquiring Human Resources
3. Analyzing Work and Designing Jobs 4. Planning for and Recruiting Human Resources 5. Selecting Employees
Part 3: Managing Talent
6. Training, Learning, and Development 7. Managing Employees' Performance
Part 4: Compensating and Rewarding Human Resources
8. Total Rewards
Part 5: Meeting Other HR Goals
9. Labour Relations 10. Managing Human Resources Globally 11. Creating and Sustaining High-Performance Organizations

SUMMARY

LO1 Define human resource management and explain how HRM contributes to and supports an organization's strategies and performance.

Human resource management consists of an organization's "people practices"—the policies, practices, and systems that influence employees' behaviours, attitudes, and performance. HRM influences who works for the organization and the experience employees have at work. The organization's human resources have the potential to be a source of sustainable competitive advantage. As part of its strategic role, HR can demonstrate the impact of human resource practices on company results by engaging in evidence-based HRM. Sustainability, organizational agility, and diversity characterize successful organizations. The organizational context is increasingly globalized and rapidly changing, requiring relevant and agile approaches to all HR functions and processes.

LO2 Summarize competencies, careers, professional accreditation, and ethics in human resource management.

Human resources professionals require substantial and varied competencies. Careers in HRM may involve specialized work in fields such as talent acquisition, total rewards, or labour relations—or work as generalists, performing a full range of HR accountabilities. Provincial/territorial associations manage the certification process and award professional designations. Work is underway throughout Canada to move HR from an unregulated to a self-regulated profession. Human resources professionals are required to uphold high ethical standards including duties to the public, profession, clients and employers, and individuals in the workplace.

LO3 Explain the role of supervisors and managers in human resource management.

Supervisors and managers must be familiar with their own important role in managing human resources and implementing HR processes. Supervisors and managers are likely to analyze work, interview job candidates, participate in selection decisions, provide training, set goals, provide coaching and feedback, provide performance feedback, and recommend pay increases. On a day-to-day basis, supervisors and managers represent the company to their employees, so they also play an important role in employee and labour relations.

LO4 Describe trends in the composition and expectations of the labour force.

Canada's labour force is aging, multi-generational, and diverse. Immigration is an important force for population and labour force growth. The Indigenous population is growing more rapidly than the non-Indigenous population and is characterized by having many young people under the age of 14 years. The educational attainment of the labour force is increasing and knowledge workers hold a position of power in the workplace.

LO5 Discuss how technology is impacting human resource management.

Technology is reshaping how we live and work. Social networking, artificial intelligence, and robotics influence many aspects of HRM. Companies continue to use Human Resource Information Systems to store data and support decision making, and mobile devices enable timely and convenient access to HR processes. Cloud computing has created capabilities for people to work collaboratively and virtual teams rely heavily on technology. In a high-performance work system, technology, structure, people, and processes work together seamlessly.

CRITICAL THINKING QUESTIONS

1. How can human resource management contribute to a company's success and sustainability?
2. Consider a job that you have (or had). What moments or critical events were most influential in contributing to your employee experience? How does (did) your employee experience impact your level of engagement? Discuss.
3. Based on this chapter's description, does a career in human resource management appeal to you? Why or why not? In your opinion, which would be more interesting—a position as an HR specialist or an HR generalist? Explain.
4. How does implementing evidence-based HRM including the use of people (human capital) analytics change the role and competency requirements of human resources professionals?
5. What skills are important for success in human resource management? Which of these skills are already strengths of yours? Which would you like to develop further?
6. Why do all managers and supervisors need knowledge and skills related to human resource management?
7. How does each of the following labour force trends affect HRM?
   a. Aging of the workforce
   b. Diversity
   c. Shift to knowledge workers
   d. Increasing levels of education of the workforce
8. Review the description of each of the generations in the workforce. Does this information match your understanding and experience? What additions or changes do you suggest to the narrative on the generation you associate most closely with?
9. Why does HR need technology and data?

EXPERIENCING HR—HOW IS HRM IMPACTED?

This chapter described trends shaping human resource management, including the aging of the workforce, the multi-generational workforce, diversity, and the impact of technology. Alone or with a partner, list two or three of the trends that interest you. Then select a manager or employee who would be willing to talk about these trends for about 15 minutes—someone in human resource management or in a different field that interests you.

With your partner if you have one, interview the person. Summarize each trend you listed, and ask your interviewee to describe any impact of that trend that they have observed at work. Take notes.

In a paragraph, summarize what you learned. In a second paragraph, analyze the impact on human resource management. If your interviewee noted specific opportunities (or challenges), suggest how HR professionals might help the organization achieve its strategy.

CASE STUDY: EVIDENCE-BASED HRM

Quantifying the Employee Experience

IBM has literally "done the math" for putting employee experience at the centre of its people management practices. Diane Gherson, chief human resources officer at IBM, explains: "Like a lot of other companies, we started with the belief that if people felt great about working with us, our clients would too. That wasn't a new thought, but it's certainly one we took very seriously, going back about four or five years. We've since seen it borne out. We've found that employee engagement explains two-thirds of our client experience scores. And if we're able to increase client satisfaction by five points on an account, we see an extra 20 percent in revenue, on average."

IBM started with an initial question, "So, what is the ideal employee experience at work?" as the starting point to explore the relationship between employee experience and client experience. This initial question was later reframed into three questions to leverage a path to improved job performance and sustained competitive advantage:

1. What is the ideal employee experience in today's workplace?
2. What impact could a positive employee experience have on key outcomes?
3. How can organizations drive more positive and human employee experiences?

To answer these questions, IBM's Smarter Workforce Institute and Globoforce's WorkHuman® Research Institute partnered to carry out a global research study consisting of three phases:

- **Phase 1**—Literature review and identification of constructs related to a positive employee experience.
- **Phase 2**—Construct measurement: implementation of a global survey of more than 23,000 IBM employees in 45 countries and territories.
- **Phase 3**—Development of an Employee Experience Index and key leadership and workplace/HR practices to enhance employee experience.

IBM used the findings to leverage changes to HR offerings and brought employees directly into the design process. For example, Millennial employees were brought in to co-design a learning platform that is individually personalized for each of IBM's 380,000 employees. This personalization includes considering how people consume content on their devices, their role, organizing content into channels, and providing a live-chat adviser.

IBM measures its HR programs and processes with a Net Promoter Score (NPS) rather than classic satisfaction ratings. NPS is a core measurement for rating customer experience and is calculated using a 0–10 scale for the question: *"How likely is it that you would recommend [brand] to a friend or colleague?"* Promoters are loyal enthusiasts (score 9–10); Passives are satisfied but unenthusiastic (score 7–8); Detractors are unhappy (score 0–6). NPS provides better feedback on what people are experiencing but it's much more difficult to get a high rating because the percentage of Detractors is subtracted from the percentage of Promoters. As a result, Net Promoter Scores range from –100 (if everyone is a Detractor) to 100 (if everyone is a Promoter). At the time of publication in 2018, IBM's learning and development NPS was 60. According to Gherson, chief human resources officer, "that's in the excellent range, but of course there's still room to improve."

Questions

1. What is your reaction to IBM's approach to "co-creating the employee experience" by bringing employees into the design process for HR programs?
2. How could smaller organizations adapt IBM's approach to evidence-based HRM to support strategy and decision making?

Sources: Lisa Burrell, "Co-Creating the Employee Experience," *Harvard Business Review*, March/April 2018, pp. 54-58; "The Employee Experience Index," *IBM Smarter Workforce & Globoforce*, September 2016, pp. 1-12; "What is Net Promoter?" www.netpromoter.com, accessed June 25, 2018.

CASE STUDY: HRM SOCIAL

Glassdoor Opens the Way to Better Communication

Anonymous employee reviews about what it's like to work for the company—does that sound like a recruiting advantage or a public relations nightmare? Employee reviews are one of the information services of Glassdoor, a job website featuring employee-provided reviews and salary information along with employer-provided job listings. Employers might see a loss of control over information sharing, but Glassdoor also lets employers respond to reviews and gather data about what people are saying and doing on the site.

Nestlé Purina PetCare, employing approximately 600 people across Canada, treats Glassdoor as a means to foster better communication with employees. Purina has a reputation for treating its employees well, with benefits including a pet-friendly work culture intended to keep business decisions focused on pets. But management understands that perks alone do not create a favourable work environment. The company also makes a practice of listening to employees and responding to their concerns.

Purina's human resource department monitors employee comments on Glassdoor and prepares a summary to include in its monthly report to executives. Steve Degnan, chief human resources officer, says Purina also investigates and responds to any complaints it sees. At one point the department noticed a pattern of employees complaining that it was difficult to balance the demands of work and their personal lives. The department responded by creating a video in which top managers acknowledged the problem and suggested ways to address it, such as being more careful to consider the timing and length of meetings. A survey after the video was distributed, showed that 40 percent of employees immediately saw "a definite change."

Questions

1. In what ways is knowledge a source of power for workers in this example? In what ways does the knowledge sharing on Glassdoor impact Purina's human resources professionals? Managers and supervisors?
2. Besides opinions about their company, what other kinds of knowledge could employees constructively share on social media (Glassdoor and other tools)?

Sources: Purina website, www.purina.ca, accessed June 23, 2018; Glassdoor website, www.glassdoor.ca, accessed June 23, 2018; Nestlé USA, "Nestlé Purina PetCare Honored as One of the Best Places to Work in 2016," news release, December 9, 2015, http://www.nestleusa.com; Angela Mueller, "Top Dogs: Why Nestlé Purina PetCare Is Consistently a Best Place to Work," *St. Louis Business Journal*, March 13, 2015, http://www.bizjournals.com; Caryn Freeman, "Value Placed on Feedback Boosts Nestlé Purina to Top of Glassdoor List," *HR Focus*, February 2015, pp. 3–4.

CHAPTER 2

The Legal Context for HRM and Creating Safe and Healthy Workplaces

WHAT DO I NEED TO KNOW?

After reading this chapter, you should be able to:

LO1	Explain the overall context and legal framework for human resource management in Canada.
LO2	Discuss major areas of employment legislation including their relevance and implications for human resource management.
LO3	Identify the requirements and implications of workplace health and safety.
LO4	Discuss the ways employers promote worker health and safety.

Harold Stiver / Alamy Stock Photo

Public Services and Procurement Canada (PSPC) serves federal departments and agencies in a variety of capacities including property management of iconic government buildings. PSPC was recently recognized as one of Canada's Best Diversity Employers.

PSPC Recognized as a Best Diversity Employer

Public Services and Procurement Canada (PSPC), which serves federal departments and agencies as "the central purchasing agent, real property manager, treasurer, accountant, pay and pension administrator, integrity adviser and linguistic authority," was recently recognized as one of Canada's Best Diversity Employers. The award is based upon a review of an organization's diversity and inclusiveness initiatives.[1]

With more than 11,000 employees in Canada, Public Services and Procurement Canada "participates in the Federal Internship for Newcomers Program, is piloting a program to eliminate language-related barriers to career advancement, offering second language scholarships to high-potential individuals, launched a Positive Space initiative, has formal guidelines for gender transition, is developing a strategy to address official languages, hosts an annual Indigenous Awareness Week, and maintains a procurement strategy to increase contracts with Aboriginal businesses."[2] Employee resource groups at Public Services and Procurement Canada include persons with disabilities, visible minorities, Aboriginal peoples, LGBTQ2+, Managers Community Network, National Youth Network, and a pilot Cancer Support project. These resource groups receive funding to host awareness events and promote initiatives for their networks.[3]

Introduction

As we saw in Chapter 1, human resource management takes place in the context of the company's goals and society's expectations for how a company should operate. In Canada, the federal, provincial, and territorial governments have set some limits on how an organization can practise human resource management. Among these limits are requirements intended to foster fairness in hiring and employment practices and to protect the health and safety of workers while they are on the job. Questions about a company's performance in these areas can result in employee turnover, human rights complaints, lawsuits, and negative publicity that will cause serious problems for a company's success and survival. Conversely, a company can gain a competitive advantage over its competitors by going beyond just legal compliance to find ways of linking fair and respectful employment and worker safety to business goals such as building a workforce that is highly motivated and attuned to customers.

One point to make at the outset is that managers often want a list of dos and don'ts that will keep them out of legal trouble. Some managers rely on strict rules such as "Don't ever ask a female applicant if she is married," rather than learning the reasons behind those rules. Clearly, certain practices are illegal or at least inadvisable, and this chapter will discuss these areas. However, managers who merely focus on how to avoid breaking the law are not thinking about how to be ethical or how to attract and engage people in the best way to carry out the company's mission. The legal landscape for human resource management is complex, evolving, and differs among jurisdictions. This chapter introduces ways to think proactively about fair employment and workplace health and safety, and provides a starting point for exploring the requirements for where you live and work.

LO1 The Legal Context for HRM in Canada

Valuing Diversity and Inclusion

As discussed in Chapter 1, Canada is a diverse nation, and becoming more so. In addition, many Canadian companies have customers and operations in more than one country. Managers differ in how they approach the opportunities and challenges related to this diversity. Some define a diverse workforce as a competitive advantage that brings a wider pool of talent and greater insight into the needs and behaviours of their diverse customers. These organizations, including Public Services and Procurement Canada described in the chapter opening, have developed a reputation for valuing *diversity* and *inclusion.*

Despite an "overwhelming strategic focus on diversity, many Canadian organizations are still reporting that, while overt racism, sexism, and homophobia are not as prevalent as they were a decade age, diversity in workplaces has not yet translated into true inclusiveness."[4] **Diversity** refers to having "people of different backgrounds and experiences represented in the workplace."[5] Diversity can be calculated, tracked, and reported—it's about *differences.* However, **inclusion** is about *behaviour* i.e. the *"how"* that creates an environment where people experience "a sense of belonging, feeling respected, valued, and seen for who we are as individuals."[6] Viewed this way, inclusion is not only the right thing to do but also the essential means to achieve higher operational performance that leverages how the organization "develops strategy, sets goals, makes decisions, runs meetings, solves problems, and engages people, and how people interact."[7]

> **diversity** Having people of different backgrounds and experiences represented in the workplace.
>
> **inclusion** A sense of belonging: feeling respected, valued, and seen for who we are as individuals.

See Table 2.1 for a sampling of diversity initiatives implemented by some of the organizations recently recognized as "Canada's Best Diversity Employers."

TABLE 2.1

Sampling of Diversity Initiatives at Some of Canada's Best Diversity Employers (2018)

Organization	Initiative
Accenture	LGBT Ally training program
Bell	Language diversity program to help employees improve their French or English
Canada Mortgage and Housing Corporation (CMHC)	Online diversity training materials on topics including mental health, unconscious bias, and second-language training
CIBC	Diversity toolkit for people managers
Government of Northwest Territories	Training on Aboriginal cultural awareness and mental health
Lafarge Canada Inc.	Hosts mock interviews and workshops on interview preparation and networking strategies in partnership with Immigrant Services Calgary
Manulife	Influencing skills for female leaders (3-day program)
Red River College	Conducted an inclusive company climate review; Aboriginal elders available for staff and students
SaskPower	Head office accessibility was reviewed in collaboration with Spinal Cord Injury SK
Shell Canada	"Lunch and Learns" on unconscious bias, disability, and Indigenous awareness
Sodexo Canada	Workshops on unconscious bias; training on inclusion and generations

Source: Richard Yerema and Kristina Leung, "Canada's Best Diversity Employers (2018)," *Mediacorp Inc.*, www.canadastop100/diversity, accessed July 4, 2018.

Culture of Workplace Health and Safety

The protection of employee health and safety is regulated by the government; however, the effective management of health and safety in the workplace includes more than legal compliance. NB Power takes a holistic approach to health and safety and makes it one of the eight integrated HR functions. The other seven functions are recruitment, compensation, diversity, leadership, relationship management, well-being, and labour relations.[8]

Increasingly, organizations are taking a strategic approach to occupational health and safety by adopting a values-based commitment to safe operations as a way to protect people. Additional benefits to business include cost savings by reducing worker injuries, fatalities, occupational disease, and property damage as well as improving employee relations, reliability, and productivity improvement.[9] Employers and employees share responsibility for creating and maintaining safe and healthy work environments. Employer–employee partnerships are put in place to create a climate and culture of safety in the organization in addition to ensuring compliance.[10] Ultimately, however, employers have a legal duty to provide their employees with a physically and psychologically safe work environment.

The Legal Framework for HRM

Federal, provincial, and territorial governments in Canada all play an important role in creating the legal environment for human resource management. Approximately 94 percent of Canadian employers and their employees are covered by provincial and territorial legislation. The remaining 6 percent are covered by federal legislation. Table 2.2 summarizes the types of organizations that fall under federal and provincial /territorial legislation.

Federal, provincial, and territorial employment-related laws tend to mirror one another; however, some differences exist. It is important for employers to be aware of and comply with all legal requirements. For organizations with workers in more than one province, territory, or industry it can be time consuming and challenging to maintain compliance with this web of legal requirements. As mentioned previously in the chapter, many proactive human resource departments and their organizations are moving beyond a mindset of compliance and are recognizing the strategic importance of valuing the various goals pursued through the legislation; for example, diversity, inclusion, privacy, and the health and safety of employees.

TABLE 2.2

What Types of Organizations Are Regulated by the Provinces and Territories versus the Federal Government?

Organizations Regulated by the Federal Government	Organizations Regulated by Provinces and Territories
Banks	All other businesses not listed. Examples include:
Marine shipping, ferry and port services	• Retail and hospitality businesses, such as a store, a restaurant, a hotel, etc.
Air transportation, including airports, aerodromes, and airlines	• Hospitals and health care providers
Railway and road transportation that involves crossing provincial or international borders	• Schools, colleges, and universities
Canals, pipelines, tunnels, and bridges (crossing provincial borders)	• Most manufacturers
Telephone, telegraph, and cable systems	
Radio and television broadcasting	
Grain elevators, feed and seed mills	
Uranium mining and processing	
Businesses dealing with the protection of fisheries	
Many First Nations activities	
Federal departments, agencies, and most federal Crown corporations	

Sources: "Federally Regulated Businesses and Industries,"https://www.canada.ca/en/employment-social-development/programs/employment-equity/regulated-industries.html, accessed July 5, 2018; "Canadian Human Rights Commission Overview," www.chrc-ccdp.ca/discrimination/federally_regulated-en.asp, accessed April 13, 2008; Anti-Discrimination Casebook, p. 1, www.chrc-ccdp.ca/legis&poli, retrieved February 18, 2004; and Human Resource Management Laws and Regulations Government of Canada, http://hrmanagement.gc.ca, accessed February 18, 2004.

LO2 Employment-related Legislation

This section will cover human rights, employment equity, privacy, employment/labour standards, and pay equity. Subsequent sections will cover employee health and safety. It is important to note that these topic areas are intertwined. For example, treating people with dignity and respect and providing a harassment-free workplace promotes psychological well-being, and the recent legalization of cannabis for recreational purposes (discussed in the health and safety section) has implications for employees' human rights and privacy at work.

Protecting Human Rights at Work

All the jurisdictions have human rights legislation, which has implications beyond employment situations; however, the focus in this chapter will be directed toward application within the workplace. The purpose of human rights legislation is to remove discrimination. **Discrimination** means "treating someone differently, negatively, or adversely because of their race, age, religion, sex, or other prohibited ground."[11]

Direct discrimination involves policies or practices that clearly make a distinction on the basis of a prohibited ground (see Figure 2.1). **Indirect discrimination** involves policies or practices that appear to be neutral but have an *adverse effect* on the basis of a prohibited ground. For example, a company that has a policy of not employing any part-time employees appears to have a policy that can be equally applied to all applicants and existing employees. However, the effect of this policy is not neutral—someone who

discrimination Treating someone differently, negatively, or adversely because of their race, age, religion, sex, or other prohibited ground.

direct discrimination Policies or practices that clearly make a distinction on the basis of a prohibited ground.

indirect discrimination Policies or practices that appear to be neutral but have an adverse effect on the basis of a prohibited ground.

FIGURE 2.1

Prohibited Grounds of Discrimination in Employment

Prohibited Ground	Federal	BC	AB	SK	MB	ON	QC	NB	NS	PEI	NL	NWT	YT	NU
Race	*	*	*	*	*	*	*	*	*	*	*	*	*	*
National or ethnic origin (place of origin)	*	*	*	*	*	*	*	*	*	*	*	*	*	*
Colour	*	*	*	*	*	*	*	*	*	*	*	*	*	*
Religion or creed	*	*	*	*	*	*	*	*	*	*	*	*	*	*
Age	*	*	*	*	*	*	*	*	*	*	*	*	*	*
Sex (gender; pregnancy; gender identity or expression)	*	*	*	*	*	*	*	*	*	*	*	*	*	*
Sexual orientation	*	*	*	*	*	*	*	*	*	*	*	*	*	*
Marital status	*	*	*	*	*	*	*	*	*	*	*	*	*	*
Family status	*	*	*	*	*	*	*	*	*	*	*	*	*	*
Disability (physical or mental)	*	*	*	*	*	*	*	*	*	*	*	*	*	*
Pardoned conviction (record of offences)	*	*				*				*	*	*	*	*
Political belief (activity or association)		*			*		*	*	*	*	*	*	*	
Source of income (social condition) e.g., receipt of public assistance		*	*	*	*	*	*		*	*	*		*	*

Note: This chart is for quick reference purposes. To ensure currency and for interpretation and/or application of specific details, refer to the relevant Human Rights Commission(s).

Sources: From "Prohibited Grounds of Discrimination in Canada," pp. 1–3, Canadian Human Rights Commission, 1998. URL: www.chrc-ccdp.ca/discrimination/grounds-en.asp, retrieved December 6, 2004. Updates: "Overview of Human Rights Code by Province and Territory in Canada," *Canadian Centre for Diversity and Inclusion,"* January, 2018, https://ccdi.ca, pp. 1–35, accessed July 5, 2018; "What is Discrimination? www.chrc-ccdp.gc.ca/eng/content/what-discrimination, retrieved March 23, 2015; "Mandatory Retirement in Canada," www.hrsdc.gc.ca/en/lp/spila/clli/eslc/19mandatory_retirement.shtml, retrieved April 13, 2008; and "Retiring Mandatory Retirement," February 21, 2008, www.cbc.ca/newsbackground/retirement/mandatory/retirement.html, retrieved April 19, 2009.

has family responsibilities would be denied employment or denied the opportunity to reduce their work hours.

In summary, all individuals have a right to an equal chance to be hired, keep a job, get a promotion, or receive other work benefit regardless of personal characteristics; for example, race, colour, national or ethnic origin, religion, sexual orientation, age, marital status, sex, family status, and physical or mental disability.

How Would You Know?

How would you know if you had been discriminated against at work? Decisions about human resources are so complex that discrimination is often difficult to identify and prove. However, legal scholars and court rulings have arrived at some ways to show evidence of discrimination.

Differential Treatment

One sign of discrimination is **differential treatment**—differing treatment of individuals, where the differences are based on a prohibited ground such as the individuals' race, colour, religion, sex, national origin, age, or disability. For example, differential treatment would include

differential treatment Differing treatment of individuals where the differences are based on a prohibited ground.

hiring or promoting one person over an equally qualified person because of the individual's race. Suppose a company fails to hire women with school-age children (claiming the women will be frequently absent) but hires men with school-age children. In that situation, the women are victims of differential treatment, because they are being treated differently on the basis of their sex.

To avoid complaints of differential treatment, companies can evaluate the questions and investigations they use in making employment decisions. These should be applied consistently. For example, if the company investigates conviction records of job applicants, it should investigate them for all applicants, not just for some applicants. Companies may want to avoid some types of questions altogether. For example, questions about marital status can cause problems, because interviewers may unfairly make different assumptions about men and women. A common stereotype about women has been that a married woman is less flexible or more likely to get pregnant than a single woman, in contrast to the assumption that a married man is more stable and committed to his work.

bona fide occupational requirement (BFOR)
A necessary (not merely preferred) requirement for performing a job.

Is differential treatment ever legal? The courts have held that in some situations, a factor such as sex or religion may be a **bona fide occupational requirement (BFOR)**, that is, a necessary (not merely preferred) qualification for performing a job. In some cases, a core function of the job may be related to a prohibited (protected) ground. For example, a reference from a Parish Priest is required to submit an application for a teaching position in the Catholic School system in Regina, Saskatchewan.[12] However, it is very difficult to think of many jobs where criteria such as sex and religion are BFORs. Although employers should seek ways to perform the job so that these restrictions are not needed, for example, a job may require a specified level of visual capability to be performed effectively and safely, thereby eliminating someone who does not meet this requirement.

It is the employer's responsibility to prove the existence of a BFOR if any complaint of discrimination should arise. In the widely publicized *Meiorin* case, Tawny Meiorin, a female forest firefighter, lost her job when she failed to meet a required aerobic fitness standard that had been established by the British Columbia Public Service Employee Relations Commission. This standard had been put in place as a minimum requirement for all firefighters. She lost her job after failing *one* aspect of a minimum fitness standard—taking 49.4 seconds too long to complete a 2.5 kilometre run.[13] She filed a complaint stating that the fitness standard discriminated against women because women usually have less aerobic capability than men. Although the employer argued the standard was a bona fide occupational requirement of the job, the Supreme Court of Canada ultimately ruled the standard was *not* a BFOR—the fitness standard was not reasonably necessary to fulfill a legitimate work-related purpose.[14] Ms. Meiorin was reinstated to her job and received compensation for lost wages and benefits.

Mandatory Retirement

The practice of forcing an employee to retire for the reason of age is a human rights issue and falls under the protection of human rights legislation. All jurisdictions in Canada have legislation that makes mandatory retirement discriminatory unless there is a bona fide occupational requirement due to a specific employment requirement.[15]

What Is the Employer's Duty to Accommodate?

duty to accommodate
An employer's duty to consider how an employee's characteristic such as disability, religion, or sex can be accommodated and to take action so the employee can perform the job.

An employer has a duty to consider how an employee's characteristic such as disability, religion, or other protected ground can be accommodated and to take action so that the employee can perform the job. See Figure 2.2. This duty is referred to as the **duty to accommodate**.

Accommodation may even require that the employee perform another job within their capabilities. Employers' duty to accommodate extends to the point of *undue hardship*—"undue" meaning only if it is so high that the very survival of the organization or business would be threatened or essentially changed.[16]

In the context of religion, this principle recognizes that for some individuals, religious observations and practices may present a conflict with work duties, dress codes, or company practices. For example, some religions require head coverings, or to be able to pray at a particular time, or individuals might need time off to observe the Sabbath or other holy days, when the company might have them scheduled to work. When the employee has a legitimate religious belief requiring accommodation, the employee should communicate this need to the employer. Assuming that it would not present an undue hardship, employers are required to accommodate such religious practices. They may have to adjust schedules so that employees do not have to work on days when their religion forbids it, or they may have to alter dress or grooming requirements.

For employees with disabilities, accommodations also vary according to the individuals' needs—increasingly, however, the emphasis is placed on *abilities* and capabilities rather than focusing on disabilities. For example, Sodexo has a "disABILITY" strategy that advances the inclusion of adults with disabilities. The organization states, "We find people with disabilities are absolutely fantastic at the jobs we put them in. They want to be part of the organization, they stay in the organization,

Adrian Wyld/TCPI/The Canadian Press

Steven Fletcher, Canada's first quadriplegic MP and Member of Cabinet was a two-time Manitoba kayaking champion and had recently graduated from geological engineering studies when in 1996, at the age of 23, his car collided with a moose while driving to work. Steven was paralyzed from the neck down; nevertheless, within one year of the accident, he was accepted into the University of Manitoba's MBA program. Two years later (1999), he was the president of the University of Manitoba Students Union; after serving for two years was elected president of the Progressive Conservative Party of Manitoba. In 2004, Steven won his competitive Winnipeg riding and became a federal member of parliament. He subsequently won the riding three more times.[17]

they grow within the organization, so it works very well for us and for those employees."[18]

Some of the accommodations employers provide include restructuring jobs, making facilities in the workplace more accessible, and modifying equipment. Innovation, Science and Economic Development Canada recently announced a new *Accessible Technology Program* to fund innovative projects that will support Canadians with disabilities to participate more fully in the digital economy. For example, the Neil Squire Society recently received $3 million in funding for "LipSync"—a project to develop and distribute mouth-operated systems that will make digital technologies like laptops and mobile devices more accessible.[19] In some situations, an individual may provide their own accommodation, which the employer permits, as in the case of an employee with vision loss who brings a service dog to work.

Protection from Harassment

Human rights legislation also prohibits all forms of **harassment**. Harassment is "a form of discrimination. It involves any unwanted physical or verbal behaviour that offends or humiliates you."[20] Research from the Queen's School of Business at Queen's University in Kingston, Ontario, found that 31 percent of female and 22 percent of male respondents "had experienced or were currently experiencing workplace harassment." These numbers had decreased slightly since 2012. Dr. Jane Raver, the study's lead, theorizes that an increased public interest in the topic evidenced from media coverage to government legislation has likely led to the decline; however, workplace harassment remains a problem in Canada. She recommends employers establish clear policies supported by education. "Actually outline a code of conduct. Do some training. Let people understand what this looks like and where people cross the line."[21]

harassment A form of discrimination that involves any unwanted physical or verbal behaviour that offends or humiliates you.

For example, following is Seneca College's Discrimination and Harassment Policy Statement:

> It is the Policy of Seneca College that all employees and students have a right to work and study in an environment that asserts the personal worth and dignity of each individual. In order to achieve this objective, Seneca College will not tolerate any form of discrimination and/or harassment in its employment, educational, accommodation or business dealings. Every member of the College community has the right to file a complaint of discrimination/harassment.[22]

Figure 2.2 discusses each of the prohibited grounds of discrimination and provides an example of an allegation of discrimination or harassment made in a work-related situation along with the settlement that the complainant received.

Sexual Harassment

The media spotlight on sexual harassment and the resulting social media hashtag #MeToo has sparked social change and provided a catalyst for leaders and HR professionals to re-examine their own organization's culture and practices. According to Suzanne Hiron, senior communications adviser at the Canadian Human Rights Commission in Ottawa, "Despite all that's been done to reduce

Martin de Jong/Shutterstock.com

"The [#MeToo] movement has given women confidence to speak up regarding inappropriate acts they may have experienced," said Shelley Martin, CEO of Nestlé Canada.[23]

FIGURE 2.2

Human Rights Allegations and Settlements (Federal Prohibited Grounds)

Prohibited Ground	Description	Allegation	Settlement
Race, colour, and national or ethnic origin	These three grounds are related, and it is often difficult to draw clear distinctions between them. They are intended to get at the societal problem referred to as "racism."	The complainant alleged that a disgruntled customer used a distasteful tone and made racial slurs. She alleged that the respondent (employer) asked her to deal with the situation by hiding whenever the customer entered her area. Her employment was subsequently terminated for poor performance.	• Letter of reference • Financial compensation for general damages • Financial compensation for pain and suffering • Reimbursement of legal fees • Assistance with job search
Religion or creed	Discrimination has occurred because of knowledge of one's religion or a perception of that religion. *Note:* When an individual alleges adverse effect discrimination from some policy or decision, the following three questions must be answered "yes": • Is the belief sincerely held? • Is it religious? • Is it the cause of the objection being made?	The complainant cannot work on Saturdays because of her religious beliefs. She alleged that, because of this, her supervisor required her to work every Saturday. Eventually, her employment was terminated.	• Financial compensation for general damages • Letter of regret
Age	The ground can refer to: • An individual's actual age. • Membership in a specific age group, e.g., over 55. • A generalized characterization of his age, e.g., too old or too young.	The complainant, who is 47 years old, alleged that he was denied education assistance normally provided to younger employees. The complainant also alleged that remarks about his age were made and written comments included in his employee file.	• Removal from the complainant's file of all reference to his age or to the number of years he could remain as an employee • Assurance that having filed a complaint will not negatively affect his employment • Financial compensation for future tuition and books • Reimbursement for tuition and books for past courses
Sex (including pregnancy, gender identity, or gender expression)	Refers to the condition of being, identifying, or expressing one's sex or gender identity.	The complainant handed in her resignation at one point because of an excessive workload, but her employer refused to accept it and she continued working. After she announced that she was pregnant two months later, she alleged that her employer suddenly decided to accept her resignation.	• Financial compensation for lost wages and general damages • Letter of recommendation

(*continued on next page*)

FIGURE 2.2

Human Rights Allegations and Settlements (Federal Prohibited Grounds) (*continued*)

Prohibited Ground	Description	Allegation	Settlement
Sexual orientation	Typically refers to: • heterosexuality • homosexuality • bisexuality	The complainant alleged that, during a job interview, he was asked inappropriate questions about his sexual orientation. In the end, the complainant got the job.	• Letter of regret • Training for all interviewers on the Canadian Human Rights Act
Marital status	Condition of being: • single • legally married • common-law spouses (opposite-sex or same-sex) • widowed • divorced	The complainant and his partner filed separate complaints alleging that the respondent did not take action against a co-worker who made defamatory and harassing remarks about their personal relationship. They allege that the respondent did not provide a harassment-free work environment. Note: This allegation included two grounds: marital status and sex.	• Development of protocol for future instances of sexual harassment • Joint management and union anti-harassment and human rights training • Posting of the respondent's human rights and employment equity policy, and relevant provisions of the collective agreement • Financial compensation for pain and suffering
Family status	Refers to the interrelationship that arises as a result of marriage, legal adoption, ancestral relationship, as well as the relationships between spouses, siblings, uncles or aunts, cousins, etc.	The complainant alleged that her employer denied her several career-enhancing opportunities when she returned to work from maternity leave, and that it ultimately terminated her employment on the pretext that it was downsizing and that her job no longer existed. Note: This allegation included two grounds: family status and sex.	• Expression of regret to the complainant • Financial compensation for general damages
Physical or mental disability	Disability is defined as being either: • Physical or mental • Previous or existing • Including dependence on alcohol or a drug Note: A disability can be either permanent or temporary (e.g., a temporary impairment as a result of an accident, or a treatable illness).	The complainant, who has multiple sclerosis, alleged that her employer, by refusing her a work schedule recommended by her doctor, failed to accommodate her disability.	• Adjustment of the complainant's work schedule to reflect the doctor's recommendations • Briefing session for employees on multiple sclerosis and non-visible disabilities • Occupational training, with half of the training program to be determined by one of the two parties • Reinstatement of leave • Letter of regret • Withdrawal of related grievances

Prohibited Ground	Description	Allegation	Settlement
Pardoned criminal conviction	A conviction for which a pardon has been granted by any authority under law.	The complainant is a truck driver who was required to travel to the United States. Although he had been granted a pardon for a conviction in Canada, he was nevertheless denied entry in the United States. Consequently, his employer laid him off on the ground that he could not fulfill all the requirements of the job.	• Financial compensation

Sources: From "Prohibited Grounds of Discrimination in Canada," pp. 1–3, Canadian Human Rights Commission, 1998. Settlement Examples, www.chrc-ccdp.ca/disputeresolution_reglementdifferends/settlements_ententes-eng.aspx; Discrimination and Harassment, www.chrc-ccdp.ca/discrimination/act_actes-eng.aspx. Canadian Human Rights Commission.

incidents of sexual harassment in the workplace, it continues to rear its ugly head."[24]

The Canada Labour Code defines sexual harassment as "any conduct, comment, gesture, or contact of a sexual nature that is likely to cause offence or humiliation to any employee; or that might, on reasonable grounds, be perceived by that employee as placing a condition of a sexual nature on employment or on any opportunity for training or promotion."[25]

Insights West recently polled 451 working women in Canada and provided the following results:[26]

- More than half of working women (54 percent) say they have "experienced conduct, comments, gestures or contact of a sexual nature that caused them offence or humiliation."
- Thirty percent say they have "experienced conduct, comments, gestures or contact of a sexual nature that they perceived as placing a condition of a sexual nature on their employment (*quid pro quo sexual harassment*) or on any opportunity they might have for training or promotion."

However, as illustrated in Figure 2.3, only 28 percent of the surveyed working women in Canada who experienced behaviour that placed a condition on their employment or future career reported it to a "superior" and/or to the HR department. And only 22 percent filed a complaint after being offended or humiliated by another person's behaviour (*hostile or poisoned work environment sexual harassment*).

Illustrative example of behaviours referred to as hostile or poisoned work environment sexual harassment include:[27]

- derogatory language and/or comments toward women (or men, depending on the circumstances);
- sex-specific derogatory names;
- leering or inappropriate staring;
- displaying or circulating pornography, sexual pictures or cartoons, or other sexual images (including online);
- sexual jokes, including circulating written sexual jokes (e.g., by email);
- unnecessary physical contact, including unwanted touching;
- rough and vulgar humour or language related to gender;
- spreading sexual rumours (including online);
- suggestive or offensive remarks or innuendo about members of a specific gender;
- bragging about sexual prowess;
- questions or discussions about sexual activities;
- paternalistic behaviour based on gender that a person feels undermines their status or position of responsibility.

As noted above, paternalistic behaviour based on gender, which a person feels undermines their status or position of responsibility, may also be determined to be sexual harassment. For example, a "tribunal found an employer's repeated use of terms including "sweetheart," "little lady," "hun," "sweetie," and "dear" to be "terms of diminishment," and that, within the broader context of his other sexualized overtures, the use of these terms created a poisoned work environment.[28] Although a large majority of sexual harassment complaints involve women being harassed by men, sexual harassment can affect anyone.

To ensure a workplace free from harassment, organizations can follow some important steps. In some jurisdictions employers are required to develop an anti-harassment policy making it very clear that harassment will not be tolerated in the workplace. Second, all employees need to

FIGURE 2.3

Who Reported Sexual Harassment to a "Superior and/or HR Department? —Insights West Survey Results

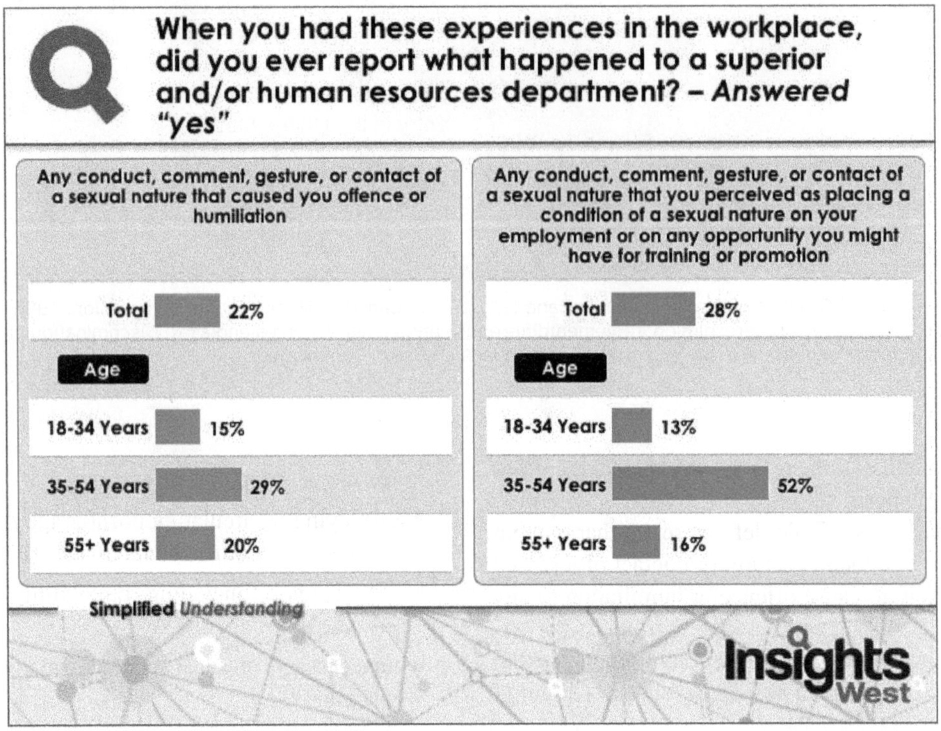

Note: Responses reflect survey respondents who answered "yes" to the question: "When you had these experiences in the workplace, did you ever report what happened to a superior and/or human resources department?"

Source: "Half of Working Women in Canada Have Endured Sexual Harassment, *Insights West,* December 6, 2017, https://insightswest.com/news/half-of-working-women-in-canada-have-endured-sexual-harassment/, accessed July 7, 2018.

be made aware of the policy and receive training. In addition, the organization can develop a mechanism for reporting harassment in a way that encourages people to speak out. Finally, management can prepare to act promptly to discipline those who engage in harassment, as well as to protect the victims of harassment. Rare is the business owner or manager who wants to wait for the government to identify that the organization has failed to meet its legal requirements to treat employees fairly. Instead, out of motives ranging from concern for employee well-being to the desire to avoid costly lawsuits and negative publicity, most companies recognize the importance of complying with these laws and creating safe and respectful workplaces. For example, attention was once again focused on the RCMP when the commissioner offered an apology and $100 million in compensation to settle class-action lawsuits that included 500 female RCMP officers and civilians for allegations that included a range of inappropriate behaviours including harassment, unwanted sexual touching, sexist comments, and rape.[29]

Often, management depends on the expertise of human resources professionals to help to ensure employees are not exposed to behaviours that could be psychologically harmful. Keeping the workplace psychologically safe and healthy will be discussed in more detail later in this chapter.

Employment Equity

Canada's federal employment equity policy was inspired by a report written in 1984 by Justice Rosalie Abella. Employment equity legislation focuses on eliminating employment barriers to the four designated groups who are viewed to have been historically disadvantaged in their employment relationships. The four designated groups are:

- *Women.*
- *Aboriginal peoples* ("An Aboriginal person is a North American Indian or a member of a First Nation, Métis, or Inuit. North American Indians or members of a First Nation include treaty, status, or registered Indians, as well as non-status and non-registered Indians.")[30]

- *Members of visible minorities* ("A person in a visible minority group is someone, other than an Aboriginal person as defined above, who is non-white in colour/race, regardless of place of birth.")[31]
- *Persons with disabilities* ("A person with a disability has a long-term or recurring physical, mental, sensory, psychiatric, or learning impairment.")[32]

Employment equity promotes equitable workforce representation for each of the designated groups. Reporting progress examines *representation*—the share of designated groups in a given labour market (e.g., the entire federally regulated private sector workforce, a specific industry, or a specific organization), relative to *labour market availability* (LMA)—the share of designated group members in the workforce from which the employer(s) could hire. Figure 2.4 provides the progress in representation over time of the four designated employment equity groups in the federally regulated private sector. Members of visible minorities have seen the most progress with their representation, which increased from 11.7 percent in 2001 to 22.2 percent in 2016, surpassing the group's LMA of 17.8 percent. This is the only designated group in the federally regulated private sector whose overall representation surpasses its LMA. The application of employment equity to workforce planning will be discussed in Chapter 4.

Protection of Privacy

Employees expect to have privacy at work; however, most people recognize that when they work for someone, the employer requires certain information about them so to ensure they receive pay and benefits and to ensure their work is being performed in a way that meets the employer's requirements. All of the jurisdictions—provinces, territories, and federal—are subject to privacy laws that regulate how personal information (e.g., personal health information and personal financial information) is handled. The following section will discuss privacy requirements that connect most directly to the employer–employee relationship.

Personal Information Protection and Electronic Documents Act (PIPEDA)
Sets the ground rules for how private-sector organizations collect, use, and disclose personal information in the course of for-profit commercial activities in Canada. It also applies to the personal information of employees of federally-regulated businesses

The **Personal Information Protection and Electronic Documents Act (PIPEDA)** "sets the ground rules for how private-sector organizations collect, use, and disclose personal information in the course of for-profit commercial activities in Canada. It also applies to the personal information of

FIGURE 2.4

Change in Representation over Time in the Federally Regulated Private Sector (Banking, Communication, Transportation, and Other)

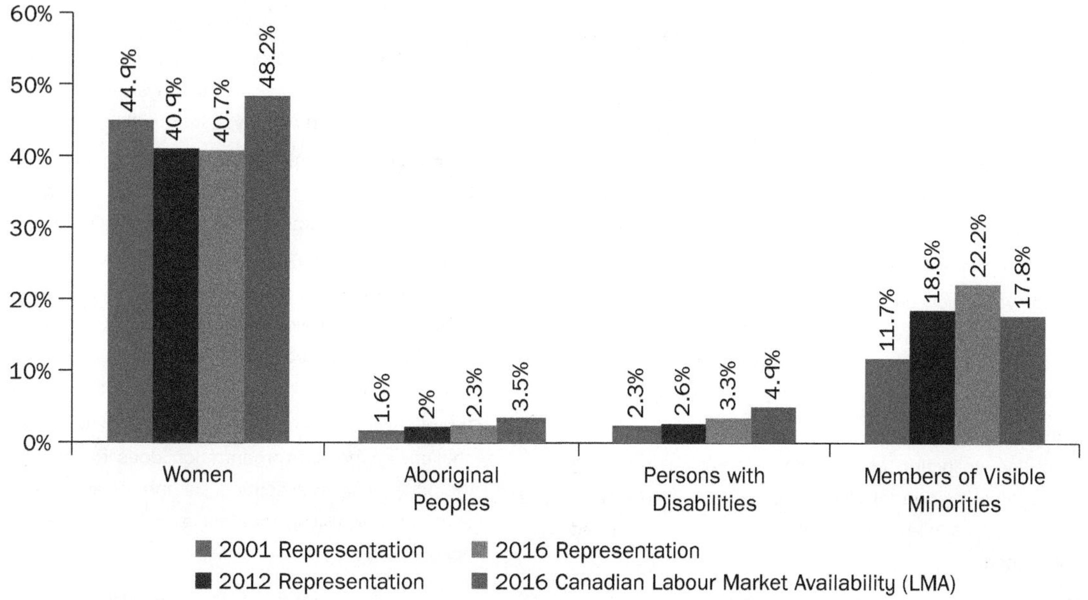

Sources: "Employment Equity Act: Annual Report 2017, Table 1: Designated Group Representation and Attainment: Role of Canadian LMA for the Federally Regulated Private Sector 2015 and 2016 (%)," *Employment and Social Development Canada,* (2018), p. 4 and "Employment Equity Act: Annual Report *2013,* Chart 1: Progress in Representation Over Time in the Federally Regulated Private Sector," *Employment and Social Development Canada,* December 11, 2014, p. 3.

employees of federally regulated businesses." Personal information includes information about your:[33]

- race;
- national or ethnic origin;
- religion
- age;
- marital status;
- medical, education, or employment history;
- financial information;
- DNA;
- identifying numbers such as your social insurance number or driver's licence;
- views or opinions about you as an employee.

This law also gives individuals the right to access and request correction of the personal information these organizations may have collected about them."[34]

PIPEDA generally applies to personal information of employees who work in private-sector organizations that conduct business in Manitoba, New Brunswick, Newfoundland and Labrador, Northwest Territories, Nova Scotia, Nunavut, Ontario, Prince Edward Island, Saskatchewan, and Yukon and always applies to federally regulated organizations that conduct business in Canada (e.g., banking, communications, transportation). PIPEDA does not apply to organizations that operate entirely within Alberta, British Columbia, or Quebec because they have privacy laws recognized as "substantially similar" to PIPEDA. In these provinces the relevant Personal Information Privacy Act (PIPA) applies, e.g., PIPA Alberta and PIPA BC. In addition, provinces and territories in Canada have their own laws that apply to government agencies.[35]

The HR How-To box illustrates responsibilities HR departments have in protecting employees' personal information.

HR How-To

Protecting Employees' Personal Information

PIPEDA's principles serve as a guide to organizations and HR professionals to maintain legal compliance when collecting and using employee information needed for administration and decision making. HR professionals need to consider the following principles when collecting and using employee personal information in the course of all HR activities:

1. **Accountability.** The employer is responsible for personal information it controls. Start by appointing a privacy officer(s).
2. **Identifying purpose.** Before collecting information, the organization needs to identify why it is collecting the information and how it will be used. Conduct a "privacy audit" to determine what information is collected and why it is collected.
3. **Consent.** The organization is responsible for ensuring that employees know and consent to the collection, use, and/or disclosure of personal information. Consider what type of consent is needed for each type of information on the basis of criteria such as the sensitivity of the information.
4. **Limiting collection.** Care must be taken to make sure that the collection of personal information is limited to what is needed for the stated purpose. Use a "reasonable person" test to determine what is considered appropriate.
5. **Limiting use, disclosure, and retention.** Personal information cannot be used or disclosed to others without consent and information can be retained only to meet the stated purpose(s) for which it was collected. Additional care must be taken when HR functions are outsourced. Create minimum and maximum retention times for information collected.
6. **Accuracy.** Information of employees must be current and correct. Keep information accurate and introduce a process to correct errors in a timely way.
7. **Safeguards.** Security protection needs to be put in place. Implement both technical and physical security measures to safeguard employee information.
8. **Openness.** Communicate privacy policies and practices. Consider developing training materials, brochures, or other means of communication about the organization's approach to privacy protection.
9. **Individual access.** Be responsive to employees when they request access to information the organization holds about them. Have a method in place to deal with employee concerns about the accuracy and completeness of information.
10. **Compliance challenges.** Individuals have the power to challenge what the organization does to comply with the principles just described. Be open to employee concerns and be willing to adapt policies and practices to ensure compliance with all aspects.

Sources: "Application of the *Personal Information Protection and Electronic Documents Act* to Employee Records, *Office of the Privacy Commissioner of Canada*, www.priv.ac.ca/resource/fs-fi/02 05 d 18 e.asp, retrieved March 25, 2015; Dianne Rinehart, "The ABC's of the New Privacy Legislation," *Small Business Canada Magazine*6, no. 2 (Spring 2004), p. 7; and "The 10 Principles of the Federal Privacy Law," *Canadian HR Reporter*, March 6, 2004, p. G7.

Privacy legislation principles establish standards for privacy practices and have implications for organizations and their responsibilities to safeguard employee privacy. Decisions made by the Office of the Privacy Commissioner of Canada have confirmed that although employers can collect information on employees about performance, attendance, and potential for advancement, there is little an employer can keep from an employee. For example, an employee of the federal public service demanded to see all the information obtained about her during an assessment review. The employee wanted to see the notes made by the contractor hired to conduct the assessment. These notes contained feedback and comments from other employees. The Office of the Privacy Commissioner of Canada ruled the employee was entitled to this information and that employees cannot be promised confidentiality when they make statements about another person.[36]

Employment/Labour Standards

Federal, provincial, and territorial laws are in place in each jurisdiction to provide minimum standards for employees. Some of the areas covered typically include:

- minimum wage
- overtime pay
- hours of work and work scheduling
- general holidays
- annual vacations
- benefits for part-time workers
- parental leave
- layoff procedures
- terminations and severance pay

A variety of far-reaching and complex changes to employment/labour standards laws have recently been made in some jurisdictions. For example, Ontario's Bill 148, "The Fair Workplaces, Better Jobs Act," provided amendments including increases to minimum wage; increased vacation; providing employees the right to refuse being on call or taking a shift unless four days notice has been provided; enhanced family medical leaves, and new provisions for access to domestic or sexual violence leave. However, some of the provisions have been amended or scrapped by Ontario's Progressive Conservative government. For example, a provision of Bill 148 requiring employers to provide the same pay scale for all employees who perform a particular job; i.e., a part-time, temporary, or casual employee must be paid similarly to those performing the job on a full-time basis (subject to differences due to seniority, merit, and other objective criteria), has been withdrawn.[37]

Alberta's "The Fair and Family-Friendly Workplaces Act," provided a variety of changes to its Employment Standards Code including increased minimum wage (became $15 per hour in October 2018); three-hour minimum shift payments, expanded parental and compassionate care leave; job-protected sick leave; and domestic violence leave.[38]

Controversies

A ongoing controversy with respect to employment/labour standards relates to the use of unpaid interns. In a variety of industries including politics, technology, fashion, and journalism, several years of unpaid labour have sometimes been needed to finally achieve "paid status." These young and inexperienced interns may be particularly vulnerable to being exploited because they are unlikely to complain due to fear of jeopardizing future employment or securing a good reference.[39] The HR Oops! feature further explores the scrutiny the federal government and other employers face over unpaid interns.

Another area of employment/labour standards controversy emerged in the form of class-action lawsuits over unpaid overtime. For example, CIBC, Scotiabank, and KPMG dealt with class-action lawsuits on behalf of employees over allegations of unpaid overtime. CIBC faced a potential $600 million lawsuit involving as many as 31,000 current and former front-line employees from across Canada. The suit alleged that front-line employees such as tellers, account executives, and commercial and personal bankers were given workloads too heavy to be handled in regular working hours and claimed that CIBC failed to pay for overtime work that was required or at least permitted, in contravention to the Canada Labour Code. Both KPMG and Scotiabank reached settlements with their current and former employees to compensate for unpaid overtime worked; however, CIBC maintained it has a "clearly defined" overtime policy that "exceeds legislative requirements," and has continued its legal battle.[40]

Another ongoing class-action lawsuit involves current and some former hockey players in the OHL, WHL, and QMJHL seeking compensation for "back-wages, overtime pay, holiday pay and vacation pay which should have been paid to them while they played in one or more of the leagues." The statement of claim alleges the players are actually employees who sign standard form league contracts and are paid only a weekly fee of between $35 and $120 per week for spending 35–40 hours of time each week on team business. "If the court decides that the players are employees, then the fee violates minimum wage legislation in every province where the teams play hockey."[41]

HR Oops!

Are Unpaid Internships a Violation of Minimum Employment Standards?

The federal government has confronted "uncomfortable questions" about extensive use of unpaid interns. A reported 961 interns have been used in federal departments between 2008 and 2014; however only 22 were actually hired after their internship terms ended. "It's shocking, it's disappointing but unfortunately it means that these opportunities aren't actually benefiting the interns," says Canadian politician, Laurin Liu. Liu estimates there are 300,000 unpaid interns in Canada. "But there is no official data from StatsCan to prove this. So if we want to deal with the issue of unpaid interns in Canada ... we need to measure the problem."

Under the Ontario Employment Standards Act, the Ontario Ministry of Labour has been cracking down on unpaid internships by establishing six criteria for an unpaid internship to be legal. If all of the criteria are not met, the intern is determined to be an employee and must be paid at least minimum wage. Magazines including *Toronto Life* and the *Walrus* have stopped "employing" unpaid interns after they were informed their practice of bringing in aspiring journalists and designers, and others, was in violation of Ontario's Employment Standards Act, and Bell Mobility scrapped its unpaid intern program in the wake of "a growing public outcry." However, other federally regulated organizations have continued to use unpaid interns.

Although promises had been made with the 2017 budget, federal government officials pushed the date back for releasing new rules on unpaid internships to Fall 2019, which would likely delay implementation until 2020.

Sources: Jordan Press, "Liberals promise to set strict rules for unpaid interns pushed to 2019," *The Canadian Press*, July 12, 2018, https://m.hrmonline.ca, accessed July 12, 2018; Liz Bernier, "Feds Facing Scrutiny Over Unpaid Interns," *Canadian HR Reporter*, February 9, 2015, pp. 1, 7; Lee-Ann Goodman, "Federal Officials to Discuss Unpaid Interns With Youth Work Advocates," *The Globe and Mail*, January 26, 2015, www.theglobeandmail.com, accessed March 26, 2015; Simon Houpt, "End to Unpaid Internships Shakes Up Magazine Industry," *The Globe and Mail*, March 27, 2014, www.theglobeandmail.com, accessed March 26, 2015; and Zane Schwartz, "Unpaid Internships Are Just Wrong," *The Globe and Mail*, May 3, 2013, www.theglobeandmail.com, accessed March 26, 2015.

Pay Equity

Pay equity legislation requires that employers are responsible to provide *equal pay for work of equal value.*

pay equity The concept of "equal pay for work of equal value."

Pay equity is a principle of nondiscrimination in wages that requires men and women doing work of equal value to the employer to be paid the same. In addition to the Federal Government of Canada, the provinces of Manitoba, Ontario, New Brunswick, Prince Edward Island, Nova Scotia and Quebec have pay equity legislation. Saskatchewan, Newfoundland, and British Columbia have implemented pay equity frameworks applicable to public-sector employees.[42]

Australia, Scandinavian countries, and many U.S. states have laws to ensure women and men working in female-dominated jobs (e.g., nursing, clerical, and retail sales) are paid fairly. The four criteria usually applied are *skill, effort, responsibility,* and *working conditions.* Chapter 8 includes a discussion of job evaluation, which applies these criteria to measure the relative value of jobs in the effort to ensure that jobs are paid fairly relative to one another within an organization.

Pay equity legislation is intended to address the *pay gap*—the difference between the earnings of women working full-time versus the earnings of men working full-time. Although some Canadians believe that the gender income gap has been successfully dealt with, the Conference Board of Canada reports the gap in income between men and women in Canada is 19 percent. This ties Canada with the United States at 11th in its peer countries (earning a "C" grade). The gender income gap ranges from a low of 8 percent (Norway) to a high of 29 percent (Japan).[43]

The federal government recently announced the intent to introduce new pay equity legislation intended to narrow the gap in the federally regulated private sector (e.g., banking, telecommunications) to 90.7 cents.[44] The irony is that men and women tend to begin their career on an approximately equal footing; however, women fall behind later—often after time away from paid employment to have children. As a result, men end up with more experience. Also, men tend to work longer hours, have more education, and are less likely than women to work part-time.[45]

Cumulatively, however, these factors do not explain the entire wage gap or earnings gap between men and women.

For example, Statistics Canada reported the results of a study of 29 universities related to the salaries of male and female professors. The study revealed that "male university professors earned on average up to $17,300 more than female colleagues."[46] According to the Canadian Association of University Teachers (CAUT), one reason for the wage gap is that women are underrepresented in the highest-paying position of full professor.[47] The University of Guelph recently provided a raise of $2,050 to more than 300 full-time faculty members who identify as female or non-male, after a "salary review found they were being paid less than their male colleagues." The salary review provided a "robust statistical analysis taking into account a wide variety of factors including gender, age, experience, hiring date, and some performance data." This follows raises provided to all female faculty at the University of Waterloo in 2016 ($2,905); McMaster University in 2015 ($3,515), and the University of British Columbia in 2013 (2 percent).[48]

Enforcement of Employment Legislation

At a minimum, employers must comply with the legal requirements of their jurisdiction. Education and consultation is available to employers and employees. Although employers have a duty to comply with all of the relevant requirements, and a collaborative discussion approach is encouraged, employee complaint processes are provided as part of the enforcement process. Typically, the recommended approach is for employees to discuss any questions or concerns directly with their employer; for example, supervisor/manager and/or HR department (and/or union representative) before filing a formal complaint.

Human Rights Commissions

The federal government, provinces, and territories have Human Rights Commissions. For example, the Canadian Human Rights Commission (CHRC) provides individuals under federal jurisdiction a means to resolve complaints of discrimination. The CHRC has the power to receive and address allegations of discrimination or harassment complaints based on the prohibited grounds outlined in the Canadian Human Rights Act. The CHRC tries to resolve complaints using mediation and conciliation; however, some complaints are resolved only by using a tribunal. Cases may also be ultimately appealed all the way to the Supreme Court of Canada for final resolution. The Canadian Human Rights Commission is also responsible for auditing federally regulated employers to ensure compliance with the federal Employment Equity Act. In addition, the CHRC enforces pay equity requirements.[49]

Privacy Commissioners

The Office of the Privacy Commissioner of Canada is responsible for ensuring compliance with federal privacy legislation including the Personal Information Protection and Electronic Documents Act (PIPEDA) and the Privacy Act. The Office of the Privacy Commissioner of Canada has the power to investigate complaints and recommend solutions to employers. To ensure compliance, the Commissioner can publicly identify organizations violating individuals' privacy rights and take the complaint to the Federal Court of Canada. If unable to resolve the complaint, the Court can order the organization to take specific actions and can also award damages.[50] Other jurisdictions also have Privacy Commissioners responsible for ensuring compliance with their respective relevant provincial legislation.

One area of interest and concern for both individuals and organizations is the growing use of social media and specifically the growing practice of HR professionals conducting social media background checks on both current and prospective employees. For example, the Office of the Information Privacy Commissioner of Alberta published "Guidelines for Social Media Background Checks" (see Table 2.3).

Employment/Labour Standards Offices

Employment/Labour Standards Offices are in place within each jurisdiction to ensure that employees are paid fairly and that other non-monetary requirements of the legislation are provided properly (e.g., work scheduling and

TABLE 2.3

Guidelines for Social Media Background Checks

1. Determine what the business purpose is for performing a social media background check. Do you reasonably require personal information that cannot be obtained through traditional means such as interviews or reference checks?
2. Recognize that any information that is collected about an individual is personal information or personal employee information and is subject to privacy laws.
3. Consider the risks of using social media to perform a background check. Conduct a privacy impact assessment to assess the risks.

Source: "Guidelines for Social Media Background Checks," Office of the Information and Privacy Commissioner of Alberta, December 2011, www.oipc.ab.ca/downloads/documentloader.ashx?id=3539, accessed July 9, 2018.

employee leaves). Officers hear complaints, conduct investigations, and make actionable rulings. Tools and resources are increasingly provided online to support both employees and employers. For example, Employment Standards—Government of British Columbia, provides an online "Self Help Kit" intended as a first step for employees and employers.[51]

LO3 Workplace Health and Safety

At the beginning of this chapter we briefly introduced the importance of taking a strategic approach to health and safety. The protection of employee health and safety is regulated by the government. Many elements are similar in all jurisdictions across Canada; however, the details of the relevant Occupational Health and Safety (OH&S) legislation and the ways the laws are enforced vary (e.g., "mandatory" vs. "discretionary").[52] The effective management of health and safety in the workplace includes more than legal compliance. Increasingly, organizations are approaching health and safety with a values-based commitment to safe operations as a way to protect people: "All workers have the right to return home each day safe and sound."[53]

© LifesizeImages/iStockPhoto

All workers have a right to work safely each day.

Internal Responsibility System

In Canada, safety in the workplace is based on the foundation of an **internal responsibility system**. The internal responsibility system is a philosophy of occupational health and safety in which employers and employees share responsibility for creating and maintaining safe and healthy work environments. Employer–employee partnerships are put in place to ensure compliance and create a culture of safety in the organization.[54]

internal responsibility system Philosophy of occupational health and safety whereby employers and employees share responsibility for creating and maintaining safe and healthy work environments.

Health and Safety Committees

Health and safety committees, a key feature of the internal responsibility system, are jointly appointed by the employer and employees at large (or union) to address health and safety issues in a workplace. For example, under federal regulations, a workplace health and safety committee is required for every workplace that has 20 or more employees. The committee must consist of at least two persons and is required to meet at least nine times a year, at regular intervals, during normal working hours.[55] The premise is that it is the people employed in a particular workplace who know the most about hazards and unhealthy conditions. Table 2.4 outlines the role of a health and safety committee.

health and safety committees A committee jointly appointed by the employer and employees at large (or union) to address health and safety issues in a workplace.

TABLE 2.4

Role of a Health and Safety Committee

The Role of a Health and Safety Committee Includes:
• Act as an advisory body
• Identify hazards and obtain information about them
• Recommend corrective actions
• Assist in resolving work refusal cases
• Participate in accident investigations and workplace inspections
• Make recommendations to the management regarding actions required to resolve health and safety concerns

Source: "OH&S Legislation in Canada—Basic Responsibilities," *Canadian Centre for Occupational Health and Safety,* www.ccohs.ca/oshanswers/legisl/responsi.html, accessed March 29, 2015.

Did You KNOW?

Top Seven Dangers for Young Workers (in BC)

Young workers are at significant risk of injury in a number of industries as a result of lifting objects; at risk of falls when working at elevated levels; and working with knives, food slicers, and hot substances or objects when employed as cooks, waiters, and food preparers in the hospitality and services industry.

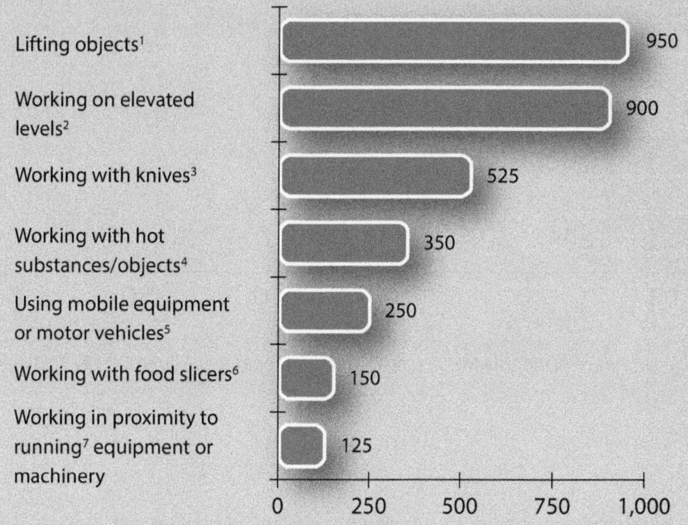

[1] Lifting objects—overexertion causing sprains, strains, tears.

[2] Working at elevated levels—sprains, strains, tears, and fractures.

[3] Working with knives—cuts and lacerations.

[4] Working with hot substances/objects—burns.

[5] Using mobile equipment or motor vehicles—sprains, strains, tears, and fractures.

[6] Working with food slicers—cuts and lacerations.

[7] Working in proximity to running equipment or machinery—cuts, lacerations, and fractures.

Source: From WorkSafeBC "Top 7 Dangers for Young Workers," www2.worksafebc.com/Topics/YoungWorker/Top-Seven-Dangers.asp, retrieved March 23, 2015. © WorkSafeBC. Used with permission. WorkSafeBC.com.

What Are the Responsibilities of Employers, Managers, and Supervisors?

Employers need to assess and be alert to workplace hazards and safety issues. Employers, managers, and supervisors have a *duty* to provide a safe workplace. An employer must:

- establish and maintain a health and safety committee, or cause workers to select at least one health and safety representative;
- take every reasonable precaution to ensure the workplace is safe;
- train employees about any potential hazards and in how to safely use, handle, store, and dispose of hazardous substances and how to handle emergencies;
- supply personal protective equipment and ensure workers know how to use the equipment safely and properly;
- immediately report all critical injuries to the government department responsible for OH&S;
- appoint a competent supervisor who sets the standards for performance, and who ensures safe working conditions are always observed.[56]

Some Contemporary Workplace Hazards and Safety Issues

Legalization of Cannabis for Recreational Use

Work safety, especially in safety-sensitive roles, is the top concern for employers when Canada became the first G7 country to legalize and regulate recreational cannabis on a national scale. The Conference Board of Canada, in its recent report, "Blazing the Trail: What the Legalization of Cannabis Means for Canadian Employers," reports that 57 percent of surveyed organizations identified "workplace safety" as their top concern about the legalization of recreational cannabis. See Figure 2.5.

FIGURE 2.5

Top Organizational Concerns about the Legalization of Recreational Cannabis

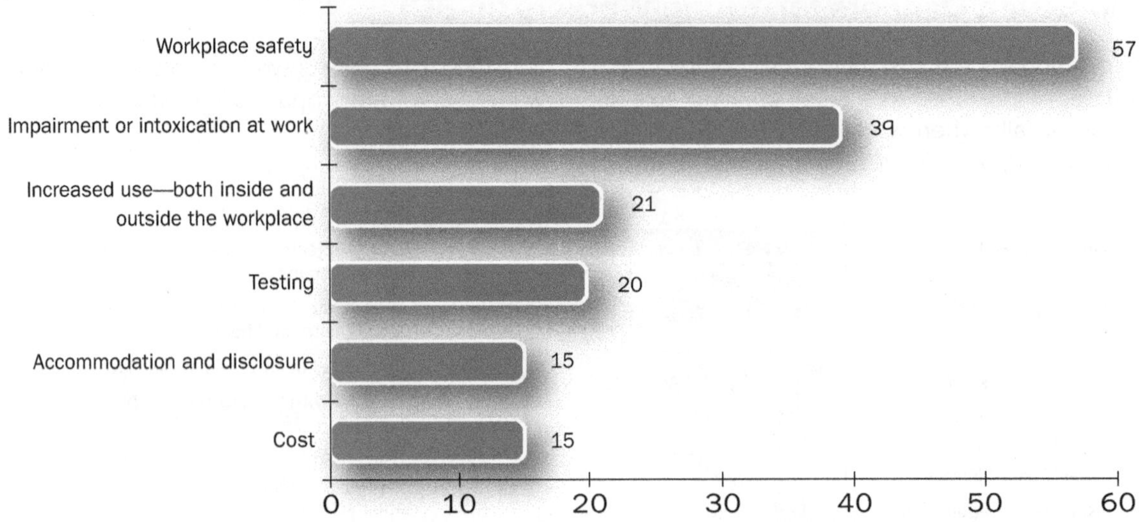

Source: Monica Haberl, "Blazing the Trail: What the Legalization of Cannabis Means for Canadian Employers," June 2018, *The Conference Board of Canada,* p. 8.

Although recreational cannabis has been legalized, employees need to understand that they must come to work unimpaired and work safely. Managers, supervisors, and HR professionals will require training and guidance in navigating the workplace impacts. For example, the report recommends that before implementing changes to alcohol or drug testing guidelines, legal partners should be consulted.[57]

Use of Mobile Devices

A study published in the *British Medical Journal* found drivers talking on a cellphone are four times more likely to be involved in a serious crash. In another study, psychologists concluded that "using a hands-free cellphone while driving could impair drivers as much as having a blood-alcohol level of 0.08 percent."[58] The Ontario Ministry of Labour also provides the cautionary finding that "when drivers take their eyes off the road for more than two seconds, their crash risk doubles."[59] However, distractions and hazards associated with the use of devices is not limited just to driving. Kevin Hayes, corporate safety manager for the Canadian operations of Acciona Infrastructure, a global construction and engineering firm explains: "There are more cellular phone subscribers in the world today than landline phone subscribers. People are communicating in real-time and, unfortunately, with this need to communicate instantly, new hazards are being created." Hayes discusses a workplace fatality he was tasked to investigate at one of his company's construction projects. A road worker had been hit and killed by a dump truck and it was concluded that cellphone use was a significant factor that resulted in the fatal accident. Hayes's company has since enforced a mobile device use policy that prescribes acceptable and unacceptable use of devices while at work. In particular, Hayes said, workers are prohibited from using their devices while performing safety-sensitive tasks.[60]

Worker Fatigue

Research findings have tended to focus on the association of workplace injuries with shift work and safety-sensitive occupations; however, Canadian researchers have also demonstrated a connection between difficulty sleeping and experiencing a workplace injury. One of the findings was that annual injury rates for workers who got less than 5 hours of sleep were almost 4 times higher than workers who got 7.0–7.9 hours of sleep. According to a recent Canadian report, organizations are encouraged to think about fatigue as a safety risk in their organizations. According to the report, 27 percent of employees report "being tired at work every day or most days during a typical week" and most employees "are affected by fatigue at least some of the time."[61]

The Nova Scotia Health Authority's Central Zone created a task force to design and implement a fatigue management program. Following an extensive literature review and engaging internal experts as well as front-line workers, guiding principles were established that focused on the importance of having a culture of safety and sharing responsibility between employees and the organization.[62]

Employee Rights and Responsibilities

All Canadian workers have three fundamental rights that are protected by occupational health and safety legislation:[63]

- *The right to refuse* unsafe work.
- *The right to participate* in the workplace health and safety activities through a health and safety committee or as a worker health and safety representative.
- *The right to know,* or the right to be informed about, actual and potential dangers in the workplace.

Employees can refuse work if they believes that the situation is unsafe to either themselves or co-workers. When an employee believes that a work refusal should be made, the employee must report to the supervisor that they are refusing the work and state why the situation is unsafe. The resulting investigation will involve the employee, supervisor, and a health and safety committee member (or employee representative). Mutual agreement that the problem is solved is needed before the employee returns to this work. However, if the problem is not resolved, a government health and safety officer/inspector will be called in to investigate and provide a written decision.[64]

Although employers and their managers and supervisors are responsible for protecting workers from health and safety hazards, employees have responsibilities as well. Employees' responsibilities include:[65]

- working in compliance with OH&S acts and regulations
- using personal protective equipment and clothing as directed by the employer
- reporting workplace hazards and dangers
- working in a manner as required by the employer and using the prescribed safety equipment.

WHMIS

The Workplace Hazardous Materials Information System (WHMIS) is related to the worker's "right to know." "WHMIS is Canada's national hazard communication program consisting of symbols and warning labels for consumers and material-specific safety data sheets that guide the handling of dangerous substances in the workplace, as well as related worker education and training."[66] WHMIS is implemented through coordinated federal, provincial, and territorial laws to ensure that hazardous products are properly labelled, used, stored, handled, and disposed of safely. In 2015, WHMIS was modified to incorporate the Globally Harmonized System of Classification and Labelling of Chemicals (GHS) for workplace chemicals and is now referred to as *WHMIS 2015*. The transition to WHMIS 2015 was accomplished in a phased approach that was fully implemented in 2018.[67]

Organizations must have **safety data sheets (SDSs)** for hazardous products that employees are exposed to. An SDS form details the hazards associated with a chemical; the chemical's producer or importer is responsible for identifying these hazards and detailing them on the form. Employers must ensure that all containers of hazardous chemicals are labelled with information about the hazards, prepare workplace labels and SDSs (as necessary), educate and train employees in safe handling of the chemicals, and ensure appropriate control methods are in place to protect the health and safety of workers.

> **safety data sheets (SDSs)** Detailed hazard information concerning a controlled (hazardous) product.

Enforcement of Occupational Health and Safety Regulations

Enforcement responsibilities exist within the federal, provincial, and territorial governments. Occupational health and safety officers/inspectors have the authority to inspect workplaces and issue orders to employers and workers. In some serious cases, charges may also be laid by law enforcement under a section of the Canada Criminal Code that was amended in 2004 to create additional legal duties on employers to ensure the safety of workers and the public. This amendment, **Bill C-45 (Westray Bill)**, named after the Nova Scotia mining disaster in 1992 that killed 26 workers, makes organizations and anyone who directs the work of others criminally liable for safety offences. Maximum fines were increased to $100,000 from $25,000 for less serious offences and the Bill provides an unlimited fine for more serious offences. Anyone who directs the work of others can also face serious charges—criminal conviction, a criminal record, and even life imprisonment for failing to provide for health and safety in the workplace.[68] Although there have been relatively few criminal convictions handed down, there have been some well-publicized cases including the case of Metron Construction Corporation, which was the first Ontario firm to be convicted under the Criminal Code after Metron's president was charged with "criminal negligence causing death" after four workers were killed and another seriously injured when a swing stage scaffold collapsed while they were repairing concrete balconies on an apartment building in Toronto.[69]

> **Bill C-45 (Westray Bill)** Amendment to the Criminal Code making organizations and anyone who directs the work of others criminally liable for safety offences.

WHMIS 2015: Pictograms of Hazard Classes & Categories

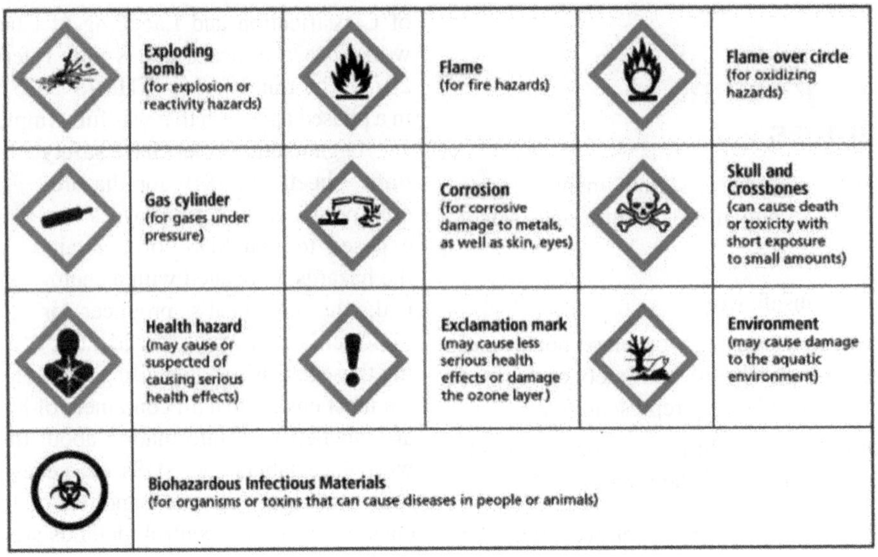
Exploding bomb (for explosion or reactivity hazards)
Flame (for fire hazards)
Flame over circle (for oxidizing hazards)
Gas cylinder (for gases under pressure)
Corrosion (for corrosive damage to metals, as well as skin, eyes)
Skull and Crossbones (can cause death or toxicity with short exposure to small amounts)
Health hazard (may cause or suspected of causing serious health effects)
Exclamation mark (may cause less serious health effects or damage the ozone layer)
Environment (may cause damage to the aquatic environment)
Biohazardous Infectious Materials (for organisms or toxins that can cause diseases in people or animals)

Source: WHMIS 2015 - Pictograms, URL: https://www.ccohs.ca/oshanswers/chemicals/whmis_ghs/pictograms.html, Canadian Centre for Occupational Health and Safety (CCOHS), 2015. Reproduced with the permission of CCOHS, 2018

Psychological Safety

Ensuring a safe physical working environment for employees has long been recognized as an essential organizational responsibility; however, psychological safety has more recently become a significant focus. As discussed earlier in the chapter, human rights legislation prohibits behaviours such as harassment. Workplace violence is a broad problem, particularly for certain occupational groups. According to the Canadian Centre for Occupational Health and Safety, health care workers, correctional officers, social service employees, teachers, and retail employees are some of the occupational groups more at risk.[70] In addition to harassment, workplace violence includes:

- threatening behaviour, e.g., throwing objects, or destroying property;
- verbal or written threats, e.g., expressing intent to inflict harm;
- verbal abuse, e.g., swearing and insults;
- physical attacks, e.g., hitting, pushing, or kicking.[71]

More than two-thirds of 1,381 EMS workers surveyed in Ontario and Nova Scotia reported being subjected to on-the-job verbal, physical, or sexual abuse.[72] Employees exposed to workplace violence, including harassment, may develop conditions considered occupational injuries (e.g., depression, anxiety, and burnout). Judges, arbitrators, and commissioners now identify that action needs to be taken under both human rights and occupational health and safety laws and regulations to protect the psychological well-being and safety of employees.[73] The case of a former British Columbia RCMP officer serves to illustrate the significant consequences. Ex-Mountie Nancy Sulz was awarded $950,000 by the B.C. Supreme Court for "damages, lost wages, and loss of future earnings" after finding her Staff Sgt. and two subordinate officers caused Sulz "serious psychological harm" related to incidents arising after the birth of a child.[74]

Through a range of programs and policies, the County of Wellington, a municipal government in southwestern Ontario, shows its employees that preserving their mental health is just as important as physical safety. The County of Wellington was the winner of the first Canada's Safest Employers Psychological Safety Award. Michele Richardson, health and safety co-ordinator, says the county puts a great deal of effort into education and communication on the importance of psychological safety. From the time they're hired, employees are trained in policies regarding a respectful workplace, verbal de-escalation, and workplace violence. Training, including online programs, continue on a regular basis. The county provides a mental health tool kit as part of mandatory training for all staff. While workers learn to report unhealthy psychological situations to their managers, managers are trained to investigate issues and, if required, take corrective action. At quarterly meetings, managers often discuss a topic regarding psychological health and safety. Absenteeism reports, worker complaints, results of exit interviews, and employee and family assistance program (EFAP) quarterly reports are used to set objectives when the health and safety team develops its psychological health and safety management system.[75]

Impact of Occupational Health and Safety Legislation

Legislation has succeeded in raising the level of awareness of occupational safety. The rate of workforce fatalities increased by more than 50 percent between 1996 and 2005; however, workplace fatalities have been reduced by almost 18 percent between 2005 and 2016 (see Figure 2.6). Although on every second day in 2016, one *fewer* person lost their life due to work than in 2005, 904 lives were lost to workplace fatalities in Canada, a terrible and tragic loss of life. There has been a relatively significant reduction in time-loss injuries experienced in recent years relative to 1996–2008 levels (Figure 2.7).

Many workplace accidents are a product of unsafe behaviours, not unsafe working conditions. Because legislation does not directly regulate employee behaviour, little change can be expected unless employees are convinced of the standards' importance.[76] Because conforming to the law alone does not necessarily guarantee their employees will be safe, many employers go beyond the letter of

FIGURE 2.6

Number of Workplace Fatalities in Canada, 1996–2016

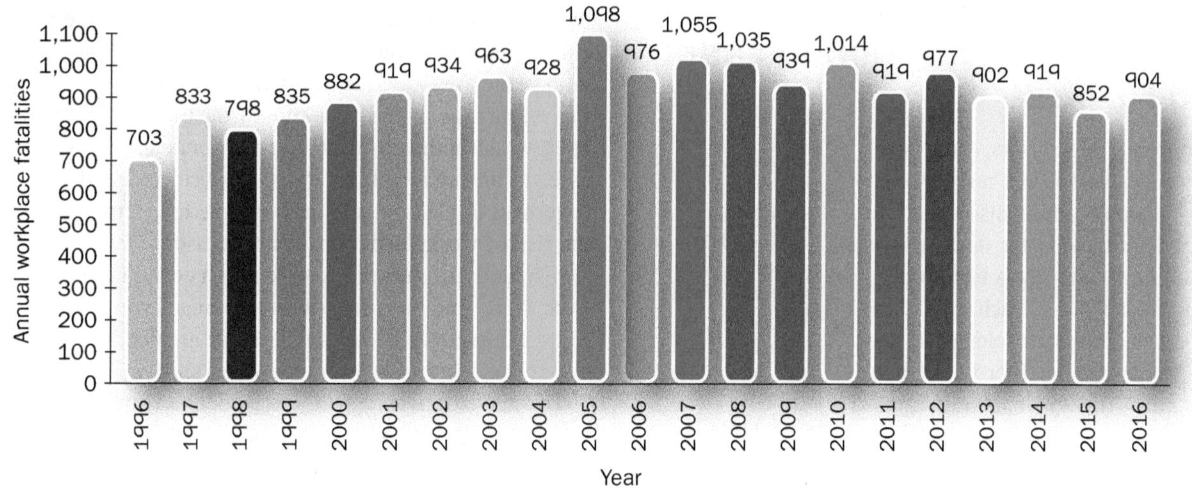

Source: "2014-2016 National Work Injury, Disease, and Fatality Statistics," *Association of Workers' Compensation Boards of Canada*, "Table 22: Number of Fatalities, by Jurisdiction 1993-2016," www.awcbc.org, accessed July 7, 2018.

FIGURE 2.7

Number of Accepted Lost-Time Claims in Canada, 1996–2016

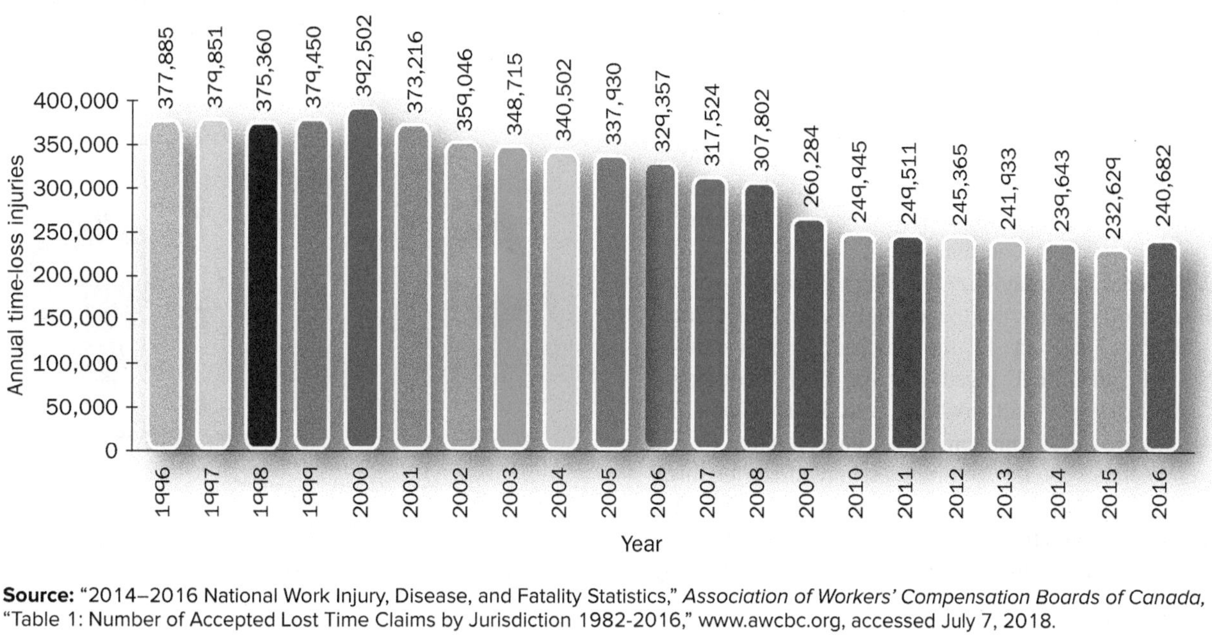

Source: "2014–2016 National Work Injury, Disease, and Fatality Statistics," *Association of Workers' Compensation Boards of Canada*, "Table 1: Number of Accepted Lost Time Claims by Jurisdiction 1982-2016," www.awcbc.org, accessed July 7, 2018.

the law. In the next section we examine various kinds of employer-initiated safety awareness programs that comply with, and in some cases exceed, legal requirements.

LO4 Employer-sponsored Health and Safety Programs

Many employers establish safety awareness programs to go beyond mere compliance with occupational health and safety regulations and attempt to instill an emphasis on safety. A safety awareness program has three primary components: identifying and communicating hazards, reinforcing safe practices, and promoting safety internationally.

Identifying and Communicating Job Hazards

Employees, supervisors, and other knowledgeable sources need to consider potential problems related to safety. One method for doing this is the **job hazard analysis technique**.[77] With this technique, each job is broken down into basic elements, and each of these is rated for its potential for harm or injury. If there is agreement that some job element has high hazard potential, the group isolates the element and considers possible technological or behaviour changes to reduce or eliminate the hazard.

job hazard analysis technique Safety promotion technique that involves breaking down a job into basic elements, then rating each element for its potential for harm or injury.

Another means of isolating unsafe job elements is to study past accidents. The **technic of operations review (TOR)** is an analysis method for determining which specific element of a job led to a past accident.[78] The first step in a TOR analysis is to establish the facts surrounding the incident. To accomplish this, all members of the work group involved in the accident give their initial impressions of what happened. The group must then, through discussion, come to an agreement on the single, systematic failure that most likely contributed to the incident, as well as two or three major secondary factors that contributed to it.

technic of operations review (TOR) Method of promoting safety by determining which specific element of a job led to a past accident.

Job analysis may be entering a new level of sophistication, thanks to the development of wearable devices that connect to the Internet. For example, Honeywell and Intel together have been developing a wearable device that contains sensors and monitors for gathering and communicating data related to the wearer's safety. The device provides immediate feedback to the wearer and the supervisor. Workers in high-risk environments could transmit data about their whereabouts, movements, and conditions in their environment, allowing supervisors to monitor employee well-being. The data collected in particular incidents also could prove useful for future safety training.[79]

To communicate with employees about job hazards, managers should talk directly with their employees about safety. Written messages are also important to restate key points and help establish a "paper trail" that can later document a history of the employer's concern regarding the job hazard. Posters, especially if placed near the hazard, serve as a constant reminder, supporting other messages. Mobile devices can provide convenient, effective channels for communicating safety messages (e.g., the use of podcasts).

In communicating risk, managers should recognize that different groups of individuals may constitute different audiences. "Young and new workers are particularly vulnerable to workplace injury or illness, many of the injuries occurring in the first month on the job."[80] "Full of energy and enthusiasm, young workers can be a valuable asset to an organization. Yet this spirit, coupled with an eagerness to please and a lack of experience, may increase the risk of workplace injuries or illnesses."[81]

A study of nurses showed a high correlation between shift work and the risk of developing Type 2 diabetes. Shift workers are also considered at greater risk for obesity. "The relationship now between shift work and Type 2 diabetes is much clearer, the evidence is much stronger and therefore, we need to start looking at ways to intervene and the workplace is an obvious place for that to start," said Jocalyn Clark, a Toronto-based senior editor at the publication, *PLOS Medicine*.[82]

Experienced employees sometimes need retraining to jar them from complacency about the dangers associated with their work.[83] This is especially the case if the hazard in question poses a greater threat to older employees. For example, accidents that involve falling off a ladder are a greater threat to older workers than to younger ones. Over 20 percent of such falls lead to a fatality for workers in the 55-to-65 age group, versus 10 percent for all other workers.[84]

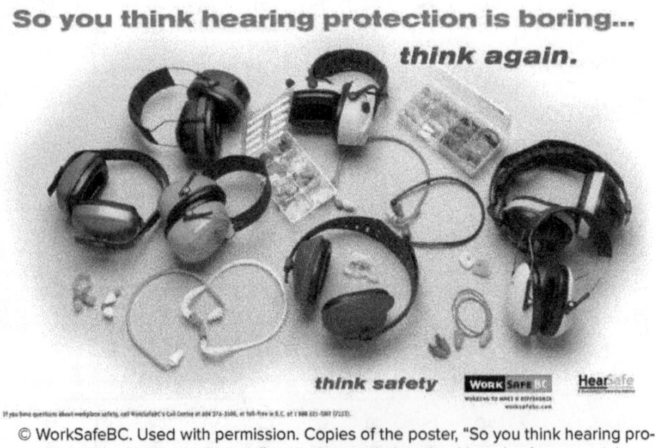

© WorkSafeBC. Used with permission. Copies of the poster, "So you think hearing protection is boring . . . think again" and other workplace health and safety materials are available free of charge at the WorkSafeBC website (WorkSafeBC.com).

WorkSafeBC produces a variety of posters and other resources to communicate job hazards and promote working safely.

Reinforcing Safe Practices

To ensure safe behaviours, employers should not only define how to work safely but also reinforce the desired behaviour. One common technique for reinforcing safe practices is implementing a *safety incentive program* to reward workers for their support of and commitment to safety goals. Such programs start by focusing on monthly or quarterly goals or by encouraging suggestions for improving safety. Goals might include good housekeeping practices, adherence to safety rules, and proper use of protective equipment. Later, the program expands to include more wide-ranging, long-term goals. Typically, the employer distributes awards in highly public forums, such as company or department meetings. Using merchandise, instead of cash, for prizes, provides a lasting symbol of achievement. A good deal of evidence suggests that such incentive programs are effective in reducing the number and cost of injuries.[85]

Besides focusing on specific jobs, organizations can target particular types of injuries or disabilities, especially those for which employees may be at risk. For example, the CNIB reports that every day 700 Canadian workers sustain eye injuries on the job, often resulting in lost time and, in some cases, either temporary or permanent vision loss.[86] Organizations can prevent such injuries through a combination of job analysis, written policies, safety training, protective eyewear, rewards and sanctions for safe and unsafe behaviour, and management support for the safety effort.

Industries and occupational groups also provide organizational safety awards. For example, the Canadian Association of Petroleum Producers—CAPP presents awards to oil and gas companies for innovative health and safety accomplishments. Talisman Energy Inc. was recognized for its "Cypress 3D Seismic Program," a large-scale, low-environmental impact, geophysical exploration program near Fort St. John, British Columbia. The program's study included the potential to improve helicopter safety while also protecting migratory birds.[87]

Employee Health and Wellness Programs

Another way to improve the well-being and overall health of employees is to offer an **employee health and wellness program**, a set of communications, activities, and facilities designed to change health-related behaviours in ways that reduce health risks. Typically, wellness programs aim at specific health risks, such as high blood pressure, high cholesterol levels, smoking, and obesity, by encouraging preventive measures such as exercise and good nutrition. However, many organizations are adopting an integrated strategic approach to wellness that promotes a corporate culture to support employees in taking responsibility for their health and overall wellness. Chapter 8 will explore employee health and wellness programs in more detail.

employee health and wellness program A set of communications, activities, and facilities designed to change health-related behaviours in ways that reduce health risks.

Organizations that place a strategic emphasis on employee health and wellness achieve economic benefits including reduced injury and disability insurance costs, enhanced productivity and service, and reduced costs due to a reduction in employee absenteeism and turnover.[88] Some organizations are also attempting to measure the return on investment (ROI) of health and wellness programs. For example, Desjardins Group reports "a return on investment of between $1.50 and $3 for every dollar invested in their program in addition to other positive employee self-reported outcomes including making healthier food choices, lower stress, and engaging in more physical activity.[89]

The Town of Conception Bay South, Newfoundland and Labrador, is a growing municipality located just minutes away from St. John's, the provincial capital. After senior leaders noted a significant increase in Workplace Health, Safety, and Compensation Commission claims and premiums, they decided to create a health and wellness program. After seeking feedback from all employees on health and wellness concerns, a health and wellness program with several components was implemented. Employees receive free use of all recreational facilities (e.g., swimming, tennis, skating, and squash); they are also encouraged to use the employee assistance program (EAP), attend luncheon sessions, and access the monthly wellness newsletters. Some of the outcomes experienced to date include annual savings of $45,000 in sick leave, significant and sustained savings in WHSCC premiums due to a significant decline in claims, and achieving a score of over 90 percent on the town's occupational health and safety audit, a considerable improvement from its initial audit score of 38 percent.[90]

Employee Assistance Programs (EAPs)

An **employee assistance program (EAP)** is a confidential, short-term counselling service for employees with personal issues that affect their work performance.[91] EAPs began in the 1950s with a focus on treating alcoholism, and in the 1980s they expanded into drug treatment. Today, many EAP providers offer a very broad range of services that may overlap with health, wellness, and lifestyle-related services (e.g., dealing with stress). To enhance inclusivity for Indigenous employees, some organizations' employee assistance programs have integrated Indigenous elders.[92]

employee assistance program (EAP) Confidential, short term, counselling service for employees with personal issues that affect their work performance.

Many organizations extend EAP services to family members. Left untreated, these issues may cause employees to lose their ability to cope and their work performance and safety may suffer. Employees must be able to feel confident the program respects their confidentiality. In addition to services provided, other considerations include proximity to counsellors, client references, and availability of effectiveness reporting measures.[93]

Promoting Safety Globally

Given the increasing focus on globalization, organizations also need to consider how to ensure the safety of their employees regardless of the nation in which they operate. Cultural differences may make this more difficult than it seems. For example, a study examined the impact of one standardized corporation-wide safety policy on employees in three different countries: the United States, France, and Argentina. The results of this study indicate that employees in the three countries interpreted the policy differently because of cultural differences. The individualistic, control-oriented culture of the United States stressed the role of top management in ensuring safety in a top-down fashion. However, this policy failed to work in Argentina, where the culture is more "collectivist" (emphasizing the group). Argentine employees tend to feel that safety is

Thinking ETHICALLY

Simple Situations Can Become Awkward

"What did you do on the weekend?" It sounds like a simple question that managers might ask their employees in order to build a team atmosphere and show interest in their lives outside work. But for LGBTQIA2+ employees (lesbian, gay, bisexual, transgender, questioning, intersex, asexual, or two-spirit employees), who may not be "out" to their work colleagues or bosses, it can be one of the hardest questions to answer. Similarly company-sponsored social events that invite partner attendance, or even casual after-hours gatherings of co-workers, can become uncomfortable or awkward for employees navigating their sexual orientation, gender identity, or gender expression in the workplace. Transgender employees may be particularly vulnerable. According to survey results from the National Center for Transgender Equality, "80 percent of the transgender population experienced harassment or mistreatment on the job, or took steps to avoid it."

Companies that promote diversity emphasize hiring, training, and retention of people protected by human rights and employment equity legislation. Some companies take diversity efforts further. For example, Loblaw Companies, Ltd. recently introduced a LGBTQ Youth Internship, and KPMG LLP provides an employee network called pride@KPMG.

When Apple CEO Tim Cook announced in a column he wrote that he "is proud to be gay," he became the first openly gay CEO of a Fortune 500 company. "I've come to realize that my desire for personal privacy has been holding me back from doing something more important," he said in *Bloomberg Businessweek*. "If hearing that the CEO of Apple is gay can help someone struggling to come to terms with who he or she is, or bring comfort to anyone who feels alone, or inspire people to insist on their equality, then it's worth the trade-off with my own privacy."

Questions

1. Are corporate diversity initiatives (e.g., the employee networks at Loblaw Companies Inc. and KPMG LLP) good business? Do they illustrate good ethics? Should a company pursue an approach to diversity that goes beyond legal requirements? Why or why not?
2. How confident are you that workplaces are increasingly becoming genuinely inclusive—so that employees are less likely to feel they need to hide their sexual orientation, gender identity, or gender expression or endure harassment?

Sources: "Lesbian, Gay, Bisexual. and Transgender Workplace Issues," *Catalyst Knowledge Center*, June 6, 2018, www.catalyst.org, accessed July 12, 2018; Diane Jermyn, "2018 Best Diversity Employers: Diversity and inclusion give these firms a competitive advantage," *Special to The Globe and Mail*, March 7, 2018, www.theglobeandmail.com, accessed July 12, 2018; Sandy E. James, Jody L. Herman Susan Rankin, et al., "The Report of the 2015 U.S. Transgender Survey," *National Center for Transgender Equality*, 2016; Sarah Dobson, "Out and Proud at Work," *Canadian HR Reporter*," December 1, 2014, pp. 1–2; Timothy Cook, "Tim Cook Speaks Up," *Bloomberg Business*, October 30, 2014, www.bloomberg.com/news/articles/2014-10-30/tim-cook-speaks-up, accessed March 30, 2014; Amanda Silliker, "LGBT Staff Still Face Bias," *Canadian HR Reporter*, December 19, 2011, pp. 1, 9; and Susan Turner, "Simple Questions and Awkward Situations: The Impact of the Closet at Work," *Canadian HR Reporter*, December 20, 2004, p. 10.

everyone's joint concern, so the safety programs needed to be defined from the bottom of the organization up.[94]

Another challenge in promoting safety globally is that laws, enforcement practices, and political climates vary from country to country. With the increasing use of offshoring, described in Chapter 1, more companies have operations in countries where employment and labour standards are far less strict than in Canada. Managers and employees in these countries may not think the company is serious about protecting workers' health and safety. In that case, strong communication and oversight will be necessary if the company intends to adhere to the ethical principle of valuing its global workers' safety as much as the safety of its workers in Canada.

SUMMARY

LO1 Explain the overall context and legal framework for human resource management in Canada.

Although the practice of valuing diversity has no single form, organizations that value diversity are likely to be mindful of the benefits and work actively to create a work environment in which individuals feel valued and able to perform to their potential. Approximately 94 percent of Canadian employees are covered by provincial and territorial legislation. The remaining 6 percent are covered by federal legislation. Although jurisdictional differences exist, laws tend to mirror one another. Increasingly, organizations are taking a strategic approach to occupational health and safety by adopting a values-based commitment to safe and healthy operations.

LO2 Discuss major areas of employment legislation including their relevance and implications for human resource management.

Employers can prevent discrimination by avoiding differential treatment of job applicants and employees. Organizations can develop and enforce practices and policies that demonstrate a high value placed on diversity and inclusion and preventing harassment. Employment equity initiatives may remove employment barriers to the designated groups.

Privacy legislation provides rules about how organizations can collect, use, and disclose information about you. Employment/ labour standards legislation deals with minimum standards. Pay equity provisions help assure equal pay for work of equal value. Human Rights Commissions, Employment/Labour Standards Offices, and Privacy Commissioners play key roles to provide education and support in addition to providing oversight and enforcement.

LO3 Identify the requirements and implications of workplace health and safety.

All jurisdictions in Canada have occupational health and safety legislation. Canada's approach to safety in the workplace is based on the internal responsibility system whereby both employers and employees are responsible for safety. Employers, managers, and supervisors have a duty to provide a safe workplace. Canada's workers have fundamental rights as well as specific responsibilities. Psychological safety has also become a significant workplace health and safety issue.

LO4 Discuss the ways employers promote worker health and safety.

Besides complying with occupational health and safety regulations, employers often establish safety awareness programs designed to instill an emphasis on safety. Employers may identify and communicate hazards through the job hazard analysis technique or the technic of operations review. They may adapt communications and training to the needs of different employees and establish incentive programs to reward safe behaviour.

CRITICAL THINKING QUESTIONS

1. Some people say that Millennials and Generation Z are more likely than other generations to "notice the absence of inclusion than when it exists." Millennials and Generation Z have also been credited as seeing inclusion as "more about varying ideas and workstyles than it is about skin colour, religion, or ethnicity."[95] Do you agree or disagree with these statements? Why or why not?
2. On the basis of your knowledge of diverse religious practices, what types of accommodations should an employer be prepared to provide?
3. What is your reaction to the #MeToo movement? Do you think it has reduced the stigma of reporting sexual harassment? Why or why not?

4. Research minimum wages across various jurisdictions in Canada; for example, Alberta, New Brunswick, and Ontario. What are your observations and conclusions about minimum wages and employer reactions to recent changes?
5. Do you think that employers violate current or prospective employees' privacy rights when they use social media sites such as LinkedIn, Instagram, or Twitter to conduct informal background checks? Why or why not?
6. Have you ever experienced harassment at work or been injured on the job?
7. What are jobs that you consider particularly hazardous? What types of hazards and hazardous activities might workers experience in these jobs? What is your advice to reduce or eliminate the hazards and hazardous activities identified?
8. Why are younger workers are more likely to be injured on the job?
9. Do you think that fatigue is a form of impairment? Why or why not? What should organizations do about worker fatigue in their efforts to provide a safe and healthy workplace for all stakeholders; e.g. employees, co-workers, customers, and the general public?
10. For each of the following occupations, identify at least one possible hazard and at least one action employees could take to minimize the risk of any injury or illness related to that hazard.
    a. Server in a restaurant
    b. House painter
    c. Data scientist
    d. Worker in a personal care home for seniors

EXPERIENCING HR—IDENTIFYING WORKPLACE HAZARDS

Form groups of three or four students. In your group, identify an office location that you can visit to identify any potential workplace hazards that may be present. If you have been given time for research, review the chapter for ideas of where to gather information about the type of workplace injuries that are most prevalent in office settings. Visit the office location you identified (ensuring you have received the necessary advance approval from the appropriate manager). Carefully document any workplace hazards and/or any unsafe behaviours you observed.

With your entire class, share your findings. What types of hazards (if any) did your team identify? Did you observe any unsafe employee behaviours? What is your advice to remove potential hazards (if any) in the office you visited? What is your advice to reduce/eliminate any unsafe behaviours you observed?[96]

CASE STUDY: EVIDENCE-BASED HRM

Sodexo Examines the Impact of Gender-balanced Leadership on Performance

Rohini Anand, global chief diversity officer at Sodexo, a global food services and facilities management company, collected, analyzed, and shared data showing the value of gender diversity. She conducted a study of the company's 50,000 managers in 80 countries from executive to site management levels to quantify the impact of gender balance in management.

Anand's findings revealed that gender balance in management significantly related to improved financial performance, employee engagement, and client retention. She found that teams with a management male–female ratio of between 40 and 60 percent delivered the consistently best results on both financial and non-financial performance indicators. Specific results of Sodexo's internal study found that gender-balanced management entities had:

- better employee engagement: +4 points
- higher gross profits: +23 percent
- stronger brand image: +5 points

Anand's study also determined that globally, 56 percent of Sodexo's employees currently work in a team with gender-balanced leadership. In Canada, Sodexo reports that 87 percent of its management teams are gender-balanced.

One of the action items moving forward, is the creation of gender-balance targets for leaders. For example, Sodexo's global CEO, Michel Landel, has set a goal that by 2025 at least 40 percent of Sodexo's 1,400 global senior leaders will be women (a total of 560 women leaders). To ensure that goal is reached, 10 percent of senior leaders' bonuses are based on their yearly progress toward that goal.

Sodexo Canada recently announced the appointment of its first female President—Suzanne Bergeron. Bergeron had been the vice-president of human resources and is based in Montreal. Sodexo Canada has more than 10,000 employees and has been recognized for five consecutive years as one of Canada's Best Diversity Employers.

Questions

1. What is your reaction to Sodexo's goal that by 2025 at least 40 of senior global leaders will be women? What could go wrong? What must go right?
2. Why do you think Sodexo teams with gender-balanced leadership have achieve higher levels of performance than teams that do not have gender-balanced leadership?

Sources: Based on J. Simons, "Workplace Diversity Efforts Get a Reboot," *Wall Street Journal,* February 15, 2017, p. B5; Sodexo Canada website, "Sodexo Canada announces the appointment of Suzanne Bergeron as new Country President," May 28, 2018, www.sodexo.com, accessed July 10, 2018; "Sodexo named Top Diversity Employer Five Years Running," *CNW Newswire,* March 2, 2018, www.newswire.ca, accessed July 10, 2018; "Case Study: Sodexo Analyzes the Impact of Gender Balance on Performance," *Gender Balance Business News,* https://ca.sodexo.com/files/live/sites/sdxcom-global/files/020_Global_Content_Master/Building_Blocks/GLOBAL/Multimedia/PDF/Diversity_and_Inclusion/SODEXO_GBBN2015_GB_WEB.pdf, accessed July 10, 2018.

CASE STUDY: HRM SOCIAL

Using Social Media in Hiring Poses Discrimination Risk

At many organizations, the people who make hiring decisions conduct an online search of social media to learn more about candidates. According to a 2017 CareerBuilder poll of 2,380 HR and hiring private-sector managers, approximately 70 percent of employers said they used social media for hiring—a significant increase from 60 percent in 2016 and 11 percent a decade ago. The objective is to gain greater insight into people's character and spot red flags that a person might behave unprofessionally. However, some recent research suggests that screening candidates with social media contributes to discriminatory hiring decisions.

In one study, researchers created fictional résumés and social-media profiles and sent the résumés to businesses that had advertised job openings. All the résumés listed the same qualifications under different names, but the social media hinted that applicants were either Christian or Muslim or that they were either gay or straight. The companies were more likely to call the applicants with the Christian-sounding profiles than the applicants who seemed to be Muslim. Broken down geographically, the difference was statistically significant. The researchers did not find a difference in response rates related to sexual orientation in this study.

To avoid discriminatory behaviour, it is important for employers to get expert advice to ensure compliance with human rights and privacy requirements. For example, employers must be sure the information they gather is related to job qualifications. Some suggest that employers consider using a third-party company to conduct background checks on social media. That agency would report only the job-related information obtained from the background check and omit protected information, such as an employee's religion, health, and pregnancy status. One recent survey found that 95 percent of social media screening is conducted internally and 5 percent is outsourced to an external vendor.

Questions

1. Explain how the findings of the research study provide an example of differential treatment.
2. For the employee characteristics protected by human rights legislation, which could you avoid revealing on a social media site? Which would be difficult or impossible to avoid disclosing?

Sources: Debbie Lamb, "Social Media Screening Continues Its Upward Trends," *Sterling Talent Solutions,* October 5, 2017, www.sterlingtalentsolutions.com, accessed July 10, 2018; "Is trawling social media the future of background checks?," *HRD,* July 6, 2017, www.hrmonline.ca, accessed July 10, 2018; Michael Bologna, "Social Media Strategies in Recruiting, Hiring Pose Legal Risks for Employers," *Bloomberg BNA,* April 21, 2014, http://www.bna.com; Jennifer Valentino-DeVries, "Bosses May Use Social Media to Discriminate against Job Seekers," *Wall Street Journal,* November 20, 2013, http://online.wsj.com.

PART 2

Preparing for and Acquiring Human Resources

CHAPTER 3

Analyzing Work and Designing Jobs

CHAPTER 4

Planning for and Recruiting Human Resources

CHAPTER 5

Selecting Employees

Blend Images/Getty Images

CHAPTER 3

Analyzing Work and Designing Jobs

WHAT DO I NEED TO KNOW?

After reading this chapter, you should be able to:

LO1 Summarize the elements of work flow analysis and how work flow relates to an organization's structure.

LO2 Discuss the significance of job analysis and identify the elements of a job analysis.

LO3 Explain how to obtain information for a job analysis and review job analysis developments.

LO4 Understand the different approaches to job design.

Ingram Publishing

Do you associate STEM education with designing a skate park?

Exceptionally Interesting Jobs in STEM?

What comes to mind when you think of a job in Science, Technology, Engineering, or Math (STEM)? Do you associate STEM jobs with lab coats and whiteboards filled with equations? How about skate park half-pipes, food trends, video games, and fireworks?

Many jobs in STEM may be unexpected and reflect the dynamic nature of work that needs to be accomplished by organizations. For example, a skate park engineer's job description may include duties such as "calculating the amount of building materials such as concrete, wood, and coping needed."

Rebecca Kapogiannis, talent acquisition and inclusion at 3M Canada, provides some additional background to explain the changing nature of jobs—"most of our STEM-educated workforce is directly in the field with our customers" (e.g., working on site to troubleshoot issues).[1]

Introduction

This chapter discusses the analysis and design of work and, in doing so, lays out some considerations that go into making informed decisions about how to create and link jobs. The chapter begins with a look at the big-picture issues related to analyzing work flow and organizational structure. The discussion then turns to the more specific issues of analyzing and designing jobs. Traditionally, job analysis has emphasized the study of existing jobs in order to make decisions such as employee selection, training, and rewards. In contrast, job design has emphasized making jobs more efficient or more motivating. However, as this chapter shows, the two activities are interrelated.

LO1 Work Flow in Organizations

Informed decisions about jobs take place in the context of the organization's overall work flow. Through the process of **work flow design**, managers analyze the tasks needed to produce a product or service. With this information, they assign these tasks to specific jobs and positions. (A **job** is a set of related duties. A **position** is the set of duties performed by one person. A school has many teaching *positions;* the person filling each of those positions is performing the *job* of teacher.) Basing these decisions on work flow design can lead to better results than the more traditional practice of looking at jobs individually.

work flow design The process of analyzing the tasks necessary for the production of a product or service.

job A set of related duties.

position The set of duties (job) performed by a particular person.

Work Flow Analysis

Before designing its work flow, the organization's planners need to analyze what work needs to be done. Figure 3.1 shows the elements of a work flow analysis. For each type of work, such as producing a product or providing a support service (accounting, legal support, and so on), the analysis identifies the output of the process, the activities involved, and three categories of inputs: raw inputs (materials and information), equipment, and human resources.

Outputs are the products of any work unit—whether a department, team, or an individual. Outputs may be identifiable objects such as a solar panel or a drivetrain for a passenger vehicle. However, an output can also be a service such as an airline flight or information (e.g., an answered question about employee benefits). In identifying the outputs of particular work units, work flow analysis considers both quantity and quality. Thinking in terms of these outputs gives HRM professionals a clearer view of how to increase each work unit's effectiveness.

Work flow analysis next considers the *work processes* used to generate the outputs identified. Work processes are the activities that a work unit's members engage in to produce a given output. They are described in terms of operating procedures for every task performed by each employee at each stage of the process. Specifying the processes helps HR professionals design efficient work systems by clarifying which tasks are necessary. Knowledge of work processes also can guide staffing changes when work is automated, outsourced, or restructured.

Finally, work flow analysis identifies the *inputs* required to carry out the work processes. As shown in Figure 3.1, inputs fall into three categories: raw inputs (materials and information), equipment, and human resources (knowledge, skills, and abilities). In the advertising industry, for example, technology has changed the relative importance of inputs. The stars of the ad business used to be the creative minds who dreamed up messages for television ads that would get people talking (and buying). But as consumers turn their attention to digital media, ad agencies need people who understand the latest in social media and who not only can generate a stream of messages but also can interpret the reaction streaming back from consumers.[2]

How Does the Work Fit with the Organization's Structure?

Work flow takes place in the context of an organization's structure. It requires the cooperation of individuals and groups. Ideally, the organization's structure brings together the people who must collaborate to produce the desired outputs efficiently. The structure may do this in a way that is highly *centralized* (i.e., with authority concentrated in a few people at the top of the organization)

FIGURE 3.1

Developing a Work Flow Analysis

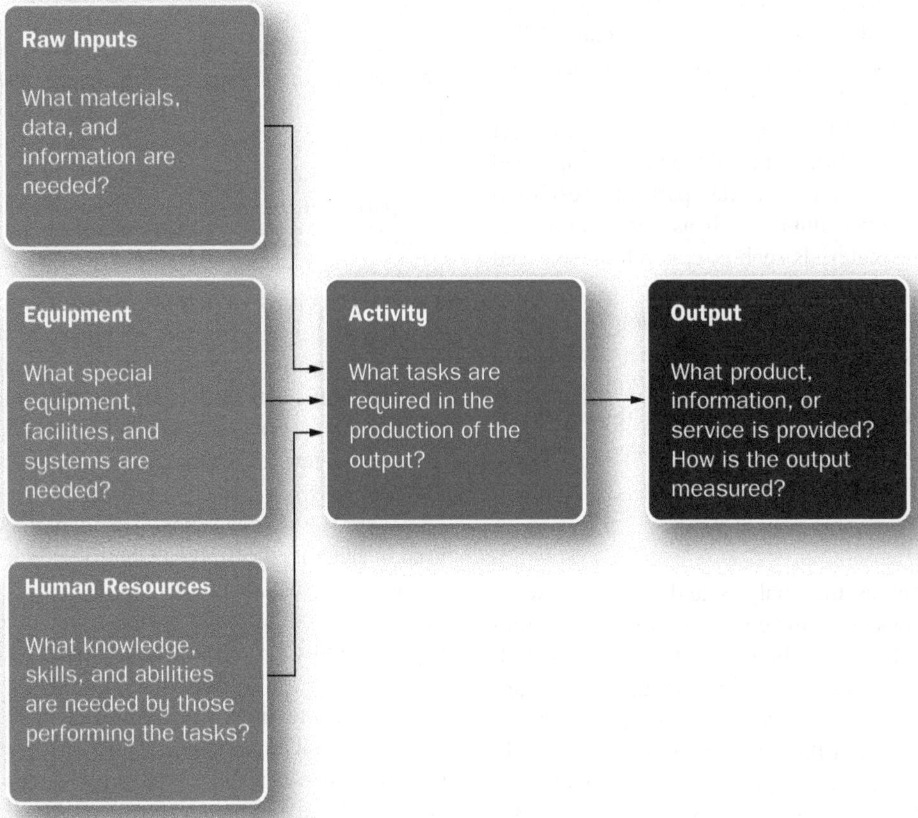

or *decentralized* (with authority spread among many people). The organization may group jobs according to functions (e.g., welding, painting, packaging), or it may set up divisions to focus on products or customer groups.

Although there are an infinite number of ways to combine the elements of an organization's structure, we can make some general observations about structure and work design. If the structure is strongly based on function, workers tend to have low authority and to work alone at highly specialized jobs. Jobs that involve teamwork or broad responsibility tend to require a structure based on divisions other than functions. When the goal is to empower employees, companies need to set up structures and jobs that enable broad responsibility, such as jobs that involve employees serving a particular group of customers or producing a particular product, rather than performing a narrowly defined function. The organization's structure also affects managers' jobs. Managing a division responsible for a product or customer group tends to require more experience and cognitive (thinking) ability than managing a department that handles a specific function. In contrast, managing a functional department requires skill in managing conflicts and aligning employees' efforts with higher-level goals, because these employees tend to identify significantly with their department or profession.[3]

Work design often emphasizes the analysis and design of jobs, as described in the remainder of this chapter. Although all of these approaches can succeed, each focuses on one isolated job at a time. These approaches do not necessarily consider how that single job fits into the overall work flow or structure of the organization. To use these techniques effectively, human resources professionals should also understand their organization as a whole.

LO2 Job Analysis

To achieve high-quality performance, organizations have to understand and match job requirements and people. This understanding requires *job analysis,* the process of getting detailed information about jobs. Analyzing jobs and understanding what is required to carry out a job provide essential knowledge for staffing, training, performance management, and many other HR activities

FIGURE 3.2

Job Analysis Provides Information for HR Processes

(see Figure 3.2). For instance, a supervisor's assessment of an employee's work should be based on performance relative to job requirements. In very small organizations, managers may perform a job analysis, but usually the work is done by a human resources professional. A large company may have a compensation management or total rewards function that includes *job analysts.* Organizations may also contract with firms that provide this service.

Importance of Job Analysis

Job analysis is so important that it has been called the building block of everything that HR does.[4] The fact is that almost every human resource management process requires some type of information gleaned from job analysis:[5]

- **Work redesign**. Often an organization seeks to redesign work to make it more efficient or to improve quality. The redesign requires detailed information about the existing job(s). In addition, preparing the redesign is similar to analyzing a job that does not yet exist.
- **Workforce planning**. As planners analyze human resource needs and how to meet those needs, they must have accurate information about the levels of skill required in various jobs, so that they can tell what kinds of human resources will be needed.
- **Talent acquisition**. To identify the applicants most likely to be the highest performers in various positions, decision makers need to know what tasks the individuals must perform, as well as the necessary knowledge, skills, and abilities.
- **Training, learning, and development**. Almost every employee hired by an organization will require training and/or development. Any learning initiative requires knowledge of the tasks performed in a job, so that the learning is related to the necessary knowledge and skills.
- **Performance management**. Performance management requires information about how well each employee is performing in order to reward employees who perform well and to improve their performance. Job analysis helps in identifying the behaviours and the results associated with effective performance.

- **Career planning**. Matching an individual's skills and aspirations with career opportunities requires that those responsible for developing career planning processes know the skill requirements of the various jobs. This facilitates matching of individuals to jobs in which they will succeed and be satisfied.
- **Job evaluation**. The process of job evaluation involves assessing the relative value of each job to the organization in order to set up fair pay structures. If employees do not believe pay structures are fair, they will become dissatisfied and may quit, or they will not see much benefit in striving for advancement. To put values on jobs, it is necessary to get information about different jobs and compare them.

Job analysis is also important from a legal standpoint. As we saw in Chapter 2, governments impose requirements related to human rights and pay equity. Detailed, accurate, objective job analysis information helps decision makers comply with these requirements by keeping the focus on tasks and abilities. Employers have a legal obligation to eliminate discrimination against employees and prospective employees requiring workplace accommodation. Job redesign may be required to meet the needs of the job applicant. When accommodation is discussed with the employee or job applicant, it is important to have a mindset and use language that focuses on the person's abilities (in contrast to "disability").[6]

Besides helping human resources professionals, job analysis helps supervisors and managers carry out their duties. Data from job analysis can help managers identify the types of work in their units, as well as provide information about the work flow process, so that managers can evaluate whether work is done in the most efficient way. Job analysis information also supports managers as they make hiring decisions, discuss performance, and recommend rewards.

EyeWire Collection/Getty Images

Careful job analysis makes it possible to define what a person in a certain job does and what qualifications are needed for the job. Firefighters use specific equipment to extinguish fires, require physical strength to do their jobs, and must possess the ability to make decisions under pressure.

Job Descriptions

job description
A list of the tasks, duties, and responsibilities (TDRs) that a particular job entails.

A key outcome of job analysis is the creation of job descriptions. A **job description** is a list of the tasks, duties, and responsibilities (TDRs) that a job entails. TDRs are observable actions. For example, a news photographer's job requires the job holder to use a camera to take photographs. If you were to observe someone in that position for a day, you would almost certainly see some pictures being taken. When a manager attempts to evaluate job performance, it is most important to have detailed information about the work performed in the job (i.e., the TDRs). This information makes it possible to determine how well an individual is meeting each job requirement.

A job description typically has the format shown in Figure 3.3. It includes the job title, an overview of the job, and a list of the main duties. Although organizations may modify this format according to their needs, all job descriptions within an organization should follow the same format. This helps the organization make consistent decisions about matters such as pay and promotions. It also helps the organization show that it makes human resource decisions fairly.

Whenever the organization creates a new job, it needs to prepare a job description. Preparation of a job description begins with gathering information about the job from people already performing the job, the supervisor or the managers creating the job, and external experts or sources of information. Based on that information, the writer of the job description identifies the essential duties of the job, including mental and physical tasks and any methods and resources required. Job descriptions should be reviewed periodically (say once a year) and updated if necessary. Performance feedback conversations can provide a good opportunity for updating job descriptions, as the employee and supervisor compare what the employee has been doing against the details of the job description.

When organizations prepare many job descriptions, the process can become repetitive and time consuming. To address this challenge, a number of companies have developed software that provides forms into which the job analyst can insert details about the specific job. Typically, the job analyst would use a library of basic descriptions, selecting one that is for a similar type of job and then modifying it to fit the organization's needs.

Organizations should provide newly hired employees with access to their job description. This helps an employee understand what is expected, but it shouldn't be presented as limiting the employee's commitment to quality and customer satisfaction. Ideally, employees will want to go above and beyond the listed duties when the situation and their abilities call for that. Many job descriptions

FIGURE 3.3

Sample Job Description

FINANCIAL AND INVESTMENT ANALYSTS (NOC 1112)

Financial and investment analysts collect and analyze financial information such as economic forecasts, trading volumes and the movement of capital, financial backgrounds of companies, historical performances, and future trends of stocks, bonds, and other investment instruments to provide financial and investment or financing advice for their company or their company's clients. Their studies and evaluations cover areas such as takeover bids, private placements, mergers, or acquisitions.

Main Duties

Financial analysts perform some or all of the following duties:

- Evaluate financial risk, prepare financial forecasts, financing scenarios, and other documents concerning capital management, and write reports and recommendations
- Plan short- and long-term cash flows and assess financial performance
- Analyze investment projects
- Advise on and participate in the financial aspects of contracts and calls for tender
- Follow up on financing projects with financial backers
- Develop, implement, and use tools for managing and analyzing financial portfolios
- Prepare a regular risk profile for debt portfolios
- Assist in preparing operating and investment budgets

Investment analysts perform some or all of the following duties:

- Collect financial and investment information about companies, stocks, bonds, and other investments using daily stock and bond reports, economic forecasts, trading volumes, financial periodicals, securities manuals, company financial statements, and other financial reports and publications
- Examine and analyze financial and investment information collected, including profiles of companies, stock and bond prices, yields, and future trends and other investment information
- Provide investment advice and recommendations to clients, senior company officials, pension fund managers, securities agents, and associates
- Prepare company, industry and economic outlooks, analytical reports, briefing notes, and correspondence

Source: Government of Canada - National Occupational Classification (NOC 2016), Financial and Investment Analysts, http://noc.esdc.gc.ca/English/NOC/QuickSearch.aspx?ver=&val65=1112, accessed January 29, 2018.

include the phrase *and other duties as required* as a way to remind employees not to tell their supervisor, "But that's not part of my job."

Job Specifications

Whereas the job description focuses on the activities involved in carrying out a job, a **job specification** looks at the qualities or requirements the person performing the job must possess. It is a list of the knowledge, skills, abilities, and other characteristics (KSAOs) a job holder must have to perform the job.

job specification
A list of the knowledge, skills, abilities, and other characteristics (KSAOs) that an job holder must have to perform a particular job

Knowledge refers to factual or procedural information necessary for successfully performing a task. For example, this course is providing you with knowledge in how to manage human resources. A *skill* is an individual's level of proficiency at performing a particular task—the capability to perform it well. With knowledge and experience, you could acquire skill in the task of preparing job specifications. *Ability,* in contrast to skill, refers to a more general enduring capability that an individual possesses. A person might have the ability to collaborate with others or to write clearly and concisely. Finally, *other characteristics* might be personality traits such as persistence or motivation to achieve. Some jobs also have legal requirements, such as licensing or certification. Figure 3.4 is a sample job specification for the job description in Figure 3.3.

FIGURE 3.4

Sample Job Specification

FINANCIAL AND INVESTMENT ANALYSTS (NOC 1112)
Employment Requirements

- A bachelor's degree in commerce, business administration, or economics *and* on-the-job training and industry courses and programs are usually required.
- A master's degree in business administration (MBA—concentration in finance) or in finance may be required.
- The Chartered Financial Analyst (CFA) designation, available through a program conducted by the Institute of Chartered Financial Analysts in the United States, may be required.

Source: Government of Canada - National Occupational Classification (NOC 2016), Financial and Investment Analysts, http://noc.esdc.gc.ca/English/NOC/ProfileQuickSearch.aspx?val=1&val1=1112&ver=16&val65=Financial%20Analyst, accessed January 29, 2018.

In developing job specifications, it is important to consider all of the elements of the KSAOs. As with writing a job description, the information can come from a combination of people performing the job, people supervising or planning for the job, trained job analysts, and external sources. A study by ACT's Workforce Development Division interviewed manufacturing supervisors to learn what they do each day and what skills they rely on. The researchers learned that the supervisors spend much of their day monitoring their employees to make sure the workplace is safe, product quality is maintained, and work processes are optimal. Also, they rely heavily on their technical knowledge of the work processes they supervise.[7] Based on this information, a job specification for a manufacturing supervisor would include skill in observing how people work, as well as in-depth knowledge of manufacturing processes and tools.

In contrast to tasks, duties, and responsibilities, KSAOs are characteristics of people and are observable only when individuals are carrying out the TDRs of the job—and afterward, if they can show the product of their work. Thus, when individuals apply for a job as a news photographer, you could not simply look at them to determine whether they can spot and take effective photos. However, you would be able to draw conclusions later about their skills by looking at examples of their photos. Similarly, many employers specify educational requirements. Meeting these requirements is treated as an indication that a person has some desired level of knowledge and skills.

Accurate information about KSAOs is especially important for making decisions about who will fill a job. A manager attempting to fill a position needs information about the characteristics required and about the characteristics of each applicant. Interviews and selection decisions should therefore focus on KSAOs.

LO3 Sources of Job Information

Information for analyzing an existing job often comes from *incumbents,* that is, people who currently hold that position in the organization. They are a logical source of information because they are most acquainted with the details of the job. Incumbents should be able to provide very accurate information.

A drawback of relying solely on incumbents' information is that they may have an incentive to exaggerate what they do to appear more valuable to the organization. Information from incumbents should therefore be supplemented with information from observers, such as supervisors. Supervisors should review the information provided by incumbents, looking for a match between what incumbents are doing and what they are supposed to do. Research suggests that supervisors may provide the most accurate estimates of the importance of job duties, while incumbents may be more accurate in reporting information about the actual time spent performing job tasks and safety-related risk factors.[8] For analyzing skill levels, the best source may be external job analysts who have more experience rating a wide range of jobs.[9]

The federal government also provides background information for analyzing jobs. Employment and Social Development Canada, working with Statistics Canada, maintains the **National Occupational Classification (NOC)** to provide standardized sources of information

National Occupational Classification (NOC) Tool created by the federal government to provide a standardized source of information about jobs in Canada's labour market.

about jobs in Canada's labour market. The NOC is a tool that uses a four-digit code to classify occupations based on the types and levels of skills required. The NOC classification system supports the needs of employers and individual job seekers, as well as career counsellors, statisticians, and labour market analysts, by providing a consistent way to identify and interpret the nature of work. A recent addition to the site is a publication titled *Job Descriptions: An Employers' Handbook* that may be particularly helpful to managers and human resource professionals.

Position Analysis Questionnaire

Position Analysis Questionnaire (PAQ) A standardized job analysis questionnaire containing 194 questions about work behaviours, work conditions, and job characteristics that apply to a wide variety of jobs.

After gathering information, the job analyst uses the information to analyze the job. One of the broadest and best-researched instruments for analyzing jobs is the **Position Analysis Questionnaire (PAQ)**, a standardized tool containing 194 items that represent work behaviours, work conditions, and job characteristics that apply to a wide variety of jobs. The questionnaire is organized into six sections concerning different aspects of the job:

1. **Information input**. Where and how a worker gets information needed to perform the job.
2. **Mental processes**. The reasoning, decision-making, planning, and information-processing activities involved in performing the job.
3. **Work output**. The physical activities, tools, and devices used by the worker to perform the job.
4. **Relationships with other persons**. The relationships with other people required in performing the job.
5. **Job context**. The physical and social contexts where the work is performed.
6. **Other characteristics**. The activities, conditions, and characteristics other than those previously described that are relevant to the job.

The person analyzing a job determines whether each item on the questionnaire applies to the job being analyzed. The analyst rates each item on six scales: extent of use, amount of time, importance to the job, possibility of occurrence, applicability, and special code (special rating scales used with a particular item). The PAQ headquarters scores the questionnaire and generates a report that describes the scores on the job dimensions.

Using the PAQ provides an organization with information that helps in comparing jobs, even when they are dissimilar. The PAQ also has the advantage that it considers the whole work process, from inputs through outputs. However, the person who fills out the questionnaire must have postsecondary-level reading skills, and the PAQ is meant to be completed only by job analysts trained in this method. In fact, the ratings of job incumbents tend to be less reliable than ratings by supervisors and trained analysts.[10] Also, the descriptions in the PAQ reports are rather abstract, so the reports may not be useful for writing job descriptions or redesigning jobs.

Fleishman Job Analysis System

Fleishman Job Analysis System Job analysis technique that asks subject-matter experts to evaluate a job in terms of the abilities required to perform the job.

To gather information about worker requirements, the **Fleishman Job Analysis System** asks subject-matter experts (typically job incumbents) to evaluate a job in terms of the abilities required to perform the job.[11] The survey is based on 52 categories of abilities, ranging from written comprehension to deductive reasoning, manual dexterity, stamina, and originality. The survey items are arranged into a scale for each ability. Each begins with a description of the ability and a comparison to related abilities. Below this is a seven-point scale with phrases describing extremely high and low levels of the ability. The person completing the survey indicates which point on the scale represents the level of the ability required for performing the job being analyzed.

Analyzing Teamwork

Work design increasingly relies on teams to accomplish an organization's objectives, so HR professionals often must identify the best ways to handle jobs that are highly interdependent. Just as there are standardized instruments for assessing the nature of a job, there are standard ways to measure the nature of teams. Three dimensions are most critical:[12]

1. **Skill differentiation**—The degree to which team members have specialized knowledge or functional capacities.
2. **Authority differentiation**—The allocation of decision-making authority among individuals, subgroups, and the team as a whole.
3. **Temporal (time) stability**—The length of time over which team members must work together.

Competency Models

These traditional approaches to job analysis are too limited for some organizational needs. When human resource management is actively engaged in talent management as a way to support strategy, organizations need to think beyond skills for particular jobs. They must identify the capabilities they need to acquire and develop in order to promote the organization's success. For this purpose, organizations develop competency models. A **competency** is an area of personal capability that enables employees to perform their work successfully.[13]

competency An area of personal capability that enables employees to perform their work successfully.

For example, success in a job or career path might require leadership strength, skill in coaching others, and the ability to bring out the best in each member of a diverse team of employees. A competency model identifies and describes all the competencies required for success in a particular occupation or set of jobs. Organizations may create competency models for occupational groups, levels of the organization, or even the entire organization. The Conference Board of Canada recently reported that almost three-quarters (72 percent) of organizations have a clearly defined set of competencies for key roles and positions. Highest use of competencies was in government (83 percent) and in organizations with 1,500–4,999 employees (88 percent).[14]

A competency model might require that all middle managers or all members of the organization be able to act with integrity, value diversity, and commit themselves to providing am excellent customer experience. Table 3.1 shows an example of a competency model for a project manager. The left side of the table lists competencies required for a project manager (organizational and planning skills; communications; and financial and quantitative skills). The right side of the table shows behaviours that might be used to determine a project manager's level of proficiency for each competency. As in this example, competency models focus more on how people work, whereas job analysis focuses more on work tasks and outcomes. By focusing on performance and development aligned with organizational strategy, competency modelling provides the potential to create a fuller integration of human resource functions than traditional job analysis that examines specific jobs.[15]

Developments in Job Analysis

As we noted in the earlier discussion of work flow analysis and competency models, organizations have been appreciating the need to analyze jobs in the context of the organization's structure, strategy, and performance. In addition, organizations are recognizing that today's workplace must be agile and adaptable, and is constantly subject to change. Thus, although we tend to think of "jobs" as something stable, they actually tend to change and evolve over time. Those who occupy or manage jobs often make adjustments to match personal preferences or changing conditions.[16] Indeed, although errors in job analysis can have many sources, most of the inaccuracy is likely to result from job descriptions being outdated. For this reason, job analysis must not only define jobs when they are created but also detect changes in jobs.

TABLE 3.1

Examples of Competencies and a Competency Model

Project Manager Competencies	Proficiency Ratings
Organizational and Planning Skills Ability to establish priorities on projects and schedule activities to achieve results.	**1—Below Expectations:** Unable to perform basic tasks. **2—Meets Expectations:** Understands basic principles and performs routine tasks with reliable results; works with minimal supervision or assistance. **3—Exceeds Expectations:** Performs complex and multiple tasks; can coach, teach, or lead others.
Communications Ability to build credibility and trust through open and direct communications with internal and external customers.	**1—Below Expectations:** Unable to perform basic tasks. **2—Meets Expectations:** Understands basic principles and performs routine tasks with reliable results; works with minimal supervision or assistance. **3—Exceeds Expectations:** Performs complex and multiple tasks; can coach, teach, or lead others.
Financial and Quantitative Skills Ability to analyze financial information accurately and set financial goals that have a positive impact on company's bottom line and fiscal objectives.	**1—Below Expectations:** Unable to perform basic tasks. **2—Meets Expectations:** Understands basic principles and performs routine tasks with reliable results; works with minimal supervision or assistance. **3—Exceeds Expectations:** Performs complex and multiple tasks; can coach, teach, or lead others.

Source: Based on R. J. Mirabile, "Everything You Wanted to Know about Competency Modeling," *Training and Development* (August 1997): pp. 73–77.

With global competitive pressures, automation, and weak demand growth, one corporate change that has affected many organizations is downsizing. Research suggests that successful downsizing efforts almost always entail changes in the nature of jobs, not just their number. Jobs that have survived downsizing tend to have a broader scope of responsibilities coupled with less supervision. In some cases, organizations preserve jobs by asking employees to get the same amount of work done during fewer hours for less pay (because of the reduced hours). These changes can succeed with the right people in the jobs, working in conditions that allow them to focus on what matters most.[17]

These changes in the nature of work, the expanded use of "project-based" organizational structures, and the increasing shift to an on-demand economy require the type of broader understanding that comes from an analysis of work flows. For example, Uber's business model relies upon independent contractors as drivers, most of whom work only a few hours per week. In this context, work analysis focused on the tasks involved in the work is likely more relevant than traditional job analysis.[18]

Because the work can change rapidly and it is impossible to rewrite job descriptions every week, job descriptions and specifications need to be flexible. At the same time, legal requirements (as discussed in Chapter 2) may discourage organizations from writing flexible job descriptions. This means organizations must balance the need for flexibility with the need for legal documentation. This presents one of the major challenges to be faced by HRM departments in the next decade. Many are meeting this challenge with a greater emphasis on careful job design.

LO4 Job Design

Although job analysis, as just described, is important for an understanding of existing jobs, organizations also must plan for new jobs and periodically consider whether they should revise existing jobs. When an organization is expanding, supervisors and human resources professionals must help plan for new or growing work units. When an organization is trying to improve quality or efficiency, a review of work units and processes may require a fresh look at how jobs are designed.

These situations call for *job design,* the process of defining the way work will be performed and the tasks that a given job requires, or *job redesign,* a similar process that involves changing an existing job design. To design jobs effectively, a person must thoroughly understand the job itself (through job analysis) and its place in the larger work unit's work flow process (through work flow analysis). Having a detailed knowledge of the tasks performed in the work unit and in the job, a manager then has many alternative ways to design a job. As shown in Figure 3.5, the available approaches emphasize different aspects of the job: the mechanics of doing a job efficiently, the job's impact on motivation, and the job's impact on both the physical and mental health and well-being of the people performing the job.

Designing Efficient Jobs

If workers perform tasks as efficiently as possible, not only does the organization benefit from lower costs and greater output per worker, but also workers should be less fatigued. This point of view has for years formed the basis

FIGURE 3.5

Approaches to Job Design

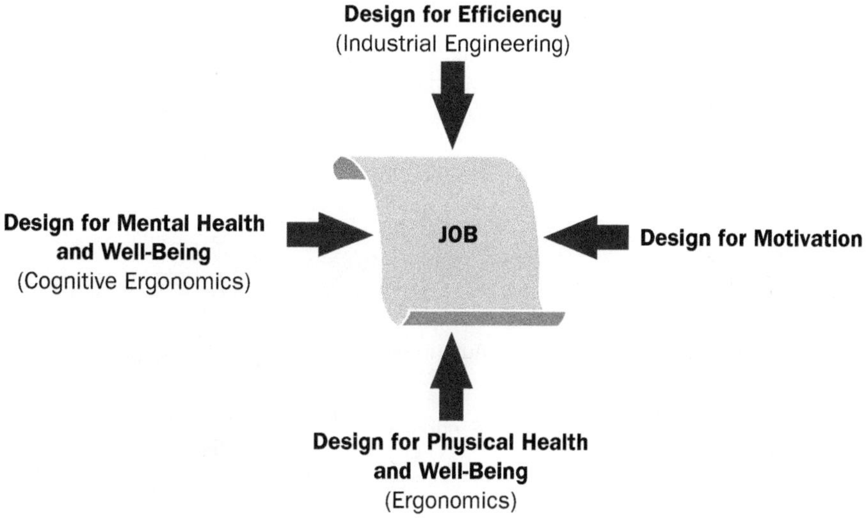

of classical **industrial engineering**, which looks for the simplest way to structure work in order to maximize efficiency. Typically, applying industrial engineering to a job reduces the complexity of the work, making it so simple that almost anyone can be trained quickly and easily to perform the job. Such jobs tend to be highly specialized and repetitive.

industrial engineering The study of jobs to find the simplest way to structure work in order to maximize efficiency.

In practice, the scientific method traditionally seeks the "one best way" to perform a job by performing time-and-motion studies to identify the most efficient movements for workers to make. Once the engineers have identified the most efficient sequence of motions, the organization should select workers based on their ability to do the job, then train them in the details of the "one best way" to perform that job. The company also should offer pay structured to motivate workers to do their best. (Chapter 8 discusses total rewards.)

Industrial engineering provides measurable and practical benefits. However, a focus on efficiency alone can create jobs that are so simple and repetitive that workers get bored. Workers performing these jobs may feel their work is meaningless. Hence, most organizations combine industrial engineering with other approaches to job design.

Designing Jobs That Motivate

Especially when organizations have to compete for employees, depend on skilled knowledge workers, or need a workforce that cares about customer satisfaction, a pure focus on efficiency will not achieve human resource objectives. Organizations need jobs that employees find interesting and satisfying, and job design should take into account factors that make jobs motivating to employees.

A model that shows how to make jobs more motivating is the Job Characteristics Model, developed by Richard Hackman and Greg Oldham. This model describes jobs in terms of five characteristics:[19]

1. **Skill variety**—The extent to which a job requires a variety of skills to carry out the tasks involved;
2. **Task identity**—The degree to which a job requires completing a "whole" piece of work from beginning to end (e.g., building an entire component or resolving a customer's issue);
3. **Task significance**—The extent to which the job has an important impact on the lives of other people;
4. **Autonomy**—The degree to which the job allows an individual to make decisions about the way the work will be carried out;
5. **Feedback**—The extent to which a person receives clear information about performance effectiveness from the work itself.

As shown in Figure 3.6, the more of each of these characteristics a job has, the more motivating the job will be, according to the job characteristics model. The model predicts that a person with such a job will be more satisfied and will produce more and better work. For an example of such a job, consider the skill variety and task significance of some of the positions companies are filling in order to have a stronger web presence. Front-end developers apply knowledge of software, design, and user behaviour to create a user interface that is clear and easy to use. Data scientists translate business problems into mathematical models they can test and then translate their

FIGURE 3.6

Characteristics of a Motivating Job

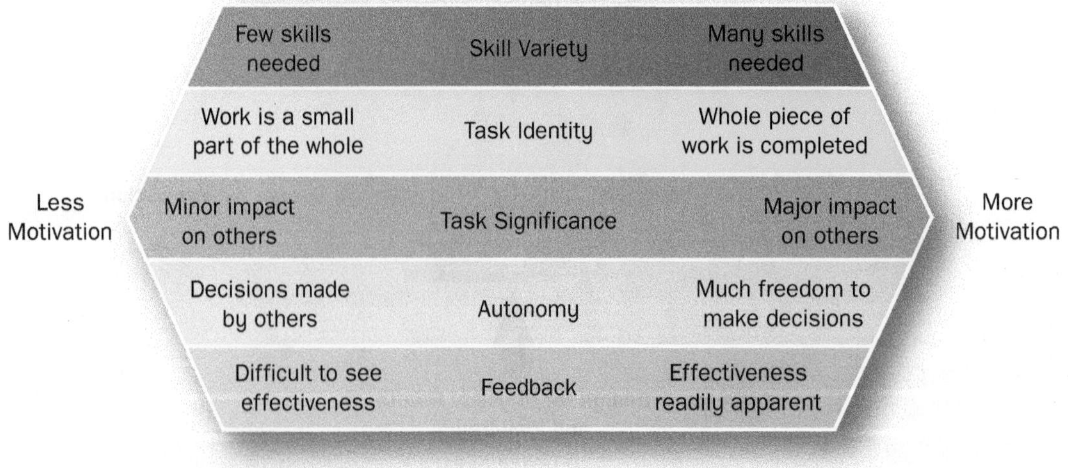

statistical test results into business solutions. Now imagine employees in jobs like this working in an environment such as Square Root, a tech company that analyzes data to help businesses improve their performance. Square Root's policies are based on a belief that employees do their best work when they have autonomy concerning their schedule and other working conditions. Its employees say the company provides great challenges and a great atmosphere—and their co-workers go above and beyond to meet goals.[20]

Applications of the job characteristics approach to job design include job enlargement, job enrichment, self-managing work teams, flexible work schedules, and remote work. In applying these methods, HR professionals should keep in mind that individual differences among workers will affect how much they are motivated by job characteristics and able to do their best work.[21] For example, someone who thrives in a highly structured environment might not actually be motivated by autonomy and would be a better fit where a supervisor makes most decisions.

Job Enlargement

In a job design, **job enlargement** refers to broadening the types of tasks performed. The objective of job enlargement is to make jobs less repetitive and more interesting. Jobs also become enlarged when organizations add new goals or ask fewer workers to accomplish work that had been spread among more people. In those situations, the challenge is to avoid crossing the line from interesting jobs into jobs that burn out employees.

> **job enlargement**
> Broadening the types of tasks performed in a job.

Organizations that use job enlargement to make jobs more motivational employ techniques such as job extension and job rotation. **Job extension** is enlarging jobs by combining several relatively simple jobs to form a job with a wider range of tasks. An example might be combining the jobs of receptionist, data entry clerk, and records clerk into jobs containing all three kinds of work. This approach to job enlargement is relatively simple, but if all the tasks are dull, workers will not necessarily be more motivated by the redesigned job.

> **job extension**
> Enlarging jobs by combining several relatively simple jobs to form a job with a wider range of tasks.

Job rotation does not actually redesign the jobs, but rather moves employees among several different jobs. This approach to job enlargement is common among production teams. During the course of a week, a team member may carry out each of the jobs handled by the team. Team members might assemble components one day and pack products into cases another day. As with job extension, the enlarged jobs may still consist of repetitious activities, but with greater variation among those activities.

> **job rotation**
> Enlarging jobs by moving employees among several different jobs.

Job Enrichment

The idea of **job enrichment**, or empowering workers by adding more decision-making authority to their jobs, comes from the work of Frederick Herzberg. According to Herzberg's two-factor theory, individuals are motivated more by the intrinsic aspects of work (e.g., the meaningfulness of a job) than by extrinsic rewards such as pay. Herzberg identified five factors he associated with motivating jobs: achievement, recognition, growth, responsibility, and performance of the entire job. Thus, ways to enrich a manufacturing job might include giving employees authority to stop production when quality standards are not being met and having each employee perform several tasks to complete a particular stage of the process, rather than dividing up the tasks among the employees. For a sales associate in a store, job enrichment might involve the authority to resolve customer problems, including the authority to decide whether to issue refunds or replace merchandise.

> **job enrichment**
> Engaging workers by adding more decision-making authority to jobs.

In practice, however, it is important to note that not every worker responds positively to enriched jobs. These jobs are best suited to employees who are flexible and responsive to others; for these employees, enriched jobs can dramatically improve motivation.[22]

Self-managed Work Teams

Instead of merely enriching individual jobs, some organizations engage employees by designing work to be done by self-managed work teams. These teams have authority for an entire work process or segment. Team members typically have authority to schedule work, hire team members, resolve problems related to the team's performance, and perform other duties traditionally handled by management. Teamwork can give a job motivating characteristics such as autonomy, skill variety, and task identity.

Because team members' responsibilities are great, their jobs usually are defined broadly and include sharing of work assignments. Team members may, at one time or another, perform every duty of the team. The challenge for the organization is to provide enough training so that the team members can learn the necessary skills. Another approach, when teams are responsible for particular work processes or customers, is to assign the team responsibility for the process or customer, then let the team decide which members will carry out which tasks.

A study of work teams at a large financial services company found that the right job design was associated with effective teamwork.[23] In particular, when teams are self-managed and team members are highly involved in decision making, teams are more productive, employees more satisfied, and managers more satisfied with performance. Teams also tend to do better when each team member performs a variety of tasks and when team members view their effort as significant.

Flexible Work Schedules

One way an organization can give employees some say in how their work is structured is to offer flexible work schedules. Depending on the requirements of the organization and the individual jobs, organizations may be able to be flexible about when employees work. As introduced in Chapter 1, types of flexibility include flextime and job sharing. Figure 3.7 illustrates alternatives to the traditional 40-hour workweek.

flextime A scheduling policy in which full-time employees may choose starting and ending times within guidelines specified by the organization.

Flextime is a scheduling policy in which full-time employees may choose starting and ending times within guidelines specified by the organization. The flextime policy may require that employees be at work between certain hours, say, 10:00 a.m. and 3:00 p.m. Employees work additional hours before or after this period in order to work the full day. One employee might arrive early in the morning in order to leave at 3:00 p.m. to pick up children after school. Another employee might need to check in on an aging parent in the morning, or prefer going to the gym before arriving for work at 10:00 a.m. and work until 6:00 or 7:00 p.m. A flextime policy may also enable workers to adjust a specific day's

Antonio Mo/Getty Images

Employees who have enriched jobs and/or work in self-managed teams are likely to be motivated and engaged when they have decision-making authority.

FIGURE 3.7

Alternatives to the 8-to-5 Job

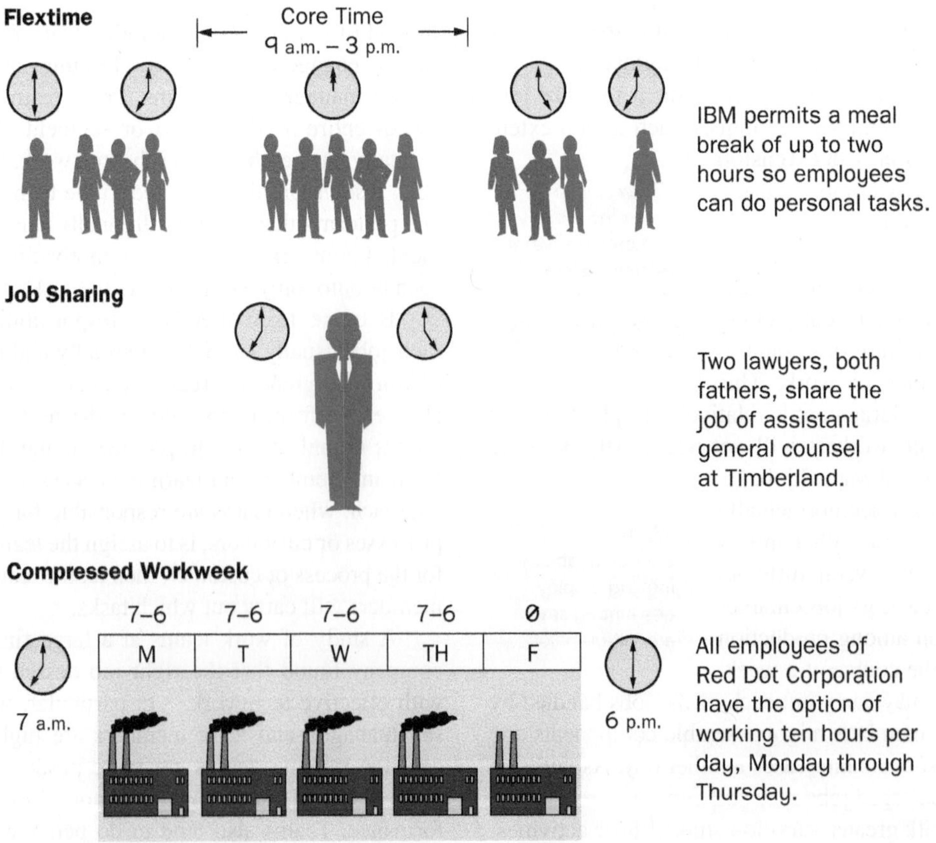
Flextime
Core Time
9 a.m. – 3 p.m.
IBM permits a meal break of up to two hours so employees can do personal tasks.
Job Sharing
Two lawyers, both fathers, share the job of assistant general counsel at Timberland.
Compressed Workweek
7–6
7–6
7–6
7–6
0
M
T
W
TH
F
7 a.m.
6 p.m.
All employees of Red Dot Corporation have the option of working ten hours per day, Monday through Thursday.

hours in order to make time for outside appointments, family activities, or volunteer work. A work schedule that allows time for personal, community, and family interests can be extremely motivating for some employees.

Job sharing is a work option in which two part-time employees carry out the tasks associated with a single position. Such arrangements can enable an organization to attract or retain valued employees who want more time to attend school, care for family members, or allocate time to personal interests. The job requirements in such an arrangement include the ability to work cooperatively and coordinate the details of one's job with another person.

job sharing
A work option in which two part-time employees carry out the tasks associated with a single position.

Although not strictly a form of flexibility on the level of individual employees, another scheduling alternative is the *compressed workweek.* A compressed workweek is a schedule in which full-time workers complete their weekly hours in fewer than five days. For example, instead of working eight hours a day for five days, the employees might complete 40 hours of work in four 10-hour days. This alternative is most common, but some companies use other alternatives, such as scheduling 80 hours over nine days (with a three-day weekend every other week) or reducing the workweek from 40 to 38 or 36 hours. Employees may appreciate the extra days available for leisure, family, or volunteer activities. An organization might even use this schedule to offer a kind of flexibility—for example, letting workers choose whether they want a compressed workweek during the summer months. This type of schedule has a couple of drawbacks, however. One is that employees may become exhausted on the longer workdays. Another is that if the arrangement involves working more than a specific number of hours during a week, employment/labour standards legislation may require the payment of overtime wages to certain groups of employees. For ideas on how to set up flexible scheduling, see HR How To.

HR How-To

Planning for Workplace Flexibility

Many companies allow for some flexibility in work arrangements, but far fewer have established formal policies for it, according to a recent survey by World at Work and FlexJobs. Providing guidelines in "print" is one important step in ensuring that such arrangements are fair and well understood. Here are some additional tips for setting up flexible arrangements:

- Set guidelines or boundaries for what is flexible. For example, employees may work any hours between Monday and Friday as long as these include at least 30 hours worked in the office each week.
- Establish performance standards that managers can track whether or not they and their employees are working in the same place at the same time.
- Recognize that some jobs are suitable for flexible work hours and locations, but others are not. Review job requirements to ensure that decisions about flexibility are related to the conditions for successful job performance.
- Avoid making any pre-conceived conclusions about which employees will value flexibility. Stereotypes might suggest that women are more concerned about having flexibility because they have more responsibilities for family care. However, surveys that ask about flexibility are finding that men also value flexibility.
- Plan what measures to use to monitor the success of any flexibility policies. For example, the company might measure employee turnover, absenteeism, and output before and after starting to offer flexibility, in order to estimate its impact on business success.
- Develop managers' understanding of and ability to support flexible arrangements. If managers are comfortable with, say flextime, employees will be more likely to use it. These policies will be more effective if managers feel confident in leading employees and measuring performance.

Sources: Ellen Galinsky, "Relationship Management: The New Flexibility," *HR Magazine,* December 2015, https://www.shrm.org; Genevieve Douglas, "Flexible Work Programs Plentiful, but Not Formalized," *HR Focus,* November 2015, pp. 13–14; Kathy Gurchiek, "Five Companies That Get Workflex Right," *HR Magazine,* October 2015, https:www.shrm.org; "Study: Men Value Flex Just as Much as Women Do," *HR Specialist: Compensation & Benefits,* January 2015, *Business Insights:* Global, http://bi.galegroup.com; Clare Benttelley, "Turn for the Better," *Employee Benefits,* March 2015, EBSCOhost, https://web.a.ebscohost.com.

HR Oops!

Neglecting Remote Workers?

Although more people are working remotely, Gallup research identifies three areas where managers fall short in engaging their fully remote workers—not recognizing or praising their good work as frequently; being less likely to have a conversation about career goals and personal growth; and not providing opportunities to connect with co-workers. And, according to a recent survey of 1,153 employees conducted by VitalSmarts, remote workers say that colleagues leave them out and even mistreat them. For example, 84 percent of remote workers report that when they experience routine workplace challenges "the concern dragged on for a few days or more." Remote workers are also more likely to report that "their colleagues don't fight for my priorities, say bad things behind my back, and make changes to a project without warning me," than on-site employees.

Questions

1. What can managers do to build trust and keep remote workers focused and high-performing?
2. What can remote workers do to maintain strong connections to their organizations?

Source: Michael Ferguson, "Stop Neglecting Remote Workers," *Harvard Business Review*, January 17, 2018, https://hbr.org; John Dujay, "Remote workers feeling excluded: Study," *Canadian HR Reporter*, 30 (21), December 11, 2017, p. 3, 10; Joseph Grenny and David Maxfield, "A Study of 1,100 Employees Found That Remote Workers Feel Shunned and Left Out," *Harvard Business Review*, November 2, 2017, https://hbr.org; Annamarie Mann, "3 Ways You Are Failing Your Remote Workers," *Gallup News*, August 1, 2017, http://news.gallup.com, accessed February 1, 2018.

Telework and Remote Work

Flexibility can extend to work locations as well as work schedules. Before the Industrial Revolution, most people worked either close to or inside their own homes. Mass production technologies changed all this, separating work life from home life, as people began to travel to centrally located factories and offices. Escalating prices for office space, combined with drastically reduced prices for computers and communication technologies, are forces working to reverse this trend. The broad term for doing one's work away from a centrally located office is *remote work, telework,* or *telecommuting;* however, it was been suggested that *remote workers* work solely from home, whereas *telecommuters* work from home an average of 1–3 days per week.[24] Wayne Berger, executive vice-president of Regus Canada, a flexible workplace provider based in Toronto, describes remote work/telework being at the highest level ever with 47 percent of Canadians working "outside the office for half the week or more."[25]

For employers, advantages of remote work include reduced need for office space and the ability to offer greater flexibility to employees. A recent report by Global Workforce Analytics and FlexJobs estimates that half-time telecommuting would reduce real estate costs by 25 percent; reduce absenteeism costs by 31 percent, and increase productivity by 15 percent.[26]

Remote work/telework can also support a strategy of sustainability because these employees do not produce the greenhouse gas emissions that result from commuting by vehicle. Remote work and telework is easiest to implement for people in managerial, professional, office, or sales jobs. A remote arrangement is generally difficult to set up for manufacturing workers and has become a hot topic in tech companies. For example, IBM, once a "remote-work pioneer" with 40 percent of its 386,000 global employees working remotely, recently informed 2,600 remote employees that the company would be calling them back to state-of-the art office spaces to inspire collaboration, innovation, and team work.[27]

Leslie Sarauer, senior vice-president of human resources at Waterloo, Ontario–based OpenText, explains that "when it comes to tech developers and engineering teams, it's helpful to have those teams working together as opposed to remotely."[28]

Designing Ergonomically Correct Jobs

The way people use their bodies when they work—whether lifting heavy furniture into a moving truck or sitting quietly before a computer screen—affects their physical well-being and may affect how well and how long they can work. The study of the interface between individuals' physiology and the characteristics of the physical work environment is called **ergonomics**. The goal of ergonomics is to minimize physical strain on

ergonomics
The study of the interface between individuals' physiology and the characteristics of the physical work environment.

the worker by structuring the physical work environment around the way the human body works. Ergonomics therefore focuses on outcomes such as reducing physical fatigue, aches and pains, and health complaints. Ergonomic research includes the context in which work takes place, such as the lighting, space, and hours worked.[29]

Ergonomic job design has been applied in redesigning equipment used in jobs that are physically demanding. Such redesign is often aimed at reducing the physical demands of certain jobs so that more people are able to perform them. In addition, many interventions focus on redesigning machines and technology—for instance, adjusting the height of a computer keyboard to minimize occupational illnesses, such as carpal tunnel syndrome. The design of chairs and desks to fit posture requirements is very important in many office jobs. One study found that having employees participate in an ergonomic redesign effort significantly reduced the number and severity of *repetitive strain injuries* (injuries that result from performing the same movement over and over), lost production time, and restricted-duty days.[30]

A more recent ergonomic challenge comes from the popularity of mobile devices. As workers find more and more uses for these devices, they are at risk from repetitive-stress injuries (RSIs). Typing with one's thumbs to send frequent text messages on a smartphone can result in inflammation of the tendons that move the thumbs. Laptop computers are handy to carry, but because the screen and keyboard may be contained in a single device, it can be difficult to create the ergonomically correct standards of screen at eye level and keyboard low enough to type with arms bent at a 90-degree angle. Frequent users of these devices must therefore trade off eyestrain against physical strain to wrists, unless they hook up their device to an external, properly positioned keyboard. Touchscreens pose their own risks. They are typically part of a flat device such as a smartphone or tablet, and these are difficult to position for optimal viewing and typing. Using vertically oriented touchscreens causes even more muscle strain than tapping on a screen lying flat. In addition, because touchscreens usually lack the tactile feedback of pressing keys on a keyboard, users tend to strike them with more force than they use on real keys. Attaching a supplemental keyboard addresses this potential source of strain. When using mobile devices or any computer, workers can protect themselves by taking frequent breaks and paying attention to their posture while they work.[31]

Did You KNOW?

Mental Illness in the Employed Is Increasing for All Age Groups

The Mental Health Commission of Canada (MHCC) reports that 1 in 5 Canadians experience a mental health or addiction problem in any given year and that mental health costs the Canadian economy about $51 billion every year. Information about a job's cognitive demands including time pressures, social interactions, and general stressors that could increase the mental stress of people performing the job is important to designing jobs and matching employees' capabilities to an organization's jobs.

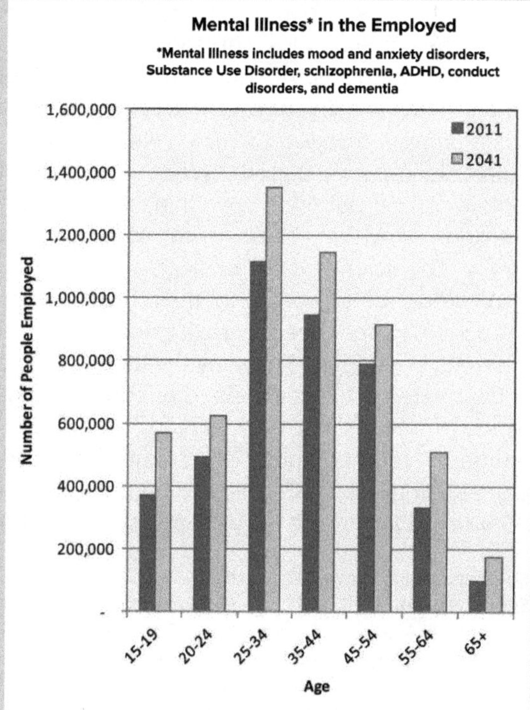

Sources: "Advancing the Mental Health Strategy for Canada: A Framework for Action 2017–2022, (2016), www.mentalhealthcommission.ca, accessed February 1, 2018; Joseph Cohen-Lyons, Samantha Seabrook, "The Rise of cognitive demands analysis," *Canadian HR Reporter*, December 12, 2016, p. 17; P. Smetanin, D. Stiff, D., C. Briante, C.E. Adair, S. Ahmad, and M. Khan, "The Life and Economic Impact of Major Mental Illnesses in Canada: 2011 to 2041," (2011), RiskAnalytica, on behalf of the Mental Health Commission of Canada.

Designing Jobs That Consider Cognitive Demands

Just as the human body has capabilities and limitations, addressed by ergonomics, the mind, too, has capabilities and limitations. As more and more work activities become information processing activities, the need to consider *cognitive ergonomics* is likely to be an emerging trend.[32] Besides hiring people with certain mental skills, organizations can design jobs so that they can be accurately and safely performed given the way the brain processes information. Generally, this means reducing the information processing requirements of a job. In these redesigned jobs, workers may be less likely to make mistakes or have accidents. Of course, less complex jobs may also be less motivating. Research has found that challenging jobs tend to fatigue and dissatisfy workers when they feel little control over their situation, lack social support, and feel motivated mainly to avoid errors. In contrast, they may enjoy the challenges of a difficult job where they have

Thinking ETHICALLY

How Can You Ethically Design a Dangerous Job?

One of the most popular professional sports in North America is football, but the Canadian Football League (CFL) and the National Football League (NFL) face new scientific evidence suggesting that injuries sustained by football players are more serious than had previously been thought. Winning a game requires aggressive play, including head collisions. Sometimes the result is a major concussion, known to be serious. But scientists have observed a link between taking less severe hits day in and day out and a condition called chronic traumatic encephalopathy (CTE). With CTE, the brain's repeated contact with the skull causes the formation of abnormal protein tangles. People with CTE suffer from headaches, memory loss, episodes of anger, and suicidal tendencies. Although the NFL has conceded there is a link between football brain injuries and brain disease, CFL Commissioner Randy Ambrosie recently stated, "We're continuing to look at all of it but right now I think the answer is we don't know yet. There is not conclusive evidence. The science is still unclear."

A group of players and their families have sued the NFL for covering up the dangers of concussions in the past. They say the league formed a committee to investigate the consequences of these injuries but downplayed the long-term dangers it learned about. The plaintiffs are seeking a settlement of $5 billion to be paid out over 25 years. One of the lawyers points out that for a business earning $9 billion a year, it could be seen as reasonable to compensate former players who are disabled by brain injuries sustained on the job. In Canada, a $200 million class action lawsuit has been filed over concussions and brain trauma.

Meanwhile, the NFL has tried modifying players' jobs by creating new rules for the game. The rules include requiring knee pads to reduce knee-to-head collisions and moving kick-offs up five yards to reduce the number of returns. Another change is that players will have fewer full-contact workouts during the preseason. In addition, when players experience symptoms associated with concussions, they may not return to play or practise until they have been cleared by a neurologist who is not affiliated with their team. These changes may reduce the injuries to players, but some players are concerned the changes will make the game less appealing to fans.

Questions

1. How do the rights of Canadian workers protected by occupational health and safety legislation (Chapter 2) apply to professional football players and the safety risks described here?
2. Will making football players' jobs safe achieve the ethical goal of the greatest good for the greatest number of people? Why or why not? Is there an ethical level of safety in football?

Sources: Devin Heroux, "It's time to say football is not a safe sport: CFL great challenges commissioner on concussions," *CBC Sports*, November 24, 2017, http://www.cbc.ca/sports; Heather Hansman, "Can This New Football Helmet Prevent Head Injuries?" *Smithsonian Magazine*, February 5, 2016, http://www.smithsonianmag.com; David DiSalvo, "Is the NFL Doing Enough to Prevent Brain Trauma? '60 Minutes' Probes for Answers," *Forbes*, November 16, 2015, http://www.forbes.com; William Weinbaum and Steve Delsohn, "Dorsett, Others Show Signs of CTE," ESPN Outside the Lines, April 5, 2014, http://espn.go.com; Joseph Serna, "Study Finds Chronic Brain Damage in Former NFL Players," *Los Angeles Times*, January 22, 2013, http://articles.latimes.com.

some control and social support, especially if they enjoy learning and are unafraid of making mistakes.[33] Because of this drawback to simplifying jobs, it can be most beneficial to simplify jobs where employees will most appreciate having the mental demands reduced (as in a job that is extremely challenging) or where the costs of errors are severe (as in the job of a surgeon or air-traffic controller). Analysis of a job's cognitive demands also provides valuable information to support employees' mental health and well-being (see Did You Know?)

There are several ways to reduce a job's mental demands. One is to limit the amount of information and memorization the job requires. Organizations can also provide adequate lighting, easy-to-understand gauges and displays, simple-to-operate equipment, and clear instructions. Often, employees try to reduce some of the mental demands of their own jobs by creating checklists, charts, or other aids. Finally, every job requires some degree of thinking, remembering, mental focus, and social interaction, so for every job, organizations need to evaluate whether their employees can meet the job's cognitive demands.

Changes in technology sometimes reduce job demands and errors, but in some cases, technology has made the problem worse. Some employees try to juggle information from several sources at once—say, browsing the Internet for information during a team member's business presentation, or repeatedly stopping work on a project to check email or text messages. In these cases, the mobile device and email or text messages are distracting the employees from their primary task. They may convey important information, but they also break the employee's train of thought, reducing performance, and increasing the likelihood of errors. The problem may be aggravated by employees downplaying the significance of these interruptions. Research by a firm called Basex, which specializes in the knowledge economy, found that a big part of the information overload problem is *recovery time;* that is, the time it takes a person's thinking to switch back from an interruption to the task at hand. The Basex researchers found that recovery time is from 10 to 20 times the length of the interruption. For example, after a 30-second pause to check a social media feed, the recovery time could be five minutes or longer.[34]

SUMMARY

LO1 Summarize the elements of work flow analysis and how work flow relates to an organization's structure.

Work flow analysis identifies the amount and quality of a work unit's outputs (products, parts of products, or services) and determines the work processes required to produce the outputs, breaking down tasks into those performed by each person. Finally, the work flow analysis identifies the inputs used to carry out the processes and produce the outputs. Within an organization, units and individuals must cooperate to create outputs, and the organization's structure brings people together for this purpose.

LO2 Discuss the significance of job analysis and identify the elements of a job analysis.

Job analysis is the process of getting detailed information about jobs. Job analysis provides the important foundation for carrying out many HRM responsibilities. Key elements of job analysis are job descriptions, which identify the tasks, duties, and responsibilities (TDRs) associated with the job, and job specifications, which provide the knowledge, skills, abilities, and other characteristics (KSAOs) that the jobs will demand of the people performing them.

LO3 Explain how to obtain information for a job analysis and review job analysis developments.

Information for analyzing an existing job often comes from incumbents and their supervisors. The federal government provides information about jobs in the National Occupational Classification (NOC), and tools such as the Position Analysis Questionnaire (PAQ) or the Fleishman Job Analysis System may be used. Analyzing teamwork and using competency models provides the potential to support talent management and facilitate a more robust integration of human resource functions with organizational strategy and performance.

LO4 Understand the different approaches to job design.

Four approaches to job design are identified including consideration of how to design (redesign) jobs that are efficient, motivating, and take into account both the physical and mental health and well-being of the people performing the jobs.

CRITICAL THINKING QUESTIONS

1. Assume you are the manager/owner of a local coffee house. What are the outputs of your work unit? What are the activities required to produce those outputs? What are the inputs?
2. Based on Question 1, consider the barista's job at the local coffee house. What are the outputs, activities, and inputs for that job?
3. Consider the "job" of university or college student. Perform a job analysis on this job. What tasks are required in the job? What knowledge, skills, abilities, and other characteristics (KSAOs) are necessary to perform those tasks?
4. Discuss how the following trends are changing the skill requirements for managerial jobs:
   - **a.** Increasing use of social media
   - **b.** Increasing global competition
   - **c.** Increasing use of remote work
5. Suppose you have taken a job as a training and learning specialist in a financial institution that has created competency models for all its positions. How could the competency models help you implement training, learning, and development initiatives for employees? How could the competency models help you succeed in your career at the financial institution?
6. Consider the job of a customer service representative for a telecommunications provider who handles calls from residential customers for billing inquiries and routine service requests. What measures can the employer take to design this job to make it efficient? What might be some drawbacks or challenges of designing this job for efficiency?
7. How might the job in Question 6 be designed to make it more motivating? Would these considerations apply to the barista's job in Question 2?
8. What ergonomic considerations might apply to each of the following jobs? For each job, what kinds of costs would result from addressing ergonomics? What costs might result from failing to address ergonomics?
   - **a.** Data scientist
   - **b.** UPS driver
   - **c.** Registered nurse
9. What are the trade-offs between the different approaches to job design? Which approach do you think should be weighted more heavily when designing jobs? Why?
10. Consider a job you hold now or have held recently. Would you want this job to be redesigned to place more emphasis on efficiency, motivation, ergonomics, or cognitive considerations? What changes would you want, and why? (Or why do you *not* want the job to be redesigned?)

EXPERIENCING HR—DEVELOPING A PROFESSOR'S JOB DESCRIPTION AND JOB SPECIFICATION

Form small working groups (3–6 students is recommended). In your group, develop a job description for your professor's job. Use your knowledge and assumptions about the job's tasks, duties, and responsibilities. If you have been given time for research, review the chapter for additional ideas on where to gather information for your job description, and use it to improve your job description. Then use your completed job description as a basis for developing a job specification for your professor's job.

With the whole class, share which tasks, duties, and responsibilities you included in your job description and what you included in your job specification. Discuss what requirements you define as important and what your professor defines as important. Ask your professor how closely your job description and job specification match the school's actual expectations. Was your professor given a job description? Would professors at your school be more effective if the school used the job description and job specification written by you and your classmates? Why or why not? How would you adjust your team's job description and specification, based on what you learned from this discussion? Turn in your job description and job specification for credit on the assignment.

CASE STUDY: EVIDENCE-BASED HRM

Analytics Drive Success at United Parcel Service (UPS)

United Parcel Service (UPS) is one of the the world's largest package-shipping companies, so saving a tiny bit of gasoline on every truck route can generate enormous savings, in both expenses and impact on the environment. For example, reducing each route by 1.6 km (1 mile) per day for a year can save the company about 162 million km (100 million miles) per year, a reduction of carbon emission of 100,000 tonnes and a cost saving of about $50 million. Thus, efficiency is a major factor in work design. UPS keeps improving its ability to gather, analyze, and apply data to making every aspect of package handling use fewer resources.

Some of its detailed requirements once included requiring drivers to hook their truck keys over one finger instead of stashing them in a pocket. This task was updated when drivers were provided with a digital-remote fob to wear on their belts. With the keyless systems, drivers stop the truck and press a button to turn off the engine and unlock the bulkhead door. This change saves 1.75 seconds at each stop. That's equivalent to an average of 6.5 minutes per driver per day. Besides saving time, the changes save motions by the driver, reducing fatigue.

Recently, the company began using a system called ORION (On-Road Integrated Optimization and Navigation). The ORION system gathers data from customers, vehicles, and drivers' handheld mobile devices. It analyzes the data—even times for pickup and delivery when customers have special requests—and designs routes for each driver to use the minimum time and fuel, driving the minimum distance.

According to UPS, once fully implemented, ORION is expected to save the company $300 to $400 million a year. The company hopes that ORION will eventually do even more to improve outcomes—for example, updating routes when accidents or construction sites cause traffic congestion. With results like these, it is easy to see why UPS invested years to develop the ORION system. The challenge for managers is to find drivers who are willing to commit to a system in which their every turn is planned by a computer and to keep those jobs engaging.

Questions

1. What benefits does UPS derive from using ORION to help it make drivers' work more efficient?
2. What challenges does the system pose for drivers and their managers?

Sources: "ORION Backgrounder," UPS Press Room, January 30, 2018, https://pressroom.ups.com; Steven Rosenbush and Laura Stevens, "At UPS, the Algorithm Is the Driver," *Wall Street Journal,* February 16, 2015, http://www.wsj.com; Thomas H. Davenport, "Big Brown Finds Big Money from Big Data," *Wall Street Journal,* April 9, 2014, http://blogs.wsj.com; Richard Waters, "Big Data Sparks Cultural Changes," *Financial Times,* March 25, 2014, http://www.ft.com; Mary Schlangenstein, "UPS Crunches Data to Make Routes More Efficient, Save Gas," *Bloomberg News,* October 30, 2013, http://www.bloomberg.com; Jennifer Levitz, "Deliver Drivers to Pick Up Pace by Surrendering Keys," *The Wall Street Journal,* September 16, 2011, http://online.wsj.com.

CASE STUDY: HRM SOCIAL

With Effective Analysis, Work Isn't *Just* a Game

Job analysis can support one of the hot trends in business, called *gamification.* To gamify work, organizations use elements of games designed to yield better results, and they apply them to jobs to enable stronger performance. For example, they observe how runners and cyclists are motivated when they can share their routes and data such as duration, distance, and speed with their friends on social media, or how teams of players collaborate to defeat an enemy in an online game. A "leaderboard" displaying a list of the top scorers also is a widely used tool to motivate players to improve and earn a place on the list.

Employers can easily create a leaderboard of top salespeople, ask employees to post their progress on a team project, or award badges for completing training modules. But when a gamification effort is just a matter of adding playful features to the company's internal website, employees may ignore it. Well-planned gamification helps employees achieve goals that are relevant to their own and their organization's success. This is where job analysis comes in, by pinpointing what employees should be accomplishing and what skills and resources they need. Gamification works when it aligns with job requirements and the learning of relevant skills. For example, Dominos has transformed its training to make pizzas into a web-based game with achievements, points, and levels.

In the United Kingdom, the Department of Work and Pensions (DWP) wanted its employees to become more active in developing useful ideas for innovation. To gamify this aspect of employees' jobs, the company set up a collaboration site on its internal network. Employees are encouraged to submit ideas and vote on the ideas they think are most valuable. As ideas earn votes, they move up a leaderboard, and the company acts on them. Coming up with an idea that wins votes is exciting; seeing it move up the leaderboard is even more motivating; and of course, seeing it make a change for the better is the best prize of all.

Questions

1. Suppose you are a human resources manager at a company that is going to gamify the job of its salespeople. How would job analysis help you advise the team on which behaviours to reward?
2. In the same scenario, how would job analysis help you advise the team on which kinds of rewards to incorporate?

Sources: M. Teresa Cardador, Gregory B. Northcraft & Jordan Whicker, "A theory of work gamification: Something old, something new, something borrowed, something cool?," *Human Resource Management Review* 27 (2017), pp. 353–365; Tony Ventrice, "What the Future of Gamification in the Workplace Looks Like," *Fast Company,* February 4, 2015, http://www.fastcompany.com; Brian Burke, "Why Gamification's Not a Game," *CIO Journal,* May 6, 2014, http://blogs.wsj.com; Farhad Manjoo, "High Definition: The 'Gamification' of the Office Approaches," *Wall Street Journal,* January 12, 2014, http://online.wsj.com; Meghan M. Biro, "Five Ways Leaders Win at Gamification Technology," *Forbes,* September 15, 2013, http://www.forbes.com; Cliff Saran, "A Business Case for Gameplay at Work," *Computer Weekly,* August 20–26, 2013, pp. 19–22.

CHAPTER 4

Planning for and Recruiting Human Resources

WHAT DO I NEED TO KNOW?

After reading this chapter, you should be able to:

LO1	Discuss how to align workforce planning with the organization's strategy.
LO2	Examine methods organizations use to deal with a labour surplus or shortage.
LO3	Explain the importance of recruiting and describe approaches to attract talent.
LO4	Compare and contrast recruitment sources.
LO5	Describe the recruiter's role.

© Hero/Corbis/Glow Images

Ride-sharing companies like Uber and Lyft seamlessly match labour demand (for rides) with labour supply (available drivers). Uber's ride-sharing rival Lyft is now also operating in Canada—competing actively for Uber's riders and drivers.

Balancing Labour Demand and Supply: Uber and Lyft

When they discuss their business model, representatives for Uber tend to focus on the technology e.g. the app that links riders with drivers and, hence, quickly and seamlessly connects a specific demand for labour with a specific supply of labour. Beyond the technology though, a big part of Uber's success can be attributed to the fact that most of the labour employed is low paid, has no job security, and is provided no benefits. Although many Uber drivers enjoy the flexibility that this work provides, they may actually receive less than minimum wage, when expenses and vehicle depreciation are taken into account. The company can do this if the drivers are classified as "independent contractors" rather than "traditional employees."

Despite facing negative publicity due to corporate scandals, regulatory issues, and its reported "fairly toxic" corporate culture, Uber's share of the ride-sharing market in North America is approximately three times that of its number one rival, Lyft. The battle between these competitors is not only for riders but also for drivers. Lyft recently chose Toronto as its first international city and has been actively working to attract drivers from Uber with policies that "treat people better—whether that's drivers, riders, or regulators." For example, Lyft offered a 25 percent bonus to its first 3,000 drivers on all rides for the first three months and $200 bonuses for providing new driver referrals. Lyft was also the first ride-sharing company to introduce tipping, a policy valued by drivers.[1]

Introduction

As this example show, when demand for a service rises (or falls), organizations will need more (or fewer) people to perform the work. When the labour market changes—as when more people pursue postsecondary education or seek greater flexibility—or when a sizeable share of the population retires—the supply of qualified workers may grow, shrink, or change in nature. Organizations are having difficulty filling some STEM (science, technology, engineering, and math)-related jobs such as data scientists, because the demand for people with skills in the discipline of analytics outstrips the supply. For example, Cameron Dow, President of SAS Canada, notes a projected need for 100,000 information-related employees to fill jobs in the Canadian economy.[2]

To prepare for and respond to these challenges, organizations engage in *workforce planning*—defined in Chapter 1 as identifying the numbers and types of employees the organization will require to meet its objectives.

This chapter describes why and how organizations carry out workforce planning and how organizations identify and attract talent. In the first part of the chapter, we lay out the steps that go into developing and implementing a workforce plan. Throughout each section, we focus especially on recent developments and practices, including downsizing, employing temporary workers, and outsourcing. The remainder of the chapter explores the process of recruiting. We discuss the importance of employer branding to attract talent, the process by which organizations look for people to fill job openings, and consider sources of job candidates. Finally, we discuss the role of recruiters.

LO1 Workforce Planning—Why, What, and How?

To meet business objectives and gain an advantage over competitors, organizations should carry out *workforce planning*. To do this, organizations need a clear idea of the strengths and weaknesses of their existing internal labour force. They also must know what they want to be doing in the future—what size they want the organization to be, what products and services it should be producing, and so on. This knowledge helps to define the number and kinds of employees they will need. Workforce planning compares the present state of the organization with its goals for the future, then identifies what changes it must make in its human resources to meet those goals. The changes may include downsizing, training existing employees in new skills, or hiring new employees. The overall goal of workforce planning is to ensure the organization has the right people with the right skills in the right places at the right time.

These activities give a general view of workforce planning and take place in the process shown in Figure 4.1. Workforce planning consists of three stages: forecasting; goal setting and strategic planning; and program implementation and evaluation.

Forecasting

The first step in workforce planning is **forecasting**, as shown in the top portion of Figure 4.1. In forecasting, the HR professional tries to determine the *supply* of and *demand* for various types of human resources. The primary goal is to predict which areas of the organization will experience labour shortages or surpluses.

forecasting The attempts to determine the supply of and demand for various types of human resources to predict areas within the organization where there will be labour shortages or surpluses.

Forecasting supply and demand can use statistical methods or human judgment. Statistical methods capture historic trends in a company's demand for labour. Under the right conditions, these methods predict demand and supply more precisely than a human forecaster can using subjective judgment. But many important events in the labour market have no precedent and require reliance on the judgments of experts to make decisions and guide changes to statistical models.

FIGURE 4.1

Overview of the Workforce Planning Process

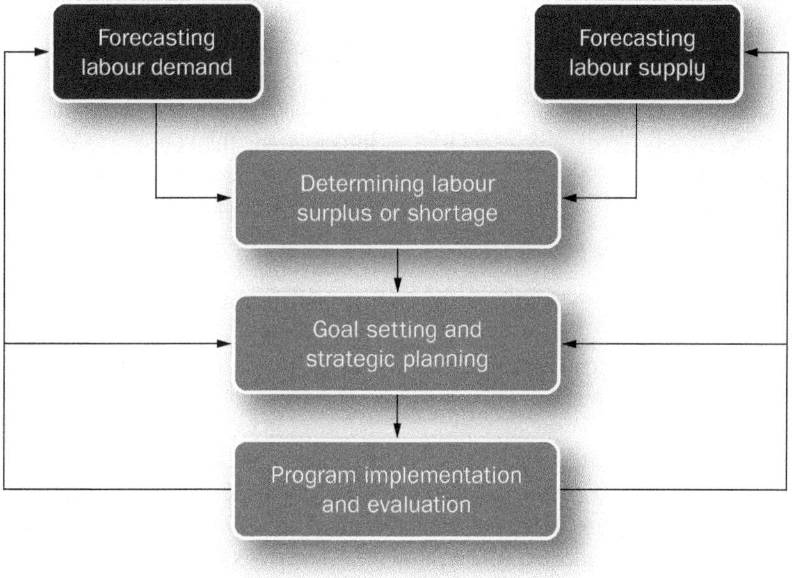

Forecasting Labour Demand

Usually, an organization forecasts demand for specific job categories or skill areas. After identifying the relevant job categories or skills, the planner investigates the likely demand for each. The planner must forecast whether the need for people with the necessary skills and experience will increase or decrease. There are several ways of making such forecasts.

At the most sophisticated level, an organization might use **trend analysis**, constructing and applying statistical models that predict labour demand for the next time period, given relatively objective statistics from the previous time period. These statistics are called **leading indicators**—objective measures that accurately predict future labour demand. They might include measures of the economy (such as sales or inventory levels), actions of competitors, changes in technology, and trends in the composition of the workforce and overall population. Recently, for example, low-interest rates on loans, relatively stable prices for fuel, and a long stretch of slow, steady growth in hiring have together made it a good time for many households to buy a vehicle. Rising demand for vehicle purchases has triggered more hiring by dealerships. But the same low oil prices leading to lower fuel prices have meant low payoffs for traditional oil-drilling projects. Therefore, in that industry, demand for labour has fallen.[3]

trend analysis
Constructing and applying statistical models that predict labour demand for the next year, given relatively objective statistics from the previous year.

leading indicators
Objective measures that accurately predict future labour demand.

Statistical planning models are useful when there is a long, stable history that can be used to reliably detect relationships among variables. However, these models almost always have to be complemented with subjective judgments of experts.

Forecasting Labour Supply

Once a company has forecast the demand for labour, it needs to understand the firm's available labour supply. Determining the internal labour supply calls for a

© Royalty-Free/Corbis/DAL

As the average age of many workers in skilled trades increases, the growing demand for workers in many trades is expected to outstrip supply. There is a potential for employers in some areas to experience a labour shortage because of this. What should HR do to avoid shortages of labour?

detailed analysis of how many people are currently in various job categories or have specific skills within the organization. The planner then modifies this analysis to reflect changes expected in the future as a result of retirements, promotions, transfers, voluntary turnover, and terminations.

One type of statistical procedure that can be used for this purpose is the analysis of a **transitional matrix**, which is a chart that lists job categories held in one period and shows the proportion of employees in each of those job categories in a future period. It answers two questions: "Where did people who were in each job category go?" and "Where did people now in each job category come from?" Table 4.1 is an example of a transitional matrix.

transitional matrix
A chart that lists job categories held in one period and shows the proportion of employees in each of those job categories in a future period.

This example lists job categories for an auto parts manufacturer. The jobs listed at the left were held in 2017; the numbers across show what happened to the people in 2019. The numbers represent proportions. For example, 0.95 means 95 percent of the people represented by a row in the matrix. The column headings under 2017 refer to the row numbers. The first row is sales manager, so the numbers under column (1) represent people who became sales managers. Reading across the first row, we see that 95 percent of the people who were sales managers in 2017 are still sales managers in 2019. The other 5 percent correspond to column (8), "Not in organization," meaning that 5 percent of people who are not still sales managers have left the organization. In the second row are sales representatives. Of those who were sales reps in 2017, 5 percent were promoted to sales manager, 60 percent are still sales reps, and 35 percent have left the organization. In row (3) half (50 percent) of sales apprentices are still in that job, but 20 percent are now sales reps, and 30 percent have left the organization. This pattern of jobs shows a career path from sales apprentice to sales representative to sales manager. Of course, not everyone is promoted, and some of the people leave instead.

Reading down the columns provides another kind of information: the sources of employees holding the positions in 2019. In the first column, we see that most sales managers (95 percent) held that same job two years earlier. The other 5 percent were promoted from sales representative positions. Skipping over to column (3), half the sales apprentices on the payroll in 2019 held the same job two years before, and the other half were hired from outside the organization. This suggests that the organization fills sales manager positions through promotions, so planning for this job would focus on preparing sales representatives. In contrast, planning to meet the organization's needs for sales apprentices would emphasize recruitment and selection of new employees.

Matrices like this are extremely useful for charting historical trends in the company's supply of labour. More important, if conditions remain somewhat constant, they can also be used to plan for the future. For example, if we believe we are going to have a surplus of labour in the production assembler job category in the next two years, we can plan to avoid layoffs. Still, historical data may not always reliably indicate future trends. Planners need to combine statistical forecasts of labour supply with expert judgments. For example, managers in the organization may see that a new training program

TABLE 4.1

Hypothetical Transitional Matrix for an Auto Parts Manufacturer

	2019							
2017	(1)	(2)	(3)	(4)	(5)	(6)	(7)	(8)
1. Sales manager	0.95							0.05
2. Sales representative	0.05	0.60						0.35
3. Sales apprentice		0.20	0.50					0.30
4. Assistant plant manager				0.90	0.05			0.05
5. Production manager				0.10	0.75			0.15
6. Production assembler					0.10	0.80		0.10
7. Clerical							0.70	0.30
8. Not in organization	0.00	0.20	0.50	0.00	0.10	0.20	0.30	

will likely increase the number of employees qualified for new openings. Forecasts of labour supply also should take into account the organization's pool of skills. Many organizations include inventories of employees' skills in an HR database. When the organization forecasts that it will need new skills in the future, planners can consult the database to see how many existing employees have those skills.

Besides looking at the labour supply within the organization, the planner should examine trends in the external labour market. The planner should keep abreast of labour market forecasts, including the size of the labour market, the employment rate, and the kinds of people who will be in the labour market. For example, we saw in Chapter 1 that the labour market is aging and that immigration is an important source of new workers. Relevant sources of data on the external labour market are available from Statistics Canada. Details and news (releases from *The Daily*) are available at the Statistics Canada site.

Determining Labour Surplus or Shortage

By analyzing the gap between forecasts of labour demand and supply, the planner can determine whether there will be a shortage or surplus of labour for each job category. Determining expected shortages and surpluses allows the organization to plan how to address these challenges. HR professionals can increase the value of this planning by developing competency in applying data and analytic techniques. For example, when an organization is deciding to expand or move to a new location, software can analyze data such as job requirements, local graduation rates, pay levels, and more to estimate the likelihood that the company can readily find and afford the necessary talent in a given location.[4]

LO2 Goal Setting and Strategic Planning

The second step in workforce planning is goal setting and strategic planning, as shown in the middle of Figure 4.1. The purpose of setting specific numerical goals is to focus attention on the issue and provide a basis for measuring the organization's success in addressing labour shortages and surpluses. The goals should come directly from the analysis of labour supply and demand. They should include a specific figure indicating what should happen with the job category or skill area and a specific timetable for when the results should be achieved.

For each goal, the organization must choose one or more human resource strategies. A variety of strategies are available for handling expected shortages and surpluses of labour. Table 4.2 shows major options for reducing an expected labour surplus, and Table 4.3 provides options for avoiding an expected labour shortage.

TABLE 4.2

HR Strategies for Addressing an Expected Labour Surplus

Options for Reducing a Surplus		
Option	Speed of Results	Amount of Suffering Caused
Downsizing	Fast	High
Pay reductions	Fast	High
Demotions	Fast	High
Transfers	Fast	Moderate
Reducing hours	Fast	Moderate
Hiring freeze	Slow	Low
Attrition	Slow	Low
Early retirement	Slow	Low
Retraining	Slow	Low

TABLE 4.3

Options for Addressing an Expected Labour Shortage

Option	Speed of Results	Ability to Change Later
Overtime	Fast	High
Temporary employees	Fast	High
Outsourcing	Fast	High
Retained transfers	Slow	High
Turnover reductions	Slow	Moderate
New external hires	Slow	Low
Technological innovation	Slow	Low

This planning stage is critical. The options differ widely in their expense, speed, and effectiveness. Options for reducing a labour surplus cause differing amounts of human suffering. The options for avoiding a labour shortage differ in terms of how easily the organization can undo the change if it no longer faces a labour shortage. For example, an organization probably would not want to handle every expected labour shortage by hiring new employees. The process is relatively slow and involves expenses to find and train new employees. Also, if the shortage becomes a surplus, the organization will have to consider laying off some of the employees. Layoffs involve another set of expenses, such as severance pay, and they are costly in terms of human suffering.

Another consideration in choosing an HR strategy is whether the employees needed will contribute directly to the organization's success. Organizations are most likely to benefit from hiring and retaining as employees who provide a **core competency**—that is, a set of knowledge and skills that provide a competitive advantage.

core competency A set of knowledge and skills that provide a competitive advantage

Organizations try to anticipate labour surpluses far enough ahead that they can freeze hiring and let *attrition* (people leaving on their own) reduce the labour force. Unfortunately for many workers, organizations often stay competitive in a fast-changing environment by responding to a labour surplus with downsizing, which delivers fast results. The impact is painful for those who lost jobs, as well as those left behind to carry on without them. To handle a labour shortage, organizations typically hire temporary employees or use outsourcing. Because downsizing, using temporary employees, and outsourcing are most common, we will look at each of these in greater detail in the following sections.

Downsizing

As discussed in Chapter 1, **downsizing** is the planned elimination of large numbers of employees with the goal of enhancing the organization's competitiveness. The primary reason organizations engage in downsizing is to promote future competitiveness. According to surveys, they do this by meeting four objectives:

downsizing The planned elimination of large numbers of employees with the goal of enhancing the organization's competitiveness.

1. **Reducing costs**—Labour is a large part of a company's total costs, so downsizing is often a top-of-mind place to start cutting costs.
2. **Replacing labour with technology**—Closing outdated factories, automating, or introducing other technological changes reduces the need for labour. Often, the labour savings outweigh the cost of the new technology.
3. **Mergers and acquisitions**—When organizations combine, they often need less administrative overhead, so they lay off managers and some professional staff members.
4. **Moving to more economical locations**—In recent years, many Canadian firms have shifted jobs to other countries, including Mexico, India, and China, where wages are usually lower.

Although downsizing has an immediate effect on costs, much of the evidence suggests that it hurts long-term organizational effectiveness. This is especially true for certain kinds of companies, such as those that emphasize research and development and where employees have extensive contact with customers.[5] The negative effect of downsizing was especially high among firms that engaged in high-involvement work practices, such as the use of teams and performance-related pay incentives. As a result, the more a company tries to compete through its human resources, the more layoffs hurt productivity.[6]

Why do so many downsizing efforts fail to meet expectations? There seem to be several reasons. First, although the initial cost savings give a temporary boost to profits, the long-term effects of an improperly managed downsizing effort can be negative. Downsizing leads to a loss of talent, and it often disrupts the social networks through which people are creative and flexible.[7]

In some organizations, the introduction of new technologies (including robotics) reduces the need for a large number of employees. This places the focus of competition on who can produce the best robots, and when it comes to this battle, Japanese manufacturers seem to be far ahead of their rivals. Japanese companies such as Fanuc and Kawasaki Heavy Industries produce over 50 percent of the world's working robots.[8]

Unless the downsizing is managed well, employees feel confused, demoralized, and even less willing to stay with the organization. Especially in an age of blogs and text messaging, the once-private practice of laying off employees is becoming increasingly transparent, and any organizational mistake that gets made in the process is likely to become highly public.[9] Organizations may not take (or even know) the steps that can counter these reactions—for example, demonstrating how they are treating employees fairly, building confidence in the company's plans for a stronger future, and showing the organization's commitment to behaving responsibly with regard to all its stakeholders, including employees, customers, and the community.[10]

Also, many companies wind up rehiring. Downsizing campaigns often eliminate people who turn out to be irreplaceable. In one survey, 80 percent of the firms that had downsized wound up replacing some of the very people they had laid off. However, recent trends in employment suggests that companies will not rehire employees for many of the jobs eliminated when they restructured, introduced automation, or moved work to lower-cost regions.[11]

Finally, downsizing efforts often fail because employees who survive the purge become self-absorbed and afraid to take risks. Motivation drops, because any hope of future promotions—or any future—with the company dies. Many employees start looking for other employment opportunities. The negative publicity associated with a downsizing campaign can also hurt the company's image in the labour market, so it is harder to recruit employees later.

Many problems with downsizing can be reduced with better planning. Instead of slashing jobs across the board, successful downsizing makes strategic cuts that improve the company's competitive position, and management addresses the problem of employees becoming demoralized.

Reducing Hours

Given the limitations of downsizing, many organizations are more carefully considering other avenues for eliminating a labour surplus (shown in Table 4.2). One alternative seen as a way to spread the burden more fairly is cutting work hours, generally with a corresponding reduction in pay. Besides the thought that this is a more equitable way to weather a slump in demand, companies choose a reduction in work hours because it is less costly than layoffs requiring severance pay, and it is easier to restore the work hours than to hire new employees after a downsizing effort.

Early- and Phased-Retirement Programs

Another popular way to reduce a labour surplus is with an early- or phased-retirement program. As we discussed in Chapter 1, the average age of the Canadian workforce is increasing. But even though many Baby Boomers are reaching traditional retirement age, indications are that this group has no intention of leaving the workforce soon.[12] Reasons include improved health and well-being, jobs becoming less physically demanding, insufficient savings, high levels of debt, lack of pensions, and enjoyment of work (especially in higher-paying occupations). Many workers fear their retirement savings and pension plans supplemented by the Canada/Quebec Pension Plan (CPP/QPP) and Old Age Security (OAS) pension will still not be enough to cover their expenses. Finally, protection from discrimination and eliminating mandatory retirement has limited organizations' ability to force older workers to retire. However, under the pressures associated with an aging labour force, many employers try to encourage older workers to leave voluntarily by offering a variety of early-retirement incentives. The more lucrative of these programs succeed by some measures. Research suggests that these programs encourage lower-performing older workers to retire.[13] Sometimes they work so well that too many workers retire.

Many organizations are moving from early-retirement programs to *phased-retirement programs.* In a phased-retirement program, the organization can continue to enjoy the experience of older workers while reducing the number of hours these employees work, as well as the cost of those employees. This option also can also provide younger employees with access to experienced mentors while offering older employees the psychological and financial benefits of a gradual transition to retirement.

Temporary Workers and Independent Contractors

While downsizing has been a popular way to reduce a labour surplus, the most widespread methods for eliminating a labour shortage are hiring temporary workers, independent contractors, and outsourcing work. Employers may arrange to hire a temporary worker through an agency that specializes in linking employers with people who have the necessary skills. The employer pays the agency that, in turn, pays the temporary worker. Employers may also contract directly with individuals, often professionals, to provide a particular service. Temporary and contract employment is popular with employers because it gives them the flexibility they need to operate efficiently when demand for their products changes rapidly.

In addition to flexibility, hiring temporary workers offers several other advantages:

- The use of temporary workers often lowers costs by freeing the firm from many administrative tasks and financial burdens associated with being the "employer of record." For example, the cost of employee benefits such as paid time off, pension plans, life insurance, and medical and dental coverage are significant expenses provided for many permanent employees.
- Small companies that cannot afford their own assessment programs often get employees who have been screened by a staffing agency.
- Many staffing agencies train employees before sending them to employers, which reduces training costs and eases the transition for both the temporary worker and the company.
- Because the temporary worker has little experience in the host firm, the person brings an objective perspective to the organization's problems and procedures that is sometimes valuable.

Besides using a staffing agency, a company can obtain workers for limited assignments by entering into contracts with them. If the person providing the services is an independent contractor, rather than an employee, the company does not pay employee benefits, such as health insurance and vacations. As with using temporary employees, the savings can be significant, even if the contractor works at a higher rate of pay.

It is useful to distinguish between temporary workers, who are part of a large employment agency and are more or less rented by the primary employer, and independent contract workers, who are more or less freelancers and not part of any organization. *Independent contractors* are unattached individuals who agree to do specific tasks for specific time periods as part of a written contract between the worker and the employer. Rather than shifting the burden to be the "employer of record" from the employer to a staffing agency, in this case, virtually all the burden associated with this distinction falls directly on the worker. In Canada, there are approximately 1.9 million people identified as self-employed and without having employees of their own, and an additional 2.3 million people classified as temporary employees.[14]

The unprecedented increase in the use of contract workers signals a shift in the supply of labour and has been termed the *gig economy,* fuelled in part by the ability of mobile apps to link employers to workers without the need to go through any other intermediary. Despite the demonstrated success associated with this business model achieved by companies like Uber Technologies Inc., ongoing legal disputes include class action lawsuits claiming that Uber drivers have been misclassified as independent contractors. This dispute has also reached Canada in the form of a proposed class-action lawsuit claiming that anyone who has driven for Uber in Ontario was actually an employee entitled to minimum wage, overtime, and vacation pay.[15]

As illustrated in this example, this strategy carries risks. If the person providing the service is a contractor and not an employee, the company is not supposed to directly supervise the worker. The company can tell the contractor what criteria the finished assignment should meet, but not, for example, where or what hours to work. This distinction is significant, because if the company treats the independent contractor as an employee, the company has certain legal obligations related to overtime pay and withholding income taxes. For example, an Ontario lawsuit claimed that Uber has control over its drivers because they must use Uber's app, they are paid by Uber directly at specified periods of time, they are subject to required inspections, and Uber "sets pay rates, methods, and work volumes."[16]

When an organization wants to consider using independent contractors, human resources professionals can help by alerting the company to the need to verify that the arrangement will meet legal requirements. A good place to start is with the advice provided at Canada Revenue Agency. In addition, the organization may need to obtain legal or financial services advice.

THE CANADIAN PRESS/Chris Young
Tim Hortons has faced criticism over employment practices related to temporary foreign workers.

Outsourcing and Immigration

Instead of using a temporary employee to fill a single job, an organization might want a broader set of services. As discussed in Chapter 1, contracting with another organization to perform a broad set of services is called *outsourcing.* Organizations use outsourcing as a way to operate more efficiently and save money. They choose outsourcing firms that promise to deliver the same or better quality at a lower cost. One reason they can do this is that the outside company specializes in the services and can benefit from economies of scale (the economic principle that producing something in large volume tends to cost less for each additional unit than producing in small volume). This efficiency is often the attraction for outsourcing human resource functions such as payroll. Costs are also lower when the outsourcing firm is located in a part of the world where wages are relatively low. For example, countries such as China, India, Jamaica, and Ireland have been creating an abundant supply of labour.

The first uses of outsourcing emphasized manufacturing and routine tasks. However, technological advances in computer networks and transmission have sped up the outsourcing process and have helped it spread beyond manufacturing areas and low-skilled jobs. For example, DuPont moved legal services associated with its $100 million asbestos case litigation to a team of lawyers working in the Philippines. The work is a combination of routine document handling and legal judgments such as determining the relevance of a document to the case. Salaries for legal professionals in the Philippines are about one-fifth the cost of their North American counterparts.[17]

Outsourcing may be a necessary way to operate as efficiently as competitors, but it does pose challenges. Quality-control problems, security violations, and poor customer service have sometimes wiped out the cost savings attributed to lower wages. To ensure success with an outsourcing strategy; companies should follow these guidelines:

- Learn about what the provider can do for the company, not just the costs. Make sure the company has the necessary skills, including an environment that can meet standards for clear communication, on-time shipping, contract enforcement, fair labour practices, and environmental protection.[18] Some companies are keeping outsourcing inside Canada in order to meet this full set of requirements.
- Do not offshore any work that is proprietary or requires tight security.[19]
- Start small and monitor the work closely, especially in the beginning, when problems are most likely.

Boeing offers a cautionary tale with its ambitious plan to have a worldwide network of suppliers build all the components for its 787 *Dreamliner.* The project eventually fell three years behind schedule and went billions of dollars over budget as various subcontractors fell behind and failed to meet exacting quality standards. Along the way, Boeing went so far as to acquire some of the suppliers to gain more control over the production process.[20]

- Look for opportunities to outsource work in areas that promote growth, for example, by partnering with experts who can help the organization tap new markets.[21]

Companies also increasingly outsource many of their HRM tasks to outside vendors that specialize in efficiently performing many of the more routine administrative tasks associated with this function. Cost savings in this area are easily obtained because rather than purchase and maintain their own specialized hardware and software, as well as specialized staff to support such systems, companies can time-share the facilities and expertise of a firm that focuses on this technology.

Another way organizations fill a labour shortage is by bringing foreign workers into the country. Immigration has always been a vital part of the Canadian economy, and many foreign workers are willing to leave their home countries and pursue work and life in Canada. For example, Canada's Temporary Foreign Worker (TFW) program allows Canadian employers to hire foreign workers to fill temporary jobs when qualified Canadians are not available.[22]

Tim Hortons and McDonald's have faced criticism about employment of temporary foreign workers at some of their Canadian franchises. In Victoria, British Columbia, Canadian employees alleged that foreign workers were "given priority status and in some cases took their jobs." Allegations from foreign temporary workers have also been made, including violation of Employment Standards requirements. For example, a foreign temporary worker from the Philippines working at a franchise in Fernie, British Columbia, claimed that he received paycheques including overtime pay but was required to pay back the franchise owner in cash. Other foreign temporary workers said they believed they would be sent back to their home country to live in poverty if they complained.[23]

Despite the types of issues discussed in the preceding examples, the number of temporary foreign workers staying in Canada has increased dramatically in recent years. Temporary foreign workers have become a significant source of permanent residents admitted to Canada. For example, Statistics Canada recently reported that 21 percent of temporary foreign workers who arrived in Canada from 2005 to 2009 had become permanent residents by the end of 2014.[24]

Overtime and Expanded Hours

Organizations facing a labour shortage may be reluctant to hire employees, even temporary workers, or to commit to an outsourcing arrangement. Especially if the organization expects the shortage to be temporary, it may prefer an arrangement that is simpler and less costly. Under some conditions, these organizations may try to garner more hours from the existing labour force, asking them to go from part-time to full-time or to work overtime.

A major downside of overtime is that the employer must pay non-management employees additional pay above and beyond their normal wages for work done as overtime. Even so, employers see overtime pay as preferable to the costs of hiring and training new employees. The preference is especially strong if the organization doubts that the current higher level of demand for its products will last long.

For a short time at least, many workers appreciate the added compensation for working overtime. Over extended periods, however, employees may experience negative physical and mental health outcomes resulting in organizational problems. Overtime is best suited for short-term labour shortages. For example, Sandi Mowat, president of the Manitoba Nurses Union, spoke at the Canadian Nursing Association biennium about the use of excessive overtime in Manitoba due to inadequate staffing, citing health and well-being concern for her members as well as patient care quality and safety.[25]

Implementing and Evaluating the Workforce Plan

For HR strategies selected, the final stage of workforce planning involves implementing the strategies and evaluating the outcomes. This stage is represented by the bottom part of Figure 4.1. When implementing the HR strategy, the organization must hold an individual accountable for achieving the goals. That person also must have the authority and resources needed to accomplish those goals. It is also important that this person issue regular progress reports, so the organization can be sure that all activities occur on schedule and that the early results are as expected.

Implementation that ties planning and recruiting to the organization's strategy and to its efforts to develop employees becomes a complete program of talent management. Today's computer systems have made talent management more practical. For example, companies can tap into databases and use analytic tools to keep track of which skills and knowledge they need, which needs have already been filled, which employees are developing experiences to help them meet future needs, and which sources of talent have met talent needs most efficiently.

In evaluating the results, the most obvious step is checking whether the organization has succeeded in avoiding labour shortages or surpluses. Along with measuring these numbers, the evaluation should identify which parts of the planning process contributed to success or failure. For example, consider a company where meeting human resource needs requires that employees continually learn new skills. If there is a gap between needed skills and current skill levels, the evaluation should consider whether the problem lies with failure to forecast the needed skills or with implementation. For example, are employees signing up for training, and is the right kind of training available?

Applying Workforce Planning to Employment Equity

As discussed in Chapter 2, many organizations have a human resource strategy that includes employment equity to support diversity goals. Meeting diversity and employment equity goals requires that employers carry out an additional level of workforce planning aimed at those goals. In other words, besides looking at its overall workforce and needs, the organization looks at the representation of specific groups in its labour force; for example, the proportion of women and visible minorities.

Employment equity plans forecast and monitor the proportion of employees who are members of various protected groups (women, Aboriginal peoples, people with disabilities, and members of a visible minority group). The planning looks at the representation of these employees in the organization's job categories and career tracks. The planner can compare the proportion of employees who are in each group with the proportion each group represents in the labour market. For example, the organization might note that in a labour market that consists of 20 percent visible minorities, 60 percent of its customer service employees are members of "visible minorities". This type of comparison is called a **workforce utilization review**. The organization can use this process to determine whether there is any specific group whose proportion in the relevant labour market differs substantially from the proportion in the job category.

workforce utilization review
A comparison of the proportion of employees in protected groups with the proportion that each group represents in the relevant labour market.

If the workforce utilization review indicates that some group—for example, if Indigenous people ("Aboriginal peoples" is the legal language of the Employment Equity Act) make up 10 percent of the relevant labour market for a job category but that this same group constitutes only 2.5 percent of the employees actually in the job category at the organization, this is evidence of *underutilization.* That situation could result from problems in selection or from problems in internal movement (promotions or other movement along a career path). One way to diagnose the situation would be to use transitional matrices, such as that shown in Table 4.1 earlier in this chapter. Figure 4.2 compares participation of the employment equity groups with workforce availability (WFA) for one of Canada's largest employers, the Federal Public Service of Canada.

The steps in a workforce utilization review are identical to the steps in the workforce planning process shown in Figure 4.1. The organization must assess current utilization patterns, then forecast how these are likely to change in the near future. If these analyses suggest the organization is underutilizing certain groups and if forecasts suggest this

FIGURE 4.2

Employment Equity Portrait in the Federal Public Service of Canada, Overall (4 boxes on the left) and for the Executive Category (4 boxes on the right)

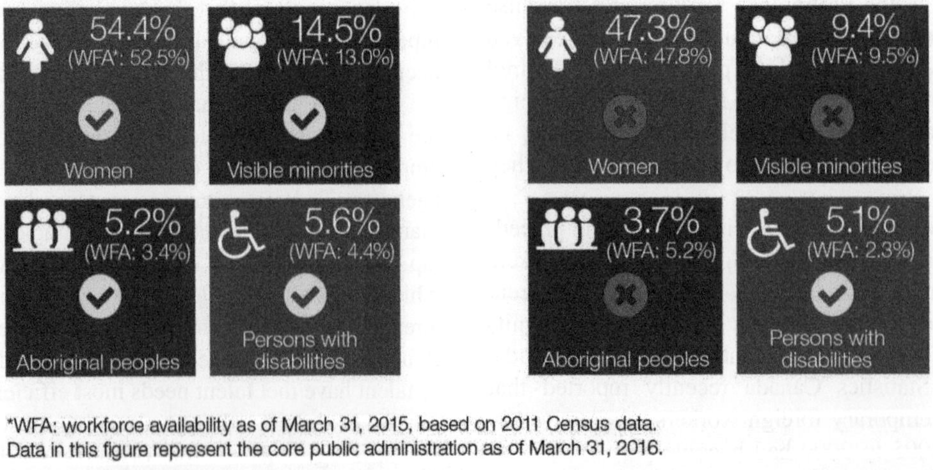

*WFA: workforce availability as of March 31, 2015, based on 2011 Census data.
Data in this figure represent the core public administration as of March 31, 2016.

Source: "Progress Update: Joint Union/Management Task Force on Diversity and Inclusion in the Public Service," Government of Canada (2017), accessed https://www.canada.ca February 13, 2018.

pattern is likely to continue, the organization may need to set goals and timetables for changing. The planning process may identify new strategies for recruitment or selection. The organization carries out these HR strategies and evaluates their success.

Succession Planning: A Type of Workforce Planning

Succession planning refers to the process of identifying and tracking high-potential employees who are capable of moving into different positions in the company resulting from planned or unplanned job openings due to turnover, promotion, or business growth. Succession planning is often discussed when considering a company's managers or top leaders, but it is an important consideration for any job. Succession planning helps organizations in several ways:[26]

succession planning The process of identifying and tracking high-potential employees who will be able to fill top management positions or other key positions when they become vacant.

- Requires senior management to systematically review leadership talent in the company;
- Ensures that top-level leadership talent is available;
- Provides a set of development experiences that leaders must complete to be considered for top management positions, helping to avoid premature promotion of managers who are not ready for upper management ranks;
- Helps attract and retain talented employees by providing development opportunities if leadership advancement is their career goal.

Succession planning focuses on **high-potential employees**, that is, employees the organization believes can succeed in higher-level positions such as general manager of a business unit, director of a function (such as marketing or finance), or chief executive officer.[27] Succession planning is usually closely linked to a development program, which may include education, executive mentoring and coaching, and rotation through job assignments. This will be discussed in more detail in Chapter 6.

high-potential employees Employees the organization believes can succeed in higher-level positions.

Despite the importance of succession planning, many companies do not do it well. A survey of company directors showed that fewer than half believed they were spending enough time on succession planning and 18 percent did not agree that their company had adequate *bench strength* in its talent pool.[28] Bench strength refers to having a pool of talented employees who are ready when needed to take on the next level.

The **HR How-To** identifies the process used to develop a succession plan.

LO3 Recruiting Human Resources

As the first part of this chapter shows, it is difficult to always predict exactly how many (if any) new employees the organization will need to hire in a given year in a given job category. The role of recruitment is to build a supply of potential new hires that the organization can draw on as the need arises. In human resource management, **recruiting** consists of any practice or activity carried on by the organization with the primary purpose of identifying and attracting potential employees.[29] It thus creates a buffer between workforce planning and the actual selection of new employees (the topic of the next chapter). The goals of recruiting (encouraging qualified people to apply for jobs) and selection (deciding which candidates will be the highest performers) are different enough that they are most effective when performed separately, rather than combined as in a job interview that also involves selling candidates on the company.[30]

recruiting Any activity carried on by the organization with the primary purpose of identifying and attracting potential employees.

Because of differences in companies' strategies, they may assign different degrees of importance to recruiting.[31] For example, at Netflix, recruiters are considered "vital contributors to building the business, and hiring managers need to treat them as business partners."[32]

As shown in Figure 4.3, all organizations have to make decisions in three areas of recruiting: (1) human resource policies, which affect the kinds of jobs the organization has to offer; (2) recruitment sources used to attract applicants, which affects who applies; and (3) the characteristics and behaviours of the recruiter. These, in turn, influence both the nature of the vacancies and the nature of the people applying for jobs in a way that shapes job choice decisions. Ultimately, an applicant's decision to accept a job offer—and the organization's decision to make the offer—depend on the match between characteristics of the vacancy and the applicant.

The remainder of this chapter explores these three aspects of recruiting: human resource policies, recruitment sources, and recruiter traits and behaviours.

Human Resource Policies

An organization's *human resource policies* are its decisions about how it will carry out human resource management, including how it will fill job openings. These policies influence the nature of the positions that are vacant. According to the research on recruitment, characteristics

HR How-To

The Process of Developing a Succession Plan

1. **Identify what positions are included in the plan.** Will the succession plan include all management positions or only certain levels of management?
2. **Identify the employees who are included in the plan.** Will only high-potential employees be included?
3. **Develop standards to evaluate positions.** Will the emphasis be on competencies or on the experiences an individual needs to have before moving into the position?
4. **Determine how employee potential will be measured.** Will employees' performance in their current jobs as well as ratings of potential be used? Will employees' position interests and career goals be considered?
5. **Develop the succession planning review.** Typically, succession planning reviews initially involve employees' managers and human resources professionals. A talent review could also include an overall assessment of leadership talent in the company, an identification of high-potential employees based on their performance and potential, and a discussion of plans to keep key people from leaving the company.
6. **Link the succession planning system with other human resource systems.** Which human resource systems require integration; for example, training, learning, and development; total rewards; performance management; and/or talent acquisition systems?
7. **Determine what feedback is provided to employees.** How much detail will be shared with employees?
8. **Measure the effectiveness of the succession plan.** What is the organization's bench strength—calculated as the ratio of successors (ready to take on the next level) to the total number of incumbents at the next level?

Sources: Based on A. Cremo & T. Bux, "Creating a Vibrant Organizational Leadership Pipeline", *TD* (July 2016): 76–77; N. Davis and W. Pina-Ramirez, "Essential Continuity," *T+D*, March 2015, pp. 45–47; D. Sims, "Five Ways to Increase Success in Succession Planning," *T+D*, August 2014, pp. 60–63; W. Rothwell, "The Future of Succession Planning," *T+D*, September 2010, pp. 51–54; B. Dowell, "Succession Planning," in Implementing Organizational Interventions, ed. J. Hedge and E. Pulaskos (San Francisco: Jossey-Bass, 2002), pp. 78–109; R. Barnett and S. Davis, "Creating Greater Success in Succession Planning," *Advances in Developing Human Resources* 10 (2008), pp. 721–39.

FIGURE 4.3

Three Aspects of Recruitment

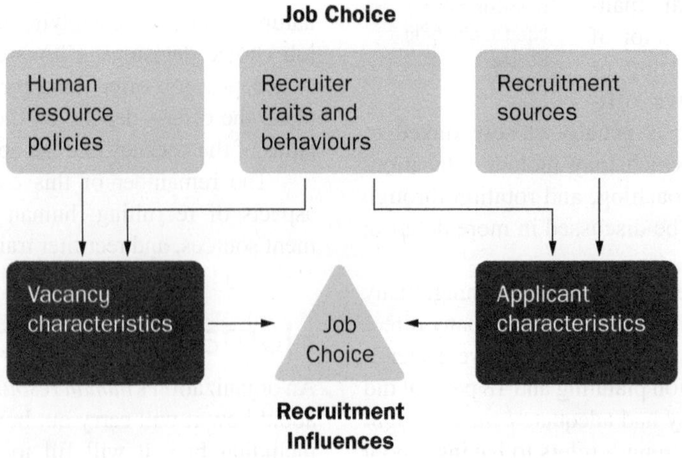

of the vacancy may be more important than recruiters or recruiting sources for predicting job choice. Several policies are especially relevant to recruitment:

- **Internal versus external recruiting**—Organizations with policies to "promote from within" try to fill vacancies by recruiting candidates internally—that is finding candidates who already work for the organization. Opportunities for advancement make a job more attractive to applicants and employees (See the Did You Know? box). Decisions about internal versus external recruiting affect the nature of jobs, recruitment sources, and the nature of applicants, as we will describe later in the chapter.
- **Lead-the-market pay strategies**—Pay is an important job characteristic for almost all applicants. Organizations have a recruiting advantage if their policy is to take a "lead the market" approach to pay—that is, pay more than the current market rate for a job. Higher pay can also make up for a job's less desirable features, such as working a night shift or outdoors in extreme weather conditions. Organizations that compete for applicants based on pay may use bonuses, stock options, and other forms of pay besides wages and salaries. Chapter 8 will take a closer look at these and other decisions about pay.
- **Employer branding**—Besides advertising specific job openings, as discussed in the next section, organizations may promote themselves as a good place to work in general. **Employer branding**, or *employment branding, or recruitment branding* is a strategic approach of attaching a visual, emotional, or cultural brand to an organization. Employer branding uses marketing techniques to attract, engage, and retain employees in the effort to become an *employer of choice*. For example, when an organization is recognized as one of "Canada's Top 100 Employers," the organization acquires the ability to use a well-known logo in various media—for example, print or a company website—to support and enhance its recruitment efforts.

employer branding A strategic approach of attaching a visual, emotional, or cultural brand to an organization.

An *employment brand* is the impression the company makes on employees and job seekers. Marketing it successfully is the same as marketing any other brand.[33] "The secret to an effective employment brand is differentiating an organization from the competition, targeting key benefits of the job to the right labour segments, and using multiple platforms to reach the right audiences."[34] This employment brand, the image an employer projects to potential hires, should be honest and paint a realistic picture of the company.[35] Just as marketers talk about the unique features of their products, employers need to first understand their own strengths and weaknesses and what they can offer top talent that their rivals cannot.[36] Employers strive to be recognized not only as one of Canada's Top 100 Employers, but also to earn a spot in one of the other targeted categories e.g., "Canada's Best Diversity Employers" or "Canada's Top Employers for Young People."

When an organization is recognized as a top employer, it is likely to experience a dramatic increase in the number of résumés it receives. Employer branding is not the exclusive domain of the private sector or even of individual organizations. "Savvy governments across the country are beginning to build and market a solid employment brand, creating catchy tag lines to grab the attention of jobseekers."[37] The tag line for Nova Scotia's public service is "DO Big Things" and the Manitoba government's job opportunities site proclaims, "Your search is over."[38]

LO4 Recruitment Sources

Another critical element of an organization's talent acquisition strategy is its decisions about where to look for applicants. The total labour market is enormous and spread over the entire globe. As a practical matter, an organization will draw from a small fraction of that total market. The methods the organization chooses for communicating its labour needs and the audiences it targets will determine the size and nature of the labour market the organization taps to fill its vacant positions.[39] Recruiting is increasingly becoming a "digital experience as candidates come to expect convenience and mobile contact."[40]

Canadian employers rely on a combination of traditional and web-based recruitment approaches to find employees for all types of jobs. Figure 4.4 provides the percentage of organizations using various recruitment sources for recruiting professional employees.[41] Each of the major sources from which organizations draw recruits has strengths and weaknesses.

Internal Sources

As we discussed with regard to human resource policies, an organization may emphasize internal or external sources of job applicants. Internal sources are employees who currently hold other positions in the organization. Organizations recruit existing employees through a **job posting**, or communicating information about the vacancy on company bulletin boards, in employee publications, on corporate intranets, and anywhere else the organization

job posting The process of communicating information about a job vacancy on company bulletin boards, in employee publications, on corporate intranets, and anywhere else the organization communicates with employees.

Did You KNOW?

Four in Ten Positions Are Filled with Insiders

In a recent survey of Canadian organizations, 62 percent of overall hires came from outside the organization. However, for senior executives as well as service and production-level jobs, 50 percent of the positions were filled by internal candidates and 50 percent were filled by external candidates.

Question

1. Would a promote-from-within policy be relevant to an organization that fills mostly entry-level jobs? Why or why not?

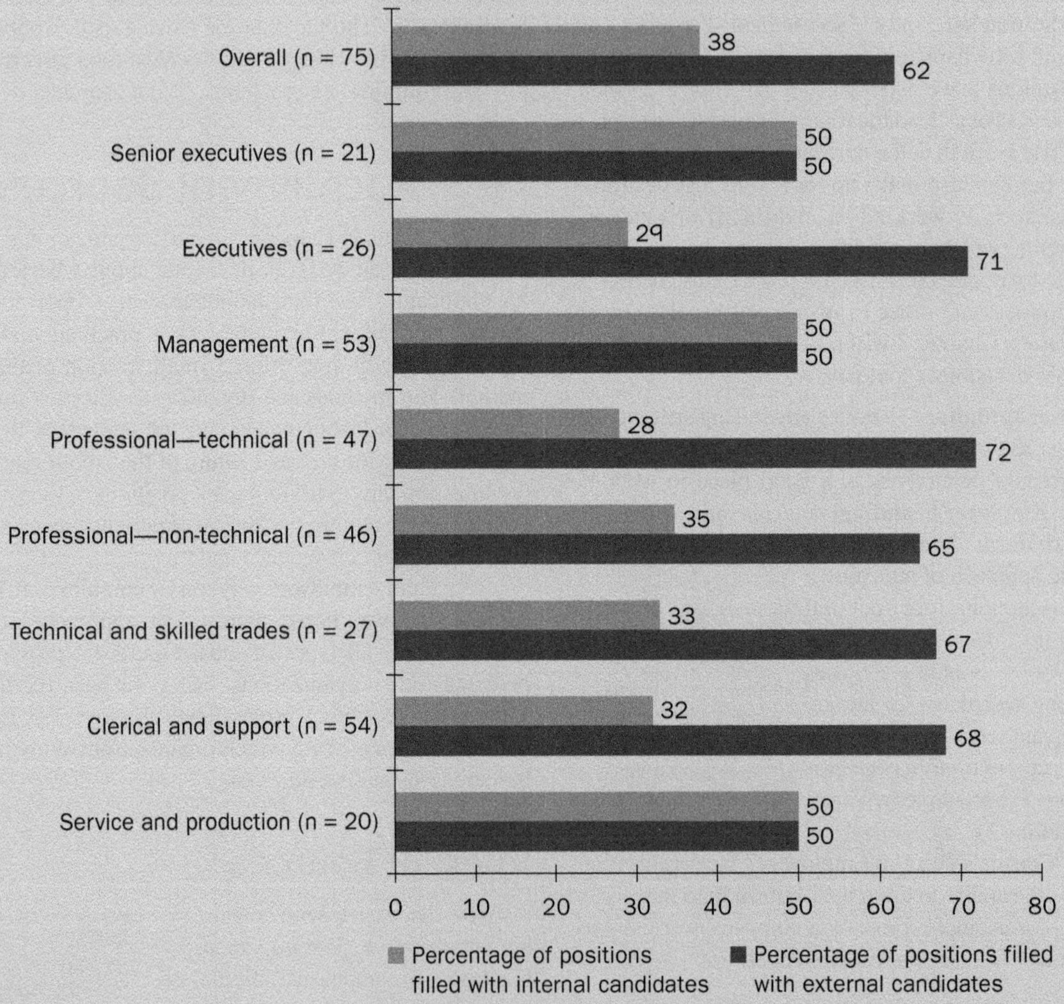

Source: Jane Cooper and Shannon Jackson, "Talent Management Benchmarking: Human Resources Trends and Metrics, Fourth Edition, Conference Board of Canada, February 2017, p. 49.

communicates with employees. Managers also may identify candidates to recommend for vacancies. Policies that emphasize promotions and even lateral moves (transfers) to achieve broader career experience can give applicants a favourable impression of the organization's jobs. The use of internal sources also affects what kinds of people the organization recruits.

For the employer, relying on internal sources offers several advantages.[42] First, it generates applicants who are well known to the organization. In addition, these applicants are relatively knowledgeable about the organization's vacancies, which minimizes the possibility they will have unrealistic expectations about the job. Finally, filling vacancies through internal recruiting

FIGURE 4.4

Sources Used for Recruiting Professionals (Technical and Non-Technical)

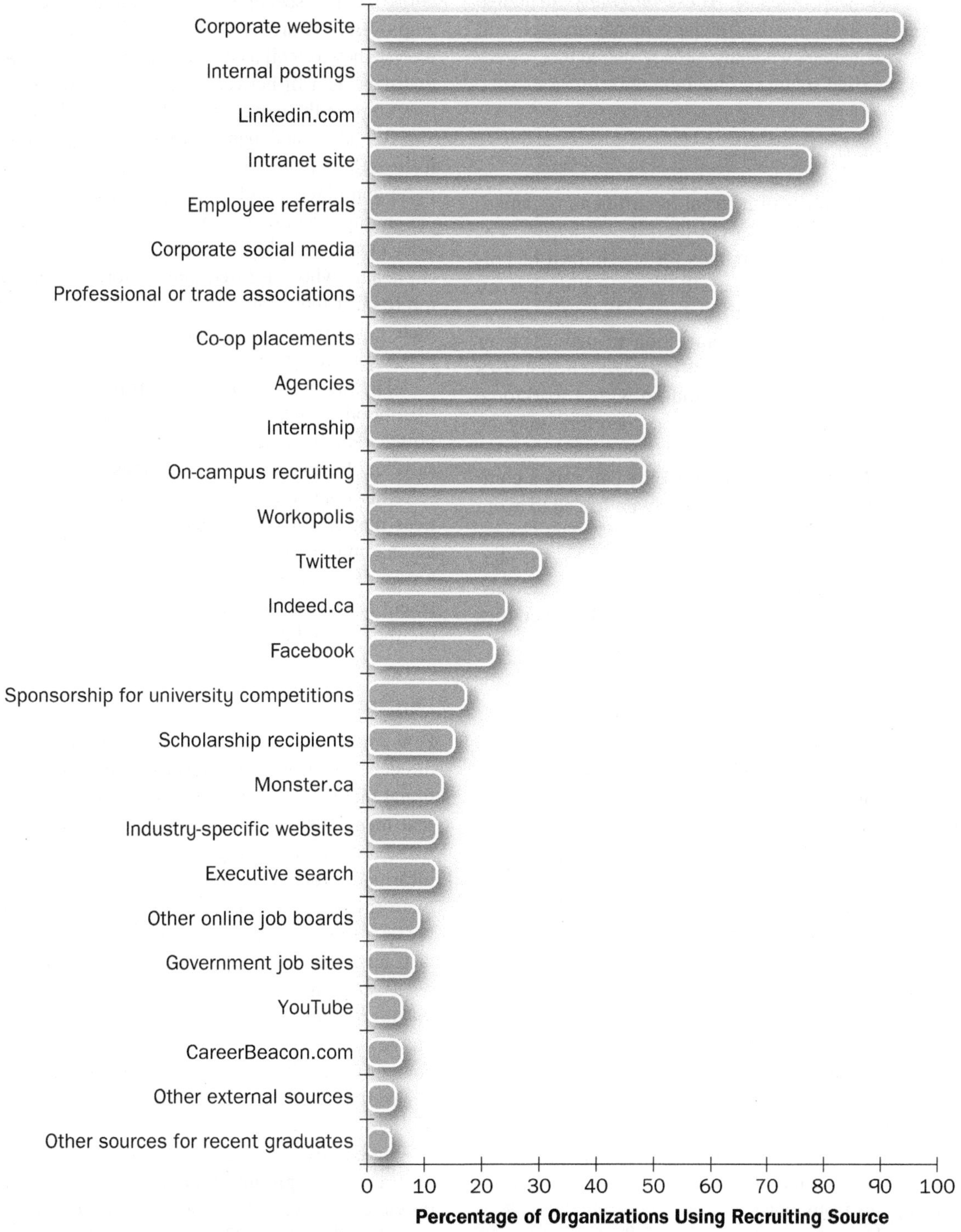

Source: Data from Jane Cooper, and Shannon Jackson, "Talent Management Benchmarking: Human Resources Trends and Metrics, Fourth Edition, *The Conference Board of Canada,* 2017, p. 42.

is generally cheaper and faster than looking outside the organization.

Chad Rabello, director of people operations at NakedWines.com, recognized these benefits and set up processes that would help the company fill more positions internally. One process helps employees build a career at the company, not just carry out a job. Rabello meets with each of the company's employees (there are fewer than a hundred) to create a career development plan, which may involve learning skills needed for the same or a different position. Another program invites employees to present new business ideas to top management; the executives pick one idea to fund. This process develops creative thinking and helps Rabello and the other executives identify employees with leadership potential. These programs encourage employees to stay, and they prepare management to fill openings with insiders who have already shared their career goals and practised solving problems creatively.[43]

External Sources

Despite the advantages of internal recruitment, organizations often have good reasons to recruit externally.[44] For entry-level positions and perhaps for specialized technical and professional positions, the organization has no internal recruits from which to draw. Also, bringing in outsiders may expose the organization to new ideas or new ways of doing business. An organization that uses only internal recruitment can wind up with a workforce whose members all think alike and therefore may be poorly suited to innovation.[45] And finally, companies that are able to grow during a slow economy can gain a competitive edge when other organizations are forced to avoid hiring, freeze pay increases, or even lay off talented people.[46] So organizations often recruit through social platforms such as LinkedIn, direct applicants and referrals, advertisements, employment agencies, and universities and colleges.

Direct Applicants and Referrals

Even without a formal effort to reach job applicants, an organization may hear from candidates through direct applicants and referrals. **Direct applicants** are people who apply for a vacancy without prompting from the organization. **Referrals** are people who apply because someone in the organization prompted them to do so.[47] The target of an organization's recruitment efforts may also involve recruiter-initiated contacts including identifying and contacting **passive job seekers**—individuals who are not actively seeking a job, but represent a significant source of top talent. These sources of recruits share characteristics that make them excellent pools from which to draw.

direct applicants People who apply for a vacancy without prompting from the organization.

referrals People who apply for a vacancy because someone in the organization prompted them to do so.

passive job seekers Individuals who are not actively seeking a job.

One advantage is that many direct applicants are to some extent already "sold" on the organization. Most have done some research and concluded there is enough fit between themselves and the vacant position to warrant submitting an application, a process called *self-selection,* which, when it works, eases the pressure on the organization's recruiting and selection systems. A form of aided self-selection occurs with referrals. Many job seekers look to friends, relatives, and acquaintances to help find employment. Using these personal networks not only helps the job seeker but also simplifies recruitment for employers.[48] Current employees (who are familiar with the vacancy as well as the person they are referring) decide that there is a fit between the person and the vacancy, so they suggest the person should apply for the job.

An additional benefit of using such sources is that it costs less than formal recruiting efforts. Considering these combined benefits, referrals and direct applications are among the best sources of new hires. Some employers offer current employees financial incentives for referring applicants who are hired and perform acceptably on the job (e.g., if they stay 180 days). Other companies rely on their good reputations in the labour market to generate direct applications.

The major downside of referrals is that they limit the likelihood of exposing the organization to fresh viewpoints. People tend to refer others who are like themselves. Furthermore, sometimes referrals contribute to hiring practices that are or that appear unfair, an example being **nepotism**, or the hiring of relatives. Employees may resent the hiring and rapid promotion of "the boss's son" or "the boss's daughter," or even the boss's friend.

nepotism The practice of hiring relatives.

Digital Recruiting Strategies

Few employers can fill all their vacant positions through direct applications and referrals, so most need to use additional methods of attracting applicants. Most often today, that means using digital recruiting strategies. Digital or web-based recruiting generally involves posting career information at the company website, using social media platforms such as LinkedIn, Twitter, and Facebook, and posting job ads on sites such as Workopolis, Monster, or Career Beacon. The popularity of some paid sites has been declining because more and more job seekers are turning to *job aggregators* such as Indeed. This type of online service gathers job information from job boards, company websites, newspaper ads, and more, making it all available through one website or mobile app. Overall, however, LinkedIn dominates online recruitment, fundamentally shifting the playing field of how companies recruit by giving them unprecedented connection to previously inaccessible passive job seekers.[49] Approximately 14 million Canadians are LinkedIn members and, globally, LinkedIn has half a billion members in 200 countries.[50]

On any of these sites, employers are competing for attention amid the flood on online information. Research by The Ladders, a jobs website, found that workers spend less than a minute and a half reading a job ad before deciding whether to apply. In that context, gaining the interest of qualified workers requires straightforward, clear job descriptions that highlight what is meaningful about the position.[51]

Most large companies and many smaller ones also make career information available at their own websites. To make that information easier to find, they may register a domain name with a "careers" or "jobs" extension such as www.starbucks.ca/careers for a link to information about careers at Starbucks and http://jobs.bce.ca to access information about careers at Bell Canada. Candidates also appreciate a response that the company has received their résumé—especially a response that gives a timetable about further communications from the company.

Accepting applications at the company website is not so successful for smaller and less well-known organizations, because fewer people are likely to visit the website. These organizations might get better results by going to the national job board websites, such as Monster and CareerBuilder, which attract a vast array of applicants. At these sites, job seekers submit standardized résumés. Employers can search the site's database for résumés that include specified key terms, and they can also submit information about their job opportunities, so that job seekers can search that information by key term. With both employers and job seekers submitting information to and conducting searches on them, these sites offer an efficient way to find matches between job seekers and job vacancies. However, a drawback is that the big job websites can provide too many leads of inferior quality, because they are so large and serve all job seekers and employers, not a select segment.

Because of this limitation of the large websites, smaller, more tailored websites called "niche boards" focus on certain industries, occupations, or geographic areas. For example, Atlantic Canada–based CareerBeacon is a job board particularly well known by applicants from Atlantic Canada. Professional and trade associations also provide career support to their members including access to job postings as well as expanded career services. For example, "Hire Authority" is the job board of Canada's largest Association of Human Resource Professionals—the Human Resources Professionals Association (HRPA).[52]

Photo courtesy of Human Resources Professionals Association (HRPA)

"Hire Authority" is the job board of the Human Resources Professionals Association (HRPA). In addition to posting employers' job openings, tweets and email broadcasts are sent to all of the HRPA's members.

Ads in Newspapers and Magazines

Although computer search tools have made electronic job lists the most popular way to advertise a job opening, some recruiters still follow the traditional route and advertise open positions in newspapers or magazines. When the goal is to find people who know the local community, advertising in a local newspaper can reach that audience. Similarly, when the goal is to find people in a specialized field, advertising in a trade, professional, or industry publication can reach a targeted subset of job candidates.

Advertising can be expensive, so it is especially important that the ads be well written. The person designing a job advertisement needs to answer two questions:

- What do we need to say?
- To whom do we need to say it?

With respect to the first question, an ad should give readers enough information to evaluate the job and its requirements, so they can make a well-informed judgment about their qualifications. Providing enough information may require long ads, which cost more. The employer should evaluate the additional costs against the costs of providing too little information: Vague ads generate a large number of applicants, including many who are not reasonably qualified. In practice, the people who write job ads tend to overstate the skills and experience required, perhaps generating too few qualified candidates.

Specifying whom to reach with the message helps the advertiser decide where to place the ad. Ads placed in the classified section of local newspapers are relatively inexpensive, yet reach many people in a specific geographic area who are currently looking for work. On the downside, this medium offers little ability to target skill levels. Typically, many of the people reading classified ads are either over- or under-qualified for the position. Also, people not looking for work rarely read the classifieds. For reaching a specific part of the labour market, including certain skill levels and more people who are employed, the organization may get better results from advertising in professional or industry journals.

Public Employment Agencies

Employers can register job vacancies at the Government of Canada's Job Bank. In addition to posting job openings, employers can access information and links to government forms, services, and programs. Prospective employees can narrow their job search by province and are also provided access to a variety of resources and career tools. *Job Match* facilitates matching of employers and job seekers based on their respective needs and profiles.

Private Staffing Companies

In addition to providing temporary employees, private staffing companies provide assistance to employers in attracting applicants for permanent positions. Job seekers

HR Oops!

Can Job Ads Perpetuate Gender Bias?

When a manager or recruiter prepares a job posting or ad, it is unlikely there is any intention to infuse it with wording that could prevent women from applying. However, researchers from the University of Waterloo and Duke University found that when job advertisements included more words stereotypically associated with men; for example, "assertive," "independent," "ambitious," and "analytical," the study participants, who were mostly students, perceived more men within these occupations, and perhaps most importantly, women found these jobs less appealing and perceived a reduced level of "belonging."

Managers and recruiters should also avoid using words like "rockstar," "guru," or "ninja" in job titles because these words tend to have masculine associations. Descriptive titles like "engineer," "project manager," and "developer" are free of gender bias so are more likely to attract the person who will be the best person for the job. According to Sara Watts-Rynard, executive director of the Canadian Apprenticeship Forum in Ottawa, "There's no purposeful attempt being made to discriminate but in an environment that's been largely made up of men for generations, this bias just comes out."

Questions

1. Why might a job posting or job ad contain language that is unintentionally "gender coded?"
2. Do adjectives matter when you are considering applying for a job?

Sources: Carmen Nobel, "How to Take Gender Bias Out of Your Job Ads," *Forbes,* December 14, 2016, www.forbes.com; Sarah Dobson, "'Male-wanted' job ads," *Canadian HR Reporter,* May 5, 2014, p. 1, 10; Danielle Gaucher, Justin Friesen, & Aaron C. Kay, "Evidence That Gendered Wording in Job Advertisements Exists and Sustains Gender Inequality," *Journal of Personality and Social Psychology,* 2011, Vol.101(1), pp. 109–128.

apply to the private staffing company and are usually screened for suitability. These companies differ significantly in the types of services provided. It is important for both job seekers and employers to research and thoroughly assess private staffing firms so as to work with the company that will best meet their needs and expectations. These companies provide their services for a fee. Usually these fees are paid by the employer.

For executives, managers, or professionals, an employer may use the services of a type of private staffing company called an *executive search firm* (ESF). People often call these agencies "headhunters," because unlike other staffing companies, they find new jobs for people almost exclusively already employed. For job candidates, dealing with executive search firms can be sensitive. Typically, executives, managers, and professionals do not want to advertise their availability, because it might trigger a negative reaction from their current employer. ESFs serve as a buffer, providing confidentiality between the employer and the potential candidate. That benefit may give an employer access to candidates it cannot recruit in other, more direct ways.

Universities and Colleges

Most universities and colleges have placement services that seek to help their students and graduates obtain employment. On-campus interviewing is an important source of recruits for entry-level professional and managerial vacancies.[53] Organizations tend to focus especially on universities and colleges that have strong reputations in areas for which they have critical needs—say petroleum engineering or accounting.[54]

Many employers have found that successfully competing for the best students requires more than just signing up prospective graduates for interview slots. One of the best ways to establish a stronger presence on a campus is with a cooperative education or internship program. These programs give an organization early access to potential applicants and let the organization assess their capabilities directly. Employers may also meet potential future employees by hosting networking events to meet scholarship recipients and providing sponsorships for university competitions. JDC West is Western Canada's largest business school competition and has corporate partners including Accenture, Canadian Western Bank (CWB), Deloitte, and KPMG.[55]

Another way of increasing the employer's presence on campus is to participate in university and college job fairs. In general, a job fair is an event where many employers gather for a short time to meet large numbers of potential job applicants. Although job fairs can be held anywhere (such as at a hotel or convention centre), campuses are ideal because of the many well-educated, not-yet-employed individuals there. Job fairs are an inexpensive means of generating an on-campus presence. They can provide one-on-one dialogue with students; however, it is also important to offer a candidate experience that includes the ability to apply for jobs with as few clicks as possible. Encouraging texting is another way for recruiters to demonstrate they are authentic and willing to answer students' questions as they come up.[56]

Evaluating Recruitment Sources

In general, there are few rules that say what recruitment source is best for a given job vacancy. Therefore, it is wise for employers to monitor the quality of all their recruitment sources. One way to do this is to develop and compare **yield ratios** for each source.[57] A yield ratio expresses the percentage of applicants who successfully move from one stage of the recruitment and selection process to the next. For example, the organization might find the number of candidates interviewed as a percentage of the total number of résumés generated by a given source (i.e., number of interviews divided by number of résumés). A high yield ratio (large percentage) means the source is an effective way to find candidates to interview. By comparing the yield ratios of different recruitment sources, HR professionals can determine which is the best or most efficient for the type of vacancy.

yield ratios
A ratio that expresses the percentage of applicants who successfully move from one stage of the recruitment and selection process to the next.

Another measure of recruitment success is the *cost per hire.* To compute this amount, find the cost of using a particular recruitment source for a particular type of vacancy. Then divide that cost by the number of people hired to fill that type of vacancy. A low cost per hire means that the recruitment source is efficient; it delivers qualified candidates at minimal cost.

To see how HR professionals use these measures, look at the examples in Table 4.4. This table shows the results for a hypothetical organization that used six kinds of recruitment sources to fill a number of vacancies. For each recruitment source, the table shows four yield ratios and the cost per hire. To fill these jobs, the best two sources of recruits were local colleges/universities and employee referral programs. Company websites generated the largest number of recruits (1,000 résumés). However, only 40 were assessed acceptable, of which only half accepted employment offers, for a cumulative yield ratio of 20/1,000, or 2 percent. Recruiting at renowned colleges and/or universities generated highly qualified applicants, but relatively few of them ultimately accepted positions with the organization. Executive search firms produced the highest cumulative yield ratio. These generated only 20 applicants, but all of them accepted interview offers, most were assessed suitable, and 75 percent of these suitable candidates took jobs with the organization. However, notice the cost per hire. The executive search firms charged $120,000 for finding these 15 employees, resulting in the largest cost per hire. In contrast, local colleges and universities provided modest yield ratios at one of the lowest costs per hire. Employee referrals provided excellent yield ratios at a slightly higher cost.

As recruiting software and social sharing applications evolve, the distinction between use of the various recruiting sources is becoming increasingly blurred. However, Chris Gould, senior director of the talent acquisition solutions group for Aon Hewitt, anticipates that "we will see more 'social sharing' applications that will integrate with mobile, social media. These apps will make it easier to share jobs and will provide the ability to track click-throughs and sources."[58]

Photo by Tibor Kolley, © Copyright The Globe and Mail Inc./CP Photo

Capt. Jen Causey, an artillery officer with the 2nd Regiment, Royal Canadian Horse Artillery, based in Petawawa, Ontario, was staffing the booth at the Women in Leadership Career Fair at the University of Toronto. She is chatting with Cora Cheng, a second-year mechanical engineering student at U of T. How do career fairs benefit employers and the students at the same time?

LO5 Recruiter Traits and Behaviours

The last part of the model presented in Figure 4.4 that we will discuss is the recruiter. Many applicants approach the recruiter with some skepticism. Knowing it is the recruiter's job to sell them on a vacancy, some applicants discount what the recruiter says, in light of what they have heard from other sources, such as friends, family, online resources, and instructors. For these and other reasons, recruiters' characteristics and behaviours seem to have less impact on applicants' job choices than we might expect.

TABLE 4.4

Results of a Hypothetical Recruiting Effort

	Recruiting Source					
	Local College/ University	Renowned College/ University	Employee Referrals	Newspaper Ad	Executive Search Firm	Company Website
Résumés generated	200	400	50	500	20	1,000
Interview offers accepted	150	100	45	400	20	80
Yield ratio	**75%**	**25%**	**90%**	**80%**	**100%**	**8%**
Applicants judged acceptable	100	95	40	50	19	40
Yield ratio	**67%**	**95%**	**89%**	**12.5%**	**95%**	**50%**
Accept employment offers	90	10	35	25	15	20
Yield ratio	**90%**	**10.5%**	**87.5%**	**50%**	**79%**	**50%**
Cumulative yield ratio	90/200 **45%**	10/400 **2.5%**	35/50 **70%**	25/500 **5%**	15/20 **75%**	20/1,000 **2%**
Cost	$30,000	$50,000	$15,000	$20,000	$120,000	$500
Cost per hire	**$333**	**$5,000**	**$429**	**$800**	**$8,000**	**$25**

Recruiters' Functional Area and Traits

Most organizations have to choose whether their recruiters are specialists in human resources or experts at particular jobs (supervisors or job incumbents). Some studies indicate that applicants perceive HR specialists as less credible and are less attracted to jobs when recruiters are HR specialists.[59] The evidence does not completely discount a positive role for HR specialists in recruiting. It does indicate, however, that these specialists need to take extra steps to ensure that applicants perceive them as knowledgeable and credible.

Two traits stand out when applicants' reactions to recruiters are examined. The first, which could be called "warmth," reflects the degree to which the recruiter seems to care about the applicant and is enthusiastic about her potential to contribute to the company. The second characteristic could be called "informativeness"—meaning the recruiter provides the kind of information the applicant is seeking. In general, applicants respond more positively to recruiters who are perceived as warm and informative. These characteristics seem more important than demographic characteristics such as age, sex, or race, which have complex and inconsistent effects on applicant responses.[60]

Recruiters' Realism

Perhaps the most well-researched aspect of recruiting deals with the level of realism that recruiters incorporate into their message. Because the recruiter's job is to attract candidates, there is some pressure to exaggerate the positive features of the vacancy while downplaying the negative features. Applicants are highly sensitive to negative information. However, if the recruiter goes too far in a positive direction, the candidate can be misled and lured into taking the job under false pretenses.

realistic job previews Background information about a job's positive and negative qualities.

Many studies have looked at how well **realistic job previews**—background information about jobs' positive and negative qualities—can get around this problem and help minimize early job turnover. On the whole, the research indicates that realistic job previews do lower expectations and can help reduce future turnover in the workforce.[61] Currently, the idea that one can go overboard in selling a vacancy to a recruit has merit. However, the belief that informing people about the negative characteristics of the job will totally "inoculate" them to such characteristics seems unwarranted, based on the research conducted to date.[62]

We conclude that an organization's decisions about policies that directly affect the job's attributes (pay, security, advancement opportunities, and so on) will probably be more important than recruiter traits and behaviours in affecting job choice.

Enhancing Recruiter Impact

Researchers have tried to find the conditions in which recruiters do make a difference. Such research suggests that an organization can increase the positive impact that recruiters have on job candidates:

- **Provide timely feedback**. Applicants react very negatively to delays in feedback, often making unwarranted attributions for the delays (such as, "The organization is uninterested in my application").[63]
- **The organization can recruit in teams rather than by individuals**. Applicants tend to view job incumbents and supervisors as more credible than HR specialists, so these kinds of recruiters should be part of any team. However, HR specialists have knowledge that is not shared by job incumbents and supervisors (who may perceive recruiting as a small part of their "real" jobs), so they necessarily play a key role on the recruiting team.

Thinking ETHICALLY

Mindsets Shift on Boomerang Employees

The hiring of boomerang employees—employees who leave and return (in contrast to alumni employees—employees who leave and don't return) is on the rise due to the changing mindset of HR professionals. According to a survey of 1,800 HR professionals, nearly half said their organization previously had a policy against rehiring former employees, but three-quarters of these HR professionals say they are now open to hiring boomerang employees.

Organizations are also using LinkedIn and Facebook to stay connected with former employees including providing a corporate alumni group experience and even announcing their accomplishments and promotions. Another strategy is to host social events to keep in touch with former employees.

In addition to knowing the organization and being known in the organization, boomerang employees can be a powerful recruiting tool because they know that the grass is definitely not greener, and they are usually very pleased to share that perspective," said Joyce Gioia, a management consultant, workforce futurist, and CEO of Employer of Choice International. "But with everything, there's a blessing and a curse," said Ilene Siscovick, a partner at global consultancy, Mercer. "There's a fundamental reason that the employee left the organization in the first place, and bringing them back in could have unintended consequences." There could also be a risk that former employees could use the alumni social media platforms and hosted events to recruit employees to their new company.

Questions

1. What are the potential benefits and risks (if any) associated with actively keeping in touch with former employees?
2. What are the potential ethical concerns that could arise if an organization decided to pursue former employees as a targeted recruitment source?

Sources: Roy Maurer, "Stay in Touch with Former Employees: One Could be Your Next Hire, Society for Human Resource Management," April 22, 2016, shrm.org; Kerry Hannon, "Welcome Back; Boomerang Employees Are on the Rise," *Forbes*, September 7, 2015, www.forbes.com; "The Corporate Culture and Boomerang Employee Study, The Workforce Institute at Knonus and WorkplaceTrends.com, September 1, 2015, https://workplacetrends.com; Abbie J. Shipp, Stacie Furst-Holloway, T. Brad Harris & Benson Rosen, "Gone Today but here Tomorrow; Extending the Unfolding Model of Turnover to Consider Boomerang Employees," *Personnel Psychology* 67 (2014), pp. 421–462.

SUMMARY

LO1 Discuss how to align workforce planning with the organization's strategy.

Workforce planning compares the present state of the organization with its goals for the future, then identifies what changes it must make in its human resources to meet those goals. Workforce planning uses labour supply and demand forecasts to anticipate labour shortages and surpluses. When done well, workforce planning can enhance the success of the organization while minimizing the human suffering resulting from poorly anticipated labour surpluses or shortages.

LO2 Examine methods organizations use to deal with a labour surplus or shortage.

Based on whether a surplus or a shortage is expected, the planner sets goals and creates a strategy for achieving those goals. The strategy also involves programs that can be utilized to reduce a labour surplus (such as downsizing and early retirement programs) and eliminate a labour shortage (such as bringing in temporary workers or expanding overtime). The organization then implements its HR strategy and evaluates the results. Succession planning identifies and tracks high-potential employees who are capable of filling future openings in key positions.

LO3 Explain the importance of recruiting and describe approaches to attract talent.

Human resource recruiting is a buffer activity that creates an applicant pool that the organization can draw from in the event of a labour shortage that is to be filled with new hires. Organizational recruitment programs affect talent acquisition outcomes through human resource policies (such as promote-from-within policies) that affect the attributes of the vacancies themselves and can also impact the types of people who apply for positions by using different recruitment sources.

LO4 Compare and contrast recruitment sources.

A critical element of an organization's talent acquisition strategy is its decisions about where to look for applicants. An organization may emphasize internal or external sources of job applicants. Increasingly, recruiting is becoming a digital experience. Employers need to evaluate recruitment sources in the effort to optimize efficiency and quality.

LO5 Describe the recruiter's role.

Through their behaviour and other characteristics, recruiters influence the nature of the job vacancy and the kinds of applicants generated. Applicants tend to perceive job experts as more credible than recruiters who are HR specialists. Recruiters can enhance their impact by being informative and authentic, providing timely feedback, and recruiting in teams.

CRITICAL THINKING QUESTIONS

1. Suppose an organization expects a labour shortage to develop in key job areas over the next few years. Recommend general responses the organization could make in each of the following areas:
   a. Recruitment
   b. Training, learning, and development
   c. Rewards (pay, employee benefits, and work environment)
2. Review the sample transitional matrix shown in Table 4.1. What jobs experience the greatest turnover (employees leaving the organization)? How might an organization with this combination of jobs reduce the turnover?
3. In the same transitional matrix, which jobs seem to rely the most on internal recruitment? Which seem to rely most on external recruitment? Why?
4. Why do organizations combine statistical and judgmental forecasts of labour demand, rather than relying on data or judgment alone? Give an example of a situation in which each type of forecast could be inaccurate.
5. Some organizations have detailed employment equity plans, complete with goals and timetables, for each of the designated groups, yet have no formal workforce plan for the organization as a whole. Why might this be the case? What does this practice suggest about the role of human resource management in these organizations?
6. Is succession planning becoming more or less important? Explain your answer.
7. Give an example of a human resource policy that would help attract a larger pool of job candidates. Give an example of a human resource policy that would likely reduce the pool of candidates. Would you expect these policies to influence the quality as well as the number of applicants? Why or why not?

8. Discuss the relative merits of internal versus external recruitment. Give an example of a situation in which each of these approaches might be particularly effective.
9. Recruiting people for jobs that require global assignments is increasingly important for many organizations. Where might an organization go to recruit people interested in such assignments?
10. What is your experience with the use of social platforms in the recruiting process; for example, LinkedIn, Facebook, Twitter, and/or YouTube? What is your advice to managers and HR professionals in using digital recruiting to attract job applicants?
11. How can organizations improve the effectiveness and impact of their recruiters?

EXPERIENCING HR—EVALUATING YOUR RÉSUMÉ AND/OR LINKEDIN PROFILE

Find a job posting for a position and company that interests you. Review and evaluate your own résumé and/or LinkedIn profile from the perspective of an HR professional or organizational leader who may be leading the recruitment process. What qualities on your résumé and profile match what the company is looking for? What words and phrases does the company use in its job posting and on its website that you could use (truthfully) to show that you would be a high performer in the job? Are there any additional experiences and/or skills you may need before you would be considered for the job?

Write a one-page paper summarizing your findings. Attach your résumé and/or details from your Linkedin profile, and turn it in for credit on the assignment.

CASE STUDY: EVIDENCE-BASED HRM

City of Edmonton Uses Podcasts in Recruitment

The City of Edmonton's HR team have successfully established a strong recruitment presence on social media over the past five years. They had even put in place an online application that allowed prospects to apply for positions as soon as they saw the job posting ad.

But the 14,000-plus employer was facing a big challenge. Typical job postings attracted a number of unqualified candidates and failed to communicate less tangible benefits, such as leadership style, business strategies, and current initiatives. Moreover, given the union's specifications for 90 percent of the job postings with the government employer, a lot of text was required on job descriptions. "We knew people wanted to know who they would be working for, what the culture was like, and to get excited about working here," says Margaret Blair, director of recruitment. "But they didn't want to read about it."

Enter Shahid Wazed, team lead of talent sourcing strategies. He had already helped the city establish 115,000 Facebook followers and 40,000 on LinkedIn on the recruiting channels alone. Now he proposed using podcasts. "Inbound marketers were using podcasts a lot and I thought, 'Why not use something like this for recruitment?'" says Wazed. "In reality, 50 percent of our candidates come through mobile devices. So why not make it easier and just embed an informative, engaging podcast right into the job posting so when top talent lands on a job posting, they get to listen to it right away before reading any text?"

Wazed initially sold the idea to both Jeff MacPherson, HR branch manager, and Margaret Blair, as well as a key pivot person in the process, Nigel Brown, team lead for the executive recruitment team. As the agency within the City of Edmonton dedicated to recruitment at the executive level (often facing unique or hard-to-fill vacancies), their portfolio was the perfect one to launch with, says Blair. "Nigel saw the value in the strategy and was key to getting buy-in from our own staff, and then directing them to us for the technical work." With Brown's nod, Wazed set about developing pilot podcasts. Since he was coming at it from scratch, he researched a number of options and settled on Garageband software to record the podcasts, and Libsyn, an online podcast hosting service, he says.

Clear communication and processes helped win over management, says Blair. Specifically, Wazed and Jessica Avila, recruitment and content marketing consultant, developed a one-page marketing document and a visual podcast process overview diagram to help hiring managers understand the process and timelines. These days, Wazed and Avila develop and share a podcast script and interview questions with the hiring manager, and conduct a quick coaching call. The final podcast is reviewed with them, and the two keep the hiring managers up to date on the number of downloads after the podcast is live.

Any instances where hiring managers might have frozen in front of a camera were eliminated with the microphone-only approach, says Blair. The approach also allowed for editing, says Wazed. "We are able to do edits, and ask them to record smaller segments, too. The first recordings would take one hour to an hour-and-a-half. Now, they take 15 or 20 minutes at the most." "The candidate response has been terrific," says Blair. "The podcasts are downloaded anywhere from 150 to 1,000 times each." This means candidates are spending the time to listen to the short five-minute podcasts before deciding whether or not to put in their application, she says.

"Not only are these inexpensive to produce, on the innovation side of things, this is the first time from a company perspective that we're enabling transparency between candidates and hiring managers." Typically, job postings limit accessibility, says Blair. "But it's important for top candidates to know what their manager's leadership style is and to see if they connect. We need them to be responsible for way more than XYZ, and the podcasts take job descriptions to the next level." Ultimately, the podcasts help make the interaction a personalized and more informative one, she says.

And the positive reception from hiring managers is a testament to its success, says Blair. Deputy city managers and city councillors have all recorded podcasts to help recruit top talent. While it's too early for the team to track the return on investment, they are tracking the number of times candidates refer to the podcast on their cover letter or during pre-screening interviews. "We've had candidates remark on how an upcoming project really excites them," says Blair. "We believe this will correlate to higher qualified candidates, too. Already we are attracting people who we would not otherwise attract."

Questions

1. How would you go about calculating the return on investment (ROI) of using podcasts in the recruitment process as described in this City of Edmonton case?
2. If you were responsible for recruiting at the City of Edmonton, what other enhancements to the recruiting process would you recommend? How would you go about calculating the ROI of each recommended enhancement?

CASE STUDY: HRM SOCIAL

Effective Talent Searches via Social Networks

Listing job openings online is an easy way to let potential employees know about positions. But these ads can generate a flood of responses from unqualified or barely interested job candidates. Most employers today are therefore opting for digital recruiting that allows more precise targeting of their messages and deeper insight into the qualifications and interest of potential candidates. That often means using social media. According to research by the Society for Human Resource Management, two-thirds of employers hired candidates they found via social media. Even more (84 percent) use social media as a recruiting method.

The social media site most often used for recruiting is LinkedIn. On this career-related networking site, employers can run searches to identify individuals whose profiles mention particular skills, interests, or areas of experience. They also can advertise openings in special-interest groups (taking care to follow each group's rules for this type of posting). Employers also can benefit from participating on social media sites that serve groups for professions or trades.

To use social media effectively, HR departments need a two-pronged approach. The first prong is to develop a favourable online "brand" as an employer. This requires not only regularly posting helpful, informative messages from the company, but also monitoring conversations in order to identify concerns and problems—and address them with solutions. When an employer's brand is favourable, workers who admire a company on Facebook might apply for a job or share a story about job openings, even if they didn't go on Facebook to look for work. Some companies view their campaigns to attract candidates as important as their advertising to customers. For example, Heineken has developed unconventional videos that focus on its employment brand and employee experience.

The second prong is to gather and analyze useful data about talented people who are or might become job candidates. Social media data can tell employers where people are talking about the brand, the company, or the industry. Searches can point recruiters to discussions on particular topics, where they can see who is making a valuable contribution. Dell's Global Talent Brand and Tools team launched a social network campaign including blog posts and videos of employees sharing their experiences working at Dell. The videos were posted to the company's career website, its YouTube channel, and other candidate- and employee-targeted sites such as Glassdoor in concert with launching an optimized job search site. The most sophisticated users of social media use analytic tools to help them find desirable candidates for key positions, so they can reach out with an offer to talk.

Questions

1. Based on this description, what are some advantages of finding a candidate via social media compared with traditional job postings on the company's website?
2. Do you think it's important to have a LinkedIn profile? Why or why not?

Sources: Brett Walsh and Erica Volini, "Rewriting the rules for the digital age," 2017 Deloitte Global Human Capital Trends, *Deloitte University Press*, dupress.deloitte.com; Joanna Stern, "Ignoring LinkedIn Is Hurting Your Career," *Wall Street Journal*, April 13, 2016, http://www.wsj.com; Desda Moss, "Talent Search," *HR Magazine*, April 2016, https://www.shrm.org; Heather Huhman, "Four Mistakes Your Social-Media Profiles May Be Committing with Job Seekers," *Entrepreneur*, February 8, 2016, http://www.entrepreneur.com; Bruce Shutan, "The Social Recruiting Journey," *Employee Benefit News*, September 15, 2015, pp. 31–32; Lindsay Stanton, "Attracting Talent with Technology: How Digital Job Descriptions Can Draw In Top Talent," *Workforce Solutions Review*, September 2015, pp. 31–33; John Zappe, "New SHRM Survey Shows Growing Reach of Hiring from Social Media," TLNT, September 2, 2015, http://www.eremedia.com/tlnt; Donna Wells, "Close the Skills Gap—Once and for All," *Chief Learning Officer*, August 2015, pp. 44–46.

CHAPTER 5

Selecting Employees

WHAT DO I NEED TO KNOW?

After reading this chapter, you should be able to:

LO1	Identify the elements and legal requirements of the selection process.
LO2	Define ways to measure the success of a selection method.
LO3	Compare some of the common methods used for obtaining and verifying candidate information.
LO4	Describe the major types of employment tests.
LO5	Discuss how to conduct effective interviews and make and communicate the selection decision.

Ingram Publishing

A Danish training and consulting firm called Specialisterne recruits people on the autism spectrum for companies in need of skilled workers.

Valuing Workers with Autism

Shawn Bolshin is a 30-year old university graduate with exemplary analytical skills. He has been working in Toronto for CIBC for the past two years in their information security department and is considered a "rising star" due to his knack for uncovering difficult to spot security breaches. "I'm not, like, that different," Shawn says hesitantly, "but I do have that ability to see those details and things and have a much tighter focus on things." Bolshin has autism spectrum disorder (ASD). Although people on the autism spectrum often demonstrate "trustworthiness, strong memories, reliability, adherence to rules, and attention to detail," social communications like interviews may be awkward and uncomfortable. And although the majority of people with autism have average or above-average intelligence, most college-educated adults with autism are underemployed.

SAP, a global software company headquartered in Germany, also recognizes the value of hiring people with autism. For example, people with ASD may have high-structured thinking patterns including careful attention to detail. For some jobs, such as writing manuals and debugging software, these ways of thinking are exactly what employers like SAP need. SAP tested its recruitment of workers with autism in Germany and India; based on the pilot program's success, it rolled out the effort to Canada, Ireland, and the United States.

A Danish training and consulting firm called Specialisterne recruits people on the autism spectrum for companies in need of skilled workers. Workshops are used to screen candidates and are focused on completing complex tasks like building and testing a robot, rather than relying on interviews. Those who pass the screening are referred to a growing list of successful organizations including CIBC, SAP, TD Canada Trust, and Shoppers Drug Mart. Luisa Delgado, a member of SAP's executive board, described the competitive advantage of her organization's experience: "Only by employing people who think differently and spark innovation will SAP be prepared to handle the challenges of the 21st century."[1]

Introduction

Recruitment (Chapter 4) together with selection occupies a central place in talent management and organizational strategy that is increasingly referred to as talent acquisition. This strategic role that recruitment and selection play in organizations has triggered many new developments and approaches that have "expanded traditional conceptualizations of recruitment and selection practices," and we will include a discussion of several of these emerging developments in this chapter.[2]

The organization's decisions about selecting people are central to its ability to survive, adapt, and grow. Selection decisions become especially critical when organizations face tight labour markets or must compete for talent with other organizations in the same industry. If a competitor keeps getting the best applicants, the remaining companies have to make do with who is left. Hiring decisions are about acquiring the talent who will perform well in the job and in the organization. Any organization that appreciates the competitive edge provided by good people must take the utmost care in choosing its members.

This chapter will familiarize you with ways to increase the effectiveness of employee selection. The chapter starts by describing the selection process, examining the importance of candidate experience, and discussing how to evaluate possible methods for carrying out the selection process. It then takes an in-depth look at the most widely used methods: applications and résumés, employment tests, and interviews. The chapter wraps up by describing the process by which organizations arrive at and communicate hiring decisions.

LO1 What Are the Steps in the Selection Process?

Through the process of selection, organizations make decisions about who will be chosen to fill job openings. Selection begins with the candidates identified through recruitment and attempts to reduce their number to the individuals who are most likely to be the best performers in the available jobs and who will support the culture of the organization. At the end of the process, the selected individuals are placed in jobs with the organization.

The process of selecting employees varies considerably from organization to organization and from job to job. At most organizations, however, selection includes the steps illustrated in Figure 5.1. First, a human resources professional reviews the applications received to see which meet the requirements of the job. For candidates who meet the requirements, the organization administers tests and reviews work samples to assess the candidates' abilities. Those with the best abilities are invited to participate in one or more interviews. Often, supervisors and team members are involved at the interview stage of the process. By this point, the decision makers are beginning to form conclusions about which candidates are likely to be the best performers. For the top few candidates, the organization should check references and conduct background checks to verify that the organization's information is correct. Then supervisors, teams, and other decision makers select a person to receive a job offer. In some cases, the candidate may negotiate with the organization regarding salary, benefits, and the like. If the candidate accepts the job, the organization places him or her in that job.

The ease of applying online has made this processing overwhelming for many recruiters. A simple job posting

FIGURE 5.1

Steps in the Selection Process

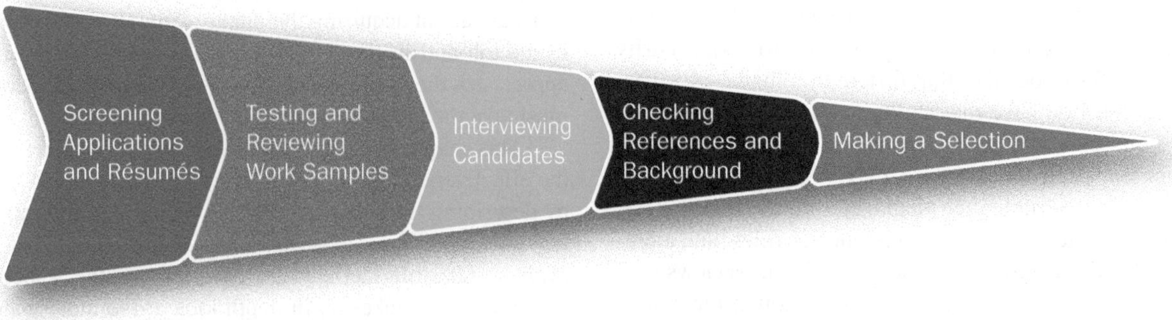

online could generate hundreds of responses in one day. Many employers are automating much of the selection process with an **applicant tracking system (ATS)**, which is a software application that streamlines the flow of information between job seekers, HR staff, and hiring managers. As organizations expand their corporate websites into interactive career centres, applicant tracking systems provide capabilities including multilingual support for global locations; pre-screening of applications and résumés for education, specific KSAOs and/or competencies, and experience; and generation of applicant confirmation letters. Applicant tracking systems also support various data handling and report generation requirements associated with hiring employees; for example, storing résumés, tracking candidate sources, and connecting applications to specific hiring managers or job openings. By automating the process to match available talent with current job opportunities, the efficiency and speed of the overall hiring process is improved. Organizations can streamline the process, build relationships with candidates, cut hiring cycle-time, and increase the probability of hiring an available and interested candidate.[3] Some even predict outcomes of hiring candidates with particular qualities.[4]

applicant tracking system (ATS) A software application that streamlines the flow of information between job seekers, HR staff, and hiring managers.

How does an organization decide which of these elements to use, and in what order? Some organizations simply repeat a selection process that is familiar. If members of the organization underwent job interviews, they conduct job interviews, asking familiar questions. However, what organizations should do is to create a selection process in support of its job descriptions and specifications. In Chapter 3, we explained that a job specifications identifies the skills and abilities required for successfully performing a job. The selection process should be set up in such a way that it lets the organization identify people who have the necessary KSAOs and/or competencies.

This kind of strategic approach to selection requires ways to measure the effectiveness of selection tools. From science, we have basic standards for this:

- The selection method provides reliable information.
- The method provides valid information.
- The information can be generalized to apply to the candidates.
- The method offers high utility (practical value).
- The selection criteria are legal.

The Candidate Experience

The **candidate experience** is a job seeker's perception of and response to an employer's talent acquisition process. In turn, candidate experience is a critical determinant of the organization's reputation and employer brand. A positive candidate experience can result in more and potentially better applicants, hires, and referrals, and reduce the hiring costs and time to fill vacancies. However, news of negative candidate experience can be rapidly shared through social media and employer review sites like Glassdoor.[5]

candidate experience A job seeker's perception of and response to an employer's talent acquisition process.

Candidate experience also impacts business results when people who have a poor candidate experience withdraw their support as a customer and tell others in their personal and professional networks. Recent research conducted by Talent Board, a non-profit organization focused on elevating and promoting quality candidate experience, reported that candidates share their positive experiences with their inner circles publicly online (social media, Glassdoor, etc.) 77 percent of the time and their negative experiences 61 percent of the time. When job seekers have a highly positive "5 Star" candidate experience, they are 74 percent more likely to increase their business relationship with the potential employer—even when they are not hired or become a finalist for the job. However, when job seekers have a negative "1 Star" candidate experience, 46 percent will sever their business relationship with the potential employer. The Evidenced-based HRM case at the end of the chapter examines research conducted by IBM's Smarter Workforce Institute about the impact of candidate experience and how Johnson & Johnson recently transformed its talent acquisition process to provide a transparent and compelling experience for job seekers.[6]

What Are the Legal Standards for Selection?

Whether selecting a new employee or promoting an employee from within the organization, the selection process needs to be conducted in a way that meets human rights and privacy requirements. Human rights legislation and privacy legislation described in Chapter 2 have implications for the selection process.

- The interview needs to be conducted in a way that candidates can be assessed without drawing out information that is not relevant to the job being filled. As summarized in Table 5.1, the organization may not ask questions on an application form or in an interview that gathers information about prohibited grounds of discrimination, even indirectly. For example, asking candidates for the dates they attended high school might indirectly gather information about applicants' age.
- Interview notes are made by interviewers to help distinguish among candidates. Even if these notes are used only by the interviewers, they cannot identify or distinguish candidates based on any of the prohibited grounds of discrimination (e.g., "black woman," "50-ish," "male with Irish accent," would be inappropriate to include in interview notes).[7]
- Candidates must provide their consent before a background or reference check can be conducted. Because background and reference checks may unearth information about protected grounds such as age or religious affiliation, or other personal information, human rights commissions recommend that the applicant should first receive a conditional job offer. The employer's conditional job offer is offered subject to a successful background and reference check.

TABLE 5.1

Guidelines for Applications and Interviews

Subject	Avoid Asking	Preferred	Comments
Name	• about name change: whether it was changed by court order, marriage, or other reason. • for maiden name.		Ask after selection if needed to check on previously held jobs or educational credentials.
Address	for addresses outside Canada.	Ask place and duration of current or recent address.	
Age	for birth certificates, baptismal records, or about age in general.	Ask applicants whether they are eligible to work under Canadian laws regarding age restrictions.	If precise age is required for benefit plans or other legitimate purposes, it can be determined after selection.
Sex	about pregnancy, childbearing plans, or child care arrangements.	Ask applicant if the attendance requirements can be met.	During the interview or after selection, the applicant, for purposes of courtesy, may be asked which of Dr., Mr., Mrs., Miss, or Ms. is preferred.
Marital status	• whether the applicant is single, married, divorced, engaged, separated, widowed, or living common-law. • whether the applicant's spouse may be transferred. • about the spouse's employment.	If transfer or travel is part of the job, the applicant can be asked whether they can meet these requirements. Ask whether there are any circumstances that might prevent completion of a minimum service commitment.	Information on dependants can be determined after selection if necessary.

(continued on next page)

TABLE 5.1

Guidelines for Applications and Interviews (*continued*)

Subject	Avoid Asking	Preferred	Comments
Family status	• about number of children or dependants. • about child care arrangements.	Ask if the applicant would be able to work the required hours and, where applicable, overtime.	Contacts for emergencies and/or details on dependants can be determined after selection.
National or ethnic origin	• about birthplace, nationality of ancestors, spouse, or other relatives. • whether born in Canada. • for proof of citizenship.	Ask if the applicant is legally entitled to work in Canada.	Documentation of eligibility to work (papers, visas, etc.) can be requested after selection.
Photographs	for photo to be attached to applications or sent to interviewer before interview.		Photos for security passes or company files can be taken after selection.
Religion	• about religious affiliation. • for references from clergy or religious leader. • whether the applicant will work a specific religious holiday.	Explain the required work shift, and ask whether such a schedule poses problems for the applicant.	Reasonable accommodation of an employee's religious beliefs is the employer's duty.
Disability	• for a list of all disabilities, limitations, or health problems. • whether the applicant drinks or uses drugs. • whether the applicant has ever received psychiatric care or been hospitalized for emotional problems. • whether the applicant has received workers' compensation.	Disclose any information on requirements or standards early in the process. Then ask whether the applicant has any condition that might affect ability to do the job.	A disability is relevant to job ability only if it: • threatens the safety or property of others. • prevents the applicant from safe and adequate job performance even when reasonable efforts are made to accommodate the disability.
Pardoned conviction	• whether an applicant has ever been convicted. • whether the applicant has ever been arrested. • whether the applicant has a criminal record.	If bonding is a job requirement, ask whether the applicant is eligible.	Inquiries about criminal record or convictions are discouraged unless related to job duties.
Sexual orientation	about the applicant's sexual orientation.		Contacts for emergencies and/or details on dependants can be determined after selection.

Note: This table provides examples and is not intended as a complete listing of all guidelines. The examples are based on federal human rights legislation; some provincial laws vary and may affect these examples.

Source: "Guide to Screening and Selection in Employment," Canadian Human Rights Commission, March 2007, pp. 6–10, www.chrc-ccdp.ca/eng/content/guide-screening-and-selection-employment. Reproduced with the permission of the Canadian Human Rights Commission.

An important principle of selection is to combine several sources of information about candidates, rather than relying solely on interviews or a single type of testing. The sources should be chosen carefully to relate to the characteristics identified in the job description (see the HR How-To). When organizations do this, they are increasing the validity of the decision criteria. They are more likely to make hiring decisions that are fair and unbiased. They also are more likely to choose the best candidates.

HR How-To

Using Data Analytics to Support Fair Hiring Decisions

As companies get increasingly sophisticated about collecting and analyzing data, they can apply those skills to employee selection. But the selection criteria need to be fair and free from illegal discrimination.

- Understand the jobs, company, and data well enough to develop a model explaining why criteria matter. A company that collects a lot of data can eventually find relationships between some variables and superior performance. Suppose you find that people from certain postal codes are less likely to quit. If you don't dig further into what it is about people from those postal codes, you could wind up making hiring choices that show a pattern of discrimination—and don't select for important qualities behind the numbers.
- Use analytics to test whether assumptions about job requirements really are relevant. A company that routinely selects for workers with a more than 85 percent postsecondary average can gather data to see whether this requirement is actually associated with success. Perhaps someone with a 75 percent average and certain experiences performs even better.
- Use analytics methods to remove irrelevant criteria from the selection process. For example, having a computer do the initial screening removes the potential for unconscious bias related to factors such as people's names or photographs.
- Create robust processes. Just knowing that you want certain characteristics doesn't mean the company will hire great people. Ensure the selection tools, including questions asked in interviews, are effective (reliable, valid, and so on). Ensure that the process is efficient and treats all candidates with respect.
- Apply the analytic methods to all applicants. If applications submitted online are screened by a computer system, then applications submitted on paper or in person should be screened using the same criteria.

Sources: Lydell C. Bridgeford, "Experts Discuss Big Data's Effect on Hiring, Bias Claims," HR Focus, September 2015, pp. 4–6; Kurt Naasz, "Advances in 'Big Data' and Analytics Can Unlock Insights and Drive HR Actions," HR Focus, May 2015, pp. 1–4; Murad Hemmadi, "The End of Bad Hiring Decisions," Canadian Business, January 2015, EBSCOhost, http://web.a.ebscohost.com.

LO2 What Are the Criteria for Evaluating Selection Methods?

Reliability

The **reliability** of a type of measurement indicates how free that measurement is from random error.[8] A reliable measurement therefore generates consistent results. Assuming that a person's intelligence is fairly stable over time, a reliable test of intelligence should generate consistent results if the same person takes the test several times. Organizations that construct intelligence tests therefore should be able to provide (and explain) information about the reliability of their tests.

reliability
The extent to which a measurement generates consistent results, i.e., is free from random error.

Usually this information involves statistics such as correlation coefficients. These statistics measure the degree to which two sets of numbers are related. A higher correlation coefficient signifies a stronger relationship. At one extreme, a correlation coefficient of 1.0 means a perfect positive relationship—as one set of numbers goes up, so does the other. If you took the same vision test three days in a row, those scores would probably have nearly a perfect correlation. At the other extreme, a correlation of −1.0 means a perfect negative correlation—when one set of numbers goes up, the other goes down. In the middle, a correlation of 0 means there is no correlation at all. For example, the correlation between weather and intelligence would be at or near 0. A reliable test would be one for which scores by the same person (or people with similar attributes) have a correlation close to 1.0.

Reliability answers one important question—whether you are measuring something accurately—but ignores another question that is as important: Are you measuring something that matters? Think about how this applies at companies that try to identify workers who will fit in well with the company's culture. Often these companies depend on teamwork, social networking, and creativity, and they expect those behaviours to prevail when workers get along well and share similar values. However, efforts to seek cultural fit often translate into favouring the most likable candidates—for example, those who make eye contact, display an interest in others, and tell engaging stories.[9]

This approach not only raises questions of reliability—for example, whether making eye contact in a job interview is a reliable predictor of a person's behaviour on the job over time—but also raises questions about the extent to which being likable really translates into effective teamwork and creative problem solving. Perhaps the prickly member of the team will be the one who opens up a new and valuable line of thinking. Additionally, making eye contact (or not) is associated with social norms that vary cross-culturally. As in this example, employers need to consider both the reliability of their selection methods and their validity, defined next.

Validity

For a selection measure, **validity** describes the extent to which performance on the measure (such as a test score) is related to what the measure is designed to assess (such as job performance). Although we can reliably measure characteristics such as weight and height, these measurements do not provide relevant information about how a person will perform in a job. One way to determine whether a measure is valid is to compare many people's scores on that measure with their job performance. For example, suppose people who score above 60 words per minute on a keyboarding test consistently get high marks for their performance in data-entry jobs. This observation suggests the keyboarding test is valid for predicting success in that job.

validity The extent to which performance on a measure (such as a test score) is related to what the measure is designed to assess (such as job performance).

As with reliability, information about the validity of selection methods often uses correlation coefficients. A strong positive (or negative) correlation between a measure and job performance means the measure should be a valid basis for selecting (or rejecting) a candidate. This information is important, not only because it helps organizations identify the best employees but also because organizations can ensure that their selection process is fair and objective. Three ways of measuring validity are criterion-related, content, and construct validity.

Criterion-related Validity

The first category, **criterion-related validity**, is a measure of validity based on showing a substantial correlation between test scores and job performance scores. In the example in Figure 5.2, a company compares two measures—an intelligence test and a university or college grade point average—with performance as a sales representative. In the left graph, which shows the relationship between the intelligence test scores and job performance, the points for the 20 sales representatives fall near the 45-degree line. The correlation coefficient is near 0.90 (for a perfect 1.0, all the points would be on the 45-degree line). In the graph at the right, the points are scattered more widely. The correlation between university or college

criterion-related validity A measure of validity based on showing a substantial correlation between test scores and job performance scores.

FIGURE 5.2

Criterion-related Measurements of a Student's Aptitude

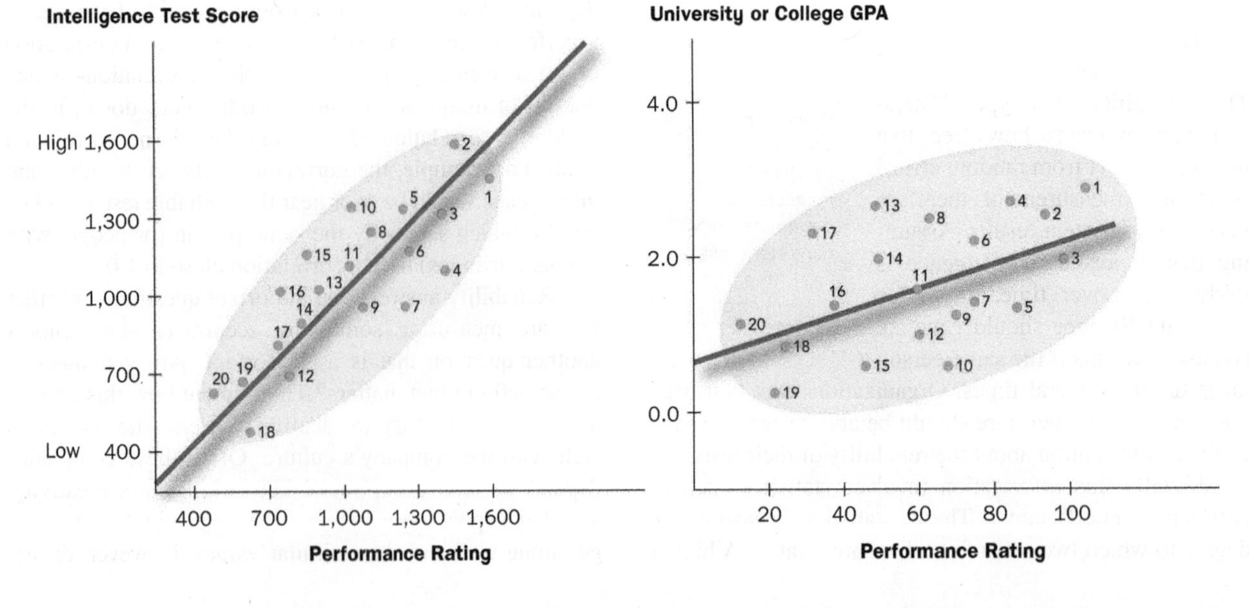

GPA and sales representatives' performance is much lower. In this hypothetical example, the intelligence test is more valid than GPA for predicting success at this job.

Two kinds of research are possible for arriving at criterion-related validity:

1. **Predictive validation**. This research uses the test scores of all applicants and looks for a relationship between the scores and future performance. The researcher administers the tests, waits a set period of time, and then measures the performance of the applicants who were hired.
2. **Concurrent validation**. This type of research administers a test to people who currently hold a job, then compares their scores to existing measures of job performance. If the people who score highest on the test also do better on the job, the test is assumed to be valid.

predictive validation
Research that uses the test scores of all applicants and looks for a relationship between the scores and future performance of the applicants who were hired.

concurrent validation
Research that consists of administering a test to people who currently hold a job, then comparing their scores to existing measures of job performance.

Predictive validation is more time consuming and difficult, but it is the best measure of validity. Job applicants tend to be more motivated to do well on the tests, and their performance on the tests is not influenced by their firsthand experience with the job. Also, the group studied is more likely to include people who perform poorly on the test—a necessary ingredient to accurately validate a test.[10]

Content and Construct Validity

Another way to show validity is to establish **content validity**—that is, consistency between the test items or problems and the kinds of situations or problems that occur on the job. A test that is "content-valid" exposes the job applicant to situations that are likely to occur on the job. It tests whether the applicant has the knowledge, skills, or ability, that is, competencies to handle such situations.

content validity
Consistency between the test items or problems and the kinds of situations or problems that occur on the job.

In the case of a company using tests for selecting a construction superintendent, tests with content validity included organizing a random list of subcontractors into the order they would appear at a construction site and entering a shed to identify construction errors that had intentionally been made for testing purposes.[11] More commonly today, employers use computer role-playing games in which software is created to include situations that occur on the job. The game measures how the candidate reacts to the situations, and then it computes a score based on how closely the candidate's responses match those of an "ideal employee".[12]

The usual basis for deciding that a test has content validity is through expert judgment. Experts can rate the test items according to whether they mirror essential functions of the job. Because establishing validity is based on the experts' subjective judgments, content validity is most suitable for measuring behaviour that is concrete and observable.

For tests that measure abstract qualities such as intelligence or leadership ability, establishment of validity may have to rely on **construct validity**. This involves establishing that tests really do measure intelligence, leadership ability, or other such "constructs," as well as showing that mastery of this construct is associated with successful performance of the job. For example, if you could show that a test measures something called "mechanical ability," and that people with superior mechanical ability perform well as assemblers, then the test has construct validity for the assembler job. Tests that measure a construct usually measure a combination of behaviours thought to be associated with the construct.

construct validity
Consistency between a high score on a test and a high level of a construct such as intelligence or leadership ability, as well as between mastery of this construct and successful performance on the job.

Ability to Generalize

Along with validity in general, we need to know whether a selection method is valid in the context in which the organization wants to use it. A **generalizable** method applies not only to the conditions in which the method was originally developed—job, organization, people, time period, and so on. It also applies to other organizations, jobs, applicants, and so on. In other words, is a selection method that was valid in one context also valid in other contexts?

generalizable
Valid in other contexts beyond the context in which the selection method was developed.

Researchers have studied whether tests of intelligence and thinking skills (called cognitive ability) can be generalized. The research has supported the idea that these tests are generalizable across many jobs. However, as jobs become more complex, the validity of many of these tests increases. In other words, they are most valid for complex jobs.[13]

Practical Value

Selection methods not only show how well individuals will perform but also should produce information that

Did You Know?

Consequences of a Bad Hire Affect the Bottom Line

Almost two-thirds (66 percent) of employers surveyed by CareerBuilder said their company had experienced negative consequences as a result of selecting someone who was not a good fit or did not perform the job well. Of these respondents, 27 percent said a poor hiring decision had cost their company more than $50,000. When asked to identify the types of consequences, respondents most often said productivity suffered.

Question

1. Do the results of this survey indicate that companies should spend up to $50,000 to select an employee for every vacant position? Why or why not?

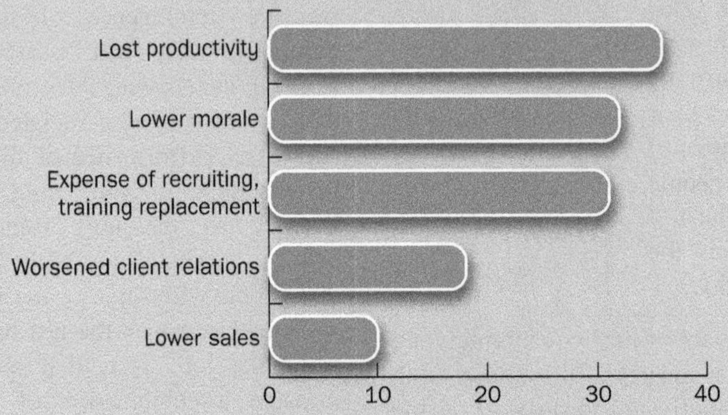

Sources: Mariah Deleon, "What Really Happens When You Hire the Wrong Candidate," Entrepreneur, April 9, 2015, https://www.entrepreneur.com; Rachel Gillett, "Infographic: How Much a Bad Hire Will Actually Cost You," Fast Company, April 8, 2014, http://www.fastcompany.com; Adecco, "Hiring Mistakes, the Cost of a Bad Hire," AdeccoUSA blog, June 10, 2013, http://blog.adeccousa.com; CareerBuilder, "More Than Half of Companies in the Top Ten World Economies Have Been Affected by a Bad Hire, according to a CareerBuilder Survey," news release, May 8, 2013, http://www.careeerbuilder.com

actually benefits the organization. Being valid, reliable, and generalizable adds value to a method. Another consideration is the cost of using the selection method. Selection procedures such as testing and interviewing cost money. However, they should cost significantly less than the benefits of hiring the new employees. Methods that provide economic value greater than the cost of using them are said to have **utility**.

utility The extent to which the selection method provides economic value greater than its cost.

The choice of a selection method may differ according to the job being filled. If the job involves providing a product or service of high value to the organization, it is worthwhile to spend more to find a top performer. At a company where salespeople are responsible for closing million-dollar deals, the company will be willing to invest more in selection decisions. At a fast-food restaurant, such an investment will not be worthwhile; the employer will prefer faster, simpler ways to select workers.

LO3 Job Applications and Résumés

Nearly all employers gather background information on applicants at the beginning of the selection process. The usual ways of gathering background information are by asking applicants to fill out application forms and provide résumés. Organizations also verify the information by checking references and conducting background checks.

Asking job candidates to provide background information is inexpensive. The organization can get reasonably accurate information by combining applications and résumés with background checks and well-designed interviews.[14] A major challenge with applications and résumés is the sheer volume of work they generate for the organization. Especially considering how easy it is for candidates to submit applications or résumés online, human resource departments need to take steps to ensure they are not swamped with more than they can carefully review.

Applications

Asking each applicant to fill out an employment application is a low-cost way to gather basic data from many applicants. It also ensures that the organization has certain standard categories of information, such as mailing address and employment history, from every applicant.

Employment applications include areas for applicants to provide several types of information:

- **Contact information.** The employee's name, address, contact number, and email address.
- **Work experience.** Companies the applicant worked for, job titles, and dates of employment.
- **Educational background.** High school, college, or university attended and diploma(s) or degree(s) awarded.
- **Applicant's signature.** Signature or verification following a statement that the applicant has provided true and complete information.

The application form may include other areas for the applicant to provide additional information, such as specific work experiences, technical skills, certifications, or memberships in professional or trade associations. Also, including the date on an application is useful for keeping up-to-date records of job applicants. The application form should not request information that might violate human rights legislation. For example, questions about an applicant's birthplace, marital status, or number of children would be inappropriate.

By reviewing application forms, HR staff can identify which candidates meet minimum requirements for education and experience. They may be able to rank applicants—for example, giving applicants with five years' experience a higher ranking than applicants with two years of experience. In this way, the applications enable the organization to narrow the pool of candidates to a number it is prepared to test and interview.

Résumés

The usual way applicants introduce themselves to a potential employer is by submitting a résumé. An obvious drawback of this information source is that applicants control the content of the information, as well as the way it is presented. This type of information is therefore oriented in favour of the applicant and may not even be accurate (although this is unethical). The Statistic Brain Research Institute reports that 53 percent of résumés contain falsifications, 33 percent include inaccurate job descriptions, and 21 percent list a fraudulent degree.[15] Some employers today see social media (e.g., LinkedIn profiles) as an alternative source of information that is more relevant or more accurate. However, this inexpensive way to gather information does provide employers with a starting point. Organizations typically use résumés as a basis for deciding which candidates to consider further.

As with employment applications, an HR staff member reviews the résumés to identify candidates meeting basic requirements such as educational background, related work performed, and types of equipment the person has used. Because résumés are created by the job applicants (or the applicants have at least approved résumés created by someone they hire), they also may provide some insight into how candidates communicate and present themselves. Employers tend to decide against applicants whose résumés are unclear, messy, or contain mistakes. For example, a recent study of recruiters found that when "applicants have strong job experience, the presence of spelling errors significantly increases the rejection rates."[16]

On the positive side, résumés may enable applicants to highlight accomplishments that might not show up in the format of an employment application. Review of résumés is most valid when the content of the résumé is assessed in terms of the elements of a job description and job specifications.

Organizations are increasingly turning to applicant tracking systems to centralize the handling of résumés and job applications from both internal and external applicants. Typically this involves completing an online application form on the employer's website and uploading a résumé. In many cases, information is electronically extracted from the résumé and inserted into the application form. Before submitting the application, the applicant verifies the information and performs any necessary edits.

The use of blind screening has been adopted by organizations including KPMG and HSBC in the effort to remove unconscious bias that may present barriers or exclude some candidates from consideration. In addition to name, this process typically removes home address, email address, and any information that could reveal applicants' ethnicity, home country, or employment equity information on an application. Studies have provided mixed results about whether or not blind screening promotes diversity. For example, the Public Service Commission of Canada recently implemented a name-blind recruitment pilot project within the federal public service. The pilot project involved more than 2,200 candidates, 685 of whom self-declared as visible minorities. The Final Report concluded that "removal of identifying information from job applications had no effect on the screening decisions of applications from members of visible minority groups."[17]

References

Application forms often ask that applicants provide the names of several references. Applicants provide the names and contact information of former employers or others who can vouch for their abilities and past job performance. In some situations, the applicant may provide letters of reference written by those people. It is then up to the organization to have someone contact the references to gather information or verify the accuracy of the information provided by the applicant.

As you might expect, references are not an unbiased source of information. Most applicants are careful to choose references who will say something positive. In addition, former employers and others may be afraid that if they express negative opinions, they will be sued. Their fear is understandable. In one case, an employee sued his former supervisor for comments about how the employee had succeeded in overcoming attendance problems related to a struggle with multiple sclerosis. The employee felt that the disclosure of his prior attendance problems was defamatory.[18] (Disclosing his medical condition also would have posed problems for the potential future employer's ability to comply with human rights legislation.) This case shows that even well-intentioned remarks can cause problems. Also problematic from the perspective of getting useful information is that some candidates fail to list people who can speak about their work history.

Usually the organization checks references after it has determined that the applicant is a finalist for the job. Questions asked in reference checks need to adhere to the same requirements as applications and interviews (see Table 5.1).[19]

Contacting references for all applicants would be time consuming, and it does put a burden on the people contacted. Part of that burden is the risk of giving information seen as too negative or too positive. If the person who is a reference gives negative information, there is a chance the candidate will claim defamation, meaning the person damaged the applicant's reputation by making statements that cannot be proved truthful.[20]

At the other extreme, if the person gives a glowing statement about a candidate, and the new employer later learns of misdeeds such as sexual misconduct or workplace violence, the new employer might sue the former employer for misrepresentation.[21] Employers have a duty to protect workers and the public from harassment or violence arising from placing an unfit or dangerous person in the workplace. **Negligent hiring** refers to a situation where an employer may be found liable for harm an employee causes to others if references and background checks were not performed adequately at the time of hiring. In these cases, the employer may be found to "have known or should have known" that an employee might cause harm to others in the workplace.

negligent hiring A situation where an employer may be found liable for harm an employee causes to others if references and background checks were not performed adequately at the time of hiring.

Because such situations occasionally arise, often with much publicity, people who give references tend to give as little information as possible. Most organizations have policies that the human resource department will handle all requests for references and that they will verify only employment dates and sometimes the employee's final salary. In organizations without such a policy, HR professionals should be careful—and train managers to be careful—to stick to observable, job-related behaviours and to avoid broad opinions that may be misinterpreted. An irony with respect to policies about the content and handling of references is that managers and colleagues in these organizations may well be actively providing highly visible and public references in the form of skills endorsements and recommendations in LinkedIn. "Human nature makes it difficult for a person, when asked, to deny the request to recommend someone. Therefore, a 'no recommending employees on LinkedIn' clause in a social media policy is helpful. It provides an ideal excuse when denying an employee that request and, it is hoped, avoids causing offence."[22]

In spite of these drawbacks of references, the risks of not learning about significant problems in a candidate's past outweigh the possibility of getting only a little information. "An HR manager may be in the interesting position of declining to give an elaborate reference for any employee who intends to leave her organization, yet demand one for a person she wishes to hire. And applicants may find themselves to be essentially unemployable, as they discover they can't be hired without a satisfactory reference from their former employer."[23]

Background Checks

A background check provides an additional means to verify that applicants are as they represent themselves to be. Unfortunately, not all candidates (or references) are open and honest. In a recent survey of HR professionals, more than half said they had caught at least one piece of false information on a résumé.[24]

Note that this is not the same as half of résumés contain lies. However, it's also possible that some professionals saw but didn't recognize misinformation. And a recent survey reported that 82 percent of Canadian HR professionals "believe that people providing references are not always honest" and "68 percent believe they've been lied to while conducting phone references."[25]

Companies like BackCheck™ specialize in employment background checks such as criminal record checks, credit inquiries, education verifications, employment verifications, driving records, identity cross-checks, and reference checks. For example, Scotiabank expanded its range of pre-employment screening with BackCheck to include criminal reference checks and identity verifications in addition to reference checking, and employment and educational verifications.[26]

Angus Stewart, vice-president of forensics and leader of corporate intelligence at KPMG in Toronto, says that knowing what to look for is key to a successful search.

"Education fraud is the most common," he says, adding that people lie about the degree they received or the institutions they attend. There is also the "diploma mill issue": people state degrees they ordered online from phony institutions. "There's quite a bit of that."[27]

Also fuelling this growing use of background checks are applicants using complex and high-tech means to fraudulently impress employers. For example, a counterfeiting ring operating from a house in Markham, Ontario, may have supplied thousands of people with forged university degrees and transcripts as well as forged immigration documents, according to York Regional Police. The police confiscated forged degrees from the University of Toronto, the University of Western Ontario, Cape Breton University, and many others. Even university officials were hard pressed to detect the fakes. "These were of such high quality that our university people had to do a double take," said Detective Fred Kerr. "From an employer point of view, you're not going to catch what's wrong with them."[28]

Before performing a background check, employers need to keep in mind they must get consent from the candidate. As discussed earlier in the chapter, conducting a background check after extending a contingent job offer can help to protect the potential employer from a discrimination claim if the applicant is not hired. Consent may also be needed to comply with privacy legislation. Employers also need to "tread carefully" when it comes to social media presence checks or random online searches. Although there are no laws that prohibit these kinds of checks, the growing trend of conducting these types of random social media background checks prompted Offices of the Privacy Commissioner of both Alberta and British Columbia to release "Guidelines for Social Media Background Checks." Employers are cautioned to follow the guidelines when using social media or Google to seek out information about potential employees. The primary dilemma is that a social media check may reveal information that extends beyond job-relevant information. Even so, job seekers need to be aware that sites such as Twitter, Instagram, and Facebook may still be making them look good or bad to potential employers. According to Louise Fox, director of Toronto's Protocol Solutions: "Don't put anything online that you wouldn't want your mom to read or have published in the newspaper."[29]

LO4 Employment Tests and Work Samples

When the organization has identified candidates whose applications or résumés indicate they meet basic requirements, the organization continues the selection process with this narrower pool of candidates. Often, the next step is to gather objective data through one or more employment tests or assessments. Increasingly, these tests and assessments can be completed on mobile devices, which represents an evolution from web-based and computer versions that were pre-dated by paper-and-pencil assessments.[30]

These tests fall into two broad categories:

1. **Aptitude tests** assess how well a person can learn or acquire skills and abilities. In the realm of employment testing, the best-known aptitude test is the General Aptitude Test Battery (GATB). The Public Service Commission of Canada also provides other employment-related tests such as the Office Skills Test (OST-200), which assesses an individual's clerical skills including: following directions, filing, performing calculations, checking, and understanding words.[31]

aptitude tests
Tests that assess how well a person can learn or acquire skills and abilities.

2. **Achievement tests** measure a person's existing knowledge and skills. For example, some organizations use interactive tests to assess applicants' skills using software such as Outlook, Excel, and PowerPoint.

achievement tests
Tests that measure a person's existing knowledge and skills.

Before using any test, organizations should investigate the test's validity and reliability. Besides asking the testing service to provide this information, it is wise to consult more impartial sources of information, such as the ones described in Table 5.2. Recent research findings have provided evidence of optimism that tests can be taken on mobile devices without harming the validity or reliability of the tests; however, HR professionals need to ensure that the content of any specific test is suitable for mobile platforms.[32]

Physical Ability Tests

Physical strength and endurance play less of a role in the modern workplace than in the past, thanks to the use of automation and current technology. Even so, many jobs still require certain physical abilities or psychomotor abilities (those connecting brain and body, as in the case of eye–hand coordination). When these abilities are essential to job performance or avoidance of injury, the organization may use physical ability tests. These evaluate one or more of the following areas of physical ability: muscular tension, muscular power, muscular endurance, cardiovascular endurance, flexibility, balance, and coordination.[33] Although these tests can accurately predict success at certain kinds of jobs, some of these tests also tend to exclude women and people with disabilities. As a result, use of physical ability tests can make the organization vulnerable to human rights complaints. It is therefore important to be certain that the abilities tested for really are essential to job

TABLE 5.2

Sources of Information About Employment Tests

Mental Measurements Yearbook	Descriptions and reviews of tests that are commercially available
Principles for the Validation and Use of Personnel Selection Procedures **(Society for Industrial and Organizational Psychology)**	Guide to help organizations evaluate tests
Standards for Educational and Psychological Tests **(American Psychological Association)**	Description of standards for testing programs
Tests: A Comprehensive Reference for Assessments in Psychology, Education, and Business	Descriptions of thousands of tests
Test Critiques	Reviews of tests, written by professionals in the field

Royal Canadian Mounted Police I Gendarmerie Royale du Canada

The RCMP's Physical Abilities Requirement Evaluation (PARE) consists of three timed stations—Obstacle Course, Push/Pull, and Weight Carry.

performance or that the absence of these abilities really does create a safety hazard.

The RCMP have invested significant effort to develop an effective test to assess candidates' physical abilities—Physical Abilities Requirement Evaluation (PARE). The PARE is a job-related physical ability test that simulates a critical incident of chasing, controlling, and apprehending a suspect.[34]

Cognitive Ability Tests

Although fewer jobs require muscle power today, brainpower is essential for most jobs. Organizations therefore benefit from people who have strong mental abilities. **Cognitive ability tests**—sometimes called "intelligence tests"—are designed to measure mental abilities such as verbal skills (skill in using written and spoken language), quantitative skills (skill in working with numbers), and reasoning ability (skill in thinking through the answer to a problem). Many jobs require all of these cognitive skills, so employers often get valid information from general tests. The Public Service Commission of Canada uses the General Competency Test Level 1 (GCT1) to measure thinking skills (understanding written material, solving numerical problems, and drawing logical conclusions) for administrative support position selection decisions. See Figure 5.3 for a sample question and answer from the General Competency Test Level 1 (GCT1). A test called the GCT2 is used to assess general cognitive abilities required for officer-level positions.[35] Many reliable tests are commercially available. The tests are especially valid for complex jobs and for those requiring adaptability in changing circumstances.[36]

cognitive ability tests Tests designed to measure mental abilities such as verbal skills, quantitative skills, and reasoning ability.

Job Performance Tests and Work Samples

Many kinds of jobs require candidates who excel at performing specialized tasks, such as operating a certain machine, handling calls from customers, or designing advertising materials. To evaluate candidates for such jobs, the organization may administer tests of the necessary skills. Sometimes the candidates take tests that involve a sample of work, or they may show existing samples of their work. Testing may involve a simulated work environment, a difficult team project, or a complex computer programming puzzle.[37] Examples of job performance tests include tests of keyboarding speed and in-basket tests. An in-basket test measures the ability to juggle a variety of demands, as in a manager's job. The candidate is presented with simulated emails and messages describing the kinds of problems that confront a person in the job. The candidate has to decide how to respond to

FIGURE 5.3

Sample Question from the Public Service Commission of Canada's General Competency Test: Level 1 (GCT1)

Government of Canada MEMORANDUM | Gouvernement du Canada NOTE DE SERVICE

TO: All employees
FROM: Manager

We are pleased to announce that our Ministry's budget has been increased and consequently we will experience an increase in staff size. Because new positions will become available, we will be holding interviews within the next few weeks.

The main focus of this memo is to indicate a change concerning:

1. better ministerial policy.
2. better budget publicity.
3. more human resources.
4. more office space.

① ② ● ④

Source: General Competency Test Level 1 (GCT1)—Instructions and Sample Questions, www.psc-cfp.gc.ca/ppc-cpp/test-examen/gct1-ecg1/index-eng.htm. Public Service Commission 2011. Reproduced with the permission of the Public Service Commission of Canada.

these messages, and in what order. Examples of jobs for which candidates provide work samples include graphic designers and writers.

Tests for selecting managers may take the form of an **assessment centre**—a wide variety of specific selection programs that use multiple selection methods to rate applicants or job incumbents on their management potential. An assessment centre typically includes in-basket tests, tests of more general abilities, and personality tests. Combining several assessment methods increases the validity of this approach. For example, the Public Service Commission of Canada uses the Human Resources Consultant Simulation Exercise, which "simulates important aspects of a human resource consultant's job." The candidate receives exercise items including memoranda, letters, and reports and is given three hours to review the items and complete a written action plan and prepare for an oral presentation. The next step is to make an oral presentation (30 minutes maximum) to the selection panel followed by questions from the panel. The final phase requires the candidate to provide assistance and advice to a manager as part of an interactive exercise.[38]

assessment centre A wide variety of specific selection programs that use multiple selection methods to rate applicants or job incumbents on their management potential.

Job performance tests have the advantage of giving applicants a chance to show what they can do, which leads them to feel that the evaluation was fair.[39] The tests also are job-specific—that is, tailored to the kind of work done in a specific job. So they have a high level of validity, especially when combined with cognitive ability tests and a highly structured interview.[40] This advantage can become a disadvantage, however, if the organization wants to generalize the results of a test for one job to candidates for other jobs. The tests are more appropriate for identifying candidates who are generally able to solve the problems associated with a job, rather than for identifying which specific skills or traits the individual possesses.[41] Developing different tests for different jobs can become expensive. One way to save money is to prepare computerized tests that can be delivered online to various locations.

Personality Inventories

In some situations, employers may also want to know about candidates' personalities. For example, one way psychologists think of personality is in terms of the "Big Five" traits: extroversion, adjustment, agreeableness, conscientiousness, and inquisitiveness (explained in Table 5.3). There is evidence that people who score high

TABLE 5.3

Five Major Personality Dimensions Measured by Personality Inventories

1. Extroversion	Sociable, gregarious, assertive, talkative, expressive
2. Adjustment	Emotionally stable, non-depressed, secure, content
3. Agreeableness	Courteous, trusting, good natured, tolerant, cooperative, forgiving
4. Conscientiousness	Dependable, organized, persevering, thorough, achievement oriented
5. Inquisitiveness	Curious, imaginative, artistically sensitive, broadminded, playful

on conscientiousness tend to excel at work, because they use self-control to pursue goals and excel at overcoming obstacles.[42] The relevance of personality dimensions may also be job specific. For example, extroverts tend to excel in sales jobs, because these jobs call upon traits associated with extroversion—notably, being gregarious and assertive.[43] Companies also are crunching their data to see which traits are associated with success at their particular organization. At JetBlue, for example, the director of talent acquisition and assessment says his company can measure specific traits to determine who will deliver the best job performance.[44]

The usual way to identify a candidate's personality traits is to administer one of the personality tests that are commercially available. The employer pays for the use of the test, and the organization that owns the test then scores the responses and provides a report about the test taker's personality. An organization that provides such tests should be able to discuss the test's validity and reliability. It is possible to find reliable, commercially available measures of each trait, but the evidence of their validity and generalizability is mixed at best.[45]

Some people don't have enough insight about themselves to answer accurately, or their personalities vary on and off the job. Also, compared with intelligence tests, people are better at "faking" their answers to a personality test to score higher on desirable traits.[46] Evidence includes higher scores for conscientiousness when people take job-related tests than when they take research-related tests. Also, candidates who don't get hired have scored much higher when they retry the test. Ways to address this problem include using trained interviewers rather than surveys, collecting information about the applicant from several sources, and letting applicants know that several sources will be used.[47]

One trend in favour of personality tests is greater use of teamwork. Because team members must work together closely, the selection of one member can affect the personality requirements for other team members. where personality conflicts can be a significant problem. Traits such as agreeableness and conscientiousness have been associated with effective teamwork.[48] An organization might try to select team members with similar traits and values in order to promote a strong culture where people work together harmoniously, or they instead might look for a diversity of personalities and values as a way to promote debate and creativity.

Honesty and Drug and Alcohol Tests

No matter what employees' personalities may be like, organizations want employees to be honest and to perform safely. Some organizations are satisfied to assess these qualities on the basis of judgments from reference checks and interviews. Others investigate these characteristics more directly through the use of tests.

The most famous kind of honesty test is the polygraph, the so-called "lie detector" test. As a result of controversies associated with the use of polygraph tests, testing services have developed other types of honesty (or integrity) tests. Generally, these tests ask applicants directly about their attitudes toward honesty and integrity and their own experiences in situations inside and outside work. Most of the research into the validity of these tests has been conducted by the testing companies, but evidence suggests they do have some ability to predict behaviour such as theft of the employer's property.[49] A recent study conducted by Canadian researchers with Canadian Armed Forces recruits provided evidence that integrity can be predicted from three of the Big Five personality factors—conscientiousness, agreeableness, and emotional stability.[50]

As concerns about workplace safety and performance due to to the use of both legal and illegal substances (e.g., alcohol, cannabis, medications, and "street" drugs) continues to grow, so has the use of drug and alcohol testing including pre-employment testing. Pre-employment testing is intended to reduce risks associated with hiring people who may put themselves and others in danger in safety-sensitive jobs.[51]

Employers considering the use of drug and alcohol tests should ensure that their testing programs comply with relevant human rights legislation for their jurisdiction. As discussed in Chapter 2, the Canadian Human Rights Act prohibits discrimination related to a disability, and dependence on drugs or alcohol is considered a disability that must be accommodated to the point of undue hardship. For example, the Canadian Human Rights Commission's Policy on Alcohol and Drug Testing describes "testing for alcohol or drugs as a form of medical examination" and "pre-employment drug or alcohol testing is permitted only in limited circumstances."[52]

Employers also have to keep in mind that testing will not uncover all problems. One recent concern is that addictive drug use increasingly relates to legal prescription painkillers and the legalization of recreational cannabis has posed a variety of issues for organizations to navigate including the need for clear policies.

The approach to pre-employment substance testing in Western Canada has tended to emphasize safety and has directly conflicted with Ontario Court of Appeal decisions. For example, the Alberta Court of Appeal upheld the employer's right to immediately terminate a new employee who failed a pre-employment drug screening test that was part of the hiring process for Kellogg Brown & Root (KBR), a subsidiary of Houston-based oil-and-gas giant Haliburton. The employee had started work and been on the job for nine days when his marijuana-positive test results came back. The Alberta Court of Appeal ruled that the terminated employee was not an addict, but rather a recreational user; therefore, he was not disabled and did not require accommodation. The Court ruled that there was no discrimination because the employer's testing policy was connected to workplace safety.[53]

Medical Examinations

Especially for physically demanding jobs, organizations may wish to conduct medical examinations to see that the applicant can meet the job's requirements. Employers may also wish to establish an employee's physical condition at the beginning of employment, so that there is a basis for measuring whether the employee has suffered a work-related disability later on. At the same time, as described in Chapter 2, organizations may not discriminate against individuals with disabilities who could perform a job with reasonable accommodations. Likewise, organizations may not use a measure of physical ability that discriminates against women, older workers, etc., unless those requirements are valid in predicting the ability to perform a job. Medical examinations must be related to job requirements and may not be given until the candidate has received a conditional job offer. Many organizations make selection decisions first, then conduct the exams to confirm that the employee will be able to meet requirements of the job, with any reasonable accommodations required. Limiting the use of medical examinations in this way also holds down the cost of what tends to be an expensive process.

LO5 Interviews

Supervisors and team members most often get involved in the selection process at the stage of employment interviews. These interviews usually bring together job applicants and representatives of the employer to obtain information and evaluate the applicant's qualifications and organizational fit. While the applicant is providing information, they are also forming opinions about what it is like to work for the organization. Most organizations use interviewing as part of the selection process. In fact, this method is used more than any other.

Interviewing Techniques

Interview techniques include choices about the type of questions to ask and the number of people who conduct the interview. Several question types are possible:

- In a **nondirective interview**, the interviewer has great discretion in choosing questions. The candidate's reply to one question may suggest other questions to ask. Non-directive interviews typically include open-ended questions about the candidate's strengths, development areas, career goals, and work experience. Because these interviews give the interviewer wide latitude, their reliability is not great and some interviewers ask questions that are not valid or even legal.

nondirective interview A selection interview in which the interviewer has great discretion in choosing questions to ask each candidate.

- A **structured interview** establishes a set of questions for the interviewer to ask. Ideally, the questions are related to job requirements and cover relevant knowledge, skills, and experiences. The interviewer is supposed to avoid asking questions that are not on the list. Although interviewers may object to being restricted, the results may be more valid and reliable than with a nondirective interview.

structured interview A selection interview that consists of a predetermined set of questions for the interviewer to ask.

- A **situational interview** is a structured interview in which the interviewer describes a situation likely to arise on the job and asks the candidate what they would do in that situation. This type of interview may have high validity in predicting job performance.[54]
- A **behavioural interview** is a situational interview in which the interviewer asks the candidate to describe how they handled a type of situation in the past. Questions about the candidates' actual experiences tend to have the highest validity.[55]

situational interview A structured interview in which the interviewer describes a situation likely to arise on the job, then asks the candidate what they would do in that situation.

behavioural interview A structured interview in which the interviewer asks the candidate to describe how they handled a type of situation in the past.

BMO Financial Group has been using behavioural interviews since the early 1990s for almost every position it fills. BMO even offers prospective employees advice about what a good answer includes. BMO Financial Group views behavioural interviews as most effective for external candidates because internal candidates have existing performance reviews and have been through the process at some point.[56]

The common setup for either a nondirective or structured interview is for an individual (an HR professional or the supervisor for the vacant position) to interview each candidate face to face. However, variations on this approach are possible. In a **panel interview**, several members of the organization meet to interview each candidate. A panel interview gives the candidate a chance to meet more people and see how people interact in that organization. It provides the organization with the judgments of more than one person, with the intent to reduce the effect of personal biases in selection decisions. However, biased decisions may actually be higher in a panel interview if the members of the panel interview have similar backgrounds or experience "groupthink." Panel interviews may be particularly intimidating for people with ADHD, autism, and other learning differences.[57]

panel interview
Selection interview in which several members of the organization meet to interview each candidate.

Alternatively, some organizations conduct an interview without any interviewers; they use a **digital interview**, a technology-based interview in which interviewees digitally record their responses to interview questions that are provided digitally, without live interaction with the interviewer.[58]

digital interview
A technology-based interview in which interviewees digitally record their responses to interview questions that are provided digitally, without live interaction with the interviewer.

Digital interviews have evolved from earlier applications of technology to improve the efficiency of the job interview process; e.g., telephone interviews and video-conference interviews. A digital interview process typically starts with a candidate receiving an email with a link to an online platform. The candidate reads the instructions on a mobile device or computer. The first interview question is provided in text form and a clock counts down available time to read the question (e.g., 60 seconds). The candidate clicks a "record" button, which opens a new browser window, and is provided time (e.g., up to 3 minutes) to answer the interview question. The candidate stops the recording and clicks "submit video." After a brief pause (e.g., 15 seconds), the next interview question is provided and the previous steps are repeated. Interviews may be rated by human raters or by machine-learning algorithms, which eliminate human influence and personal bias. Additional benefits of digital interviews include flexibility, standardization, and analytical capabilities; however, downsides include no ability to ask follow-up questions, no ability for interviewees to ask questions, as well as the potential for negative candidate reactions including opting out of the process.[59]

HireVue, the largest provider of digital interviews in North America worked with Hilton Hotels & Resorts, which hires thousands of team members annually for its more than 5,000 properties in 103 countries and territories globally. Amber Weaver, who heads up the high-volume talent acquisition team at Hilton, partnered with HireVue to revamp Hilton's traditional hiring process, which was taking approximately six weeks to fill a training class of 25 new hires. Hilton's multi-step process was transformed into a single video assessment using "predictive analytics to assess a candidate's vocabulary, intonation, and nonverbal gestures" relative to top performers and cut the time to fill a training class to 5 days.[60]

Air Canada President and CEO Calin Rovinescu recently explained how Air Canada will be introducing artificial intelligence and facial recognition programs to to evaluate potential employees for skills such as linguistic abilities—reducing the interview process from eight to three steps for selecting flight attendants.[61]

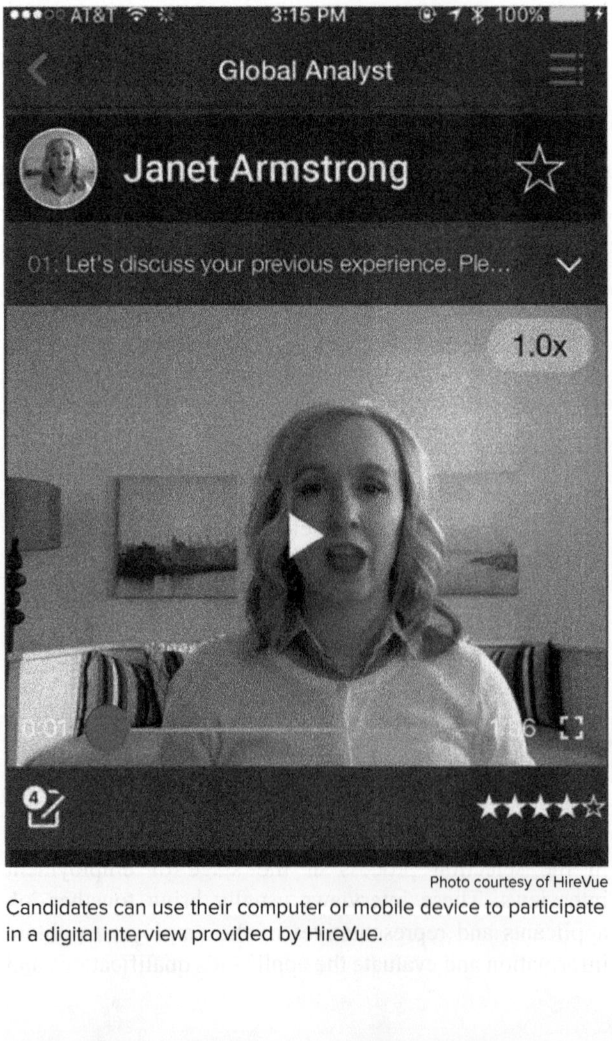

Photo courtesy of HireVue

Candidates can use their computer or mobile device to participate in a digital interview provided by HireVue.

Advantages and Disadvantages of Traditional Interviewing

The wide use of traditional in-person interviewing is not surprising. People naturally want to see prospective employees firsthand. As we noted in Chapter 1, the top qualities that employers seek in new hires include communication skills and interpersonal skills. Talking face to face can provide evidence of these skills. Interviews can give insights into candidates' personalities and interpersonal styles. They are more valid, however, when they focus on job knowledge and skill. Interviews also provide a means to check the accuracy of information on the applicant's résumé or job application. Asking applicants to elaborate about their experiences and offer details reduces the likelihood of a candidate being able to invent a work history.[62]

Despite these benefits, in-person interviewing is not necessarily the most accurate basis for making a selection decision. Research has shown that interviews can be unreliable, low in validity,[63] and biased against a number of different groups.[64] Interviews are also costly. They require that at least one person devote time to interviewing each candidate, and the applicants typically have to be brought to one geographic location. Interviews are also subjective, so they place the organization at greater risk of discrimination complaints by applicants who were not hired, especially if those individuals were asked questions not entirely related to the job.

Organizations can avoid some of these pitfalls.[65] Human resources staff should keep the interviews focused, structured, and standardized. The interview should focus on accomplishing a few goals, so that at the end of the interview, the organization has ratings on several observable measures, such as ability to express ideas. As noted earlier, situational and behavioural interviews are especially effective for doing this. The interview should not try to measure abilities and skills—for example, cognitive intelligence—that tests can measure better. Organizations can prevent problems related to subjectivity by training interviewers and using more than one person to conduct interviews. Training typically includes focusing on the recording of observable facts, rather than on making subjective judgments, as well as developing interviewers' awareness of their biases.[66] Using a structured system for taking notes or scoring responses may help reduce subjectivity and help the interviewer remember and explain an evaluation later.[67] Finally, to address costs of interviewing, some organizations also use applications with video chat capabilities (e.g., Skype).

Marconobre/Dreamstime.com

When interviewing candidates, it's valid to ask about willingness to travel if that is a requirement of the job. Interviewers might ask questions about previous business travel experiences and/or how interviewees handled situations requiring flexibility and self-motivation (qualities that would be an asset in someone who is travelling alone and solving business problems remotely).

Preparing to Interview

Organizations get the greatest benefits from in-person interviewing if they prepare carefully. A well-planned interview should be standardized, comfortable for the participants, and focused on the job and the organization. The interviewer should have a quiet place in which to conduct interviews without interruption. This person should be trained in how to ask objective questions, what subject matter to avoid, and how to detect and handle their own personal biases or other distractions in order to fairly evaluate candidates.

The interviewer should have enough documents to conduct a complete interview. These should include a list of the questions to be asked in a structured interview. When the questions are prepared, it is also helpful to determine how the answers will be assessed. For example, if questions are asked about how interviewees have handled certain situations, consider what responses are best in terms of meeting job requirements. If the job requires someone who develops new and creative solutions to problems, then a response that shows innovative behaviour would receive a higher score. The interviewer also should have a copy of the interviewee's employment application and résumé to review before the interview and refer to during the interview. If possible, the interviewer should also have information on hand about the organization and the job. Near the beginning of the interview, it is a good idea to go over the job specifications, organizational policies, and so on, so that the interviewee has a clearer understanding of the organization's needs and expectations.

The interviewer should schedule enough time to review the job requirements, discuss the interview questions, and give the interviewee a chance to ask questions. Interviewers need to be well prepared to answer interviewee questions. For example, a highly skilled candidate may ask, "How is your company supporting Indigenous communities?" If the interviewers do not have an answer, they potentially miss the opportunity to hire the candidate who may have multiple competing employment opportunities.[68]

HR Oops!

Red Flags During Job Interviews

When managers or HR professionals select candidates to interview, they are trying to find the candidates with basic qualifications, who are likely to be the highest performers. Sometimes, unfortunately, what happens in an interview signals a troubling lack of motivation or business sense. For example, interviewers are unimpressed with someone who arrives at an interview after making no effort to learn anything about the company or prepare any questions to ask.

Sometimes candidates' behaviour demonstrates such poor motivation and lack of judgment that it resembles a bad comedy routine. Interviewers have complained of candidates checking Facebook or wearing headphones during an interview; one even took a phone call about a job at another company. Some make odd statements: one told an interviewer she had taken "too much Valium" beforehand, and another said his personal hero was himself.

Some memorable incidents reported by interviewers are downright frightening. One applicant had a car accident—hitting the employer's building. Another tried making a secret recording of the interview. And a third applicant, responding to an interviewer's prompt to "impress me," lit the interviewer's newspaper on fire.

Questions

1. With a multiple-hurdle model, interviewing typically comes late in the selection process. Based on what you know about the steps in the process, why do you think the candidates described here made it past the earlier hurdles? (For example, might they have other qualifications, or might there be problems with the process?)
2. In the compensatory model, a high score on one type of assessment can make up for a low score on another. Assuming the candidates described here had low scores on their interviews, can you think of a situation in which a high score on some other measure could make these candidates the best choice for a position? Explain.

Sources: "Top 10 Unbelievable Interview Blunders," CareerBuilder, http://employer.careerbuilder.com, accessed April 11, 2016; Ryan Caldbeck, "These Five Interview Blunders Will Probably Kill Your Job Prospects," Entrepreneur, March 14, 2014, http://www.entrepreneur.com; Adam Auriemma, "Fire, Valium, Dentures: Job Interviews Gone Wild," Wall Street Journal, January 16, 2014, http://blogs.wsj.com; CareerBuilder, "Employers Share Most Memorable Interview Blunders," news release, January 16, 2014, http://www.careerbuilder.com.

To close the interview, the interviewer should thank the candidate and provide information about what to expect—for example, that the organization will contact a few finalists within the next week or that a decision will be made by the end of the week.

Selection Decisions

After reviewing applications, scoring tests, conducting interviews, and checking references, the organization needs to make decisions about which candidates will be provided a job offer. In practice, most organizations find more than one qualified candidate to fill an open position. The selection decision typically combines ranking based on objective criteria along with subjective judgments about which candidate will likely be the highest performer.

How Organizations Select Employees

The selection decision should not be a simple matter of whom the supervisor likes best or which candidate will take the lowest offer. Also, observing confidence in job candidates does not necessarily mean they are competent. Rather, the people making the selection decision should look for the best fit between candidate and position. In general, the person's performance will result from a combination of ability and motivation. Often, the selection is a choice among a few people who possess the basic qualifications. The decision makers therefore have to decide which of those people have the best combination of ability and motivation to perform well in the position and in the organization as a whole.

The usual process for arriving at a selection decision is to gradually narrow the pool of candidates for each job. This approach, called the **multiple-hurdle model**, is based on a process such as the one shown earlier in Figure 5.1. Each stage of the process is a hurdle, and candidates who overcome a hurdle continue to the next stage of the process. For example, the organization reviews applications and/or résumés of all candidates, conducts some tests on those who meet minimum requirements, conducts initial interviews with those who had the highest test scores, follows up with additional interviews or testing, and then selects a candidate from the few who successfully navigated this process. Another, more expensive alternative is to take most applicants through all steps of the process and then review all the scores to find the most desirable candidates. With this alternative, decision makers may use a **compensatory model**, in which a very high score on one type of assessment can make up for a low score on another. Think about how each of these two models would apply.

multiple-hurdle model Process of arriving at a selection decision by eliminating some candidates at each stage of the selection process.

compensatory model Process of arriving at a selection decision in which a very high score on one type of assessment can make up for a low score on another.

Whether the organization uses a multiple-hurdle model or conducts the same assessments on all candidates, the decision maker or makers need criteria for choosing among qualified candidates. An obvious strategy is to select the candidates who score highest on tests and interviews. However, employee performance depends on motivation as well as ability. It is possible that a candidate who scores very high on an ability test might be "overqualified"; that is, the employee might be bored by the job the organization needs to fill, and a less-able employee might actually be a better performer in the job. Similarly, a highly motivated person might learn some kinds of jobs very quickly, potentially outperforming someone who has the necessary skills. Furthermore, some organizations have policies of developing employees for career paths in the organization. Such organizations might put less emphasis on the skills needed for a particular job and more emphasis on hiring candidates who share the organization's values.

Finally, organizations have choices about who will make the decision. Sometimes the immediate supervisor or manager makes the final decision, often alone. This person may couple knowledge of the job with a judgment about who will contribute the most to the department. The decision could also be made by a human resources professional using standardized, objective criteria. Especially in organizations that value teamwork, selection decisions may be made by a work team or other panel of decision makers. As noted in the HR How To feature and in the discussion of digital interviews, organizations are increasingly turning to data-driven methods to inform and/or make hiring decisions. This approach is an application of people (human capital) analytics (see Chapter 1) to make evidence-based hiring decisions. A **hiring algorithm** is a mathematical model that predicts which job candidates are most likely to be high performers once hired. The use of this type of predictive model is intended to improve the quality of hiring decisions by reducing the human errors associated with biases and other perceptual distortions.

hiring algorithm Mathematical model that predicts which job candidates are most likely to be high performers after being hired.

Timing of the decision is also important. "Hiring managers are busy but the best candidates don't stay on the market long. And often the best candidate is lost in the process if the hiring manager takes too long to make a decision or if there's too much back-and-forth between the hiring manager and HR," explains Ken Graham, director of training and professional services at Adecco in Toronto.[69]

Communicating the Decision

The human resource department is often responsible for notifying applicants about the results of the selection process. When a candidate has been selected, the organization should communicate the offer to the candidate. The offer should include the job responsibilities, work schedule, rate of pay, starting date, and other relevant details. If placement in a job requires that the applicant complete a medical examination, the offer should state that contingency. The person communicating the offer should also indicate a date by which the candidate should reply with an acceptance or rejection of the offer. For some jobs, such as management and professional positions, the candidate and organization may negotiate pay, benefits, and work arrangements before they arrive at a final employment agreement.

The person who communicates this decision should keep accurate records of who was contacted, when, and for which position, as well as of the candidate's reply. The HR department and the immediate supervisor also should be in close communication about the job offer. Organizations would like to be able to hire their first-choice candidates, but this does not always happen, particularly when labour markets are tight. The Conference Board of Canada's "Trends and Metrics Survey, Fourth Edition" recently collected information from 150 Canadian organizations and reported results by job category. For example, on average, only 72 percent of executive vacancies were filled with first-choice candidates, whereas, 90 percent of management, technical and skilled trades, and clerical and support positions were filled with first-choice candidates.[70]

When an applicant accepts a job offer, the HR department must notify the supervisor, so that they can be well prepared for the new employee's arrival.

Thinking Ethically

What Is an Employer's Ethical Duty to Check Facts?

A survey of hiring professionals found that a majority recalled seeing a lie on a candidate's résumé. The most common lies involved exaggerating skills and responsibilities, and some were startling—for example, attendance at a nonexistent university or employment in two cities during the same time period.

Why would job seekers take a chance that they won't be caught? One reason might be they see or imagine that employers won't take the information seriously. Survey results indicate that more than two-thirds of those reviewing a résumé devote less than five minutes to the task—and many of them spend less than two minutes. Also, employers aren't necessarily giving out accurate information themselves if they paint overly rosy pictures during interviews and on their websites or fail to keep job descriptions up to date. Candidates may conclude that the selection process is one of manipulation, not honesty.

Besides doing their part to make the selection process transparent, employers can protect themselves against misrepresentations by job seekers. These efforts generally involve some kind of background check. Methods include contacting current and former employers to verify employment; this is where most discrepancies with résumés are detected. Other checks may look at a candidate's education, credit record, driving abstract, and other available information, as long as these methods are legal and relevant.

Companies might rely on interviews to catch gaps. This requires a high level of skill; the average person barely does better than guessing at random when it comes to detecting a gap. For example, many people assume that lack of eye contact is a sign of lying, but the evidence doesn't support that assumption. For example, in Indigenous cultures, eye contact is generally avoided because it is perceived to be too assertive. A more effective approach is to ask neutral questions and listen carefully for details and inconsistencies. Ideally, the candidate offers details that can be verified later through objective methods.

Questions

1. Who is affected by an employer's decision to skip background checks? Discuss whether such a decision achieves the greatest good for the greatest number of individuals.
2. How can employers meet the standards of being fair and equitable when they conduct background checks?

Sources: "What is Culture and Why Does it Matter," First Nations Construction," http://www.aboriginalconstructioncareers.ca/toolkit/what-culture-and-why-does-it-matter,; Andre Lavoie, "What Happens When Your Hiring Process Is Founded on Deceit?" Entrepreneur, March 1, 2016, http://www.entrepreneur.com; Martin Berman-Gorvine, "Multiple Background Checks Suggested for Candidates," HR Focus, December 2015, pp. 10–11; "Liar, Liar, Résumé on Fire," HR Magazine, October 2015, https://www.shrm.org; Dennis McCafferty, "The Worst Jaw-Dropping Résumé Blunders," CIO Insight, August 27, 2015, http://www.cioinsight.com; Martin Bermine-Gorvine, "The Notion That It's Easy to Spot a Liar Is Itself a Lie," HR Focus, August 2015, pp. 10–13.

SUMMARY

LO1 Identify the elements and legal requirements of the selection process.

Selection typically begins with a review of candidates' employment applications and résumés, then tests are administered, followed by one or more interviews. Reference and background checks may be conducted to verify the accuracy of information provided by candidates. A candidate is selected and placed in the position The selection process must comply with human rights and privacy legislation and be conducted in a fair and consistent manner. To provide a positive candidate experience, each step in the selection process must be handled effectively.

LO2 Define ways to measure the success of a selection method.

One criterion is reliability, which indicates the method is free from random error, so that measurements are consistent. A selection method should also be valid, meaning that performance on the measure (such as a test score) is related to what the measure is designed to assess (such as job performance). A selection method also should be generalizable, so that it applies to more than one specific situation. Each selection method should have utility, meaning it provides economic value greater than its cost.

LO3 Compare some of the common methods used for obtaining and verifying candidate information.

Nearly all organizations gather information through employment applications and résumés. These methods are inexpensive, and job applications standardize basic information received from all applicants. The information is not necessarily reliable, because each applicant provides the information. References and background checks help to verify the accuracy of the information.

LO4 Describe the major types of employment tests.

Employment tests and work samples may be used to narrow the applicant pool. Any test or assessment must measure abilities associated with successful job performance. Increasingly, employment tests are conducted on mobile devices.

Physical ability tests need to be job related. Cognitive ability tests, or intelligence tests, tend to be valid and available at low cost. Job performance tests, review of work samples, personality, and integrity tests, may also be used. Under certain circumstances it may be possible to conduct pre-employment substance tests. A medical examination should be conducted only after making a conditional job offer.

LO5 Discuss how to conduct effective interviews and make and communicate the selection decision.

Interviews are widely used in the selection process. Structured, situational, and behavioural interviews provide greater validity than unstructured interviews. Interviews are costly and may introduce bias into the selection process; however, preparation and training as well as applications of technology are increasingly being used to make interviewing more efficient and effective.

Hiring decisions need to be based on objective criteria and may be made by supervisors, managers, or HR professionals, or through data-driven methods.

CRITICAL THINKING QUESTIONS

1. What activities are involved in the selection process? Think of the last time you were hired for a job. Which of those activities were used in selecting you? Should the organization that hired you have used other methods as well? What advice do you have to the organization about providing an excellent candidate experience?
2. Why should the selection process be designed to align with the organization's job descriptions and specifications?
3. Suppose a manufacturer using analytics to support their hiring decisions, learns that employees who graduated from one Polytechnic/College/Institute of Technology take longer to get up to speed than employees who graduated from another Polytechnic/College/Institute of Technology. How might applying the data to hiring decisions increase the risk of discrimination? How could the manufacturer use the information in a non-discriminatory way? Consider the HR How-To in preparing your responses.
4. Choose two of the selection methods identified in this chapter. Describe how you can compare them in terms of reliability, validity, ability to generalize, utility, and compliance with human rights legislation.
5. Suppose your organization needs to hire a data scientist, and you are reviewing LinkedIn profiles of candidates who have applied for the available position. What kinds of information will you want to review about the candidates' work experience? What kinds of information will you want to consider about their education? How important are the candidates' "Summary"? What methods would you use for verifying or exploring this information? Why would you use those methods?
6. For each of the following jobs, select two kinds of tests you think would be most important to include in the selection process. Explain why you chose those tests.
   a. City bus driver
   b. Pharmaceutical sales representative
   c. HR professional
   d. Barista
7. Suppose you are a human resources professional at a large retail chain. You want to improve the company's hiring process by standardizing interviews, so that every time someone is interviewed for a particular job category, that applicant answers the same questions. You also want to make sure the questions asked are relevant to the job and comply with

human rights legislation. Think of three questions to include in interviews for each of the following jobs. For each question, state why you think it should be included.

   a. Front-line sales person at one of the company's stores
   b. Store manager
   c. Accounts payable clerk at company headquarters

8. How can organizations improve the quality of their interviewing so that interviews provide valid information?

9. The following questions are favourites of three seasoned hiring managers. For each of the following questions provide your opinion of:

   i. what you think the interviewer was after.
   ii. the "best" answer.
   iii. the "worst" answer.

   a. Del Rollo, director of hospitality, Jackson-Triggs Niagara Estate, Niagara-on-the-Lake asks, "What is the greatest service experience you've had?"
   b. Gary Hellard, manager of recruiting, WestJet Airlines, Calgary asks, "Tell us what began as your most frustrating or tough day, and what you did so that it ended up being your most productive day."
   c. Nancy Blair, office leader, Egon Zehnder International Inc., Calgary asks, "What do you hope this job is not?

10. Some organizations set up a selection process that is long and complex. In some people's opinion, this kind of selection process not only is more valid but also has symbolic value. What can the use of a long, complex selection process symbolize to job seekers? How do you think this would affect the organization's ability to attract the best employees?

Source: Question 9 is based on: Tony Martin, "Why Are They Asking Me This?" Report on Business, The Globe and Mail, September 26, 2007, www.theglobeandmail.com, retrieved September 27, 2007.

EXPERIENCING HR—ELEVATING CANDIDATE EXPERIENCE

To get a sense of what it is like to perform work of an HR professional, conduct research about how to create a positive candidate experience. Summarize the advice and recommendations provided by various credible sources and organize your key points to align with the steps in the selection process illustrated in Figure 5.1. Do your recommendations and advice provide a comprehensive map of a candidate's journey through each stage of a selection process? Who would be accountable for designing, implementing, and sustaining the talent acquisition practices and processes recommended (e.g., HR professional, supervisor/manager, executive leader)? Identify two or three things that could be implemented quickly and cost-effectively, and have a significant effect on candidate experience. How would you measure the impact and/or results? Be prepared to share your findings and insights in a class discussion.

CASE STUDY: EVIDENCE-BASED HRM

Assessing the Impact of the Candidate Experience

The IBM Smarter Workforce Institute examined information from more than 7,000 job applicants across a variety of industries and from thousands of organizations in 45 countries and territories to determine the evidence-based outcomes associated with satisfying and dissatisfying candidate experiences.

Research revealed that applicants who were satisfied with their candidate experience, regardless of whether they received a job offer, "are more than twice as likely to recommend the hiring organization to others who were not satisfied (62 percent vs. 28 percent)" and are "twice as likely to become a customer of the hiring organization." Additionally, candidates' experiences are "amplified"—more than 60 percent "talk about their experiences with friends and family."

The research also revealed that the candidate experience had far-reaching impacts. For organizations aspiring to hire their first-choice candidates—research findings included that "candidates who were satisfied with their experience are 38 percent more likely to accept a job offer." These findings provide evidence of the organizational benefits associated with providing a positive and satisfying candidate experience.

Johnson & Johnson, the global pharmaceutical and health care company, recently conducted a series of surveys and focus groups and learned that candidates experienced frustration with their hiring process. Sjored Gehring, global vice-president of talent acquisition, and his team established a bold vision to reimagine their talent acquisition process. That was no small task given that Johnson & Johnson receives approximately one million applications for more than 25,000 job openings annually. "We've started to see in job candidates the same expectations for a consumer-like experience that they're getting elsewhere," explained Gehring. Gehring and his team developed a transparent, mobile-friendly hiring platform, J & J Shine, that provides candidates with transparency including the ability to track their applications in real time—like Amazon customers can track their packages. J & J Shine is seamlessly integrated to an applicant tracking system that measures applicants' satisfaction rate with their job-seeking process using "Net Promoter Score," a metric extensively used to measure customer experience and predict business growth.

Questions

1. Is candidate experience a metric that should be used to assess an organization's selection process? Why or why not?
2. For each of the steps in the selection process (Figure 5.1), identify what job seekers would likely want in a positive candidate experience.
3. How can candidate experience translate into business performance?

Sources: Haiyan Zhang and Sheri Feinzig, "The far-reaching impact of candidate experience," IBM Smarter Workforce Institute, (2017), pp. 1-7; Ayn-Monique Kiahre, "3 Ways Johnson & Johnson is Taking Talent Acquisition to the Next Level," August 29, 2017, https://www.jnj.com; and Andrew R. McIlvaine, "Johnson & Johnson Takes Steps to Make Hiring Shine," Recruiting Trends, October 24, 2017, www.recruitingtrends.com; and "What is Net Promoter?" https://www.netpromoter.com.

CASE STUDY: HRM SOCIAL

Conducting Background Checks via Social Media

Searching for a job candidate's name online is so easy that it seems like an obvious way to check the person's background. Public information could show, for example, whether the person really is vice-president of marketing at XYZ Corporation or has done something that could later embarrass the employer. Indeed, research indicates that employers are interested. A survey by CareerBuilder found that 39 percent use social media to research candidates, and a survey by recruiting firm Challenger, Grey and Christmas, found even greater use: 22 percent said they always review social media, and another 38 percent said they sometimes do so.

Employers need to proceed with caution, however. A particular concern is to protect candidates' privacy and avoid discrimination, yet the very nature of social media encourages sharing the kinds of information related to prohibited grounds of discrimination. For example, photos and descriptions of activities can tell or suggest a person's age, gender identity, sexual orientation, religion, marital status, family status, ethnicity, and disabilities. Employers can try to avoid discrimination and privacy violations by postponing their search of social media until after they have identified a candidate they want to hire.

A better way to use social media is to involve someone who is not the decision maker. The company can use a designated HR employee or contract with a service that specializes in screening job candidates. The service uses criteria from the employer—for example, screening out candidates who misrepresent their experience or education. It gathers information about the candidate and reports to the employer only the job-related information gathered. Before using a service such as this or conducting any background check, employers should obtain permission from the candidate.

Finally, a few companies have sought greater insight than what is available publicly by asking candidates for their passwords, so the employer can look at a candidate's private information. Experts advise against this practice, which is invasive, probably violates media sites' terms of use, and is likely to alienate many good candidates.

Questions

1. How well does searching social media fulfill the requirements of providing reliable, valid, high-utility, and legal information for selection decisions?
2. What would show up in a search of public information about your name? What is your advice to others about the importance of managing their online presence?

Sources: Ed Lieber, "How to Use Social Media to Find Employees," Small Business Trends, September 27, 2015, http://smallbusinesstrends.com; Catey Hill, "Your Boss Doesn't Care about Your Facebook, Twitter Profiles," MarketWatch, May 19, 2014, http://www.marketwatch.com; Rebecca Weiss, "Social Media's Impact on Hiring, Management and Discipline: What Every Employer Needs to Know," Lexology, September 2, 2013, http://www.lexology.com; CareerBuilder, "More Employers Finding Reasons Not to Hire Candidates on Social Media, Finds CareerBuilder Survey," news release, June 27, 2013, http://www.careerbuilder.com; Steve Bates, "Use Social Media Smartly When Hiring," Society for Human Resource Management, HR Topics and Strategy, March 19, 2013, http://www.shrm.org.

PART 3

Talent Management

Blend Images/Getty Images

CHAPTER 6

Training, Learning, and Development

WHAT DO I NEED TO KNOW?

After reading this chapter, you should be able to:

LO1	Discuss how to link training, learning, and development to organizational needs and strategy.
LO2	Explain how to carry out the steps in a complete instructional design process.
LO3	Describe methods for employee onboarding and supporting diversity and inclusion.
LO4	Discuss the approaches organizations use for employee development.
LO5	Explore the steps in the career management process including creating a development plan and consideration of high-potential employees.

KAIROS Canada

An Indigenous-focused learning experience, called the Blanket Exercise, is part of the training of all RCMP cadets.

The Blanket Exercise—An Indigenous Learning Experience

The Blanket Exercise, created by social justice group KAIROS Canada, is now part of the training of all RCMP cadets. The Blanket Exercise is a "powerful tool in building empathy and opening minds and hearts to ongoing learning about First Nations, Inuit, and Metis people." In the 90-minute exercise, blankets, representing the land that eventually became Canada, are laid out on the floor and participants are invited to step on to them as Indigenous peoples prior to European contact. Blankets are folded and moved, symbolizing the loss of territory, with participants being relocated or removed during treaty making, colonization, resistance, and other eras and events that have profoundly impacted Indigenous peoples' land, culture, and way of life. Facilitators guide the exercise and serve as narrators while participants become part of the experience by reading scrolls and carrying cards that determine their ultimate outcomes. For example, during the exercise, some participants are asked to leave the blankets to represent people who died due to diseases such as smallpox brought by European colonizers.

The blanket exercise is a reconciliation tool and is based on a holistic Indigenous approach to learning—"engaging the mind, and moving the bodies, opening hearts, and deepening relationships to others." The exercise educates participants on 500 years of Indigenous history while creating a context for understanding critical issues including residential schools and missing and murdered Indigenous women. According to Nathalie Fehr, curriculum designer at the RCMP Academy: "We felt that the Blanket Exercise would be a great experiential exercise, giving the cadets some Indigenous history while understanding how it impacts the communities we serve." Cadet Matt Plaskett of Troop 10, the first troop to experience the blanket exercise said, "When we started getting pushed off our blankets, it turned into a real emotional moment for all of us. It gave me a perspective I've never had before." And his troopmate, Cadet Habeeb Shah, added, "I want to carry the knowledge and the empathy I got today with me going forward. More than ever, I'm inspired to build bridges between this uniform and Indigenous people."[1]

LO1 Introduction

Training refers to a planned effort by an organization to facilitate employees' learning of job-related knowledge, skills, and behaviours. The goal of training is for employees to master the knowledge, skills, and behaviours emphasized in training and apply them to their day-to-day activities. Traditionally, companies have relied on formal training through a course, a program, or an event to teach employees the knowledge, skills, and behaviours they need to successfully perform their jobs. **Formal training** refers to talent development programs, courses, and events that are developed and organized by the organization. Typically employees are required to attend or complete these programs, which can include face-to-face training programs (such as instructor-led courses) as well as online programs.

> **training** Planned effort by an organization to facilitate employees' learning of job-related knowledge, skills, and behaviours.

> **formal training** Talent development programs, courses, and events that are developed and organized by the organization.

Informal learning is also important for facilitating knowledge and skill acquisition.[2] **Informal learning** refers to learning that is learner-initiated, involves action and doing, is motivated by an intent to develop, and does not occur in a formal learning setting.[3] Informal learning occurs without an instructor, and its breadth, depth, and timing are controlled by the employee. It occurs on an as-needed basis and may involve an employee learning alone or through face-to-face or technology-aided social interactions. Informal learning can occur through many different ways, including casual unplanned interactions with peers, email, informal mentoring, or company-developed or publicly available social networking websites such as Instagram or Facebook. The application of social media from a marketing strategy to a learning strategy and the availability of Web 2.0 technologies such as social networks, microblogs, and wikis give employees easy access to social learning through collaboration and sharing with one or two or more people.[4] One estimate is that informal learning may account for up to 75 percent of learning within organizations.

> **informal learning** Learning that is learner initiated, involves action and doing, is motivated by an intent to develop, and does not occur in a formal learning setting.

To fully benefit from employees' strengths and skills, managers also provide for **employee development**—the combination of formal education, job experiences, relationships, and assessment of personality and abilities to help employees prepare for the future of their careers. Human resource management establishes a process for employee development that prepares employees to help the organization meet its goals. Table 6.1 summarizes the traditional differences between training and development.

> **employee development** The combination of formal education, job experiences, relationships, and assessment of personality and abilities to help employees prepare for the future of their careers.

In this chapter, we emphasize the conditions through which training and development practices can help organizations gain competitive advantage. We begin by examining

TABLE 6.1

Training versus Development

	Training	Development
Focus	Current	Future
Use of work experiences	Low	High
Goal	Preparation for current job	Preparation for changes
Participation	Required	Voluntary

the connection of talent development to organizational needs and strategy. Next, a systematic and effective approach to instructional design is provided including needs assessment, planning, design, implementation, and evaluation. Orienting and onboarding new employees and the management of diversity and inclusion are also discussed. The chapter also looks at development approaches, including formal education, assessment, job experiences, interpersonal relationships, and career management. The chapter concludes with exploring career management systems, high-potential employee considerations, and creating development plans.

LO2 Training, Learning, and Development Linked to Organizational Needs and Strategy

Workplace training and employee development are key ingredients in the competitiveness of firms and ultimately of national competitiveness.[5] A recent survey of Canadian organizations identified their top three strategic goals for learning and development:[6]

- improving organizational performance
- enhancing individual employee performance
- developing organizational leaders.

Rapid change, especially in the area of technology, requires that employees continually learn new skills. **Continuous learning** refers to a learning system that requires employees to understand the entire work system; acquire new skills, apply them on the job, and share what they have learned with other employees.[7]

continuous learning Learning system that expects employees to acquire new skills, apply them on the job, and share what they have learned with other employees.

For example, Jiffy Lube relies on continuous learning to support their business strategy. Jiffy Lube has more than 2,000 service centres in Canada and the United States and services approximately 24 million customers each year. Jiffy Lube's strategic goals focus on developing growth opportunities for franchisees and providing a world-class customer experience. Training and certification of service technicians is provided through Jiffy Lube University (JLU). It is estimated that employees participated in more than two million learning hours in the previous two years. Learning for employees and franchisees is offered using face-to-face and virtual instruction, as well as online self-paced modules. Jiffy Lube has also established partnerships with colleges to allow service centre employees to transfer credits from courses earned through JLU to earn an undergraduate certificate in management foundations. Learners can access an online roadmap, which shows how training is helping them advance their careers. Jiffy Lube provides video cameras so that store employees can capture best practices and ideas. These videos have focused on customer service, team building, operational excellence, and safety. Jiffy Lube instructors edit the videos and make them available to all employees on YouTube.[8]

The new psychological contract, described in Chapter 1, has created the expectation that employees invest in their own career development, including engaging in learning opportunities. Growing reliance on teamwork creates a demand for the ability to solve problems in teams, an ability that often requires formal training. Finally, the diversity of the Canadian population, coupled with the globalization of business, requires that organizations create inclusive work environments and support employees to work effectively with each other.

Some organizations are developing their employer brand and reputation for talent development and creating a positive employee experience. These organizations emphasize training, career, and development opportunities as a means to gaining competitive advantage.[9] These organizations may be described as having a strong learning culture. **Learning culture** is "an organizational commitment to ongoing learning, and the processes of sharing, support, communication, and understanding that move the organization forward." In an increasingly competitive, complex, and global economy, organizations with strong learning cultures are more likely to be agile and resilient. There is also evidence that organizations reporting strong learning cultures have higher levels of performance compared to weak learning cultures: leadership performance (41.0 percent difference); employee performance (39.0 percent difference); communication within the organization (35.0 percent difference); and productivity (32.0 percent difference).[10]

learning culture An organizational commitment to ongoing learning, and the processes of sharing, support, communication, and understanding that move the organization forward.

Did You Know?

More Learning Time in Companies Exhibiting a Strong Learning Culture

A recent Conference Board of Canada survey found that organizations committed to learning and development invested both more money and time in learning. Organizations exhibiting strong learning cultures reported the highest average of 34 hours of learning (per employee) annually, 10 hours more than employees in organizations with a weak learning culture.

Hours of Learning, by Learning Culture
(mean number of hours annually)

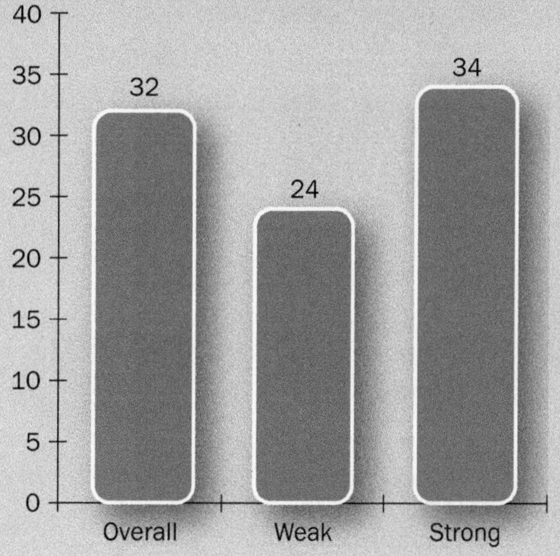

Question

1. In your opinion, which is more important, increasing hours of learning or investing more dollars in learning? Why?

Source: S. Cotsman and C. Hall, *Learning Cultures Lead the Way: Learning and Development Outlook,* 14th Edition, Ottawa: The Conference Board of Canada, 2018, p. 23.

As shown in the Did You Know? box, organizations with strong learning cultures tend to provide employees with more hours of learning than organizations with weak learning cultures.

How are Canadian firms investing in and supporting learning? The Conference Board of Canada explores these and other questions in its *Learning and Development Outlook, Learning Cultures Lead the Way,* 14th Edition (2018). The report reveals that 50 percent of responding organizations strongly agreed or agreed that learning is a top priority. This priority appears to be evidenced in increased investment in training, learning, and development. For example, on average, direct investment on training and development across all industries in Canada was $889 per employee in 2016–17, was up from $800 per employee in 2014–15. Canadian organizations are closing the gap with the United States in learning and development investments. In 2016–17, Canadian organizations spent 81 cents for every $1.00 by U.S. organizations, representing a significant increase from 51 cents for every $1.00 by U.S. organizations in 2006.[11]

With talent development so essential in modern organizations, it is important to provide training that is effective. An effective training program actually teaches what it is designed to teach, and participants learn skills and behaviours that will help the organization achieve its goals. Training programs may increase employees' competence and performance, enable the organization to respond to change, reduce turnover, enhance worker safety, improve customer service and product design, and meet many other goals. To achieve those goals, HR professionals approach training through **instructional design**—a process of systematically developing training to meet specified needs.[12]

instructional design A process of systematically developing training to meet specified needs.

A complete instructional design process includes the steps shown in Figure 6.1. It begins with an assessment of needs—what the organization requires that its people learn. Next, the organization ensures that employees are ready in terms of their attitudes, motivation, basic skills, and work environment. The third step is to plan the program, including the program's objectives, instructors, and methods. The organization then implements the program. Finally, evaluating the results provides feedback for planning future programs.

Needs Assessment

needs assessment The process of evaluating the organization, individual employees, and employees' tasks to determine what kinds of training, if any, are necessary.

Instructional design logically should begin with a **needs assessment**, the process of evaluating the organization, individual employees, and employees' tasks to determine what

FIGURE 6.1

Stages of Instructional Design

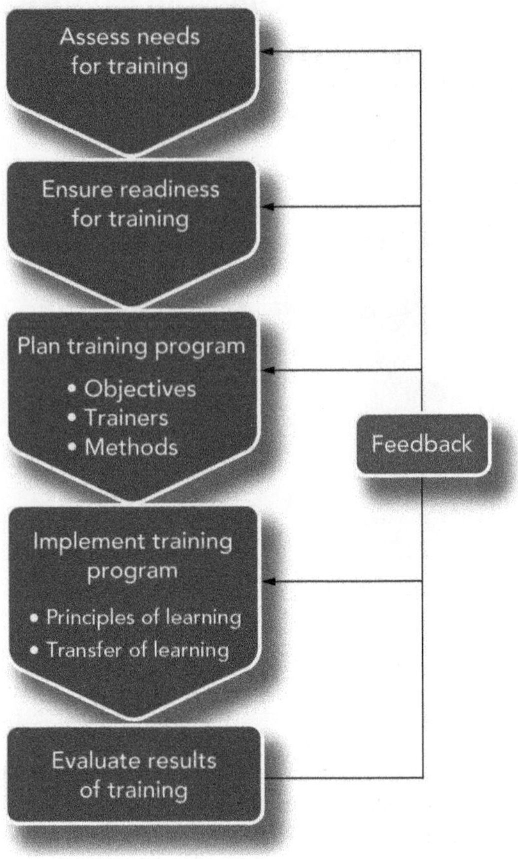

kinds of training and learning, if any, are necessary. As this definition indicates, the needs assessment answers questions in the three broad areas:[13]

1. *Organization*—What is the context in which learning will occur?
2. *Person*—Who needs the learning?
3. *Task*—What topics should be covered?

The answers to these questions provide the basis for planning an effective program.

A variety of conditions may prompt an organization to conduct a needs assessment. Figure 6.2 shows the causes and outcomes resulting from needs assessment. As the figure illustrates, varying types of "pressure points" may suggest that training is necessary. Some of these pressure points are performance gaps, new technology, internal or external customer requests for training, job redesign, new legislation, changes in customer preferences, and new products, as well as support for the company's business strategy (e.g., growth, global business expansion). Many of these conditions should prompt a needs assessment because these changes tend to require new skills.

What outcomes result from a needs assessment? The outcome of the needs assessment is a set of decisions about how to address the issues that prompted the needs assessment. These decisions do not necessarily include a training program, because some issues should be resolved through methods other than training—for example, plans for enhanced rewards to improve motivation, better hiring decisions, and safety precautions. As shown in Figure 6.2, needs assessment shows who needs training and what trainees need to learn, including the tasks in which they need to be trained plus knowledge, skill, behaviour, or other job requirements. Needs assessment helps determine whether the company should contract with an external provider or develop training resources internally.

Usually, the needs assessment begins with the **organization analysis**. This is a process for determining the appropriateness of training by evaluating the characteristics of the organization. The organization analysis looks at training needs in light of the organization's strategy, resources available, and management's support for learning activities.

organization analysis A process for determining the appropriateness of training by evaluating the characteristics of the organization.

Training needs will vary depending on whether the organization's strategy is based on growing or shrinking its workforce, whether it is seeking to serve a broad customer base or focusing on the specific needs of a narrow market segment, or various other scenarios. An organization that concentrates on serving a niche market may need to continually update specialized skills of its workforce. A company cutting costs with a downsizing strategy may need to provide employees with job search skills. The employees who remain following a downsizing may need cross-training so they can handle a wider variety of responsibilities.

Anyone planning a training program must consider whether the organization has the budget, time, and expertise for training. Even if training fits the organization's strategy, it can be viable only if the organization is willing to support the investment. Managers increase the success of training when they support it through actions such as helping trainees see how they can use their newly learned knowledge, skills, and behaviours on the job.[14] Conversely, the managers will be most likely to support training if the people planning it can show that it will solve a significant problem or result in a significant improvement, relative to its cost. Managers appreciate proposals with specific goals, timetables, budgets, and methods for measuring success.

Person Analysis

Following the organizational assessment, needs assessment turns to the remaining areas of analysis: person and task. The **person analysis** is a process for determining individuals'

person analysis A process for determining individuals' needs and readiness for learning.

FIGURE 6.2

The Needs Assessment Process

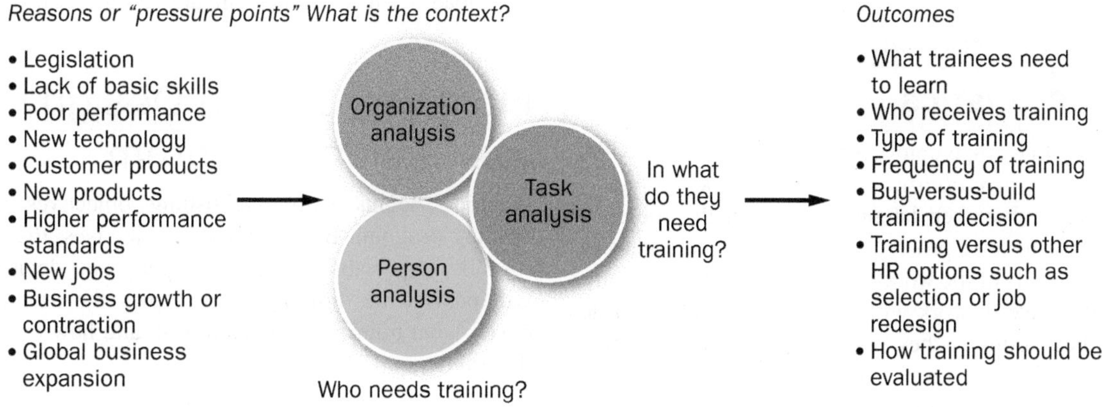

needs and readiness for learning. It involves answering several questions:

- Do performance gaps result from a lack of knowledge, skill, or ability? (If so, training is appropriate; if not, other solutions are more relevant.)
- Who needs training?
- Are these employees ready?

The answers to these questions help the manager identify whether training is appropriate and which employees need training. In certain situations, such as the introduction of a new technology or service, all employees may need training. However, when needs assessment is conducted in response to a performance issue, training is not always the best solution.

The person analysis is critical when training is considered in response to a performance issue. In assessing the need for training, the manager should identify all the variables that can influence performance. The primary variables are the person's ability and skills, their mindset and motivation, the organization's input (including clear directions, necessary resources, and freedom from interference and distractions), performance feedback, and positive consequences to encourage good performance. Of these variables, only ability and skills can be affected by training. Therefore, before planning a training program, it is important to be sure that any performance issue results from a deficiency in knowledge and skills. Otherwise, investment will be wasted, because the training is unlikely to have much effect on performance.

The person analysis also should determine whether employees are ready to undergo training. In other words, the employees to receive training not only should require additional knowledge and skill, but also must be willing and able to learn. (After our discussion of the needs assessment, we will explore the topic of employee readiness in greater detail.)

Task Analysis

The third area of needs assessment is **task analysis**, the process of identifying the tasks, knowledge, skills, and behaviours that training should emphasize. Usually, task analysis is conducted along with person analysis. Understanding shortcomings in performance usually requires knowledge about the tasks and work environment as well as the employee.

task analysis The process of identifying the tasks, knowledge, skills, and behaviours that training should emphasize.

To carry out the task analysis, the HR professional looks at the conditions in which tasks are performed. These conditions include the equipment and environment of the job, time constraints (e.g., deadlines), safety considerations, and performance standards. These observations form the basis for a description of work activities, or the tasks required by the person's job. For a selected job, the analyst interviews employees and their supervisors to prepare a list of tasks performed in that job. Then the analyst validates the list by showing it to employees, supervisors, and other subject-matter experts and asking them to complete a questionnaire about the *importance, frequency,* and *difficulty* of the tasks. The information from these questionnaires is the basis for determining which tasks will be the focus of the training. Logically, training is most needed for tasks that are important, frequent, and at least moderately difficult.

Readiness for Learning

Effective training requires not only a program that addresses real needs but also a condition of employee readiness. **Readiness for learning**

readiness for learning A combination of employee characteristics and positive work environment that permit learning.

is a combination of employee characteristics and positive work environment that permit learning. It exists when employees are able and eager to learn and their organizations encourage learning.

Employee Readiness Characteristics

To be ready to learn, employees need basic learning skills, especially *cognitive ability,* which includes being able to use written and spoken language, solve math problems, and use logic to solve problems. However, recent forecasts of the skill levels of the workforce indicate that many companies will have to work with employees who lack basic skills.[15] For example, they may need to provide literacy training before some employees will be ready to participate in job-related training.

Employees learn more when they are highly motivated to learn—that is, when they really want to learn the content of the training program.[16] Employees tend to feel this way if they believe they are able to learn, see potential benefits from the training program, are aware of their need to learn, see a fit between the training and their career goals, and have the basic skills needed for participating in the program. Managers can influence a ready attitude by providing encouraging feedback, establishing rewards for learning, and communicating with employees about the organization's career paths and future needs. In a recent survey of 1,000 employees, 88 percent of those with supervisor support for training and development said they are "motivated to do their best work" and 86 percent said they "are satisfied with their job."[17]

Work Environment

Readiness also depends on two broad characteristics of the work environment: situational constraints and social support.[18] *Situational constraints* are the limits on training's effectiveness that arise from the situation or the conditions within the organization. Constraints can include a lack of money for training, lack of time for training or practising, and failure to provide proper tools and materials for learning or applying the lessons of training. For example, it is estimated that 80 percent of the global workforce are "deskless workers" who do not work in offices or at desks, nor have consistent access to a computer. These workers are employed in a variety of industries ranging from food services to health care. Training and development can be challenging to implement due to lack of access to training infrastructure available to office workers.[19]

Social support refers to the ways the organization's people encourage training, including giving trainees positive feedback and encouragement, sharing information about participating in training programs, and expressing positive attitudes toward the organization's training programs. Readiness for learning is greater in an organization where employees share knowledge, encourage one another to learn, and have a positive attitude about carrying the extra load when co-workers are attending classes.

How to Plan and Design the Training Program

Planning begins with establishing objectives for the training program. Based on those objectives, the planner (usually a specialist in the HR department) decides who will provide the training, what topics the training will cover, what training methods to use, and how to evaluate the training.

Objectives of the Program

Formally establishing objectives for the training program has several benefits. First, a training program based on clear objectives will be more focused and more likely to succeed. Employees learn best when they know what the training is supposed to accomplish. Finally, down the road, establishing objectives provides a basis for measuring whether the program succeeded, as we will discuss later in this chapter.

Effective training objectives have three components:

- They include a statement of what the employee is expected to do, the quality or level of performance that is acceptable, and the conditions under which the employee is to apply what they learned (for instance, physical conditions, mental stresses, or equipment failure).[20]
- They include performance standards that are measurable.
- They identify the resources needed to carry out the desired performance or outcome. Successful training requires employees to learn and employers to provide the necessary resources.

A related issue at the outset is who will participate in the training program. Some training programs are developed for all employees of the organization or all members of a team. Other training programs identify individuals who lack required skills or have potential to be promoted, then provide training in the areas of need that are identified for the particular employees. When deciding whom to include in training, the organization has to avoid illegal discrimination as a minimum requirement. The organization must not—intentionally or unintentionally—exclude anyone due to a prohibited ground of discrimination, for example, age, sex, or disability. Inclusive programs are likely to significantly exceed basic legal requirements by supporting a range of learners with differing abilities.[21]

In-House or Contracted Out?

An organization can provide an effective training program, even if it lacks expertise in training. Many companies and consultants provide training services to organizations. Colleges, universities, technical institutes, and polytechnics often work with employers to train employees in a variety of skills.

To select a training service, an organization can post a *request for proposal (RFP),* a document outlining the type of service needed, the type and number of references needed, the number of employees to be trained, the date by which the training is to be completed, and the date by which proposals should be received. A complete RFP also indicates funding for the project and criteria for the vendor selection process. Use of a request for proposal is time consuming but worthwhile because it helps the organization clarify its objectives, establish accountabilities, compare vendors, and measure results.

The cost of purchasing training from a contractor can vary substantially. In general, it is much costlier to purchase specialized training tailored to the organization's requirements than to participate in a seminar or training course that teaches general skills or knowledge. Even in organizations that send employees to outside training programs, someone in the organization may be responsible for coordinating the overall training program. Called *training administration,* this is typically the responsibility of a human resources professional. Training administration includes activities before, during, and after training sessions.

Selecting Training Methods

Regardless of the training method, for training to be effective it needs to be based on the instructional design model shown in Figure 6.1. Needs assessment, a positive learning environment, and transfer of learning are critical for program effectiveness. Training methods fall into the broad categories described in Table 6.2: presentation, hands-on, and group- or team-building methods.

A number of different methods can help employees acquire new knowledge, skills, and behaviours. Figure 6.3 shows the percentages of companies using various broad categories of delivery methods. Although instructor-led classroom (face-to-face) delivery continues to be the most dominantly used method, it has gradually lost ground to other methods. In 2000, 80 percent of all learning time was instructor-led classroom (face-to-face); this was reduced to 58 percent in 2010 and 48 percent in 2017.[22]

Presentation Methods

presentation methods
Methods in which learners are passive recipients of information.

Presentation methods refer to methods in which learners are passive recipients of information. Presentation methods include traditional classroom instruction, distance learning, and audiovisual training. They can include the use of personal computers and mobile devices including smartphones and tablets. These methods are useful for presenting new facts, information, different philosophies, and alternative problem-solving solutions or processes.

Instructor-led Classroom Instruction

Classroom instruction typically involves an instructor leading a group. In many cases, the lecture is supplemented with question-and-answer periods, discussion, or case studies. Classroom instruction remains a popular training method despite new technologies such as interactive video and computer-assisted instruction. Traditional classroom instruction is one of the least expensive, least time-consuming ways to present information on a specific topic to many learners. The more active participation,

TABLE 6.2

Categories of Training Methods

Method	Techniques	Applications
Presentation methods: learners receive information provided by others	Lectures, workbooks, video clips, podcasts, websites	Conveying facts or comparing alternatives
Hands-on methods: learners are actively involved in trying out skills	On-the-job training, simulations, role-plays, computer games	Teaching specific skills; showing how skills are related to job or how to handle interpersonal issues
Group- or Team-building methods: learners share ideas and experiences, build group identities, learn about interpersonal relationships and the group	Group discussions, experiential programs, team training	Establishing teams or work groups; managing performance of teams or work groups

FIGURE 6.3

Delivery Methods as Percentage of Overall Learning Time, 2012–2013; 2014-2015; and 2016–2017

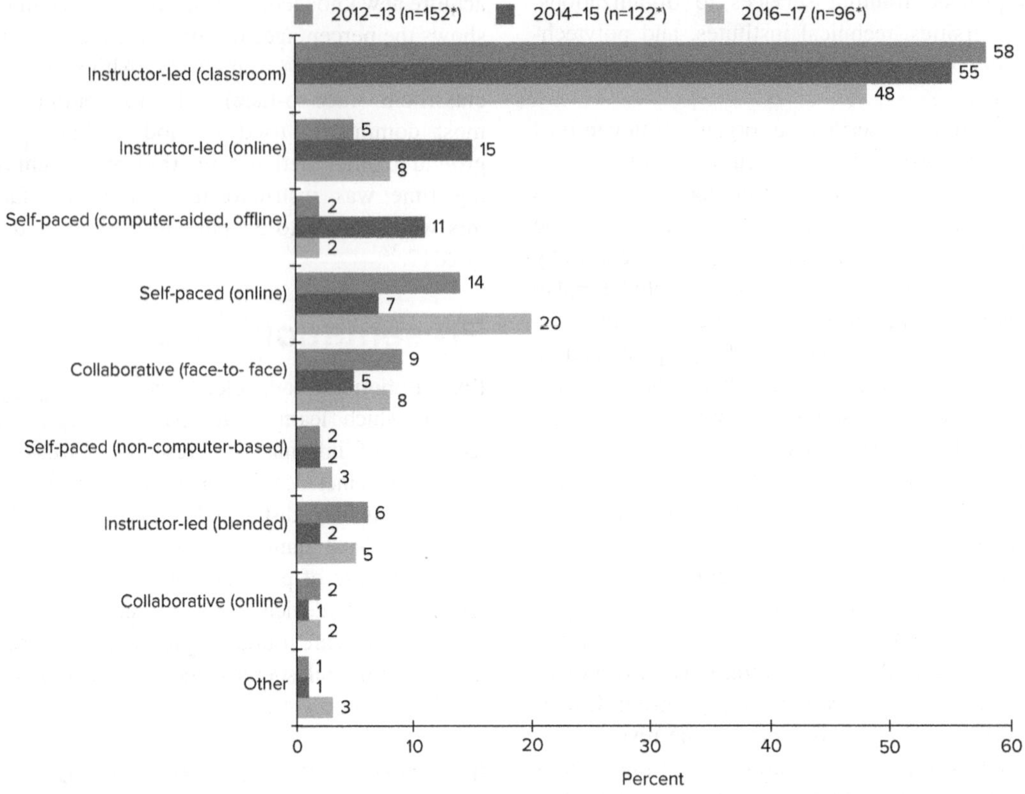

Source: S. Cotsman, & C. Hall, "Learning Cultures Lead the Way: Learning and Development Outlook, 14th Edition," Ottawa: The Conference Board of Canada, 2018, p. 42.

job-related examples, and exercises that the instructor can build into traditional classroom instruction, the more likely trainees will learn and use the information presented on the job.

Distance Learning

Distance learning is used by geographically dispersed companies to provide information about new products, policies, or procedures as well as skills training and expert lectures to field locations.[23] Distance learning features two-way communications between people.[24] With distance learning, learners at different locations attend programs online, using their computers or mobile devices to view lectures, participate in discussions, and share information. Distance learning provides many of the benefits of classroom training without the cost and time of travel to a shared location. The major disadvantage is that interaction between the instructor and participants may be limited. However, tools including videoconferencing, blogs, wikis, email, instant messaging, document-sharing software, online communities of practice, and web cameras increase interaction and engagement.

Audiovisual Training

Presentation methods need not require learners to attend a class. Learners can work independently, using materials in workbooks or on the Internet. Audiovisual training can easily be made available on computers and mobile devices. These devices allow users to access the materials at any time or place. They also allow instruction to include videos, podcasts, charts and diagrams, learning points, and lectures to emphasize learning points, real-life experiences. and examples. This supports learning by appealing to a variety of the participants' senses and by both communicating and demonstrating knowledge, skills, and behaviours.

With audiovisual training, learners often have some control over the presentation. They can review material and may be able to slow down or speed up the lesson. Videos can show situations and equipment that cannot be easily demonstrated in a classroom. Another advantage of audiovisual presentations is that they give learners a consistent presentation. The problems associated with these methods may include trying to present too much material, poorly written dialogue, overuse of features such as

© The McGraw-Hill Companies, Inc./Lars A. Niki, photographer/DAL

Mobile technology is useful for not only entertainment but also employees who are need to be in touch with the office. Smartphones, tablets, and laptop computers give employees additional flexibility in how and when they participate in training programs.

humour or music, and drama that distracts the key points. Well-written and carefully produced content can overcome such problems.

Hands-on Methods

Hands-on methods are training methods that require the learner to be actively involved. Hands-on methods include on-the-job training, simulations, business games and case studies, behaviour modelling, interactive video, and Web-based training. These methods are ideal for developing specific skills, understanding how skills and behaviours can be transferred to the job, experiencing all aspects of completing a task, and dealing with interpersonal issues that arise on the job.

hands-on methods Training methods that require the learner to be actively involved.

On-the-job training (OJT) refers to methods in which a person with job experience and skill guides learners in practising job skills at the workplace. This type of training takes various forms. OJT can be useful for training newly hired employees, upgrading experienced employees' skills when new technology is introduced, cross-training employees within a department or work unit, and onboarding transferred or promoted employees to their new jobs.

on-the-job training (OJT) Training methods in which a person with job experience and skill guides trainees in practising job skills at the workplace.

For example, the OJT program at Canadian Air Transport Security Authority (CATSA) provides a structured approach supported by job knowledge experts. After completing extensive classroom training including role-plays and hands-on practice in a training lab, screening officers participate in live-line-on-the-job training. Point leaders pay careful attention to the screening officers while they conduct various searches and investigations of passengers and their belongings. One class of trainees intercepted an item that looked like a rocket-propelled grenade on the X-ray machine. After the police responded and searched the bag, it turned out to be cologne. Ten minutes later, on the same screening line, the search of a passenger's carry-on bag yielded over $30,000 in U.S. currency. Local police and Canadian Border Services Agency officers attended the checkpoint and conducted their investigations. Through this live-line OJT, trainees received invaluable first-hand experience of how to deal with the discovery of contraband at the screening checkpoint and work with stakeholders such as police, airport security, air carriers, and airport authorities.[25]

An **apprenticeship** is a work–study training method that teaches job skills through a combination of on-the-job training and classroom training. The OJT component of an apprenticeship involves the apprentice assisting a certified journeyperson in the workplace. Typically, the technical training is provided by polytechnics, local trade schools, high schools, community colleges, or other technical institutes. On average, 85 percent of the apprentice's two-to-five-year training is spent in the workplace; the rest is spent at a training institution.[26] Some apprenticeship programs are sponsored by individual companies, others by employee unions. Apprenticeship programs are usually administered by provincial and territorial government departments with support from advisory bodies such as apprenticeship and certification boards. Obtaining a "Red Seal" endorsement after completing an interprovincial standards exam provides journeypersons mobility to practise their trade anywhere in Canada.[27] For trainees, a major advantage of apprenticeship is the ability to earn an income while learning a trade; that is, "earning while learning." In addition, training through an apprenticeship is usually effective because it involves hands-on learning and extensive practice. For example, Nestlé, the global food and beverage company, recently formalized a customized apprenticeship program as a talent development strategy for maintenance mechanics and technicians working at individual factories.[28]

apprenticeship A work–study training method that teaches job skills through a combination of on-the-job training and classroom training.

An **internship** is on-the-job learning sponsored by an educational institution as a component of an academic program. Students are placed in paid positions where they can gain experience related to their area of study. If interns perform

internship On-the-job learning sponsored by an educational institution as a component of an academic program.

well, many companies offer them full-time positions after they complete their studies.

Co-operative education is a plan of higher education that incorporates paid work experience as an important component of academic studies. Co-operative education is being readily accepted by government, business, and industry in Canada and throughout the world. Universities, colleges, polytechnics, other technical schools, and high schools are offering co-op programs to thousands of students in a growing number of disciplines.[29]

co-operative education A plan of higher education that incorporates paid work experience as an integral part of academic studies.

A **simulation** is a training method that represents a real-life situation, with learners' decisions resulting in outcomes that mirror what would happen if they were on the job. Simulations, which allow trainees to see the impact of their decisions in an artificial, risk-free environment, are used to teach production and process skills as well as management and interpersonal skills. Although simulations are expensive to develop and keep updated, they are an excellent method when the risks of a mistake on the job are great. For example, airlines purchasing Boeing's 787 *Dreamliner* use simulators to train the pilots who will fly it. Although the 787 flight deck is designed with the same layout as the familiar 777, it has a new feature called the head-up display (HUD). When flying conditions are poor, this small see-through screen drops down in pilots' line of vision to provide information to help them navigate. Pilots need to practise with the simulator until they are accustomed to landing the jet while using the HUD.[30]

simulation A training method that represents a real-life situation, with learners' decisions resulting in outcomes that mirror what would happen if they were on the job.

One way to enhance simulations is through virtual reality. **Virtual reality** is a computer-based technology that provides an interactive three-dimensional (3D) learning experience. Using specialized equipment or viewing the virtual model on the computer screen, learners move through the simulated environment and interact with its components.[31] Technology is used to stimulate multiple senses of the trainee.[32] Devices relay information from the environment to the senses. For example, audio interfaces, gloves that provide a sense of touch, treadmills, or motion platforms are used to create a realistic, artificial environment. Devices also communicate information about the trainee's movements to a computer. These devices allow the trainee to experience the perception of actually being in a particular environment. For example, a company called Vantage Point is testing 30-minute virtual training modules designed to replicate unfolding stories of sexual harassment with the goal to deeply engage learners' empathy and improve their ability to make appropriate decisions about how to respond and/or intervene appropriately.[33]

virtual reality A computer-based technology that provides an interactive three-dimensional (3D) learning experience.

Although virtual reality (VR) may require the purchase of expensive special equipment, another form of immersive technology, *augmented reality (AR)* can be provided in a highly accessible way using specialized glasses or even on an employee's own Apple or Google device. AR can provide an additional layer of information in the form of captions, labels, or other overlays to the scenario or equipment being used in the workplace. For example, aim your phone at a complicated piece of equipment in your workplace and get "real-time holographic guidance on how to operate it." [34]

Training programs use *business games and case studies* to develop employees' skills. A case study is a detailed description of a situation that learners study and discuss. Cases are designed to develop higher-order thinking skills, such as the ability to analyze and evaluate information. They also can be a safe way to encourage learners to take appropriate risks, by giving them practice in weighing and acting on uncertain outcomes. There are many sources of case studies, including the Richard Ivey School of Business, Wilfrid Laurier University, and Harvard Business School. One dilemma associated with the use of case studies is that they often require more time (or attention span) than the audience has available. The *mini case study* is intended to be delivered with less time (e.g., 30 minutes) but still offers a powerful and engaging learning tool, albeit with less detail.[35]

With business games, learners gather information, analyze it, and make decisions that influence the outcome of the game. For instance, the Marketing Business simulation, Markstrat, integrated into a marketing course, requires participants to use strategic thinking (such as analyzing competitors) to increase their share of the market.[36] Games stimulate learning because they actively involve participants and mirror the competitive nature of business. A realistic game may be more meaningful to trainees than techniques such as classroom instruction.

Gamification, "applying principles of digital and computer games," is a growing development in learning. Work gamification is also a growing movement in performance management to "direct and energize desired work behaviours" and will be discussed in Chapter 7.[37] Games enhance learning by providing a fun way to learn, use leaderboards to increase learners' motivation by capitalizing on their competitiveness, and incorporate levels that require learners to demonstrate they are competent in prerequisite knowledge and skills (by achieving certain scores) before learning more challenging knowledge and skills.

gamification Applying principles of digital and computer games.

Games stimulate learning because participants are actively involved and they mirror the competitive nature of business. The types of decisions that participants make in games include all aspects of management practice, including human resource management (such as pay increases), marketing (the price to charge for a new product), and finance (financing the purchase of new technology). A realistic game or case may stimulate more learning than presentation methods (such as classroom instruction) because it is more meaningful.

For example, KFC recently gamified their training for limited time promotions—new products available at stores for brief periods of time. Most learners are hourly employees and training needs to deliver high impact in a limited amount of time. Game challenges were integrated into assessment questions to test knowledge. Learners drag and drop images to virtually build and then pack the product. In one pirate-themed course, learners earned jewels after each game activity and at the end of the course used their jewels to decode an important message on the last screen.[38]

Research suggests that one of the most effective ways to teach interpersonal skills is through *behaviour modelling*.[39] This involves training sessions in which participants observe other people demonstrating the desired behaviour, then have opportunities to practise the behaviour themselves. For example, a training program could involve several days of four-hour sessions, each focusing on one interpersonal skill, such as communicating or coaching. At the beginning of each session, participants hear the reasons for using the key behaviours, then they watch a video of an expert performing the key behaviours. They practise through role-playing and receive feedback about their performance. In addition, they evaluate the performance of the expert in the video and discuss how they can apply the behaviour on the job.

E-Learning, *computer-based training, online learning,* and *web-based training* refer to instruction and delivery of training by computer through the Internet or an organization's intranet.[40] To enhance learning, this method can include and integrate the following into instruction: text; interaction using simulations and games; video; collaboration using blogs, wikis, and social networks; and hyperlinks to additional resources. In some types of computer-based training, content is provided using standalone software with no connection to the Internet. Trainees can still interact with the training content, answer questions, and choose responses regarding how they would behave in certain situations, but they cannot collaborate with other learners. For ideas about applying wearable technology to learning, see the HR How To.

e-learning
Instruction and delivery of training by computer through the Internet or an organization's intranet.

Many employees use their mobile devices for training because of their ease of use, dynamic displays, ability to connect to the web, access to social media, and availability of powerful apps and video streaming capabilities. For example, PwC provides employees with an app that enables them to access course materials, complete course prerequisites, and access materials on an as-needed basis. PwC reported that more than 36,000 hours of learning were completed by employees on their mobile devices in a recent 12-month time period.[41]

An **electronic performance support system (EPSS)** is a technology platform that provides access to skills training, information, and expert advice.[42] Employees needing guidance can use the EPSS to look up the particular information they need, such as detailed instructions on how to perform an unfamiliar task. Using an EPSS is faster and more relevant than attending classes, even classes offered online. It also can make training available to a global workforce. Cisco Systems, with 15,000 services team employees spread around the world, built a software platform to host training resources online. Employees use their computers or mobile devices to visit the Cisco Career Connections page, where they can take online courses, sign up for classroom training, submit questions, get advice from mentors, read blogs, watch videos, post knowledge to share, and engage in social networking with other team members.[43]

electronic performance support system (EPSS)
A technology platform that provides access to skills training, information, and expert advice.

These digital platforms may embed data analytics and learning science to provide personalized or *adaptive learning* capabilities. Instructional content can be personalized to respond to individual learners' actions and outcomes. For example, as a learner progresses in an adaptive course, the platform collects data about the learner's time, accuracy, and confidence, and automatically guides learners to new content and learning experiences.[44]

Many companies are moving to a *hybrid, or blended, learning* approach because of the limitations of e-learning related to technology (e.g., insufficient bandwidth, lack of high-speed Web connections), learner preferences for face-to-face contact with instructors and colleagues, and employees' inability to find unscheduled time during their workday to devote to learning from their desktops or devices. **Blended learning** refers to combining technology methods, such as e-learning, simulations, or social media, with face-to-face instruction, for delivery of learning content and instruction. ADP's training program for new hires includes one week of in-person workshops, eight simulations, and collaborative, self-paced online learning.[45] This allows the new hires to spend more time on hands-on training (which includes online virtual instructor-led classes focused on product training), working with their mentor, and networking with their peers.

blended learning
Combining technology methods, such as e-learning, simulations, or social media, with face-to-face instruction, for delivery of learning content and instruction.

HR How-To

Using Wearable Technology to Support Training

As soon as wearable technologies like fitness trackers and smart watches and eyeglasses became available, businesses envisioned ways to use them. More recent developments include electronic sensing badges, which can track employees' interaction patterns in the workplace, and sensor-equipped desks that measure employee keystrokes and mouse-clicks, so it's not surprising that some employers are experimenting with ways to use these technologies to help their employees learn to work more efficiently and safely. Here are some guidelines for using these technologies in support of training goals:

- Keep the focus on how to support business and employee objectives, not on how cool a new device is. For example, employees on the move might benefit from hands-free, instant access to an online guide. At Ericsson, workers' locations are tracked using an app and this information is used to facilitate connections to the closest subject-matter expert "on duty" when needed. Similarly, motion sensors can offer helpful feedback for learning to perform a job that involves physical motions.
- Monitor technology trends, such as augmented reality. With augmented reality delivered by a device such as smart eyeglasses, information is projected in the user's line of sight. Imagine, for example, that trainees learning to service a type of equipment can use augmented-reality displays labelling the parts of the machine they are looking at.
- Respect privacy concerns. Wearables that track an employee's steps, hand motions, or even interactions with others might provide valuable information for improving performance. They also might feel like an intrusion into the learner's privacy. Employers should prepare for these concerns by ensuring that employees know what data is being collected and consent to having their data analyzed. Policies for how the data will be used (for example, looking only at patterns at the departmental level, rather than individuals' actions), how to keep private data from becoming public, and why use of the data could help employees (say, protecting their safety or helping them meet goals by integrating multiple sources of data to gain insight about what high-performing employees do differently from their colleagues)—are also essential.
- Protect the company's data. A company that equips its employees with easily portable technology that gathers data might open itself up to the employee recording meetings or saving other information that might be private. Therefore, employers need measures in place to guard against the information falling into the wrong hands.

Questions

1. Identify two possible risks and two possible advantages of collecting and analyzing employee data collected by wearable technologies.
2. How might data collected by wearable technologies be used to determine employee learning needs?

Sources: Patty Gaul, "Big Data: Using People Analytics to improve Leadership Development," *TD*, March 2018, pp. 29-33; Alex Moore, "Learning Meets the Internet of Things," *TD*, December 2017, pp. 18-20; Lorri Freifeld, "Wearables at Work," *Training*, September/October 2015, pp. 18–21; Christopher Pappas, "Seven Ways Wearable Technology Could Be Used in Corporate Training," *eLearning Industry*, August 25, 2015, http://elearningindustry.com; Kate Everson, "Learning Is All in the Wrist," *Chief Learning Officer*, April 2015, pp. 18–21; Bill Barlow, "Wear It Well," *Training*, November 14, 2014, https://trainingmag.com.

A **learning management system (LMS)** refers to a technology platform that can be used to automate the administration, development, and delivery of all of a company's training programs. An LMS can provide employees, managers, and instructors with the ability to manage, deliver, and track learning activities.[46] LMSs have become popular for several reasons. An LMS can help companies reduce travel and other costs related to training, reduce time for program completion, increase employees' accessibility to training across the business, and provide administrative capabilities to track program completion and course enrolments. For example, an organization's LMS can serve as a central place for all of the company's learning programs and materials, including user-generated content from managers, employees, and other subject-matter experts.

learning management system (LMS) A technology platform that can be used to automate the administration, development, and delivery of all of a company's training programs.

Group- or Team-building Methods

Group- or team-building methods are training methods designed to improve team or group effectiveness. Training is directed at improving the participants' skills as well as team effectiveness. In group- or team-building methods, learners share ideas and experiences, build team identity, understand the dynamics of interpersonal relationships, and get to know their own strengths and weaknesses and those of their co-workers. Group techniques focus on helping teams increase their skills for effective teamwork. All involve examination of feelings, perceptions, and beliefs about the functioning of the team; discussion; and development of plans to apply what was learned to the team's performance in the work setting. Group- or team-building methods fall into three categories: experiential programs, team training, and action learning.

group- or team-building methods Training methods that help learners share ideas and experiences, build team identity, understand the dynamics of interpersonal relationships, and get to know their own strengths and weaknesses and those of their co-workers.

Experiential programs are training programs in which participants learn concepts and apply them by simulating behaviours involved, analyzing the activity, and connecting it with real-life situations.[47]

experiential programs Training programs in which participants learn concepts and apply them by simulating behaviours involved and analyzing the activity, connecting it with real-life situations.

Experiential training programs should follow several guidelines. A program should be related to a specific business problem. Participants should feel challenged and move outside their comfort zones but within limits that keep their motivation strong and help them understand the purpose of the program.

One form of experiential program, called **adventure learning**, uses challenging, structured physical activities, which may include difficult sports such as dogsledding or mountain climbing. Other activities may be structured tasks like climbing walls, completing rope courses, climbing ladders, or making "trust falls" (in which each trainee falls backward into the arms of other group members). The impact of adventure learning programs has not been rigorously tested, but participants report they gained a greater understanding of themselves and the ways that the organization insist that entire work groups participate together. This encourages people to see, discuss, and change the kinds of behaviour that keep the group from performing well.

adventure learning A teamwork and leadership training program based on the use of challenging, structured physical activities.

Before requiring employees to participate in experiential programs, the organization should consider the possible drawbacks. Because these programs are usually physically demanding and often require participants to touch each other, companies face certain risks. Some employees may be injured or may feel that they were sexually harassed or that their privacy was invaded. Also, human rights and employment equity legislation (discussed in Chapter 2) raises questions about requiring employees with disabilities to participate in physically demanding training experiences.

Team training coordinates the performance of individuals who work together to achieve a common goal. An organization may benefit from providing such training to groups when group members must share information and group performance depends on the performance of the individual group members. Success depends on individuals coordinating their activities to make decisions, perhaps in dangerous work situations performed in crews or teams; for example, at a nuclear generating station or in the military. Ways to conduct team training include cross-training and coordination training.[48] In **cross-training**, team members understand and practise each other's skills so they are prepared to step in and take another member's place.

cross-training Team training in which team members understand and practise each other's skills so that they are prepared to step in and take another member's place.

For example, Toronto Hydro cross-trains supervisors so they can work across specializations. Toronto Hydro's manager of organizational development and performance says, "This enhances their skills. It's a great retention strategy; it gives them more variety and makes their job more meaningful."[49]

Coordination training trains the team in how to share information and decisions to obtain the best team performance. This type of training is especially important for teams including commercial aviation and surgical teams. Both of these kinds of teams must monitor different aspects of equipment and the environment while sharing information to make the most effective decisions regarding patient care or aircraft safety and performance.

coordination training Team training that teaches the team how to share information and make decisions to obtain the best team performance.

Training may also target the skills needed by the teams' leaders. **Team leader training** refers to

team leader training Training in the skills necessary for effectively leading the organization's teams.

© David Pu'u/Corbis

One of the most important features of organizations today is teamwork. Experiential programs, including team-building exercises like wall climbing and rafting, help build trust and cooperation among employees.

training people in the skills necessary for team leadership. For example, the training may be aimed at helping team leaders learn to resolve conflicts or coordinate activities.

action learning
Training in which teams get an actual problem, work on solving it, commit to an action plan, and are accountable for carrying it out.

In **action learning**, teams or work groups get an actual problem, work on solving it, commit to an action plan, and are accountable for carrying out the plan. Ideally, the project is one for which the efforts and results will be visible not only to participants but also to others in the organization. The visibility and impact of the task are intended to make participation exciting, relevant, and engaging. To heighten the learning, organizations can get their best leaders involved as mentors and coaches to the participants. The effectiveness of action learning has not been formally evaluated. This type of training seems to result in a great deal of learning, however; and employees are able to apply what they learn, because it involves actual problems the organization is facing. The group approach also helps teams identify behaviours that interfere with problem solving.

Implementing and Evaluating the Training Program

Learning can permanently change behaviour. For employees to acquire knowledge and skills in the training program and apply what they have learned in their jobs, the training program must be implemented in a way that applies what we know about how people learn.

Principles of Learning

Researchers have identified a number of ways employees learn best.[50] Table 6.3 summarizes ways training can best encourage learning. In general, effective training communicates learning objectives clearly, presents information in distinctive and memorable ways, and helps learners link the subject matter to their jobs.

Employees are most likely to learn when training is linked to their current job experiences and tasks.[51] There are a number of ways to make this link. Training sessions should present material using familiar concepts, terms, and examples. As far as possible, the training context—such as the physical setting or the images presented on a computer—should mirror the work environment. Along with physical elements, the context should include emotional elements, for example, by providing interactions that require authenticity including emotional realism.

To fully understand and remember the content of the training, employees need a chance to demonstrate and practise what they have learned. Actively involving the learners, practising repeatedly, and completing tasks within a time that is appropriate in light of the learning objectives is critical. Practice requires physically carrying out the desired behaviours, not just describing them. People tend to benefit most from practice that occurs over several sessions, rather than one long practice session.[52] Sessions should offer feedback so that learners understand whether or not they are succeeding. Effective feedback focuses on specific behaviours and is delivered as soon as possible after the learners practise or demonstrate what they have learned.[53]

Well-designed training helps people remember the content. Training programs need to break information into chunks that people can remember. Research suggests that people can attend to no more than four to five items at a time. If a concept or procedure involves more than five items, the training program should deliver information in shorter sessions or chunks.[54] Other ways to make information more memorable include presenting it with visual images and practising some tasks enough that they become automatic. Use of **microlearning**, "small chunks of learning, less than 15 minutes in duration," is expected to increase significantly in the effort to keep employees' attention in the context of competing distractions by providing only the most critical information.[55]

microlearning
Small chunks of learning, less than 15 minutes in duration.

Written materials should have an appropriate reading level. A simple way to assess readability—the difficulty level of written materials—is to look at the words being used and at the length of sentences. If training materials are too difficult to understand, several adjustments can help. The basic approach is to revise the material looking for ways to simplify it:

- Substitute simple, concrete words for unfamiliar or abstract words.
- Divide long sentences into two or more short sentences.

TABLE 6.3

Ways That Training Helps Employees Learn

Training Activity	Ways to Provide Training Activity
Communicate the learning objective(s)	Demonstrate the performance to be expected. Give examples of questions to be answered.
Use distinctive, attention-getting messages	Emphasize key points. Use pictures, not just words.
Limit the content of training	Group lengthy material into chunks. Provide a visual image of the course material. Provide opportunities to repeat and practise material.
Guide trainees as they learn	Use words as reminders about sequence of activities. Use words and pictures to relate concepts to one another and to their context. Prompt trainees to evaluate whether they understand and are using effective tactics to learn the material.
Elaborate on the subject	Present the material in different contexts and settings. Relate new ideas to previously learned concepts. Practise in a variety of contexts and settings.
Provide memory cues	Suggest memory aids. Use familiar sounds or rhymes as memory cues.
Transfer course content to the workplace	Design the learning environment so that it has elements in common with the workplace. Require learners to develop action plans that apply training content to their jobs. Use words that link the course to the workplace.
Provide feedback about performance	Tell trainees how accurately and quickly they are performing their new skill. Show how trainees have met the objectives of the training.

Sources: Adapted from R. M. Gagne, "Learning Processes and Instruction," *Training Research Journal 1* (1995/96), pp. 17–28; and Traci Sitzmann, "Self-Regulating Online Course Engagement," *T&D,* March 2010, Business & Company Resource Center, http://galenet.galegroup.com.

- Divide long paragraphs into two or more short paragraphs.
- Add lists (like this one) and illustrations to clarify the text.

Another approach is to substitute video, hands-on learning, or other nonwritten methods for some of the written material. A longer-term solution is to use assessments to identify employees to improve their reading levels and to provide that training first.

Choosing the Training Method

Given the large number of available training methods, the task of choosing may seem difficult. One way to choose a training method is to compare methods. The first step in choosing a method is to identify the type of learning outcome the training is to influence. These outcomes include verbal information, intellectual skills, cognitive strategies, attitudes, motor skills, or some combination. Training methods may influence one or several learning outcomes.

There is considerable overlap between learning outcomes across the training methods. Group team-building methods are unique because they focus on individual as well as team learning (e.g., improving group processes). Some of the group team-building methods (e.g., experiential learning, team training, action learning) would be appropriate if the goal is to improve the effectiveness of groups or teams. Second, comparing the presentation methods to the hands-on methods illustrates that most hands-on methods provide a better learning environment and transfer of training than do the presentation methods.

Online learning or blended learning can be an effective training method for geographically dispersed trainees. Online learning and other technology-driven training methods have higher development costs, but travel and housing cost savings will likely offset development costs over time. A blended learning approach can take advantage of the positive features of both face-to-face and technology-based instruction.

A final but important consideration is the training budget. If the budget for developing new training methods is limited, then structured on-the-job training is a good choice. It is a relatively inexpensive yet effective hands-on method. Hands-on methods that facilitate transfer of training, such as simulations, are feasible with a larger budget.

Transfer of Learning

Ultimately, the goal of implementation is **transfer of learning**, or on-the-job use of knowledge, skills, and behaviours learned in training. Transfer of learning requires that employees actually learn the content of the program. For employees to apply what they learned, certain conditions are important: social support, technical support, and self-management. According to a recent survey of Canadian organizations, employees are viewed to have primary accountability to apply learning to the job, followed by supervisor/manager accountability, and then instructor accountability.[56]

transfer of learning On-the-job use of knowledge, skills, and behaviours learned in training.

Social support, as we saw in the discussion of readiness for training, includes support from the organization and from learners' colleagues. The organization can formally provide peer support by establishing **communities of practice**—groups of employees who work together, learn from each other, and develop a common understanding of how to get work accomplished. For example, group members can share how they coped with challenges related to what they learned. Schlumberger, which provides oil field services, sets up online communities of practice, where geologists, physicists, managers, engineers, and other employees around the world can trade knowledge to solve problems.[57] Organizations can also assign experienced employees as mentors to learners, providing advice and support.

communities of practice Groups of employees who work together, learn from each other, and develop a common understanding of how to get work accomplished.

Transfer of learning is greater when organizations also provide technical resources that help people acquire and share information. Technical support may come from the electronic performance support system (EPSS) or learning management system (LMS) described earlier. Knowledge management systems including online and database tools also make it easy for employees to look up information they want to review or consult later.

Organizations are beginning to provide a strong combination of social and technical support for transfer of learning by setting up social media applications. When participants use social media to share with other employees what they are learning or discuss questions posted by instructors, it can reinforce lessons and build the whole group's motivation to learn.

As applications of artificial intelligence (AI) continue to evolve, **chatbots** (also referred to as *AI bots*), "automated, personalized conversations between software and human users" are transforming from personal productivity tools to workplace implementation including leveraging employee learning.[58] Chatbots that tap into organizational sources of information can be used to "provide conversational answers and serve as a quick reference guide."[59]

chatbot Automated, personalized conversation between software and human users.

For example, a chatbot can be designed to send engaging and friendly messages through preferred channels similar to those that friends or colleagues would use. In the orientation and onboarding discussion that follows in the next section, an illustration of a sample chatbot conversation with a new employee is provided as an illustrative example. When a learning program concludes with the participant creating a meaningful goal to apply the content to to the job, a chatbot can even become the learner's "accountability partner" by asking about progress and providing additional resources.[60]

Measuring Results of Training

After a training program ends, or at intervals during an ongoing training program, organizations should ensure that the training is meeting objectives. The stage to prepare for evaluating a training program is when the program is being developed. Along with designing course objectives and content, the planner should identify how to measure achievement of objectives. Depending on the objectives, the evaluation can use one or more of Kirkpatrick's evaluation levels:[61]

- Level 1: Learner reactions
- Level 2: Demonstration of learning
- Level 3: Behaviour change
- Level 4: Business results
- Level 5: Cost–benefit analysis

There has been a significant decline in conducting training evaluation. Although 89 percent of organizations conducted evaluations in 2002, in 2016/2017 only 45 percent of organizations reported that they conducted evaluations. However, organizations with strong learning cultures are more likely to conduction evaluations—60 percent conducting Level 1 evaluations; 46 percent conducting Level 2 evaluations; 37 percent conducting Level 3 evaluations; 16 percent conducting Level 4 evaluations; and 9 percent conducting Level 5 evaluations.[62]

The usual way to measure whether participants have acquired information is to administer tests on paper or electronically. Instructors or supervisors can observe

HR Oops!

Measurement of Training Effectiveness Earns a Bad Grade

In a recent survey of more than 200 chief learning officers, roughly three-quarters reported a need to improve their company's measurement of training effectiveness. Worse, the numbers have been heading in the wrong direction. In four years of asking this question, the researchers have seen the share of executives who are satisfied with measurement decline, while the dissatisfied share has been rising.

One source of dissatisfaction may be that the most common measurements used at respondents' companies are not directly tied to business success. Most companies measure the amount of training they do: number of courses, number of students, hours of training. A majority of companies also ask participants if they are satisfied with training they participated in. Less than half ask about employee performance or impact of the training on the company's business results.

In this context, training professionals can give their company an edge by linking training programs to business strategy. Ideally, whenever considering a training program, they would start by determining how the company's performance should change as a result of the employees learning new information or skills. They would establish training content to make that performance improvement possible, and they would measure whether the desired results indeed have followed the training program.

Questions

1. Suppose you are a training leader at a manufacturing company, and you have been asked to deliver a report about the value of your department's work. You report the number of training hours provided by your staff and the number of employees trained. How do you think the company's business managers would react to this report?
2. Give examples of a few measures that might be more relevant to these managers.

Sources: Cushing Anderson, "Bad Measurement Affects Training Impact," *Chief Learning Officer,* May 2014, pp. 44–46; James D. Kirkpatrick and Wendy K. Kirkpatrick, "Creating a Post-Training Evaluation Plan," *T+D,* June 2013, pp. 26–28; David Zahn, "No Excuse for Not Measuring Training's Impact," *Connecticut News,* June 10, 2013, http://blog.ctnews.com.

whether participants demonstrate the desired skills and behaviours. Changes in company performance have a variety of measures, many of which organizations keep track of for preparing performance appraisals, annual reports, and other routine documents, in order to demonstrate the highest measure of success: business results and cost–benefit analysis.

Evaluation of training should evaluate *effectiveness,* that is, *outcomes*—what (if anything) has changed as a result of the training. The relevant training outcomes are those related to the organization's goals for the training and its overall performance. Possible outcomes include the following:

- learner satisfaction with the training program (reaction);
- information such as facts, techniques, and procedures that learners can recall after the training (learning);
- changes in behaviour related to the content of the training; for example, concern for safety or support of diversity (behaviour change);
- improvements in individual, group, or company performance; for example, higher customer satisfaction, more sales, fewer defects (business results); and
- calculation to determine if the monetary benefits of the training program outweigh the costs (cost–benefit analysis). Note: *Return on investment (ROI)* refers to the monetary benefits of the investment compared to the amount invested, expressed as a percentage.

For any of these methods to measure effectiveness, the most accurate but most costly way to evaluate the training program is to assess performance, knowledge, or behaviours among all employees before the training, then to train only some of the employees. After the training is complete, the performance, knowledge, or behaviour are again assessed, and the trained group is compared to the untrained group. A simpler but less accurate way to assess the training is to conduct a *pre-test* and *post-test* on all trainees, comparing their performance, knowledge, or behaviours before and after the training. This form of measurement does not rule out the possibility that change resulted from something other than training (e.g., a change in the rewards system). The simplest approach is to use only a post-test. Of course, this type of measurement does not enable accurate comparisons, but it may be sufficient, depending on the cost and purpose of the training.

Training is a significant part of many organizations' budgets and many organizations are also concerned about measuring efficiency in addition to effectiveness. Examples of efficiency measures include:[63]

- number of employees trained by each training, learning, and development staff member;
- total number of employees trained annually; and
- time to implement a new learning initiative.

The purpose of evaluating training is to help with future decisions about the organization's training programs. Using the evaluation, the organization may identify a need to modify the training and gain information about the kinds of changes needed. The organization may decide to expand on successful areas of training and cut back on training that has not delivered significant benefits.

Unfortunately—as described in the HR Oops!—organizations sometimes fail to gain the insights that come from careful evaluation.

LO3 Applications of Training

Two categories of training that have become widespread are orientation and onboarding of new employees and training in how to effectively support workforce diversity and inclusion.

Orientation and Onboarding of New Employees

Many employees receive their first training during their first days on the job. This training is the organization's **orientation** program—its training designed to prepare employees to perform their jobs effectively, learn about the organization, and establish work relationships. Organizations provide orientation because employees need to become familiar with job tasks and learn the details of the organization's practices, policies, and procedures.

orientation Training designed to prepare employees to perform their jobs effectively, learn about their organization, and establish work relationships.

Increasingly, employers understand that success in today's work environment requires more than employees being able to complete an orientation program, follow rules, and navigate around the workplace. These employers have taken orientation to the next level with the process of **onboarding**, which aims to prepare and socialize new employees for full participation in the organization. Onboarding is a "process that focuses on transferring organizational, team, and role-specific knowledge" to new employees.[64]

onboarding Process that focuses on transferring organizational, team, and role-specific knowledge to new employees.

In so doing, onboarding also helps new employees adjust to both the social and the performance aspects of their jobs so they can quickly become productive contributors to the organization.[65] As Figure 6.4 shows, a comprehensive onboarding process prepares employees in four areas: complying with policies and rules, clarifying job requirements, understanding the organization's culture, and connecting with co-workers. To achieve these objectives, onboarding activities address social as well as task-related aspects of work. Onboarding is an ongoing process with follow-up to ensure the new employees are making a successful transition. Onboarding processes may combine various training methods such as printed and audiovisual materials, classroom instruction, on-the-job training, e-learning, and even chatbots as discussed earlier in the chapter. The following dialogue is a sample of a

FIGURE 6.4

Goals for a Four-Stage Onboarding Process

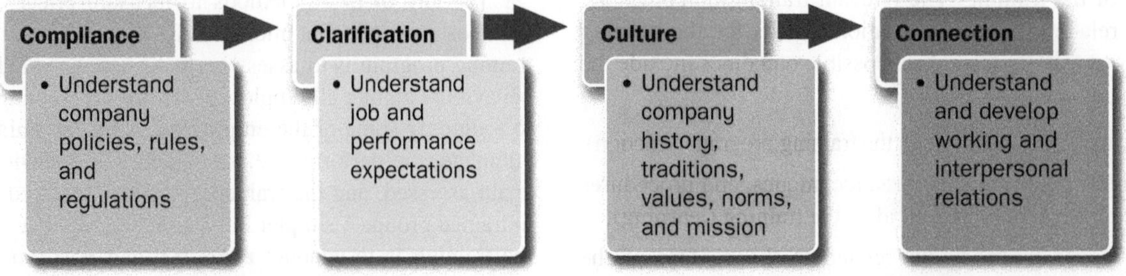

Sources: Based on Tayla N. Bauer, *Onboarding New Employees: Maximizing Success, Effective Practice Guidelines* (Alexandria, VA: SHRM Foundation, 2010); G. Chao, A. O'Leary-Kelly, S. Wolf, H. Klein, and P. Gardner, "Organizational Socialization: Its Content and Consequences," *Journal of Applied Psychology* 79 (1994): 730–743.

chatbot-initiated conversation with a new employee near the conclusion of their first week on the job:[66]

> ***Chatbot:*** *"Hi Ragbavi, I just wanted to check in on your first week! Were you able to complete your onboarding paperwork?"*
>
> ***Raghavi:*** *"I did. What else do I need to get done before my first month is up?"*
>
> ***Chatbot:*** *"Nice! Way to take the initiative. Before your first month is over, you also need to finish your first two workplace safety training modules."*

Everyone is likely to vividly readily recall their onboarding experiences and John Deere strives to create highly positive and memorable moments for new employees:

- As soon as the job offer is accepted, the new hire immediately receives an email from a colleague at John Deere, who provides a personal welcome and a personal photo to be easily recognized when they meet at the entrance on the new hire's first day.
- Fast forward to Day 1—the new employee is greeted by the colleague and enters the building—observing a large greeting and welcome sign. The colleague takes the new hire to their office, making introductions along the way.
- The new employees logs into their computer and a message from the CEO is waiting, describing John Deere's vision and strategic goals.
- People drop by throughout the day to provide introductions and a warm welcome.
- The new employee's peers join them for lunch to create additional connections and a sense of belonging and welcome.[67]

Supporting Diversity and Inclusion

Diversity can be considered to be any dimension that differentiates one person from another.[68] Diversity is a reality in labour and customer markets and is a social expectation and value. **Inclusion** refers to creating an environment in which employees share a sense of belonging, mutual respect, and commitment from others so that they can perform their best work. Inclusion allows organizations to capitalize not only on the diversity of their employees but also with their customers, suppliers, and community partners.

> **inclusion** An environment in which employees share a sense of belonging, mutual respect, and commitment from others so that they can perform their best work.
>
> **diversity training** Learning efforts designed to change employee attitudes about diversity or to develop skills needed to work with a diverse workforce.

Diversity training refers to learning efforts designed to change employee attitudes about diversity or to develop skills needed to work with a diverse workforce. However, training alone is insufficient to capitalize on the strengths of a diverse workforce.[69] **Managing diversity and inclusion** involves creating an environment that enables all employees to contribute to organizational goals and experience personal growth. The company must develop employees who are comfortable embracing differences such as age, ethnicity, education, sexual orientation, religion, work style, race, and gender. However, it is increasingly recognized that these factors are only some of the most apparent differences between people. The next frontier of diversity relates to applying understanding of differences resulting from lived experiences and our neural makeup. For example, considering generational diversity and thought diversity in an organization's inclusivity efforts are likely to create conditions where innovation and creativity thrive.[70]

> **managing diversity and inclusion** Creating an environment that allows all employees to contribute to organizational goals and experience personal growth.

Research shows that diversity training can impact cognitive (acquiring knowledge), affective (attitudes), and behavioural outcomes.[71] For example, the Blanket Exercise discussed in the chapter opening is a learning experience that provides RCMP cadets with historical knowledge while building empathy and understanding to strengthen relationships with Indigenous peoples. Diversity training is most effective when it is part of a larger effort to manage diversity and inclusion rather than a standalone program. This means that a company will see the success of its diversity efforts only if it makes a long-term commitment to an inclusive workplace culture.

LO4 Approaches to Employee Development

The definition of employee development provided near the beginning of this chapter indicates that it is future oriented. Development implies learning that is not necessarily related to the employee's current job.[72] Instead, it prepares employees for other positions in the organization and increases their ability to move into jobs that may not yet exist.[73] Development also may help employees prepare for changes in responsibilities and requirements in their current jobs, such as changes resulting from new technology, work designs, or customers.

Development for Careers

The concept of a career has changed in recent years. In the traditional view, a career consists of a sequence of positions within an occupation or organization.[74] For example, an engineer might start as a staff engineer, then with greater experience earn promotions to the positions of advisory engineer, senior engineer, and vice-president of engineering. In these examples, the career resembles a set of stairs from the entry to a profession or organization to the senior levels.

Recently, however, changes such as downsizing and restructuring have become the norm, so the concept of a career has become more fluid. Today's employees are more likely to have a **protean career**, one that frequently changes based on changes in the person's interests, abilities, and values and in the work environment. For example, an engineer might decide to take a sabbatical from her position to become a manager with Engineers without Borders, so she can develop managerial skills and decide whether she likes being a manager. As in this example, employees in protean careers take responsibility for managing their careers. This concept is consistent with the current *psychological contract* described in Chapter 1. Employees look for organizations to provide not job security and a career ladder to climb but, instead, development opportunities and flexible work arrangements.

protean career
A career that frequently changes based on changes in the person's interests, abilities, and values and in the work environment.

To remain marketable, employees must continually develop new skills. Beyond knowing job requirements, employees need to understand the business in which they are working and be able to cultivate valuable relationships with co-workers, managers, suppliers, and customers. They also need to follow trends in their field and industry, so they can apply technology and knowledge that will match emerging priorities and needs. Learning such skills requires useful job experiences as well as effective training programs. More employees will follow a spiral career path in which they cross the boundaries between specialties and organizations. As organizations provide for employee development (and as employees take control of their own careers), they will need to (1) determine their interests, skills, and areas of needed development, and (2) seek development experiences involving jobs, relationships, and formal courses. As discussed later in the chapter, organizations can meet these needs through a system for *career management* or *development planning*. Career management helps employees select development activities that prepare them to meet their career goals. It helps employers select development activities in line with their human resource needs.

The many approaches to employee development fall into four broad categories: formal education, assessment, job experiences, and interpersonal relationships.[75]

Figure 6.5 summarizes these four methods. Many organizations combine these approaches.

FIGURE 6.5

Four Approaches to Employee Development

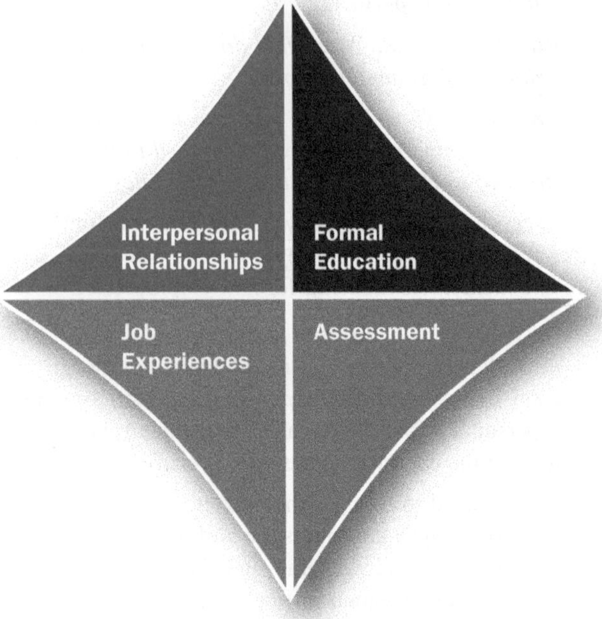

Formal Education

Organizations may support employee development through a variety of formal educational programs, either at the workplace or off-site. These may include workshops designed specifically for the organization's employees, short courses offered by consultants, colleges, or universities, and MBA and Executive MBA programs. These programs may involve methods including lectures by business experts, business games and simulations, and experiential programs.

Many companies have centralized talent development facilities that offer in-house training. Universities including Queen's University, the University of Western Ontario, the University of Alberta, and UBC as well as colleges such as George Brown College, Humber College, Conestoga College, Durham College, and Seneca College, offer leadership and professional development programs to organizations. A growing number of companies and educational institutions are also using distance learning and other e-learning options to reach their audiences. Another trend in executive education is for employers and the education provider to create offerings with content designed specifically for the organization.

Assessment

Another way to provide for employee development is **assessment**—collecting information and providing feedback to employees about their behaviour, communication style, or skills.[76] Information for assessment may come from the employees, their peers, managers, and customers. The most frequent uses of assessment are to identify employees with leadership potential to measure current

assessment
Collecting information and providing feedback to employees about their behaviour, communication style, or skills.

employees' strengths and areas for development. Organizations also use assessment to identify leaders with potential to move into higher-level executive positions. Organizations that assign work to teams may use assessment to identify the strengths and weaknesses of individual team members and the effects of the team members' decision-making and communication styles on the team's performance.

For assessment to support development, the information must be shared with the employee being assessed. Along with that assessment information, the employee needs suggestions for enhancing current skills and addressing any skill or behavioural gaps. The suggestions might be to participate in training courses or develop skills through new job experiences. Based on the assessment information and available opportunities, employees should develop action plans to guide their development efforts.

It is increasingly recognized that excellent technical skills are not enough for individuals or organizations to be successful. "Strong people skills are equally important to attracting clients, building lasting relationships with both clients and colleagues, and expanding business."[77] As a result, organizations vary in the methods and sources of information they use in developmental assessment. Organizations with sophisticated development systems may use psychological tests to measure employees' skills, personality types, and communication styles. They may collect self, peer, and manager ratings of employees' behaviour and style of working with others. The tools used for these assessment methods may include the *Myers-Briggs Type Indicator (MBTI),* a popular psychological inventory, assessment centres, and 360-degree feedback. In addition, assessment of emotional intelligence (EQ) increases employees' self-awareness and facilitates their development with respect to interpersonal skills, adaptability, and handling of stress.[78] Applying this kind of information about employees' preferences or tendencies helps organizations understand the communication, motivation, teamwork, work styles, and leadership of the people in their groups.

Myers-Briggs Type Indicator

Myers-Briggs Type Indicator (MBTI) Psychological test that identifies individuals' preferences for source of energy, means of information gathering, way of decision making, and lifestyle, providing information for team building and leadership development.

The most popular psychological inventory for employee development is the **Myers-Briggs Type Indicator (MBTI)**. This assessment identifies individuals' preferences for source of energy, means of information gathering, way of decision making, and lifestyle. The assessment consists of more than 100 questions about how the person feels or prefers to behave in different situations (such as "Are you usually a good 'mixer' or rather quiet and reserved?"). The assessment describes these individuals' preferences in the four areas:

1. The *energy* dimension indicates where individuals gain interpersonal strength and vitality, measured as their degree of introversion or extroversion. Extroverted types (E) gain energy through interpersonal relationships. Introverted types (I) gain energy by focusing on inner thoughts and feelings.
2. The *information-gathering* dimension relates to the preparations individuals make before making decisions. Individuals with a Sensing (S) preference tend to gather the facts and details to prepare for a decision. Intuitive types (N) tend to focus less on the facts and more on possibilities and relationships among them.
3. In *decision making,* individuals differ in the amount of consideration they give to their own and others' values and feelings, as opposed to the hard facts of a situation. Individuals with a Thinking (T) preference try always to be objective in making decisions. Individuals with a Feeling (F) preference tend to evaluate the impact of the alternatives on others, as well as their own feelings; they are more subjective.
4. The *lifestyle* dimension describes an individual's tendency to be either flexible or structured. Individuals with a Judging (J) preference focus on goals, establish deadlines, and prefer to be conclusive. Individuals with a Perceiving (P) preference enjoy surprises, are comfortable with changing a decision, and dislike deadlines.

The alternatives for each of the four dichotomies result in 16 possible combinations. Applying this kind of information about employees' preferences or tendencies helps organizations understand the communication, motivation, teamwork, work styles, and leadership of the people in their groups. For example, salespeople or executives who want to communicate better can apply what they learn about their own personality styles and the way other people perceive them. For team development, the MBTI can help teams match team members with assignments based on their preferences and thus improve problem solving.[79]

Research on the validity, reliability, and effectiveness of the MBTI is inconclusive.[80] People who take the MBTI find it a positive experience and say it helps them change their behaviour. However, MBTI scores are not necessarily stable over time. Studies in which the MBTI was administered at two different times found that as few as one-quarter of those who took the assessment were classified as exactly the same type the second time. Still, the MBTI is a valuable tool for understanding communication styles and the ways people prefer to interact with others. It is not appropriate for measuring job performance or as the only means of evaluating promotion potential.

Assessment Centres

In addition to their use as a type of employment test to screen candidates, as discussed in Chapter 5, assessment centres may engage multiple evaluators (assessors) to evaluate current employees' performance on a number of exercises.[81] Usually an off-site location such as a conference centre is used, and 6 to 12 employees participate at one time. The primary use of assessment centres for development is to identify whether employees have the personality characteristics, administrative skills, and interpersonal skills needed for managerial jobs. Organizations also use assessment centres to determine whether employees have the skills needed for working in teams.

The types of exercises used in assessment centres include leaderless group discussions, interviews, in-baskets, and role-plays.[82] In a **leaderless group discussion**, a team of five to seven employees is assigned a problem and must work together to solve it within a certain time period. The problem may involve buying and selling supplies, nominating an employee for an award, or assembling a product. Interview questions typically cover each employee's work and personal experiences, skill strengths and weaknesses, and career plans. In-basket exercises, discussed as a selection method in Chapter 5, simulate the requirements of a manager's job, and interest and aptitude tests may be used to evaluate an employee's vocabulary, general mental ability, and reasoning skills. Personality tests may be used to assess employees' tolerance for uncertainty, and other traits related to success as a manager or team member.

leaderless group discussion An assessment centre exercise in which a team of five to seven employees is assigned a problem and must work together to solve it within a certain time period.

As we mentioned in Chapter 5, research suggests that assessment centre ratings are valid for predicting performance, salary level, and career advancement.[83] Assessment centres may also be useful for development because of the feedback that participants receive about their attitudes and skill strengths.[84]

360-Degree Feedback

As we will discuss in more detail in Chapter 7, a recent trend in performance appraisals is *360-degree feedback*—performance measurement by the employee's supervisor, peers, direct reports, and customers. Often the feedback involves rating the individual in terms of skills, competencies, and work-related behaviours. For development purposes, the rater identifies an area of behaviour as a strength of that employee or an area requiring further development. The results presented to the employee show how they were rated on each item and how self-evaluations differ from other raters' evaluations. The individual reviews the results, seeks clarification from the raters, and sets specific development goals based on the strengths and areas of development identified.[85]

There are several benefits of 360-degree feedback. Organizations collect multiple perspectives of performance, allowing employees to compare their own personal evaluations with the views of others. This method also establishes formal communications about behaviours and skill ratings between employees and their internal and external customers. Several studies have shown that performance improves and behaviour changes as a result of participating in upward feedback and 360-degree feedback systems.[86] The organization can make it more likely that 360-degree feedback will yield benefits by having the results delivered by a trained person and to hold the employees accountable in follow-up meetings with their manager or coach.[87]

Potential limitations of 360-degree feedback include the significant amount of time for raters to complete the evaluations. If raters, especially peers or direct reports, provide negative feedback, some managers might try to identify and punish them. A facilitator is needed to help interpret results. Finally, simply delivering ratings to a manager does not provide ways to act on the feedback (for example, development planning, meeting with raters, or taking courses). As noted earlier, any form of assessment should be accompanied by suggestions for improvement and development of an action plan.

One way to develop employees is to begin with an assessment, which may consist of assigning an activity to a team and seeing who brings what skills and strengths to the team. How can this assessment help employees?

Job Experiences

job experiences
The combination of relationships, problems, demands, tasks, and other features of an employee's job.

Most employee development occurs through **job experiences**[88] the combination of relationships, problems, demands, tasks, and other features of an employee's job. Using job experiences for employee development assumes that development is most likely to occur when the employee's skills and experiences do not entirely match the skills required for the employee's current job. To succeed, employees must stretch their skills. In other words, they must learn new skills, apply their skills and knowledge in new ways, and master new experiences.[89]

The usefulness of job experiences for employee development varies depending on whether the employee views the experiences as positive or negative sources of stress. When employees view job experiences as positive stressors, the experiences challenge them and stimulate learning. When they view job experiences as negative stressors, employees may suffer from high levels of harmful stress. Of the job demands studied, managers were most likely to experience negative stress from creating change and overcoming obstacles (adverse business conditions, lack of management support, lack of personal support, or a difficult boss). Research suggests that all job demands except obstacles are related to learning.[90] Organizations should offer job experiences that are most likely to increase learning, and they should consider the consequences of situations that involve negative stress.

Various job assignments can provide for employee development. The organization may enlarge the employee's current job or move the employee to different jobs. Lateral moves include job rotation, transfer, or temporary assignment to another organization. The organization may also use downward moves or promotions as a source of job experience. Figure 6.6 summarizes these alternatives.

Job Enlargement

As Chapter 3 discussed in the context of job design, *job enlargement* involves adding challenges or new responsibilities to employees' current jobs. Examples include completing a special project, switching roles within a work team, or researching new ways to serve customers. An accountant might join a task force developing new career paths for professional employees. The work on the project could give the accountant a leadership role through which he or she learns about the company's career development system while also practising leadership skills to help the

FIGURE 6.6

How Job Experiences Are Used for Employee Development

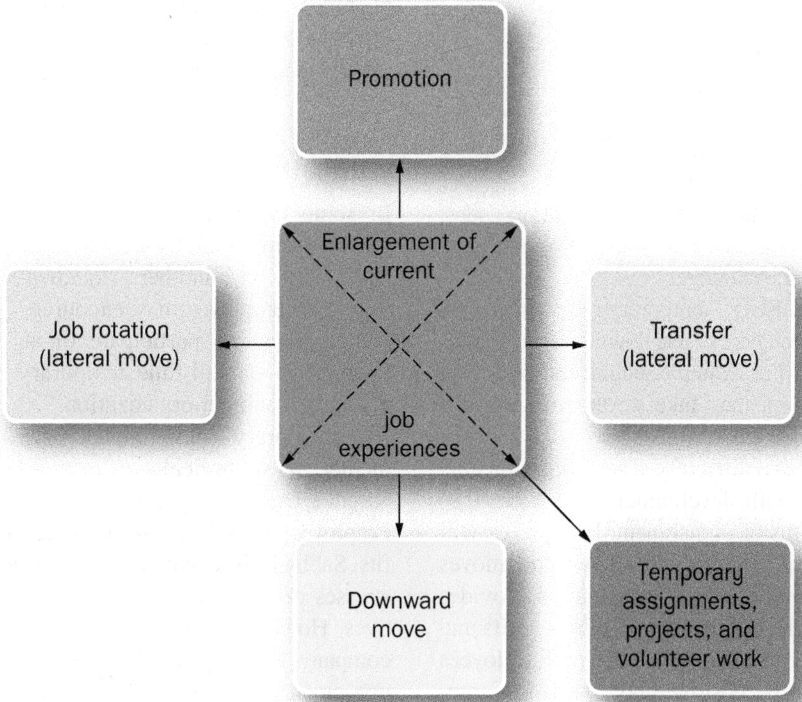

task force reach its goals. In this way, job enlargement not only makes a job more interesting but also creates an opportunity for employees to develop new skills.

Job Rotation

Another job design technique that can be applied to employee development is *job rotation,* moving employees through a series of job assignments in one or more functional areas. At Purdy's Chocolates in British Columbia, employees are provided development opportunities. Plant workers are given the chance to run a shift to see if they have the potential to replace a lead hand or become a warehouse manager in the future.[91]

Job rotation helps employees gain an appreciation for the company's goals, increases their understanding of different company functions, develops a network of contacts, and improves problem-solving and decision-making skills.[92] However, the rotation of employees through a department may hurt productivity and increase the workload of those who remain after employees are rotated out.

© Radius Images/Alamy RF

Working outside one's home country is the most important job experience that can develop an employee for a career in the global economy.

Transfers, Promotions, and Downward Moves

transfer Assignment of an employee to a position in a different area of the company, usually in a lateral move.

Most companies use upward, downward, and lateral moves as an option for employee development. In a **transfer**, the organization assigns an employee to a position in a different area of the company. Transfers do not necessarily increase job responsibilities or compensation. They are usually lateral moves; that is, moves to a job with a similar level of responsibility. They may involve relocation to another department, location, or even to another country.

downward move Assignment of an employee to a position with less responsibility and authority.

A **downward move** occurs when an employee is given less responsibility and authority. The organization may demote an employee because of poor performance or move the employee to a lower-level position in another function so that the employee can develop different skills. The temporary cross-functional move is the most common way to use downward moves for employee development. For example, engineers who want to move into management may take a role such as shift supervisor to develop their leadership skills.

Many employees have difficulty associating transfers and downward moves with development; these changes may feel more like forms of punishment. Employees will be more likely to accept transfers and downward moves as development opportunities if the organization provides information about the change and its possible benefits and involves the employee in planning the change. Employees are also more likely to be positive about such a recommendation if the organization provides clear performance objectives and frequent feedback.

promotion Assignment of an employee to a position with greater challenges, more responsibility, and more authority than in the previous job, usually accompanied by a pay increase.

A **promotion** involves moving an employee into a position with greater challenges, more responsibility, and more authority than in the previous job. Usually promotions include pay increases. Because promotions improve the person's pay, status, and feelings of accomplishment, employees are more willing to accept promotions than lateral or downward moves.

Temporary Assignments with Other Organizations

externship Employee development through a full-time temporary position at another organization.

sabbatical A leave of absence from an organization to renew or develop skills.

In some cases, an employer may benefit from the skills an employee can learn at another organization. The employer may encourage the employee to participate in an **externship**—a full-time temporary position at another organization.

Temporary assignments can include a **sabbatical**—a leave of absence from an organization to renew or develop skills. Employees on sabbatical often receive full pay and benefits. Sabbaticals let employees get away from the day-to-day stresses of their jobs and acquire new skills and perspectives. How employees spend their sabbaticals varies from company to company. Some employees may work for a non-profit agency, others may study at a college or university, or travel to a developing economy and provide their skills to an initiative or project.

Interpersonal Relationships

Employees can also develop skills and increase their knowledge about the organization and its customers by interacting with a more experienced organization member. Increasingly, these interactions are also taking place online with social media tools (e.g., LinkedIn offers discussion groups as well as a multitude of groups to follow).

Two types of relationships used for employee development are *mentoring* and *coaching*.

Mentors

A **mentor** is an experienced, productive senior employee who helps develop a less experienced employee, called the *protégé* or *mentee.* Most mentoring relationships develop informally as a result of interests or values shared by the mentor and protégé. According to research, the employees most likely to seek and attract a mentor have certain personality characteristics: emotional stability, ability to adapt their behaviour to the situation, and high needs for power and achievement.[93] Mentoring relationships also can develop as part of the organization's planned effort to bring together successful senior employees with less experienced employees.

mentor An experienced, productive senior employee who helps develop a less experienced employee (a protégé or mentee).

One major advantage of formal mentoring programs is that they ensure access to mentors for all employees, regardless of gender or other background. A mentoring program also can ensure that high-potential employees are matched with experienced mentors in key areas—and that mentors are hearing the challenges facing employees who have less authority, work directly with customers, or hold positions in other parts of the organization.[94] However, in an artificially created relationship, mentors may have difficulty providing counselling and coaching.[95] One practical way employees can address this shortcoming is to look for more than one mentor, including informal relationships with interested people outside the organization. Employees also should accept the limits of mentoring relationships. Mentoring is not, for example, a substitute for other necessary support: a mentor might offer tips for navigating a business presentation, whereas a counsellor is a better choice for someone who needs help with persistent anxiety.[96]

Mentoring programs tend to be most successful when they are voluntary and participants understand the details of the program. Rewarding managers for employee development is also important because it signals that mentoring and other development activities are worthwhile. In addition, the organization should carefully select mentors based on their interpersonal and technical skills, train them for the role, and evaluate whether the program has met its objectives.[97]

Mentors and protégés (mentees) can both benefit from a mentoring relationship. Table 6.4 summarizes the advantages of mentoring programs to both protégés (mentees) and mentors. Protégés (mentees) receive career support, including coaching, protection, sponsorship, challenging assignments, and visibility among the organization's managers. They also receive benefits of a positive relationship—a friend and role model who accepts them, has a positive opinion toward them, and gives them a chance to talk about their worries. Employees with mentors are also more likely to be promoted, earn higher salaries, and have more influence within their organization.[98] Acting as a mentor gives managers a chance to develop their interpersonal skills and increase their feelings that they are contributing something important to the organization. Working with a technically trained protégé on matters such as new research in the field

TABLE 6.4

Advantages of Mentoring Programs

For Protégés/Mentees	For Mentors
Breaks down "silos" throughout the organization	Maintains a pulse on the organization by keeping regular contact and communication with employees
Increases communication	Enhances interpersonal and leadership competencies
Supports continuous learning throughout all levels of the organization	
Enhances career development and growth	
Improves employee satisfaction and engagement	
Fosters a culture where employees support and help one another	

Source: Adapted from Conference Board of Canada, "Mentoring—Low Cost, Big Benefits," www.conferenceboard.ca/humanresource/mentoring-inside.htm, retrieved February 24, 2005.

may also increase the mentor's technical knowledge. Recent research sponsored by MentorcliQ, has found that providing training to mentors is associated with high effectiveness. "Organizations that train mentors before or during the mentoring program were significantly more likely than those that do not train mentors to report that they were highly effective at meeting learning goals."[99]

Coaching

coach A peer or manager who works with an employee to provide a source of motivation, help him or her develop skills, and provide reinforcement and feedback.

A **coach** is a peer or manager who works with an employee to provide a source of motivation, help him or her develop skills, and provide reinforcement and feedback. Coaches may play one or more of three roles:[100]

1. Working one-on-one with an employee, as when giving feedback.
2. Helping employees learn for themselves—for example, helping them find experts and teaching them to obtain feedback from others.
3. Providing resources such as mentors, courses, or job experiences.

William Gray, president of Mentoring Solutions Inc. and former UBC professor, draws a distinction between mentoring and coaching. Gray describes mentoring as developing the "whole person" whereas coaching involves developing a specific skill set.[101] Coaching cultures can benefit the entire organization.[102]

Coaches may be internal to the organization, external resources, or a combination. Internal coaches allow the organization to "start small" and may allow more people to access coaching resources. Use of internal coaching resources may also enhance affordability and availability, and provide the context for the use of specific workplace examples. However, external coaches, because they are removed from the client's organization, may be less likely to hold any biases as they support their clients and may offer more experience and proficiency, as well as confidentiality, particularly if performance issues have prompted the coaching relationship.[103] Artificial intelligence-driven coaching apps developed by companies including VoiceVibes, Butterfly.ai, and Orai, can be useful supplements to human coaches and may be particularly appealing to Millennials seeking frequent and targeted feedback feedback. For example, Orai has developed a public speaking app that not only listens and counts the speaker's pauses and use of filler words but also tracks tone, speed, and energy level. Then it provides a report with specific data on the various metrics along with focused development advice.[104]

Researchers from the Human Capital Institute define a *strong coaching culture* as meeting at least five of the following criteria:[105]

- employees value coaching;
- senior leaders value coaching;
- the organization has a dedicated budget for coaching;
- coaching is available to all employees;
- accredited coaching training is provided to managers, leaders, or internal coaches;
- internal coaches, external coaches, and leaders or managers using coaching skills are all present in the organization.

Often, managers are eager to coach their employees but don't really know how. Table 6.5 provides suggestions on how to coach employees to support development.

TABLE 6.5

Coaching Employees

- **Distinguish coaching from delivering performance feedback.** Coaching invites personal reflection; feedback provides information. Feedback often sounds like this: "Here's what went wrong and what you should do next time." A coach asks questions: "How do you think that went? What would you want to do differently? What resources do you need in order to make those changes?"
- **Ask questions with a purpose.** Plan a broad set of questions that support employee development, and tailor them to the person and situation. For example, cover four development-related topics:
  - *Employee's goal* (What is your next career goal?);
  - *Reality* (Where are you now, in terms of your strengths and areas needing improvement or change?);
  - *Options* (What changes would enable you to take the next step?)
  - *Way forward* (What step will you take to start making the needed changes?)
- **Ensure that employees understand that receiving coaching entails responsibilities.** Employees receiving coaching need to reflect on questions, come up with ideas, and try the ideas. The coach's role is not to solve problems for the employee, but the coach can help the employee develop better problem-solving skills.

Sources: Monique Valcour, "People Won't Grow If You Think They Can't Change," *Harvard Business Review,* April 21, 2016, https://hbr.org; Rosanna Nadeau, "Managers Need to Coach," *New Hampshire Business Review,* December 25, 2015, http://www.nhbr.com; Renée Robertson, "Five Ways to Develop a Culture of Coaching," *Fast Company,* June 30, 2015, http://www.fastcompany.com.

LO5 Career Management Systems

Employee development is most likely to meet the organization's needs if it is part of a human resource system of career management. In practice, organizations' career management systems vary. Some rely heavily on informal relationships, while others are sophisticated programs. As shown in Figure 6.7, a basic career management system involves four steps: data gathering, feedback, goal setting, and action planning and follow-up. Ways to make this system more effective include gathering data in areas associated with success, keeping feedback confidential and specific, involving higher-level management in planning and follow-up, and crafting action plans that are realistic and targeted to building expertise needed for the person's career path.[106] Human resources professionals can also contribute to the system's success by ensuring it is linked to other HR practices such as performance management, training, and recruiting.

Data Gathering

In discussing the methods of employee development, we highlighted several assessment tools. Such tools may be applied to the first stage of career development. **Self-assessment** refers to the use of information by employees to determine their career interests, values, aptitudes, and behavioural tendencies.

self-assessment The use of information by employees to determine their career interests, values, aptitudes, behavioural tendencies, and development needs.

Self-assessment tools often include psychological tests such as the Myers-Briggs Type Inventory (described earlier in the chapter), the Strong-Campbell Interest Inventory, and the Self-Directed Search. The Strong-Campbell Inventory helps employees identify their occupational and job interests. The Self-Directed Search identifies employees' preferences for working in different kinds of environments—sales, counselling, and so on. Tests may help employees identify the relative value they place on work and leisure activities. Additional data may be collected by keeping a daily journal of work experience and reflecting on emerging themes and observations.[107]

Self-assessment can help an employee consider their current career status, future plans, and the fit between the career and current situation and resources. Some organizations provide counsellors to help employees in the self-assessment process and to interpret the results of psychological tests.

Feedback

In the next step of career management, **feedback**, employees receive information about their competencies and where these assets fit into the organization's plans. The employee's responsibility is to identify what skills they could realistically develop in light of the opportunities available. Opportunities might include promotions and transfers. Some organizations develop and communicate **career paths**—the identified

feedback Information employers give employees about their skills and knowledge and where these assets fit into the organization's plans.

career paths The identified pattern or progression of jobs or roles within an organization.

FIGURE 6.7

Steps in the Career Management Process

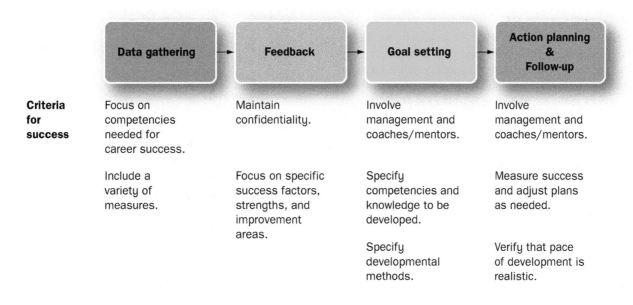

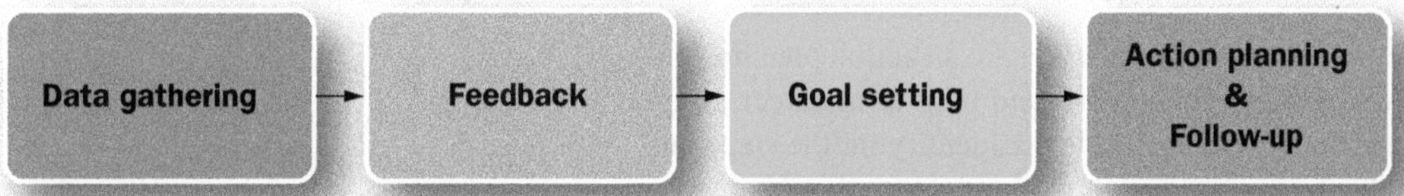

	Data gathering	Feedback	Goal setting	Action planning & Follow-up
Criteria for success	Focus on competencies needed for career success.	Maintain confidentiality.	Involve management and coaches/mentors.	Involve management and coaches/mentors.
	Include a variety of measures.	Focus on specific success factors, strengths, and improvement areas.	Specify competencies and knowledge to be developed.	Measure success and adjust plans as needed.
			Specify developmental methods.	Verify that pace of development is realistic.

pattern or progression of jobs or roles within an organization to provide clarity about how an employee may progress into more senior positions. Career paths may include a wide variety of jobs or may provide specific information related to cumulative responsibilities for a managerial, technical, or professional career. Career-path information can also enhance the discussion of opportunities between employees and their managers by providing consistent language related to how jobs and roles are defined in the organization.[108]

Goal Setting

On the basis of the information from the self-assessment and feedback, the employee sets short- and long-term career objectives. These goals usually involve one or more of the following categories:

- Desired roles, such as becoming a team leader within three years.
- Level of competency to apply; for example, to apply one's budgeting skills to improve the unit's cash flow.
- Work setting; for example, to move to corporate marketing within two years.
- Skill acquisition, such as learning how to use data and other evidence-based approaches to enhance client experience.

As in these examples, the goals should be specific, and they should include a date by which the goal is to be achieved. It is the employee's responsibility to identify the goal and the method of determining their progress toward each goal. Usually the employee discusses the goals with their manager. The organization's responsibilities are to ensure that the goal is specific, challenging, and achievable, and to help the employee reach the goal.

Action Planning and Follow-Up

In the final step, employees prepare an action plan for *how* they will achieve their short- and long-term career goals. The employee is responsible for identifying the steps and timetable to reach the goals. The employer should identify resources required, including learning needs, work experiences, and relationships. The employee and the manager should meet in the future to discuss progress toward career goals.

Action plans may involve any one or a combination of the development methods discussed earlier in the chapter—training, assessment, job experiences, or the help of a mentor or coach. The approach used depends on the particular developmental needs and career objectives. For example, suppose the program manager in an information systems department uses feedback from clients to determine that greater knowledge of project management software is needed. The manager plans to increase that knowledge by reading articles (formal education), meeting with software vendors, and contacting the vendors' customers to ask them about the software they have used (job experiences). The manager and his supervisor agree that six months will be the target date for achieving the higher level of knowledge through these activities.

The outcome of action planning often takes the form of a *development plan.* Figure 6.8 is an example of a development plan for a project manager. Development plans usually include descriptions of strengths and areas for development, career goals, and training, learning, and development activities for reaching each goal.

High-Potential Employees

As discussed in Chapter 4, *succession planning*—the process of identifying and tracking high-potential employees—is usually closely linked to a development program. A typical approach to development of high-potential employees is to have them complete an individual development program including education, executive mentoring and coaching, and rotation through job assignments. Job assignments are based on the successful career paths of the organizational leaders whom the high-potential employees are preparing to replace. High-potential employees may also receive special assignments, such as making presentations and serving on committees and task forces. The Thinking Ethically feature explores the advantages and pitfalls associated with telling employees they are "high-potential."

Research shows that an effective program for developing high-potential employees has three stages:[109]

1. **Selection of high-potential employees**—Organizations may select outstanding performers and employees who have completed elite academic programs, such as earning a master's degree in business administration. Organizations may also use the results of psychological tests such as assessment centres.
2. **Developmental experiences**—As employees participate in developmental experiences, the organization identifies those who succeed in the experiences. The organization looks for employees who continue to show qualities associated with success in senior roles, such as communication skills, leadership talent, and inclusivity.
3. **Active involvement with senior leadership**—High-potential employees become actively involved with senior leaders in the organization, providing them with

FIGURE 6.8

Development Plan

Name: **Title:** Project Manager **Immediate Manager:**

Competencies

Please identify your three greatest strengths and areas for development.

Strengths

- Strategic thinking and execution (confidence, command skills, action orientation).
- Results orientation (creating a motivating work environment, perseverance).
- Spirit for winning (building team spirit, customer focus, respect colleagues).

Areas for Development

- Written communications (ability to write clearly and succinctly).
- Concern for people (too much focus on successful completion of projects rather than developing relationships with individuals involved in the projects).

Career Goals

Please describe your overall career goals.

- *Long-term.* Accept positions of increased responsibility to a level of general manager (or beyond). The areas of specific interest include but are not limited to product and brand management, technology and development, strategic planning, and marketing.
- *Short-term.* Continue to improve my skills in marketing and brand management while utilizing my skills in product management, strategic planning, and global relations.

Next Assignments

Identify potential next assignments (including timing) that would help you develop toward your career goals.

- Manager or director level in planning, development, product, or brand management. Timing estimated to be Fall 2020.

Training, Learning, and Development Needs

List both training, learning, and development activities that will either help you develop in your current assignment or provide overall career development.

- Master's degree classes will allow me to practise and improve my written communications skills. The dynamics of my current position, teamwork, and reliance on other individuals allow me to practise patience and to focus on individual team members' needs along with the success of the project.

Employee ____________________ **Date** ________
Immediate Manager ____________________ **Date** ________
Mentor ____________________ **Date** ________

a greater understanding of the organization's culture. The development of high-potential employees may be a slow process. Reaching stage 3 may take several years. which may include education, mentoring, and coaching, as well as rotation through job assignments.

A good example is the effort at ADP, which provides software and services for payroll and other HR functions. Several years ago, ADP conducted a formal study of its spending on training and development and found that most of its spending was aimed at training to meet immediate needs. The company determined that it needed to invest more in preparing for the future, especially in the sales function. Now it operates a formal sales development program that is meeting the company's demand for leaders who can deliver superior sales.[110]

Thinking Ethically

Should Companies Tell Employees They Have High Potential?

Employee development programs aimed at meeting future leadership needs typically start by identifying high-potential employees and offering them an opportunity to participate in the program. In so doing, a company is setting apart certain employees for special treatment. What are the consequences of this practice?

For the employees identified as having high potential, the immediate impact of being called high potential is that they feel valued. They may increase their commitment to the company and want to stick around to contribute more. Their enthusiasm to build on their strengths may translate into fast development of skills in leadership, time management, and decision making. Furthermore, these employees are likely already contributing at a high level, and holding back the information might cause them to think they have a better future elsewhere. Nevertheless, despite these advantages, some managers worry about telling employees they have such high potential, on the grounds that these employees might take the label as permission to coast, feeling secure in their favoured status.

Other negatives involve the employees who are left out. When they see that the organization does not consider them to have high potential, they may feel devalued. They may give up on their own development or start looking for a job at a company that will value them more.

Organizations that want to continue leadership development programs can take some steps to minimize the downside of the "high-potential" label. With regard to the high-potential employees, organizations should emphasize that the designation is more than a signal of high status; it is a challenge to take on greater responsibility and contribute more. The label shouldn't come with any implied promises about promotions or special status. For the other employees, the company should provide other avenues for development, with the message that employees can increase their potential as they gain skills and experience. For all employees, it is beneficial to have clear, objective standards for how the company measures their potential.

Questions

1. Can a leadership development program for high-potential employees be fair and equitable? If so, how? If not, why not?
2. If the company has identified high-potential employees, should managers tell these employees that they have high potential? Why or why not?

Sources: CEB, "High-Potential Employees: Why You Should Tell Them They're HIPOs," corporate blog, September 16, 2015, https://cebglobal.com; Gail Dutton, "High Potentials: Tell Them or Not?," *Training,* July/August 2015, https://trainingmag.com; Claudia Hill and James Peters, "Tell or Don't Tell? Talking Talent with Your Employees," *Korn Ferry Institute,* January 2015, http://www.kornferryinstitute.com.

SUMMARY

LO1 Discuss how to link training, learning, and development to organizational needs and strategy.

Organizations pursue strategic goals for training, learning, and development that include enhancing employee and organizational performance and developing leaders. Organizations with strong learning cultures appear to have increased ability to achieve these strategic goals. Some organizations make significant investments in talent development including utilizing a comprehensive approach to instructional design.

LO2 Explain how to carry out the steps in a complete instructional design process.

The instructional design process begins with a needs assessment, then ensures readiness for training, plans a training program, implements the program, and evaluates the results based on effectiveness and efficiency.

LO3 **Describe methods for employee onboarding and supporting diversity and inclusion.**

Employee orientation and onboarding is designed to prepare new employees to perform their job effectively, learn about the organization, and establish work relationships. To achieve the benefits of diversity, learning initiatives may be used to support the provision of inclusive work environments where all employees are able to contribute to organizational goals and experience personal growth.

LO4 **Discuss the approaches organizations use for employee development.**

Employee development is a future-oriented approach that prepares for change. Organizations may use formal educational programs, assessments, job experiences, and interpersonal relationships including coaching and mentoring to prepare employees for changing requirements in their current jobs or for future roles and responsibilities.

LO5 **Explore the steps in the career management process including creating a development plan and consideration of high-potential employees.**

Career management is a process that includes data gathering; feedback; goal setting; and action planning and follow-up. Although employees have primary responsibility, the success of career management depends on manager support and connecting the system to other HR practices and processes. The outcome may include creating a development plan. High-potential employees are typically supported by development programs that include a combination of development approaches.

CRITICAL THINKING QUESTIONS

1. Is it important for an organization to have a strong learning culture? Why or why not?
2. "Melinda!" bellowed Toran to the company's HR specialist, "I've got a problem, and you've got to solve it. I can't get people in this plant to work together as a team. As if I don't have enough trouble with our competitors and our past-due accounts, now I have to put up with running a zoo. You're responsible for seeing that the staff gets along. I want a training proposal on my desk by Monday." Assume you are Melinda.
   a. Is training the solution to this problem? How can you determine the need for training?
   b. Summarize how you would conduct a needs assessment.
   c. How do Toran's comments suggest readiness (or lack of readiness) for learning?
3. Many organizations turn to e-learning as a less expensive alternative to instructor-led classroom training. What are some other advantages of substituting e-learning for instructor-led classroom training? What are some disadvantages? Would you prefer a blended form of delivery? Why or why not?
4. What can companies do to encourage informal learning?
5. What features of games may motivate learning?
6. Choose a job you are familiar with. Design a new employee onboarding program for that job. Explain how your program contributes to effective socialization, performance, and employee retention.
7. What is the difference between diversity and inclusion? Why do organizations provide diversity and inclusion training? What kinds of goals are most relevant?
8. What are the four broad categories of development methods? Why might it be beneficial to combine all of these methods into a formal development program?
9. Many people feel that mentoring relationships should occur naturally, in situations where organizational leaders choose to play that role. What are some advantages of setting up a formal mentoring program, rather than letting organizational leaders decide how and whom to help?
10. How is a coach different than a mentor? Do artificial intelligence "bots" have a useful role to play in coaching employees? Why or why not?
11. What are the manager's roles in a career management system? Which role do you think is most difficult for the typical manager? Why might managers want to be involved in career management?
12. Would you want to know that you had been identified as a "high-potential" employee? Why or why not?

EXPERIENCING HR—ASSESSING A LEARNING VIDEO

Go to eHow, YouTube, or another site recommended by your instructor. Use the site's search function to look up a lesson on how to do one of the following tasks:

- Conduct a job interview
- Dress business casual
- Give a presentation
- Cook chili
- Clean a laptop computer
- Handle an upset customer

View the presentation you selected, taking notes to help you recall its content and methods. Then write a one-page review of the presentation. Rate the presentation's content (was it relevant and understandable?) and methods (was it engaging and effective?). Also, note whether the presentation provided a means for assessing what was learned. Finally, suggest how the presentation could have been improved. What could make it more effective as part of an employer's training program?

CASE STUDY—EVIDENCE-BASED HRM

Talent Development Enables Diversity and Inclusion at Sodexo

Sodexo is the leading food and facilities management company in the world, employing 427,000 employees in 80 countries and serving 100 million customers daily. Sodexo has 10,000 employees in Canada—over 65 percent of employees are women, 33 percent are visible minorities, 5.5 percent are Indigenous, 3.2 percent have a disability, and 87 percent of Sodexo's Canadian management teams are gender balanced.

A policy of inclusion is not an option or a choice—it is a business necessity. Sodexo is committed to providing all employees "the best possible work–life experience regardless of age, gender, nationality, culture or personal characteristics" and positions diversity and inclusion as the cornerstone of culture and a fundamental component of overall growth strategy. Sodexo's culture of diversity and inclusion extends beyond its workforce and community partnerships, and into its supply chain. Sodexo Canada works with 200 small and medium-sized enterprises, 84 Indigenous suppliers, and 24 women-owned businesses.

Diversity and inclusion are core competencies at Sodexo. Diversity and inclusion are part of employees' training and managers' annual performance assessment. New employee orientation and onboarding emphasizes Sodexo's values and expectations regarding diversity and inclusion.

At Sodexo, diversity training is part of the managing diversity strategy. Top management is involved in and committed to managing diversity. The senior executives program includes ongoing classroom training that is reinforced with community involvement, sponsoring employee groups, and mentoring diverse employees. Executives are engaged in learning the business case for diversity and are personally held accountable for the company's diversity agenda. The one-day Spirit of Inclusion session, mandatory for all managers, focuses on building awareness and skills around diversity and inclusion. Sodexo's diversity training includes learning labs focused on skill building and diversity awareness. Examples of these learning labs include Generations in the Workplace, Disability Awareness Training, Cross-cultural Communications, and Improving Team Effectiveness through Inclusion. The company's learning and development team develops customized learning solutions for different functions and work teams. For example, a course related to selling to a diverse client base was developed and offered to the sales force, and a cross-cultural communication program was provided for recruiters.

To emphasize the importance of diversity for the company, at Sodexo each manager has a diversity scorecard that evaluates their success in recruitment, retention, promotion, and development of all employees. The scorecard includes both quantitative goals as well as evaluation of behaviours such as participating in training, mentoring, and doing community outreach. A proportion of a manager's pay bonus is determined by success in these areas.

Sodexo has found that its commitment to diversity and inclusion is positively affecting the business in several ways. Its mentoring program has led to increased productivity, engagement, and retention. There was an estimated return on investment of $19 for every dollar spent on the program. Sodexo has found that gender-balanced teams—those with 40–60 percent women in management—outperform non-balanced teams on measures of global engagement, brand awareness, client retention, and positive profit and growth.

Sodexo also has been awarded several new business contracts and retained clients because of its involvement in managing diversity. Sodexo has been recognized for its diversity and inclusion efforts, which helps attract talented employees by signalling that the company cares about the well-being of all of its employees. For example, Sodexo Canada continues to receive recognition for its efforts, earning recognition in 2018 by MediaCorp. as one of Canada's Best Diversity Employers—Sodexo Canada has received this distinction for five consecutive years. Sodexo is also a Gold Certified Progressive Aboriginal Relations (PAR) Company, and has been a Top Employer for Young People for six years running.

Questions

1. What training, learning, and development methods does Sodexo use, according to the information provided?
2. Suppose Sodexo Canada continues to grow and asks you to advise senior leadership on how to maintain its focus on providing employee training, learning, and development related to diversity and inclusion. Suggest two or three methods from the chapter, and explain why you recommend each.

Sources: "Fort McKay First Nation Named as Recipient of 2018 CCAB Award Celebrating Economic Development in Canada," March 14, 2018, www.newswire.ca; "Diversity and Inclusion: Our Priorities," https;//ca.sodexo.com; Sodexo Named Top Diversity Employer Five Years Running," March 2, 2018, www.newswire.ca; "Sodexo Among Canada's 2018 Top Employers for Young People," February 9, 2018, www.newswire.ca; "Corporate Responsibility," www.sodexousa.com; "Report Highlights Diversity and Inclusion as a Core Competency of Sodexo Business Growth Strategy," February 6, 2017, www.sodexousa.com; "2016 Global Diversity and Inclusion Report," www.sodexousa.com; M. Landel, "How We Did It...Sodexo's CEO on Smart Diversification," *Harvard Business Review,* March 5, 2015, pp. 41-44; R. Emelo, "Peer Collaboration Enhances Diversity and Inclusion, *T+D,* December 2014, pp. 48-52; R. Anand and M. Winters, "A Retrospective View of Corporate Diversity Training from 1964 to the Present," *Academy of Management Learning and Education* 7 (2008), pp. 556-572.

CASE STUDY—HRM SOCIAL

Just-in-Time Technology-driven Learning at Janssen Pharmaceutical

The Janssen Pharmaceutical Companies of Johnson & Johnson develop and sell drugs to treat and cure diseases such as cancer, Alzheimer's, and HIV. Salespeople need to learn about drugs and other products before they can sell them to doctors, pharmacies, and hospitals. The faster that salespeople are trained on new drugs, the sooner that patients can gain access to them. However, because they are located around the world and often on the road, salespeople don't have the time to learn in a classroom environment. To facilitate a culture of learning, Janssen relies on digital resources that enable employees to access information on products when and where they need it. For example, before the company introduced a new diabetes drug, it had to train 2,000 salespeople in less than two months. Using a virtual classroom, Janssen was able to provide training four days after the drug received government approval.

Other sales training has been delivered using mobile devices. This training includes video case studies and podcasts. Janssen also provides employees with a performance support tool, known as YouLearn, that allows them to acquire skills and knowledge on their own time. Janssen helps to ensure that technology-delivered learning is in sync with the employees and the company's learning needs through in-person coaching and development planning. Managers are required to have at least five development conversations with employees each year, and each employee completes an individual development plan.

Questions

1. How does Janssen's use of technology for training support a continuous learning strategy?
2. Why is it necessary for Janssen to provide several types of training, learning, and development approaches?

Source: F. Kalman, "Janssen Pharmaceuticals: Ahead of the Curve," *Chief Learning Officer,* June 2016, pp. 32–33; Janssen Pharmaceuticals, "About Us," www.janssen.com.

CHAPTER 7

Managing Employees' Performance

WHAT DO I NEED TO KNOW?

After reading this chapter, you should be able to:

LO1	Describe the relevance, purpose, and criteria associated with an effective performance management system.
LO2	Identify the activities involved in performance management.
LO3	Compare the major performance management methods and sources of information.
LO4	Explain how to minimize rating errors and effectively provide performance feedback.
LO5	Discuss some of the legal, ethical, and privacy issues that impact performance management.

Carlos Osorio/Toronto Star via Getty Images.

Rather than ratings, Deloitte uses "performance snapshots" to identify candidates who need particular kinds of responses, such as development opportunities or clarification of job responsibilities. Managers can review snapshots over time or for their team as a whole to interpret any patterns in the data.

Changing Performance Management at Deloitte

As a business consulting firm, Deloitte has been well aware of managers' complaints about performance management systems: they're too slow, they don't promote employee engagement, and the connection to business results is hard to find. Deloitte's HR leaders had to admit that those criticisms might apply to the firm's own performance management process. Objectives were set for each employee at the beginning of the year. Managers rated employee performance every time a project ended and then used the data to arrive at ratings for each employee at the end of the year. Finally, managers discussed the results in calibration meetings and then with employees. Employees liked the fairness of the approach, but the year-long timeline made the process hard to use for employee development. Furthermore, the managers were rating employees' skills, which are difficult to observe, so the ratings varied according to who was evaluating the employees.

The HR team set out to design an approach better suited to today's fast-paced business environment. They started by applying some of the firm's own research about the conditions most common on its highest-performing teams. Most notably, teams performed best when employees said they had a chance to use their strengths each day. Based on this, the HR team determined that it needed a system that would help its people use their strengths while also providing a source of reliable data about performance.

The HR team identified questions managers could answer reliably: four questions about their plans for the person—specifically, using a scale to rate how strongly they want to reward the employee; how much they want the person on their team in the future; whether the person is at risk for low performance; and whether the person is ready for promotion. Managers answer these questions at the end of each project or at least quarterly. The data yields a "performance snapshot" rather than a rating. Along with the process of creating performance snapshots each year, Deloitte's managers are expected to check in with each employee on their team frequently, say, every week or two. The check-ins are meant to be focused on the future—an opportunity to set goals and priorities, provide feedback about recent work, and address any needs for change.[1]

Introduction

Performance management is the process through which managers ensure that employees' activities and outputs contribute to the organization's goals. This process requires knowing what activities and outputs are desired, observing whether they occur, and providing feedback to help employees meet expectations. In the course of providing feedback, managers and employees may identify performance issues and establish ways to resolve those issues.

In this chapter we examine a variety of approaches to performance management. We begin by exploring the relevance and purpose of performance management, including the criteria for effective performance management, and how performance management is changing. Next, we describe the steps in the performance management process as well as the various sources of performance information, including the strengths and weaknesses of each. The next section explores the kinds of errors that commonly occur during the assessment of performance, as well as ways to reduce those errors. Then we describe ways of giving performance feedback effectively and intervening when performance must improve. Finally, we discuss legal, ethical, and privacy issues affecting performance management.

LO1 Relevance of Performance Management to Organizational Strategy and Performance

"Performance management practices have recently come under scrutiny regarding their relevance for organizational effectiveness and other outcomes."[2]

- 81 percent of Canadian organizations report their performance management system or process has been changed within the last three years or is under consideration for change.[3]
- The majority of Canadian organizations are "questioning the effectiveness of their performance management process."[4]
- Only 41 percent of Canadian organizations say their performance management system is "effective" or "very effective."[5] See Figure 7.1.
- In a survey of 164 chief financial officers (CFOs), performance management emerged as a top priority; 73 percent said that, within their first 100 days on the job, "they were expected to come up with a new plan for performance management."[6]

To contribute to high performance and be strategically relevant, performance management is necessarily a "dynamic business process that enables performance and drives organizational and individual success.[7] Deloitte's rationale for changing its approach to performance management was described in the chapter opener. Patagonia, the outdoor apparel and provisions company, also recently introduced "a more agile and adaptive performance approach," in support of its culture. Patagonia replaced its year-end evaluation-focused approach to a more continuous one that includes "quarterly stretch goals, quarterly check-in conversations, and continuous crowd-sourced feedback."[8]

A relevant and dynamic approach to performance management also requires integration with other human resource management practices including workforce and succession planning, hiring and promotion decisions, learning,

FIGURE 7.1

Effectiveness of Performance Management System

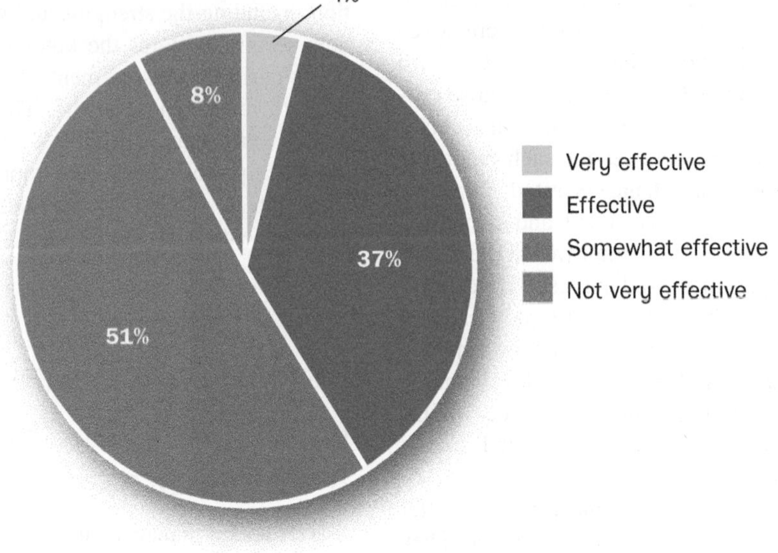

Source: Jane Cooper and Shannon Jackson, "Talent Management Benchmarking: Human Resources Trends and Metrics, Fourth Edition," Ottawa: The Conference Board of Canada, 2017, p. 57.

development planning, and rewards.[9] Performance management systems are more likely to be effective when they are perceived by employees to be fair, and when employees participate in the development and implementation of a performance management system, perceptions of fairness increase.[10]

IBM recently introduced a new performance management system that was co-created with employees. The co-creation process started when Diane Gherson, IBM's chief human resources officer, blogged to employees to ask for input on an initial design concept and received 18,000 responses overnight. Discussion groups were set up and prototypes continued to evolve, ultimately involving about 100,000 employees. Employees were also asked to name the new performance management system and tens of thousands of employees voted to narrow down to three names, from which "Checkpoint" was chosen. Gherson says the new performance management system "was cited as the top reason engagement improved."[11]

Purposes of Performance Management

Figure 7.2 explains the ways in which performance management has changed. The most frequent changes to performance management systems are adopting coaching, ongoing feedback, and developmental focus. Despite these changes, organizations continue to establish performance management systems to meet three broad purposes: strategic, administrative, and developmental.

Strategic Purpose

Strategic purpose means effective performance management helps the organization achieve its business objectives. It does this by helping to link employees' behaviour with the organization's goals. As discussed in the following section, performance management starts with defining what the organization expects from each employee. It measures each employee's performance to identify where those expectations are and are not being met. This enables the organization to take corrective action, such as training, incentives, or discipline. Performance management can achieve its strategic purpose only when measurements are truly aligned with the organization's goals and when the goals and feedback about performance are communicated to employees. For example, at Maple Leaf Foods employee performance is based on not only achieving specific outcomes but also demonstrating behaviours that are consistent with the corporate values. This focus on *how* results are achieved includes things like "Do What's Right" (act with integrity, behave responsibly, and treat people with respect) and "Dare to be Transparent" (have the courage to be candid and direct, and communicate openly).[12]

Administrative Purpose

The *administrative purpose* of a performance management system refers to how organizations use the system to provide information for day-to-day decisions about salary,

FIGURE 7.2

How Performance Management Has Changed
(percentage of organizations responding)

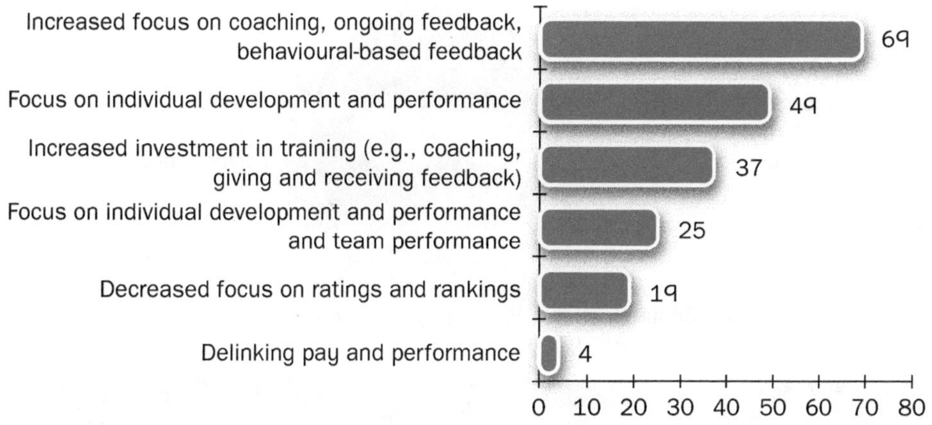

Note: Responses do not total to 100 as more than one option could be chosen.
Source: Jane Cooper and Shannon Jackson, "Talent Management Benchmarking: Human Resources Trends and Metrics, Fourth Edition," Ottawa: The Conference Board of Canada, 2017, p. 59.

benefits, and recognition programs. Performance management can also support decision making related to employee retention, termination for poor performance, and hiring or layoffs. Because performance management supports these administrative decisions, the information in a performance appraisal can have a great impact on the future of individual employees. Managers recognize this, which is the reason they may feel uncomfortable conducting performance appraisals when the appraisal information is negative and therefore, likely to lead to a layoff, disappointing pay increase, or other negative outcome.

Developmental Purpose

Finally, performance management has a *developmental purpose,* meaning that it serves as a basis for developing employees' knowledge and skills. Even employees who are meeting expectations can become more valuable and high performing when they receive and discuss performance feedback. Effective performance feedback and coaching make employees aware of their strengths and of the areas in which they can improve.

Criteria for Effective Performance Management

In Chapter 5, we saw that there are many ways to predict performance of a job candidate. Similarly, there are many ways to measure the performance of an employee. For performance management to achieve its goals, its methods for measuring performance must be effective. Selecting these measures is a critical part of planning a performance management system. Several criteria are associated with effectiveness:

- *Fit with strategy*—A performance management system should aim at achieving employee behaviour and mindset that support the organization's strategy, goals, and culture. If a company emphasizes customer service, then its performance management system should define the kinds of behaviour that contribute to excellent customer service. Performance appraisals should measure whether employees are engaging in those behaviours. Feedback should help employees enhance their performance in those areas. When an organization's strategy changes, human resources professionals should help managers assess how the performance management system should change to serve the new strategy.
- *Validity*—As we discussed in Chapter 5, *validity* is the extent to which a measurement tool actually measures what it is intended to measure. In the case of performance appraisal, validity refers to whether the appraisal measures all the relevant aspects of performance and omits irrelevant aspects of performance. Figure 7.3 shows two sets of information. The circle on the left represents all the information in a performance appraisal; the circle on the right represents all relevant measures of job performance. The overlap of the circles contains the valid information. Information that is gathered but irrelevant is *contamination.* Comparing salespeople on the basis of how many calls they make to customers could be a contaminated measure. Making a lot of calls does not necessarily improve sales or customer satisfaction, unless every salesperson makes only

FIGURE 7.3

Contamination and Deficiency of a Job Performance Measure

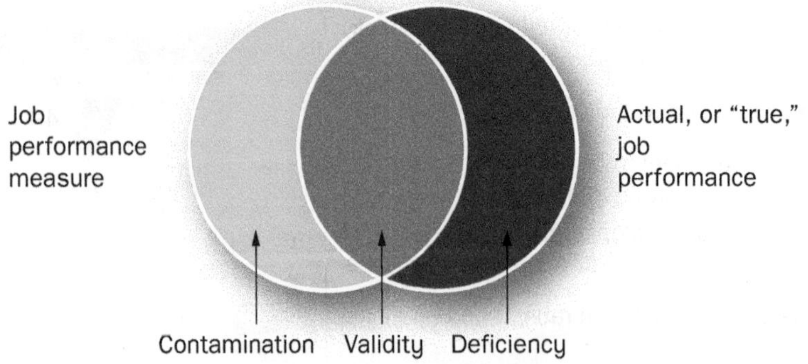

HR Oops!

Unclear Expectations

Common sense would suggest that for employees to *do* what is expected of them, they have to *know* what is expected. It's surprising, then, that when Gallup asked employees to rate their agreement with a statement that they understand what is expected of them on the job, only half said they strongly agree. Far smaller groups strongly agree that their managers help them set performance goals (13 percent) and work priorities (12 percent).

One place to start is to write and communicate clear job descriptions. Unfortunately, a consultant with law firms has found that written job descriptions are uncommon—and when they do exist, the leadership rarely updates or refers to them. Furthermore, this consultant finds that most of these descriptions outline areas of responsibility in generalities rather than saying what the person in the position is supposed to accomplish.

The lack of clarity goes beyond job descriptions. A full understanding of expectations also includes knowing how one's tasks contribute to the organization's success and engaging in dialogue with one's managers about how to contribute. In this last area, some research suggests that female employees operate at a disadvantage. A review of performance evaluations found that performance feedback for men and women differed. Praise for men more often mentioned specific accomplishments, whereas women were praised in general terms (e.g., "You had a great year"). Managers reviewing men's performance tended to identify specific technical areas for development, whereas women tended to be told simply that they needed to improve their communication style. Of course, all areas of development are important, but focusing on technical skills makes it easier to identify assignments and promotions for development; a focus on communication skills rarely suggests any such opportunities. To the extent that this is occurring in organizations, it is harder for female employees to apply feedback in a way that enables them to contribute more to the organization's performance.

Questions

1. What problems will an organization experience if its employees don't fully understand what is expected of them?
2. For the developmental purpose of performance management, a company might search through its database of performance feedback to find employees with accomplishments that make them good candidates for projects or promotions. How would specific (instead of general) feedback support this purpose?

Sources: Shelley Correll and Caroline Simard, "Research: Vague Feedback Is Holding Women Back," *Harvard Business Review*, April 29, 2016, https://hbr.org; "Job Expectations Are Unclear to Many Employees," *TD*, January 2016, https://www.td.org; Patrick J. McKenna, "When Job Descriptions Don't Do the Job," *Of Counsel*, May 2015, pp. 15–18.

well-planned calls. Information that is not gathered but is relevant represents a *deficiency* of the performance measure. For example, suppose a company measures whether employees have good attendance records but not whether they work efficiently. This limited performance appraisal is unlikely to provide a full picture of employees' contribution to the company. Performance measures should minimize both contamination and deficiency.

- *Reliability*—With regard to a performance measure, reliability describes the consistency of the results that the performance measure will deliver. *Interrater reliability* is consistency of results when more than one person assesses performance. Simply asking a supervisor to rate an employee's performance on a scale of 1 to 5 would likely have low interrater reliability; the rating will differ depending on who is assessing the employees. *Test–retest reliability* refers to consistency of results over time. If a performance measure lacks test–retest reliability, determining whether an employee's performance has truly changed over time will be impossible.
- *Acceptability*—Whether or not a measure is valid and reliable, it must meet the practical standard of being acceptable to the people who use it. For example, the people who use a performance measure must believe that it is not too time consuming. Likewise, if employees believe the measure is unfair, they will not use the feedback as a basis for improving their performance.
- *Specific feedback*—A performance measure should specifically tell employees *what* is expected of them and *how* they can meet those expectations. Being specific helps performance management meet the goals of supporting strategy and developing employees. Being specific may also mean the performance measure can be defined in quantitative terms. If a measure does not specify what an employee must do to help the organization achieve its goals, it does not support the strategy. If the measure fails to point out performance gaps, employees will not know how to improve. For more on this, see the HR Oops! feature.

LO2 The Process of Performance Management

How performance management is handled is a key part of the employee experience. As organizations make changes to their process, including moving away from annual ratings and formal performance evaluation (appraisals), there is also an emerging discussion that perhaps there is a middle ground to consider.[13] Facebook used focus groups and surveys to discover that 87 percent of its employees preferred to keep performance ratings to provide for fairness, transparency, and development. This discussion can be summarized as performance is always rated—"if you don't have formal evaluations, the ratings will be hidden in a black box."[14]

So despite costs and specific criticisms, effective performance management can deliver many benefits. Effective performance management can tell top performers that they are valued, encourage communication between managers and employees, establish uniform standards for evaluating employees, and help the organization identify its highest performers. Performance evaluations, properly done, meet an "ethical obligation of leadership" by providing information that all members of an organization want to know so they can succeed: "What do you expect of me? How am I doing to meet your expectations?"[15] And, according to a SHRM Globoforce Employee Recognition Survey, 83 percent of employees who are satisfied with their reviews are also satisfied with their jobs overall (versus only 55 percent for those dissatisfied).[16]

Figure 7.4 shows a performance management process that consists of six steps. As shown in the model, feedback and formal performance evaluation are important parts of the process; however, they are not the only critical components. An effective performance management process contributes to the company's overall competitive advantage and must be given visible support by the CEO and other senior managers. This support ensures that the process is consistently implemented across the company, evaluations are timely, and giving and receiving ongoing performance feedback are recognized as an important aspect of the company's culture.

Step 1 and Step 2 involve identifying what the company is trying to accomplish (its goals or objectives) and developing employee goals and actions to achieve these outcomes. Typically, the outcomes benefit customers, the employee's colleagues or team members, and the organization itself. The goals, behaviours, and activities should be measurable and become part of the employee's job description.

Step 3 in the process—organizational support—involves providing employees with training, necessary resources and tools, and ongoing feedback between the employee and manager that focuses on accomplishments as well as issues and challenges that influence performance. For effective performance management, both the manager and the employee have to value feedback and exchange it on a regular basis, not just once or twice a year. Also, the manager needs to make time to provide ongoing feedback to the employee and learn how to give and receive it.

Step 4 involves evaluating performance; that is, when the manager and employee discuss and compare targeted goals and supporting behaviour with actual results. This step includes formal performance evaluation or appraisal.

The final steps involve both the employee and manager identifying what the employee can do to capitalize on performance strengths and gaps, if any (**Step 5**) and providing consequences for achieving (or failing to achieve) performance outcomes; for example, pay increases, bonuses,

FIGURE 7.4

Steps in the Performance Management Process

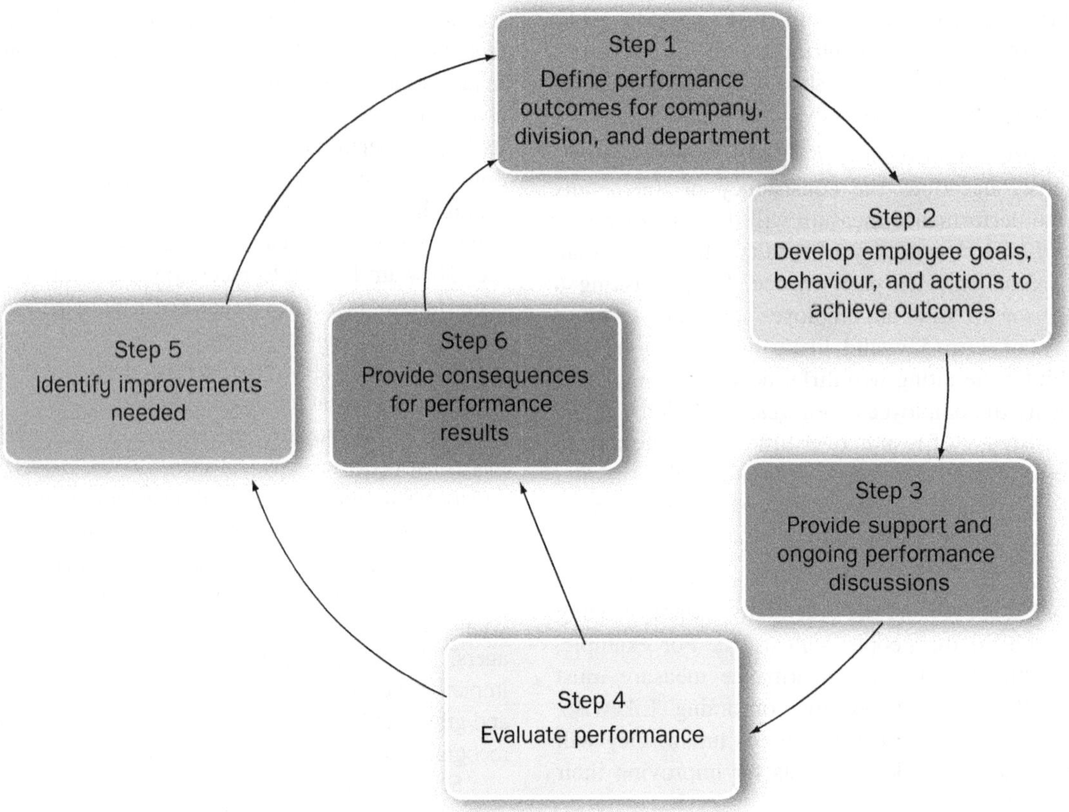

Sources: Based on E. Pulakos, R. Hanson, S. Arad, and N. Moye, "Performance Management Can Be Fixed: An On-the-Job Experiential Learning Approach for Complex Behavior Change," Industrial and Organizational Psychology, March 2015, pp. 51–76; E. Pulakos, R. Mueller-Hanson, R. O'Leary, and M. Meyrowitz, Building a High-Performance Culture: A Fresh Look at Performance Management (Alexandria, VA: SHRM Foundation, 2012); H. Aguinis, "An Expanded View of Performance Management," in J. W. Smith and M. London (eds.), Performance Management (San Francisco: Jossey-Bass, 2009), pp. 1–43; J. Russell and L. Russell, "Talk Me through It: The Next Level of Performance Management," T + D, April 2010, pp. 42–48.

or action plans (**Step 6**). This includes identifying training needs; adjusting the type or frequency of feedback the manager provides to the employee; clarifying, adjusting, or modifying performance outcomes; and discussing behaviours or activities that need improvement.

LO3 Methods for Measuring Performance

Organizations have developed a wide variety of methods for measuring performance. Some methods rank each employee to compare employees' performance. Other methods break down the evaluation into ratings of individual attributes, behaviours, or results. Many organizations use a measurement system that includes a variety of these measures. Table 7.1 compares these methods in terms of four criteria for effective performance management.

Making Comparisons

The performance appraisal method may require the rater to compare one individual's performance with that of others. This method involves some form of ranking, in which some employees are the highest performers, some are fully meeting expectations, and others are not. The usual techniques for making comparisons are simple ranking, forced distribution, and paired comparison.

Simple ranking requires managers to rank employees in their group from the highest performer to the lowest performer. In a variation on this approach, *alternation ranking,* the manager works from a list of employees. First, the manager decides which employee is the highest performer and crosses that

simple ranking
Method of performance measurement that requires managers to rank employees in their group from the highest to the lowest performer.

TABLE 7.1

Basic Approaches to Performance Management

	Criteria				
Approach	**Fit with Strategy**	**Validity**	**Reliability**	**Acceptability**	**Specificity**
Comparative	Poor, unless manager takes time to make link	Can be high if ratings are done carefully	Depends on rater, but usually no measure of agreement used	Moderate; easy to develop and use but resistant to normative standard	Very low
Attribute	Usually low; requires manager to make link	Usually low; can be fine if developed carefully	Usually low; can be improved by specific definitions of attributes	High; easy to develop and use	Very low
Behavioural	Can be quite high	Usually high; minimizes contamination and deficiency	Usually high	Moderate; difficult to develop, but accepted well for use	Very high
Results	Very high	Usually high; can be both contaminated and deficient	High; main problem can be test–retest—depends on timing of measure	High; usually developed with input from those to be evaluated	High regarding results, but low regarding behaviours necessary to achieve them

person's name off the list. From the remaining names, the manager selects the lowest-performing employee and crosses off that name. The process continues with the manager selecting the second-highest, second-lowest, third-highest, and so on until all the employees have been ranked. The major downside of ranking involves validity. To state a performance measure as broadly as "highest" or "lowest" doesn't define what exactly is effective or ineffective about the person's contribution to the organization. Ranking therefore raises questions about fairness.

Another way to compare employees' performance is with the **forced-distribution method**. This type of performance measurement assigns a certain percentage of employees to each category in a set of categories. For example, the organization might establish the following percentages and categories:

forced-istribution method Method of performance measurement that assigns a certain percentage of employees to each category in a set of categories.

- Outstanding—5 percent
- Exceeds expectations—20 percent
- Meets expectations—55 percent
- Developmental—15 percent
- Below expectations—5 percent

The manager completing the performance evaluation would rate 5 percent of employees as outstanding, 20 percent as exceeding expectations, and so on. A forced-distribution approach works best if the members of a group really do vary this much in terms of their performance. It overcomes the temptation to rate everyone high in order to avoid conflict. Research simulating some features of forced rankings found that they improved performance when combined with goals and rewards, especially in the first few years, when the system eliminated the lowest performers.[17] However, a manager who does very well at selecting, creating a motivating work environment, and training employees will be more likely to have a group of high performers. This manager would have difficulty assigning employees to the lower categories. In that situation, saying that some employees are "below expectations" or "developmental" may not only be inaccurate but also will hurt morale.

The Conference Board of Canada reports that although only 11 percent of surveyed organizations use a forced-distribution performance management system, an additional 42 percent of surveyed organizations have guidelines or recommendations to ensure a normal distribution of performance ratings.[18] Figure 7.5 illustrates these findings.

Another variation on rankings is the **paired-comparison method**. This approach involves comparing each employee with each other employee to establish rankings.

paired-comparison method Method of performance measurement that compares each employee with each other employee to establish rankings.

FIGURE 7.5

Forced Performance Distribution and Guidelines

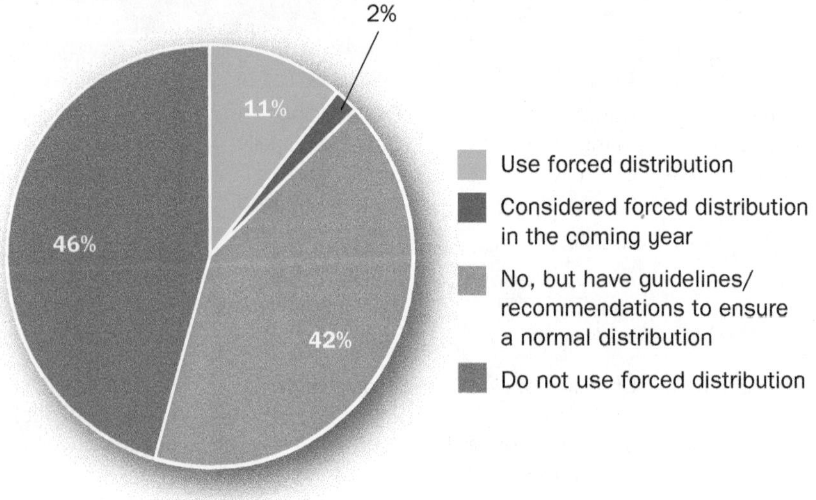

Note: Total does not add to 100 due to rounding
Source: Heather McAteer, "Compensation Planning Outlook 2018," (Ottawa: Conference Board of Canada, October 2017), p. 33.

Suppose a manager has five employees, Jaida, Ramat, Skylar, Ming, and Mohammed. The manager compares Jaida's performance to Ramat's and assigns one point to whichever employer is the higher performer. Then the manager compares Jaida's performance to Skylar's, then to Ming's, and finally to Mohammed's. The manager repeats this process with Ramat, comparing his performance to Skylar's, Ming's, and Mohammed's. When the manager has compared every pair of employees, the manager counts the number of points for each employee. The employee with the most points is considered the top-ranked employee. Clearly, this method is time consuming if a group has more than a few employees. For a group of 15, the manager must make 105 comparisons.

In spite of the drawbacks, ranking employees offers some benefits. It counteracts the tendency to avoid controversy by rating everyone favourably or near the centre of the scale. Also, if some managers tend to evaluate behaviour more strictly (or more leniently) than others, a ranking system can erase that tendency from performance scores. Therefore, ranking systems can be useful for supporting decisions about how to distribute pay raises or layoffs. Some ranking systems are easy to use, which makes them acceptable to the managers who use them. A major drawback of rankings is that often they are not linked to the organization's goals. Also, a simple ranking system leaves the basis for ranking open to interpretation. In that case, the rankings are not helpful for employee development and may hurt morale or result in legal challenges.

Rating Individuals

Instead of focusing on arranging a group of employees from highest to lowest performance, performance measurement can look at each employee's performance relative to a uniform set of standards. The measurement may evaluate employees in terms of attributes (characteristics, traits, or competencies) believed necessary for success in the job or in the organization. Or the measurements may identify whether employees have *behaved* in desirable ways, such as helping co-workers or working safely. The performance management system must identify the desired attributes or behaviours, then provide a form on which the manager can rate the employee in terms of those attributes or behaviours. Typically, the form includes a rating scale, such as a scale from 1 to 5, where 1 is the lowest level of performance and 5 is the highest.

Rating Attributes

The most widely used method for rating attributes is the **graphic rating scale**. This method lists attributes and provides a rating scale for each. The employer uses the scale to indicate the extent to which the employee being rated displays the attributes. The rating scale may provide points to circle (as on a scale going from 1 for "below expectations" to 5 for

graphic rating scale Method of performance measurement that lists attributes and provides a rating scale for each attribute; the employer uses the scale to indicate the extent to which an employee displays each attribute.

FIGURE 7.6

Example of a Graphic Rating Scale

The following areas of performance are significant to most positions. Indicate your assessment of performance on each dimension by circling the appropriate rating.

PERFORMANCE DIMENSIONS	RATING				
	OUTSTANDING	EXCEEDS EXPECTATIONS	MEETS EXPECTATIONS	DEVELOPMENTAL	BELOW EXPECTATIONS
Client service	5	4	3	2	1
Communication	5	4	3	2	1
Leadership	5	4	3	2	1
Professionalism	5	4	3	2	1
Teamwork	5	4	3	2	1
Interpersonal skills	5	4	3	2	1
Initiative	5	4	3	2	1
Creativity	5	4	3	2	1
Problem solving	5	4	3	2	1

"outstanding") or it may provide a line representing a range of scores, with the manager marking a place along the line. Figure 7.6 shows an example of a graphic rating scale that uses a set of ratings from 5 to 1. A drawback of this approach is that it leaves to the particular manager the decisions about what is "outstanding teamwork" or "exceeds expectations" in problem solving. The result is low reliability, because managers are likely to arrive at different assessments.

Rating attributes is the most popular way to measure performance in organizations. In general, attribute-based performance methods are easy to develop and can be applied to a wide variety of jobs and organizations. If the organization is careful to identify which attributes are associated with high performance, and to define them carefully on the appraisal form, these methods can be reliable and valid. However, appraisal forms often fail to meet this standard. In addition, measurement of attributes may not be clearly linked to the organization's strategy. Furthermore, employees tend, perhaps rightly, to be defensive about receiving a mere numerical rating on some attribute. How would you feel if you were told you scored 2 on a 5-point scale of initiative or communication skill? The number might seem arbitrary, and it doesn't tell you how to improve.

Rating Behaviours

One way to overcome the drawbacks of rating attributes is to assess employees' behaviour. To rate behaviours, the organization begins by defining which behaviours are associated with success on the job. Which kinds of employee behaviour help the organization achieve its goals? The appraisal requires the manager to rate an employee in terms of each of the identified behaviours.

One way to rate behaviours is with the **critical-incident method**. This approach requires managers to keep a record of specific examples of the employee behaving in ways that are either effective or ineffective. Here's an example of a critical incident in the performance evaluation of an appliance repair person:

critical-incident method Method of performance measurement based on managers' records of specific examples of the employee behaving in ways that are either effective or ineffective.

> A customer called in about a refrigerator that had stopped dispensing water. The technician prediagnosed the cause of the problem based on known issues with the particular make and model of refrigerator, and checked her truck for the necessary parts. When she found she did not have them, she checked the parts out from inventory so that the customer's refrigerator would be repaired on her first visit and the customer would be satisfied promptly.

This incident provides evidence of the employee's knowledge of refrigerator repair and concern for efficiency and customer satisfaction. Evaluating performance in this specific way gives employees feedback about what they do well and what requires improvement. The manager can also relate the incidents to how the employee is helping the company achieve its goals. Keeping a daily or weekly log of critical incidents requires significant effort, however, and managers may resist this requirement. Also, critical incidents may be unique, so they may not support comparisons among employees.

A **behaviourally anchored rating scale (BARS)** builds on the critical incident approach. The BARS method is intended to define performance dimensions specifically, using statements of behaviour that describe different levels of performance.[19] (The statements are "anchors" of the performance levels.) The scale in Figure 7.7 shows various performance levels for "listening, understanding, and responding." The statement at the top (rating 5) describes the highest level of listening, understanding, and responding. The statement at the bottom describes behaviour associated with ineffective or counterproductive performance. These statements are based on data about past performance. The organization gathers many critical incidents representing effective and ineffective performance, then classifies them from most to least effective. When experts about the job agree the statements clearly represent levels of performance, they are used as anchors to guide the rater. Although BARS can improve interrater reliability, this method can bias the manager's memory. The statements used as anchors can help managers remember similar behaviours, but at the expense of other critical incidents.[20]

behaviourally anchored rating scale (BARS) Method of performance measurement that rates behaviour in terms of a scale showing specific statements of behaviour that describe different levels of performance.

FIGURE 7.7

BARS Rating Dimension: Customer Service Representative

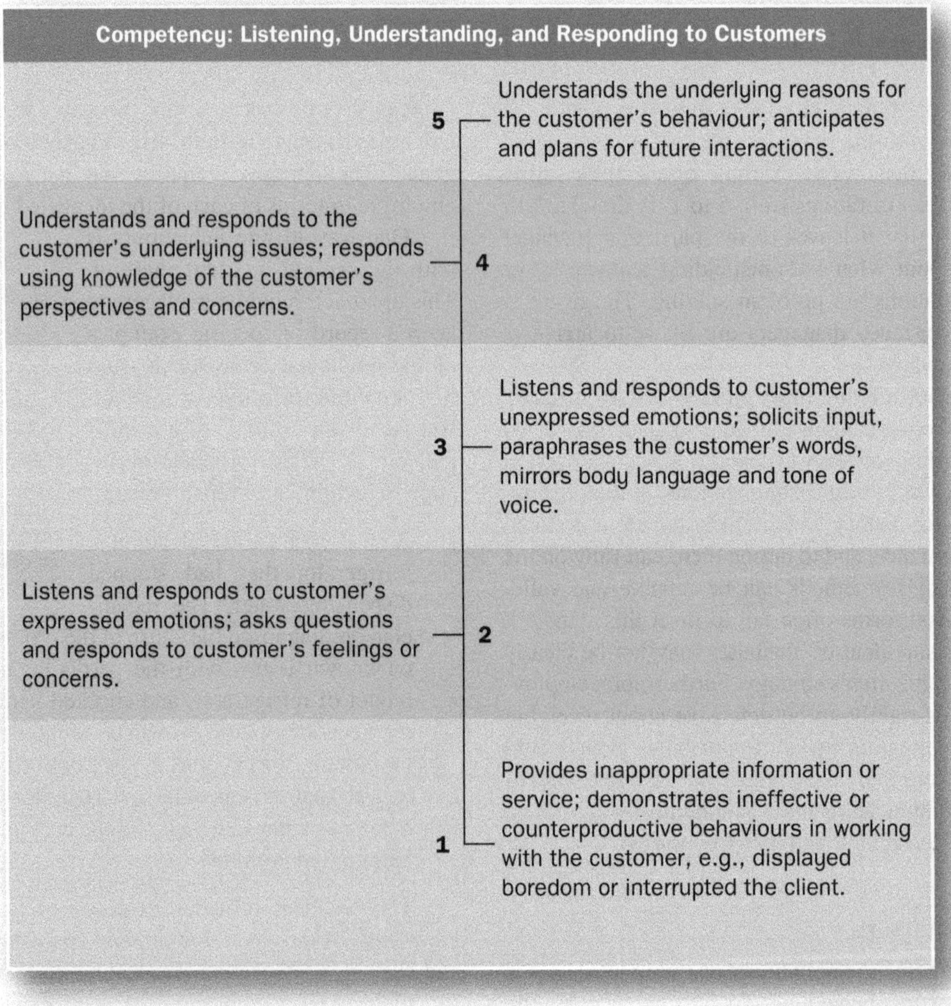
Competency: Listening, Understanding, and Responding to Customers
5
Understands the underlying reasons for the customer's behaviour; anticipates and plans for future interactions.
Understands and responds to the customer's underlying issues; responds using knowledge of the customer's perspectives and concerns.
4
3
Listens and responds to customer's unexpressed emotions; solicits input, paraphrases the customer's words, mirrors body language and tone of voice.
Listens and responds to customer's expressed emotions; asks questions and responds to customer's feelings or concerns.
2
1
Provides inappropriate information or service; demonstrates ineffective or counterproductive behaviours in working with the customer, e.g., displayed boredom or interrupted the client.

Source: Adapted from "Manager's HR Toolkit," BC Public Service Agency.

A **behavioural observation scale (BOS)** is a variation of a BARS. Like a BARS, a BOS is developed from critical incidents.[21] However, while a BARS discards many examples in creating the rating scale, a BOS uses many of them to define all behaviours necessary for effective performance (or behaviours that signal ineffective performance). As a result, a BOS may use 15 behaviours to define levels of performance. Also, a BOS asks the manager to rate the frequency with which the employee has exhibited the behaviour during the rating period. These ratings are averaged to compute an overall performance rating. Figure 7.8 provides a simplified example of a BOS for assessing a supervisor's behaviour "overcoming resistance to change."

behavioural observation scale (BOS) A variation of BARS, which uses all behaviours necessary for effective performance to rate performance at a task.

A major drawback of this method is the amount of information required. A BOS can have 80 or more behaviours, and the manager must recall how often the employee exhibited each behaviour in a 6-to-12-month rating period. This is taxing enough for one employee, but managers often must assess ten or more employees. Even so, compared to BARS and graphic rating scales, managers and employees have said they prefer BOS for ease of use, providing feedback, maintaining objectivity, and suggesting training needs.[22]

Another approach to assessment builds directly on a branch of psychology called *behaviourism,* which holds that individuals' future behaviour is determined by their past experiences—specifically, the ways in which past behaviours have been reinforced. People tend to repeat behaviours that have been rewarded in the past. Providing feedback and reinforcement can therefore modify individuals' future behaviour. Applied to behaviour in organizations, **organizational behaviour modification (OBM)** is a plan for

organizational behaviour modification (OBM) A plan for managing the behaviour of employees through a formal system of feedback and reinforcement.

FIGURE 7.8

Example of a Behavioural Observation Scale

Overcoming Resistance to Change

Directions: Rate the frequency of each behaviour from 1 (Almost Never) to 5 (Almost Always).

1. Describes the details of the change to employees.
   Almost Never 1 2 3 4 5 Almost Always
2. Explains why the change is necessary.
   Almost Never 1 2 3 4 5 Almost Always
3. Discusses how the change will affect the employee.
   Almost Never 1 2 3 4 5 Almost Always
4. Listens to the employee's concerns.
   Almost Never 1 2 3 4 5 Almost Always
5. Asks the employee for help in making the change work.
   Almost Never 1 2 3 4 5 Almost Always
6. If necessary, specifies the date for a follow-up meeting to respond to the employee's concerns.
   Almost Never 1 2 3 4 5 Almost Always

Score: Total number of points = ______________________

Performance

Points	*Performance Rating*
6–10	Below expectations
11–15	Developmental
16–20	Meets expectations
21–25	Exceeds expectations
26–30	Outstanding

Scores are set by management.

managing the behaviour of employees through a formal system of feedback and reinforcement. Specific OBM techniques vary, but most have four components:[23]

1. Define a set of key behaviours necessary for job performance.
2. Use a measurement system to assess whether the employee exhibits the key behaviours.
3. Inform employees of the key behaviours, perhaps in terms of goals for how often to exhibit the behaviours.
4. Provide feedback and reinforcement based on employees' behaviour.

OBM techniques have been used in a variety of settings. For example, a community health agency used OBM to increase the rates and timeliness of critical job behaviours by showing employees the connection between job behaviours and the agency's accomplishments.[24] This process identified job behaviours related to administration, record keeping, and service provided to clients. Feedback and reinforcement improved staff performance. OBM also increased the frequency of safety behaviours in a processing plant.[25]

Behavioural approaches such as organizational behaviour modification and rating scales can be very effective. These methods can link the company's goals to the specific behaviour required to achieve those goals. Behavioural methods also can generate specific feedback, along with guidance in areas requiring improvements. As a result, these methods tend to be valid. The people to be measured often help develop the measures, so acceptance tends to be high as well. When raters are well trained, reliability also tends to be high. However, behavioural methods do not work as well for complex jobs in which it is difficult to see a link between behaviour and results or there is more than one good way to achieve success.[26]

For example, women studied in high-tech and professional-services firms tended to get feedback emphasizing how they communicate. This could be relevant in light of research where peers (male and female) judged women harshly when they spoke forcefully.[27] But focusing on communication style overlooks the value of the communicator's messages. Does the problem behaviour in communication breakdowns lie with the speaker, the hearers, or both?

Measuring Results

Performance measurement can focus on managing the objective, measurable results of a job or work group. Results might include sales, costs, or productivity (output per worker or per dollar spent on production), among many possible measures. Two of the most popular methods for measuring results are measurement of productivity and management by objectives.

Productivity is an important measure of success, because getting more done with a smaller amount of resources (money or people) increases the company's profits. Productivity usually refers to the output of production workers, but it can be used more generally as a performance measure. To do this, the organization identifies the outcomes it expects a group or individual to accomplish. At a repair shop, for instance, the desired outcome might be something like "quality of repair." The next step is to define how to measure quality of repair. The repair shop could track the percentage of items returned because they still do not work after a repair and the percentage of quality-control inspections passed. For each measure, the organization decides what level of performance is desired. Finally, the organization sets up a system for tracking these measures and giving employees feedback about their performance in terms of these measures. This type of performance measurement can be time consuming to set up, but research suggests it can improve productivity.[28]

Management by objectives (MBO) is a system in which people at each level of the organization set goals in a process that flows from top to bottom, so employees at all levels are contributing to the organization's overall goals. These goals become the standards for evaluating each employee's performance. An MBO system has three components:[29]

1. Goals are specific, difficult, and objective. The goals listed in the second column of Table 7.2 provide two examples for a financial institution.

management by objectives (MBO) A system in which people at each level of the organization set goals in a process that flows from top to bottom, so employees at all levels are contributing to the organization's overall goals; these goals become the standards for evaluating each employee's performance.

TABLE 7.2

Management by Objectives: Two Objectives for a Financial Institution

Key Result Area	Objective	% Complete	Actual Performance
Loan portfolio management	Increase portfolio value by 5% over the next 6 months	90	Increased portfolio value by 4.5% over the past 6 months
Sales	Generate fee income of $15,000 over the next 6 months	150	Generated fee income of $22,500 over the past 6 months

2. Managers and their employees work together to set the goals.
3. The manager gives objective feedback through the rating period to monitor progress toward the goals. The two right-hand columns in Table 7.2 are examples of feedback given after six months.

MBO can have a very positive effect on an organization's performance. In 70 studies of MBO's performance, 68 showed that productivity improved.[30] The productivity gains tended to be greatest when top management was highly committed to MBO. Also, because staff members are involved in setting goals, it is likely that MBO systems effectively link individual employees' performance with the organization's overall goals.

In general, evaluation of results can be less subjective than other kinds of performance measurement. This makes measuring results highly acceptable to employees and managers alike. Results-oriented performance measurement is also relatively easy to link to the organization's goals. However, measuring results has problems with validity, because results may be affected by circumstances beyond each employee's performance. Also, if the organization measures only final results, it may fail to measure significant aspects of performance that are not directly related to those results. If individuals focus only on aspects of performance that are measured, they may neglect significant skills or behaviours. For example, if the organization measures only productivity, employees may not be concerned enough with customer service. The outcome may be high efficiency (costs are low) but low effectiveness (sales are low, too).[31] Finally, focusing strictly on results does not provide guidance on how to improve.

To increase the accuracy and amount of data and to obtain more frequent employee evaluations, mobile technology offers a promising application, referred to as *event capturing,* which would enable managers to make short descriptive entries (e.g., limit the number of characters) to capture behaviours, outcomes, or performance on an ongoing basis throughout the year. Alternatively, a less sophisticated variation would require managers to send themselves emails with employee observations they save for later retrieval. These frequent, technology-enabled observations not only increase the accuracy and amount of data but also reduce the effect of the recency emphasis error that will be discussed later in the chapter.[32]

Balanced Scorecard

The **balanced scorecard** is an organizational approach to performance management that integrates strategic perspectives including financial, customer, internal business processes, and learning and growth. Robert S. Kaplan and David P. Norton developed this widely adopted approach, illustrated in Figure 7.9. The basic idea is that managers are encouraged to go beyond meeting just traditional financial targets, and recognize and simultaneously monitor the progress of other important goals such as customer

balanced scorecard An organizational approach to performance management that integrates strategic perspectives including financial, customer, internal business processes, and learning and growth.

FIGURE 7.9

The Balanced Scorecard

Source: © Kheng Guan Toh | Dreamstime.com

THE CANADIAN PRESS/Jason Franson

A coach provides feedback to their team just as a manager provides feedback to employees. Feedback is important so that individuals know what they are doing well and what areas they may need to work on.

and employee satisfaction.[33] Use of a balanced scorecard provides the means to align strategy at all levels of the organization and serves as "an excellent guide to measure and manage the performance of all employees."[34] Balanced scorecards are widely used in both the public and private sector. A sampling of the organizations that use balanced scorecards as part of their strategic management and performance management systems includes J. D. Irving Ltd., Canadian Cancer Society, Carleton University, Nova Scotia Power Inc., Cooperators, and Great-West Life Assurance Company.

Sources of Performance Information

All the methods of performance measurement require decisions about who will collect and analyze the performance information. To qualify for this task, a person should have an understanding of the job requirements and the opportunity to see the employee doing the job. The traditional approach is for managers to gather information about their employees' performance and arrive at performance ratings. However, many sources are possible. Possibilities of information sources include managers, peers, direct reports, self, and customers.

Using just one person as a source of information poses certain problems. People tend to like some people more than others, and those feelings can bias how an employee's efforts are perceived. Also, one person is likely to see an employee in a limited number of situations. A supervisor, for example, cannot see how an employee behaves when the supervisor is not there—for example, when a service technician is at the customer's facility. To get as complete an assessment as possible, some organizations combine information from most or all of the possible sources, in what is called a *multi-rater* or **360-degree performance appraisal**.

360-degree performance appraisal
Performance measurement that combines information from the employee's managers, peers, direct reports, self, and customers.

The John Molson School of Business at Montreal's Concordia University conducted a study to learn about the experiences of 101 large Canadian organizations with 360-degree programs. The study found that 43 percent of the organizations surveyed used 360-degree, that is, multi-rater approaches. Companies are using 360-degree performance reviews because of advantages including increased measurement accuracy and perceived fairness. Respondents also identified challenges such as resistance from individuals because of concerns about the process being time, cost, and energy consuming; trust issues including anonymity of feedback; and the need to ensure a clear purpose and link to organizational strategy are in place before implementing 360-degree performance appraisal.[35] Netflix instituted informal 360-degree performance reviews when they stopped doing formal performance reviews. The 360-degree reviews were kept simple, people were asked to "identify things that colleagues should stop, start, or continue." Initially, an anonymous software system was used, but later that shifted to the use of signed feedback, and now many teams hold their 360-degree reviews face-to-face.[36]

Managers and Supervisors

The most-used source of performance information is the employee's manager or supervisor. It is usually safe for organizations to assume that managers have extensive knowledge of the job requirements and that they have enough opportunity to observe their employees. In other words, managers possess the basic qualifications for this responsibility. Another advantage of using supervisors and managers to evaluate performance is that they have an incentive to provide accurate and helpful feedback, because their own success depends so much on their employees' performance.[37] Finally, when supervisors and managers try to observe employee behaviour or discuss performance issues in the feedback session, their feedback can improve performance, and employees tend to perceive the appraisal as accurate.[38]

Still, in some situations, problems can occur with using managers and supervisors as the source of performance information. For employees in some jobs, the manager or supervisor does not have enough opportunity to observe the employee performing job duties. A sales manager with many offsite sales associates cannot be with the sales associates on many visits to customers. Even if the sales manager does make a point of travelling with sales associates for a few days, they are likely to be on their best behaviour while the manager is there. The manager cannot observe how they perform at other times.

Peers

Another source of performance information is the employee's peers or co-workers. Peers are an excellent source of information about performance in a job where the supervisor does not often observe the employee. Examples include law enforcement and sales. For these and other jobs, peers may have the most opportunity to observe the employee in day-to-day activities. Peers have expert knowledge of job requirements. They also bring a different perspective to the evaluation and can provide extremely valid assessments of performance.[39]

Peer evaluations obviously have some potential disadvantages. Friendships (or rivalries) have the potential to bias ratings. Research, however, has provided little evidence that this is a problem.[40] Another disadvantage is that when the evaluations are done to support administrative decisions, peers are uncomfortable with rating employees for decisions that may affect themselves. Generally, peers are more willing to participate in reviews to be used for employee development.[41]

Direct Reports

For evaluating the performance of managers, direct reports are an especially valuable source of information. Direct reports—the people reporting to the manager—often have the best chance to see how well a manager treats employees. At HCL Technologies, for example, managers not only receive reviews from their employees but also are expected to publish the reports on the company's internal website to create a climate that values open communication and personal development. Sanjeev Nikore, a vice-president who did this, learned that his employees found him resistant to delegating. He acknowledged he needed to improve his people skills, made some changes, and earned a key promotion.[42]

Direct-report evaluations have some potential problems because of the power relationships involved. Direct reports are reluctant to say negative things about the person to whom they report; they prefer to provide feedback anonymously. Managers, however, have a more positive reaction to this type of feedback when the employees are identified. When feedback requires that the direct reports identify themselves, they tend to give the manager higher ratings.[43] Another problem is that when managers receive ratings from direct reports, the employees have more power, so managers tend to emphasize employee satisfaction, even at the expense of productivity. This issue arises primarily when the evaluations are used for administrative decisions. Therefore, as with peer evaluations, direct report evaluations are most appropriate for developmental purposes. To protect employees, the process should be anonymous and use at least three employees to rate each manager.

Despite these challenges, direct report ratings of managers could become even more widespread for the simple reason that individuals are growing used to the experience of using social media to publish online ratings of everything from movies and restaurants to professors and doctors.

Self

No one has a greater chance to observe the employee's behaviour on the job than does the employee themself. Self-ratings are rarely used alone, but they can contribute valuable information. A common approach is to have employees evaluate their own performance before the feedback session. This activity gets employees thinking about their accomplishments and performance. Areas of disagreement between the self-appraisal and other evaluations can be fruitful topics for the feedback session. At an Australia-based software company called Atlassian, self-appraisals are part of weekly performance feedback. Employees use an online app that displays performance-related questions such as, "How often have you stretched yourself?" and lets employees move a dot along a scale with a range of possible answers. The responses then serve as a catalyst for discussion in meetings between each employee and their supervisor.[44]

The obvious problem with self-ratings is that individuals have a tendency to inflate assessments of their performance. Especially if the ratings will be used for administrative decisions, exaggerating one's contributions has practical benefits. Also, social psychologists have found that, in general, people tend to blame outside circumstances for their failures while taking a large part of the credit for their successes. Supervisors can reduce this tendency by providing frequent feedback, but, because people tend to perceive situations this way, self-appraisals are not appropriate as the basis for administrative decisions.[45]

Customers and Clients

Services are often produced and consumed on the spot, so the customer or client is often the only person who directly observes the service performance and may be the best source of performance information. Many companies in service industries have introduced customer evaluations of employee performance. Marriott provides a customer satisfaction survey to a random sample of its hotel customers. Whirlpool's Consumer Services Division conducts surveys of customers after factory technicians have serviced their appliances. These surveys allow the company to evaluate an individual technician's customer-service behaviours while in the customer's home.

Using customer evaluations of employee performance is appropriate in two situations.[46] The first is when an employee's job requires direct service to the customer or linking the customer to other services within the organization. Second, customer evaluations are appropriate when the organization is interested in gathering information to determine what products and services the customer wants. That is, customer evaluations contribute to the organization's goals by enabling HRM to support the organization's marketing activities. In this regard, customer evaluations are useful both for evaluating an employee's performance and for helping to determine whether the organization can improve customer service by making changes in HRM activities such as training or compensation.

The weakness of using customer feedback for performance measurement is the expense. The expenses of a traditional survey can add up to hundreds of dollars to evaluate one individual. Many organizations therefore limit the information gathering to short periods once a year.

Crowdsourcing Performance Appraisal

The collaborative tools of social media can allow individuals to work together by contributing small pieces to a bigger project. Especially when this is done on a large scale, it is known as *crowdsourcing*. With regard to performance management, crowdsourcing can apply to gathering and using data from all of an employee's co-workers or all of a manager's employees to develop an appraisal—a variation of 360-degree performance appraisal, discussed previously in this chapter. Similarly, one attraction of this approach is that the information will be more complete so employees may consider the resulting appraisal to be more accurate and fair.

Gathering performance data through an online app could further improve the timeliness, accuracy, and completeness of information by inviting employees to post performance information whenever they observe it. The company might even open up the submission of feedback to the whole organization. Suppose a salesperson is trying to solve a customer problem and gets valuable help from one of the engineers; the salesperson could visit the appraisal site and post an appreciative comment describing the situation. Assuming that employees can read the feedback about themselves as it is posted, this type of information gathering also provides positive recognition—or in the case of negative comments, early warning of problems to correct.

A growing number of companies are attracted to the potential and are beginning to use some form of crowdsourced appraisals. However, the approach does raise some concerns. One is that employees may not be motivated to provide careful feedback about their co-workers. They might, for example, find it easier to rate employees based on likability. Another is that bringing everyone into the appraisal process can conflict with legal requirements. As described later in this chapter, performance appraisals are used as evidence to show that employment decisions have not been discriminatory. If courts see appraisals as too subjective, employers defending a discrimination claim could run into trouble. Still, the idea that more voices add more information, and that more information will increase accuracy, continues to attract favourable attention. Employers are motivated to overcome the concerns about fairness and legal requirements, so crowdsourcing may indeed be part of the future of appraisals.

LO4 Errors in Performance Measurement

Research consistently reveals that humans have tremendous limitations in processing information. Because we are so limited, we often use "heuristics," or simplifying mechanisms, to make judgments, whether about investments or about people.[47] These heuristics, which appear often in subjective measures of performance, cause unconscious bias, which can lead to rater errors and incorrect attributions or reasons we use to explain an employee's performance. **Unconscious bias** is a judgment outside our consciousness that affects decisions based on background, culture, and personal experience. We are all subject to unconscious bias. For example, research has found that, compared to men, women receive two and one-half times more feedback about having an aggressive communication style.[48] Also, men tend to receive more feedback linked to a business outcome than do women. It doesn't matter whether the manager conducting the performance evaluation was a man or a woman. Biases may result in gender-based double standards—women need to outperform men to be evaluated the same or that a situation is viewed positively or negatively based on gender. For example, in a pair of performance evaluations the manager noted the female's *analysis paralysis* but a similar behaviour demonstrated by a male was considered *appropriately careful:*

unconscious bias A judgment outside our consciousness that affects decisions based on background, culture, and personal experience.

- "Simone seems paralyzed and confused when facing tight deadlines to make decisions."
- "Cameron seems hesitant in making decisions, yet he is able to work out multiple alternative solutions and determine the most suitable one."[49]

Types of Rating Errors

Table 7.3 shows the different types of rating errors. The "similar to me" error is based on stereotypes the rater has about how individuals with certain characteristics are expected to perform.[50] Leniency, strictness, and central tendency are known as distributional errors because the rater tends to use only one part of the rating scale.

Appraisal politics refer to evaluators purposefully distorting a rating to achieve personal or company goals. Research suggests that several factors promote appraisal politics. These factors are inherent in the appraisal system and the company culture. Appraisal politics are most likely to occur when raters are accountable to the employee being rated, there are competing rating goals, and a direct link exists between performance appraisal and highly desirable rewards. Also, appraisal politics are likely to occur if top executives tolerate distortion or are complacent toward it.

appraisal politics Evaluators purposefully distorting a rating to achieve personal or company goals.

What Can Be Done to Reduce Errors?

Approaches to reducing performance measurement errors include rater error training, rater accuracy training, unconscious bias training, and calibration meetings.

Rater Error Training

Rater error training attempts to make managers aware of rating errors and helps them develop strategies for minimizing those errors.[51] These programs may consist of having the participants view video-recorded vignettes designed to elicit rating errors such as "contrast." They then make their ratings and discuss how the error influenced the ratings. Finally, they get tips to avoid committing those errors. This approach has been shown to be effective for reducing errors, but there is evidence that reducing rating errors can also reduce accuracy.[52]

Rater Accuracy Training

Rater accuracy training, also called *performance dimension training* or *frame-of-reference training,* attempts to emphasize the multidimensional nature of performance and to get raters to understand and use the same idea of high, medium, and low performance when making evaluations. This involves providing examples of performance for each dimension and then discussing the actual or "correct" level of performance that the example represents.[53] Accuracy training seems to increase accuracy, provided that the raters are held accountable for ratings, job-related rating scales are used, and raters keep records of the behaviours they observe.[54]

Unconscious Bias Training

In addition to these approaches many companies, such as Microsoft, Google, Facebook, and Dow Chemical, are

TABLE 7.3

Types of Rating Errors

Rating Error	Description
"Similar to me" error	Individuals who are similar to us in race, gender, background, interest, beliefs, and the like receive higher ratings than those who are not.
Contrast error	Ratings are influenced by comparison between individuals instead of an objective standard (e.g., employee receives lower-than-deserved ratings because they are compared to outstanding peers).
Strictness	Rater gives low ratings to all employees regardless of their performance.
Leniency	Rater gives high ratings to all employees regardless of their performance.
Central tendency	Rater gives middle or average ratings to all employees despite their performance.
Halo	Rater gives employee high ratings on all aspects of performance because of an overall positive impression of the employee.
Horns	Rater gives employee low ratings on all aspects of performance because of an overall negative impression of the employee.
Recency emphasis	Rater bases an annual or longer-term rating only on the employee's most recent work.

requiring employees to participate in training programs to reduce the potential influence of unconscious bias in performance evaluations and other work-related decisions (e.g., promotions).[55] These training programs focus on helping employees become aware of unconscious bias and reducing its impact by slowing down decision making and carefully considering reasons behind and language used in decisions about people.

Calibration Meetings

calibration meetings Meeting at which managers discuss employee performance ratings and provide evidence supporting their ratings with the goal of eliminating the influence of rating errors.

An important way to help ensure that performance is evaluated consistently across managers and to reduce the influence of unconscious bias and rating errors is to hold calibration meetings.[56] **Calibration meetings** provide a way to discuss employees' performance with the goal of ensuring that similar standards are applied to their evaluations. These meetings include managers responsible for conducting performance appraisals and their managers; they are facilitated by an internal HR representative or an external consultant. In the meetings, each employee's performance rating and the manager's reasons for the ratings are discussed. Managers have the opportunity to discuss the definition of each performance rating and ask questions. The calibration meetings help managers identify if their ratings are too positive or negative or tend to be based on employees' most recent performance. Managers are more likely to provide accurate evaluations that are well documented when they know they may have to justify them in a calibration meeting. Calibration meetings can also help eliminate politics by discussing how performance ratings relate to business results.

Using Data Analytics, Analysts, and Ratee training

Besides training raters, a growing number of organizations are bringing *data analytics* into the rating process. When mobile apps and wearable devices can track employees' activities, analytic software can find patterns in what employees do, as well in the messages they post within the organization's computer network and beyond. Some organizations, including Facebook, use *analysts* to look for evidence of bias in performance evaluations. For example, are words like "abrasive" being used more frequently to describe women than men? And what effect might this have on their evaluations, opportunities for advancement, and/or pay?[57]

Performance management experts also tend to advocate for *ratee training* in addition to rater training to improve both rating accuracy and acceptance of the performance management system.[58]

Performance Feedback

Once the manager (and others) have assessed an employee's performance, this information needs to be shared with the employee. Although the feedback stage of performance management is essential, it may be uncomfortable to managers and employees and may even undermine employee engagement and commitment if not handled effectively. In a productive and meaningful performance feedback session both parties need to feel heard, understood, and respected even if they don't necessarily agree on all of the points discussed.[59] And many employees apparently appreciate the importance of performance reviews. Results of a Ceridian Canada and Harris Decima survey stated that 71 percent of employees said their performance review made them feel valued and 91 percent said their performance reviews either met (79 percent) or exceeded (12 percent) their expectations.[60]

Effective Performance Feedback

Feedback Should Be Given Frequently, Not Once a Year

Performance feedback should be a regular, expected management activity. The practice or policy at many organizations is to give formal performance feedback once or twice a year. But annual or even semi-annual feedback is not enough to support employees to maintain high levels of performance or deal with any performance gaps. Another reason for frequent performance feedback is that feedback is most effective when the information does not surprise the employee. If employees have to wait for up to a year to learn what the manager thinks of their work, employees will wonder whether they are valued and fully meeting

TABLE 7.4

Examples of Questions that Start a Collaborative Ongoing Performance Conversation

- What's working?
- Where did you get stuck?
- How can I help?
- What have you learned?
- What would you do differently next time?
- What skills would you like to develop?
- What would you like to discuss today?
- What do you see as the next steps?
- When can I check in with you next?

Source: Based on M. Buckingham, "Out With the Old In With. . .," *TD*, August 2016, pp. 44–48; "Goodyear Performance Management Optimization Case Study," presented on September 6, 2016, to MHR 4328 Performance Management class, The Ohio State University.

expectations. Employees should instead receive feedback so often that they know what the manager will say during formal annual/semi-annual performance evaluations.

Generational differences in the workplace may contribute to different perspectives about what is *timely* feedback. Millennials may expect immediate feedback because their reference points are often built around short time frames and accomplishments.[61] Ernst and Young created an online "Feedback Zone," where employees can request or submit performance feedback at any time beyond the formal evaluations required twice a year. The Conference Board of Canada found that almost half of both Generation X employees and Millennials indicated they preferred feedback "as needed," in contrast to less than 10 percent stating a preference for annual feedback. These results support existing research indicating that "Millennials expect leaders to be freely available to give frequent feedback."[62]

Social media tools similar to Facebook and Twitter are increasingly being used to deliver timely feedback. **Social performance management** refers to systems similar to Facebook, LinkedIn, and Yammer, and apps that allow employees to quickly exchange information, talk to each other, provide coaching, and receive recognition. Social performance management is especially valued by Millennials and Generation Z employees, who have grown up connecting to others through social networking via smartphones and computers.[63]

social performance management Social media and microblogs similar to Facebook, LinkedIn, and Yammer that allow employees to quickly exchange information, talk to each other, provide coaching, and receive feedback and recognition.

© Ryan McVay/Getty Images

When giving performance feedback, do it in an appropriate meeting place. Meet in a setting that is neutral and free of distractions. What other factors are important for a feedback session?

Create the Right Context for the Discussion

The manager should create the appropriate context for the discussion. Being well prepared and choosing a distraction-free neutral location for the feedback session are important. Managers should describe the meeting as an opportunity to discuss the role of the employee, the role of the manager, and the relationship between them. Managers should also authentically approach feedback sessions with a mindset of curiosity, appreciation, and openness to creating dialogue.

Ask the Employee to Rate Their Performance Before the Session

Managers should also enable the employee to be well prepared for a formal feedback session. For example, the manager could ask the employee to complete a self-assessment in advance. The self-assessment requires employees to think about their performance over the past rating period and to be aware of their strengths and areas for improvement, so they can participate more fully in the discussion. Also, differences between the manager's and the employee's rating may be fruitful areas for discussion.

Have Ongoing, Collaborative Performance Conversations

Managers should use a "problem-solving" or collaborative approach to work with employees to address performance gaps in an atmosphere of respect and encouragement. Table 7.4 provides examples of questions that managers can use to start a collaborative ongoing performance conversation with their employees.When employees participate in the feedback session, they are consistently satisfied with the process. (Recall the discussion of fairness earlier in this chapter.) Participation includes allowing employees to voice their opinions of the evaluation, as well as to discuss performance goals and development needs.

Moving to an ongoing collaborative performance conversation is necessary to reduce the anxiety, uncertainty, and feelings of lack of fairness and control that employees typically experience in a manager-driven "tell-and-sell" or "tell-and-listen" approach.[64] This approach to performance feedback is consistent with creating a coaching culture to manage, assess, and develop employees and requires managers to have well-developed coaching skills.[65]

Provide Balanced, Accurate Feedback That Emphasizes Behaviour and Goal Setting

Feedback should include a balanced and accurate assessment of how the employee is doing. The discussion should include a specific discussion of areas in which the employee's performance met, exceeded, and fell short of expectations. As shown in the Did You Know?, Millennial and Generation X employees tend to prefer positive feedback.

Did You KNOW?

Millennials and Generation X Employees Prefer Praise to Corrective Feedback

Given the choice, both Millennials and Generation X employees are more than twice as likely to prefer feedback that focuses on work done well rather than work done poorly.

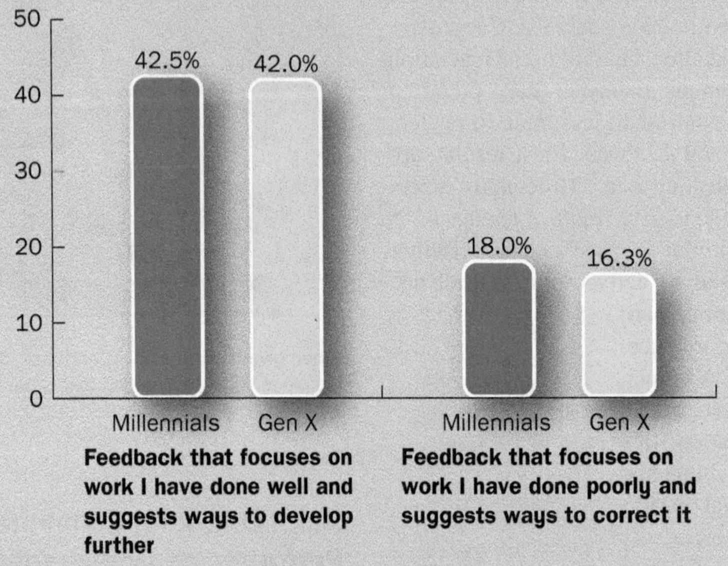

Source: Naoko Hawkins, Jane Vellone, and Ruth Wright, "Workplace Preferences of Millennials and Gen X: Attracting and Retaining the 2020 Workforce," Table 5: Type of Feedback on Job Performance Preferred by Millennials and Gen X, June 2014, *The Conference Board of Canada*, p. 25.

Any areas of required improvement should lead to problem solving. The content of the feedback should emphasize behaviour, not personalities. For example, "Why was the deadline missed?" can open a conversation about what needs to be done differently, but "You're not motivated" is likely to result in the employee feeling defensive and angry. The feedback session should end with goal setting and a decision about when to follow up. The HR How-To box provides additional guidance on providing performance feedback.

Performance Improvement

When performance evaluation indicates that an employee's performance is below expectations, the feedback process should launch an effort to address the performance gap. Even when the employee is meeting current standards, the feedback session may identify areas in which the employee can improve in order to contribute more to the organization in a current or future job. The final feedback stage of performance management involves identifying areas for improvement and ways to improve performance in those areas.

The most effective way to improve performance varies according to the employee's ability and motivation. In general, when employees have high levels of ability and motivation, they perform at or above expectations. But when an employee lacks ability, motivation, or both, corrective action is needed. The type of action called for depends on what is missing:

- **Lack of ability**—When a motivated employee lacks knowledge, skills, or abilities in some area, the manager may offer training and more detailed feedback. Sometimes it is appropriate to restructure the job so the employee can meet the job demands.
- **Lack of motivation**—Managers with an unmotivated employee can explore ways to demonstrate that the employee is valued. The solution may be as simple as delivering more positive feedback. Employees may also benefit from a referral for counselling or help with stress management.

HR How-To

Discussing Employee Performance

Employees and managers often dread feedback sessions, because they expect some level of criticism, and criticism feels uncomfortable. However, there are ways to structure communication about employee performance so that it is constructive. Here are some ideas for talking about employee performance in a way that is clear, honest, and fair:

- **Use specific, concrete examples.** Statements about "attitude" or "commitment" require some mind reading, and employees may feel misunderstood. In contrast, references to specific accomplishments and examples of behaviour are more objective. Even if the supervisor is concerned about attitude, talking about behaviours can open a discussion of the real changes that might be needed: "Several customers commented that you seemed angry when you spoke to them. Let's talk about what's happening in those conversations so you can come across to customers as supportive."
- **Listen as well as talk.** Especially when the reviewer is nervous, the instinct is to fill up the meeting time with comments. However, the feedback session is a valuable opportunity for the supervisor to learn about the employee's expectations and hopes for learning and advancement. Also, ahead of the meeting, invite the employee to reflect on their accomplishments. Open the meeting by inviting the employee to talk about these accomplishments.
- **Be candid.** If performance is not acceptable, don't pretend that it is. Pretending is disrespectful of the employee and could get the organization in legal trouble if the employee is later let go and believes the company discriminated. If the employee asks a question and the supervisor is unsure of the answer, candour and honesty are the wisest course. Guessing at an answer related to an employee's future is another way to create problems for the organization, as well as for the supervisor's relationship with the employee.
- **Be positive.** Be positive within the parameters of honesty and authenticity. Instead of negative expressions like "You shouldn't," use positive language such as "What if we tried." Demonstrate appreciation by thanking employees for their contributions.
- **Prepare for success.** Look forward to the future as well as backward at past performance. For areas where you expect a change in performance, help the employee arrive at a plan for how to make that change. Furthermore, either take time to discuss goals for career development or plan a time to do so.

Sources: Eric Kilponen, "How to Talk Your Way to Better Employee Performance," Insperity blog, http://www.insperity.com, accessed May 9, 2016; Kristi Hedges, "How to Give Concise Positive Feedback," *Forbes*, October 7, 2015, http://www.forbes.com; Scott Halford, "Five Steps for Giving Productive Feedback," *Entrepreneur*, http://www.entrepreneur.com, accessed June 20, 2016; Bureau of National Affairs, "For Better Reviews, Discuss Money First, Avoid 'Compliment Sandwiches'" *HR Focus*, June 2013, pp. 8–9; Andrea Murad, "How to Deliver Feedback to Employees Without Squashing Morale," *Fox Business*, May 24, 2013, http:www.foxbusiness.com.

- **Lack of both**—Employees whose performance is below expectations because they have neither the motivation nor the ability to perform the job may not be a good fit for the position or even the organization.

A documented performance improvement plan may be introduced by the manager as a means to discuss and reach agreement on next steps. A **performance improvement plan** is a summary of the performance gap(s) and includes an action plan mutually agreed to by the employee and manager with specific dates to review progress. If the employee does not authentically respond by changing mindset, behaviour, and performance results, the organization may have to demote or terminate the employee.

performance improvement plan Summary of performance gaps and includes an action plan mutually agreed to by the employee and supervisor with specific dates to review progress.

LO5 Legal, Ethical, and Privacy Issues

In developing and using performance management systems, human resources professionals and managers need to ensure that these systems meet legal requirements and thoughtfully address ethical considerations and privacy requirements.

Legal Requirements for Performance Management

Because performance measures play a central role in decisions about pay, promotions, and discipline, employment-related legal challenges may be directed at an organization's performance management system. Legal challenges related to performance management usually involve charges of illegal discrimination, and unjust or constructive dismissal.

Claims often allege that the performance management system discriminated against employees on the basis of one of the protected grounds identified in human rights legislation such as age or sex (gender), or ethnicity. Many performance measures are subjective, and measurement errors, such as those described earlier in the chapter, can easily occur.

With regard to lawsuits filed on the grounds of unjust or constructive dismissal, the usual claim is that the person was dismissed for reasons besides the ones that the employer states. In this type of situation, courts generally focus on the employer's performance management system, looking to see whether the dismissal could have been based on poor performance. The employer needs a performance management system that provides evidence to support its employment decisions.

To protect against these legal challenges, it is important to have a performance management system based on valid job analysis, as described in Chapter 3, with the requirements for job success clearly communicated to employees. Performance measurement should evaluate behaviours or results on the basis of objective criteria. The organization should use multiple raters (including self-appraisals) and train raters (and ratees) in how to use the system. The organization should provide for a review of all performance ratings by upper-level managers and set up a system for employees to appeal when they believe they were evaluated unfairly. Along with feedback, the system should include a process for coaching or training employees to help them improve, rather than simply dismissing poor performers.

Supervisors and managers must also be careful to ensure performance feedback does not go beyond

Thinking ETHICALLY

What Are the Ethical Boundaries of Tracking Employee Activities?

Mobile and wearable devices are making it easier than ever to track what employees do at work. True, measuring physical motions of workers goes back to the Industrial Age. But motion-sensing devices (think Fitbit or Xbox Kinect for the workplace) make data collection precise and affordable. Add to this the ease of data entry via smartphones and tablets, as well as computers positioned on workstations, and there are almost no limits to what employers can know about employees' activities.

Examples of how employers are using the technology include the measurement of computer keystrokes, employee traffic patterns as they walk, and driving patterns of employees who travel or make deliveries in company vehicles. An ad agency has employees sign in each day by posting selfies on a designated social-media service; it says the advantage is that it can easily keep attendance when employees are working off-site.

Along with the ability to gather data come questions about whether some kinds of data are or should be off-limits. Although employers have some legal latitude to observe employees on the job, monitoring has to be in working areas during work hours. Also, employers should be careful to use monitoring consistently. Employers also need to consider ethical boundaries such as fairness, consent, and mutual respect.

One relevant consideration is that data can empower employees as well as management. In one situation, an employee juggling home and work responsibilities asked to start work at 10 a.m. The company was reluctant, but when it measured her performance, it found that this employee was significantly more productive on the days she started later. Armed with the data, the employee made the case for a flexible work arrangement.

Questions

1. What is your perspective on the use of tech-enabled collection of performance data?
2. Imagine you work for a hospital that wants to track the travel patterns of its nurses to ensure they work efficiently and that each patient is visited a certain number of times each day. What measures would you recommend to promote fairness in the way the system is implemented?

Sources: "The Future of Wearables in the Workplace," *Management Today*, December 2015/January 2016, pp. 52–55; Chitra Narayanan, "Roll Call on Twitter," *Business Today*, July 19, 2015, pp. 34–35; Lee Michael Katz, "Big Employer Is Watching," *HR Magazine*, June 2015, pp. 67–74.

"reasonable criticism." The Ontario Court of Appeal provided guidance to what a supervisor can and cannot do in the context of performance appraisal and performance improvement in the case of Viren Shah, a 12-year employee at Xerox Canada. The court determined that Shah's manager passed beyond the "bounds of reasonableness" when Shah received critical performance reviews that were not based on any substantiated concerns and the manager's behaviour was described as "authoritarian, impatient, and intolerant."[66] As discussed in Chapter 2, provinces including Ontario, Saskatchewan, and Quebec have legislation that expands the definition of harassment, but employees in other provinces also have protection from employers who go too far in their criticism of employees.[67]

Ethical and Privacy Issues

Companies increasingly rely on electronic tracking and monitoring systems to ensure that employees are working when and how they should be and to block access to certain websites (such as those containing inappropriate images). These systems include handprint and fingerprint recognition systems; global positioning systems (GPS), software that can track employees using smartphones and notebook computers; and wearables.

For example, in the trucking industry, drivers are monitored continually.[68] An onboard computer records whether the driver is on or off duty, documents the driver's gas mileage, and tells them where to get fuel. If the truck stops while the driver is on duty, they are asked to provide an explanation. The electronic monitoring system built in to the computer tells the driver which route to follow and records even slight deviations from the route due to traffic or accidents. UPS uses a computer analysis program to monitor its delivery drivers. This helps them avoid wasting time and fuel on left-hand turns on their routes. It also helps promote driver safety by documenting seat belt usage and how many feet a driver backs up, which is a dangerous manoeuvre. Uber uses an app that includes sensors in a driver's smartphone to detect when the driver moves or touches their phone, such as during texting. The app also tracks when drivers speed, cut corners, or brake severely. The purpose of the app is to help drivers improve by providing them with more detailed data than the ratings they receive from customers. The data also provide a record that can protect them from groundless customer complaints.[69]

Companies are also using software that analyzes employees' computers and creates a profile.[70] Over time, the software is able to create a baseline of normal behaviour, including where they log in, what programs and databases they use, and which external websites they browse. It also provides a score for users (a risk score) based on what dangers they may pose to the company, such as stealing data or new product designs or viewing pornography. Software applications can be used to evaluate the content of employees' email and other communications. The software scans for variations in language usage in the emails such as an increase in the use of a phrase such as "missed payment," which may mean the employee is at an increased risk for stealing.

Wearables allow us to track our sleep, steps, and exercise levels. Companies offer health-tracking wearables to employees as part of wellness programs designed to reduce health care costs. For example, IBM distributes Fitbits to employees to encourage them to exercise and maintain a healthy lifestyle.[71] Despite the potential increased productivity and efficiency benefits that can result from these systems, they still present privacy concerns.[72] Critics argue that these systems threaten to reduce the workplace to an electronic sweatshop in which employees are treated as robots that are monitored to maximize productivity for every second they are at work. Also, electronic monitoring systems threaten employees' perceived rights and dignity to work without being monitored.

Some critics argue that electronic tracking systems are needlessly surveilling and tracking employees when there is no reason to believe that anything is wrong. Good managers know what their employees are doing, and electronic systems should not be a substitute for good management. Critics also argue that such systems result in less productivity and motivation, demoralize employees, and create unnecessary stress. A mentality is created that employees always have to be at their desks to be productive. Wearable devices have the potential to gather a much broader range of information than other types of monitoring technology. But most employees don't know what data are being collected, and health and personal data collected by a wearable are not necessarily private or secure. Even when participation in company wellness programs is voluntary and the adoption of wearables is optional, employees may feel pressure to participate and resent the need to do so.

However, electronic monitoring can ensure that time is not abused, it can improve scheduling, and it can help motivate workers and improve performance.[73] To avoid the potential negative effects of electronic monitoring, managers must communicate to employees why they are being monitored. Monitoring may be used more positively to gather information for coaching employees and helping them develop their skills.

Although electronic monitoring can improve productivity, it also generates privacy concerns. Critics point out that an employer should not monitor employees when it has no reason to believe that anything is wrong. Critics complain that monitoring systems threaten to make the workplace an electronic sweatshop in which employees are treated as robots, robbing them of dignity. Some note that employees' performance should be measured by accomplishments, not just time spent at a desk or workbench. Electronic systems should not be a substitute for careful management.

As discussed in Chapter 2, privacy legislation (e.g., the federal Personal Information Protection and Electronic Documents Act [PIPEDA]) has additional implications for performance management. Organizations are required to ensure that personal information including an employee's performance review is securely protected, retained only for a specified time, and accessible to the employee.

SUMMARY

LO1 Describe the relevance, purpose, and criteria associated with an effective performance management system.

Many organizations are questioning and scrutinizing the effectiveness of their performance management systems. As a result, organizations are transforming their approaches to performance management. The most frequent change to performance management systems is adopting a feedback, coaching, and developmental focus. Performance management systems are intended to meet three broad purposes: strategic, administrative, and developmental.

LO2 Identify the activities involved in performance management.

How performance management is handled is a key part of the employee experience. Performance management is the process through which managers ensure that employees' activities and outputs contribute to the organization's goals. The organization begins by specifying which aspects of performance are relevant; the relevant aspects of performance are measured through performance appraisal; and in performance feedback sessions, employees receive information about their performance.

LO3 Compare the major performance management methods and sources of information.

The methods for measuring performance include approaches that compare employees' performance or look at each employee's performance individually by rating attributes or behaviours, or by measuring results. Performance information may come from an employee's self-appraisal or from others including the employee's manager, peers, direct reports, and/or customers and clients. Each option has associated strengths and weaknesses. Performance management systems may integrate several of these sources in the form of 360-degree performance appraisal or crowdsourcing.

LO4 Explain how to minimize rating errors and effectively provide performance feedback.

Performance measurement can be distorted by unconscious bias, rating errors, and appraisal politics. Performance measurement errors can be reduced by providing rater error training, rater accuracy training, unconscious bias training, and calibration meetings, as well as using data analytics and analysts, and providing training to employees (ratees). Performance feedback should be a regular, scheduled management activity, carried out in a way that both parties feel heard, understood, and respected.

LO5 Discuss some of the legal, ethical, and privacy issues that impact performance management.

Legal issues related to performance management usually involve claims of discrimination, psychological harassment, and constructive or unjust dismissal. Managers must make sure that performance management systems and decisions treat employees fairly, without regard to their age, sex (gender), ethnicity, or other prohibited grounds. An ethical issue of performance management is the use of electronic tracking and monitoring systems.

CRITICAL THINKING QUESTIONS

1. Why are companies changing their performance management systems? Is this a good idea? Explain your answer.
2. Give two examples of an administrative decision that would be based on performance management information. Give two examples of developmental decisions based on this type of information.
3. Consider how you might rate the performance of three instructors from whom you are currently taking a course. (If you are currently taking fewer than three courses, consider this one and two you recently completed.)
   a. Would it be more difficult to *rate* the instructors' performance or to *rank* their performance? Why?
   b. Prepare two items to use in rating the instructors—one each to rate them in terms of a behaviour and an outcome.
   c. Which measure in (b) do you think is most valid? Most reliable? Why?
   d. Many universities and colleges use surveys or questionnaires to gather data from students about their instructors' performance. Would it be appropriate to use the data for administrative decisions? Developmental decisions? Other decisions? Why or why not?
4. What do you think is the most important step shown in the performance management process? Explain your answer.
5. Do you think performance ratings are necessary? Why or why not?
6. Explain what fairness has to do with performance management.
7. Why might a manager unintentionally distort performance ratings or the reasons used to explain

an employee's performance? What would you recommend to minimize this problem?

8. Describe a time when you received performance feedback that resulted in you feeling valued. What aspects of effective performance feedback discussed in this chapter contributed to this positive feedback experience?

9. How can the use of technology enhance the performance management process? What concerns or issues could arise?

10. Can electronic monitoring and tracking of performance ever be acceptable to employees? Explain.

EXPERIENCING HR—IS IT AGEISM OR A PERFORMANCE ISSUE?

You are an HR Business Partner (HR Generalist). One of your clients is Gretchen, a first-time manager who was recently promoted to the position of Supervisor–Technical Writing. She has called you seeking your advice. Note: The Supervisor—Technical Writing position is accountable for several writers who write, revise, and maintain technical policy and procedure documents for a telecommunications company.

Gretchen: "I am enjoying the new job and would value your advice about one of the writers. I get frustrated with her periodically, and she happens to be the oldest person on my team. it's Rachel—she's in her 60s, I guess. There's a lot of things that seem to come easily to all the other writers but with Rachel, I have to keep asking her for her content updates and ideas. Everyone else on the team comes up with a monthly set of plans and priorities but Rachel says she needs me to give her ideas. I've been letting this slide with her because of some personal problems she's been struggling with but also because I'm worried that perhaps at least some of my frustration comes from ageism. Rachel is not quick to respond to emails, she struggles with using digital tools on the new authoring platform, and gets defensive when I give her feedback. Rachel is a very kind person and sometimes she turns in really good work but I'm concerned that she's not happy to have a supervisor who is so much younger: Rachel's younger sister went to high school with my mother! I'm considering lightening her work load in the coming weeks to take off some strain and see if that makes a difference. I value your perspective. Is this a valid performance issue or is this a reality check for me—that I could be guilty of being too hard on Rachel because of her age?

What evidence would you look for to help you understand whether Gretchen is "guilty" of ageism? What behaviours (e.g., words or action) would be associated with a supervisor demonstrating ageism? What behaviours (e.g., words or actions) would be associated with a supervisor demonstrating an appropriate approach to dealing with an employee's performance gap? Write a one-page summary of your findings that you will use to guide your follow-up conversation with Gretchen. What credible and current sources did you access to inform your findings?

Based on: Alison Green, "Am I Guilty of Age Discrimination at Work?" *The Cut*, April 17, 2018, https://www.thecut.com; Kate Rockwood, "Hiring in the Age of Ageism," *HR Today*, February 2018, https://www.shrm.org; Sarah Dobson, "Older Tech Workers Face Ageism in Hiring," *Canadian HR Reporter*, October 30, 2017, pp. 3, 16.

CASE STUDY: EVIDENCE-BASED HRM

Encouraging Frequent and Productive Performance Conversations

Adobe Systems Inc. provides multimedia and creativity software products including Photoshop, Adobe Acrobat, and Adobe Acrobat Reader. Adobe was experiencing an increase in turnover, which it discovered was related to employees' dissatisfaction with the performance review process, a lack of recognition, and the lack of regular feedback about their performance. Like other companies, Adobe used a performance review system in which managers provided an overall rating of each employee on a scale from 1 to 4, based on how the employee's performance compared to that of other employees. This created a competitive work environment, rather than the collaborative one that Adobe values. Each year after employees received their reviews, HR saw a spike in voluntary turnover, which was especially concerning because Adobe was losing good employees.

To improve performance management, Adobe decided to abandon annual ratings and introduced a new system called Check-In. Check-In emphasizes ongoing feedback. Instead of managers discussing performance with employees only during the formal performance review, as tended to occur in the old system, Check-In encourages managers and employees to have informal performance discussions at least every other month. Managers are asked to focus performance discussions around employees' performance objectives or goals and what resources they need to succeed. Also, employees' career development needs are part of the conversations. Managers are given complete freedom to decide how often and in what ways they want to set goals and provide feedback. The discussion is future focused. That is, both the employee and the manager consider what to change to increase the likelihood that performance will be effective. Employees are evaluated on the basis of how they have performed against their goals rather than how they compare to other employees. More frequent performance feedback is especially important to Millennial employees, who are used to real-time communications through texting and postings.

Managers no longer have to complete lengthy performance evaluation forms and submit them to HR. HR's role is to provide managers with consulting and tools to help with performance discussions rather than policing to see if reviews are completed or discussions have occurred. Both managers and employees can access a resource centre that provides materials about coaching, giving feedback, and personal and professional development. For example, managers might use the resource centre to help them with tough performance conversations such as those involving giving employees difficult feedback. HR relies on what is known as a skip-level process to ensure that performance discussions are occurring throughout the year. This means that the manager's own boss holds the manager accountable for having performance discussions. The boss asks employees if discussions are occurring and if they have a development plan.

There are several indications that Check-In is effective. HR includes questions about performance management in its annual employee survey. Survey results show that 80 percent of employees responded that they had regular performance meetings with their managers and felt supported by them. Since Check-In was introduced, voluntary turnover has decreased by 25 percent. Also, it is estimated that Check-In saves Adobe managers 80,000 hours each year that were previously spent completing employee performance evaluation forms.

Questions

1. What steps should managers take to ensure that performance discussions are effective?
2. What are the benefits and potential disadvantages of more frequent performance discussions between managers and employees?
3. Which purpose of performance management will be more difficult to achieve for companies like Adobe that decide to eliminate ranking or rating employee performance?

Sources: Based on R. Feintzeig, "The Trouble with Grading Employees," *Wall Street Journal,* April 22, 2015, pp. B1, B7; D. Meinert, "Reinventing Reviews," *HR Magazine,* April 2015, pp. 36–40; J. Ramirez, "Rethinking the Review," *Human Resource Executive,* July/August 2013, pp. 16–19.

CASE STUDY: HRM SOCIAL

Apps Make Giving and Receiving Feedback Quick and Easy

IBM's Checkpoint performance management app allows employees to set short-term performance goals and managers to provide feedback on their progress. Employees and managers at Mozilla can use an app to send each other colourful "badges" to recognize good performance. The badges include slogans such as "you rock" or "kicking butt." Also, employees can receive feedback and coaching from peers and managers by posting short questions about their performance, such as "What did you think about my speech?"

The availability of apps used to ask for and give feedback may not always be positive. Amazon's Anytime Feedback Tool can be used secretly by office workers to praise or critique their colleagues. The peer evaluations can be submitted to members of the management team at any time, using the company's internal directory. Many workers used the app in a dysfunctional way. They described making agreements with colleagues to comment negatively on the same co-worker or to heap high praise on each other. Some employees felt sabotaged by the negative comments from unidentified colleagues. In some cases, the negative comments were copied directly into employees' performance reviews (known as "the full paste.").

Questions

1. Does the use of apps for feedback help or hinder performance management? Explain.
2. Can a performance management app replace the need for a regularly scheduled performance evaluation? Why or why not?

Sources: Based on H. Clancy, "How Am I Doing?" *Fortune,* March 1, 2017, p. 34; D. MacMillan, "Uber to Monitor Actions by Drivers in Safety Push," *Wall Street Journal,* June 30, 2016; M. Weinstein, "Annual Review under Review," *Training,* July/August 2016, pp. 22–29; C. Zillman, "IBM Is Blowing Up Its Annual Performance Review," *Fortune,* February 1, 2016; B. Hassell, "IBM's New Checkpoint Reflects Employee Preferences," *Workforce,* April 2016, p. 12; J. Kantor and D. Streitfeld, "Inside Amazon: Wrestling Big Ideas in a Bruising Workplace," *New York Times,* August 16, 2015, p. A1; E. Goldberg, "Performance Management Gets Social," *HR* Magazine, August 2014, pp. 35–38.

PART 4

Compensating and *Rewarding Human Resources*

CHAPTER 8

Total Rewards

Blend Images/Getty Images

CHAPTER 8

Total Rewards

WHAT DO I NEED TO KNOW?

After reading this chapter, you should be able to:

LO1 Discuss how organizations implement a "total rewards" approach to compensating and rewarding employees.

LO2 Identify the kinds of decisions and influences involved in providing base pay to employees.

LO3 Describe how organizations recognize individual, team, and organizational performance with incentives.

LO4 Summarize the role of employee benefits and the types of benefits offered by employers.

LO5 Review the importance of effectively communicating the organization's approach to total rewards.

LO6 Examine issues related to compensating and rewarding executives.

Ovais Iqbal/ Cisco.

Cisco's Time2Give provides full-time employees with five days of paid leave each year to volunteer with a non-profit or charity organization.

Cisco Provides Time2Give

Time2Give is the formal volunteering policy of the global IT and networking firm Cisco. The policy provides all full-time employees with five days of paid time each year to volunteer at a non-profit organization or charity of their choice. David Heather, vice-president of HR for Canada explains, "Employees were volunteering on their own time and taking some time off personally. We wanted to make the commitment to our employees that they could have five days of paid leave that wouldn't affect their benefits."

Cisco employees can schedule the time in increments such as two hours twice a month or take the five days as a block of time. Employees let their managers know and book their time in the company tracking system, similar to how they book vacation time. The volunteer projects vary from judging a local science fair, to scuba diving to clear debris, to building schools in Africa. "We leave it open to our employees," says Heather. "It's their passion; it's their choice."

With his time from "Time2Give," Toronto-based Ovais Iqbal, director of systems engineering, recently travelled to Turkey for one week to volunteer with the Canadian charity Minhaj Welfare Foundation. The Foundation provides aid and distributes food to people displaced by the violence in Syria and was exploring the feasibility of building an orphan care home in Reyhanli, a town near the Syrian border. Iqbal shared his experience on a Cisco blog: "There is no doubt that this trip has changed me. I feel grateful to live in Canada and to work for a company that believes we have a responsibility to be our better selves and help those in need, no matter where they are in the world."[1]

LO1 Introduction

Many organizations are recognizing the strategic value of adopting a comprehensive approach to compensating and rewarding employees, frequently referred to as **total rewards**. Figure 8.1 shows how a total rewards strategy reflecting the organization's culture, business strategy, and HR strategy is a powerful tool to attract, motivate, engage, and retain employees while achieving organizational performance and results.

> **total rewards** A comprehensive approach to compensating and rewarding employees.

RBC defines its approach to employee compensation and benefits to take into account the "overall work experience provided to employees."[2] Organizations with this total rewards approach create a *value proposition* for current and prospective employees that considers the total value they receive for contributing their time and energy to the company. Because compensation, benefits, and the work experience have a major impact on employee attitudes and behaviours, total rewards influence what kinds of employees are attracted to (and remain with) the organization. A survey on strategic rewards and pay practices reported that Canadian companies cited the primary reason for developing a total rewards strategy was to align rewards with the business strategy.[3] As shown in Figure 8.2, the Conference Board of Canada's Compensation Planning Outlook 2018 identified the top rewards activities and priorities for the next 12 to 18 months as maintaining competitive position; reviewing strategy and ensuring alignment with business objectives; retaining talent, attracting talent; and connecting pay and performance.[4]

FIGURE 8.1

Total Rewards Model

Sources: Contents © 2018. Reprinted with permission from WorldatWork. Content is licensed for use by purchaser only. No part of this article may be reproduced, excerpted or redistributed in any form without express written permission from WorldatWork. WorldatWork website: www.worldatwork.org

FIGURE 8.2

Top Rewards Activities and Priorities

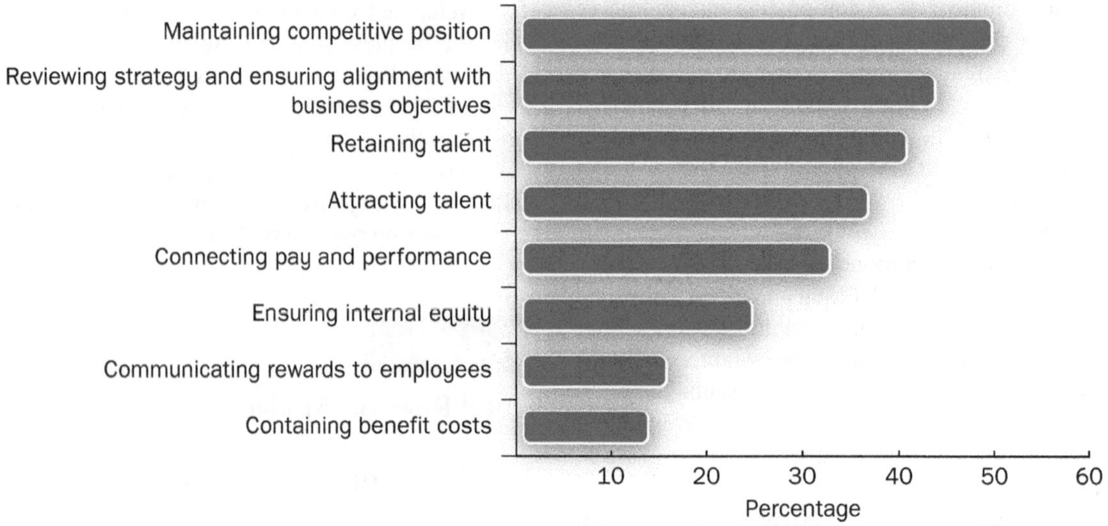

Source: Heather McAteer, "Compensation Planning Outlook 2018" (Ottawa: Conference Board of Canada, October 2017), p. 19. Reprinted with permission by the Conference Board of Canada.

Employees care about policies affecting their compensation, benefits, and the work experience itself because these policies affect not only their income but also their overall well-being and security. Also, employees consider these elements a sign of status and success. They attach great importance to compensation and rewards when they evaluate their relationship and satisfaction with their employers. As the workforce becomes increasingly diverse, the definition of what employees expect in exchange for their work will become increasingly complex. For example, Table 8.1 provides some generational total rewards preferences for consideration. This chapter addresses total rewards; however, the primary emphasis will be on forms of **total compensation**, that is, direct and indirect compensation including base pay, incentives, and benefits received in exchange for the employee's contribution of time, talent, effort, and results.[5] In addition, Chapter 1 discussed (and Chapter 11 will discuss) attributes of work environments where employees are more likely to experience satisfaction and engagement, Chapter 6 explored training, learning, and development opportunities provided to employees, and Chapter 7 examined performance processes. A comprehensive "Total Rewards Inventory" checklist outlining elements that could be included in an organization's value proposition is provided in Figure 8.3.

total compensation All types of financial rewards and tangible benefits and services employees receive as part of their employment.

direct compensation Financial rewards employees receive in exchange for their work.

This chapter opens by describing the role of **direct compensation**—all types of financial rewards employees

TABLE 8.1

Generational Emphasis within Total Rewards

Baby Boomers	High-visibility projects, promotions, support around work/life issues, personal learning and development, onsite facilities, industry recognition
Gen X	Training, learning, and development; challenging tasks/stretch assignments; independent work environment; project variety; work/life balance; flexible work arrangements; variable pay
Millennials (Gen Y)	Meaningfulness of work/projects, manager feedback, casual work environment, daily work/life balance, access to senior leaders, mentoring, social activities, community involvement, flextime

Source: Adapted from Adwoa K. Buahene and Giselle Kovary, "The Great Divide," *HR Professional*, October/November 2007, p. 27.

FIGURE 8.3

Total Rewards Inventory

Compensation

Base Wages
- ☐ Salary Pay
- ☐ Hourly Pay
- ☐ Piece Rate Pay

Premium Pay
- ☐ Shift Differential Pay
- ☐ Weekend/Holiday Pay
- ☐ On-Call Pay
- ☐ Call-In Pay
- ☐ Hazard Pay
- ☐ Bilingual Pay
- ☐ Skill-Based Pay

Variable Pay
- ☐ Commissions
- ☐ Team-Based Pay
- ☐ Bonus Programs
  - ☐ Referral Bonus
  - ☐ Hiring Bonus
  - ☐ Retention Bonus
  - ☐ Project Completion Bonus
- ☐ Incentive Pay
  - Short-Term:
    - ☐ Profit Sharing
    - ☐ Individual Performance–Based Incentives
    - ☐ Performance-Sharing Incentives
  - Long-Term:
    - ☐ Restricted Stock
    - ☐ Performance Shares
    - ☐ Performance Units
    - ☐ Stock Options/Grants

Benefits

Legally Required/Mandated
- ☐ Employment Insurance
- ☐ Workers' Compensation Insurance
- ☐ Canada Pension Plan/Quebec Pension Plan

Health & Welfare
- ☐ Medical Plan
- ☐ Dental Plan
- ☐ Vision Plan
- ☐ Prescription Drug Plan
- ☐ Flexible Spending Accounts (FSAs)
- ☐ Health Reimbursement Accounts (HRAs)
- ☐ Health Savings Accounts (HSAs)
- ☐ Life Insurance
- ☐ Spouse/Dependent Life Insurance
- ☐ AD&D Insurance
- ☐ Short-Term/Long-Term Disability Insurance

Retirement
- ☐ Defined Benefit Plan
- ☐ Defined Contribution Plan
- ☐ Profit-Sharing Plan
- ☐ Hybrid Plan

Pay for Time Not Worked
- ☐ Vacation
- ☐ Holiday
- ☐ Sick Leave
- ☐ Bereavement Leave
- ☐ Leaves of Absence (personal, medical, family)

Work/Life

Workplace Flexibility/Alternative Work Arrangements
- ☐ Flextime
- ☐ Flexible Schedules
- ☐ Telecommuting
- ☐ Alternative Work Sites
- ☐ Compressed Workweek
- ☐ Job Sharing
- ☐ Part-Time Employment
- ☐ Seasonal Schedules

Paid and Unpaid Time Off
- ☐ Maternity/Family Leave
- ☐ Sabbaticals

Health and Wellness
- ☐ Employee Assistance Programs
- ☐ On-Site Fitness Facilities
- ☐ Discounted Fitness Club Rates
- ☐ Preventive Care Programs
- ☐ Weight Management Programs
- ☐ Smoking Cessation Assistance
- ☐ On-Site Massages
- ☐ Stress Management Programs
- ☐ Voluntary Immunization Clinics
- ☐ Wellness Initiatives
- ☐ Health Screenings
- ☐ Nutritional Counselling
- ☐ On-Site Nurse
- ☐ Business Travel Health Services
- ☐ Occupational Health Programs
- ☐ Disability Management
- ☐ Return-to-Work Programs
- ☐ Reproductive Health/Pregnancy Programs

Community Involvement
- ☐ Community Volunteer Programs
- ☐ Matching Gift Programs
- ☐ Shared Leave Programs
- ☐ Disaster Relief Funds
- ☐ Sponsorships/Grants
- ☐ In-Kind Donations

Caring for Dependants
- ☐ Dependant Care Reimbursement Accounts
- ☐ Dependant Care Travel-Related Expense Reimbursement
- ☐ Dependant Care Referral and Resource Services
- ☐ Dependant Care Discount Programs or Vouchers
- ☐ Emergency Dependant Care Services
- ☐ Childcare Subsidies
- ☐ On-Site Caregiver Support Groups
- ☐ On-Site Dependant Care
- ☐ Adoption Assistance Services
- ☐ After-School Care Programs
- ☐ University and college/Scholarship Information
- ☐ Scholarships
- ☐ Mother's Privacy Rooms
- ☐ Summer Camps and Activities

Financial Support
- ☐ Financial Planning Services and Education
- ☐ Adoption Reimbursement
- ☐ Transit Subsidies
- ☐ Savings Bonds

Voluntary Benefits
- ☐ Long-Term Care
- ☐ Auto/Home Insurance
- ☐ Pet Insurance
- ☐ Legal Insurance
- ☐ Identity Theft Insurance
- ☐ Employee Discounts
- ☐ Concierge Services
- ☐ Transit Passes
- ☐ Parking

Culture Change Initiatives
- ☐ Work Redesign
- ☐ Team Effectiveness
- ☐ Diversity/Inclusion Initiatives
- ☐ Work Environment Initiatives

Performance & Recognition

Performance
- ☐ Manager/Employee 1:1 Meetings
- ☐ Performance Reviews
- ☐ Project Completion/Team Evaluations
- ☐ Performance Planning/Goal-Setting Sessions

Recognition
- ☐ Service Awards
- ☐ Retirement Awards
- ☐ Peer Recognition Awards
- ☐ Spot Awards
- ☐ Managerial Recognition Programs
- ☐ Organization-Wide Recognition Programs
- ☐ Exceeding Performance Awards
- ☐ Employee of the Month/Year Awards
- ☐ Appreciation Luncheons, Outings, Formal Events
- ☐ Goal-Specific Awards (quality, efficiency, cost savings, productivity, safety)
- ☐ Employee Suggestion Programs

Development & Career Opportunities

Learning Opportunities
- ☐ Tuition Reimbursement
- ☐ Tuition Discounts
- ☐ Corporate Universities
- ☐ New Technology Training
- ☐ On-the-Job Learning
- ☐ Attendance at Outside Seminars and Conferences
- ☐ Access to Virtual Learning, Podcasts, Webinars
- ☐ Self-Development Tools

Coaching/Mentoring
- ☐ Leadership Training
- ☐ Exposure to Resident Experts
- ☐ Access to Information Networks
- ☐ Formal or Informal Mentoring Programs

Advancement Opportunities
- ☐ Internships
- ☐ Apprenticeships
- ☐ Overseas Assignments
- ☐ Internal Job Postings
- ☐ Job Advancement/Promotion
- ☐ Career Ladders and Pathways
- ☐ Succession Planning
- ☐ On/Off Ramps Through Career Lifecycle
- ☐ Job Rotations

Source: Based on WorldatWork "Your Total Rewards Inventory," p. 4, retrieved May 5, 2008. Contents © 2018. Reprinted with permission from WorldatWork. Content is licensed for use by purchaser only. No part of this article may be reproduced, excerpted or redistributed in any form without express written permission from WorldatWork. WorldatWork website: www.worldatwork.org

receive as part of their employment—and defines the kinds of influences on those making pay-level decisions. We describe methods of evaluating jobs and market data to develop effective pay structures. Next, we look at the elements of incentive pay systems. The many kinds of incentive pay fall into three broad categories: incentives linked to individual, team, or organizational performance. Choices from these categories should consider not only their strengths and weaknesses, but also their fit with the organization's goals. This chapter also looks at **indirect**

compensation—the benefits and services employees receive in exchange for their work—including the important role benefits play. The chapter also covers why and how organizations should effectively communicate with employees about their total rewards. Finally, this chapter looks at an issue also linked to organizational performance—executive compensation.

indirect compensation The benefits and services employees receive in exchange for their work.

LO2 Decisions about Base Pay

Because pay is important both in its effect on employees and its cost, organizations need to plan what they will pay employees in each job. An unplanned approach, in which each employee's pay is independently negotiated, will likely result in unfairness, dissatisfaction, and rates that are either overly expensive or so low that positions are hard to fill. Organizations make decisions about two aspects of pay structure: job structure and pay level. **Job structure** consists of the relative pay for different jobs within the organization. It establishes relative pay among different functions and different levels of responsibility. For example, job structure defines the difference in pay between an entry-level accountant and an entry-level assembler, as well as the difference between an entry-level accountant, a senior accountant, and a director of accounting. **Pay level** is the average amount (including wages, salaries, and incentives) the organization pays for a particular job. Together, job structure and pay levels establish a **pay structure** that helps the organization achieve goals related to employee motivation, cost control, and the ability to attract and retain talented people.

job structure The relative pay for different jobs within the organization.

pay level The average amount (including wages, salaries, and incentives) the organization pays for a particular job.

pay structure The pay policy resulting from job structure and pay-level decisions.

The organization's job structure and pay levels are policies of the organization. Establishing a pay structure simplifies the process of making decisions about individual employees' pay by grouping together employees with similar jobs. As shown, in Figure 8.4, human resource professionals develop this pay structure based on legal requirements, market forces, and the organization's goals, such as attracting a high-quality workforce and meeting principles of fairness.

What Are the Legal Requirements?

All of an organization's decisions about compensation and rewards need to at least *comply* with the applicable laws. As discussed in Chapter 2, although these laws differ

FIGURE 8.4

Considerations in Developing a Pay Structure

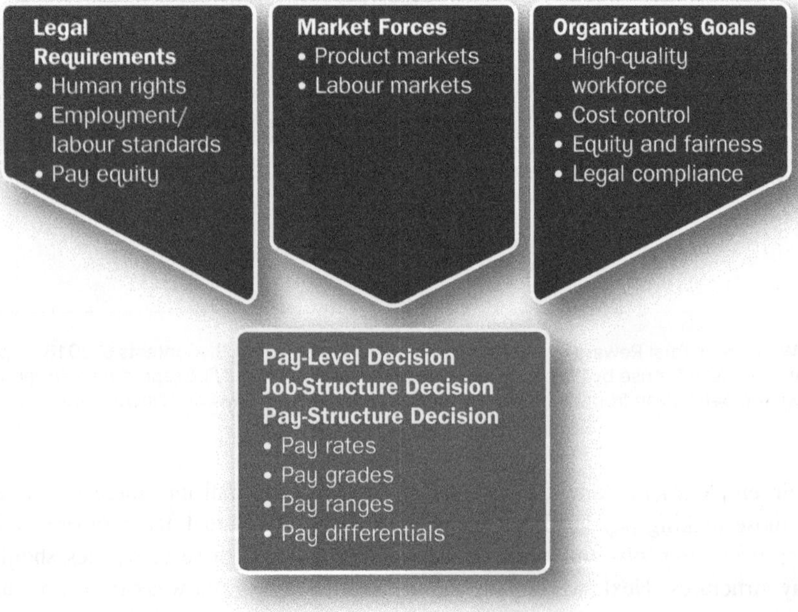

across federal, provincial, and territorial jurisdictions, a common core of legal requirements including human rights legislation, employment labour standards acts, and pay equity legislation exists. Ontario's pay transparency legislation is also provided as an illustrative example of an emerging attention.

- **Human rights legislation**—Employers may not base differences in rewards on an employee's age, sex, race, or other prohibited ground of discrimination. Any differences in pay must instead be tied to business-related considerations such as job responsibilities or performance.
- **Employment/labour standards acts**—The Canada Labour Code and the relevant provincial and territorial laws include minimum requirements for wages, hours of work, overtime pay, vacation, and statutory holidays, as well as other specific provisions. Adopting a $15 per hour minimum wage has stimulated controversy as described later in the chapter in HR Oops. Alberta's minimum hourly wage increased to $15 on October 1, 2018, and British Columbia has announced a $15.20 minimum hourly wage effective June 1, 2021.[6] Executives, professionals, administrative, and outside sales employees are usually considered "exempt" employees and are not eligible for certain provisions such as overtime pay that "non-exempt" employees receive.
- **Pay equity legislation**—In addition to the Federal Government of Canada, pay equity legislation is in place in several provinces, and attempts to address the wage gap between female- and male-dominated jobs to ensure that jobs of equal value within the organization receive similar rates of pay. Organizations use job evaluation (described later in the chapter) to establish the worth of an organization's jobs in terms of criteria such as their difficulty and their importance to the organization. The employer then compares the evaluation points awarded to each job with the pay for each job. If jobs have the same number of evaluation points, they should be paid equally. As discussed in Chapter 2, pay equity remains a highly relevant issue driven through public, political, and organizational awareness and efforts to disrupt gender-based pay gaps.
- **Pay transparency legislation (Ontario)**—Ontario's Pay Transparency Act, 2018, effective January 1, 2019, disrupts the stigma (and fear of potential retaliation) of discussing salary with co-workers and others and reducing the wage gap between female and male employees. Requirements on provincially regulated employers in Ontario include:[7]
    - all publicly advertised job openings must include a salary rate or range.
    - job candidates cannot be asked about past compensation received.
    - employees who discuss their compensation cannot be disciplined or face reprisals.
    - some employers are required to monitor and report "compensation gaps based on gender and/or other diversity characteristics."

Economic Influences on Pay

An organization cannot make spending decisions independent of the economy. Organizations must keep costs low enough that they can sell their products profitably, yet they must be able to attract workers in a competitive labour market. Decisions about how to respond to the economic forces of product markets and labour markets limit an organization's choices about pay structure.

Product and Labour Markets

The organization's *product market* includes organizations that offer competing goods and services—competing to serve the same customers. Organizations under pressure to cut labour costs may respond by reducing staff levels, freezing pay levels, postponing hiring decisions, or requiring employees to bear more of the cost of benefits such as insurance premiums. However, organizations also compete to obtain human resources in *labour markets*—competing with other firms to hire the same skilled employees.

Pay Level: Deciding What to Pay

Although legal requirements and economic influences limit organizations' choices about pay levels, there is a range within which organizations can make decisions.[8] The size of this range depends on the details of the organization's competitive environment. If many workers are competing

Ron Levine/Getty Images

Two employees who do the same job cannot be paid differently because of gender, race, age, or other prohibited grounds of discrimination. Only if there are differences in their experience, skills, seniority, or job performance are there legal reasons their pay might be different.

for a few jobs, employers will have more choice; however, in tight labour markets workers will have more employment options.

When organizations have a broad range in which to make decisions about pay, they can choose to pay *at, above,* or *below* the rate set by market forces. Economic theory holds that the most profitable level, all things being equal, would be at the market rate. Often, however, all things are *not* equal from one employer to another. For instance, an organization may gain an advantage by paying above the market rate if it uses the higher pay as one means to attract top talent and then uses these excellent employees' knowledge to be more innovative, produce higher quality, or work more efficiently.

This approach is based on the view of employees as resources. Higher pay may be an investment in superior human resources. Having higher labour costs than your competitors is not necessarily bad if you also have the best and most effective workforce, which produces more products of better quality. Pay policies are one of the most important human resource tools for encouraging desired employee behaviours. Therefore, organizations must evaluate pay as more than a cost—but rather as an *investment* that can generate returns in attracting, retaining, and motivating a high-quality workforce. Of course, employers do not always have this much flexibility. Some companies are under intense pressure to charge low prices for their products, and some companies are trying to draw workers from a pool that is too small to satisfy all employers' needs.

Gathering Information about Market Pay

To compete for talent, organizations use **benchmarking**, a procedure in which an organization compares its own practices against those of successful competitors. In terms of compensation, benchmarking involves the use of pay surveys that provide information about the going rates of pay at competitors in the organization's product and labour markets. An organization can conduct its own surveys, but the federal government and other organizations make a great deal of data readily available.

benchmarking
A procedure in which an organization compares its own practices against those of successful competitors.

For example, the federal government's Job Bank site provides earnings data by city or postal code for occupations listed in the National Occupational Classification (NOC). Many industry, trade, and professional groups also collect wage and salary data. Employers should check with the relevant groups to see what surveys are available. Consulting firms also will provide data, including the results of international surveys, and can tailor data to an organization's particular needs. Human resource professionals need to determine whether to gather data focusing on particular industries, regions, or job categories.

How Do Employees Judge Pay Fairness?

In developing a pay structure, it is important to keep in mind employees' perceptions about fairness. If employees perceive their pay as unfair, they may experience pay dissatisfaction and be less motivated to achieve organizational goals. Employees evaluate their pay relative to the pay of other employees. Social scientists have studied this kind of comparison and developed *equity theory* to describe how people make judgments about fairness.[9] According to equity theory, people measure outcomes such as pay in terms of their inputs. For example, an employee might think of her pay in terms of her degree, her three years of experience, and her 45+ hour workweeks. To decide whether a certain level of pay is equitable, the person compares her ratio of outcomes and inputs with other people's outcome/input ratios. The person in this example might notice that an employee with less education or experience is earning more than she is (unfair) or that an employee who works 55 hours a week is earning more (fair). In general, employees compare their pay and contributions using several considerations:

- What they think employees in other organizations earn for doing the same job.
- What they think other employees holding different jobs within the organization earn for doing work at the same or different levels.
- What they think other employees in the organization earn for doing the same job.

How employees respond to their impressions about equity can have a great impact on the organization. Typically, if employees see their pay as equitable, their attitudes and behaviour continue unchanged. If employees see themselves as receiving an advantage, they usually rethink the situation to see it as equitable. But if employees conclude that they are under-rewarded, they are likely to make up the difference in one of three ways—putting forth less effort (reducing their inputs), finding a way to increase their outcomes (e.g., asking for a raise), or withdrawing by leaving the organization or withholding their best ideas.

As work becomes more collaborative and the emphasis on knowledge-sharing increases, it becomes more likely that information about pay will also be shared. Social media and sites such as Glassdoor are contributing to this trend.

Job Structure: Relative Value of Jobs

Along with market forces and principles of fairness, organizations consider the relative contribution each job should make to the organization's overall performance. One typical way of doing this is with a **job evaluation**, an administrative procedure for measuring the relative internal worth of the organization's jobs. Usually, the organization does this by assembling and training a job evaluation committee, consisting of people familiar with the jobs to be evaluated. The committee often includes a human resource specialist and, if its budget permits, may hire an outside consultant.

job evaluation
An administrative procedure for measuring the relative internal worth of the organization's jobs.

To conduct a job evaluation, the committee identifies each job's *compensable factors,* meaning the characteristics of a job that the organization values and chooses to pay for. As shown in Table 8.2, an organization might consider the effort required and skill requirements of people performing information technology-related jobs. Other compensable factors might include working conditions and responsibility. Based on the job attributes defined by job analysis (discussed in Chapter 3), the jobs are rated for each factor. The rater assigns each factor a certain number of points, giving more points to factors when they are considered more important and when the job requires a high level of that factor. Often the number of points comes from one of the *point manuals* published by trade groups and management consultants. If necessary, the organization can adapt the scores in the point manual to the organization's situation or even develop its own point manual. As in the example in Table 8.2, the scores for each factor are totalled to arrive at an overall evaluation for each job.

Job evaluations provide the basis for decisions about *relative internal worth*—the value of the job within the organization necessary to meet pay equity requirements as discussed in Chapter 2. According to the sample assessments in Table 8.2, the job of business systems analyst is worth more to this organization than the job of database administrator. Therefore, the organization would be willing to pay significantly more for the work of a business systems analyst than it would for the work of a database administrator.

The organization may limit its pay survey to jobs evaluated as *key jobs.* These are jobs that have relatively stable content and are common among many organizations, so it is possible to obtain survey data about what people earn in these jobs. Organizations can make the process of creating a pay structure more practical by defining key jobs. Research for creating the pay structure is limited to the key jobs that play a significant role in the organization. Pay for the key jobs can be based on survey data, and pay for the organization's other jobs can be based on the organization's job structure. A job with a higher evaluation score than a particular key job would receive higher pay than that key job.

Pay Structure: Putting It All Together

The pay structure reflects decisions about how much to pay (pay level) and the relative value of each job (job structure). The organization's pay structure should reflect what the organization knows about market forces, as well as its own unique goals and the relative contribution of each job to achieving the goals. By balancing this external and internal information, the organization's goal is to set levels of pay that employees will consider fair and motivating. Organizations typically apply the information by establishing some combination of pay rates, pay grades, and pay ranges. Within this structure, they may state the pay in terms of a rate per hour, commonly called an **hourly wage**; a rate of pay for each unit produced, known as a **piecework rate**, or a rate of pay per week, month, or year worked, called a **salary**.

hourly wage
Rate of pay per hour worked.

piecework rate
Rate of pay for each unit produced.

salary Rate of pay for each week, month, or year worked.

Pay Rates

If the organization's main concern is to match what people are earning in comparable jobs, the organization can base pay directly on market research into as many of its key jobs as possible. To do this, the organization looks for survey data for each job title. If it finds data from more

TABLE 8.2

Job Evaluation of Three Jobs with Four Compensable Factors

	Compensable Factors				
Job Title	Skill	Effort	Responsibility	Working Conditions	Total
Database administrator	60	40	30	30	130
Software developer	80	60	50	20	210
Business systems analyst	110	70	70	20	270

than one survey, it must weight the results according to their quality and relevance. In light of that knowledge, the organization decides what it will pay for the job.

The next step is to determine salaries for the non-key jobs, for which the organization has no survey data. Instead, the person developing the pay structure creates a graph like the one in Figure 8.5. The vertical axis shows a range of possible pay rates, and the horizontal axis measures the points from the job evaluation. The analyst plots points according to the job evaluation and pay rate for each key job. Finally, the analyst fits a line, called a **pay policy line**, to the points plotted. (This can be done statistically, using a procedure called regression analysis.) Mathematically, this line shows the relationship between job evaluation and rate of pay. Using this line, the analyst can estimate the market pay level for a given job evaluation. Looking at the graph gives approximate numbers, or the regression analysis will provide an equation for calculating the rate of pay. For example, using the pay policy line in Figure 8.5, a job with 315 evaluation points would have a predicted salary of $7,783 per month.

pay policy line
A graphed line showing the mathematical relationship between job evaluation points and pay rate.

The pay policy line reflects the pay structure in the market, which does not always match rates in the organization (see key job F in Figure 8.5). Survey data may show that people in certain jobs are actually earning significantly more or less than the amount shown on the pay policy line. For example, some kinds of expertise are in short supply. People with that expertise can command higher pay, because they can easily leave one employer to get higher pay somewhere else. Suppose, in contrast, that local businesses have laid off many warehouse employees. Because so many of these workers are looking for jobs, organizations may be able to pay them less than the rate that job evaluation points would suggest.

When job structure and market data conflict in these ways, organizations have to decide on a way to resolve the two. One approach is to stick to the job evaluations and pay according to the employees' worth to the organization. Organizations that do so will be paying more or less than they have to, so they will likely have more difficulty competing for customers or employees. A way to moderate this approach is to consider the importance of each position to the organization's goals.[10] If a position is critical for meeting the organization's goals, paying more than competitors pay may be worthwhile.

At the other extreme, the organization could base pay entirely on market forces. However, this approach also has some practical drawbacks. One is that employees may conclude that pay rates are unfair. Two vice-presidents or two supervisors will expect to receive similar pay because their responsibilities are similar. If the differences between their pay are large, because of different market rates, the lower-paid employee will likely be dissatisfied. Also, if the organization's development plans include rotating managers through different assignments, the managers will be reluctant to participate if managers in some departments receive lower pay. Organizations therefore must weigh all the objectives of their pay structure to arrive at suitable rates.

FIGURE 8.5

Pay Policy Lines

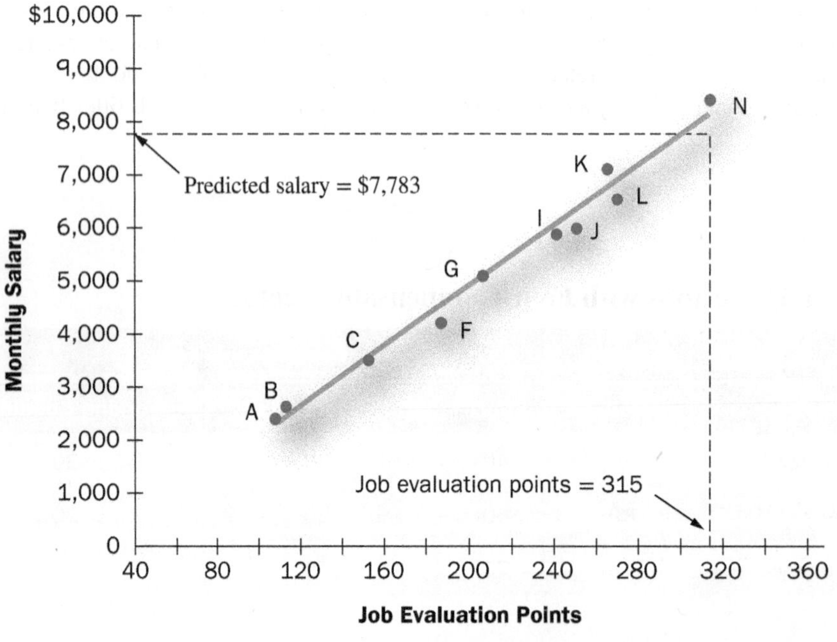

Pay Grades

pay grades Sets of jobs having similar worth or content, grouped together to establish rates of pay.

A large organization could have hundreds or even thousands of different jobs. Setting a pay rate for each job would be extremely complex. Therefore, many organizations group jobs into **pay grades**—sets of jobs having similar worth or content, grouped together to establish rates of pay. For example, the organization could establish five pay grades, with the same pay available to employees holding any job within the same grade.

A drawback of pay grades is that grouping jobs will result in rates of pay for individual jobs that do not precisely match the levels specified by the market and the organization's job structure. Suppose, for example, that the organization groups together its accountants (with a job evaluation of 255 points) and its business systems analysts (with a job evaluation of 270 points). Surveys might show that the market rate of pay for business systems analysts is higher than that for accountants. In addition, the job evaluations give more points to business systems analysts. Even so, for simplicity's sake, the organization pays the same rate for the two jobs, because they are in the same pay grade. The organization would have to pay more than the market requires for accountants or pay less than the market rate for business systems analysts (so it would probably have difficulty recruiting and retaining them).

Pay Ranges

Usually, organizations want some flexibility in setting pay for individual jobs. They want to be able to pay the most valuable employees the highest amounts and to give rewards for performance. Flexibility also helps the organization balance conflicting information from market surveys and job evaluations. Therefore, pay structure usually includes a **pay range** for each job or pay grade. In other words, the organization establishes a *minimum, maximum,* and *midpoint* of pay for employees holding a particular job or a job within a particular pay grade or band. Employees holding the same job may receive somewhat different pay, depending on where their pay falls within the range.

pay range A set of possible pay rates defined by a minimum, maximum, and midpoint of pay for employees holding a particular job or a job within a particular pay grade or band.

A typical approach is to use the market rate or the pay policy line as the midpoint of a range for the job or pay grade. The minimum and maximum values for the range may also be based on market surveys of those amounts. Pay ranges are most common for professional and administrative jobs and for jobs not covered by union contracts. Figure 8.6 shows an example of pay ranges based on the pay policy line in Figure 8.5. Notice that the jobs are grouped into five pay grades, each with its own pay range.

FIGURE 8.6

Sample Pay Grade Structure

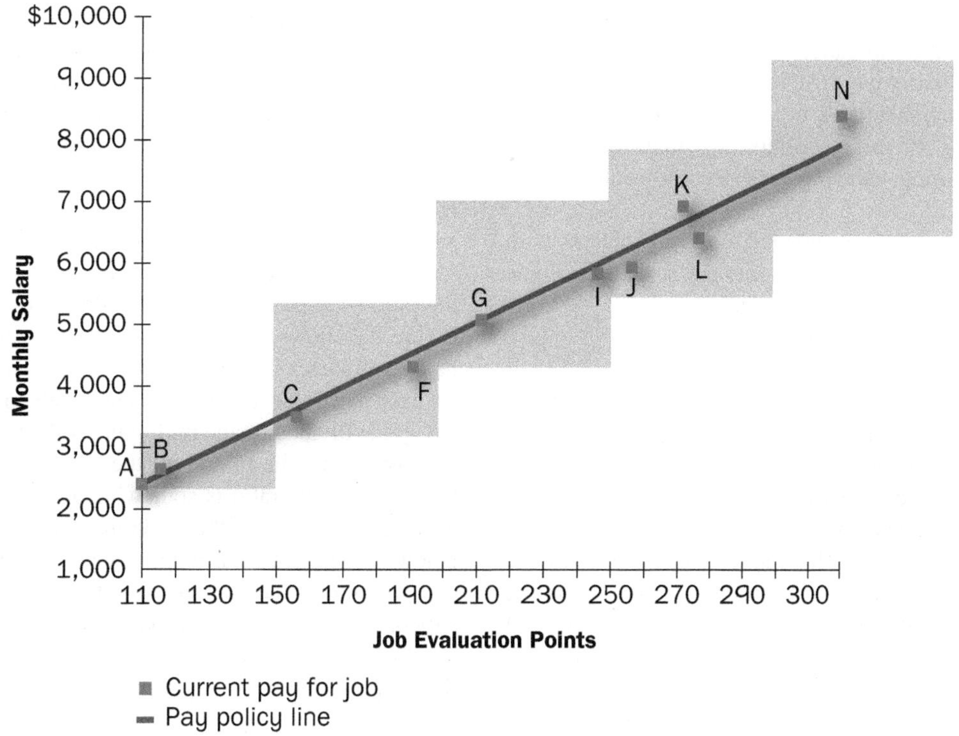

In this example, the range is widest for employees who are at higher levels in terms of their job evaluation points. That is because the performance of these higher-level employees will likely have more effect on the organization's performance, so the organization needs more latitude to reward them. For instance, as discussed earlier, the organization may want to select a higher point in the range to attract an employee who is more critical to achieving the organization's goals.

Usually pay ranges overlap somewhat, so that the highest pay in one grade is somewhat higher than the lowest pay in the next grade. Overlapping ranges gives the organization more flexibility in transferring employees among jobs, because transfers need not always involve a change in pay. On the other hand, the less overlap, the more important it is to earn promotions in order to keep getting raises. Assuming the organization wants to motivate employees through promotions (and assuming enough opportunities for promotion are available), the organization will want to limit the overlap from one level to the next.

Alternatives to Job-based Pay

The traditional and most widely used approach to developing a pay structure focuses on setting pay for jobs or groups of jobs.[11] This emphasis on jobs has some limitations. The precise definition of a job's responsibilities can contribute to a mindset that some activities "are not in my job description," at the expense of flexibility, innovation, quality, and customer service. Organizations may avoid change because it requires repeating the time-consuming process of creating job descriptions and related paperwork. Another change-related problem is that when the organization needs a new set of competencies, the existing pay structure may be rewarding the wrong behaviours. Finally, a pay structure that rewards employees for winning promotions may discourage them from gaining valuable experience through lateral career moves.

Organizations have responded to these problems with a number of alternatives to job-based pay structures. Some organizations have found greater flexibility by **broadbanding**, a pay structure that consolidates pay grades into a few "broad bands," thereby reducing the number of pay ranges in the organization's pay structure. For example, back in the 1990s IBM changed from a pay structure with 5,000 job titles and 24 salary grades to one with 1,200 jobs and 10 bands. Broadbanding reduces the opportunities for promoting employees, but this type of pay structure tends to encourage and provide flexibility for employees to make lateral career moves.

broadbanding A pay structure that consolidates pay grades into a few "broad bands."

Another way organizations have responded to the limitations of job-based pay has been to move away from the link to jobs and toward pay structures that reward employees based on their knowledge and skills (competencies).[12] **Competency-based pay systems** (also known as *skill-based pay systems*) are pay structures that set pay according to the employees' level of skill or knowledge and what they are capable of doing. Paying for competencies makes sense at organizations where changing technology requires employees to continually widen and deepen their knowledge. Competency-based pay also supports efforts to involve employees and enrich jobs because it encourages employees to add to their knowledge so they can make decisions in many areas. In this way, competency-based pay helps organizations become more flexible and innovative. More generally, competency-based pay can encourage a climate of learning and adaptability and give employees a broader view of how the organization functions.

competency-based pay systems Pay structures that set pay according to the employees' levels of skill or knowledge and what they are capable of doing.

A disadvantage associated with this type of pay system is that it rewards employees for acquiring skills but does not provide a way to ensure that employees actually *use* their new skills.[13] The result may be that the organization is paying employees more for learning skills that the employer is not benefiting from. The challenge for HRM is to design work so that the work design and pay structure support one another.

Pay Structure and Actual Pay

Usually the human resource department is responsible for establishing the organization's pay structure. But building the structure is not the end of the organization's decisions about pay structure. The structure represents the organization's policy, but what the organization actually does may be different. As part of its management responsibility, the HR department therefore should compare actual pay to the pay structure, ensuring that policies and practices match.

A common way to do this is to measure a *compa-ratio,* the ratio of average pay to the midpoint of the pay range. Figure 8.7 shows an example. Assuming the organization has pay grades, the organization would find a compa-ratio for each pay grade: the average paid to all employees in the pay grade divided by the midpoint for the pay grade. If the average equals the midpoint, the compa-ratio is 1. More often the compa-ratio is somewhat above 1 (meaning the average pay is above the midpoint for the pay grade) or below 1 (meaning the average pay is below the midpoint).

Assuming that the pay structure is well planned to support the organization's goals, the compa-ratios should be close to 1. A compa-ratio greater than 1 suggests that the organization is paying employees more than planned

FIGURE 8.7

Finding a Compa-Ratio

Pay Grade: 1
Midpoint of Range: $4,675 per month

Salaries of Employees in Pay Grade	
Employee 1	$5,306
Employee 2	$4,426
Employee 3	$5,223
Employee 4	$5,114

Compa-Ratio

$$\frac{\text{Average}}{\text{Midpoint}} = \frac{\$5{,}017.25}{\$4{,}675.00} = 1.07$$

Average Salary of Employees
$5,306 + $4,426 + $5,223 + $5,114 = $20,069
$20,069 ÷ 4 = $5,017.25

and may have difficulty keeping costs under control. A compa-ratio less than 1 suggests that the organization may be underpaying employees and may have difficulty attracting and retaining qualified employees.

LO3 Incentive Pay

The first part of this chapter discussed the framework for total rewards and setting pay for jobs. Now we focus on using pay to recognize and reward employees' contributions to the organization's success.

In contrast to decisions about pay structure, organizations have wide discretion in setting performance-related pay, called **incentive pay** or *pay for performance.* Organizations can tie incentive pay to individual performance, profits, or many other measures of success. They select incentives based on their costs, expected influence on performance, and fit with the organization's broader HR and company policies and goals.

incentive pay Forms of pay linked to an employee's performance as an individual, group member, or organization member.

Many organizations offer incentive pay in the effort to energize, direct, or influence employees' behaviour. According to the Conference Board of Canada, 82 percent of Canadian organizations have at least one short-term incentive plan. These plans are particularly popular in the private sector—91 percent of companies reported having one or more short-term incentive plans and 53 percent of public-sector organizations also have one or more short-term incentive plans.[14] Incentive pay is influential because the amount paid is linked to certain predefined behaviours or outcomes. For example, an organization can pay a salesperson a *commission* for closing a sale, or the members of a production department can earn a *bonus* for meeting a monthly production goal. Knowing they can earn extra money for closing sales or meeting departmental goals, the employees often try harder or get more creative than they might without the incentive pay. In addition, the policy of offering higher pay for higher performance may make an organization attractive to high performers.[15]

For incentive pay to motivate employees to contribute to the organization's success, the plans must be well designed. In particular, effective plans meet the following requirements:

- Performance measures are linked to the organization's goals.
- Employees believe they can meet performance standards.
- The organization gives employees the resources they need to meet their goals.

Adam121/Dreamstime.com/GetStock.com

Many sales associates in the auto industry earn a straight commission, meaning that 100 percent of their pay comes from commission instead of a salary. What type of individual might enjoy a job like this?

- Employees value the rewards given.
- Employees believe the reward system is fair.
- The plan takes into account that employees may ignore any goals that are not rewarded.

Because incentive pay is linked to particular outcomes or behaviours, the organization is encouraging them to demonstrate those desired outcomes and behaviours. As obvious as that may sound, the implications are more complicated. If incentive pay is extremely rewarding, employees may focus on only the performance measures rewarded under the plan and ignore measures that are not rewarded. Many call centres pay employees based on how many calls they handle, as an incentive to work quickly and efficiently. However, speedy call handling does not necessarily foster good customer relationships. Organizations may combine a number of incentives so employees do not focus on one measure to the exclusion of others.

Although most, if not all, employees value pay, it is important to remember that earning money is not the only reason people try to do a good job. As discussed in other chapters (see Chapters 1, 6, and 11), people also want interesting work, appreciation for their efforts, flexibility, and a sense of belonging to the work group—not to mention the inner satisfaction of work well done. Therefore, a complete plan for compensating and rewarding employees has many components, from pay to work design to developing managers so they can provide effective leadership.

We will now identify elements of incentive pay systems. We consider each option's strengths and limitations with regard to these principles. The many kinds of incentive pay fall into three broad categories: incentives linked to individual, team, or organizational performance. Choices from these categories should consider not only their strengths and weaknesses, but also their fit with the organization's goals. The choice of incentive pay may affect not only the level of motivation but also the kinds of employees who are attracted to and stay with the organization. For example, there is some evidence that organizations with team-based rewards will tend to attract employees who are more team oriented.[16]

Pay for Individual Performance

Although individual pay for performance can "foster an individualistic culture or a culture of entitlement,"[17] organizations reward individual performance with a variety of incentives.

- **Piecework rates**—As an incentive to work efficiently, some organizations pay production workers a piecework rate, a wage based on the amount they produce. The amount paid per unit is set at a level that rewards employees for above-average production volume. A clear advantage of piece rates is the direct link between how much work the employee does and the amount the employee earns. However, for complex jobs or jobs with hard-to-measure outputs, piecework plans do not apply very well. Also, unless a plan is well designed to include performance standards, it may not reward employees for focusing on quality or customer satisfaction if it interferes with the day's output. In Figure 8.8, the employees quickly realize they can earn huge bonuses by writing software "bugs" and then fixing them, while writing bug-free software affords no chance to earn bonuses.
- **Standard hour plans**—Another quantity-oriented incentive for production workers is the **standard hour plan**, an incentive plan that pays workers extra for work done in less than a preset "standard time." The organization determines a standard time to complete a task, such as tuning up a car engine. If the mechanic completes the work in less than the standard time, the mechanic receives an amount of pay equal to the wage for the full standard time. Suppose the standard time for tuning up an engine is 2 hours. If the

FIGURE 8.8

How Incentives Sometimes "Work"

Source: DILBERT, reprinted by permission of United Features Syndicate, Inc.

mechanic finishes the tune-up in 1.5 hours, the mechanic receives 2 hours of pay for 1.5 hours worked. Working that fast over the course of a week could add significantly to the mechanic's pay. In terms of pros and cons, standard hour plans are much like piecework plans. They encourage employees to work as fast as they can, but not necessarily to care about quality or customer service.

- **Merit pay**—Almost all organizations have established some program of **merit pay**—a system of linking pay increases to ratings on performance appraisals. An advantage of merit pay is that it provides a method for rewarding performance in all of the dimensions measured in the organization's performance management system. If that system is appropriately designed to measure all the important job behaviours, then the merit pay is linked to the behaviours the organization desires. This link seems logical, although so far there is little research showing the effectiveness of merit pay.[18] A drawback of merit pay, from the employer's standpoint, is that it can quickly become expensive. Managers at a majority of organizations rate most employees' performance in the top two categories (out of four or five).[19] Therefore, the majority of employees are eligible for the biggest merit increases, and their pay rises rapidly. Another drawback of merit pay is that it assumes that performance is based on employees' ability and motivation; however, performance may be enhanced or reduced by factors beyond the employees' control (e.g., economic conditions or a manager's rating bias).

standard hour plan An incentive plan that pays workers extra for work done in less than a preset "standard time."

- **Performance bonuses**—Like merit pay, performance bonuses reward individual performance, but bonuses are not rolled into base pay. The employee must re-earn them during each performance period. In some cases, the bonus is a one-time reward. For example, the nearby Did You Know? discusses the use of "spot" bonuses. Bonuses may also be linked to objective performance measures rather

merit pay A system of linking pay increases to ratings on performance appraisals.

Did You KNOW?

Awarding Spot Bonuses

A majority of companies (60 percent) paid *spot bonuses*—bonuses delivered on the spot for special recognition—most frequently to reward performance above and beyond expectations or upon the completion of a project. In organizations that award these bonuses, maximum payouts to managers, supervisors, and professionals are typically in the range of $2,500 to $5,000.

Questions

1. From the perspective of an employer, how could you determine whether the increase in the use of spot bonuses makes good business sense?

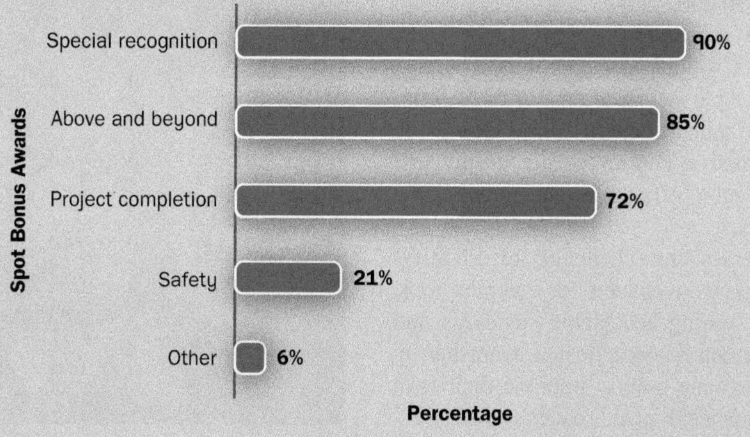

Source: "Bonus Programs and Practices," June 2014, pp. 6, 9, and 19. Contents © 2018. Reprinted with permission from WorldatWork. Content is licensed for use by purchaser only. No part of this article may be reproduced, excerpted or redistributed in any form without express written permission from WorldatWork. WorldatWork website: www.worldatwork.org

than potentially subjective ratings. Bonuses for individual performance can be extremely effective and give the organization great flexibility in deciding what kinds of behaviour to reward. All this flexibility makes it essential to be sure that bonuses are tied to behaviour that makes a difference for the organization's overall performance and to ensure that employees have some control over achieving the bonus requirements.

- **Commissions**—A variation on piece rates and bonuses is the payment of **commissions**, or pay calculated as a percentage of sales. For instance, a flooring sales consultant might earn commissions equalling 6 percent of the price of the flooring the person sells during the period. In a growth-oriented organization, sales commissions need not be limited to salespeople.

commissions Incentive pay calculated as a percentage of sales.

Pay for Team Performance

Employers may address the drawbacks of individual incentives by including team incentives in the organization's compensation plan. To earn team incentives, employees must cooperate and share knowledge so that the entire team can meet its performance targets. Widely used team incentives include gainsharing, bonuses, and team awards.

Gainsharing

Organizations that want employees to focus on efficiency may adopt a **gainsharing** program, which measures increases in productivity and effectiveness and distributes a portion of each gain to employees. For example, if a factory enjoys a productivity gain worth $30,000, half the gain might be the company's share. The other $15,000 would be distributed among the employees in the factory. Knowing that they can enjoy a financial benefit from helping the company be more productive, employees supposedly will look for ways to work more efficiently and improve the way the factory operates.

gainsharing Team incentive program that measures improvements in productivity and effectiveness and distributes a portion of each gain to employees.

Gainsharing addresses the challenge of identifying appropriate performance measures for complex jobs. Even for simpler jobs, setting acceptable standards and measuring performance can be complicated. Gainsharing frees employees to determine how to improve their own and their team's performance. It also broadens employees' focus beyond their individual interests. But in contrast to profit sharing, discussed later, it keeps the performance measures within a range of activity that most employees believe they can influence. Organizations can enhance the likelihood of a gain by providing a means for employees to share knowledge and make suggestions, as we will discuss later in this chapter.

Gainsharing is most likely to succeed when organizations provide the right conditions. Among the conditions identified, the following are among the most common:[20]

- management commitment
- need for change or strong commitment to continuous improvement
- management acceptance and encouragement of employee input
- high levels of cooperation and interaction
- employment security
- information sharing on productivity and costs
- goal setting
- commitment of all involved parties to the process of change and improvement
- performance standards and calculations that employees understand and consider fair and that are closely related to managerial objectives
- employees who value working in teams

Team Bonuses and Awards

In contrast to gainsharing plans, which typically reward the performance of all employees at a facility, bonuses for team performance tend to be for smaller work groups.[21] These bonuses reward the members of a group for attaining a specific goal, usually measured in terms of physical output. Team awards are similar to team bonuses, but they are more likely to use a broad range of performance measures, such as cost savings, successful completion of a project, or even meeting deadlines.

Robert Churchill/Getty Images

Team members who meet a sales goal or a product development team that meets a deadline or successfully launches a product may be rewarded with a bonus for team performance. What are some advantages and disadvantages of team bonuses?

Both types of incentives have the advantage that they encourage group or team members to cooperate and collaborate so that they can achieve their goal. However, depending on the reward system, competition among individuals may be replaced by competition among teams. Competition may be healthy in some situations, as when teams try to outdo one another in satisfying customers. On the downside, competition may also prevent necessary cooperation among teams. To avoid this, the organization should carefully set the performance goals for these incentives so that concern for costs or sales does not obscure other objectives, such as quality, customer service, and ethical behaviour.

Pay for Organizational Performance

Two important ways organizations measure their performance are in terms of their profits and their stock price. In a competitive marketplace, profits result when an organization is efficiently providing products that customers want at a price they are willing to pay. Stock is the owners' investment in a corporation; when the stock price is rising, the value of that investment is growing. Rather than trying to figure out what performance measures will motivate employees to do the things that generate high profits and a rising stock price, many organizations offer incentive pay tied to those organizational performance measures. The expectation is that employees will focus on what is best for the organization.

These organization-level incentives can motivate employees to align their activities with the organization's goals. At the same time, linking incentives to the organization's profits or stock price exposes employees to a high degree of risk. Profits and stock price can soar very high very fast, but they can also fall. The result is a great deal of uncertainty about the amount of incentive pay each employee will receive in each period. Therefore, these kinds of incentive pay are likely to be most effective in organizations that emphasize growth and innovation, which tend to need employees who thrive in a risk-taking environment.[22]

Profit Sharing

With **profit sharing**, payments are a percentage of the organization's profits and do not become part of the employees' base salary. Organizations use profit sharing for a number of reasons. It may encourage employees to think more like owners, taking a broad view of what they need to do in order to make the organization more effective. Employees are more likely to cooperate and less likely to focus on narrow self-interest. Also, profit sharing has the practical advantage of costing less when the organization is experiencing financial difficulties. If the organization has little or no profit, this incentive pay is small or nonexistent, so employers may not need to rely as much on layoffs to reduce costs.[23]

profit sharing Incentive pay in which payments are a percentage of the organization's profits and do not become part of the employees' base salary.

An organization setting up a profit-sharing plan should consider what to do if profits fall. If the economy slows and profit-sharing payments disappear along with profits, employees may become discouraged or dissatisfied. If profit sharing is offered to all employees but most employees think only management decisions about products, price, and marketing have much impact on profits, they will conclude that there is little connection between their actions and their rewards. In that case, profit sharing will have little impact on employee behaviours. This problem is even greater when employees have to wait months before profits are distributed. The time lag between high performance, behaviour, and financial rewards is sometimes simply too long to be motivating.

Given the limitations of profit-sharing plans, one strategy is to use them as a component of a pay system that includes other kinds of pay more directly linked to individual behaviour. This increases employees' commitment to organizational goals while addressing concerns about fairness.

Stock Ownership

While profit-sharing plans are intended to encourage employees to "think like owners," a stock ownership plan actually makes employees part owners of the organization. Like profit sharing, employee ownership is intended as a way to encourage employees to focus on the success of the organization as a whole. The drawbacks of stock ownership as a form of incentive pay are similar to those of profit sharing. Specifically, it may not have a strong effect on individuals' motivation. Employees may not see a strong link between their actions and the company's stock price, especially in larger organizations. The link between pay and performance is even harder to appreciate because the financial benefits mostly come when the stock is sold—typically when the employee leaves the organization. Ownership programs usually take the form of *stock options* or *employee stock ownership plans.* These are illustrated in Figure 8.9.

Stock Options

One way to distribute stock to employees is to grant **stock options**—the right to buy a certain number of shares of stock at a specified price. (Purchasing the stock is called *exercising* the option.) Suppose that in 2019 a company's employees received options to purchase the company's stock at $10 per share. The employees will benefit if the stock price rises above $10 per share, because they can pay $10 for something

stock options Rights to buy a certain number of shares of stock at a specified price.

FIGURE 8.9

Types of Pay for Organizational Performance

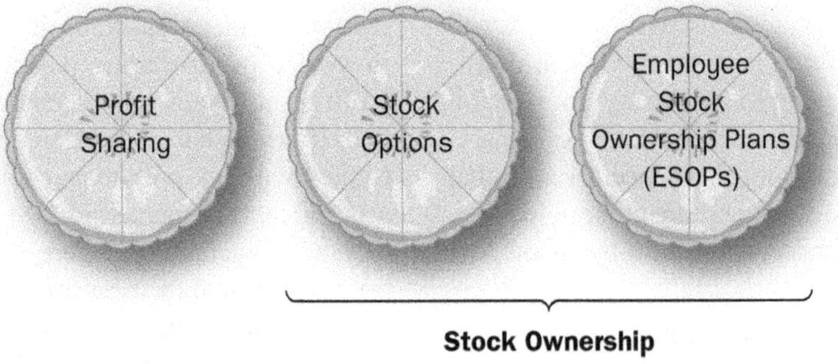

(a share of stock) that is worth more than $10. If in 2024 the stock is worth $18, they can exercise their options and buy stock for $10 a share. If they want to, they can sell their stock for the market price of $18, receiving a gain of $8 for each share of stock. Of course, stock prices can also fall. If the 2024 stock price is only $8, the employees would not exercise the options.

Traditionally, organizations have granted stock options to their executives. In recent years, many organizations pushed eligibility for options further down in the organization's structure. Some studies suggest that organizations perform better when a large percentage of top and middle managers are eligible for long-term incentives such as stock options.[24]

Recent scandals have drawn attention to another challenge of using stock options as incentive pay. As with other performance measures, employees may focus so much on stock price that they lose sight of other goals, including ethical behaviour. Ideally, managers would bring about an increase in stock price by adding value in terms of efficiency, innovation, and customer satisfaction. But there are other, unethical ways to increase stock price by tricking investors into thinking the organization is more valuable and more profitable than it actually is. Hiding losses and inflating the recorded value of revenues are just two ways some companies have boosted stock prices, enriching managers until these misdeeds come to light.

Employee Stock Ownership Plans

employee stock ownership plan (ESOP) An arrangement in which the organization distributes shares of stock to all its employees by placing it in a trust.

While stock options are most often used with top management, a broader arrangement is the **employee stock ownership plan (ESOP)**. In an ESOP, the organization distributes shares of stock to its employees by placing the stock into a trust managed on the employees' behalf. Employees receive regular reports on the value of their stock, and when they leave the organization, they may sell the stock to the organization or (if it is a publicly traded company) on the open market. For example, WestJet's Share Purchase Program enables WestJetters to receive up to 20 percent of their salaries in WestJet shares. Shares can be purchased as common shares or can be directed into RRSPs with WestJet matching the employee's contributions.[25]

Although ESOPs are the most common form of employee ownership, they raise a number of issues. On the negative side, they carry a significant risk for employees. Problems with the company's performance therefore can take away significant value from the ESOP. Many companies set up ESOPs to hold retirement funds, so these risks directly affect employees' retirement income.

Still, ESOPs can be attractive to employers. Along with tax and financing advantages, ESOPs give employers a way to build pride in and commitment to the organization. Employees have a right to participate in votes by shareholders (if the stock is registered on a national exchange, such as the TSX).[26] This means employees participate somewhat in corporate-level decision making.

LO4 What Is the Role of Employee Benefits?

Employees at almost every organization receive more than cash in exchange for their efforts. They also receive a package of **employee benefits**—compensation in forms other than cash (indirect compensation). Examples include paid vacation time, tuition reimbursement, and pension plans, among a wide range of possibilities.

employee benefits Compensation in forms other than cash.

As part of the total rewards provided to employees, benefits serve functions similar to pay. Benefits contribute to attracting, retaining, and motivating employees. The variety of possible benefits also helps employers tailor their offerings to the kinds of employees they need. Employers

HR How-To

Rewarding Workers When Raises Are Not an Option

You want to reward good performance, but there's hardly any money in the budget for raises and bonuses. That's the situation facing many HR managers in today's business climate. Here are some suggestions for making the most of whatever you can spend:

- Make sure that merit pay is truly related to performance gains. Raises are expensive and widely used, so high-performing employees expect to earn significantly more than average. Therefore, it is essential to be sure that performance measures used as the basis for raises are tied to business success and that the organization measures performance accurately.
- Offer modest but frequent incentives as quick rewards for accomplishments. An unexpected $100 one-time award for delighting a customer can have more impact, at a lower cost, than a $100 per month raise.
- Implement other strategies to reward performance that can also serve as employee incentives, such as flexible schedules, interesting and unique projects, and formal recognition. These are particularly useful for companies that don't have large budgets to provide meaningful year-end or spot bonuses.
- If the organization cannot afford to give everyone—or even all the above-average performers—a raise, it should target pay increases to the top performers. Explain that merit pay is for doing something exceptional, not just performing one's job. When expressed clearly, this message actually can strengthen employees' understanding of the connection between performance and incentive pay.
- Set and communicate clear, measurable targets for earning incentive pay. Employees want to understand what they have to do to earn a raise or bonus. They also appreciate knowing the size of the incentive they are eligible to earn.
- Accept that employees who do not achieve the requirements for earning incentive pay may leave. If the system is working properly, the employees who leave will be the ones who contribute the least. If good performers also are leaving, make sure the organization is providing employees with the resources they need—including training and empowerment—for meeting performance targets.

Sources: Stephen Miller, "Flat Salary Increase Budgets Spur Promotions for Pay Raises," *Society for Human Resource Management*, November 19, 2015, https://www.shrm.org; Yian Q. Mui, "Companies Have Found Something to Give Their Workers Instead of Raises," *Washington Post*, July 28, 2015, https://www.washingtonpost.com; "28 Ways to Reward and Recognize Your Employees," *Titan HR*, February 28, 2015, http://titanhr.com; Juan Pablo Gonzalez, Kate Richardson, and Hemali Desai, "Get More Bang for Your Comp Program Buck Despite Stagnant Salary Budget Increases," *Compensation Focus* (WorldatWork), October 2013, http://www.worldatwork.org.

need to examine their benefits package regularly to see whether they still meet employees' needs and expectations. Even if employers spend large sums on benefits, if employees do not understand how to use them or why they are valuable, the cost of the benefits will be largely wasted.[27] Employers need to communicate effectively so that the benefits are understood and appreciated by employees.

Employees have come to expect that benefits will help them maintain economic security. Canada Pension Plan/Quebec Pension Plan, company pension plans, and retirement savings plans help employees prepare for their retirement. Insurance plans help to protect employees from costs such as unexpected medical expenses. The important role that benefits serves is a reason that some benefits are required by law, e.g., Employment Insurance.

Even though many kinds of benefits are not required by law, they have become so common that today's employees expect them. Many employers find that attracting qualified workers requires them to provide health and retirement benefits of some sort. A large employer without such benefits would be highly unusual and would have difficulty competing in the labour market. A national survey conducted by Ipsos-Reid found that Canadian employees value their health benefits. As reported by Benefits Canada, 91 percent of survey respondents said that other than salary, a "good job" was defined as having a good benefits package—"benefits are serving as a proxy or a marker for a good workplace."[28] And a Sanofi Canada Healthcare Survey reveals that Millennial employees are more likely than their older co-workers to see benefits as a right—63 percent of Baby Boomers see health benefits as a perk or privilege, whereas only 50 percent of Millennial employees see health benefits as a perk or privilege.[29]

Like other forms of compensation and rewards, benefits impose significant costs. On average, out of every dollar spent on compensation, more than 31 cents go to benefits and this share has been steadily rising.[30] An organization managing its labour costs must pay careful attention to the cost of its employee benefits.

Overall, employers are concerned about balancing various issues related to benefits provided to employees. Several forces have made benefits a significant part of compensation packages. One is that laws require employers to provide certain benefits, such as contributions to Canada Pension Plan and Employment Insurance. Also, tax laws can make benefits favourable. For example, employees do not pay income taxes on most benefits they receive, but they pay income taxes on cash compensation. Therefore, an employee who receives a $1,000 raise "takes home" less than the full $1,000, but an employee who receives an additional $1,000 worth of non-taxable benefits receives the full benefits. Another cost advantage of paying benefits is that employers, especially large ones, often can get a better deal on insurance or other programs than employees can obtain on their own.

Finally, some employers assemble creative benefits packages to set them apart in the competition for talent. For example, Netflix offers unlimited vacation time (within reason). This policy is in keeping with its HR strategy of "hiring adults"—experts who already have a history of success, love movies, and can manage their time. Since the company's success comes from people driven by a passion for what they do and what they can accomplish, offering freedom as a benefit contributes to attracting and keeping the right talent.[31] Apple and Facebook attracted media attention when they offered female employees $20,000 toward "egg freezing" as part of their comprehensive benefits package (the same benefit is offered to men by covering the cost of sperm freezing).[32]

What Benefits Are Required by Law?

Governments require various forms of security to protect workers from financial hardships. Because these benefits are required by law, employers cannot gain an advantage in the labour market by offering them, nor can they design the nature of these benefits.

Canada Pension Plan (CPP)/Quebec Pension Plan (QPP) A contributory, mandatory plan that provides retirement pensions, disability benefits, and survivor benefits.

- **Canada Pension Plan (CPP)/ Quebec Pension Plan (QPP).** These plans cover all workers in Canada who are age 18 and older and have annual income exceeding $3,500. CPP/QPP is a mandatory **contributory plan** that provides retirement pensions, disability benefits, and survivor benefits. Workers who meet eligibility requirements receive benefits according to their age and earnings history.[33]

contributory plan All costs of the plan are funded by employees, employers, and the plan's own investments.

Employment Insurance (EI) A federally mandated program to provide temporary financial assistance to non-working Canadians.

- **Employment Insurance (EI).** This federally mandated program provides temporary financial assistance to non-working eligible people who have lost their jobs through no fault of their own, while they look for another job or upgrade their skills. Coverage is also extended to include a variety of situations; for example, to those who are ill; are providing compassionate care to a gravely ill family member; are pregnant, are parents caring for a newborn or adopted child, or are parents caring for a critically ill child.[34]

Workers' Compensation Acts Provincial programs that provide benefits to workers who suffer work-related injuries or illnesses.

- **Workers' Compensation Acts.** These provincial programs provide benefits to workers who suffer work-related injuries or illnesses. Workers' compensation operates under a principle of *no-fault liability,* meaning that an employee does not need to show that the employer was grossly negligent in order to receive compensation, and the employer is protected from lawsuits. The benefits fall into three major categories: wage-loss benefits, medical services, and rehabilitative services. Workers' compensation is entirely funded by employers—neither workers nor the government contribute. The amount employers pay depends on the industry and kinds of occupations involved as well as the size of the employer's payroll. Organizations can minimize the cost of this benefit by keeping workplaces safe and making employees and their managers conscious of safety issues, as discussed in Chapter 2.

What Optional Benefits Do Some Employers Provide?

Other types of benefits are optional. These include various kinds of insurance, retirement plans, and paid leave. Part-time workers often receive fewer benefits than full-time employees. The most widely offered benefits are paid leave for vacations and holidays (that exceed the legally required minimums specified in employment/labour standards legislation), life and medical insurance, and retirement plans. The extent to which the employer pays for the benefit varies widely among organizations. Some organizations require employees to pay a significant percentage of the premiums for insurance plans such as dental coverage. Other organizations pick up 100 percent of the premiums.

Benefits such as health insurance usually extend to employees' spouses and dependants. To ensure an employer does not face a charge of discrimination related to sexual orientation and/or marital status as a protected ground of discrimination, employers cover different-sex as well as same-sex partners.

Paid Leave

Employment/labour standards legislation outlines minimum entitlements (e.g., bereavement leave and paid holidays); however, many employers provide vacation and holidays in addition to the minimum legislated requirements. Some organizations also offer additional days off for personal reasons or to contribute their time to a charitable organization. For example, Cisco Systems' Time2Give formal volunteering policy, which provides all full-time employees with five days of paid time each year to volunteer at a nonprofit organization or charity of their choice was discussed in the chapter opening.

Sick leave programs pay employees for time not worked because of health issues. The amount of sick leave is often based on length of service, so that it accumulates over time; for example, one day added to sick leave for each month of service. Employers have to decide how many paid leave days to grant and whether to let them continue accumulating year after year. As reported by the Conference Board of Canada, the overall absenteeism rate has increased from an average of 6.0 days per employee in 2006–2007 to 6.6 days in 2016–2017. Absenteeism in the public sector averages 8.8 days per employee in contrast to 5.4 days in the private sector.[35]

An organization's policies for time off may include other forms of paid and unpaid leave. For a workforce that values flexibility, the organization may offer paid *personal days,* days off employees may schedule according to their personal needs, with the supervisor's approval. Typically, organizations offer a few personal days in addition to sick leave. *Floating holidays* are paid holidays that vary from year to year. The organization may schedule floating holidays so that they extend a Tuesday or Thursday holiday into a long weekend. Organizations may also give employees discretion over the scheduling of floating holidays.

Employers should establish policies for leaves without pay; for example, leaves of absence to pursue nonwork goals or to meet family needs. Unpaid leave is also considered an employee benefit because the employee usually retains seniority and benefits during the leave.

Group Insurance and Benefits

As we noted earlier, rates for group insurance are typically lower than for individual policies. Also, insurance benefits are not subject to income tax, as wages and salaries are. When employees receive insurance as a benefit, rather than higher pay so they can buy their own insurance, employees can get more for their money. Because of this, most employees value group insurance. The most common types of insurance and benefits offered as employee benefits are medical, life insurance, and disability insurance.

- **Medical insurance.** The policies typically cover medical expenses that are incurred over and above provincially funded medical coverage. Some employers offer additional coverage, such as dental care, vision care, and prescription drug programs. Employers must also make choices about coverage of so-called "lifestyle drugs," that is, drugs considered "cosmetic" or "discretionary." Examples are medical treatments for obesity, infertility, erectile dysfunction, male pattern baldness, and smoking cessation.[36] With legalization of recreational cannabis, more companies are covering medical cannabis as part of their benefits coverage. For example, Sun Life Financial includes medical marijuana in its group benefits plan.[37]

  An alternative (or in addition) to traditional employer-provided medical insurance is a **health spending account**, in which an employer puts aside a specific amount of money per employee to cover health-related costs. Employees decide what health care services they will purchase with their allocation.

  health spending account A specific amount of money set aside per employee by the employer to cover health-related costs.

- **Employee health and wellness programs.** As discussed in Chapter 2, an employee wellness program is a set of communications, activities, and facilities designed to change health-related behaviours in ways that reduce risks. *Passive* programs provide information and services, but no formal support or motivation to use the program (e.g., health education and fitness facilities). *Active* wellness programs assume that behaviour change requires support and reinforcement along with awareness and opportunity (e.g., counsellors who tailor programs or coach individual employees). The Canadian Automobile Association's (CAA) health and wellness program has been recognized at the Benefits Canada Workplace Benefits Awards for its multi-faceted approach to engage all employees including remote workers. For example, its step challenge—offering a Fitbit subsidy as well as organizing learn-to-run clinics and running groups—has seen 63 percent of employees achieve a daily recommended amount of physical activity, up from 28 percent before the step challenge.[38]

Many organizations are adopting an integrated strategic approach to wellness that promotes a corporate culture to support employees in taking responsibility for their health and overall wellness including *financial wellness.*

Shutterstock / Daxiao Productions

Companies that value employee health and wellness may provide fitness equipment or even fully functional gym facilities.

For example, Microsoft offers employees one-on-one financial coaching sessions and uses a web-based app called FiTage, which uses data about each employee's income and assets to identify the age at which the person will become financially independent. Two months after rolling out the FiTage app, more than one-fifth of the company's employees had used it. Among the initial results, employees lowered their average FiT age by more than a year. Microsoft added incentives for using the app, and participation increased to half the workforce.[39]

- **Employee assistance program (EAP).** As discussed in Chapter 2, an employee assistance program (EAP) provides confidential counselling services to employees experiencing personal problems. Many organizations also extend these services to family members. Left untreated, personal problems may cause employees to lose their ability to cope and work performance will suffer. Employees must be able to feel confident the program respects their confidentiality. Other considerations include the range of offerings provided (some EAP providers offer a very broad range of services that may overlap with health, wellness, and lifestyle-related services); proximity to counsellors; client references; and availability of effectiveness reporting measures.[40]
- **Life insurance.** Employers may provide life insurance to employees or offer the opportunity to buy coverage at low group rates. With a *term life insurance* policy, if the employee dies during the term of the policy, the employee's beneficiaries receive a payment called a death benefit. In policies purchased as an employee benefit, the usual death benefit is a multiple of the employee's yearly pay. The policies may provide additional benefits for accidental death. Along with a basic policy, the employer may give employees the option of purchasing additional coverage, usually at a nominal cost.
- **Disability insurance.** Employees risk losing their income if a disability makes them unable to work. Disability insurance provides protection against this loss of income. Typically, **short-term disability insurance** provides benefits for six months or less. **Long-term disability insurance** provides benefits after that initial period, potentially for the rest of the disabled employee's life. Disability payments are a percentage of the employee's salary—typically 50 to 70 percent. Payments under short-term plans may be higher. Often the policy sets a maximum amount that may be paid each month. Because its limits make it more affordable, short-term disability coverage is offered by more employers.

short-term disability insurance Insurance that pays a percentage of a disabled employee's salary as benefits to the employee for six months or less.

long-term disability insurance Insurance that pays a percentage of a disabled employee's salary after an initial period and potentially for the rest of the employee's life.

Retirement Plans

Employers have no obligation to offer retirement plans beyond the protection of CPP/QPP security, but many offer some form of pension or retirement savings plan. As depicted in Figure 8.10, almost 6.2 million employees in Canada have registered pension plans (RPPs). A breakdown of registered pension plans and members by type of plan is provided.

An additional issue facing employers' approaches to retirement plans is a growing interest in **phased retirement**, a gradual transition into full retirement by reducing hours or job responsibility.[41] Employers are facing an increasing demand for phased retirement programs from employees who are healthier, living longer, and have personal or financial reasons to continue working in some capacity. Employers also benefit from retaining older workers with valued skills and experience who wish to retire gradually. Phased retirement also provides the employer with more time to transfer knowledge and skills to younger employees;[42] however, many employers are worried about the implications and costs of providing benefits coverage to older employees.

phased retirement A gradual transition into full retirement by reducing hours or job responsibility.

Most pension plans are either a defined benefit plan or a defined contribution plan.

- **Defined benefit plans.** Employers have a choice of using registered retirement plans (RPPs) that define the amount to be paid out after retirement or plans that define the amount the employer will invest each year.

FIGURE 8.10

Membership in Registered Pension Plans by Type of Plan and Sector

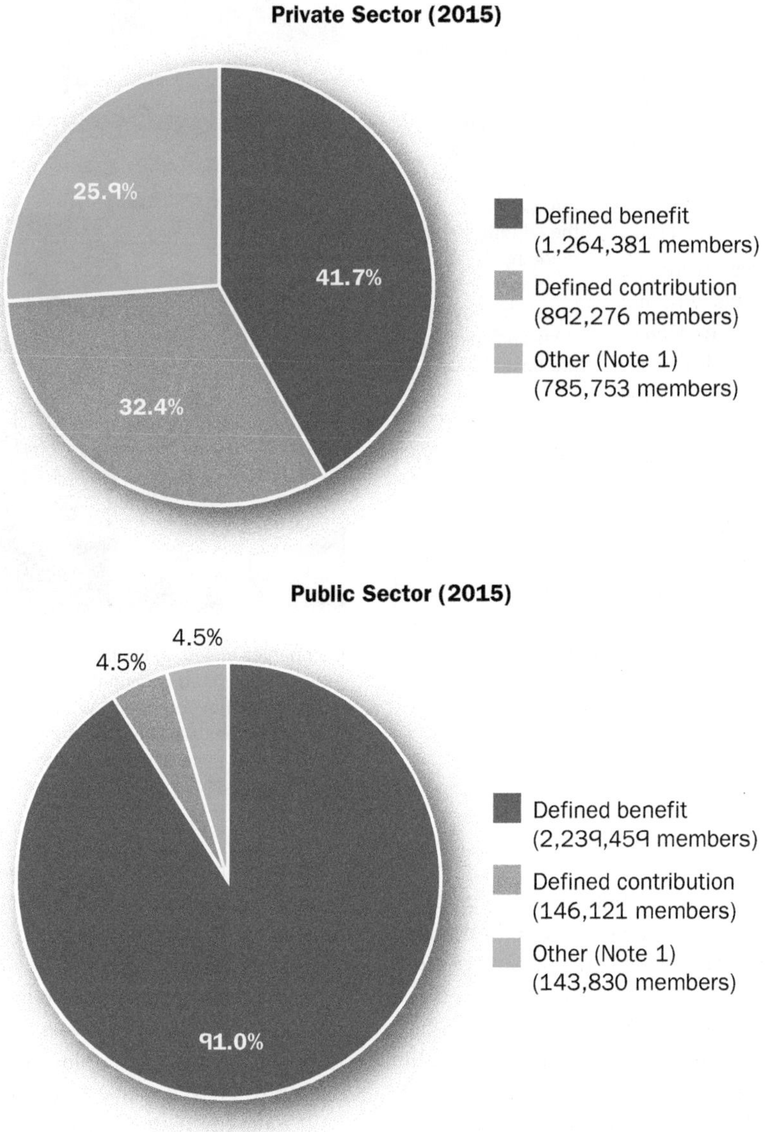

Note 1: Other plans include having a hybrid, composite, defined benefit/defined contribution, and other component.

Source: Statistics Canada, "Table 1: Registered pension plan membership, by sector and type of plan," *The Daily*, July 21, 2017, CANSIM Table 280–116, www.statcan.gc.ca/daily-quotidien/170721/t001d.htm, retrieved May 19, 2018.

defined benefit plan A pension plan that defines the benefits to be paid according to a formula stipulated in the plan.

A **defined benefit plan** defines the benefits to be paid according to a formula stipulated in the plan.[43] Usually the amount of this defined benefit is calculated for each employee based on the employee's years of service, age, and earnings (e.g., a percentage of the average of the employee's five highest-earnings years). These calculations typically result in pension payments that may provide 70 percent of pre-retirement income for a long-service employee. Using years of service as part of the basis for calculating benefits gives employees an incentive to stay with the organization so it can help to reduce voluntary turnover. Overall, 67.1 percent of employees in Canada with an RPP (in 2015) were in a defined benefit pension plan; however, this represents a decline from more than 85 percent in 2001,[44] largely due to the migration of new and existing private-sector employees to defined contribution plans. For example, in 2012, RBC stopped offering new Canadian hires access to its defined benefit plan. Existing employees can remain in RBC's defined benefits plan or switch to the defined contribution plan, which was made attractive through features such as higher employer contributions.[45]

- **Defined contribution plans.** An alternative to defined benefits is a **defined contribution plan**, which specifies the contributions made by the employer, as well as the employee. Pension benefits are based upon the accumulated contributions and investment returns achieved.[46] These plans free employers from the risks that investments will not perform as well as expected. They put the responsibility for wise investing squarely on the shoulders of each employee. A defined contribution plan is also easier to administer. Considering the advantages to employers, it is not surprising that a growing share of retirement plans in the private sector are defined contribution plans. Defined contribution plans do not penalize employees for changing jobs; however, these plans provide less assurance of financial security in retirement.

defined contribution plan A retirement plan that specifies the contributions made by the employer as well as the employee; pension benefits are based upon the accumulated contributions and investment returns achieved.

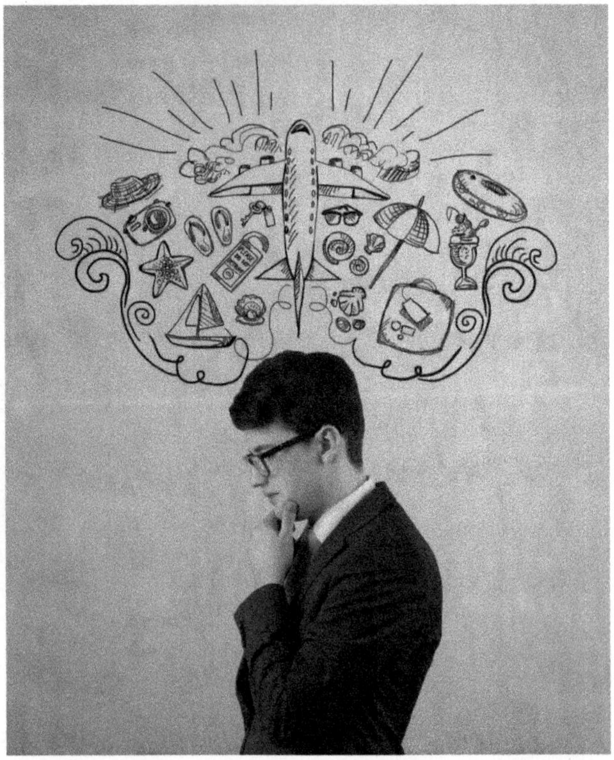

Denisismagilov/Dreamstime.com/GetStock.com

Companies including Netflix and Virgin America have implemented "unlimited vacation" policies described as "Take what you want, take what you need." What type of organizational culture and employees are likely to be the best fit to adopt this approach? Do you think this will be a successful "HR experiment" for these organizations?"

Family-friendly Benefits and Services

As employers have recognized the importance of employees' need to balance their work and outside commitments including the care of family members, pursuit of education, personal development, and volunteer activities, many have implemented "family-friendly" HR practices. Options such as flextime and telework were discussed in Chapter 1. In addition, some organizations provide benefits and services including child and/or elder care, parental leave top-up, and adoption assistance. For example, Simon Fraser University provides maternity and parental leave top-up payments (up to 100 percent of salary for 35 weeks) and the National Energy Board provides new mothers a full year of maternity top-up payments (to 93 percent of salary) and adoptive parents and new fathers parental leave top-up to 93 percent of salary for 35 weeks.[47]

According to Statistics Canada, approximately 2.7 million Canadians provide unpaid care to people 65 years and older. Many of these people have been referred to as the *sandwich generation*—with dual responsibility of raising children and providing care for aging parents or relatives. Due to the aging of the Baby Boomers this segment is expected to grow, resulting in increased stress and demands on employees.[48] Some employers have responded by providing benefits and services including access to counselling, flexible schedules, referral services, and access to information and other resources available in the community or region.

Some companies even recognize that pets are "family" and provide employees with paid time off when they get a pet or are coping with the death of a pet. For example, at Shopper's Drug Mart employees can take paid days off if they have a loss in the family, and that includes a pet.[49] The value of family-friendly benefits accrues to not only employees but also employers in the form of increased productivity, enhanced commitment, and reduced stress.[50]

Other Benefits

The scope of possible employee benefits is limited only by the imagination of the organization's decision makers. Organizations have developed a wide variety of benefits to meet the needs of employees and to attract and keep the kinds of workers who will be of value to the organization.

To encourage learning and attract the kinds of employees who wish to develop their knowledge and skills, many organizations offer *tuition reimbursement* programs. A typical program covers tuition and related expenses for courses that are relevant to the employee's current job or future career at the organization. Employees are reimbursed for these expenses after they demonstrate they have completed an approved course. Tuition reimbursement is an important benefit at many organizations on top employer lists.

Selecting Employee Benefits

Although the government requires certain benefits, employers have wide latitude in creating the total benefits package they offer employees.[51] Decisions about which benefits to include should take into account the organization's goals, its budget, and the expectations of the organization's current employees and those it wishes to recruit in the future. Employees have come to expect certain things from employers. An organization that does not offer the expected benefits will have more difficulty attracting and keeping talented workers. Also, if employees believe their employer feels no commitment to their well-being and security, they are less likely to feel committed to their employer.

An Organization's Objectives

A logical place to begin selecting employee benefits is to establish objectives for the benefits package. This helps an organization select the most effective benefits and monitor whether the benefits are doing what they should. Unfortunately, research suggests that most organizations do not have written objectives for benefits.

Among companies that do set goals, the most common objectives include controlling the cost of health care benefits and retaining employees.[52] The first goal explains the growing use of wellness programs and employee-directed health plans. For the second goal, employers need to learn what employees care about. In some cases, the approach may be indirect, helping the company distinguish itself as an employer that certain kinds of employees will be attracted and committed to. A company that establishes itself as committed to the environment could offer benefits in line with that goal—say bicycle storage and vouchers for taking the bus to work.[53] For example, Sparkrock, a software development firm, encourages employees to commute via

HR Oops!

Protests at Tim Hortons after Cuts to Employee Benefits

Employees at a Cobourg, Ontario Tim Hortons, owned by the son and daughter of the chain's co-founders, say were told to "sign a document acknowledging they are losing paid breaks, paid benefits, and other incentives as a result of the province's minimum wage hike." "Breaks will no longer be paid. A 9 hour shift will be paid for 8 hours and 20 minutes." The document also stated that employees with six months to five years of service would have to pay 75 percent of the cost of their benefits. Employees with more than five years of service would have to pay 50 percent of the cost of benefits. An employee said that benefits had previously been "covered 100 percent by the company."

Public backlash was swift and included a social media boycott campaign, #NoTimmysTuesday, with rallies in 15 cities and towns organized by the Ontario Federation of Labour. Former Ontario Premier Kathleen Wynne called the franchisees' actions "a clear act of bullying." An official statement from Tim Hortons' corporate office stated, "These recent actions by a few restaurant owners. . . . do not reflect the values of our brand, the views of our company, or the views of the overwhelming majority of our hardworking restaurant owners."

Questions

1. Is it any surprise that employee benefits are important and highly valued by Tim Hortons employees? Explain your answer.
2. Suggest what the franchise owners could have done differently to provide an approach to employee total rewards that would be viewed as fair and reasonable for employees and other Tim Hortons franchise owners.

Source: Josie Kao, "Protests hit local Tim Hortons as franchises cut workers' benefits," *The Varsity*, January 15, 2018; "Demonstrators picket Time Hortons after cuts to employee benefits," *CBC News*, January 10, 2018, www.cbc.ca; Tara Deschamps and Shawn Jeffords, "'Reckless': Tim Hortons blasts franchisees' cuts to paid breaks and benefits," *Financial Post*, January 8, 2018, http://business.financialpost.com; Martha Porado and Ryan Murphy, "Benefits cuts by Tim Hortons franchises premature: NDP critic," *Benefits Canada*, January 5, 2018, www.benefitscanada.com; Aaron Saltzman, "Tim Hortons heirs cut paid breaks and worker benefits after minimum wage hike, employees say," *CBC News*, January 3, 2018, www.cbc.ca.

bicycle to its Toronto office by providing bike parking and a $5 per day incentive, as well as hosting seasonal tune-up clinics.[54]

Employees' Expectations and Values

Employees expect to receive benefits that are legally required and widely available, and they value benefits they are likely to use. To meet employee expectations about benefits, it can be helpful to see what other organizations offer. Employers should also consider that the value employees place on various benefits is likely to differ from one employee to another. As outlined earlier in the chapter, a basic demographic factor such as age can influence the kinds of benefits employees want. However, these are only general observations; organizations should check which considerations apply to their own employees and identify more specific needs and differences.

The choice of benefits may influence current employees' satisfaction and may also affect the organization's recruiting, in terms of both the ease of recruiting and the kinds of employees attracted to the organization. The HR Oops! box discusses the public relations fiasco faced by Tim Hortons when some franchisees cut valued employee benefits.

Flexible Benefits

Organizations can address differences in employees' needs and engage their employees by offering **flexible benefits plans** in place of a single benefits package for all employees. These plans, often called flexible benefits or *flex benefits,* offer employees a set of alternatives from which they can choose the types and amounts of benefits they want. The plans vary. Some impose minimum levels for certain benefits, such as health care coverage; some allow employees to receive money in exchange for choosing a "light" package; and some let employees pay extra for the privilege of receiving more benefits. For example, some plans let employees give up vacation days for more pay or to purchase extra vacation days in exchange for a reduction in pay.

flexible benefits plans Benefits plans that offer employees a set of alternatives from which they can choose the types and amounts of benefits they want.

Flexible benefits plans have a number of advantages.[55] The selection process can make employees more aware of the value of the benefits, particularly when the plan assigns each employee a sum of money to allocate to benefits. Also, the individual choice in a flexible benefits plan enables each employee to match their needs to the company's benefits, increasing the plan's actual value to the employee.

A drawback of flexible benefits plans is that they have a higher administrative cost, especially in the design and startup stages. Organizations can avoid some of the higher cost, however, by using software packages and standardized plans that have been developed for employers wishing to offer flexible benefits. Another possible drawback is that employee selection of benefits will increase rather than decrease costs, because employees will select the kinds of benefits they expect to need the most. For example, an employee expecting to need a lot of dental work is more likely to sign up for a dental plan. The heavy use of the dental coverage would then drive up the employer's premiums for that coverage. Costs can also be difficult to estimate when employees select their benefits. Organizations frequently respond by requiring employees to share in the costs of benefits.

LO5 Communicating Total Rewards to Employees

"Communication is often a weak link. An average program well-communicated will do better than an outstanding program poorly communicated."[56] A comprehensive communications strategy is required to help employees understand the total value the organization is investing in its approach to compensating and rewarding employees. This is essential so that total rewards can achieve their objectives including focusing employees on organizational goals, attracting and retaining employees, and creating a motivating environment.

Because they interact with their employees each day, managers play a significant role in communication. The HR department should prepare managers to explain to employees why the organization's approach to compensating and rewarding is designed as it is, and to determine whether employee concerns indicate a need for change. Employees are interested in their compensation and rewards and they need a great deal of detailed information. It follows that technology and supporting databases can play a significant role. More employers are using technology to provide employees with tools and information related to both communication and administration of employee compensation and rewards. Employees and job applicants often lack a clear sense of the market value of total rewards that an organization offers. For example, research asking employees about their benefits has shown that employees significantly underestimate the cost and value of their benefits.[57]

Employers have many options for communicating information about their total rewards. Research from Sun Life showed that different generational groups have different preferences for receiving information from their employers about rewards—Baby Boomers are most likely to prefer paper-based communications, Gen X appreciates online communication, and Millennials prefer online

Did You KNOW?

Benefits Are Important to Employees

The Society for Human Resource Management has found that benefits consistently ranked in the top five contributors to employees' job satisfaction.

Question

How does the data shown here support the view that HR managers should actively communicate with employees about their benefits?

Employees Rating Benefit Important or Very Important

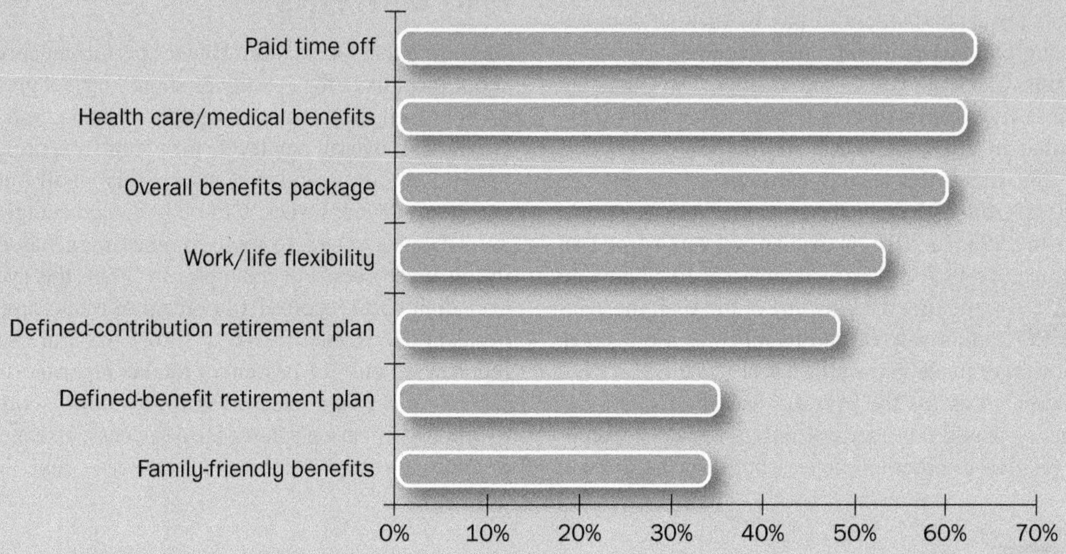

Sources: Society for Human Resource Management, *Employee Job Satisfaction and Engagement: Revitalizing a Changing Workforce*, April 2016, http://www.shrm.org; Debra Cohen, "Employee Engagement," *People and Strategy* 36, no. 4 (2014): 13–14; Frank Giancola, "How Important Are Benefit Plans to Your Employees and How Satisfied Are They with Your Offerings?" *Employee Benefit Plan Review*, July 2013, pp. 27–30.

communication to anything else.[58] To increase the likelihood that employees will receive and understand the messages, employers can combine several media, such as videos, brochures, question-and-answer meetings, intranet site, memos, presentations, email and messaging applications.

Communication efforts are also moving beyond ensuring employees receive and understand the messages to "driving action, enabling employees to make the best possible use of the programs available to them," according to Diane McElroy, a senior vice-president with Aon Hewitt in Toronto. McElroy adds that some employers provide *total rewards statements* for prospective employees as part of the job offer. "Some organizations are providing these statements when they make offers to job candidates. That way, if the potential new hire receives another offer—especially one with a higher base salary—he or she can make an informed comparison and determine whether a bigger paycheque really does mean great compensation."[59] In summary, an investment of creativity in employee communication can reap great returns in the form of committed, satisfied employees, and the achievement of organizational objectives including employee attraction and retention.

LO6 Executive Compensation and Rewards

Pay for Executives

The media have drawn public attention to the issue of executive compensation and rewards. The issue attracts notice because of the very high pay that the top executives of major North American companies have received in recent years; see Table 8.3 for Canada's highest-paid executives. In 2016, the average CEO total compensation of Canada's top 100 highest paid executives was $10.4 million.[60]

Notice also that as shown in Figure 8.11, only a small share of the average compensation paid to CEOs is in the form of a salary. Most CEO compensation takes the form of performance-related pay, such as bonuses and stock. This variable pay causes the pay of executives to vary much more widely than other employees earnings.

Although these high amounts apply to only a small proportion of the total workforce, the issue of executive pay is relevant to pay structure in terms of equity theory. As we discussed earlier in the chapter, employees draw conclusions about the fairness of pay by making comparisons among employees' inputs and outcomes. By many comparisons, Canadian CEOs' pay is high. The Canadian Centre for Policy Alternatives, a public policy think tank, reported that in 2016, Canada's 100 highest-paid CEOs received 209 times the annual earnings of an average Canadian, up from 105 times the average Canadian worker's wage in 1998. In 2016, Canadian workers earned an average wage of $49,738.[61] For example, by 10.57 a.m. on January 2, 2016, the first working day of the year, the average top CEO had already earned as much as the average Canadian worker made in the entire year.[62]

However, to assess the overall fairness of this ratio, equity theory would consider not only the size of executive pay relative to other employees but also the amount the CEOs contribute. CEOs likely have a much greater effect on the organization's performance than the average employee. But if they do not seem to contribute 209 times more, employees may see the compensation as unfair. However, according to Carleton University professor Ian Lee, CEO "compensation is justified and shouldn't be compared to an average worker's salary." Lee explains that top players in sports, entertainment, and business always make more than the average person because "they offer rare and sought-after talent."[63]

Executive Incentives and Benefits

Assuming that incentives influence performance, decisions about incentives for executives should have a great impact on how well the executives and the organization perform. Along with overall pay levels for executives, organizations need to create incentive plans for this small but important group of employees. CEO pay is increasingly moving away from a salary to total compensation based primarily on incentives. For example, in 2008, the average top Canadian CEO received 14 percent of total compensation in salary. However, in 2016, as shown in Figure 8.11 salary represented only 11 percent of total compensation.[64]

To encourage executives to develop a commitment to the organization's long-term success, executive compensation often combines short-term and long-term

TABLE 8.3

Canada's Highest Paid CEOs (2016)

Rank	Company	Title	Name	Base Salary	Other Compensation†	Total Compensation
1	Valeant Pharmaceuticals International Inc	CEO	Joseph Papa*	$1,299,990	$81,831,262	$83,131,252
2	Magna International Inc	CEO	Donald Walker*	$430,781	$28,183,681	$28,614,462
3	Rogers Communications Inc	Former President & CEO	Guy Laurence	$1,029,711	$23,573,282	$24,602,993
4	Macdonald Dettwiler & Associates Ltd	Former President & CEO	Daniel Friedmann	$266,831	$21,160,422	$21,427,253
5	Canadian Pacific Railway Ltd	CEO	Hunter Harrison	$2,904,595	$15,925,199	$18,829,794

† Other Compensation includes: cash bonuses, stock-based bonuses, options-based bonuses, pension value, and any other payments other than base salary.

Sources: David Macdonald, "Climbing Up and Kicking Down: Executive Pay in Canada," *Canadian Centre for Policy Alternatives*, January 1, 2018, p 17; and CB Staff, "Canada's Top 100 highest-paid CEOs," Canadian Business, January 2, 2018, www.canadianbusiness.com.

FIGURE 8.11

Breakdown of CEO Pay

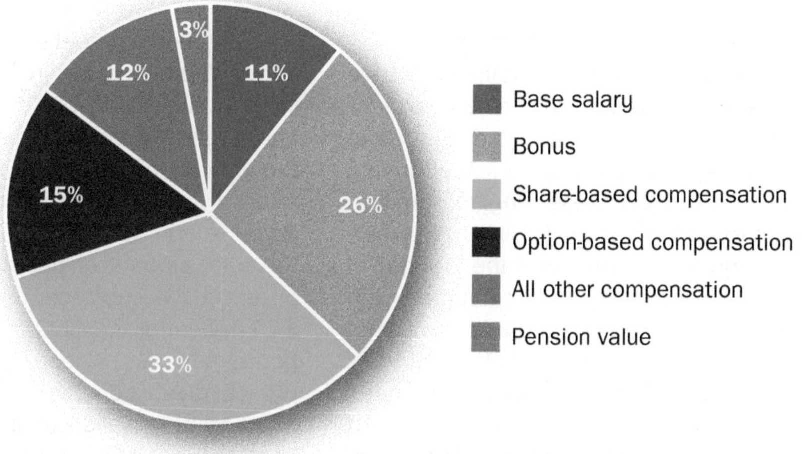

Source: David Macdonald, "Climbing Up and Kicking Down: Executive Pay in Canada," Figure 2, *Canadian Centre for Policy Alternatives,* January 1, 2018, p 10. Copied under licence from Access Copyright. Further reproduction, distribution or transmission is prohibited except as otherwise permitted by law.

incentives. *Short-term incentives* include bonuses based on the year's profits, return on investment, or other measures related to the organization's goals. Sometimes, to gain tax advantages, the actual payment of the bonus is deferred (e.g., by making it part of a retirement plan). *Long-term incentives* include stock options and stock purchase plans. The rationale for these long-term incentives is that executives will want to do what is best for the organization because that will cause the value of their stock to grow. A corporation's shareholders—its owners—want the corporation to encourage managers to act in the owners' best interests. They want managers to care about the company's profits and stock price, and incentive pay can encourage this interest. One study has found that relying on such long-term incentives is associated with greater profitability.[65]

As well as legally required benefits and the benefits extended to other employees in the organization, executives often receive extra benefits and services. These executive benefits and services may include such far-reaching benefits as use of corporate aircraft, company-provided or subsidized homes, memberships and tickets to sporting and cultural events, in addition to benefits such as company vehicles, sabbaticals, and extended vacations.

Performance Measures for Executives

The balanced scorecard approach discussed in Chapter 7 is also useful in designing executive pay. Table 8.5 shows how the choice of performance measures can be guided by a desire to balance shareholder, customer, and employee objectives. Financial results can be seen as a lagging indicator that tells the company how it has done in the past, whereas customer and employee metrics like those in Table 8.5, used by the global biopharmaceutical company Merck, are leading indicators that tell the company how its financial results will be in the future.

TABLE 8.5

Merck Performance (Balanced) Scorecard—CEO

Financial 1. Revenue vs. plan 2. Earnings per share vs. plan 3. Value of growth (e.g., ROI vs. plan)	60
Customer 1. Merck customer service level (% orders delivered on time) 2. Merck Trust & Value Customer Survey	14
Key Business Drivers 1. Cost structure (operating expense vs. plan) 2. Revenue growth in high-priority areas	16
Culture (high performance, sustainable) 1. Employee Culture Survey	10
Total	100

Source: Proxy Statement, Merck & Co., Inc., April 14, 2014, www.merck.com/finance/proxy/pr2014.pdf.

Thinking Ethically

Volkswagen Changes How It Pays

Volkswagen (VW) has an integrity problem. Volkswagen was discovered to have installed software that sensed when an engine was being tested for emissions and (temporarily) reduced emissions to a level that would pass the test. In actual driving conditions, however, VW diesel engines emitted emissions up to 40 times the legal limit. VW's marketing campaign had emphasized the wonder of the diesel engine's performance combined with environmental benefits, even though it was not true. That campaign in turn was a vital part of VW's Strategy 2018 growth plan to bypass General Motors and Toyota to become the world's largest automaker. Employees were subjected to tremendous pressure and intimidation from the top cascading down to every level to do whatever was necessary to achieve this growth goal (and keep their jobs). This apparently included engineers "willing to commit crimes to defraud the public."

As a result of this scandal, multiple legal actions have been brought against the company. VW has entered into settlements of civil lawsuits brought by drivers who found themselves stuck with noncompliant vehicles. This includes the largest class action settlement ever. The company has also paid criminal fines that together total nearly $25 billion (so far).

In an effort to avoid such problems in the future and to "quell investor ire" that executives earned large bonuses (despite their role in the scandal and large VW losses), the company is changing the way it pays. No bonuses will be paid in the future if certain financial objectives are not met. Base salary will be increased 30 percent, but the total amount of base salary plus bonus that an executive can receive will now be capped at $10 million for the CEO and $5.5 million for other board members. Also, for the first time, executives will be given company stock, presumably in an effort to better align their interests with those of shareholders. It appears that this stock-based compensation is not subject to the caps. Thus, if shareholders do well, executives can still do quite well.

Questions

1. What caused the Volkswagen scandal? What can you infer about the nature of its former pay strategy and the role it may have played?
2. Consider Volkswagen's revised pay strategy. How well do you think it will succeed going forward? Do you have suggestions for other changes? Explain.

Sources: W. Boston, "VW Revamps Pay, Imposes Caps," *Wall Street Journal*, February 25/26, 2017; S. Randazzo, "U.S. Court Gives Initial Approval to Volkswagen Vehicle Emissions Settlement," *Wall Street Journal*, February 14, 2017; J. Rothfeder, "The Volkswagen Settlement: How Bad Management Leads to Big Punishment," *The New Yorker*, July 1, 2016

SUMMARY

LO1 Discuss how organizations implement a "total rewards" approach to compensating and rewarding employees.

Many organizations are recognizing the strategic value of taking a comprehensive approach to compensating and rewarding employees. This "total rewards" approach frequently involves creating a value proposition for current and prospective employees that clearly identifies all of the aspects that are valued by employees in exchange for their time and expertise. Companies take a total rewards approach to attract and retain valued employees and improve capacity to meet organizational goals.

LO2 Identify the kinds of decisions and influences involved in providing base pay to employees.

Organizations make decisions to define a job structure or relative pay for different jobs within the organization. Organizations must also establish pay levels, based on the organization's goals, market data, legal requirements, and principles of fairness. Together job structure and pay level establish a pay structure policy. Organizations typically begin with a job evaluation to measure the relative worth of their jobs. To obtain more flexibility, organizations may reduce the levels in the organization's job structure. Other organizations reward employees according to their competencies.

LO3 Describe how organizations recognize individual, team, and organizational performance with incentives.

Organizations may recognize individual performance through incentives such as piecework rates, standard hours plans, merit pay, sales commissions, and bonuses for meeting individual performance objectives. Common team incentives include gainsharing, bonuses, and team awards. Incentives for meeting organizational objectives include profit sharing and stock ownership.

LO4 Summarize the role of employee benefits and the types of benefits offered by employers.

Like pay, benefits and services help employers attract, retain, and provide a source of motivation for employees. Employees expect at least a minimum level of benefits, and providing more than the minimum helps an organization compete in the labour market. Benefits and services are also a significant expense, but employers provide benefits and services because employees value them and many are required by law.

LO5 Review the importance of effectively communicating the organization's approach to total rewards.

A comprehensive communications strategy is needed to help employees understand and value all the components in an organization's approach to total rewards. Managers and the human resource department share responsibility for this important requirement. Technology can provide employees access to information and other tools associated with administration of compensation and rewards. Employers have many options for communicating information about total rewards.

LO6 Examine issues related to compensating and rewarding executives.

Executive compensation has drawn public scrutiny because top executive compensation is much higher than the average worker's pay. Executive compensation is complicated, contains a variety of elements, and is increasingly based on incentives rather than base salary.

CRITICAL THINKING QUESTIONS

1. Some individuals evaluate prospective employers' job offers based only on direct pay considerations. What additional factors should be considered when evaluating job offers from employers?
2. Why might an organization choose to pay employees more than the market rate? Why might it choose to pay less? What are the consequences of paying more or less than the market rate?
3. What are the advantages of establishing pay ranges, rather than specific pay levels, for each job? What are the drawbacks of this approach?
4. Suppose a small start-up business wants to establish a competency-based pay structure. What would be some advantages of this approach? List the issues the company should be prepared to address in setting up this system. Consider the kinds of information needed and the ways employees may react to the new pay structure.
5. With some organizations and jobs, pay is primarily wages or salaries, and with others, incentive pay is more important. For each of the following jobs, state whether you think the pay should emphasize base pay (wages and salaries) or incentive pay (bonuses, profit sharing, and so on). Give a reason for each.
   - **a.** An accountant at a manufacturing company
   - **b.** A salesperson for a software company
   - **c.** A mechanic for a major airline
   - **d.** A marketing manager for a communications company
   - **e.** A recruitment specialist for the federal government
6. Why do some organizations link incentive pay to the organization's overall performance? Is it appropriate to use stock performance as an incentive for employees at all levels? Why or why not?
7. Why do employers provide benefits, rather than providing all employee compensation in the form of pay and letting employees buy the benefits they want?
8. Of the benefits discussed in this chapter, list the ones you consider essential—those benefits you would require in any job offer. Why are these benefits important to you?
9. Why is it important to communicate information about total rewards? Suppose you work in the HR department of a company that has decided to add employee financial wellness counselling services to its total rewards. How would you recommend communicating this change? What information should your messages include? How would you know if your communication strategy was successful?
10. Do you think executive total compensation is too high? Why or why not?

EXPERIENCING HR—HOW TO ASSESS ROI OF A WELLNESS PROGRAM

Form groups of four or five. (Alternatively, your instructor may ask students to complete the research independently and discuss their findings in class.) You have been asked by your manager to be part of a workplace task force that will examine how to assess the return on investment (ROI) of a corporate wellness program.

Conduct research using recent academic (e.g., *ACSM's Health & Fitness Journal*) *and* HR practitioner publications (e.g., *Benefits Canada*) *and* credible websites (e.g., the website for the Canadian Centre for Occupational Health and Safety. Discuss your findings about how to determine the ROI of a corporate wellness program. Write a one-page report or make a brief class presentation summarizing your findings.

CASE STUDY: EVIDENCE-BASED HRM

Improving the Quality and Reducing the Cost of Employee Health Benefits

The new Health Transformation Alliance, a collaboration of 38 companies employing 6 million workers (including American Express and Johnson & Johnson) will use data and technology to improve the quality and reduce the cost of health benefits for its employees. The Alliance hopes to save as much as $600 million on drug spending, representing a reduction of approximately 15 percent. Part of the savings comes from the Alliance's bargaining power. However, another part of the plan is to change how care is delivered for conditions like diabetes, hip and knee replacements, and lower back pain.

IBM's Watson software will be used to "help" select drugs that provide the best value for the money and to predict which employees are most likely to develop conditions such as diabetes so as to take preventive action sooner. To perform these analyses, the goal is to use four years of data on pharmacy and insurance claims and electronic employee health records from each company.

Other companies are taking similar steps, sometimes focusing on particular issues that are most critical to them. For example, engine maker Cummins, Inc. is devoting considerable attention to the misuse of prescription opioid painkillers and is working to find alternative pain control methods for employees. Cummins notes the need for caution as most pain medication is legally prescribed and control of pain is critical. At the same time, use of such medication raises safety issues on the job and also can imperil employees' long-term health. According to one estimate, annual medical expenses for opioid abusers are about twice as high as the employer cost for other employees. Cummins relies on programs that use drug-test data and works with a pharmacy-benefits manager to track data on opioid prescriptions and attempts to detect pill shopping. The company recently opened a new facility at its headquarters that provides services such as massage, acupuncture, physical therapy, and a full-time pharmacist, all in the interest of finding better and safer ways to control pain. Cummins has also trained supervisors on how to identify employees who may be having problems with painkillers and has trained plant managers on how to triage employees having an overdose.

Questions

1. As an employee, what would your reaction be to these initiatives? Explain.
2. Do you have ideas for other ways to use data to improve the cost effectiveness and quality of health-related employee benefits?

Sources: J. Walker, "Alliance of Companies Unveil First Steps Aimed at Cutting Health-Care Costs," *Wall Street Journal*, March 7, 2017; R. E. Silverman, "One Employer Fights against Prescription-Drug Abuse," *Wall Street Journal*, November 15, 2016.

CASE STUDY: HRM SOCIAL

Bell Gets Social to Get Healthy

One of the big challenges with a wellness program is motivation—especially motivating the employees who would benefit the most. Typically, many employees never complete the health assessment used for entering these programs and then even fewer sign up for activities that would improve the health issues identified in the assessment. An important consideration is that wellness programs work best when they are part of an integrated strategy that combines realistic goals with incentives, clear communication, and a supportive culture.

Some of that education and support can come through social media tools. The knowledge-sharing function of social media readily lends itself to educating employees about health. For example, the employer could feature healthy items on the cafeteria menu each week or a page to share ideas for managing stress or working exercise into one's daily routine.

In the area of support, just as employees might use the company's computer network to find colleagues with knowledge, the company could set up web pages or a Twitter feed for groups with health-related interests such as a group that walks during lunch breaks or a weight-loss challenge group. While the company cannot disclose personal health information, it could reward team successes. For example, employees could form teams and see which team logs the most steps during a challenge period.

Bell has a walking challenge that starts during the company's mental health week in May. Marie-Josée Boivin, vice-president of human resources describes the initiative: "So our employees could either join a team or create a team, but for a full month, people were counting their steps and we were encouraging them to go out for a walk, to walk as colleagues and so on. It was a way to say it's good to keep an active lifestyle, and we also linked it to mental health, because if you're healthier up here, if you take time to relax at lunch time, at the end of the day and so on, then you have a better lifestyle."

As part of the challenge, Bell has an internal website where employees taking part can post about themselves, write comments, and compete with one another, says Boivin. " . . . In HR, we had two teams and, I have to admit, we had a very nice, happy competition going on. I think it brought a lot of the team together. We even had people writing on the wall that they ended up connecting with people they didn't know through that challenge. So they created walking groups."

Questions

1. Would you expect participation in wellness programs to be greater if they have a social media component? Why or why not?
2. How might the ideas described here be applied to a stop-smoking program for an organization's employees?

Sources: Ryan Murphy, "Bell walks toward wellness," *Benefits Canada,* April 23, 2018, www.benefitscanada.ca, accessed May 23, 2018; Stephen Walkiewicz, "Don't Go It Alone: Social Media Can Help You Quite Smoking," *Men's Fitness,* http://www.mensfitness.com, accessed June 8, 2016; Lindsay Rothfeld, "7 Companies with Amazingly Unique Wellness Programs," *Mashable,* May 5, 2015, http://mashable.com; Barb Hendrickson, "Increasing Employee Participation in Corporate Wellness Programs," *Occupational Health and Safety,* September 1, 2013, http://ohsonline.com; David Roddenberry, "Six Keys to Maximize the Value of Wellness Incentive Programs," *EHS Today,* February 2013, pp. 37–38.

PART 5

Meeting Other HR Goals

CHAPTER 9

Labour Relations

CHAPTER 10

Managing Human Resources Globally

CHAPTER 11

Creating and Sustaining High-Performance Organizations

Blend Images/Getty Images

CHAPTER 9

Labour Relations

WHAT DO I NEED TO KNOW?

After reading this chapter, you should be able to:

LO1	Define unions and labour relations and their role in organizations.
LO2	Identify the labour relations goals of management, unions, and society.
LO3	Summarize laws and regulations that affect labour relations.
LO4	Describe the union organizing process.
LO5	Explain how management and unions negotiate and administer collective agreements.
LO6	Describe more cooperative and collaborative approaches to labour–management relations.

Plane: © Ricky Deacon | Dreamstime.com, Vote sign: VectorPic/Shutterstock.com

WestJet's flight attendants recently voted in favour of unionization. CUPE (Canadian Union of Public Employees) represents WestJet's flight attendants and the Air Line Pilots Association represents WestJet's pilots.

Unionization is in the Air at WestJet

WestJet has built a reputation for having a culture and work environment that is caring and fun, providing an excellent guest experience, and sustaining a successful and profitable business that shares profits with its employees, "WestJetters." However, WestJet narrowly averted a strike of its unionized pilots, and media reports cited "growing anger among WestJet flight attendants about a compensation model that restricts hourly wages to time actually spent in the sky." For example, a full-time flight attendant (who spends half of an eight-hour day in the air) at a starting wage of $25.29 per hour of flying time, is reported to receive the equivalent of $12.64 per hour—because the other four hours of the shift are on the ground performing required but unpaid tasks such as preparing the airplane for service, and boarding and deplaning passengers.

WestJet's 3,000 cabin crew are now members of the new CUPE Local 4070. Executives including a President and Vice-President have been elected and the Bargaining Committee that will negotiate a first collective agreement with WestJet's Labour Relations team representing management, is in place.

During the unionization battle, WestJet management had argued against unionization saying, "It would harm the unique culture of the airline and its financial position." However, following certification of the union representing cabin crew, WestJet CEO Ed Sims provided a statement saying: "We are disappointed by this outcome but respect the rights of our employees to choose their representation." Sims added: "We now shift our focus to working effectively with CUPE in the interest of success for WestJet as a whole."[1]

Introduction

The presence of unions in a government agency or business changes some aspects of human resource management by directing more attention to the interests of employees as a group. In general, employees and employers share the same interests. They both benefit when the organization is strong and growing, providing employees with jobs and employers with profits. But although the interests of employers and employees overlap, they obviously are not identical. In the case of pay, workers benefit from higher pay, but high pay cuts into the organization's profits, unless pay increases are associated with higher productivity or better customer experience. Workers may negotiate differences with their employers individually, or they may form unions to negotiate on their behalf. This chapter explores human resource activities in organizations where employees belong to unions or where employees are seeking to organize unions.

We begin by formally defining unions and labour relations, and then describe the history, scope, and impact of union activity. We next summarize government laws and regulations affecting unions and labour relations. The following two sections detail types of activities involving unions: union organizing, as well as collective agreement negotiation and administration. Finally, we identify ways in which unions and management are working together in arrangements that are more cooperative and collaborative than the traditional labour–management relationship.

LO1 Role of Unions and Labour Relations

In Canada, most workers act as individuals to select jobs that are acceptable to them and to negotiate pay, benefits, flexible hours, and other work conditions. Especially when there is competition for labour and employees have hard-to-find skills, this arrangement produces satisfactory results for most employees. At times, however, workers have believed their needs and interests do not receive enough consideration from management. One response by workers is to act collectively by forming and joining labour **unions**, organizations formed for the purpose of representing their members' interests and resolving conflicts with employers.

> **unions**
> Organizations formed for the purpose of representing their members' interests in dealing with employers.

Unions have a role because some degree of conflict is inevitable between workers and management.[2] For example, managers can increase profits by lowering workers' pay, but workers benefit in the short term if lower profits result because their pay is higher. Still, this type of conflict is more complex than a simple trade-off, such as wages versus profits. Rising profits can help employees by driving up profit sharing or other benefits, and falling profits can result in layoffs and a lack of investment. Although employers can use programs like profit sharing to help align employee interests with their own, some remaining divergence of interests is inevitable. Labour unions represent workers' interests, and the collective bargaining process provides a way to clarify and systemize conditions of employment rather than relying on management's discretion.

As unionization of workers became more common, universities and colleges developed training in how to manage union–management interactions. This specialty, called **labour relations**, emphasizes skills that managers and union leaders can use to cultivate effective labour–management cooperation, minimize costly forms of conflict (such as strikes), and seek win–win solutions to disagreements. Labour relations involve three levels of decisions:[3]

> **labour relations**
> A field that emphasizes skills managers and union leaders can use to minimize costly forms of conflict (such as strikes) and seek win–win solutions to disagreements.

1. **Labour relations strategy.** For management, the decision involves how the organization will work with unions or develop (or maintain) non-union operations. This decision is influenced by outside forces such

as public opinion and competition. For unions, the decision involves whether to resist changes in how unions relate to the organization or accept new kinds of labour–management relationships.

2. **Negotiating collective agreements.** As we will describe later in the chapter, collective agreement negotiations in a union setting involve decisions about pay structure, job security, work rules, workplace safety, and many other issues. These decisions affect workers' and the employer's situation for the term of the contract.
3. **Administering collective agreements.** These decisions involve day-to-day activities in which union members and the organization's managers may have disagreements. Issues include complaints of work rules being violated or workers being treated unfairly in particular situations. A formal grievance procedure is typically used to resolve these issues.

Later sections in this chapter describe how managers and unions carry out the activities connected with these levels of decisions, as well as the goals and legal constraints affecting these activities.

Types of Unions and Affiliations

Most union members belong to a national or international union. Figure 9.1 shows the number of workers covered by Canada's ten largest unions.

FIGURE 9.1

Canada's Top-Ten Labour Organizations

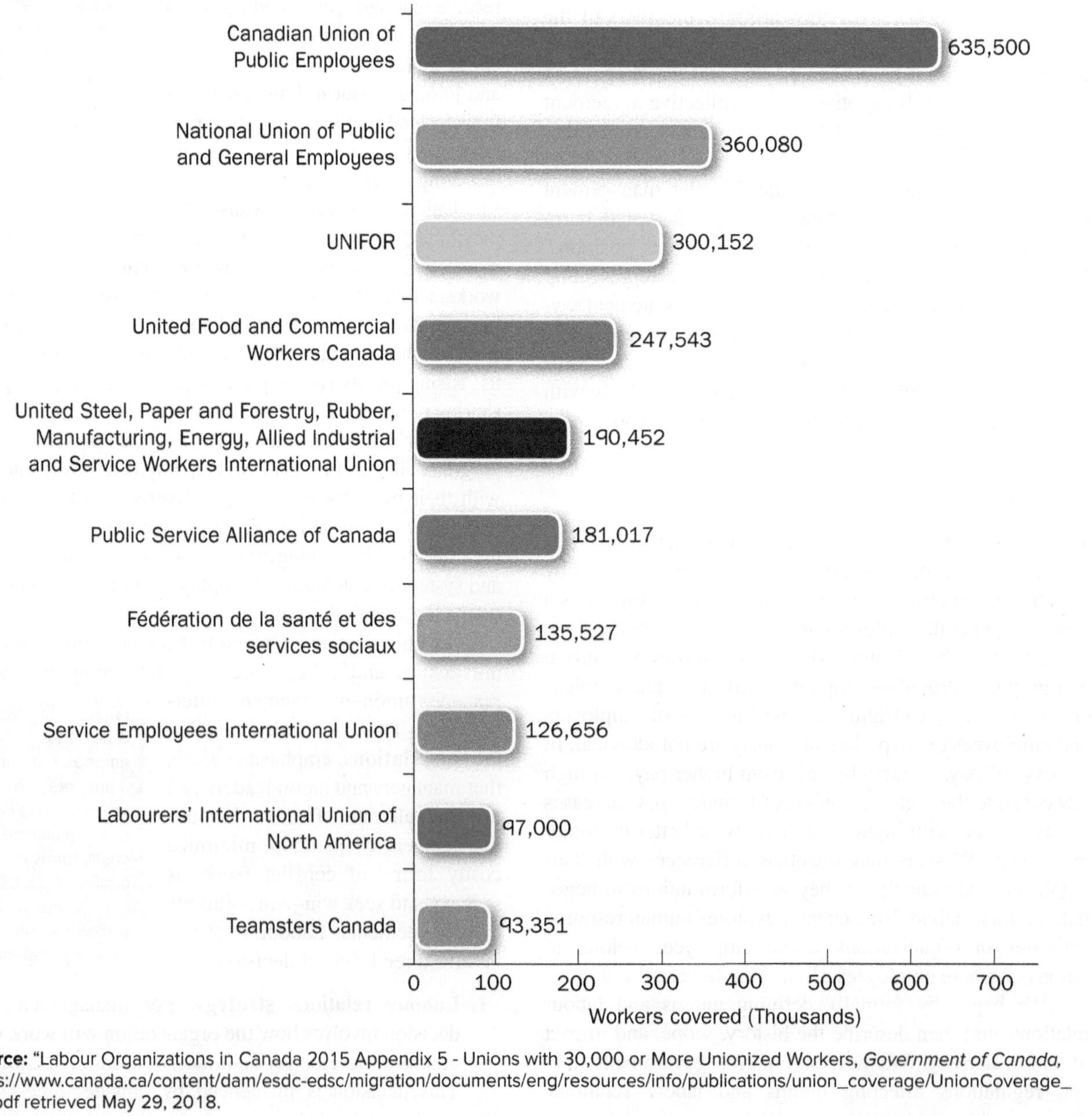

Source: "Labour Organizations in Canada 2015 Appendix 5 - Unions with 30,000 or More Unionized Workers, *Government of Canada,* https://www.canada.ca/content/dam/esdc-edsc/migration/documents/eng/resources/info/publications/union_coverage/UnionCoverage_EN.pdf retrieved May 29, 2018.

Traditionally, unions were characterized by being either *craft* or *industrial* unions. Members of a craft union had a particular skill or occupation, e.g., the International Brotherhood of Electrical Workers representing electricians (IBEW); whereas industrial unions comprised members who were linked by their work in a particular industry. These distinctions between types of unions are less clear today. For example, some "locals" of the IBEW now represent a variety of types of employees in the electrical industry and UNIFOR, Canada's largest private-sector union (created in 2013 with the merger of the Canadian Auto Workers and the Communications, Energy, and Paperworkers Union of Canada), has members who work in every major sector of the Canadian economy.[4] In addition, *public-sector unions* represent employees who work in the public sector. For example, the Public Service Alliance of Canada (PSAC) represents more than 180,000 members from every province and territory in Canada who hold diverse roles in federal government departments, airports, casinos, Indigenous communities, and the security sector, among others.[5]

Unions affiliate with labour congresses for assistance at national and international levels. The **Canadian Labour Congress (CLC)** is Canada's largest labour organization. The CLC is the umbrella organization for dozens of affiliated Canadian and international unions, as well as provincial and territorial federations of labour and regional labour councils. The CLC represents more than 3.3 million workers—more than two-thirds of unionized workers covered by collective agreements.[6] An important responsibility of the CLC is to represent labour's interests in issues such as wages and benefits, ensuring safe and healthy workplaces, environmental sustainability, and respect for human rights in Canada and throughout the world.[8] The CLC also provides information, support, and analysis that member unions can use in their activities.

Canadian Labour Congress (CLC) The umbrella organization for dozens of affiliated Canadian and international unions, as well as provincial federations of labour and regional labour councils.

THE CANADIAN PRESS/Ryan Remiorz

Hassan Yussuff, president of the Canadian Labour Congress (CLC), recently called on the federal government to take additional steps to protect workers from workplace harassment and violence. "In the era of #metoo and #timesup, we need to talk about the impacts these hazards can have in the workplace."[7]

Local Unions

National unions consist of multiple union locals, the basic units of union organization. The **union local** consists of the unionized workers from a particular department, location, industry or sector that are covered by a specific collective agreement. For example, CUPE Local 4098 represents the more than 1,000 Air Canada Rouge Flight Attendants based in Toronto, Montreal, and Vancouver.[9] Even when a national union plays the most critical role in negotiating the terms of a collective agreement, negotiation occurs at the local union level for work rules and other issues that are determined for a particular location. In addition, administration of the agreement largely takes place at the union local level. As a result, most day-to-day interaction between labour and management involves the union local.

union local The basic unit of union organization consisting of the unionized workers from a particular department, location, industry, or sector that are covered by a specific collective agreement.

Typically, the union local elects *officers,* such as president, vice-president, director, and/or secretary-treasurer. The officers may be responsible for negotiation of the collective agreement, or the local may form a bargaining committee for that purpose. When the union is engaged in bargaining, the national union provides help, including providing background data about other settlements, technical advice, and the leadership of a representative from the national office.

Individual members participate in local unions in various ways. At meetings of the local union, they elect officials and vote on resolutions. Most of workers' contact is with the **union steward**, an employee elected by union members to represent them in ensuring that the terms of the agreement are adhered to. The union steward helps to investigate any complaints and represents employees to supervisors and other managers when an employee files a grievance alleging a term of the collective agreement was violated.[10] It is valuable for managers to cultivate positive working relationships with union stewards because the stewards also have close involvement with employees.

union steward An employee elected by union members to represent them in ensuring that the terms of the collective agreement are enforced.

History and Trends in Union Membership

Unionism in Canada had early ties to Britain, as tradesmen active in the British trade union movement immigrated to Canada and settled in Atlantic Canada. The first national labour organization, a forerunner of the Canadian Labour Congress, was formed in 1873. During the early 1900s, labour activities escalated as workers demanded better wages, shorter workdays, and improved working conditions. Strikes involving large numbers of workers were frequent, with the Winnipeg General Strike in 1919 being perhaps the most well known. As labour politics developed, unionization was supported by the Co-operative Commonwealth Federation (CCF), which later became the New Democratic Party (NDP). Collective bargaining was first recognized in 1937. Post–World War II, U.S. unions began to spread into Canada and influenced Canada's labour legislation. In 1967, the federal government passed legislation that extended collective bargaining rights to government workers, and today the majority of government workers have the right to unionize.[11] During the 1960s and 1970s, unions were highly visible champions for occupational health and safety as well as accessible and paid maternity leave benefits.

Unionization levels continued to grow in both the private and public sectors until the mid-1990s despite pressures on unions that labour costs had not kept pace with productivity.[12] Union membership in Canada peaked in 1994, reaching 36.1 percent of employees.[13] In 2016, labour organizations reported that 4.83 million workers in Canada paid dues to a union in Canada.[14] The overall unionization rate or *union density* has remained relatively stable in Canada in recent years because a decrease in unionization in the private sector has been largely offset due to increased unionization in the public sector.[15]

In Canada, unionization is much higher in the public sector than the private sector—72.0 percent for the public sector, in contrast to 14.6 percent for the private sector.[16] As illustrated in Figure 9.2, union membership is concentrated in public administration, utilities, educational services, health care, and social assistance. Among the least unionized sectors are agriculture; professional, scientific, and technical services; and accommodation and food services.

Figure 9.3 illustrates the significant variation in rates of union membership among the provinces. Newfoundland and Labrador (38.7 percent) and Quebec (38.4 percent) have the highest rates of unionization. Alberta (25.0 percent) and Ontario (26.8 percent) have the lowest rates of union density. Unionization also varies by firm size. Unionization is most common in large organizations.

FIGURE 9.2

Unionization Rate (Density) in Canada by Industry

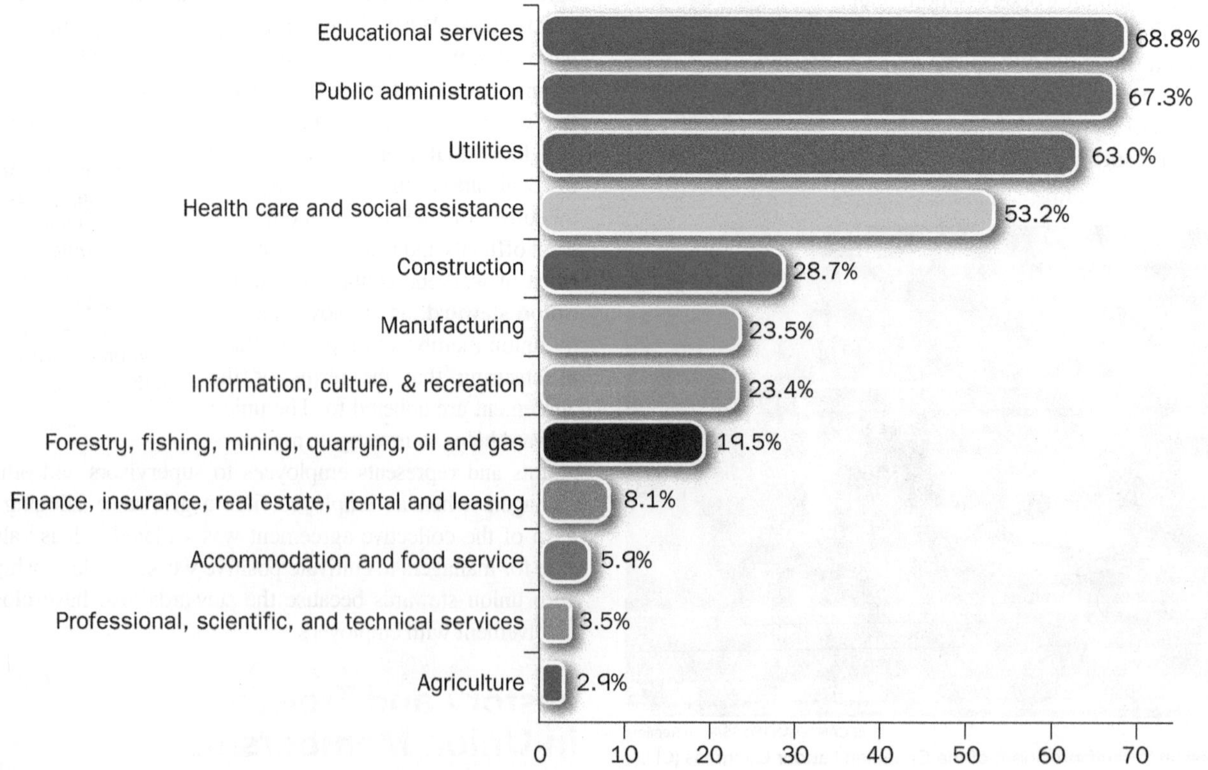

Source: Monica Haberl, "Industrial Relations Outlook 2017: Striking a Balance, Table 1: Rates of Unionization in Canada by Industry 2005–2015," December 2016, p. 9, Conference Board of Canada.

FIGURE 9.3

Unionization Rate by Province

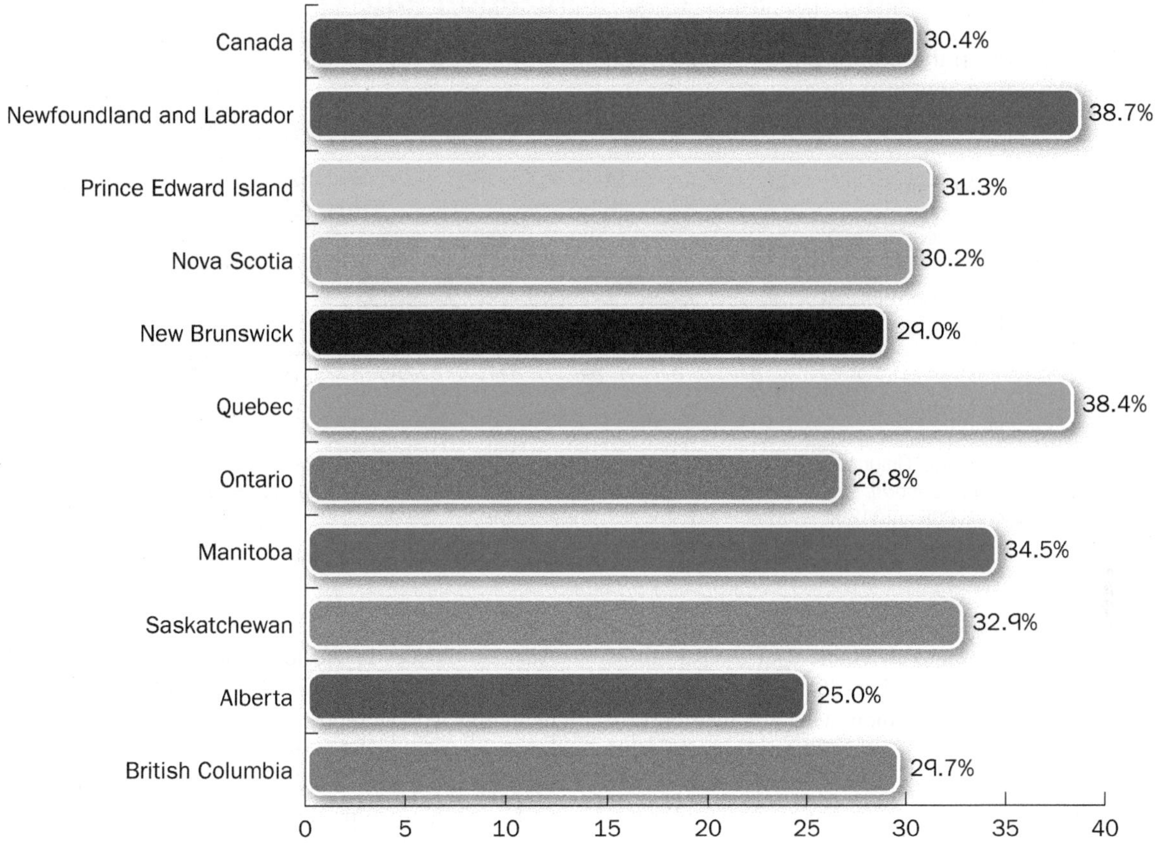

Note: Data for 2017.

Source: "Union coverage rate in Canada in 2017, by provinces, *Statista 2018,* https://www.statista.com/statistics/442980/canada-union-coverage-rate-by-province/, retrieved May 28, 2018. Data from Statistics Canada.

The overall decline in union membership has been attributed to several factors:[17]

- **Change in the structure of the economy**—Much recent job growth has occurred in the service sector of the economy, while union strength has traditionally been among urban blue-collar workers. Service industries such as finance, insurance, and real estate have lower union representation than manufacturing.
- **Management efforts to control costs**—On average, unionized workers receive higher pay than their non-unionized counterparts, and the pressure to control costs is increasing because of global competition. In the past, union membership across an industry such as automobiles or steel resulted in similar wages and work requirements for all competitors. Today, North American producers have to compete with companies that have entirely different pay scales and work rules, often putting the North American companies at a disadvantage.
- **Human resource practices**—Another way management may be contributing to the decline in union membership is by adopting human resource practices that increase employees' commitment to their job and employer. Competition for scarce human resources can lead employers to offer much of what employees traditionally sought through union membership.
- **Government regulation**—Stricter regulation in areas such as workplace safety and human rights leaves fewer areas in which unions can show an advantage over what employers must already offer.

Unions have made strategic decisions in recent years to organize the growing private-service sector. This sector includes workers employed in hotels, home care agencies, and offices. Often, these employees are women. As reported by Statistics Canada, in 2014, 30.5 percent of women were members of unions in contrast to 27.2 percent of men.[18] See Did You Know? The percentage of women who are members of

Did You Know?

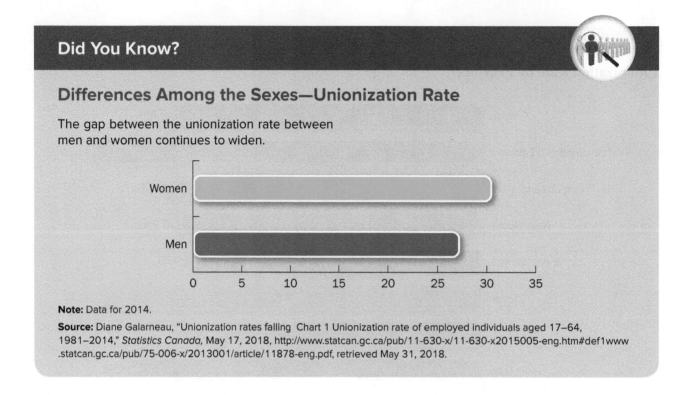

Differences Among the Sexes—Unionization Rate

The gap between the unionization rate between men and women continues to widen.

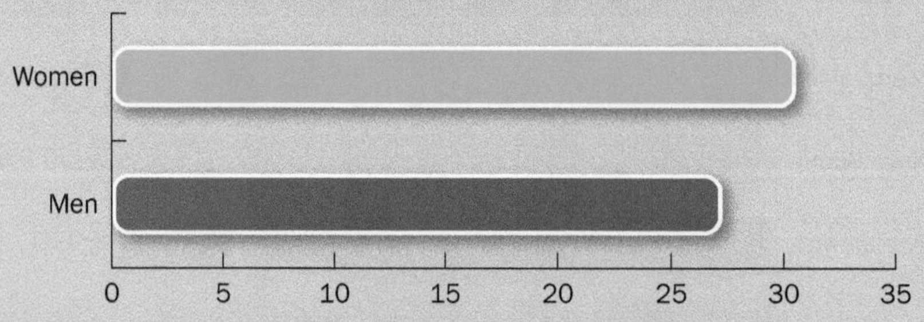

Note: Data for 2014.

Source: Diane Galarneau, "Unionization rates falling Chart 1 Unionization rate of employed individuals aged 17–64, 1981–2014," *Statistics Canada*, May 17, 2018, http://www.statcan.gc.ca/pub/11-630-x/11-630-x2015005-eng.htm#def1www.statcan.gc.ca/pub/75-006-x/2013001/article/11878-eng.pdf, retrieved May 31, 2018.

unions has remained relatively stable over the past three decades (31.4 percent in 1981 to 30.5 percent in 2014), whereas the percentage of men who are members of unions has declined significantly (42.1 percent in 1981 to 27.2 percent in 2014).[19]

The mindset of younger workers about collective action and unionization is an important consideration for union leaders. Prem Benimadhu, Conference Board of Canada, suggests that younger workers are less likely to want or need union representation—"Once workers figure out that they can negotiate successfully on their own behalf, it will be hard for unions to convince them to join up and pay dues for the same service," he concluded.[20]

The unionization rate of younger workers (17–24 years of age) has significantly declined[21]:

- In 2014, 13.4 percent of women aged 17–24 years were unionized—dropping from 23.1 percent in 1981.
- In 2014, 14.9 percent of men aged 17–24 years were unionized—dropping from 29.2 percent in 1981.

As Figure 9.4 indicates, the percentage of Canadian workers who belong to unions, although much higher than in the United States, is lower than some other countries. More dramatic is the difference in "coverage"—the percentage of employees whose terms and conditions of employment are governed by a union contract, whether or not the employees are technically union members. In Western Europe, it is common to have coverage rates of 80 to 90 percent, so the influence of labour unions far outstrips what membership levels would imply.[22] Also, employees in Western Europe tend to have a larger formal role in decision making than in Canada. This role, including worker representatives on boards of directors, is often mandated by the government. But as markets become more and more global, pressure to cut labour costs and increase productivity is likely to be stronger in every country. Unless unions can help companies improve productivity or organize new production facilities opened in lower-wage countries, union influence may decline in countries where it is now strong.

Impact of Unions on Company Performance

Organizations are concerned about whether union organizing and bargaining will hurt their performance, particularly unions' impact on productivity, profits, and stock performance. Researchers have studied the general relationship between unionization and these performance measures. Through skillful labour relations, organizations can positively influence outcomes.

There has been much debate regarding the effects of unions on productivity.[23] One view is that unions decrease productivity because of work rules and limits on workloads set by union contracts and production lost to union actions such as strikes and work slowdowns. At the same time, unions can have positive effects on productivity.[24] They can reduce turnover by giving employees a route for resolving problems.[25] Unions emphasize pay systems based on seniority, which remove incentives for employees to compete rather than cooperate. The introduction of

FIGURE 9.4

Union Membership Rates in Selected Countries (2016)

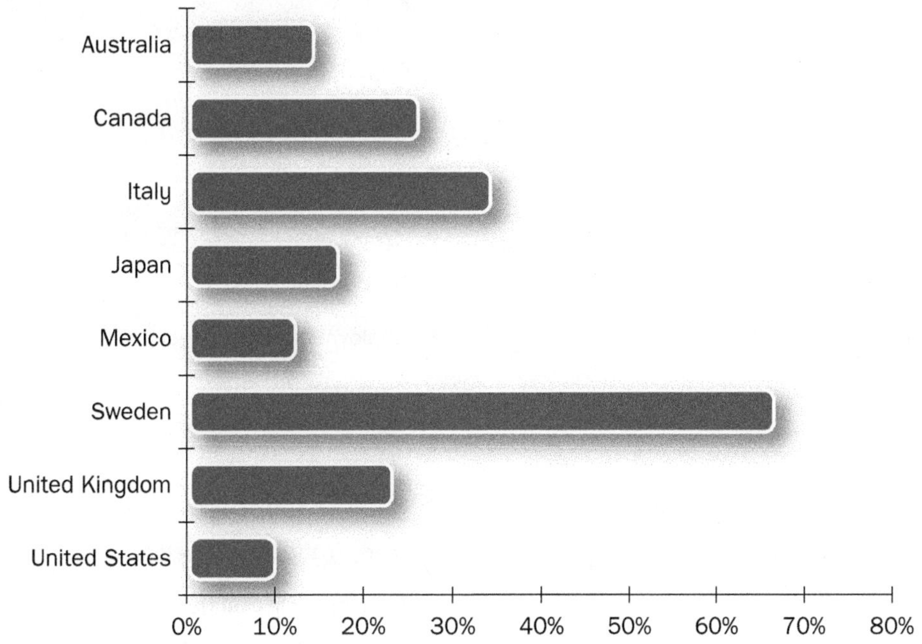

Source: Organization for Economic Co-operation and Development, OECD.Stat, http://stats.oecd.org, accessed May 30, 2018.

a union also may force an employer to improve its management practices and pay greater attention to employees' ideas.

Although there is evidence that unions have both positive and negative effects on productivity, most studies have found that union workers are more productive than non-union workers. Still, questions remain. Are highly productive workers more likely to form unions, or does a union make workers more productive? The answer is unclear. In theory, if unions caused greater productivity, we would expect union membership to be rising in the private sector, not falling as it has been.[26]

Even if unions do raise productivity, a company's profits and stock performance may still suffer if unions raise wage and benefits costs by more than the productivity gain. On average, union members receive higher wages and more generous benefits than non-union workers, and evidence shows that unions have a large negative effect on profits. Also, union coverage tends to decline faster in companies with a lower return to shareholders.[27] In summary, companies wishing to become more competitive must continually monitor their labour relations strategy. These studies look at the average effects of unions, not at individual companies or innovative labour relations. Some organizations excel at labour relations, and some have worked with unions to meet business needs. Labour management cooperation and collaboration is discussed later in the chapter.[28]

LO2 Goals of Management, Unions, and Society

Working together in a positive way is usually best accomplished when the parties involved understand each other's goals. Although individual cases vary, we can draw some general conclusions about the goals of labour unions and management. Table 9.1 provides a summary of priority issues from the perspective of management and unions. Society, too, has goals for labour and business, given form in the laws regulating labour relations.

Management Goals

Management goals are to increase the organization's profits and/or increase productivity. Managers tend to prefer options that lower costs and raise output. A concern is that a union will create higher costs in wages and benefits, as well as raise the risk of work stoppages. Managers may also fear that a union will make managers and workers into adversaries or limit management's discretion in making business and employment decisions.

When an employer has recognized a union, management's goals continue to emphasize reducing costs and improving output. Managers continue to prefer to keep the organization's operations flexible, so they can adjust activities to meet competitive challenges and customer

TABLE 9.1

Current Negotiation Issues

Management Issues	Union Issues
1. Wages	1. Wages
2. Flexible work practices	2. Employment security
3. Productivity	3. Health benefits
4. Business competitiveness	4. Outsourcing and contracting out
5. Health benefits	5. Pensions
6. Organizational change	6. Employment and pay equity
7. Outsourcing and contracting out	7. Organizational change
8. Pensions	8. Flexible work practices
9. Employment and pay equity	9. Variable pay
10. Employment security	10. Training and skills development
11. Technological change	11. Technological change
12. Training and skills development	12. Productivity
13. Variable pay	13. Business competitiveness
14. Other (e.g., vacation, type of work, etc.)	14. Other (e.g., vacation, type of work, etc.)

Note: Respondents were given a list of 14 possible choices and asked to indicate the top three negotiation issues for both management and union.

Source: Heather McAteer, "Compensation Planning Outlook 2018, Table 23: Current Negotiation Issues," October 2017, The Conference Board of Canada, p. 40.

demands. Therefore, in their labour relations, managers prefer to limit increases in wages and benefits and to retain as much discretion as they can over work rules, schedules, and other workplace decisions.

Union Goals

In general, unions have the goals of obtaining pay, job security, and working conditions that satisfy their members, and of giving members a voice in decisions that affect them. Traditionally, they obtain these goals by gaining power in numbers. The more workers who belong to a union, the greater the union's power. More members translates into greater ability to halt or disrupt operations. Larger unions also have greater financial resources for continuing a strike; the union can help to make up for the wages the workers lose during a strike. The threat of a long strike—stated or implied—can make an employer more willing to meet the union's demands.

As mentioned earlier, union membership is linked to better compensation. Statistics Canada reports that in April 2018 the average hourly wage of employees with union coverage was $30.46 per hour, almost 19.5 percent more than the $25.50 per hour earned by employees without union coverage. However, from April 2017 to April 2018, employees *without* union coverage received a larger pay increase—4.3 percent in contrast to unionized employees who received only a 2.4 percent increase.[29] Benefits packages also tend to be more generous for union members.

Unions typically want to influence the *way* pay and promotions are determined. Unlike management, which tries to consider employees as individuals so that pay and promotion decisions relate to performance differences, unions try to build group solidarity and avoid possible arbitrary treatment of employees. To do so, unions try to have any pay differences based on seniority, on the grounds that this measure is more objective than performance evaluations. As a result, where workers are represented by a union, it is common for all employees in a particular job classification to be paid at the same rate. The Thinking Ethically at the end of the chapter discusses the perceptions of fairness associated with the use of seniority provisions.

As well as working to advance the interests of members, unions often engage in **social unionism**, that is, activities intended to influence social and economic policies of government. For example, Unifor's Action Campaigns include addressing labour conditions in Mexico as a part of a renegotiated trade agreement, and advocating for universal prescription drug coverage.[30]

social unionism
A type of unionism that attempts to influence social and economic policies of government.

Ultimately, the survival and security of a union depends on its ability to ensure a regular flow of new members and member dues to support the services it provides. In 1946, Supreme Court of Canada Justice Ivan Rand brought down a significant decision that affected union financial security in Canada. The case came about as part of an arbitrated settlement of a labour dispute between the Ford Motor Company and the United Auto Workers. The **Rand Formula** is a union security provision that makes the payment of labour union dues mandatory even if the worker is not a member of the union. The rationale for the principle was that every employee benefits from union representation.[31] Unions typically place high priority on negotiating two types of contract provisions with an employer that are critical to a union's security and viability: checkoff provisions and provisions relating to union membership or contribution.

Rand Formula
A union security provision that makes payment of labour union dues mandatory even if the worker is not a member of the union.

checkoff provision
A requirement that the employer, on behalf of the union, automatically deducts union dues from employees' paycheques.

Under a **checkoff provision**, the employer, on behalf of the union, automatically deducts union dues from employees' paycheques (and remits the funds to the appropriate union). The HR Oops! describes issues encountered with

HR Oops!

Public Service Union Says It's Owed $10 Million Due to Payroll Fiasco

The federal government's new computerized pay system, Phoenix, went live on February 24, 2016. Since then, "tens of thousands of workers have been burned" and the "growing list of victims" includes "countless spouses and dependants who have also had to bear the financial—and often emotional—burden" of the system that has caused employees to go unpaid.

In addition, the Public Service Alliance of Canada (PSAC), which represents 170,000 employees, says, "The federal government now owes more than $10 million in union dues due to ongoing problems with the Phoenix payroll system." The union has stated that "a financial shortfall of this magnitude affects our ability to carry on operations and properly fulfill our statutory mandate." Debi Daviau, president of the Professional Institute of the Public Service of Canada (PIPSC) also says that her union "can't afford not to receive accurate union dues collected by the federal government's troubled new payroll system."

Despite commitments provided in the 2018 federal budget to take action to reimburse missing and inaccurate dues owed to public-sector unions, PSAC officials claim they have not yet recovered any money. Michael Aubry, communications officer with the PSAC, explains the issue: "Phoenix is causing errors for the union, the government, and federal workers, so there's no easy way to do a proper accounting of dues owed."

Unions representing federal workers are also taking a stand for their members by requesting a payroll fix that ensures workers "are paid accurately and on time." In addition, union leaders are requesting employee compensation for "the suffering they have endured and continue to face."

Questions

1. Do you anticipate the issues described will affect the long-term relationship and bargaining climate for the federal government and its unionized employees? Why or why not?
2. What is your advice to these public sector unions? Are they doing enough to support their members?

Source: Julie Ireton, "Public service union says it's owed $10M due to Phoenix," *CBC News*, March 19, 2018, www.cbc.ca, retrieved June 1, 2018; Julie Ireton, "As federal Phoenix payroll fiasco hits 2-year mark, families continue to bear brunt of it," *CBC News*, February 21, 2018, www.cbc.ca, retrieved June 2, 2018; "Pay public servants for Phoenix stress, unions tell PM," *CBC News*, February 16, 2018, www.cbc.news, retrieved June 2, 2018.

the federal government's payroll system that have resulted in errors and delays in compensating employees and unions. The strongest union security arrangement is a **closed shop**, under which a person must be a union member before being hired or the **union shop**, an arrangement that requires an employee to join the union within a certain time after beginning employment.

closed shop
A union security arrangement under which a person must be a union member before being hired.

union shop
A union security arrangement that requires employees to join the union within a certain amount of time after beginning employment.

These provisions are ways to address unions' concern about "free riders"—employees who benefit from union activities without belonging to a union. By law, all members of a bargaining unit, whether union members or not, must be represented by the union. If a union was required to offer services to all bargaining unit members even though some of them do not pay dues, it may not have enough financial resources to operate successfully.

Society's Goals

The activities of unions and management take place within the context of society, with society's values driving the laws and regulations that affect labour relations. As long ago as the late 1800s and early 1900s, industrial relations scholars saw unions as a way to make up for individual employees' limited bargaining power.[32] At that time, clashes between workers and management could be violent, and many people hoped that unions would replace the violence with negotiation. Since then, observers have expressed concern that unions in certain industries have become too strong, achieving their goals at the expense of employers' ability to compete or meet other objectives. Overall, however, societal goals for government include ensuring that neutral rules exist to ensure balance is maintained between the powers of unions and employers and that the public interest is protected.

Rather than being left to the activities of unions and management, many societal goals are also enforced through laws and regulations. As discussed in Chapter 2 clashes between workers and management could be violent, and many people hoped that unions would replace the violence with negotiation. Since then, observers have expressed concern that unions in certain industries have become too strong, achieving their goals at the expense of employers' ability to compete or meet other objectives. Overall, however, societal goals include ensuring that neutral rules exist to ensure balance is maintained between the powers of unions and employers and that the public interest is protected.

LO3 Laws and Regulations Affecting Labour Relations

The laws and regulations pertaining to labour relations affect unions' size and bargaining power, so they significantly affect the degree to which unions, management, and society achieve their varied goals. These laws and regulations set limits on union structure and administration and the ways in which unions and management interact.

Canada's overall labour relations legal framework is decentralized and relatively complex. Responsibility for labour relations is primarily a provincial/territorial responsibility; however, federal labour legislation covers federally regulated employers. Distinct federal, provincial, and territorial laws cover their respective public-sector employees, and additional labour statutes apply to essential occupations such as law enforcement, firefighters, and health care professionals.

Although some differences exist among jurisdictions, the main features of labour legislation in Canada can be summarized as follows:

- methods to certify a union that will represent a group of employees
- requirement of the employer to recognize the union chosen by the majority of its employees and to accept the union as the employees' exclusive representative for bargaining purposes
- responsibility to bargain in good faith with the intention to reach an agreement
- requirement of the employer to deduct union dues from employees
- minimum length of a collective agreement (at least one year)
- regulation of strike and lockout activities
- creation of a labour relations board (or specialized tribunal) to interpret and enforce the labour laws in their jurisdiction
- prohibition of identified **unfair labour practices** by management and labour (see the HR How-To)

unfair labour practices
Prohibited conduct of an employer, union, or individual under the relevant labour legislation.

There is a **Labour Relations Board (LRB)** (or similar structure) in each jurisdiction that serves as a specialized quasi-judicial tribunal with authority to interpret and enforce the labour laws in its jurisdiction.

Labour Relations Board (LRB)
A specialized tribunal with authority to interpret and enforce the labour laws in its jurisdiction.

HR How-To

Avoiding Unfair Labour Practices

A common core of labour legislation prohibits employers, unions, and individuals from engaging in unfair labour practices. Each jurisdiction in Canada has specific provisions dealing with unfair labour practices by management and unions.

Some of the most common examples of unfair labour practices that management must not engage in are the following:

- interfering in the formation of a union or contributing to it financially (although there have been allowances for the providing of an office for the union to conduct business and for paid leave for union officials conducting union business)
- discriminating against an employee because the individual is or is not a member of a union
- discriminating against an employee because the individual chooses to exercise rights granted by labour relations law
- intimidating or coercing an employee to become or not become a member of a union

Activities that a union is not permitted to engage in include:

- seeking to compel an employer to bargain collectively with the union if the union is not the certified bargaining agent;
- attempting at the workplace and during working hours to persuade an employee to become or not become a union member;
- intimidating, coercing, or penalizing an individual because they have filed a complaint or testified in any proceeding pursuant to the relevant labour law;
- engaging in, encouraging, or threatening illegal strikes; or
- failing to represent employees fairly.

Source: Hermann Schwind, Hari Das, and Terry Wagar, Canadian Human Resource Management, 11th ed. (Toronto: McGraw-Hill Ryerson, 2016), p. 616.

Prevention of Unfair Labour Practices

When someone believes that an unfair labour practice has taken place, they may file a complaint with the appropriate Labour Relations Board for the jurisdiction. All parties are provided a copy of the complaint and the process usually involves the Labour Relations Board conducting a preliminary investigation to determine if the complaint has merit and if it may be possible for the parties to resolve the complaint themselves. If the Labour Relations Board finds the complaint has merit and determines the complaint cannot be resolved through the parties, the Labour Relations Board will conduct a formal hearing with the parties present. Either the case can be dismissed at this point or the Labour Relations Board has the authority to issue orders to halt unfair labour practices. If the union or employer does not comply with the Labour Relations Board order, the order can be referred to the courts for enforcement.[33]

LO4 What Is the Union Organizing Process?

Unions begin their involvement with an organization's employees by conducting an organizing campaign. To meet its objectives, a union needs to convince a majority of workers that they should receive better pay or other employment conditions and that the union will help them do so. The employer's objectives will depend on its strategy—whether it seeks to work with a union or convince employees that they are better off without union representation.

The Process of Organizing

The organization process begins with a membership application. Union representatives contact employees, present their message about the union, and invite them to sign an application for membership. By signing the application and paying a nominal fee; for example, \$5, employees indicate they want the union to represent them.

When the necessary number of employees have signed membership applications, the union will apply to the appropriate Labour Relations Board for certification. Requirements differ among jurisdictions. For example, in some jurisdictions a local union can be certified without an overall representation vote if a certain threshold of signed membership applications is provided.

Management Strategies

Sometimes an employer will recognize a union after a majority of employees have signed membership applications. More often, there is a hotly contested election campaign. During the campaign, unions try to persuade employees that their wages, benefits, treatment by employers, and chances to influence workplace decisions are too poor or small and that the union will be able to obtain improvements in these areas. As described in the chapter opening, management typically responds with its own messages providing an opposite point of view.

Management messages may say the organization has provided a valuable package of wages and benefits and has treated employees well. Management may also argue that the union will not be able to keep its promises but will instead create costs for employees, such as union dues and lost income during strikes. Employers use a variety of methods to avoid unionization in organizing campaigns.[34] Their efforts range from hiring consultants to distributing letters to presenting the company's viewpoint at meetings of employees. Some management efforts go beyond what the law permits, especially in the eyes of union organizers.

Supervisors have the most direct contact with employees. Thus, as Table 9.2 indicates, it is critical that they establish good relationships with employees even before there is any attempt at union organizing. Supervisors also must know what *not* to do if a union drive takes place.

Can a Union be Decertified?

Union members' right to be represented by unions of their own choosing also includes the right to vote out an existing union. The action is called *decertifying* the union. Decertification follows the same process as a representation election. An application to decertify a union may not be acted upon during a legal strike or lockout. In some jurisdictions when a collective agreement is in place, decertification applications may be filed only during specified "open periods." Laws in some jurisdictions require the employer to post and annually circulate information related to union decertification.

TABLE 9.2

What Supervisors Should and Should Not Do to Reduce the Likelihood of Unionization

What to Do
Report any direct or indirect signs of union activity to a core management group.
Deal with employees by carefully stating the company's response to pro-union arguments. These responses should be coordinated by the company to maintain consistency and to avoid threats or promises. Take away union issues by following effective management practices all the time:
• Deliver recognition and appreciation.
• Solve employee problems.
• Protect employees from harassment or humiliation.
• Provide business-related information.
• Be consistent in treatment of employees.
• Accommodate special circumstances where appropriate.
• Ensure due process in performance management.
• Treat all employees with dignity and respect.
What to Avoid
• Threatening employees with harsher terms and conditions of employment or employment loss if they engage in union activity.
• Interrogating employees about pro-union or anti-union sentiments that they or others may have or reviewing union authorization cards or pro-union petitions.
• Promising employees that they will receive favourable terms or conditions of employment if they forgo union activity.
• Spying on employees known to be, or suspected of being, engaged in pro-union activities.

Source: J. A. Segal, "Unshackle Your Supervisors to Stay Union Free," in HR Magazine, June 1998.

LO5 Collective Bargaining

When a union has been certified, that union represents employees during collective agreement (contract) negotiations. In **collective bargaining**, a union negotiates on behalf of its members with management representatives to reach an agreement (contract) defining conditions of employment and to establish methods to resolve its interpretation for the term of the collective agreement. Typical collective agreements include provisions for pay, benefits, work rules, and resolution of workers' grievances. Table 9.3 shows typical provisions negotiated in collective agreements.

collective bargaining Negotiation between union representatives and management representatives to arrive at an agreement defining conditions of employment for the term of the agreement and to administer that agreement.

Collective bargaining differs from one situation to another in terms of *bargaining structure*—that is, the range of employees and employers covered by the contract. An agreement may involve a narrow group of employees in a craft union or a broad group in an industrial union. Agreements may cover one or several facilities of the same employer, or the bargaining structure may involve several employers. Many more interests must be considered in collective bargaining for an industrial union with a bargaining structure that includes several employers than in collective bargaining for a craft union in a single facility.

The majority of collective agreement negotiations take place between unions and employers that have been through the process before. In the typical situation,

TABLE 9.3

Typical Provisions in Collective Agreements

Rights of Parties	*Recognition of Union Security* • Union membership • Union security • Leave for union business • Restrictions on contracting out *Management Rights to Test* • Drug and alcohol testing • Intelligence and aptitude testing • Electronic surveillance • Internet/telephone monitoring • Medical examinations • Other tests *Employee Rights/Security* • Harassment protection • Employment equity program • Assistance programs, e.g., drugs and alcohol treatment
Organization of Work	*Technological Change* • Advance notice • Obligation to provide training, instruction, or retraining • Layoff protection • Wage protection • Special leaves, severance pay, and/or retirement offers *Distribution of Work* • Flexibility in work assignment • Job rotation • Semi-autonomous work groups or teams • Job sharing
Labour Relations	• Grievance procedures • Bargaining method or approach • Application of the agreement • Job evaluation (position evaluation) • Joint committees • Participation (other than committees)

continued on next page

TABLE 9.3

Typical Provisions in Collective Agreements *(continued)*

Education, Training, and Development	• Leave • Reimbursement for tuition fees and resources • Multiskilling, i.e., flexibility for the employee • Contribution to a training fund • Apprenticeship programs
Conditions of Work	*Work Schedule* • Normal hours of work • Type of work schedules • Special provisions *Overtime* • Clause limiting the use of overtime • Compensatory days in lieu of pay (banking) • Overtime pay • Meal allowance (overtime)
	Job Security and Termination • No layoffs while the agreement is in effect • Layoffs by seniority • Bumping rights • Retention of seniority • Work sharing (reduction in hours to avoid layoffs) • Education/training with pay • Supplementary employment insurance benefit *Pay* • Cost-of-living allowance • Wage guarantees *Leaves and Vacations* • Paid holidays • Annual vacation • Parental leave • Paid sick leave • Personal emergency, domestic, or sexual violence leave • Job-protected unpaid leave *Benefits* • Private group insurance plans • Pension plans (funding, administration) *Provisions Relating to Part-Time Workers* • Maximum hours of work normally allowed • Ratio of part-time to full-time workers • Holidays, vacations, sick leave, benefits, pension plan, seniority

Source: Based on "Collective Agreement Provisions," General Overview, The Labour Program—Working For You, www.hrsdc.gc.ca/eng/labour/overview.shtml. Human Resources and Skills Development website, www.hrsdc.gc.ca. Retrieved: November 2, 2004.

management has come to accept the union as an organization to work with. The situation can be very different when a union has just been certified and is negotiating its first collective agreement. For example, in Alberta, the Fair and Family Friendly Workplaces Act will permit employers and unions to apply to the Labour Relations Board for first-contract arbitration. If bargaining has not been successfully completed in 90 days, the first collective agreement can be imposed through a binding arbitration process.[35] Arbitration is discussed later in this chapter.

Bargaining over New Collective Agreements

Clearly, the outcome of collective agreement negotiations can have important consequences for labour costs, productivity, the organization's ability to compete, and creating positive conditions in the workplace. Therefore, unions and management need to prepare carefully for collective bargaining. Preparation includes establishing objectives for the agreement, reviewing the old agreement, gathering data (such as compensation paid by competitors and the company's ability

Steve Russell/Toronto Star via Getty Images

York University contract professors and teaching assistants on the picket line in 2018—the longest strike at an English-speaking university in Canada.

to survive a strike), predicting the demands to be made, and establishing the cost of meeting the demands.[36] Shifting demographics and priorities must also be carefully considered in developing a plan for how and what to negotiate. For example, it is crucial for both employers and unions to engage and understand Millennials and to be mindful of cultural differences and inclusivity opportunities arising from a workforce that is increasingly diverse.

Negotiations go through various stages.[37] In the earliest stages, many more people are often present than in later stages. On the union side, this may give all the various internal interest groups a chance to participate and voice their goals. Their input helps communicate to management what will satisfy union members and may help the union achieve greater solidarity. At this stage, union negotiators often present a long list of proposals, partly to satisfy members and partly to introduce enough issues that they will have flexibility later in the process. Management may or may not present proposals of its own. Sometimes management prefers to respond to the union's proposals.

During the middle stages of the process, each side must make a series of decisions, even though the outcome is uncertain. How important is each issue to the other side? How likely is it that disagreement on particular issues will result in a labour disruption? When and to what extent should one side signal its willingness to compromise? In addition, both employers and unions have an interest in providing meaningful responses to changing social and economic conditions. Table 9.4 provides some examples of recently negotiated innovative collective agreement clauses.

In the final stage of negotiations, pressure for an agreement increases. Public negotiations may be only part of the process. Negotiators from each side may hold one-on-one meetings or small-group meetings where they escape some public relations pressures. A neutral third party may act as a go-between or facilitator. In some cases, bargaining breaks down as the two sides find they cannot reach a mutually acceptable agreement. The outcome depends partly on the relative bargaining power of each party. That power, in turn, depends on each party's ability to withstand a labour disruption that costs the workers their pay and costs the employer lost production and possibly lost customers.

TABLE 9.4

Innovative Clauses in Collective Agreements

Leave Clause
• HyLife Foods and the UFCW agreed on a new "citizenship leave." Employees who have applied to become Canadian citizens will be granted one paid day of leave to take their oath of citizenship.
Protection from Harassment
• Loblaws Supermarkets Limited and the UFCW created a new policy on harassment, stating that there will be "zero tolerance" for customer rudeness, impropriety, and abuse. Under this policy, no employee shall be required to continue to serve a customer who has engaged in any of these behaviours and management shall take proactive steps to discourage improper customer behaviour.
Alternative Dispute Resolution
• In Chapel Island, Nova Scotia, Indigenous fishermen represented by the UFCW negotiated a clause that introduces a new conflict resolution approach. The fishermen, who are citizens of the Potlotek First Nation, will have the option of resolving contract disputes through a process called the Kisikuewey Wantaqo'suti Procedure, which permits mediation by Band Elders.
Transfer between Employees
• Yukon College and the Public Service Alliance of Canada negotiated a new provision that allows workers to transfer unused vacation time to other employees on compassionate grounds.

Sources: "Overview of Collective Bargaining in Canada, - 2015, *Government of Canada,* https://www.canada.ca/en/employment-social-development/services/collective-bargaining-data/reports/collective-bargaining.html#innovative, retrieved June 1, 2018; "Overview of Collective Bargaining in Canada, 2013," *Government of Canada Labour Program,* www.labour.gc.ca/eng/resources/info/publications/collective_bargaining/collective_bargaining.shtml, pp. 7–8, retrieved April 12, 2015.

What Happens When Bargaining Breaks Down?

The intended outcome of collective bargaining is an agreement with terms acceptable to both parties. If one or both sides determine that negotiation alone will not produce such an agreement, bargaining breaks down. To bring this impasse to an end, the union may strike, the employer may lock out employees, or the parties may bring in outside help to resolve their differences.

Strikes and Lockouts

strike A collective decision by union members not to work or to slow down until certain demands or conditions are met.

A **strike** is a collective decision of the union members not to work or to slow down until certain demands or conditions are met. The union members vote, and if the majority favours a strike, they all go on strike at that time or when union leaders believe the time is right. Strikes are typically accompanied by *picketing*—the union stations members near the work site with signs indicating the union is on strike. During the strike, the union members do not receive pay from their employer, but the union may be able to make up for some of the lost pay. The employer loses production unless it can hire replacement workers, and, even then, productivity may be reduced. Often, other unions support striking workers by refusing to cross their picket line—for example, refusing to make deliveries to a company during a strike. A **lockout**, on the other hand, is initiated by the employer. A lockout is a closure of a place of employment or refusal of the employer to provide work as a way to compel employees to agree to certain demands or conditions.

lockout A closure of a place of employment or refusal of the employer to provide work as a way to compel employees to agree to certain demands or conditions.

The vast majority of labour–management negotiations do not result in a work stoppage; i.e., strike or lockout. Figure 9.5 shows a chronological perspective of work stoppages in Canada for 1984–2017. The estimated number of person-days lost through work stoppages has also fluctuated significantly, ranging from more than 4.1 million in 2005 to 0.6 million in 2016. More than 1.2 million person-days were lost through work stoppages in 2017. In summary, from 2013–17, Canada's economy lost almost 7 million days of time not worked due to labour disruptions.[38]

Not only do workers lose wages and employers lose production, but also the negative experience of a strike or lockout can make the union–management climate strained and uncooperative. When strikes or lockouts do occur, the conduct of each party during the strike can do lasting harm to labour–management relations. Violence by either side or threats of job loss or actual job loss because jobs went to replacement workers can make future relations difficult.

FIGURE 9.5

Number of Work Stoppages and Workers Involved (000s), 1984–2017

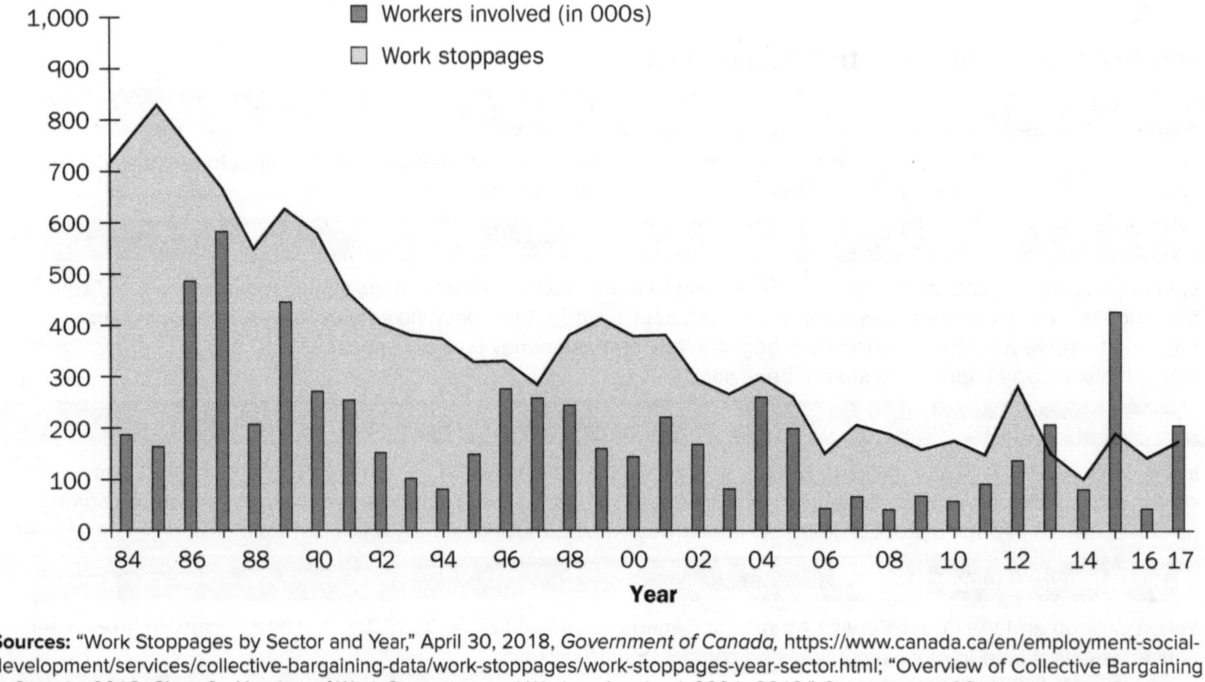

Sources: "Work Stoppages by Sector and Year," April 30, 2018, *Government of Canada*, https://www.canada.ca/en/employment-social-development/services/collective-bargaining-data/work-stoppages/work-stoppages-year-sector.html; "Overview of Collective Bargaining in Canada, 2013, Chart 9—Number of Work Stoppages and Workers Involved, 2004–2013," *Government of Canada Labour Program*, www.labour.gc.ca/eng/resources/info/publications/collective_bargaining/collective_bargaining.shtml, retrieved April 12, 2015; and Sharanjit Uppal, "Unionization 2011," Statistics Canada, Table 4, "Major Wage Settlements, Inflation and Labour Disputes," www.statcan.gc.ca/pub/75-001-x/2011004/tables-tableaux/11579/tbl04-eng.htm, retrieved May 21, 2012.

Alternatives to Strikes and Lockouts

Because strikes and lockouts are so costly and disruptive, unions and employers generally prefer other methods for resolving conflicts. Three of the most common alternatives are mediation, conciliation, and arbitration. All of these rely on a neutral third party, who usually is appointed by the federal or provincial minister of labour.

The least formal and most widely used of these procedures is **mediation**, in which a third party or *mediator* hears the views of both sides and facilitates the negotiation process. The mediator has no formal authority to impose a resolution, so a labour disruption remains a possibility. In a survey studying negotiations between unions and large businesses, mediation was used in almost four out of ten negotiation efforts.[39]

> **mediation**
> Conflict resolution procedure in which a mediator hears the views of both sides and facilitates the negotiation process but has no formal authority to impose a resolution.

> **conciliation**
> Conflict resolution procedure in which a third party to collective bargaining reports the reasons for a dispute, the views and arguments of both sides, and possibly a recommended settlement, which the parties may decline.

Conciliation, most often used for negotiations with government bodies, typically reports on the reasons for the dispute, the views and arguments of both sides, and (sometimes) a recommended settlement, which the parties may decline. The public nature of these recommendations may pressure the parties to reach a settlement. Even if they do not accept the conciliator's recommended settlement, the hope of this process is that the conciliator will identify or frame issues in a way that makes agreement easier. Sometimes merely devoting time to this process gives the parties a chance to reach an agreement. In most jurisdictions in Canada, conciliation is mandatory before a strike or lockout can be called. Again, however, there is no guarantee that a strike or lockout will be avoided.

> **arbitration**
> Conflict resolution procedure in which an arbitrator or arbitration board determines a binding settlement.

The most formal type of outside intervention is **arbitration**, under which an arbitrator or arbitration board determines a settlement that is *binding,* meaning the parties have to accept it. There is wide acceptance of "rights arbitration," which focuses on enforcing or interpreting agreement terms, but arbitration in the writing of collective agreements or setting of agreement terms has traditionally been reserved for special circumstances such as negotiations between unions and government agencies, where strikes may be illegal or especially costly. Occasionally, arbitration has also been used with businesses in situations where strikes have been extremely damaging. For example, when back-to-work legislation is imposed by a minister of labour, a provision to impose a settlement through arbitration is likely to be included.

Collective Agreement Administration

Although the process of negotiating a collective agreement (including strikes or lockouts—or the threat of these actions) receives the most publicity, other union–management activities occur far more often. Bargaining over a new contract typically occurs only about every three years, but administering labour agreements goes on day after day, year after year. The two activities are linked, of course. Vague or inconsistent language in the agreement can make administering the agreement more difficult. The difficulties can create conflict that spills over into the next round of negotiations.[40] Events during negotiations—strikes, lockouts, the use of replacement workers, or violence by either side—also can lead to difficulties in working successfully under a conflict.

The duration of collective agreements in Canada has been increasing. In 1984, the average length of a collective agreement was 19.6 months; however, in both 2016 and 2017, the average length of a new collective agreement was more than 3.5 years.[41]

Longer agreements may result in either the employer or the union requesting amendments before the expiration of the contract. For example, Air Canada and its pilots recently agreed to an amendment of their 10-year collective agreement, which is not set to expire until 2024.[42]

Collective agreement administration includes carrying out the terms of the agreement and resolving conflicts over interpretation or violation of the agreement. Under a collective agreement, the process for resolving these conflicts is called a **grievance procedure**. A grievance procedure may be started by an employee or discharged employee who believes the employer violated the agreement or by a union representative on behalf of a group of workers or union representatives.

> **grievance procedure**
> The process for resolving union–management conflicts over interpretation or violation of a collective agreement.

For grievances launched by an employee, a typical grievance procedure follows the steps shown in Figure 9.6. The grievance may be settled during any of the four steps. In *Step 1,* the employee talks to their immediate supervisor/manager about the problem. If this conversation is unsatisfactory, the employee may involve the union steward in further discussion. The union steward and employee decide whether the problem has been resolved and, if not, whether it is a violation of the collective agreement. If the problem was not resolved and does seem to be an agreement violation, the union moves to *Step 2,* putting the grievance in writing and submitting it to the next level of management. The union steward meets with the management representative to try to resolve the problem. Management consults with the labour relations staff and puts its response in writing too at this second stage. If Step 2 fails to resolve the problem, the union appeals the grievance to top management and representatives of the labour

FIGURE 9.6

Steps in an Employee-initiated Grievance Procedure

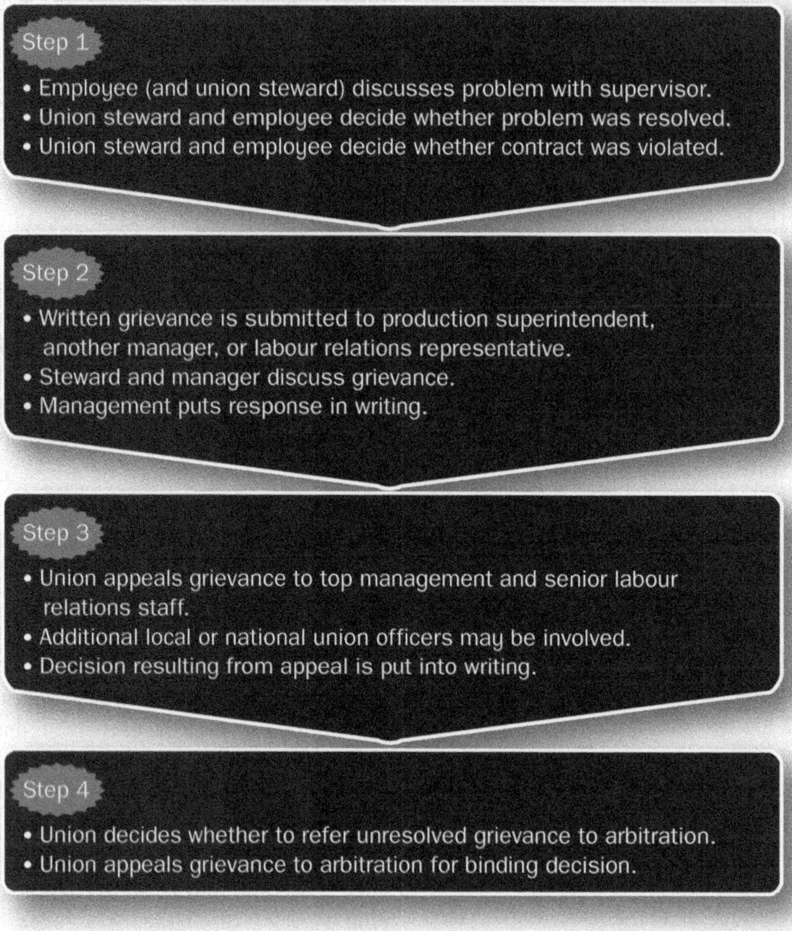
Step 1
• Employee (and union steward) discusses problem with supervisor.
• Union steward and employee decide whether problem was resolved.
• Union steward and employee decide whether contract was violated.
Step 2
• Written grievance is submitted to production superintendent, another manager, or labour relations representative.
• Steward and manager discuss grievance.
• Management puts response in writing.
Step 3
• Union appeals grievance to top management and senior labour relations staff.
• Additional local or national union officers may be involved.
• Decision resulting from appeal is put into writing.
Step 4
• Union decides whether to refer unresolved grievance to arbitration.
• Union appeals grievance to arbitration for binding decision.

Sources: J. W. Budd, *Labor Relations,* 4th ed. (Burr Ridge, IL: McGraw-Hill/Irwin, 2013); T. A. Kochan, *Collective Bargaining and Industrial Relations* (Homewood, IL: Richard D. Irwin, 1980), p. 395; and J. A. Fossum, *Labor Relations* (Boston: McGraw-Hill/Irwin, 2002), pp. 448–52.

relations staff. The union may involve more local or national officers in discussions at this stage (see *Step 3* in Figure 9.6). The decision resulting from the appeal is put into writing. If the grievance is still not resolved, the union may decide (*Step 4*) to appeal the grievance to an arbitrator. If the grievance involves a discharged employee, the process may begin at Step 2 or 3, however, and the time limits between steps may be shorter. Grievances filed by the union on behalf of a group may begin at Step 1 or Step 2.

The majority of grievances are settled during the earlier steps of the process. This reduces delays and avoids the costs of arbitration. If a grievance does reach arbitration, the arbitrator makes the final ruling in the matter.

Employers can assess the grievance procedure in terms of various criteria:[43]

- **Effectiveness**—how well day-to-day questions about the collective agreement are resolved.
- **Efficiency**—whether issues are resolved at a reasonable cost and without major delays.
- **Adaptability**—how well the grievance procedure adapts to changing circumstances. For example, if sales drop off and the company needs to cut costs, how clear are the provisions related to layoffs and subcontracting of work?
- **Allows for resolving local issues**—in the case of collective agreements covering multiple business units, the procedure should allow for resolving local contract issues, such as work rules at a particular facility.
- **Fairness**—whether employees are treated equitably and are provided a voice in the process.

From the point of view of employees, the grievance procedure is an important means of getting fair treatment in the workplace. Its success depends on whether it provides for all the kinds of issues that are likely to arise (such as how to handle a business slowdown); whether employees feel they can file a grievance without being punished for it; and whether employees believe their union representatives will follow through. Too many grievances may indicate a problem—for example, the union members or managers do not understand how to uphold the collective agreement or have no desire to do so. At the same time, a very small number of grievances may also signal a problem. A very low grievance rate may suggest a fear of filing a grievance, a belief that the system does not work, or a belief that employees are poorly represented by their union.

LO6 Labour–Management Cooperation and Collaboration

The traditional understanding of union–management relations is that the two parties are adversaries, meaning each side is competing to win at the expense of the other. There have always been exceptions to this approach. And, since at least the 1980s, there seems to be wider acceptance of the view that greater cooperation and collaboration can increase employee commitment and motivation while making the workplace more flexible.[44] Also, evidence suggests that employees who worked under traditional labour relations systems and then under the new, more cooperative systems prefer the cooperative approach.[45]

Employers build positive relationships by the way they treat employees—with respect and fairness, in the knowledge that attracting talent and minimizing turnover are in the employer's best interests. Opportunities to create a more collaborative workplace culture are needed to provide for the sustainability of business for the long term.[46]

Cooperation and collaboration between labour and management may feature employee involvement in decision making, self-managing employee teams, joint labour–management committees, broadly defined jobs, and sharing of financial gains and business information with employees.[47] The search for a win–win solution requires that unions and their members understand the limits on what an employer can afford in a competitive marketplace.

Without the union's support, efforts at employee empowerment are less likely to survive and less likely to be effective if they do survive.[48] Unions have often resisted employee empowerment programs, precisely because the programs try to change workplace relations and the role that unions play. Union leaders have often feared that such programs will weaken unions' role as independent representatives of employee interests.

An effective day-to-day relationship between labour and management is critical to achieving cooperation and collaboration. In an adversarial type of environment, union–management communication consists of dealing with grievances; however, a cooperative or collaborative model requires effective communication, trust, and mutual respect as the foundation for the day-to-day relationship. Many management and union leaders recognize that new approaches are needed to handle mutual concerns.

Improved labour–management relations may benefit both employers and unions by creating a work environment that is more appealing to younger workers by being less bureaucratic and rule-bound. HR has a significant role to play in creating these conditions; for example, reducing the complexity of the language used in collective agreements and working with senior leadership to avoid taking a "hard-line approach" on grievance arbitration and collective bargaining.[49]

A recent example that contrasts with the strained relationship between WestJet and its pilots discussed in the opening feature is provided by Air Canada. Benjamin Smith, president, Passenger Airlines, at Air Canada described recent amendments to Air Canada's historic long-term (2014–24) collective agreement with its 3,500 pilots represented by the Air Canada Pilots Association (ACPA): "These amendments voted on and ratified by our pilots further emphasize our pilots' alignment with Air Canada's successful business strategy to compete effectively in the highly competitive airline industry, and make adjustments of mutual benefit as the competitive environment evolves." This ten-year agreement was Air Canada's first deal with pilots since 1996, negotiated without arbitration or a strike.[50]

Labour–management committees provide a relatively flexible approach to labour–management cooperation and collaboration in the workplace. Over the past two decades, the use of *joint labour–management committees* has been growing. More than 80 percent of labour and management respondents to a Conference Board of Canada study reported that they have experience in using joint labour–management committees. The most common issues that such committees deal with are summarized in Table 9.5.

TABLE 9.5

Most Common Joint Labour–Management Committee Issues

1. Pay; benefits; pensions
2. Business issues and updates
3. General labour relations
4. Training; apprenticeships
5. Job evaluation; classifications; postings
6. Operations; technology
7. Hours of work; scheduling

Source: Judith Lendvay-Zwicki, "The Canadian Industrial Relations System: Current Challenges and Future Options," Conference Board Document, April 2004, p. 17, www.conferenceboard.ca, retrieved April 19, 2004.

An example of cooperation and collaboration in the organized construction industry takes the form of apprenticeships that are administered through labour unions and employer partnerships. Building-trades unions, along with their employer partners, have created Joint Apprenticeship Committees (JACs) in most provinces and territories. These partnerships are financed by industry training trust funds that own and operate training facilities.[51]

And in the public sector, employers and unions are finding common ground when focusing on workplace mental health. Younger employees are credited with making the topic of mental health less stigmatized and a topic of conversation, which is motivating employers and unions to make mental health a priority. The Public Service Alliance of Canada (PSAC) and the federal government recently created a joint committee to study mental health, and it is anticipated that language addressing mental health will be included in forthcoming collective agreements.[52]

The federal government's Joint Union Management Task Force on Diversity and Inclusion provides another recent example of collaboration under the joint leadership of the president of the Treasury Board and the heads of the bargaining agents. The task force recently released 44 far-reaching recommendations based on a

Thinking Ethically

Is the Seniority System Fair?

Traditionally, union contracts have called for pay and promotion systems that reward employees with higher pay and advancement as they achieve greater seniority; that is, more years on the job. In a company with a unionized workforce, employees with comparable amounts of experience would have comparable earnings. Employees with greater seniority would earn more than newer employees and employees with the most seniority would be promoted if they met the minimum requirements of the job opportunity.

Some people question whether tying pay and advancement to seniority is effective or even fair. For example, top-performing, recently hired employees with educational qualifications that exceed the requirements of a desired job may become frustrated when they are not even selected for an interview because many employees with greater seniority applied. However, many union leaders view the seniority clause as the means to ensure fairness in how employees are rewarded in an organization. This dilemma connects to balancing the needs of both older and younger workers to remain relevant. Younger workers tend to "have shorter tenure in organizations than older workers and are therefore less likely to benefit from seniority clauses."

In a survey of Canadian organizations, consulting firm Watson Wyatt found that one of the top five reasons that employees quit their jobs is dissatisfaction with promotional opportunities. In addition to promotion decisions, seniority clauses also affect other aspects of employees' experience at work including who receives a pay increase, who is eligible for a transfer, and when vacations can be taken. For example, participants in a recent roundtable discussion said that "younger workers do not want to wait until they are more established in their careers to have occasional weekends off or be able to take time off in the summer."

Questions

1. Why do you think unions have traditionally favoured a system of linking pay, advancement, and scheduling to seniority? Who benefits? Why do you think management might favour a system of linking pay, advancement, and scheduling to performance? Who benefits?
2. What employee rights and expectations does a seniority-based pay, promotion, and scheduling system fulfill?
3. What employee rights and expectations does a performance-based pay, promotion, and scheduling system fulfill? What standards for ethical behaviour does it meet?

Sources: Monica Haberl, "Industrial Relations Outlook 2018: The Changing Face of Labour," December 2017, *Conference Board of Canada*, p. 17; Yaseem Hemeda, "Attracting, engaging young workers," *Canadian HR Reporter*, December 14, 2015, p. 19; Virginia Galt, "Stress, Not Money, Main Cause of Turnover," *The Globe and Mail*, December 15, 2007, p. B10.

year-long consultative process that generated almost 12,000 responses to an online survey and 22 discussion forums with more than 500 participants. The recommendations are intended to provide a critical step to achieving the stated Task Force's diversity inclusion vision for the public service: "A world-class public service representative of Canada's population, defined by its diverse workforce and welcoming, inclusive and supportive workplace, that aligns with Canada's evolving human rights context and that is committed to innovation and achieving results."[53]

SUMMARY

LO1 Define unions and labour relations and their role in organizations.

A union is an organization formed for the purpose of representing its members in resolving conflicts with employers. Labour relations is the management specialty emphasizing skills that managers and union leaders can use to minimize costly forms of conflict and to seek win–win solutions to disagreements.

LO2 Identify the labour relations goals of management, unions, and society.

Management have goals to increase the organization's profits and/or productivity. Managers generally expect that unions will make these goals harder to achieve. Unions have the goal of obtaining pay and working conditions that satisfy their members. Society's values have included the view that the existence of unions will replace conflict or violence between workers and employers with fruitful negotiation.

LO3 Summarize laws and regulations that affect labour relations.

Laws and regulations affect the degree to which management, unions, and society achieve their varied goals. Canada's overall labour relations legal framework is decentralized with responsibility for labour relations shared among the federal, provincial, and territorial governments.

A common core of labour legislation exists that includes prohibiting unfair labour practices by management and labour. Labour relations boards or similar quasi-judicial tribunals exist within each jurisdiction to administer and enforce labour laws.

LO4 Describe the union organizing process.

Organizing begins when union representatives contact employees and invite them to sign a membership application. When the required numbers of employees have signed membership applications, the union will apply to the appropriate labour relations board for certification. Requirements for certification differ among federal, provincial, and territorial jurisdictions.

LO5 Explain how management and unions negotiate and administer collective agreements.

Negotiations take place between representatives of the union and the management bargaining unit. The process begins with preparation, including research into the other side's strengths and demands. If bargaining breaks down, the impasse may be broken with a strike, lockout, mediation, conciliation, or arbitration.

Collective agreement administration is a daily activity under the collective agreement. It includes carrying out the terms of the agreement and resolving conflicts over interpretation or violation of the agreement.

LO6 Describe more cooperative and collaborative approaches to labour–management relations.

In contrast to the traditional view that labour and management are adversaries, some organizations and unions work more cooperatively and collaboratively. This relationship may feature employee involvement in decision making, self-managing employee teams, joint labour–management committees, broadly defined jobs, and sharing of financial gains and business information with employees.

CRITICAL THINKING QUESTIONS

1. Why do employees join unions? Have you ever belonged to a union? If you did, do you think union membership benefited you? If you did not, do you think a union would have benefited you? Why or why not?
2. Why do managers at most companies prefer that unions not represent their employees? Can unions provide benefits to an employer? Explain.
3. Can highly effective human resource management practices make unions unnecessary? Explain.

4. How has union membership in Canada changed over the past few decades? How does union membership in Canada compare with union membership in other countries? How might these patterns in union membership affect the HR decisions of a global company?
5. What legal responsibilities do employers have regarding unions? What are the legal requirements affecting unions?
6. "Management gets the kind of union it deserves." Discuss.
7. If the parties negotiating a collective agreement are unable to reach a settlement, what actions can resolve the situation?
8. Why are most negotiations settled without a strike or lockout? Under what conditions might management choose to accept a strike?
9. What are the usual steps in a grievance procedure? What are the advantages of resolving a grievance in the first step? What skills would a supervisor need so grievances can be resolved in the first step?
10. Can the presence of a union enhance employees' experience at work? What advice would you provide to union leaders to make unionization more relevant to younger employees?

EXPERIENCING HR—APPRECIATING SHARED NEEDS AND INTERESTS

Divide into groups of six students. List your names in order of your birthdates (month and day). The first half of the students on the list will be the management team in this exercise, and the second half of the students will be the union team. (If the class size results in a group with an odd number of members, the last person on the list in that group can choose which team to join.)

Imagine that you work for an employer that is interested in working with its union representatives to address areas of mutual interest in a cooperative and collaborative way. Your instructor will assign one of the following priorities to your management and union team:

- needs of LGBTQ2+ employees
- needs of Indigenous employees
- needs of employees who have experienced domestic violence or violence on the job
- needs of employees who have a critically ill child

Spend 10 minutes in your separate teams to identify some of the needs and priorities that may be particularly important to address. Review Table 9.3 as a starting point to identify areas of a collective agreement that may be relevant. Then spend 15 minutes together, seeking areas of mutual interest. After this discussion, work independently to write your own assessment: Do you think your company and union can arrive at a set of agreed-to needs and priorities? Why or why not? What have you learned about yourself or others from this exercise?

CASE STUDY: EVIDENCE-BASED HRM

Random Drug Testing at the Toronto Transit Commission (TTC)

The Supreme Court of Canada has tended to accept drug testing when there is reasonable cause or following an incident; however, *random* drug testing has tended to be more controversial. The Toronto Transit Commission (TTC) recently implemented random drug testing, which met with opposition from the Amalgamated Transit Union (ATU) Canada. However, the judge resisted the injunction request from the ATU, based on expert evidence provided by the TTC that oral fluid technology has the ability to determine impairment due to drug use. The TTC's website provides a list of specific drugs the random drug tests are targeting; for example, cocaine, amphetamines, oxycodone, and marijuana/cannabis. These drugs were targeted for testing because they "inhibit someone's ability to perform their job safely and productively."

The legalization of cannabis for recreational use in Canada has become a top-of-mind issue for both management and unions, and language in collective agreements that address its use likely requires revision. According to Linda Silas from the Canadian Federation of Nurses Unions (CFNU): "We as unions—but I think for employers too—are going to have to be very careful for a few years until the evidence is clear . . . the evidence is not there on what cannabis will do, how long it stays in your system, and what impairment [is]."

In addition to recreational users, it is estimated that "450,000 Canadians will be using cannabis for medical purposes by 2024," however, many organizations do not currently have bargained language in place.

Questions

1. What data and information do unions and employers need in order to develop effective collective agreement language related to worker impairment associated with drug use/abuse (including prescriptions for opioids and cannabis)?
2. Once negotiated, what data and information do employers and unions need to assess whether collective agreement language related to drug use/abuse is supporting workplace health and safety?

Sources: Monica Haberl, "Industrial Relations Outlook 2018: The Changing Face of Labour," *Conference Board of Canada,* December 2017, pp. 7–12; Nicole Brockbank, "Half of TTC employees who failed random drug test in first 6 months tested positive for pot," November 15, 2017, *CBC News,* www.cbc.ca, retrieved June 4 2018; Jane Cooper, Shannon Jackson, and Lisa Irish, "Evidence-based labour relations," *Canadian HR Reporter,* October 30, 2017, p. 14; "Random drug and alcohol testing at the TTC – Information Guide 2017," www.ttc.ca, retrieved June 4, 2018.

CASE STUDY: HRM SOCIAL

UFCW Canada Uses Social Media to Engage with Young Workers

UFCW Canada has launched a new initiative called INCITE to engage and educate young workers about their rights at work. The INCITE activist team has a website and is also active on Twitter and Instagram (@incitemore), as well as Facebook (incitemore). The INCITE team was launched when it hosted a display and a series of in-class presentations to engage with students during George Brown College's week-long Labour Fair. The goal of the INCITE team is "to improve the working and living conditions of young workers across Canada by providing knowledge and tools to address the realities and challenges that young workers face"; for example, unpredictable scheduling. Various social media platforms are used for advocacy and engagement.

UFCW Canada describes itself as "Canada's leading union for young workers" and explains that INCITE builds upon its other young worker initiatives such as Students Against Migrant Exploitation (SAME) and the Youth Internship Program (YIP). The INCITE website and social media recently promoted upcoming Youth Internship sessions in Moncton, New Brunswick; Barrie, Ontario; Gimli, Manitoba; and Harrison, British Columbia. The UFCW Canada website also features "Think Forward: Young Workers Blog" as well as a YouTube channel with videos targeted to young workers; for example, Students go #AllOut to #TossTuition.

Questions

1. What is your reaction to UFCW Canada's efforts to engage with, support, and educate young workers? Do these efforts change your perspectives about the relevance of unions to young workers? Explain.
2. Do you think social media is an effective way to attract young workers to attend in-person events? Why or why not?

Sources: "UFCW Canada launches Incite initiative," www.ufcw.ca, retrieved June 1, 2018, "Think Forward; Young Workers Blog," www.ufcw.ca, retrieved June 3, 2018, https://www.youtube.com/user/UFCWCanada, retrieved June 3, 2018.

CHAPTER 10

Managing Human Resources Globally

WHAT DO I NEED TO KNOW?

After reading this chapter, you should be able to:

LO1	Summarize how the growth in international business activity affects human resource management.
LO2	Identify the factors that most strongly influence HRM in global markets.
LO3	Discuss how international operations impact human resource practices including workforce planning, selection, training and development, performance management, total rewards, and labour relations.
LO4	Explain how employers manage and prepare employees for international assignments and for their return home.

THE CANADIAN PRESS/Pawel Dwulit

Tim Hortons has its sights set on continued global growth.

Tim Hortons' Launch into China

Tim Hortons recently announced plans to open more than 1,500 restaurants in China over the next 10 years through a joint venture of its parent company, Restaurant Brands International (RBI) and Cartesian Capital Group. RBI is following the global expansion business model it used to bring 900 Burger King establishments to China. "China's population and vibrant economy represent an excellent growth opportunity for Tim Hortons in the coming years," said Tim Hortons' President Alex Macedo. Tim Hortons has more than 4,700 restaurants located in Canada and the United States as well as several other countries including Ireland, Saudi Arabia, Qatar, United Arab Emirates, Mexico, the Philippines, and the United Kingdom.

But these plans for global expansion are coming at a time when Tim Hortons' reputation has been "taking a beating as it sinks in another ranking" according to a report from New York–based Reputation Institute, and research organization Legér Marketing. Tim Hortons received a 50th ranking, well behind MEC and Canadian Tire, which both earned "Top 20" status.

However, the expansion to China likely cannot come soon enough for former University of Waterloo student Deng Yongning Nui, who is now back in China. "The coffee and doughnuts of Tim Hortons are amazing. I miss the Tim Hortons French Vanilla so much now."[1]

Introduction

This chapter discusses the HR issues that organizations must address in a world of global competition. We begin by describing how the global nature of business is affecting human resource management in organizations. Next, we identify how global differences among countries affect organizations' decisions about human resources. In the following section we explore various HRM practices in international settings. Finally, we examine considerations for managing and preparing employees for global assignments and their return.

LO1 HRM in a Global Environment

The environment in which organizations operate is rapidly becoming a global one. More and more companies are entering international markets by exporting their products, building facilities in other countries, and entering into alliances with international companies. At the same time, companies based in other countries are investing in setting up operations in Canada. Indeed, most organizations now function in the global economy. The HRM function needs to continuously reexamine its role in supporting this expanding pace of business globalization. This requires HRM to:

- align HRM processes and functions with global requirements
- adopt a *global mindset* including a thorough understanding of the global environment and the impact on managing people worldwide
- enhance its own capabilities and competencies to become a business partner in acting on global business opportunities[2]

What is behind the trend toward expansion into global markets? Global expansion can provide a business with new markets in which there are millions or billions of new customers; developing countries often provide such markets, but developed countries do so as well. In addition, companies may set up operations in other countries to achieve lower labour costs. Together, this mix of advantages can cause the location of business activities to flow from one country to another. For example, low wages drew many manufacturing operations to China, but then competition in the labour markets pushed up wages. In the textile and clothing industries, many companies moved to Vietnam to take advantage of lower wage rates, although the Chinese government has held on to others by offering subsidies and other incentives to stay.[3] In other cases, Chinese companies have followed the Japanese and U.S. pattern of improving efficiency and flexibility, so they can compete on customer service as well as cost. These companies are staying in place but offering higher-value services.[4]

Finally, due to advances in telecommunications and information technology, companies can more easily spread work around the globe, wherever they find the right mix of labour costs and abilities. Teams with members in different time zones can keep projects moving around the clock,

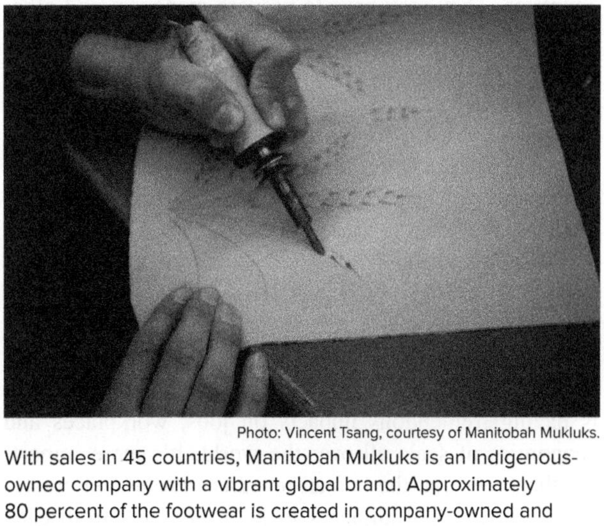

Photo: Vincent Tsang, courtesy of Manitobah Mukluks.

With sales in 45 countries, Manitobah Mukluks is an Indigenous-owned company with a vibrant global brand. Approximately 80 percent of the footwear is created in company-owned and supplied ethical factories overseas—mostly in Vietnam. The remaining 20 percent is made in Winnipeg, Manitoba.[5]

or projects can be assigned according to regions with particular areas of expertise.

Global activities are simplified and encouraged by trade agreements among nations. For example, most countries in Western Europe belong to the European Union (EU) and share a common currency, the euro. Canada, Mexico, and the United States encouraged trade among themselves with the North American Free Trade Agreement (NAFTA), and the Trans-Pacific Partnership (TPP) brought together 12 countries including Canada, the United States, Australia, Brunei, Japan, Malaysia, Vietnam, and others as trading partners. However, these trade agreements have recently faced disruptions:[6]

- **Brexit (Britain + exit)**—Although the June 2016 referendum had a narrow margin of support from U.K. voters, the United Kingdom is scheduled to leave the EU as of March 29, 2019, with a full transition to occur by December 31, 2020.
- **Trade tariffs** and **NAFTA becomes USMCA**—Trade tariffs were imposed by the United States on its NAFTA partners (as well as other global trading partners) in 2018. Retaliatory tariffs followed and NAFTA was recently revamped and renamed USMCA (United States–Mexico–Canada Agreement).
- **TPP became the CPTPP (Comprehensive and Progressive Agreement for Trans-Pacific Partnership)**—The United States announced that it would be exiting from the TTP. Canada and the other 10 other nations signed a new deal in 2018.

As these trends and arrangements impact international trade, they increase and change the demands on human resource management. Organizations with customers or suppliers in other countries need employees who understand those customers or suppliers. Organizations that operate facilities internationally need to understand the laws and customs that apply to employees in those countries. They may have to prepare managers and other employees to take international assignments. They have to adapt their human resource plans and policies to different settings. Even if some practices are the same worldwide, the company now has to communicate them to its international workforce. A variety of international activities requires managers to understand HRM principles and practices prevalent in global markets.

CPHR Canada (Chartered Professionals in Human Resources Canada) and the United States Society of Human Resources Management (SHRM) recently signed a collaborative certification agreement. Anthony Ariganello, CEO of CPHR Canada, explained: "Globalization is having tremendous impacts on jobs, workplaces and economies of scale all over the world. It's more important than ever that the human resources profession creates these international alliances to help members from each other's country get certified, if they so choose. Members can be recognized as internationally qualified, which then helps position our members to better serve employers and employees."[7]

And to specifically meet the complex and challenging requirements of employee mobility, the Canadian Employee Relocation Council (CERC) created the Canadian Global Mobility Professional (CGMP) designation. The program consists of three levels of study with each level providing a specific designation. The Level III designation focuses on global mobility and is called "Essentials of International Relocation."[9]

Employees in an International Workforce

When organizations operate globally, their employees are very likely to be citizens of more than one country. Employees may come from the employer's home country, a host country, or a third country. The **home country** is the country in which the organization's headquarters is located. For example, Canada is the home country of Fairmont Hotels and Resorts, because Fairmont's headquarters are in Toronto. A Fairmont employee who is a Canadian citizen and works at Fairmont's headquarters or one of its Canadian properties is therefore a *home-country national.*

home country
The country in which an organization's headquarters is located.

A **host country** is a country (other than the home country) in which an organization operates a facility. Barbados is a host country of Fairmont because Fairmont has operations there. Any Barbadian workers hired to work at a Fairmont Barbados property would be *host-country nationals;* that is, employees who are citizens of the host country.

host country
A country (other than the home country) in which an organization operates a facility.

A **third country** refers to a country that is neither the home country nor the host country. (The organization may or may not have a facility in the third country.) In the example of Fairmont's operations in Barbados, the company could hire an Australian manager to work there. The Australian manager would be a *third-country national,* because the manager is neither from the home country (Canada) nor from the host country (Barbados).

third country
A country that is neither the home country nor the host country of an employer.

When organizations operate globally, they need to decide whether to hire home-country nationals, host-country nationals, or third-country nationals for the international operations. Usually, they hire a combination of these. In general, employees who take assignments in other countries are called *expatriates.* In the Fairmont

The Washington Post/Getty Images

Founded in 1998, Vancouver-based athleisure giant Lululemon continues its aggressive plans for global growth. International sales are projected to contribute $1 billion of annual revenue by 2020.[8]

example, the Canadian and Australian managers working in Barbados would be expatriates during those assignments.

The extent to which organizations use home-country, host-country, or third-country nationals varies. Groupon, for example, tried using home-country employees for its expansion into the Chinese market. Unfortunately, while these employees may have understood the online deals site's business model, they didn't understand their Chinese suppliers, customers, and competitors well enough to build the relationships necessary for success. Conversely, Disney struggled with its original intention to hire host-country nationals to work as chefs in Euro Disneyland, located outside Paris. French chefs assumed that a theme park would not serve fine food, and they were reluctant to take jobs far from the city. Therefore, before Disney had established a local reputation for great service, it turned to recruiting at Dutch culinary schools and North American hotel chains.[10]

Employers in the Global Marketplace

Just as there are different ways for employees to participate in international business—as home-country, host-country, or third-county nationals—so there are different ways for employers to do business globally, ranging from simply shipping products to customers in other countries to transforming the organization into a truly global one, with operations, employees, and customers in many countries. Figure 10.1 shows the major levels of global participation.

Most organizations begin by serving customers and clients within a domestic marketplace. Typically, a company's founder has an idea for serving a local, regional, or national market. The business must recruit, hire, train, and compensate employees to produce the product, and these people usually come from the business owner's local labour market. Selection and training focus on employees' technical abilities and, to some extent, on interpersonal skills. Pay levels reflect local labour conditions. If the product succeeds, the company might expand operations to other domestic locations, and HRM decisions become more complex as the organization draws from a larger labour market and needs systems for training and engaging employees in several locations. As the employer's workforce grows, it is also likely to become more diverse. Even in small domestic organizations, a significant share of workers are from other countries. In this way, even domestic companies are affected by issues related to the global economy.

FIGURE 10.1

Levels of Global Participation

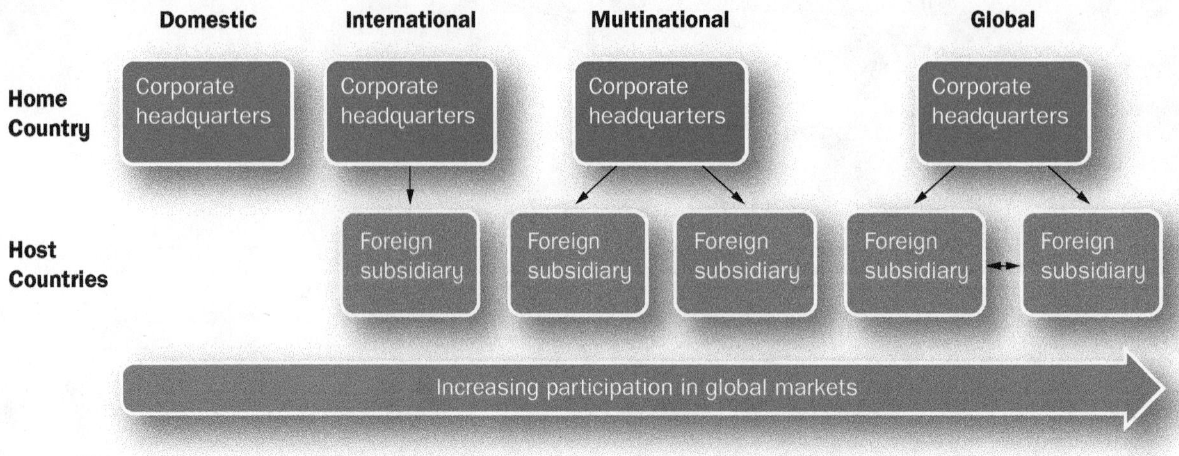

Source: Proxy Statement, Merck & Co., Inc., April 14, 2014, www.merck.com/finance/proxy/pr2014.pdf.

As organizations grow, they often begin to meet demand from customers in other countries. The usual way that a company begins to enter global markets is by *exporting,* or shipping domestically produced items to other countries to be sold there. Eventually, it may become economically desirable to set up operations in one or more foreign countries. An organization that does so becomes an **international organization**. The decision to participate in international activities raises a host of HR issues, including the basic question of whether a particular location provides an environment where the organization can successfully acquire and manage human resources.

international organization An organization that sets up one or a few facilities in one or a few foreign countries.

While international companies build one or a few facilities in another country, **multinational companies** expand on a broader scale. They build facilities in a number of different countries as a way to keep production and distribution costs to a minimum. In general, when organizations become multinationals, they move production facilities from relatively high-cost locations to lower-cost locations. The lower-cost locations may have lower average wage rates, or they may reduce distribution costs by being nearer to customers. The HRM challenges faced by a multinational company are similar but larger than those of an international organization, because more countries are involved. More than ever, the organization needs to hire people who can function in a variety of settings, give them necessary training, and provide flexible compensation systems that take into account the different pay rates, tax systems, and costs of living from one country to another.

multinational company An organization that builds facilities in a number of different countries in an effort to minimize production and distribution costs.

At the highest level of involvement in the global marketplace are **global organizations**. These flexible organizations compete by offering top products tailored to segments of the market while keeping costs as low as possible. A global organization locates each facility based on the ability to effectively, efficiently, and flexibly produce a product or service, using cultural differences as an advantage. Rather than treating differences in other countries as a challenge to overcome, a global organization treats different cultures as a source of competitive advantage. It may have multiple headquarters spread across the globe, so decisions are more decentralized. This type of organization needs HRM practices that encourage flexibility and agility and are based on an in-depth knowledge of differences among countries. Global organizations must be able to recruit, develop, retain, and fully utilize employees who can get results across national boundaries.

global organizations Organizations that choose to locate a facility based on the ability to effectively, efficiently, and flexibly produce a product or service, using cultural differences as an advantage.

A global organization needs a **transnational HRM system**[11] that features decision making from a global perspective, managers from many countries, and ideas contributed by people from a variety

transnational HRM system Type of HRM system that makes decisions from a global perspective, includes managers from many countries, and is based on ideas contributed by people representing a variety of cultures.

of cultures. Decisions that are the outcome of a transnational HRM system balance uniformity (for fairness) with flexibility (to account for cultural and legal differences). This balance and the variety of perspectives should work together to improve the quality of decision making. The participants from various countries and cultures contribute ideas from a position of equality, rather than the home country's culture dominating.

LO2 What Factors Affect HRM in International Markets?

Whatever their level of global participation, organizations that operate in more than one country must recognize that the countries are not identical and differ in terms of many factors. To simplify this discussion, we focus on four major factors:

- culture
- education and skill levels
- economic system
- political–legal system

Culture

By far the most important influence on global HRM is the culture of the country in which a facility is located. *Culture* is a community's set of shared assumptions about how the world works and what ideals are worth striving for.[12] Cultural influences may be expressed through customs, languages, religions, and so on.

Culture is important to HRM for two reasons. First, it often determines the other three global influences. Culture can greatly affect a country's laws, because laws often are based on the culture's definitions of right and wrong. Culture also influences what people value, so it affects people's economic systems and efforts to invest in education.

Even more important for understanding human resource management, culture often determines the effectiveness of various HRM practices. Practices that are effective in Canada, for example, may fail or even backfire in a country with different beliefs and values.[13] Consider the six dimensions of culture that Geert Hofstede identified in his study of culture:[14]

© Ilmagemore Co., Ltd./Corbis

In Taiwan, a country that is high in collectivism, co-workers consider themselves more as group members instead of individuals.

1. *Individualism/collectivism* describes the strength of the relation between an individual and other individuals in the society. In cultures that are high in individualism, such as Canada, the United States, and the Netherlands, people tend to think and act as individuals rather than as members of a group. In cultures that are high in collectivism, such as Columbia, Pakistan, and Taiwan, people think of themselves mainly as group members. They are expected to devote themselves to the interests of the community, and the community is expected to protect them when they are in trouble.
2. *Power distance* concerns the way the culture deals with unequal distribution of power and defines the amount of inequality that is normal. In countries with large power distance, including India and the Philippines, the culture defines it as normal to maintain large differences in power. In countries with low power distance, such as Denmark and Israel, people try to eliminate inequalities. One way to see differences in power distance is in the way people talk to one another. In the high-power distance countries of Mexico and Japan, people address one another with titles (e.g., Señor Smith, Smith-san). At the other extreme, in Canada, in most situations people use one another's first names—behaviour that would be disrespectful in some other cultures.
3. *Uncertainty avoidance* describes how cultures handle the fact that the future is unpredictable. High uncertainty avoidance refers to a strong cultural

preference for structured situations. In countries such as Greece and Portugal, people tend to rely heavily on religion, law, and technology to give them a degree of security and clear rules about how to behave. In countries with low uncertainty avoidance, including Singapore and Jamaica, people seem to take each day as it comes.

4. *Masculinity/femininity* is the emphasis a culture places on practices or qualities that have traditionally been considered masculine or feminine. A "masculine" culture is a culture that values achievement, money making, assertiveness, and competition. A "feminine" culture is one that places a high value on relationships, service, care for others, and preserving the environment. In this model, Germany and Japan are examples of masculine cultures, and Sweden and Norway are examples of feminine cultures.
5. *Long-term/short-term orientation* suggests whether the focus of cultural values is on the future (long term) or the past and present (short term). Cultures with a long-term orientation value saving and persistence—which tend to pay off in the future. Many Asian countries, including Japan and China, have a long-term orientation. Short-term orientation, as in the cultures of Canada, the United States, and Nigeria, promote respect for past tradition, and for fulfilling social obligations in the present.
6. *Indulgence/restraint* describes whether the culture encourages satisfying or suppressing gratification of human drives. A culture with an indulgent orientation encourages having fun and enjoying life. Restraint-orientation cultures use strict social norms to suppress gratification. In this dimension, Australia, Canada, and the United States have cultures characterized as indulgent, whereas India and China promote restraint.

Cultural characteristics such as these influence the ways members of an organization behave toward one another, as well as their mindsets regarding various HRM practices. For instance, cultures differ strongly in their opinions about how managers should lead, how decisions should be handled, and what employees find motivating.

HR Oops!

Cross-Cultural Management Blunders

When Andrew Pickup left his home country of the United Kingdom to take a management position in Singapore, he did not expect to have to adjust his style of gathering performance information. As Pickup analyzed the situation, he was travelling to a former British colony where people spoke English and had grown used to British ways of doing business. He assumed that his direct style of getting and sharing information would work well. Instead, when he invited feedback, employees were startled and quiet. In Singapore, people consider it polite to be subtle. Pickup learned to take his time and develop relationships, and eventually he was better able to get the information he needed.

Australian Debbie Nicol has a job that involves training others. When she arrived in Dubai for a six-year assignment, she experienced an embarrassment in the middle of a training session. One of the attendees suddenly stood up and headed for the door, and she felt she had failed to hold his interest in the subject. She asked why he was leaving. He said he was going to pray. After that, Nicol learned to build prayer breaks into training schedules at the appropriate times of day.

Pickup and Nicol quickly learned from their experiences. Managers and employees can succeed in cross-cultural situations if they are flexible and adaptable. Like Nicol, they may change their practices to suit an important cultural norm. Or, like Pickup, they may persevere in demonstrating their own practices when these are most beneficial. Either way, it is important to behave respectfully and with an effort at genuine understanding. Success also is more likely for a person who is aware of and transparent about their own cultural norms and values.

Questions

1. Based on the information provided, how respectfully and effectively did Andrew Pickup handle his mistake in seeking feedback?
2. How respectfully and effectively did Debbie Nicol handle her mistake in the training schedule?

Sources: Culture Crossing Guide, "Singapore: Basics and Business," http://guide.culturecrossing.net, accessed June 24, 2016; Andrea Murad, "Expat Angst: Four Expats Reveal Cultural Surprises," *BBC*, September 4, 2013, http://www.bbc.com; Paula Caligiuri, "Develop Your Cultural Agility," *T+D*, March 2013, pp. 70–72.

In Germany, managers achieve their status by demonstrating technical skills, and employees look to managers to assign tasks and resolve technical problems. In the Netherlands, managers focus on seeking agreement, exchanging views, and balancing the interests of the people affected by a decision.[15] Clearly, differences like these would affect how an organization selects and develops its leaders and measures their performance.

Cultures strongly influence the appropriateness of HRM practices. For example, the extent to which a culture is individualistic or collectivist will affect the success of compensation and rewards. Compensation tied to individual performance may be seen as fairer and more motivating by members of an individualistic culture; a culture favouring individualism will be more accepting of great differences in pay between the organization's highest- and lowest-paid employees. Collectivist cultures tend to have much flatter pay structures.

The success of HRM decisions related to job design, benefits, performance management, and other systems related to employee motivation also will be shaped by culture. In an interesting study comparing call centre workers in India (a collectivist culture) and the United States (an individualistic culture), researchers found that in the United States, employee turnover depended more on person–job fit than on person–organization fit. In the United States, employees were less likely to quit if they felt that they had the right skills, resources, and personality to succeed on the job. In India, what mattered more was for employees to feel they fit in well with the organization and were well connected to the organization and the community.[16]

Despite cultural differences, the factors that engage workers are relatively similar across cultures. Table 10.1 provides a look at what engages employees in four countries. Finally, cultural differences can affect how people communicate and how they coordinate their activities. In collectivist cultures, people tend to value group decision making, as in the previous example. When a person raised in an individualistic culture works closely with people from a collectivist culture, communication problems and conflicts often occur. People from the collectivist culture tend to collaborate heavily and may evaluate the individualistic person as unwilling to cooperate and share information with them.

Cultural differences in communication affected the way an agricultural company embarked on employee involvement at its facilities in North America and Brazil.[17]

TABLE 10.1

What Keeps Foreign Workers Engaged?

United States	China
Confidence they can achieve career objectives	Sense of personal accomplishment
Sense of personal accomplishment	Fair pay, given performance
Confidence organization will be successful	Comparable benefits to industry
Quality is a high priority	Confidence in senior management
Opportunity for growth and development	IT systems support business needs
Information and assistance to manage career	Opportunities for training
United Kingdom	**Brazil**
Sense of personal accomplishment	Sense of personal accomplishment
Confidence in senior management	Confidence in senior management
Opportunities for training	Opportunities for training
Fair pay, given performance	Fair pay, given performance
Good reputation for customer service	Good reputation for customer service
Regular feedback on performance	Comparable benefits to industry

Sources: Mercer HR Consulting, *Engaging Employees to Drive Global Business Success: Insight from Mercer's What's Working Research*, www.mercer.com/referencecontent.htm?idContent=1288115, retrieved September 14, 2008, quoted in Lesley Young, "Attracting, Keeping Employees Overseas," *Canadian HR Reporter*, April 7, 2008, www.hrreporter.com, retrieved May 26, 2008.

Employee involvement requires information sharing, but in Brazil, high power distance leads employees to expect managers to make decisions, so they do not desire information that is appropriately held by managers. Involving the Brazilian employees required engaging managers directly in giving and sharing information to show that this practice was in keeping with the traditional chain of command. Also, because uncertainty avoidance is another aspect of Brazilian culture, managers explained that greater information sharing would reduce uncertainty about their work. At the same time, greater collectivism in Brazil made employees comfortable with the day-to-day communication of teamwork. The individualistic North American employees needed to convinced on this aspect of employee involvement.

Because of these challenges, organizations must prepare both managers and employees to recognize and handle cultural differences. They may recruit managers with knowledge of other cultures or provide training, as described later in the chapter. For expatriate assignments, organizations may need to conduct an extensive selection process to identify individuals who can adapt to new environments. At the same time, it is important to be wary of stereotypes and avoid exaggerating the importance of cultural differences. Recent research that examined Hofstede's model of cultural differences found that differences among organizations within a particular culture were sometimes larger than differences from country to country.[18] This finding suggests that it is important for an organization to match its HR practices to its values; individuals who share those values are likely to be interested in working for the organization. Mark Chang, founder and CEO of the Malaysia-based jobs portal JobStreet.com, notes that in Asian cultures, where it often is rude to speak up for oneself and assert one's views, spotting employees' contributions takes more effort. Chang urges employees to avoid letting this become a barrier; instead, they should make the extra effort to ask questions and uncover the "quiet talents."[19]

Education and Skill Levels

Countries also differ in the degree to which their labour markets include people with education and skills of value to employers. As discussed in Chapter 1, Canada suffers from a shortage of skilled workers in many occupations, and the problem is expected to increase. On the other hand, the labour markets in many countries are very attractive because they offer high skills and low wages.

Educational opportunities also vary from one country to another. In general, spending on education is greater per student in high-income countries than in economically challenged countries. Poverty, diseases such as HIV/AIDS, and political turmoil keep children away from school in some areas. At the same time, global poverty is highest in countries where the birth rates are also highest, so the number of schoolchildren is growing. This creates both an opportunity and a challenge for these countries to foster economic development by expanding access to education, thus creating a large trained workforce. As these relatively large populations of young people attain working age, they can then contribute to building a more productive economy.[20]

Companies with international operations locate in countries where they can find suitable employees. The education and skill levels of a country's labour force affect how and the extent to which companies want to operate there. In countries with a lower levels of educational attainment, companies will limit their activities to low-skill, low-wage jobs. In contrast, India's large pool of well-trained technical workers is one reason that the country has become a popular location for outsourcing computer programming jobs.

Economic System

A country's economic system as well as the government's involvement in the economy through taxes or compensation, price controls, and other activities, influences human resource management practices in a number of ways.

As with all aspects of a region's or country's life, the economic system and culture are likely to be closely tied, providing many of the incentives or disincentives for developing the value of the labour force. Socialist economic systems provide ample opportunities for educational development because the education system is free to students. At the same time, socialism may not provide economic rewards (higher pay) for increasing one's education. In capitalist systems, students bear more of the cost of their education, but employers reward those who invest in education.

The health of an economic system affects human resource management. In developed countries with great wealth, labour costs are relatively high. Such differences show up in compensation systems and in recruiting and selection decisions.

In general, socialist systems take a higher percentage of each worker's income as the worker's income increases. Capitalist systems tend to let workers keep more of their earnings. In this way, socialism redistributes wealth from high earners to the less well-off, while capitalism apparently rewards individual accomplishments. The amount of take-home pay a worker receives after taxes may thus differ from country to country. In an organization that pays two employees in two countries $100,000 each, the employee in one country might take home more than the employee in the other country. Such differences make pay structures more complicated when they cross national boundaries, and they can affect recruiting of candidates from more than one country.

Political–Legal System

A country's political–legal system—its government, laws, and regulations—strongly impacts human resource management. The country's laws often dictate the requirements for certain HRM practices, such as training, compensation, selection, and labour relations. For example, dissatisfaction with the European Union's principle of free movement of labour across member countries, which led to high immigration rates in the United Kingdom, was undoubtedly an important consideration by UK voters in their support of the 2016 referendum to leave the EU (Brexit). The separation process will likely result in changes in HR practices there, such as work-visa requirements for European employees who are not UK citizens, as well as disruptions in employment, recruiting, and staffing.[21]

As we noted in the discussion of culture, the political–legal system arises to a large degree from the culture in which it exists, so laws and regulations reflect cultural values. For example, Canada has been a leader in eliminating discrimination in the workplace. Because the value of diversity is important in Canadian culture, legal safeguards such as human rights laws discussed in Chapter 2 exist, which affect hiring and other HRM decisions. As a society, Canada also has strong beliefs regarding the fairness of pay systems. Thus, pay equity legislation (discussed in Chapter 2), provides for equal pay for work of equal value. Other laws and regulations dictate much of the process of negotiation between unions and management. All these are examples of laws and regulations that affect the practice of HRM in Canada. When Canadian companies employ workers in other countries, the workers are usually covered by the employment laws in their own countries. Employment laws in many countries offer workers less protection than Canadian legislation provides.

Similarly, laws and regulations in other countries reflect the norms of their cultures. In Western Europe, where many countries have had strong socialist parties, some laws have been aimed at protecting the rights and benefits of workers. The European Union has agreed that employers in member nations must respect certain rights of workers, including workplace health and safety; protection against discrimination based on sex, race, religion, age, disability, and sexual orientation; and labour laws set standards for work hours and other conditions of work.

An organization that expands internationally must gain expertise in the host-country's legal requirements and ways of dealing with its legal system, often leading organizations to engage an international relocation consulting firm or hire one or more host-country nationals to help in the process. Some countries have laws requiring that a certain percentage of the employees of any foreign-owned subsidiary be host-country nationals, and in the context of our discussion here, this legal challenge to an organization's HRM may hold an advantage if handled creatively.

© Paul Almasy/Corbis

Students at the University of Warsaw in Poland are provided with a government-supported education. In general, former Soviet countries tend to be generous in funding education, so they tend to have highly educated and skilled labour forces. Countries such as Canada and the United States generally leave higher education up to individual students to pay for, but the labour market rewards students who earn a college diploma or university degree.

LO3 Workforce Planning in a Global Economy

As economic and technological change creates a global environment for organizations, workforce planning is involved in decisions about participating as an exporter or as an international, multinational, or global company. Even purely domestic companies may draw talent from the international labour market. For example, Saskatchewan health care officials and the provincial health recruitment agency actively recruited and hired hundreds of registered nurses from the Philippines to help cope with identified shortages of nurses in the province.[22] As organizations consider decisions about their level of international activity, HR professionals should provide information about the relevant human resource issues, such as local market pay rates and labour laws. When organizations decide to operate internationally or globally, workforce planning involves decisions about where and how many employees are needed for each international facility.

Decisions about where to locate include HR considerations such as the cost and availability of qualified workers. In addition, HR specialists need to work with other members of the organization to weigh these considerations against financial and operational requirements.

Increasingly, advances in technology are making automation a viable low-cost option for getting work done. A case in point is work handled by call centres. Many companies, including Accenture and American Express, have located call centres in the Philippines, where they found a large supply of English-speaking workers at relatively low wages. Now computer systems are being developed to automate customer phone calls. As these systems replace call centre employees in the Philippines, these workers will need to develop more advanced skills and hope that businesses will see them as good candidates for higher-value work.[23]

Other location decisions involve outsourcing, described in Chapter 1. Many companies have boosted efficiency by arranging to have specific functions performed by outside contractors. Many—but not all—of these arrangements involve workers outside North America in lower-wage countries.

In Chapter 3, we saw that workforce planning includes decisions to hire and lay off workers to prepare for the organization's expected needs. Compared with other countries, Canada allows employers wide latitude in reducing their workforce, giving Canadian employers the option of hiring for peak needs, then laying off employees if needs decline. Other governments put more emphasis on protecting workers' jobs. European countries, and France in particular, tend to be very strict in this regard.

Selecting Employees in a Global Labour Market

Many companies, such as Fairmont, have headquarters in Canada as well as facilities in locations around the world. To be effective, employees at Fairmont's Nairobi property need to understand that region's business and social culture. Organizations often meet this need by hiring host-country nationals to fill most of their foreign positions. A key reason is that a host-country national can more easily understand the values and customs of the local workforce than someone from another part of the world can. Also, training for and transporting families to international assignments is more expensive than hiring people locally. Employees may be reluctant to take an international assignment because of the difficulty of relocating internationally. Sometimes the move requires the employee's partner to quit a job, and some countries will not allow the employee's partner to seek work, even if jobs might be available.

Even so, organizations fill many key international positions with home-country or third-country employees. Sometimes a person's technical and human relations skills outweigh the advantages of hiring locally.

In other situations, Canada's local labour market simply does not offer enough qualified people to fill available jobs in Canada. At organizations where temporary workers are needed and no Canadian citizens or permanent residents are available to perform the job, it may be possible to hire foreign nationals under either Canada's *Temporary Foreign Worker Program (TFWP),* or the *International Mobility Program (LMIA).*[25]

Whether the organization is hiring employees from other countries to work domestically or selecting home-country or third-country nationals for global assignments, some basic principles of selection apply. Selection of employees for international assignments should reflect criteria that have been associated with success in working globally:

- competency in the employee's area of expertise;
- ability to communicate verbally and nonverbally in the foreign country;

CGMP Canadian Global Mobility Professional

Courtesy of CERC

Developed in partnership with Centennial College, the Canadian Employee Relocation Council provides a program leading to the Canadian Global Mobility Professional designation. Level III certification is a 14-week online program that follows Levels I and II and focuses on the practices and laws of other countries and how to create and administer international relocations and assignments.[24]

© Rob Brimson/The Image Bank/Getty Images

Qualities associated with success in international assignments are communication skills, adaptability, enjoying a challenging situation, and support from family members. What would influence you to take a global assignment?

- flexibility, tolerance of ambiguity, and sensitivity to cultural differences;
- motivation to succeed and enjoyment of challenges;
- willingness to learn about the foreign country's culture, language, and customs;
- support from family members.[26]

Qualities of flexibility, motivation, agreeableness, and conscientiousness are so important because of the challenges involved in entering another culture. The emotions that accompany an international assignment tend to follow steps like those in Figure 10.2[27] For a month or so after arriving, the foreign worker enjoys a "honeymoon" of fascination and euphoria as they enjoy the novelty of the new culture and compare its interesting similarities to or differences from the employee's own culture. Before long, the employee's mood declines as they notice more unpleasant differences and experience feelings of isolation, criticism, stereotyping, and even hostility. As the mood reaches bottom, the employee is experiencing **culture shock**, the disillusionment and discomfort that occur during the process of adjusting to a new culture and its norms, values, and perspectives. Eventually, if employees persist and continue learning about their host country's culture, they develop a greater understanding and a support network. As the employee's language skills and comfort increase, their mood should improve as well. Eventually, the employee reaches a stage of adjustment in which they accept and enjoy the host country's culture.

culture shock
Disillusionment and discomfort that occur during the process of adjusting to a new culture.

Employers often have difficulty persuading candidates to accept international assignments. Not only do the employee and employee's family have to contend with culture shock, but also the employee's partner commonly loses a job when an employee makes an international move. Some organizations solve this problem with **virtual expatriates**, or employees who manage an operation abroad without locating permanently in that country.[28] They may take frequent trips to the foreign country, and use technology to collaborate. An assignment as a virtual expatriate may be less inconvenient to family members and less costly to the employer. The arrangement, sometimes referred to as a *commuter assignment,* does have disadvantages. Most notably, by limiting personal contact to sporadic trips, the virtual expatriate will likely have a harder time building relationships.

virtual expatriates
Employees who manage an operation abroad without permanently locating in the country.

Selection practices widely accepted in Canada may pose challenges for Canadian employers who are hiring host-country or third-country nationals. For example, background checking is widely accepted in many parts of Europe and Australia, and has recently become more accepted as a best practice in India. However, in Japan and the United States, cultural and legal differences influence how the request will be perceived and what information is accessible.[29]

Selecting Expatriate Managers

The challenge of selecting expatriate managers begins with determining which individuals in the organization are most capable of handling an assignment in another country. Expatriate managers need technical competence in the area of operations, in part to help them earn the respect of the people they will be managing. Of course, many other skills are also necessary for success in any leadership role, especially one that involves working globally. Depending on the nature of the assignment and the culture where it is located, the organization should consider each candidate's skills, learning style, and approach to problem solving. Each of these should be related to achievement of the organization's goals, such as solving a particular problem, transferring knowledge to host-country employees, or developing future leaders for the organization.[30]

A successful expatriate manager must be sensitive to the host-country's cultural norms, flexible enough to adapt to those norms, and strong enough to survive the culture shock of living in another culture. In addition, if the manager has a family, the family members must be able

FIGURE 10.2

Emotional Stages Associated with a Global Assignment

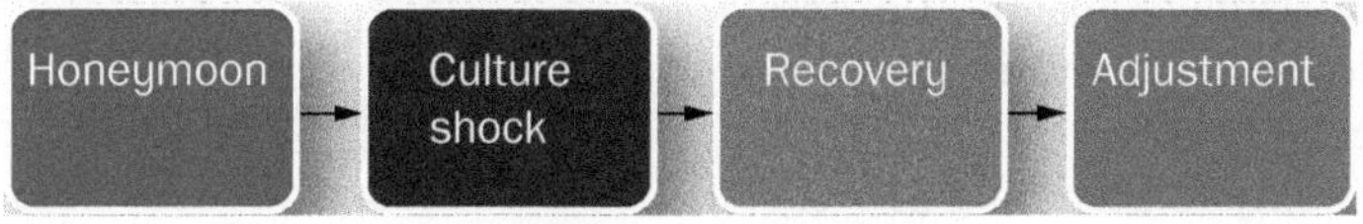

Sources: Debra Bruno, "Repatriation Blues: Expats Struggle with the Dark Side of Coming Home," *Wall Street Journal,* April 15, 2015, http://blogs.wsj.com; Delia Flanja, "Culture Shock in Intercultural Communication," *Studia Europaea* (October 2009), Business & Company Resource Center, http://galenet.galegroup.com.

HR How-To

Meeting the Need for Leadership Talent

Developing nations have been an important location for global and multinational companies because of their economic growth and relatively low cost of labour. From an HRM perspective, an organization with a global strategy should see the human resources in these locations as potential sources of talent. Here are some ideas for tapping the leadership potential of employees in developing countries:

- Along with expertise in business, look for candidates who are adaptable and interested in other cultures. For example, the company might administer a personality assessment to candidates for development programs.
- Build and evaluate relationships. People with a traditional outlook may take a relatively suspicious view of inquiries from strangers and prefer making connections through recommendations and introductions. These connections can become a key means of accomplishing goals.
- Recognize which kinds of developmental assignments are consistent with the local experience. For example, some employees might be used to deferring to authority, rather than volunteering to take over a work assignment.
- Keep abreast of changing conditions in local labour markets. For example, a few years ago, ambitious employees from China were eager to work for foreign companies and gain international experience. More recently, China's growing middle class has opened up opportunities for career development through leading efforts in previously untapped local markets. Some candidates will be best suited for assignment to another country; others will have the entrepreneurial spirit needed to build up a business in a newly developing area of their own country.
- Reconsider high-potential employees for foreign assignments at different times in their careers. For example, an executive with a Swiss pharmaceutical company in Asia wanted to postpone a transfer to another country until her daughter was a bit older.

Sources: T. Morrison, J. Pearce, S. Kounkel, M. Szuhaj, and I. Gantcheva, "Emerging Market Talent Strategies," *Deloitte University Press*, http://dupress.com, accessed June 26, 2016; Neal Goodman, "Training Chinese Leaders to Go Global," *Training*, November/December 2015, pp. 66–67; Winter Nie, "HR Challenges: Why One-Size-Fits-All Doesn't Work in China," *Forbes*, June 1, 2015, http://www.forbes.com; Archanta Mehta, "Made in China: A Chinese Approach to Talent Management," *HRCI Certified* (HR Certification Institute), vol. 1, 2015, pp. 34–37; Alex Eymieu, "The Ins and Outs of Hiring Local Senior Executives," *China Business Review*, January 1, 2012, http://www.chinabusinessreview.com.

to adapt to a new culture. Adaptation requires three kinds of skills:[31]

1. ability to maintain a positive self-image and feeling of well-being
2. ability to foster relationships with the host-country nationals
3. ability to perceive and evaluate the host-country's environment accurately

In a study that drew on the experience of people holding international assignments, expatriates told researchers that the most important qualities for an expatriate manager are in order of importance: family situation, flexibility and adaptability, job knowledge and motivation, relational skills, and openness to other cultures.[32]

To assess candidates' ability to adapt to a new environment, interviews should address topics such as those listed in Table 10.2. The interviewer should be certain to give candidates a clear and complete preview of the assignment and the host-country culture. This helps the candidate evaluate the assignment and consider it in terms of their family situation, so the employer does not violate the employee's privacy.[33]

Training and Developing a Global Workforce

In an organization whose employees come from more than one country, some special challenges arise with regard to training, learning, and development:

1. Training and development programs should be effective for all participating employees, regardless of their country of origin;
2. When organizations hire employees to work in a foreign country or transfer them to another country, the employer needs to provide training in how to handle the challenges of working in the foreign country.

TABLE 10.2

Selected Topics for Assessing Candidates for International Assignments

Motivation
• What are the candidate's reasons and degree of interest in wanting an international assignment? • Does the candidate have a realistic understanding of what is required in working and living internationally? • What is the partner's/spouse's mindset toward an international assignment?
Health
• Are there any health issues with the candidate or family members that might impact the success of the international assignment?
Language Ability
• Does the candidate have the potential to learn a new language? • Does the candidate's partner/spouse have the ability to learn a new language?
Resourcefulness and Initiative
• Is the candidate able to meet objectives and produce positive results with available employees and facilities regardless of challenges that might arise in an international business environment? • Can the candidate operate without a clear definition of responsibility and authority? • Will the candidate be able to explain the goals of the company and its mission to local managers and workers? • Does the candidate possess sufficient self-discipline and self-confidence to handle complex problems?
Adaptability
• Is the candidate collaborative and open to the opinions of others? • How does the candidate react to new situations? Does the candidate demonstrate efforts to understand and appreciate cultural differences? • How does the candidate react to feedback? • Will the candidate be able to make and develop contacts with peers in another country? • Does the candidate demonstrate patience when dealing with problems? Is the candidate resilient and able to move forward after setbacks?
Career Planning
• Does the candidate consider the assignment more than a temporary international trip? • Is the international assignment consistent with the candidate's career development plans? • What is the candidate's overall attitude toward the company? • Is there any history or indication of interpersonal problems with this candidate?
Financial
• Are there any current financial and/or legal considerations that might affect the assignment? • Will undue financial pressures be put upon the candidate and/or family as a result of the international assignment?

Sources: P. Caligiuri, *Cultural Agility: Building a Pipeline of Successful Global Professionals* (San Francisco: Jossey-Bass, 2012); P. Caligiuri, D. Lepak, and J. Bonache, *Managing the Global Workforce* (West Sussex, United Kingdom: John Wiley & Sons, 2010); M. Shaffer, D. Harrison, H. Gregersen, S. Black, and L. Ferzandi, "You Can Take It with You: Individual Differences and Expatriate Effectiveness," *Journal of Applied Psychology* 91 (2006): 109–125; P. Caligiuri, "Developing Global Leaders," *Human Resource Management Review* 16 (2006): 219–228; P. Caligiuri, M. Hyland, A. Joshi, and A. Bross, "Testing a Theoretical Model for Examining the Relationship between Family Adjustment and Expatriates' Work Adjustment," *Journal of Applied Psychology* 83(1998): 598–614; David M. Noer, *Multinational People Management: A Guide for Organizations and Employees* (Arlington, VA: Bureau of National Affairs, 1975).

Training Programs for an International Workforce

Developers of effective training programs for an international workforce must ask certain questions.[34] The first is to establish the objectives for the training and its content. Decisions about the training should support those objectives. The developers should next ask what training techniques, strategies, and media to use. Some will be more effective than others, depending on the learners' language and culture, as well as the content of the training. For example, in preparation for training, Canadian employees might expect to discuss and ask questions about the training content, whereas employees from other cultures might consider this level of participation to be disrespectful, so for them some additional support might be called for. Language differences will require translations and perhaps an interpreter at training activities. Next, the developers should identify any other interventions and conditions that must be in place for the training to meet its objectives. For example, training is more likely to meet its objectives if it is linked to performance management and has the full support of management. Finally, the developers of a training program should identify who in the organization should be involved in reviewing and approving the training program.

The plan for the training program must consider global differences among participants. For example, economic and educational differences might influence employees' ability to access mobile or online training. Cultural differences may influence whether participants will consider it appropriate to ask questions and whether the facilitator is expected to spend time becoming acquainted with employees or to get down to business immediately. Table 10.3 provides examples of how cultural characteristics can affect training design.

Training and Development for Global Relocation

cross-cultural preparation Training to prepare employees and their family members for an assignment in a foreign country.

When an organization selects an employee for a position in another country, it must prepare the employee for the assignment. This kind of training is called **cross-cultural preparation**, preparing employees to work across national and cultural boundaries, and it often includes family members who will accompany the employee on the assignment. The training is necessary for all three phases of an international assignment:

1. Preparation for *departure*—language instruction and an orientation to the foreign country's culture.
2. The *assignment* itself—some combination of a formal program and mentoring relationship to provide ongoing further information about the foreign country's culture.
3. Preparation for the *return* home—providing information about the employee's community and home-country workplace (from company newsletters, local newspapers, and so on).

The chapter-ending HRM Social case addresses how social media can support cross-cultural preparation during an assignment.

Methods for providing this training may range from lectures for employees and their families to visits to culturally diverse communities.[35] Employees and their families may also spend time visiting a local family from the country where they will be working. In many organizations, cross-cultural training is mandatory. In the later section

TABLE 10.3

Effects of Culture on Training Design

Cultural Dimension	Impact on Training
Individualism	Culture high in individualism expects participation in exercises and questioning to be determined by status in the company or culture.
Uncertainty avoidance	Culture high in uncertainty avoidance expects formal instructional environments. Less tolerance for more casual facilitative style.
Masculinity	Culture low in masculinity values relationships with fellow trainees. Female trainers less likely to be resisted in low-masculinity cultures.
Power distance	Culture high in power distance expects trainer to be an expert. Trainer expected to be an authority and in careful control of session.
Time orientation	Culture with a long-term orientation will have trainees who are likely to accept development plans and assignments.

Source: Based on B. Filipczak, "Think Locally, Act Globally," *Training*, January 1997, pp. 41-48.

on managing expatriates, we provide more detail about such preparation.

Cross-cultural preparation is important. Research links it to lower turnover among expatriates, greater willingness to accept another international assignment, and greater perceived contribution to business outcomes.[36]

Canadian-based companies sometimes need to be reminded that employees who come to Canada from another country need cross-cultural preparation as much as Canadian employees sent on global assignments.[37] In spite of the many benefits of living in Canada, relocation can be challenging. As with expatriates, organizations can prepare employees from other countries by providing information about getting the resources they need to live and work safely and comfortably in their new surroundings. For example, when Maple Leaf Foods hired 40 new foreign workers from El Salvador and Honduras for its operations in Brandon, Manitoba, employees' needs were actively considered to help make an effective transition to Canada. Plant Manager Morgan Curran-Blaney described the process to help the new recruits. "We have . . . basic living training, so living in Canada, this is what you can expect. We help them set up bank accounts here in town; we give them sort of a welcome package, the necessities that you would need to start out in Canada." Maple Leaf also arranged housing, including furnishing the houses and apartments.[38]

At global organizations, international assignments are a part of many career paths. The organization benefits most if it applies the principles of employee development in deciding which employees should be offered jobs in other countries. Career development helps employees make the transitions to and from their assignments and helps the organization apply the knowledge the employees obtain from these assignments.

Performance Management across National Boundaries

The general principles of performance management may apply in most countries, but the specific methods that work in one country may not work well in another. Therefore, organizations have to consider legal requirements, local business practices, and national cultures when they establish performance management methods in other countries. Differences may include which behaviours are rated, how, and the extent to which performance is measured; who performs the rating; and how feedback is provided.[39]

For example, National Rental Car uses a behaviourally based rating scale for customer service representatives. To measure the extent to which customer service representatives' behaviours contribute to the company's goal of improving customer service, the scale measures behaviours such as smiling, making eye contact, greeting customers, and solving customer problems. Depending on the country, different behaviours may be appropriate. In Japan, culturally defined standards for polite behaviour include the angle of bowing as well as proper back alignment and eye contact. In Ghana and many other African nations, appropriate measures include behaviours that reflect loyalty and repaying of obligations as well as behaviours related to following regulations and procedures.

The extent to which managers measure performance may also vary from one country to another. In rapidly changing regions, such as Southeast Asia, the organization may have to update its performance plans more often than once a year.

Feedback is another area in which differences can occur. Employees around the world appreciate positive feedback, but Canadian employees are much more used to receiving direct feedback than are employees in many other countries. In Mexico, managers are expected to provide positive feedback before focusing the discussion on behaviours the employee needs to improve.[40] At the Thai office of Singapore Airlines managers resisted giving negative feedback to employees because they feared this would cause them to have bad karma, contributing to their reincarnation at a lower level in their next life.[41] The airline therefore allowed the managers to adapt their feedback process to fit local cultures.

Managing Expatriates' Performance

Performance management of expatriates requires clear goals for the assignment and frequent evaluation of whether the expatriate employee is on track to meet those goals. Communication technologies and social media platforms provide a variety of ways for expats' managers to keep in touch with these employees to discuss and diagnose issues before they can interfere with performance. In addition, before employees leave for a global assignment, HR should work with managers to develop criteria for measuring the success of the assignment.[42] Measures such as productivity should take into account any local factors that could make expected performance different in the host country than in the company's home country. For example, a country's labour laws or the reliability of the electrical supply could affect the facility's output and efficiency.

Compensating and Rewarding an International Workforce

Chapter 8 explained that *total rewards* includes decisions about pay structure, incentive pay, employee benefits and services, and even development and career opportunities and other characteristics of the work environment such as

Did You KNOW?

The 10 Most Expensive Cities Are Located on Three Continents

Expatriates spend more for housing, transportation, food, clothing, and other living expenses in Hong Kong than in any other major city, according to a survey by Mercer Human Capital Consulting. Hong Kong is notable for its very high housing prices and rental rates. Three other nearby cities, Singapore, Seoul, and Tokyo, join Hong Kong in the top five, posing challenges for companies that want to do business in the relatively fast-growing economies in Southeast Asia. The remaining top-five city, Zurich, is in Europe.

The most expensive Canadian cities were Vancouver and Toronto (tied for 109th spot).

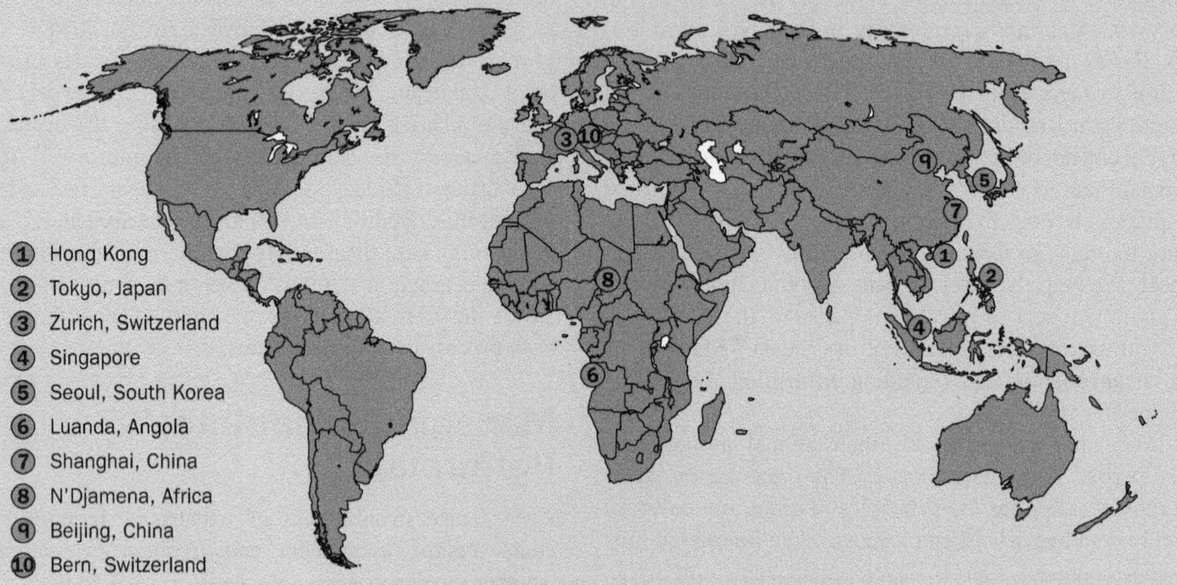

Sources: Mercer, "Mercer's 24th Annual Cost of Living Survey finds Asian, European, and African cities most expensive locations for employees working abroad," Mercer Newsroom, June 26, 2018, www.mercer.ca. and Enda Curran, "These Are the World's Most Expensive Cities for Expats," *Bloomberg*, June 25, 2018. https://www.bloomberg.com.

work–life balance. All these decisions become more complex when an organization has an international workforce. Johnson & Johnson meets the challenge by creating a global compensation strategy for its pharmaceutical, consumer, and medical-device businesses with employees in 70 countries. J&J developed the strategy at its U.S. headquarters because compensation expertise at the company varied from one region to another. However, it had representatives from each region serve on the project teams so the company would be familiar with local issues, such as the need for frequent salary reviews in Venezuela and Argentina, where high inflation rates take a toll on buying power.[43]

Pay Structure

As Figure 10.3 shows, market pay structures can differ substantially across countries in terms of both pay level and the relative worth of jobs. For example, compared with the labour market in Germany, the market in Mexico provides much lower pay levels overall. In Germany, the pay differences between jobs are less dramatic than in South Korea; for example, the relative pay of teachers is much higher than in South Korea. One reason for big pay differences in some countries is a shortage of talent in local labour markets. In Brazil, for example, companies have trouble finding enough managers with technical expertise because big construction projects and oil drilling tend to produce heavy demand for those positions. In addition, the Brazilian economy has drawn many multinationals to locate facilities in Brazil, further increasing the demand for managers there. Finally, Brazilian managers tend to be loyal employees, so recruiters need to offer especially tempting compensation packages to lure them away.[44]

Differences such as these create a dilemma for global companies: Should pay levels and differences reflect what workers are used to in their own countries? Or should

FIGURE 10.3

Earnings in Selected Occupations in Three Countries

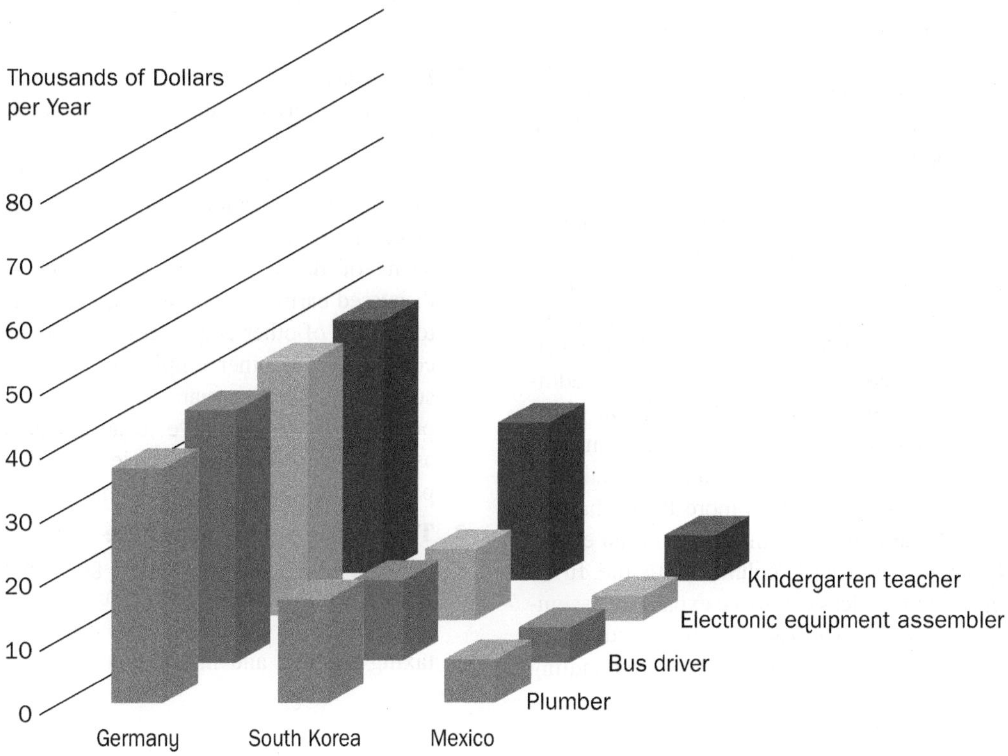

Source: Wage and hour data from International Labour Organization, LABORSTA Internet, http://laborsta.ilo.org, accessed June 20, 2016.

they reflect the earnings of colleagues in the country of the facility, or earnings at the company headquarters? For example, should a German engineer posted to Mumbai be paid according to the standard in Germany or the standard in Mumbai? If the standard is Germany, the engineers in Mumbai will likely see the German engineer's pay as unfair. If the standard is Mumbai, the company will likely find it impossible to persuade a German engineer to take an assignment in Mumbai. Dilemmas such as these make a global compensation strategy important as a way to show employees that the pay structure is designed to be fair and related to the value that employees bring to the organization.

These decisions affect a company's costs and ability to compete. The average hourly labour costs in industrialized countries such as Canada, the United States, Germany, and Japan are far higher than these costs in newly industrialized countries such as Mexico, Brazil, and Taiwan.[45] As a result, we often hear that North American labour costs are too high to compete effectively unless the companies shift operations to low-cost foreign subsidiaries. That conclusion oversimplifies the situation for many companies. Merely comparing wages ignores differences in education, skills, and productivity.[46] If an organization gets more or higher-quality output from a higher-wage workforce, the higher wages may be worth the cost. Besides this, if the organization has many positions requiring highly skilled workers, it may need to operate in (or with people from) a country with a strong educational system, regardless of labour costs. In addition, labour costs may be outweighed by other factors, such as transportation costs or access to resources or customers. Finally, increasing automation of processes is reducing the demand for labour and the significance of differences in labour costs.

Cultural and legal differences also can affect pay structure. Some countries, including Colombia, Greece, and Malaysia, require that companies provide salary increases to employees earning minimum wage. In Venezuela, employers must provide employees with a meal allowance. In Mexico and Puerto Rico, employers must pay holiday bonuses. Organizations with a global pay strategy must adjust the strategy to account for local requirements and determine how pay decisions for optional practices will affect their competitive standing in local labour markets.[47]

Most organizations use a *balance sheet approach* to determine the total amount of the package. This approach adjusts the employee's compensation so that it gives the employee the same standard of living as in the home country plus extra pay for any hardships of locating globally. As is shown in Figure 10.4, the balance sheet approach begins by determining the purchasing power of compensation for the same type of job in the employee's own country—that is, how much a person can buy, after taxes, in terms of housing, goods and services, and a reserve for savings. Next, this amount is compared with the cost (in dollars, for a Canadian company) of these same expenses in the foreign country.

In Figure 10.4, the greater size of the second column means the costs for a similar standard of living in the foreign country are much higher in every category except the reserve amount. This situation would be likely in one of the cities identified in Did You Know? For the expatriate in this situation, the employer would pay the additional costs, as shown by the third column. Finally, the expatriate receives additional purchasing power from premiums and incentives. Because of these added incentives, the expatriate's purchasing power is more than what the employee could buy at home with the salary for an equivalent job. (Compare the fourth column with the first.) These compensation practices can make expatriate assignments very expensive. Not surprisingly, then, a survey of human resources practitioners responsible for handling international moves of employees found that cost reduction is a priority at their companies. The most common solution has been to reduce global assignments.[48]

After setting the total pay, the organization divides this amount into the four components of a *total compensation* package:

1. **Base salary**—determining the base salary is complex because different countries use different currencies (dollars, yen, euros, and so on). The exchange rate—the rate at which one currency may be exchanged for another—constantly shifts in response to a host of economic forces, so the real value of a salary in terms of dollars is constantly changing. Also, as discussed earlier, the base salary may be comparable to the pay of other employees in the home country or comparable to other employees at the international subsidiary. Because many organizations pay a salary premium as an incentive to accept an international assignment, expatriates' salaries are often higher than pay for staying in the home country.
2. **Tax equalization allowance**—"Tax equalization holds that the worker neither gains nor loses with regards to tax liability as a result of an international assignment."[49] Countries have different systems for taxing income, and in some countries, tax rates are

FIGURE 10.4

The Balance Sheet for Determining Expatriate Compensation

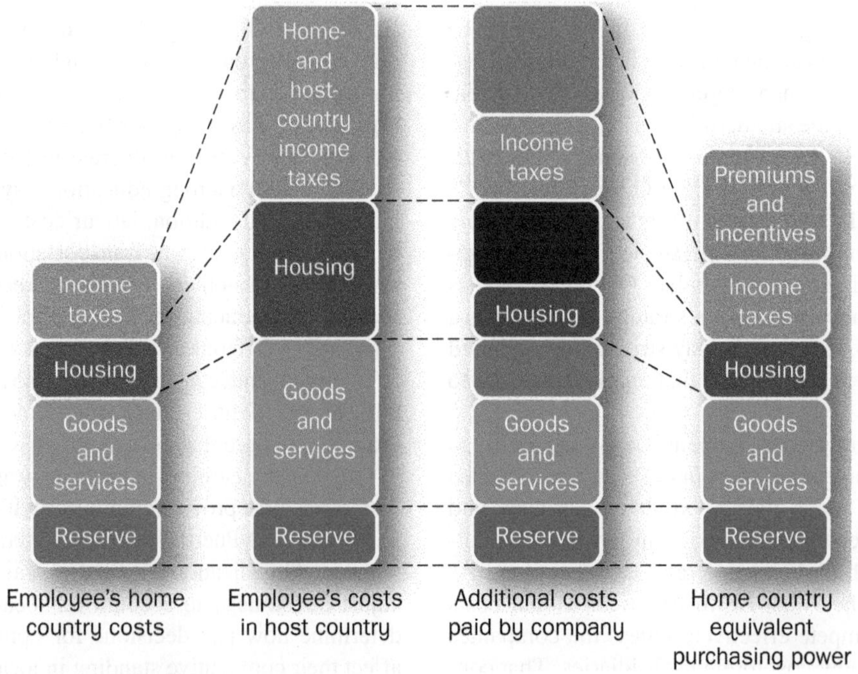

Source: C. Reynolds, "Compensation of Overseas Personnel," in J. J. Famularo, ed., *Handbook of Human Resource Administration*, 2nd ed. (New York: McGraw-Hill, 1986), p. 51. Reprinted with permission. Copyright © 1986 by The McGraw-Hill Companies higher than in Canada. Usually, the employer of an expatriate withholds the amount of tax to be paid in the home country, then pays all of the taxes due in the country where the expatriate is working.

3. **Incentives, benefits, and services**—Most of these issues have to do with whether an employee will receive similar incentives and benefits during the international assignment. For example, if an expatriate has been contributing to a pension plan in Canada, does this person have a new pension plan in the foreign country? Or can the expatriate continue to contribute to the Canadian pension plan? Similarly, health benefits may involve receiving care at certain health facilities. While the person is assigned globally, does the same health plan cover services received in another country? In one case, flying an employee back to Canada for certain procedures actually would have cost less than having the procedures done in the country where the person was working. But the company's health plans did not permit this alternative. Incentive pay and employee benefits and services are discussed in greater detail under the next headings.
4. **Allowance to make a global assignment more attractive**—Cost-of-living allowances make up the differences in expenses for day-to-day needs. Housing allowances ensure the expatriate can maintain the same standard of living as in Canada. Education allowances reimburse expatriates who pay tuition for their children to attend private schools. Relocation allowances cover the expenses of making the move to the foreign country, including transportation, shipping or storage of possessions, and expenses for temporary housing until the employee can rent or purchase a home.

Photo by Patrick Robert/Corbis via Getty Images

Taking an international assignment, especially in a volatile or potentially dangerous climate, requires the challenge of adjusting to life in a new country, so many companies pay employees higher salaries to compensate for this hardship.

Incentive Pay

Besides setting a pay structure, the organization must make decisions with regard to incentive pay, such as bonuses and stock options. Although stock options became a common form of incentive pay in North America during the 1990s, European businesses did not begin to embrace this type of compensation until the end of that decade. However, Canada and Europe differ in the way they award stock options. European companies usually link the options to specific performance goals, such as the increase in a company's share price compared with that of its competitors.

Employee Benefits and Services

As in Canada, total rewards packages in other countries include benefits and services. Decisions about benefits and services must take into account the laws of each country involved, as well as employees' expectations and values in those countries. Some countries require lengthy paid parental leave, and some countries, in addition to Canada, have nationalized health care systems, which would affect the value of private health insurance in a rewards package. An employer may offer expatriates additional benefits to address the problem of uprooting a partner when assigning an employee overseas. Availability of partner relocation assistance is a differentiator for many organizations in attracting employees to global assignments. For example, some organizations provide the "trailing partner" with educational and career assistance. Pension plans are more widespread in parts of Western Europe than in Canada, the United States, or Japan. Over 90 percent of workers in Switzerland have pension plans, as do all workers in France. Among workers with pension plans, Canadian workers are significantly less likely to have defined benefit plans than workers in Japan or Germany.

Paid vacation, also discussed in Chapter 8, tends to be more generous in Western Europe than in North America. Figure 10.5 compares the number of hours the average employee works in various countries. Of these countries, workers in Mexico, Greece, the United States, and Japan put in more hours than Canadian workers. In the other countries, the norm is to work fewer hours than a Canadian worker over the course of a year.

International Labour Relations

Companies that operate across national boundaries will increasingly need to work with unions in more than one country. Organizations establish policies and goals for labour relations, overseeing labour agreements, and monitoring labour performance (e.g., output and productivity).[50] The day-to-day decisions about labour relations are usually handled by each foreign subsidiary. The reason is that labour relations on an international scale involve

FIGURE 10.5

Average Hours Worked in Selected Countries (2017)

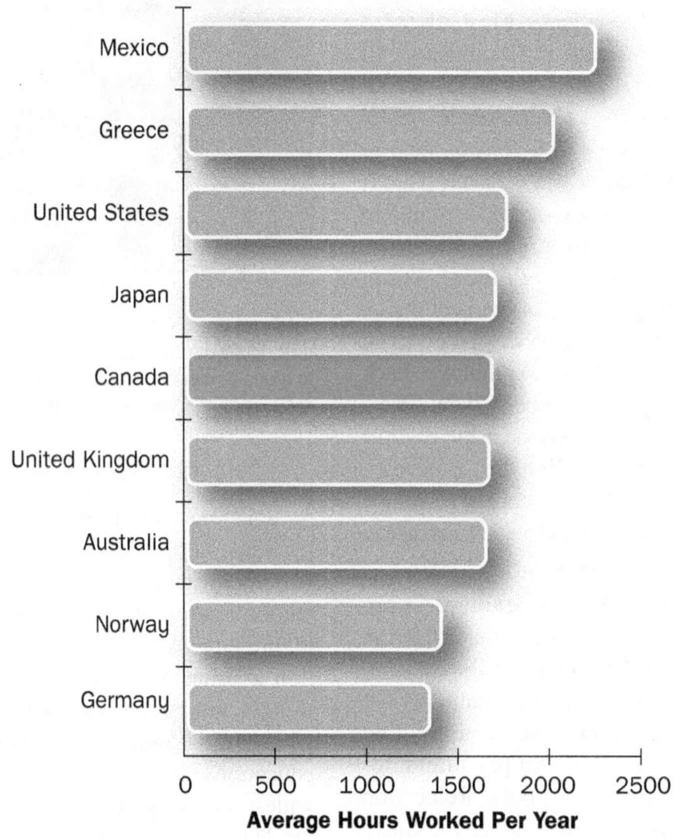

Source: Organisation for Economic Co-operation and Development, "Average annual hours actually worked per worker," OECD.Stat, https://stats.oecd.org/index.aspx?DataSetCode=ANHRShttp://stats.oecd.org, accessed July 20, 2018.

differences in laws, attitudes, and economic systems, as well as differences in negotiation styles.

At least in comparison with European organizations, North American organizations exert more centralized control over labour relations in the various countries where they operate.[51] Management therefore must recognize differences in how various countries understand and regulate labour relations. For example, in Canada, collective bargaining usually involves negotiations between a union local and an organization's management, but in Sweden and Germany collective bargaining generally involves negotiations between an employer's organization and a union representing an entire industry's employees.[52]

China's only legal labour union—and the world's largest union—is the All-China Federation of Trade Unions (ACFTU), which is controlled by the government. The Chinese government limits the workers' rights to collective bargaining and striking, and it appoints leaders of the ACFTU. At some companies in recent years, workers have begun to conduct strikes and protests seeking greater rights.[53]

Legal differences range from who may form a union to how much latitude an organization is allowed in laying off workers. In some situations, governments get involved to protect workers. After an eight-storey factory collapsed in Dhaka, Bangladesh, killing more than 1,100 people, the government of Bangladesh eased rules that had made it difficult for the country's workers to unionize. Until then, workers had to obtain permission from factory owners before forming unions.[54]

International labour relations must also take into account that negotiations between labour and management take place in a different social context, not just different economic and legal contexts. Cultural differences that affect other interactions come into play in labour negotiations as well. Negotiators will approach the process differently depending on whether the culture views the process as primarily cooperative or competitive and whether it is local practice to negotiate a deal by starting with the specifics or agreeing on overall principles.[55] Working with host-country nationals can help organizations navigate such differences in negotiation style.

LO4 Preparing and Managing Expatriates

At some point, most international and global organizations assign employees to foreign posts. These assignments give rise to significant human resource requirements, from selecting employees for these assignments to preparing them, compensating them, helping them adjust and remain safe, providing support, and preparing for return home. The same kinds of HRM principles that apply to domestic positions can help organizations avoid mistakes in managing expatriates: planning and goal setting, selection aimed at achieving the HR goals, and performance management that includes evaluation of whether the global assignment delivered value relative to the costs involved.[56]

Global Relocation Success Factors

Respondents to the Global Mobility Policy and Practice survey listed "inability of the family to adjust" (61 percent) as the number-two reason assignments fail. It is eclipsed only by "changing business conditions" (63 percent) as a reason for assignment failure. The importance of family is reinforced by the fact that 76 percent of respondents rated "family or personal circumstances" as the number-one reason employees turn down global assignments."[57] Providing "trailing partner" career transition services may make the difference whether or not an international assignment will be accepted. Personality may also be important. Research has found successful completion of international assignments to be most likely among employees who are extroverted (outgoing), agreeable (cooperative and tolerant), and conscientious (dependable and achievement oriented).[58] Researchers have concluded that organizational support is associated with the necessary cross-cultural adjustment required for expatriate effectiveness.[59] And because expatriate success depends so much on the entire family's adjustment, the employee's partner should be included in the preparation activities. Employees selected for expatriate assignments already have job-related skills, so preparation for expatriate assignments often focuses on cross-cultural training—that is, training in what to expect from the host-country's culture. The general purpose of cross-cultural training is to create an appreciation of the host-country's culture so expatriates can behave appropriately.[60] Paradoxically, this requires developing a greater awareness of one's own culture, so that the expatriate can recognize differences and similarities between the cultures and, perhaps, home-culture biases.

Reducing culture shock was also discussed previously in this chapter; however, on a more specific level, cross-cultural training for global assignments should additionally include the details of how to behave in business settings in another country—the ways people behave in meetings, how employees expect managers to treat them, and so on. As an example, Germans value promptness for meetings to a much greater extent than do Latin Americans—and so on. How should one behave when first meeting one's business counterparts in another culture? The "outgoing" personality style so valued in North America may seem quite rude in other parts of the world.[61] Ideally, the company also provides training for an expatriate's team in the host country, so that all colleagues can learn about one another's cultural practices and values.[62]

Employees preparing for an international assignment also need information about practical matters such as housing, schools, recreation, shopping, and health care facilities in the country where they will be living. This is a crucial part of the preparation. Communication in another country often requires a determined attempt to learn a new language. Some employers try to select employees who speak the language of the host country, and a few provide language training. Most companies assume that employees in the host country will be able to speak the host-country's language. Even if this is true, host-country nationals are not necessarily fluent in the home-country's language, so language barriers often remain. This is true even when employees move to a country that nominally speaks the same language. For example, a Canadian employee working in England might be surprised to discover that when a project suddenly goes awry, it has "hit the buffers," while if it is proceeding smoothly, it is "on cam." And a client who says, "Give me a bell," isn't requesting an unusual sort of gift but rather a phone call.[63]

Along with cross-cultural training, preparation of the expatriate should include career development activities. Before leaving for a global assignment, expatriates should discuss with their managers how the assignment fits into their career plans and what types of positions they can expect upon their return. This prepares the expatriate to develop valuable skills during the assignment and eases the return home. Coaching during the assignment also can improve the likelihood that the expatriate will be successful.

The use of a well-written *international assignment letter* is a helpful means to clarify the rights and responsibilities of both the employer and employee for a relocation and subsequent return. Table 10.4 describes some considerations about what to include in an international assignment letter.

When the employee leaves for the assignment, the preparation process should continue. Expatriate colleagues, coaches, and mentors can help the employee learn to navigate challenges as they arise. For example, workers in a new culture sometimes experience internal conflict when the culture where they are working expects them to behave in a way that conflicts with values they learned from their own culture. For example, an Italian manager had difficulty motivating the workforce in India because the employees were used to authoritarian leadership, and

TABLE 10.4

What to Include in an International Assignment Letter

Assignment	• Location
	• Duration of assignment
Remuneration	• Base salary
	• Incentives and benefits
	• Pension plans
	• Currency of payment
Tax Issues	• Tax equalization
	• Tax advice
	• Tax reporting
Host Country	• Housing
Relocation Program	• Home and automobile sale
	• Family allowances (if family doesn't relocate)
	• House hunting
	• Moving
	• Schooling
	• Elder care
	• Language training
	• Cultural acclimatization programs
Vacation and Home Leave	• Number of trips
	• Emergency and compassionate travel provisions
Repatriation	• Timing (e.g., to coincide with family needs such as school terms)
	• Employment opportunities upon the employee's return
	• Assignment debriefing
	• Financial counselling
	• Dealing with dismissal or resignation

Sources: Joyce Head, "How Paper Can Protect International Relocations," *Canadian HR Reporter*, March 13, 2006, p. 14; and Margaret Sim and Liam Dixon, "Unraveling Comp, Benefits for Expatriates," *Canadian HR Reporter*, December 3, 2007, p. 23.

the manager felt as if that style was harsh and disempowering. By talking over the problem with experienced expatriates, the manager came to understand why the situation was so awkward and frustrating for him. He identified specific ways in which he could be more direct and calm, so that his employees in India would better understand what was expected of them. Practising a new style of leadership became more satisfying as the manager realized that the employees valued his style and that he was becoming a more capable cross-cultural leader.[64]

Helping Expatriates Return and Minimizing Turnover

As the expatriate's assignment nears its end, the human resource department faces a final challenge: helping the expatriate make the transition back to their home country. The process of preparing expatriates to return home from a foreign assignment is called **repatriation**. According to a study by a partnership between Pricewaterhouse-Coopers and Cranfield University School of Management, more than 25 percent of repatriated employees leave the company within one year after an international assignment ends.[65] Repatriation issues should be discussed even before the candidate accepts an international assignment. Reentry is not as simple as it might sound. Culture shock takes place in reverse. The experience has changed the expatriate, and the company's and expatriate's home culture may have changed as well. Also, because of differences in economies and compensation levels, a returning expatriate may experience a decline in living standards. The standard of living for an expatriate in many countries includes household help, a car and driver, private schools, and club memberships.

Companies are increasingly making efforts to help expatriates through this transition and take steps to ensure expatriates stay with the company after their return. Two activities help to encourage retention: *communication* and *validation*.[66] Communication refers to the expatriate receiving information and recognizing changes while abroad. The more the organization keeps in contact with the expatriate, the more effective and satisfied the person is likely to be upon return. The expatriate plays a role in this process as well. Expatriates should work at maintaining important contacts in the company and industry. Communication related to performance and career development before and during the international assignment also should help the employee return to a choice of positions that are challenging and interesting. Validation means giving the expatriate recognition for the international service when they return home. Expatriates who receive family repatriation support and recognition from colleagues and top managers for their international service and future contribution have fewer troubles with reentry than those whose contributions are disregarded. Validation should also include planning for how the returning employee will contribute to the organization. What skills will they bring back? What position will they fill? The new skills may be much more than knowledge of a particular culture. For example, the person may have learned how to lead or negotiate with a diverse group of people.[67]

repatriation The process of preparing expatriates to return home from a foreign assignment.

Furthermore, for the employees and their organizations to get maximum value from the global assignment, returning employees should have opportunities to share what they learned. The company might set up meetings for returning employees and their colleagues; make returning expats available for panel discussions; invite them to blog about their experience during and after the assignment; and include data about global assignments in online databases used for promotions, employee development, and knowledge sharing.[68]

Thinking ETHICALLY

How Can Employers Support LGBTQ2+ Employees in Expat Assignments?

When LGBTQ2+ employees are offered an assignment in another country, they face some considerations about how their sexual orientation or gender identity will be treated in the new country. While some countries have inclusive attitudes, dozens frown on or even criminalize same-sex relationships and expressions of gender identity. An assignment in one of those countries could be uncomfortable at best and dangerous at worst. In countries that outlaw same-sex relationships, punishments include prison and, in a few cases, the death penalty. Even where the laws aren't enforced, they contribute to a climate in which people don't report violence against or blackmail of LGBTQ2+ persons. With this in mind, LGBTQ2+ employees sometimes turn down international assignments in order to protect themselves and their families.

LGBTQ2+ employees who accept these assignments can expect some extra surprises or challenges. A challenge—easier for single and childless employees perhaps—is a choice to hide one's sexual orientation or gender identity. While working in Nigeria, an employee of a British company asked her British HR department not to share with her local colleagues that her next of kin was her wife, because she expected problems could result. On the positive side, some employees find warm and welcoming communities that help them navigate the new culture where they are posted. And some find that being an expat already marks them as "different" in the eyes of locals, so sexual orientation or gender identity doesn't matter much.

Given that LGBTQ2+ employees may be treated differently in international assignments, employers have to determine what the organization's role will be in offering the assignments. For example, they might offer LGBTQ2+ employees global assignments only in countries where they believe these employees can travel and live safely. Or they might ensure that their cross-cultural training touches on these issues, regardless of any assumptions about employees' sexual orientation or gender identity, so that all employees can make informed decisions. Some companies with a commitment to diversity and inclusion go further and try to influence change in the countries where they operate—for example, by pointing out that anti-LGBTQ2+ laws make the countries less attractive to multinational businesses.

Questions

1. How would you apply the principle of justice and fairness to employers' decisions about offering international assignments to LGBTQ2+ employees?
2. What would be the most ethical way for employers to address the safety risks of asking a LGBTQ2+ employee to work in a country such as Dubai, Russia, or Uganda where laws may create difficult living and working conditions?

Sources: Emma Jacobs, "LGBT employees face hurdles at home and school," *The Financial Times,*" May 7, 2018, https://www.ft.com, Ronald Alsop, "Is This the Most Dangerous Expat Assignment?" *BBC,* March 31, 2016, http://www.bbc.com; Debra Bruno, "When the Closet Travels with You: For Gay Expats, Life Abroad Brings Challenges," *Wall Street Journal,* October 11, 2015, http://blogs.wsj.com; Lisa Johnson, "Integrating LGBT Expats," *Talent Management,* October 8, 2015, http://www.talentmgt.com; Jamie Waddell, "Same-Sex Expat Experiences," *ExpatBriefing.com,* May 9, 2014, http://www.expatbriefing.com.

SUMMARY

LO1 Summarize how the growth in global business activity affects human resource management.

More and more companies are entering global markets by exporting to and operating in other countries. Organizations therefore need employees who understand customers, suppliers, and local laws in other countries and are able to adapt to local situations. Organizations may operate on the scale of an exporter or an international, global, or multinational organization. A global organization needs a transnational HRM system, which makes decisions from a global perspective, includes employees from many countries, and is based on ideas contributed by people representing a variety of cultures.

LO2 Identify the factors that most strongly influence HRM in global markets.

By far the most important influence is the culture of each market—its set of shared assumptions about how the world works and what ideals are worth striving for. Countries also differ in the degree to which their labour markets include people with education and skills of value to employers. Another influence on international HRM is the foreign country's political–legal system—its government, laws, and regulations. Finally, a country's economic system, as well as the government's involvement in the country's economy, is a strong factor determining HRM practices.

LO3 Discuss how international operations impact human resource practices including workforce planning, selection, training and development, performance management, total rewards, and labour relations.

When organizations decide to operate internationally or globally, workforce planning involves decisions about where and how many employees are needed for each international facility. Organizations prepare the employees (and often their families) through training. The general principles of performance management may apply in most countries, but the specific methods that work in one country may not work well in another. Pay structures can differ substantially among countries, and labour relations involve differences in laws, attitudes, economic systems, and negotiation styles.

LO4 Explain how employers manage and prepare employees for international assignments and for their return home.

When an organization has selected an employee for an international assignment, extensive preparations are required before departure. Preparation of the expatriate should include cross-cultural training and career development activities to help the individual acquire valuable career skills during the international assignment and at the end of the assignment to handle repatriation successfully. Communication of changes at home and validation of a job well done abroad help the expatriate through the repatriation process.

CRITICAL THINKING QUESTIONS

1. Identify the home country, host country(ies), and third country(ies) in the following example: A global soft-drink company called Cold Cola has headquarters in Halifax, Nova Scotia. It operates production facilities in the United States, and in Jakarta, Indonesia. The company has assigned a manager from Moncton, New Brunswick, to head the U.S. facility and a manager from Hong Kong to manage the Jakarta facility.
2. Think of the different levels of global participation. What companies that you are familiar with exhibit the different levels of participation?
3. What are some HRM challenges that arise when a Canadian company expands from domestic markets by exporting? When it changes from simply exporting to operating as an international company? When an international company becomes a global company?
4. In recent years, many North American companies have invested in Russia and sent Canadian managers there in an attempt to transplant North American–style management. According to Hofstede, Canadian culture has low power distance, moderate uncertainty avoidance, short-term orientation, high individualism, moderate masculinity, and high indulgence. Russia's culture has high power distance, high uncertainty avoidance, long-term orientation, low individualism, low masculinity, and low indulgence. In light of what you know about cultural differences, how well do you think Canadian managers can succeed using each of the following HRM practices? (Explain your reasons.)
    a. Selection decisions based on extensive assessment of individual abilities
    b. Performance feedback and reviews based on individual performance
    c. Systems for gathering suggestions from workers
    d. Self-managing work teams
    e. Unlimited vacation time
5. Besides cultural differences, what other factors affect human resource management in an organization with international operations?

6. Suppose you work in the HR department of a company that is expanding into a country where the law and culture make it difficult to lay off employees. How should your knowledge of that requirement affect workforce planning for the international operations?
7. Suppose an organization decides to improve collaboration and knowledge sharing by developing an intranet to link its global workforce. It needs to train employees in several different countries to use this system. List the possible cultural issues you can think of that the training program should take into account.
8. Think of a time when you successfully navigated another country's cultural norms (e.g., for work or on a vacation). What factors made your experience a positive one? Did you face any major obstacles? Is there anything you would do differently next time?
9. What types of skills do you need to be able to manage in today's global workforce? Where do you expect to get those skills? What classes and/or experiences will you need?
10. In the past, a large share of expatriate managers from Canada have returned home before successfully completing their international assignments. Suggest some possible reasons for the high "failure" rate. What can HR departments do to increase the success of expatriates?

EXPERIENCING HR—GLOBAL IMPLICATIONS OF HRM

In groups of four or five students, imagine that you are the Human Resources team of Manitobah Mukluks, the Indigenous-owned manufacturer of footwear based in Winnipeg and briefly discussed earlier in the chapter. Review this chapter, including the photo and caption, about Manitobah Mukluks and do some online research to learn more about this company. Check out the article "Mukluks Company Steps into Global Success" on the Canadian Trade Commissioner Service website for additional information about how Manitobah Mukluks has successfully navigated global growth to sell more than 200,000 pairs of moccasins and boots and achieved annual sales of more than $15 million.

As a group, discuss and summarize the story of Manitobah Mukluks and describe its level of global participation. What are the most important factors that impact HRM as it relates to the company's global operations and sales? What is your advice to Manitobah Mukluks about the global implications of HR practices including workforce planning, selection, training, performance management, and compensation and rewards?

Be prepared to summarize your finding and HR advice for Manitobah Mukluks in class (or, if your instructor directs, write a one-page summary of your discussion).

CASE STUDY: EVIDENCE-BASED HRM

How "Good Things Happen to Costco"

Talking to a reporter, Costco's Chief Executive Craig Jelinek had a habit of stating the conditions in which "good things will happen to you." To summarize Costco's retail strategy, Jelinek said, "As long as you continue to take care of the customer, take care of employees, and keep your expenses in line, good things are going to happen to you." Indeed, good things *have* happened to Costco, which stands out from other retailers by remaining profitable and avoiding layoffs.

Although Costco has a growing online presence, the company is mainly a chain of warehouse stores that charges consumers a membership fee to enjoy rock-bottom prices. Although Costco is a U.S. company, almost 30 percent of its warehouses are in international markets, which include Canada, Mexico, Korea, Japan, United Kingdom, Australia, Taiwan, Spain, France, and Iceland. This international market segment is reported to contribute approximately one-quarter of Costco's total revenues and is expected to become its fastest-growing segment with $36 billion in revenues forecast by 2020.

By ordering in bulk packages, displaying goods on pallets and steel shelving, and setting markups just a sliver over costs, Costco lures shoppers with low prices. It makes most of its profits from selling memberships. Consumers like the arrangement: the renewal rate in international countries is over 80 percent. Costco's commitment to shaving expenses carries over to its plain headquarters but not to the way it treats employees. Since the 1980s, Costco has increased pay rates every three years, keeping compensation well above industry norms. Even during the financial crisis in 2009, Costco announced raises. Costco reported that 88 percent of its employees had company-sponsored health insurance plans, compared with Walmart's statement saying "more than half" of employees were covered. Costco also has resisted layoffs. For example, as other companies downsized store workforces and installed self-checkout lanes, Costco determined that its employees were more efficient and better suited to its customer service goals.

These decisions assume that satisfied employees will build a stronger company by being more committed to the organization and less likely to quit. Costco has a low rate of employee turnover (the percentage who quit each year): 5 percent among employees with at least a year on the job, or about one-quarter the industry average. The company therefore spends less to recruit and train new employees, and employees have more experience they can apply to providing great service. Costco also utilizes store employees as its main source of management talent. It pays tuition for hourly workers to pursue their education and move up the corporate ladder. By way of example, CEO Craig Jelinek joined Costco in 1984 and had many varied positions with the company before taking over the CEO job from Costco founder James Sinegal in 2012.

Costco's executives credit the treatment of employees with helping the company thrive. Its sales and stock price have been surging over the past few years. Costco also recently began selling in China using the dedicated e-commerce channel Tmall Global, and analysts predict that its first physical location in China could be coming soon.

Questions

1. What would you describe as Costco's basic strategy as a global retailer? How do its human resource practices support that strategy?
2. Instead of asking, "How can we make the customer pay more for this?" Costco asks, "Could this be less expensive for the customer?" What evidence from the case suggests that Costco's approach to people management supports this business priority?

Sources: Barbara Farfan, "Costco's Retail Innovation Craze," *The Balance Small Business,* April 16, 2018, www.thebalancesmb.com, Trefis Team, "How Will Costco's International Business Perform Going Forward?," *Nasdaq,* January 2, 2018, https://www.nasdaq.com; Nat Berman, "10 Things You Didn't Know About Craig Jelinek," *Money Inc.,* January 2018, https://moneyinc.com; Shannon Pettypiece, "Costco Will Raise Minimum Wage as Competition for Workers Grows," *Bloomberg Business,* March 3, 2016, http://www.bloomberg.com; Elizabeth A. Harris, "Walmart Will Lay Off 2,300 Sam's Club Workers," *New York Times,* January 24, 2014, http://www.nytimes.com; Caroline Fairchild, "Bulking Up Abroad," *Fortune,* January 16, 2014, http://money.cnn.com; Brad Stone, "Costco CEO Craig Jelinek Leads the Cheapest, Happiest Company in the World," *Bloomberg Businessweek,* June 6, 2013, http://www.businessweek.com; Anne Fisher, "A Blueprint for Creating Better Jobs—and Bigger Profits," *Fortune,* December 12, 2013, http://management.fortune.cnn.com.

CASE STUDY: HRM SOCIAL

Online Communities Support Expats' Spouses

A common reason cited for the failure of an international assignment is that the expatriate's spouse was dissatisfied. The role of an accompanying spouse is difficult; often this person is not legally allowed to work in the host country, so it is more difficult to find new friends and meaningful activities.

Employers can help the accompanying spouse make connections. An employer, especially one with a lot of expatriate employees, might set up its own network for spouses. In The Netherlands, Eindhoven University of Technology recruits one-third of its employees from other countries but found that many left after a short period because spouses were unhappy there. It began offering spouses a "Get in Touch" program of weekly meetings to exchange information and visit places of interest. Between meetings, the spouses can keep in contact by joining the group's Facebook community. After the three-month program ended, many of the participants didn't want to stop participating, so the university added a "Stay in Touch" program.

Another approach is to provide information about non-company-related social networks for expatriate spouses. Spouses may appreciate the chance to build their own circle of friends. One example is the Trailing Spouse Network, a LinkedIn group where people can share ideas, advice, and support. The Trailing Spouse Network also has a Facebook page.

Increasingly often, the accompanying spouse is male. Some men have had an especially hard time making connections, because support services have been geared to women. Male spouses might especially welcome information about social networks. In Belgium, for instance, a group of men set up a group called STUDS (for Spouses Trailing under Duress Successfully), which offers activities and keeps members connected online with a blog. Even after leaving Belgium, friends who met in STUDS can keep in touch by posting news and questions on the blog's website.

Questions

1. What pros and cons do you see in having an organization set up its own social network for accompanying spouses and partners?
2. What pros and cons do you see in referring an accompanying spouse or partner to an outside social network?

Sources: Brookfield Global Relocation Services, *2016 Global Mobility Trends Survey,* http://knowledge.brookfieldgrs.com; Kendra Mirasol, "Following Her Job to Tokyo? Challenges Facing the Expat Male Trailing Spouse," IOR Global Services, http://www.iorworld.com, accessed June 24, 2016; Portable Career Network, "Trailing Spouse Network," http://www.portablecareer.net, accessed June 24, 2016; "STUDS (Spouses Trailing under Duress Successfully)," (A)way Magazine, http://www.awaymagazine.be, accessed June 24, 2016; Roy Stevenson, "The Trials & Triumphs of a Male Expat Trailing Spouse," *Global Living,* March/April 2014, http://globallivingmagazine.com; Willem G. van Hoorn and Carola L. L. Eijsenring, "Setting Up a Social Support Program for Accompanying Spouses of International Knowledge Workers," *People & Strategy* 36, no. 4 (2014): 60–61, 64.

CHAPTER 11

Creating and Sustaining High-Performance Organizations

WHAT DO I NEED TO KNOW?

After reading this chapter, you should be able to:

LO1 Define high-performance work systems and identify the elements, outcomes, and conditions associated with such a system.

LO2 Explain how human resource management can contribute to high performance.

LO3 Summarize ways to measure the effectiveness and impact of human resource management.

LO4 Describe how technology can be used to improve the effectiveness and impact of human resource management.

LO5 Discuss the future for human resources professionals and the role of the chief human resources officer (CHRO).

Photo courtesy of EllisDon

Construction and building services company EllisDon breaks ground on Clayton Community Centre in Surrey, British Columbia. With offices throughout Canada as well as globally, EllisDon completes more than $3.5 billion worth of contracts annually. The Halifax Central Library; Parq Vancouver; Rogers Centre; the Ivey School of Business; Toronto's Skydome; the National Gallery of Canada; and the Water's Edge, a $650 million residential construction project in Abu Dhabi scheduled for completion in 2020 are some of EllisDon's projects.[1]

EllisDon Builds a High-Performance Culture

Over just five years, the employee-owned Canadian construction company EllisDon more than doubled in size to about 2,500 employees, enabling it to take on more complex jobs in a wider geographic area. This success posed some human resource challenges. Having more people spread out in different locations increased the likelihood that individuals would feel disconnected and unsure of their role in the business. Those are conditions in which high performers might seek opportunities elsewhere and others might show less commitment to their work. But CEO Geoff Smith decided to address employee engagement personally.

Smith visited each of the company's 11 offices and talked with all employees about what they needed to work effectively and feel satisfied. In these small-group sessions, he learned that they wanted easy ways to communicate with others in the organization when they had questions or problems. So EllisDon used Google+ Communities to set up groups where employees can ask questions, share ideas, and socialize across specialties and locations. This effort is emblematic of a leadership style that emphasizes responsiveness and respect. That style promotes loyalty, measured by a turnover rate of roughly half the industry norm. In addition, Smith says, "From a moral point of view, as well as from a very pragmatic point of view . . . if you put your employees first . . . then the clients get great experiences and the shareholders get great returns."[2]

Introduction

Every organization must meet the challenges of managing high-performing and low-performing employees. Organizations want to keep their high-performing employees. Research provides evidence that retaining employees helps retain customers and increase sales.[3] Organizations with low turnover and satisfied employees tend to perform better.[4] EllisDon doesn't report performance results such as profits and client satisfaction to the public because the company is employee owned, but we can expect that high quality of service and satisfied clients contribute to the business growth and repeat client business it does report.

This chapter summarizes the role of human resource management in creating an organization that achieves a high level of performance, measured in terms such as long-term profits, quality, and customer satisfaction. We begin with a definition of high-performance work systems and a description of these systems' elements and outcomes. Next, we identify the conditions that contribute to high performance including how to assess the employee experience as well as employee satisfaction and engagement. We explain how the various HRM functions can contribute to high performance, introduce ways to measure the effectiveness and impact of HRM, and discuss how technology can enhance HRM effectiveness. Finally, we conclude with a discussion of the future for HR professionals including the role of chief human resources officer (CHRO).

LO1 What Is a High-Performance Work System?

The challenge facing managers today is how to make their organizations into *high-performance work systems* with the right combination of people, technology, and organizational structure to make full use of resources and opportunities in achieving their organization's goals. To function as a high-performance work system, each of these elements must fit well with the others in a smoothly functioning whole. Many manufacturers use the latest in processes including flexible manufacturing technology and just-in-time inventory control (meaning parts and supplies are automatically restocked as needed), but, of course, these processes do not work on their own; they must be run by skilled people. Organizations have to determine what kinds of people fit their needs, and then locate, train, and motivate those special people.[5] According to research, organizations that introduce integrated high-performance work practices usually experience increases in productivity and long-term financial performance.[6]

Creating a high-performance work system contrasts with traditional management practices. In the past, decisions about technology, organizational structure, and human resources were treated as if they were unrelated. An organization might acquire a new information system, restructure jobs, or add an office in another country without considering the impact on its people. More recently, managers have realized that success depends on how well all the elements work together.

Elements of a High-Performance Work System

As shown in Figure 11.1, in a high-performance work system, the elements that must work together include organizational structure, task design, people (the selection, training, and development of employees), reward systems, and information systems. Human resource management plays an important role in establishing all these.

Organizational structure is the way the organization groups its people into useful divisions, departments, and reporting relationships. The organization's top management makes most decisions about structure; for instance, how many employees report to each supervisor, and whether employees are grouped according to the functions they carry out or the customers they serve. Such decisions affect how well employees coordinate their activities and

FIGURE 11.1

Elements of a High-Performance Work System

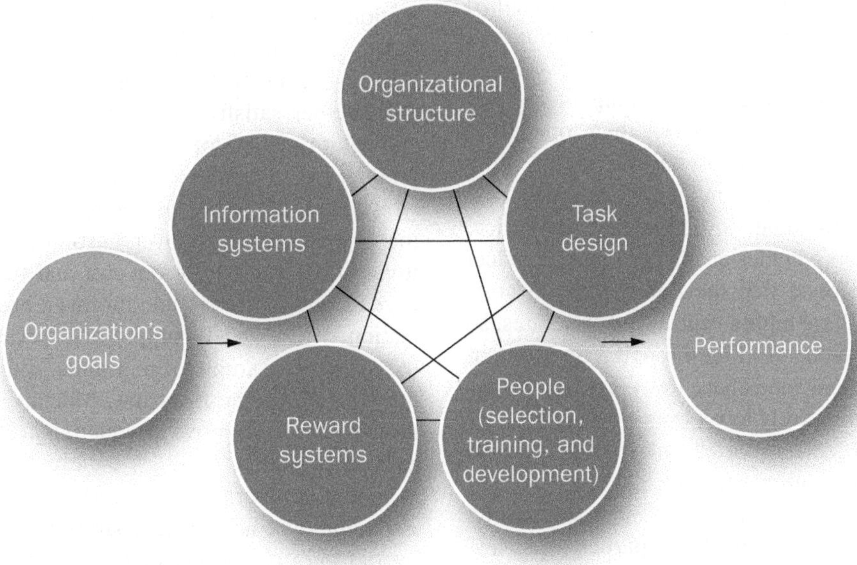

respond to change. In a high-performance work system, organizational structure promotes collaboration, learning, innovation, and accountability.

Task design determines how the details of the organization's necessary activities will be grouped, whether into jobs or team responsibilities. In a high-performance work system, task design makes jobs efficient while encouraging high-quality results. In Chapter 3, we discussed how to carry out this HRM function through job analysis and job design.

The right *people* are a key element of high-performance work systems. HRM has a significant role in providing people who are well suited to and well prepared for their jobs. Human resources professionals help the organization recruit and select people with the needed qualifications. Training, learning, development, and career management ensure that these people are able to perform their current and future jobs with the organization.

Reward systems contribute to high performance by encouraging people to strive for objectives that support the organization's overall goals. Reward systems consider the performance measures by which employees are assessed, the methods of measuring performance, and the incentive pay and other rewards linked to success. Human resource management plays an important role in developing and administering reward systems, as we saw in Chapter 8.

The final element of high-performance work systems is the organization's *information systems.* Managers make decisions about the types of information to gather and the sources of information. They also must decide who in the organization should have access to the information and how they will make the information available. Information systems (including the Internet) have enabled organizations to share information widely. For example, well over a decade ago, EllisDon had already received national recognition for information technology leadership—receiving the Canadian Information Productivity Award (CIPA) for developing and implementing a proprietary web-based project management system that enabled project staff, architects, consultants, and subcontractors to collaborate by managing documents, knowledge, and workflow.[7] HR departments also use information-sharing technologies to provide employees with access to information about benefits, training opportunities, job openings, and more, as we will describe later in this chapter.

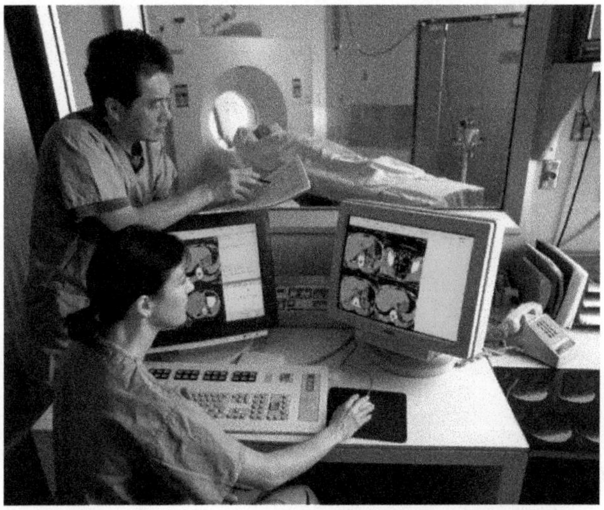

In a high-performance work system, all the elements—people, technology, and organizational structure—work together for success.

Outcomes of a High-Performance Work System

Consider the practices of steel minimills (self-contained production facilities that produce steel to make a limited quantity of products for industrial customers). Some minimills have strategies based on keeping their costs below competitors' costs; low costs let them operate at a profit while winning customers with low prices. Other steel minimills focus on "differentiation," meaning they set themselves apart in some way other than low price; for example, by offering higher quality or unique product lines. Research has found that the minimills with cost-related goals tend to have highly centralized structures, so managers can focus on controlling through a tight line of command. These organizations have low employee participation in decisions, relatively low wages and benefits, and wages highly contingent on performance.[8] At minimills that focus on differentiation, structures are more complex and decentralized, so authority is more spread out. These minimills encourage employee participation and have higher wages and more generous benefits. They are high-performance work systems. In general, these differentiator mills enjoy higher productivity, lower scrap rates, and lower employee turnover than the mills that focus on low costs.

Outcomes of a high-performance work system thus include higher productivity and efficiency. These outcomes contribute to higher profits. A high-performance work system may have other outcomes, including high product quality, great customer experience and satisfaction, and low employee turnover. Some of these outcomes meet intermediate goals that lead to higher profits (see Figure 11.2). For example, high quality contributes to customer satisfaction, and customer satisfaction contributes to growth of the business. Likewise, improving productivity lets the organization do more with less, which satisfies price-conscious customers and may help the organization win over customers from its competitors. Other ways to lower cost and improve quality are to reduce absenteeism and turnover, providing the organization with a steady supply of experienced workers. In the previous example of minimills, some employers keep turnover and scrap rates low. Meeting those goals helps the minimills improve productivity, which helps them earn more profits.

In a high-performance work system, the outcomes of each employee and work group contribute to the system's overall high performance. The organization's individuals and groups work efficiently, provide high-quality goods and services, and so on, and in this way, they contribute to meeting the organization's goals. When the organization adds or changes goals, people are flexible and make changes as needed to meet the new goals.

FIGURE 11.2

Outcomes of a High-Performance Work System

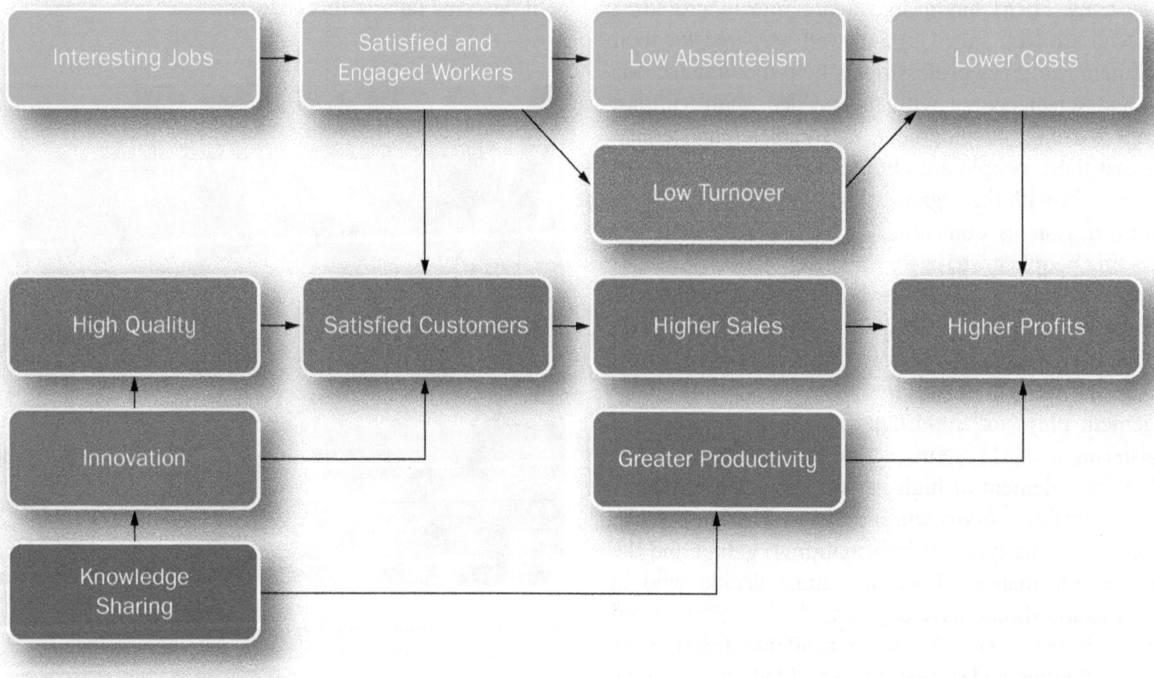

Conditions That Contribute to High Performance

Certain conditions underlie the formation of a high-performance work system:[9]

- Teams perform work.
- Employees participate in selection.
- Employees receive formal performance feedback and are actively involved in the performance improvement process.
- Ongoing training is emphasized and rewarded.
- Employees' rewards and compensation relate to the company's financial performance.
- Equipment and work processes are structured and technology is used to encourage maximum flexibility and interaction among employees.
- Employees participate in planning changes in equipment, layout, and work methods.
- Work design allows employees to use a variety of skills.
- Employees understand how their jobs contribute to the finished product or service.
- Ethical behaviour is encouraged.

Practices involving rewards, employee empowerment, and jobs with variety contribute to high performance by giving employees skills, incentives, knowledge, and autonomy—as well as satisfaction and engagement—conditions associated with high performance. Ethical behaviour is a necessary condition of high performance because it contributes to good long-term relationships with employees, customers, and the public.

Employee Experience

Employees "expect a productive, engaging, enjoyable work experience"[10] and the Conference Board recently reported that "enhancing employee experience" is a core element required for the HR function to be "an agile proactive contributor to the business."[11] In Chapter 1, *employee experience* was defined as the set of perceptions that employees have about their experiences at work in response to their interactions with the organization.

Through research described in the Evidenced-based HRM Case Study in Chapter 1, IBM developed its "Employee Experience Index," which is summarized in Table 11.1. Although ownership for driving employee experience is shared with managers across the organization, HR is increasingly called upon to "co-lead organization-wide efforts to enhance employee experience."[12]

The following conditions that contribute to high performance are also linked to positive employee experience.

TABLE 11.1

IBM's Employee Experience Index

Dimension	Description
Belonging	Feeling part of a team, group, or organization.
Purpose	Understanding why one's work matters.
Achievement	A sense of accomplishment in the work that is done.
Happiness	The pleasant feeling arising in and during work.
Vigour	The presence of energy, enthusiasm, and excitement at work.

Source: "The Employee Experience Index," *IBM Smarter Workforce Institute,* September 2016, p. 3, http://www.globoforce.com/wp-content/uploads/2016/10/The_Employee_Experience_Index.pdf. Used with permission. Industrial-organizational psychologists and experts in HR consulting from both the IBM Smarter Workforce Institute and the Globoforce WorkHuman Analytics and Research Institute undertook a large-scale research project to understand and measure what makes an optimal working experience for employees. This research resulted in the creation of the Employee Experience Index (EXI) that measures employees' personal experiences at work in terms of belonging, purpose, achievement, happiness, and vigor. The IBM and Globoforce research found that employee experience is positively associated with employee work performance, discretionary effort, and turnover intention.

We will also consider HRM's integrated contribution to high performance later in the chapter. This also provides an additional opportunity to review how the various HR functions contribute to enhancing employee experience in consideration of the entire employee journey starting even before Day 1 on the job; for example, creating a positive candidate experience was discussed in Chapter 4.

Employee Empowerment

employee empowerment Giving employees responsibility and authority to make decisions regarding all aspects of product development or customer service.

To completely benefit from employees' knowledge and skills, organizations need a management style that focuses on development and empowering employees. **Employee empowerment** means giving employees responsibility and authority to make decisions regarding all aspects of product development or customer service.[13] Employees are then held accountable for products and customer service. In return, they share the resulting rewards (or losses). Employee empowerment can also extend to innovation. Employees at all levels are encouraged to share their ideas

Did You KNOW?

Empowerment Associated with Positive Employee Experience

In a recent survey, "employees who feel their ideas and suggestions matter are more than twice as likely to report a positive employee experience than those who don't (83 percent vs. 34 percent). A similar pattern emerged among employees who have the freedom to decide how to do their work (79 percent vs. 42 percent)."

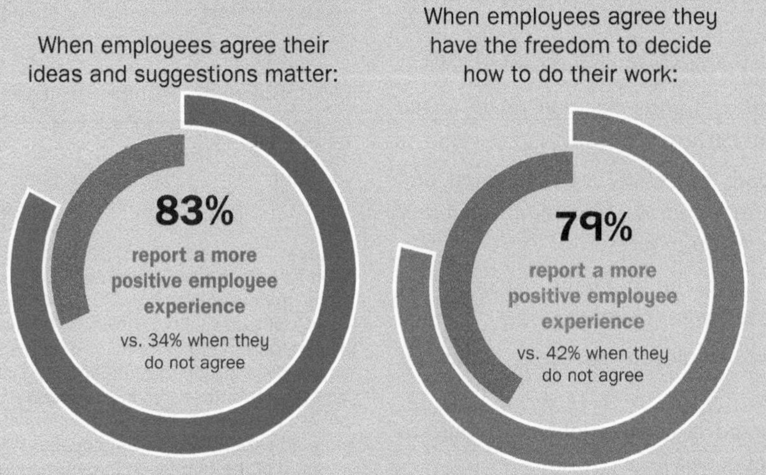
When employees agree their ideas and suggestions matter:
83%
report a more positive employee experience
vs. 34% when they do not agree
When employees agree they have the freedom to decide how to do their work:
79%
report a more positive employee experience
vs. 42% when they do not agree

Sources: "The Employee Experience Index," *IBM Smarter Workforce Institute,* September 2016, p. 8, http://www.globoforce.com/wp-content/uploads/2016/10/The_Employee_Experience_Index.pdf. Used with permission. Industrial-organizational psychologists and experts in HR consulting from both the IBM Smarter Workforce Institute and the Globoforce WorkHuman Analytics and Research Institute undertook a large-scale research project to understand and measure what makes an optimal working experience for employees. This research resulted in the creation of the Employee Experience Index (EXI) that measures employees' personal experiences at work in terms of belonging, purpose, achievement, happiness, and vigor. The IBM and Globoforce research found that employee experience is positively associated with employee work performance, discretionary effort, and turnover intention.

for satisfying customers better and operating more efficiently and safely. This is empowering when management listens to the ideas, implements valuable ones, and rewards employees for their innovations.

As illustrated in the Did You Know? box, employees are more than twice as likely to report a positive work experience when they have the "freedom to decide how to do their work" and when "their ideas and suggestions matter."

HRM practices such as performance management, training, work design, and compensation are important for ensuring the success of employee empowerment. Jobs must be designed to give employees the necessary latitude for making a variety of decisions. Employees must be properly trained to exert their wider authority and use information resources and communication tools. Employees also need feedback to help evaluate their successes. Pay and other rewards should reflect employees' authority and be related to successful handling of their responsibility. In addition, for empowerment to succeed, managers must be trained to link employees to resources within and outside the organization, such as customers, and co-workers in other departments, with needed information. Managers must also encourage employees to interact with colleagues throughout the organization, ensure that employees have access to the resources they need, and reward collaboration. Employee empowerment shifts the recruiting focus away from technical skills and toward general cognitive and interpersonal skills. Employees who have accountability for a final product or service must be able to listen to customers, adapt to changing needs, and creatively solve a variety of problems.

Teamwork

Modern technology places the information that employees need for improving quality and providing customer service right at the point of sale or production. As a result, the employees who engage in selling and producing must also be able to make decisions about how to do their work.

© Getty Images/Photodisc/DAL
It's important for companies to capture and share the knowledge of workers who have had years to learn their specialty.

Organizations need to set up work in a way that gives employees the authority and ability to make those decisions. One of the most popular ways to increase employee responsibility and control is to assign work to teams. **Teamwork** is the assignment of work to groups of employees with various skills who interact to assemble a product or provide a service. Work teams often assume many activities traditionally reserved for managers, such as selecting new team members, scheduling work, and coordinating work with customers and other units of the organization. Work teams also contribute to total quality by performing inspection and quality-control activities while the product or service is being completed.

teamwork The assignment of work to groups of employees with various skills who interact to assemble a product or provide a service.

In some organizations, technology is enabling teamwork even when workers are at different locations or work at different times. These organizations use *virtual teams*—teams that rely on communications technology to keep in touch and coordinate activities. Teamwork can motivate employees by making work more interesting and significant. At organizations that rely on teamwork, labour costs may be lower as well. Spurred by such advantages, a number of companies are reorganizing assembly operations—abandoning the assembly line in favour of operations that combine mass production with jobs in which employees perform multiple tasks, use many skills, control the pace of work, and assemble the entire final product. Witnessing the resulting improvements, companies in the service sector also have moved toward greater use of teamwork.

Teamwork is a necessary component of more and more computer programming tasks. Companies that develop software are increasingly using an approach they call *agile,* which involves weaving the development process more tightly into the organization's activities and strategies. In agile software development, self-directed teams of developers and programmers work directly with the business users of the software, using as much face-to-face communication as possible. Rather than devoting endless hours to negotiating contracts and documenting processes, the teams focus on frequently delivering usable components of the software. Throughout the development process the team is open to changing requirements and computer code as a result of their communication with users. Users of agile software development say it increases customer satisfaction and speeds up the time from concept to usable software.[14]

Knowledge Sharing

For more than two decades, managers have been interested in creating a **learning organization**, that is, an organization in which the culture values and supports lifelong learning by enabling all employees to continually acquire and share knowledge. The people in a learning organization have resources for training and development, and they are encouraged to share their knowledge with colleagues. Managers take an active role in identifying training needs and encouraging the sharing of ideas.[15] An organization's information systems, discussed later in this chapter, have an important role in making this learning activity possible. Information systems capture knowledge and make it available even after individual employees who provided the knowledge have left the organization. Ultimately, people are the essential ingredients in a learning organization. They must be committed to learning and willing to share what they have learned. A learning organization has several key features:[16]

learning organization An organization that supports lifelong learning by enabling all employees to acquire and share knowledge.

- It engages in **continuous learning**, each employee's and each group's ongoing efforts to gather information and apply the information to their decisions. In many organizations, the process of continuous learning is aimed at improving quality. To engage in continuous learning, employees must understand the entire work system they participate in, the relationships among jobs, their work units, and the organization as a whole. Employees who continuously learn about their work system are adding to their ability to improve performance.
- Knowledge is *shared.* Therefore, to create a learning organization, one challenge is to shift the focus of training away from merely teaching skills and toward a broader focus on generating and sharing knowledge.[17] In this view, training is an investment in the organization's human resources; it increases employees' value to the organization. Also, training content should

continuous learning Each employee's and each group's ongoing efforts to gather information and apply the information to their decisions in a learning organization.

be related to the organization's goals. Human resource departments can support the creation of a learning organization by planning training programs that meet these criteria, and they can help to create both face-to-face and electronic systems for employee collaboration to create, capture, and share knowledge. Increasingly, this includes providing employees with social media tools for knowledge sharing, as well as using digital file sharing and collaboration platforms like Dropbox, Google Drive, and Microsoft Sharepoint.

- Critical, systemic thinking is *widespread.* This occurs when organizations encourage employees to see relationships among ideas and to test assumptions and observe the results of their actions. Reward systems can be set up to encourage employees and teams to think in new ways.
- The organization has a *learning culture*—a culture in which learning is rewarded, promoted, and supported by managers and organizational objectives. This culture may be reflected in performance management systems and pay structures that reward employees for gathering and sharing more knowledge. A learning culture creates the conditions in which managers encourage *flexibility* and *experimentation.* The organization should encourage employees to take risks and innovate, which means it cannot be quick to punish ideas that do not work out as intended.
- Employees are *valued.* The organization recognizes that employees are the source of its knowledge. It therefore focuses on ensuring the development and well-being of each employee.

Continuous learning and knowledge sharing can support an environment of employee empowerment. For example, some organizations are giving employees access to software that monitors their productivity on the assumption that if they know data about their performance, they can use the data to improve their own productivity. Software called RescueTime measures how much time is spent on each website and application for both computer and mobile devices. One employee who used this type of tool discovered that he was most productive when he switched tasks periodically, so he set up the software to remind him every 20 minutes to do something different. A programmer who assumed that chatting online was making him less productive tested that assumption and found that time chatting was associated with writing *more* lines of code. Armed with that information, the programmer gave a higher priority to networking with co-workers and customers. Notice in these examples that the workers had latitude to discover how they work best and to control how they applied what they learned.[18]

Meaningful Work

An employee's work experience is enhanced when on-the-job roles and projects are connected to the worker's core values and create a sense of meaning and purpose. People sign on to help charitable causes for little or no pay simply because of the value they place on making a meaningful difference. The Alzheimer's Association hires staff members who are passionate about its mission of promoting research to end Alzheimer's disease and enhance care for those affected by the disease. Leadership keeps staff up-to-date on progress toward the goals, encourages employees to share ideas, and celebrates successes. CEO Harry Johns conveys a message that all employees "make our advances possible for the people we serve."[19]

Fostering pride and engagement through the opportunity to make a difference is also being promoted by governments across the country. For example, the Nova Scotia government promotes pride in the public sector through the slogan "Do Big Things" as part of its strategy to attract, engage, and retain employees.[20]

Ethics

In the long run, a high-performance organization meets high ethical standards. Ethics, defined in Chapter 1, establishes fundamental principles for behaviour, such as honesty and fairness. Organizations and their employees must meet these standards if they are to maintain positive long-term relationships with their employees, customers, and community.

Ethical behaviour is most likely to result from values held by the organization's leaders combined with systems that promote ethical behaviour. A number of organizational systems can promote ethical behaviour.[21] These include a written code of ethics that the organization distributes to employees and requires them to use in decision making. Publishing a list of ethical standards is not enough, however. The organization should reinforce ethical behaviour. For example, performance measures should include ethical standards. The organization should provide channels employees can use to ask questions about ethical behaviour or to seek help if they are expected to do something they believe is wrong. Organizations also can provide training in ethical decision making, including training for supervisors in how to handle employees' concerns about ethical matters.

As these examples suggest, ethical behaviour is a human resource management concern. The systems that promote ethical behaviour include HRM functions such as training, performance management, and discipline policies. In today's business climate, ethical behaviour can also help a company attract workers—and customers—who share those high standards.

Corporate Social Responsibility

Corporate social responsibility (CSR) is an evolving concept integrating social, environmental, and economic concerns into an organization's values, culture, decision making, strategy, and operations in a way that creates wealth and improves society.[22] Canada is recognized as a leader in

Shutterstock / Olha Afanasieva

Did office spacesharing company WeWork go too far in reducing its impact on the environment when it recently introduced a policy of not serving pork, poultry, or red meat nor allowing employees to expense those meats to the company?[23]

social responsibility and "CSR remains a concept that is openly embraced by a strong majority of Canadians."[24]

For example, research firm GlobeScan found that 92 percent of Canadians said that the "the more socially and environmentally responsible a company is, the more likely they are to purchase its products or services." Additionally, "91 percent of Canadians surveyed said they prefer to work for a company that is socially and environmentally responsible." The more socially and environmentally responsible a company is, the more attractive it becomes an an employer.[25]

Job Satisfaction

A condition underpinning any high-performance organization is that employees experience *job satisfaction*—they experience their jobs as fulfilling or allowing them to fulfill one's important job values.[26] Several aspects of job satisfaction are the following:

- Job satisfaction is related to a person's *values,* defined as "what a person consciously or unconsciously desires to obtain."
- Different employees have different views of which values are *important,* so the same circumstances can produce different levels of job satisfaction.
- Job satisfaction is based on *perception,* not always on an objective and complete measurement of the situation. Individuals compare the job situation to their values, and people are likely to differ in what they perceive.

Research supports the idea that employees' job satisfaction and job performance are related.[27] Higher performance at the individual level should contribute to higher performance for the organization as a whole. In sum, values, perceptions, and ideas of what is important are the three components of job satisfaction. As shown in Figure 11.3 organizations can contribute to job satisfaction in several ways.

Employee Engagement

A condition underpinning any high-performance organization is that employees are fully engaged with their work. As discussed in Chapter 1, *employee engagement* refers to the extent that employees experience full involvement in their work and commitment to the job and organization. Engagement has both an emotional and cognitive

FIGURE 11.3

Increasing Job Satisfaction

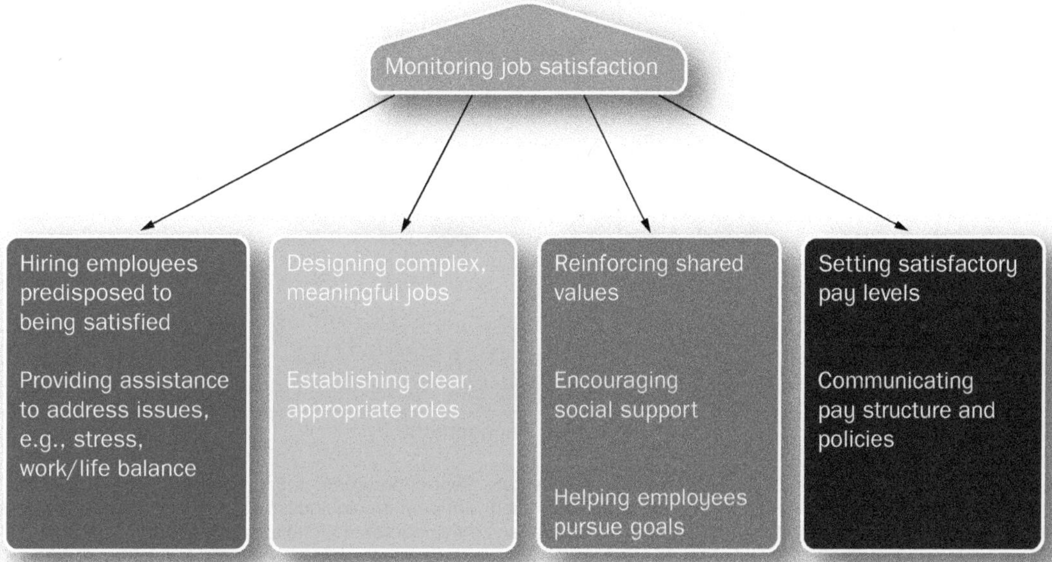

component and is evidenced through employee behaviours. For example, employees are engaged when they:[28]

- Speak positively about the organization to co-workers, potential employees, and customers;
- Have an intense desire to be a member of the organization;
- Exert extra effort and are dedicated to doing the very best job possible to contribute to the organization's business success.

Employees who are engaged in their work and committed to the company they work for provide a clear competitive advantage to that firm, including higher productivity, better customer service, and lower turnover.[29] Consultants at Gallup have found that the organizations with the most engaged employees have significantly greater customer satisfaction, productivity, and profitability.[30]

Aon, another major consulting firm, has measured an association between employee engagement and business performance. Companies scoring high in employee engagement tend to report superior sales, strong operating margins, and returns to shareholders, especially at companies that have strong leadership, positive reputations, and a focus on performance management.[31]

Companies that sustain and improve engagement levels systematically gather feedback from employees, analyze their responses, and implement changes. In these companies, engagement measures are considered as important as customer service or financial data. Employee engagement tends to require job satisfaction.

As shown in Figure 11.4, together employee engagement and employee experience provide a broader picture. When employees have high engagement and a positive employee experience, they are passionate about their work; however, when employees have low engagement and a negative employee experience, they are apathetic.

Globally, Aon has found that the practices that do the most to promote employee engagement are opportunities for career progress, recognition for accomplishments, and brand alignment. **Brand alignment** is the process of ensuring that HR policies, practices, and programs support or are congruent with an organization's overall culture or brand, including its products and services. One way to ensure HR policies align with a company's strategic vision is to educate employees about the company's brand and their role in bringing that brand to life as part of everyday work activities. Some companies discuss brand alignment as part of employee orientation programs while others develop in-depth training programs about the company's brand and how each employee is an important contributor to the company's overall success. Employers have the most impact on brand alignment by providing career opportunities, using effective performance management systems, and maintaining a positive reputation.[32]

brand alignment The process of ensuring that HR policies, practices, and programs support or are congruent with an organization's overall culture (or brand), products, and services.

FIGURE 11.4

High Engagement and Positive Experience Results in Passion for Work

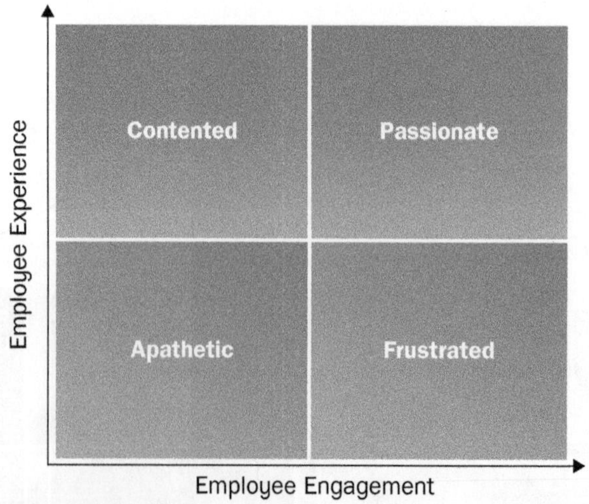

Source: "The Employee Experience Index," IBM Smarter Workforce Institute, September 2016, p. 8, http://www.globoforce.com/wp-content/uploads/2016/10/The_Employee_Experience_Index.pdf. Used with permission. Industrial-organizational psychologists and experts in HR consulting from both the IBM Smarter Workforce Institute and the Globoforce WorkHuman Analytics and Research Institute undertook a large-scale research project to understand and measure what makes an optimal working experience for employees. This research resulted in the creation of the Employee Experience Index (EXI) that measures employees' personal experiences at work in terms of belonging, purpose, achievement, happiness, and vigor. The IBM and Globoforce research found that employee experience is positively associated with employee work performance, discretionary effort, and turnover intention.

Disengaged and Overwhelmed Employees

Organizations need employees who are fully engaged and committed to their work; however, according to a Deloitte Human Capital Trends Study, "Companies are struggling to engage our modern, 21st century workforce."[33] Gallup research "shows that only 13% of employees around the world are actively engaged at work, and more than twice that number are so disengaged they are likely to spread negativity to others."[34] It was also recently reported that "two-thirds of today's employees feel overwhelmed." For example, workers say they "would like to work fewer hours, they are too distracted (mobile device users check their phones 150 times per day), and they are flooded with too many emails, conference calls, meetings, and other distractions."[35]

job withdrawal A set of behaviours with which employees try to avoid the work situation physically, mentally, or emotionally.

The organization needs to prevent a broader negative condition, called **job withdrawal**—or a set of behaviours with which employees try to avoid the work situation physically, mentally, or emotionally. Job withdrawal results when circumstances such as the nature of the job, supervisors and co-workers, pay levels, or the employee's own disposition cause the employee to become dissatisfied with the job. As shown in Figure 11.5, this job dissatisfaction produces job withdrawal. Job withdrawal may take the form of behaviour change, physical job withdrawal, or psychological withdrawal. Some researchers believe employees engage in the three forms of withdrawal behaviour in that order, while others think they select from these behaviours to address the particular sources of job dissatisfaction they experience.[36] Although the specifics of these models vary, the consensus is that withdrawal behaviours are related to one another and are at least partially caused by job dissatisfaction.[37]

The problem is compounded when employees offer evasive explanations for their physical job withdrawal, as described in the HR Oops!

HR Oops!

Employees Say Anything to Stay Away from Work

Employers understand that even satisfied employees are refreshed by a vacation or need to stay home when they're sick. But when employees invent excuses to stay away from work, it raises some questions. And it raises even more questions when the excuses are bizarre: Is this a sign of a dysfunctional relationship between employee and supervisor?

An annual survey by CareerBuilder found that a majority of employees have worked when sick, but 40 percent of employees admitted to calling in sick when they were well, up from 35 percent in the previous year. The main reasons for sick days when well were doctor's appointments (cited by 30 percent), just not wanting to work (23 percent), feeling a need to relax (20 percent), and needing to catch up on sleep (15 percent).

What do employees tell their supervisor when they just don't feel like working? They might claim to be sick, but one employee expressed her condition more creatively: She said she was not sure how the solar eclipse would affect her so needed to say home. Another blamed his absence on not having gas to get to work. Yet another claimed that a bear was in the yard and they were too afraid to come out, and one said her dog swallowed her car keys so she had to wait for the keys to come out.

Not all employers are willing to look the other way. More than one in four have caught an employee lying by checking their social media posts. And one in four have dismissed a worker who was found to have given a fake excuse for an absence.

Questions

1. Does a bizarre excuse potentially signal a greater degree of job dissatisfaction? Why or why not?
2. Why should companies care about employees' reasons for absences? If you worked for a company's HR department, what reasons for absences would you be most concerned about?

Sources: Dennis McCafferty, "Bosses Question Workers' Excuses for Missing Work," *Baseline,* December 14, 2015, http://www.baselinemag.com; Kevin McCoy, "'Grandma Poisoned Me with Ham' and Other Excuses for Missing Work," *Indianapolis Star,* October 16, 2015, http://www.indystar.com; CareerBuilder, "Increased Number of Workers Calling in Sick When They Aren't, Finds CareerBuilder Annual Survey," news release, November 16, 2017, http://www.prnewswire.com.

FIGURE 11.5

Job Withdrawal Process

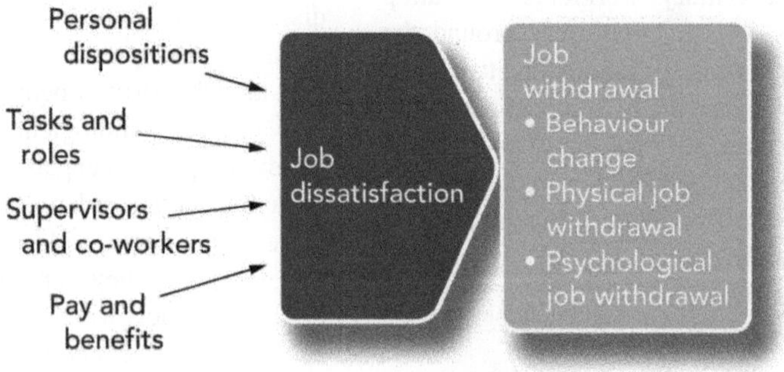

How Is Employee Experience Assessed?

The usual way to assess employee experience, including satisfaction and engagement, is with some kind of survey. A systematic, ongoing program of employee surveys should be part of the organization's human resource strategy. This allows the organization to monitor trends. IBM's ambitious research to understand the ideal employee experience at work included developing an "Employee Experience Index" that was discussed in this chapter as well as in Chapter 1.

Although the types of questions asked in employee job satisfaction and engagement surveys may vary, some of the common themes generally measured include pride and satisfaction with employer; opportunity to perform challenging work; recognition and positive feedback for contributions; personal support from supervisor; and understanding of the link between one's job and the company's overall mission. For example, if satisfaction with promotion opportunities has been falling over several years, the trend may signal a need for better career management (a topic of Chapter 6). An organizational change, such as a merger, also might have important consequences for employee job satisfaction and engagement. In addition, ongoing surveys give the organization a way to measure whether practices adopted to enhance employee satisfaction and engagement are working. Organizations can also compare results from different departments to identify groups with successful practices that may apply elsewhere in the organization. Another benefit is that some scales provide data that organizations can use to compare themselves to others in the same industry. This information will be valuable for creating and reviewing human resource policies that enable organizations to attract and retain employees in a competitive job market.

To obtain a survey instrument, an excellent place to begin is with one of the many established scales. For example, the validity and reliability of many satisfaction scales have been tested, so it is possible to compare the instruments. The main reason for an organization to create its own scale would be that it wants to measure aspects of work specific to the organization (such as satisfaction with a particular benefits plan). Surveys can be prepared and managed by using easily accessible online tools such as SurveyMonkey.

A widely used measure of job satisfaction is the Job Descriptive Index (JDI). The JDI emphasizes specific aspects of satisfaction—pay, the work itself, supervision, co-workers, and promotions. Figure 11.6 shows several items from the JDI scale. Other scales measure general satisfaction using broad questions such as, "All in all, how satisfied are you with your job?"[38] Some scales avoid language altogether, relying on pictures. Other scales exist for measuring more specific aspects of satisfaction. For example, the Pay Satisfaction Questionnaire (PSQ) measures satisfaction with specific aspects of pay, such as pay levels, structure, and raises.[39]

However, critics describe the traditional employee satisfaction feedback process as: "The individual has his or her moment of self-expression, a fleeting participation in the great collective search for truth,

Photo courtesy of Best Buy Canada

Employees from a high-performing Best Buy store receive a surprise "Be Amazing Ambush" from a senior executive to recognize and reward their accomplishments. How important are moments like this to create a positive and memorable employee experience?

then silence, nada, frustration as the status quo prevails."[40] With this in mind, the Gallup Organization set about to create a better employee feedback process that linked the elements of employee engagement to improved business outcomes; for example, sales growth, productivity, customer loyalty, and the generation of value.[41] Table 11.2 identifies Gallup's questions for measuring employee engagement.

In spite of surveys and other efforts to retain employees, some employees inevitably will leave the organization.

FIGURE 11.6

Example of a Job Descriptive Index (JDI)

Instructions: Think of your present work. What is it like most of time? In the blank beside each word given below, write

__Y__ for "Yes" if it describes your work
__N__ for "No" if it does NOT describe your work
__?__ if you cannot decide

Work Itself	**Pay**	**Promotion Opportunities**
_____ Routine	_____ Less than I deserve	_____ Dead-end job
_____ Satisfying	_____ Highly paid	_____ Unfair policies
_____ Good	_____ Insecure	_____ Based on ablility

Supervision	**Co-workers**
_____ Impolite	_____ Intelligent
_____ Praises good work	_____ Responsible
_____ Doesn't supervise enough	_____ Boring

Source: W. K. Balzar, D. C. Smith, D. E. Kravitz, S. E. Lovell, K. B. Paul, B. A. Reilly, and C. E. Reilly, *User's Manual for the Job Descriptive Index (JDI)* (Bowling Green, OH: Bowling Green State University, 1990).

TABLE 11.2

Measuring Employee Engagement: Gallup's 12 Questions

To identify the elements of worker engagement, Gallup conducted hundreds of focus groups and many thousands of worker interviews in all kinds of organizations, and at all levels, in most industries, and in many countries. The result was 12 key employee expectations that, when satisfied, form the foundation of strong feelings of engagement.
1. Do you know what is expected of you at work?
2. Do you have the materials and equipment you need to do your work right?
3. At work, do you have the opportunity to do what you do best every day?
4. In the last seven days, have you received recognition or praise for doing good work?
5. Does your supervisor, or someone at work, seem to care about you as a person?
6. Is there someone at work who encourages your development?
7. At work, do your opinions seem to count?
8. Does the mission/purpose of your company make you feel your job is important?
9. Are your associates (fellow employees) committed to doing quality work?
10. Do you have a best friend at work?
11. In the last six months, has someone at work talked to you about your progress?
12. In the last year, have you had opportunities at work to learn and grow?

Source: John Thackeray "Feedback for Real," March 15, 2001, https://news.gallup.com/businessjournal/811/feedback-real.aspx.

This presents another opportunity to gather information for retaining employees: the **exit interview**—a meeting of the departing employee with the employee's supervisor and/or a human resources specialist to discuss the employee's reasons for leaving. A well-conducted exit interview can uncover reasons that employees leave and perhaps set the stage for some of them to return. HR professionals can help make exit interviews more successful by arranging for the employee to talk to someone from the HR department (rather than the departing employee's supervisor) in a neutral location or over the phone.[42] Questions should start out open-ended and general, to give the employee a chance to name the source of the dissatisfaction or explain why leaving is attractive.

exit interview
A meeting of a departing employee with the employee's supervisor and/or human resources specialist to discuss the employee's reasons for leaving.

A recruiter armed with information about what caused a specific person to leave may be able to negotiate a return when the situation changes. And when several exiting employees give similar reasons for leaving, management should consider whether this indicates a need for change. A recent twist on the exit interview is a **stay interview**—a meeting with an employee to explore their thoughts and feelings about the job and to uncover issues in the effort to prevent that employee from becoming disgruntled.[43]

stay interview
A meeting with an employee to explore their thoughts and feelings about the job and to uncover issues in the effort to prevent that employee from becoming disgruntled.

In the long run, a high-performance organization fosters the kind of work culture that encourages high levels of motivation, satisfaction, commitment, and engagement.

Net Promoter Score (NPS), discussed in Chapter 1, was developed to assess client experience; however, its methodology is equally applicable to measuring and improving employee experience. NPS is calculated using a 0–10 scale for the question: "How likely is it that you would recommend [organization] to a friend or colleague?" *Promoters* are loyal enthusiasts (score 9–10); *Passives* are satisfied but unenthusiastic (score 7–8); *Detractors* are unhappy (score 0–6). NPS provides better feedback on what people are experiencing but it's much more difficult to get a high rating because the percentage of Detractors is subtracted from the percentage of Promoters. As a result, Net Promoter Scores range from –100 (if everyone is a Detractor) to 100 (if everyone is a Promoter). Figure 11.7, provides a sample calculation.[44]

LO2 HRM's Contribution to High Performance

Management of human resources plays a critical role in determining companies' success in meeting the challenges of a rapidly changing, highly competitive environment.[45] Total rewards, staffing, training and development, performance management, and other HRM practices are investments that directly affect employees' motivation and ability to provide products and services that are valued by customers. Table 11.3 lists examples of HRM practices that contribute to high performance.

FIGURE 11.7

Net Promoter Score (NPS) Calculation

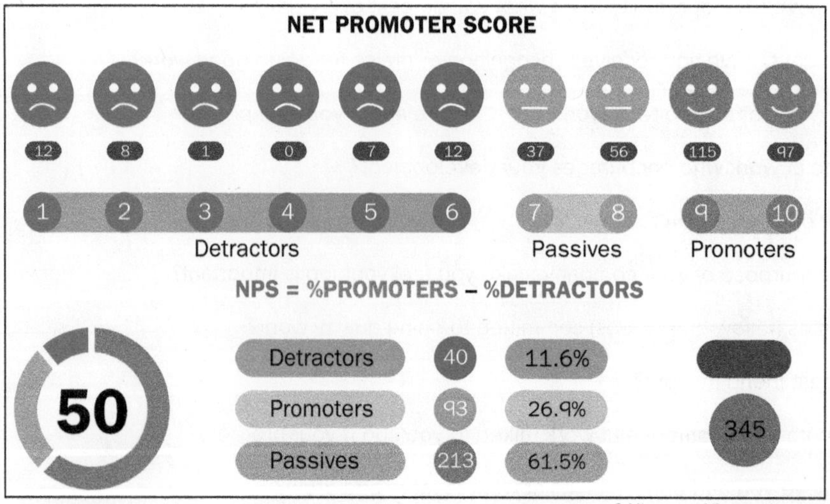

© Microvone | Dreamstime.com

TABLE 11.3

HRM Practices That Can Help Organizations Achieve High Performance

HRM practices match organization's goals.	Performance management system measures customer satisfaction and quality.
Individuals and groups share knowledge.	Organization monitors employee experience, satisfaction, and engagement.
Work is performed by teams.	Discipline system is progressive.
Organization encourages continuous learning.	Reward systems reward skills and accomplishments.
Work design permits flexibility in where and when tasks are performed.	Skills and values of a diverse workforce are valued and used.
Selection system is job related, objective, and legal.	Technology reduces time and costs of tasks while preserving quality.

Research suggests that it is more effective to improve HRM practices as a whole than to focus on one or two isolated practices, such as the organization's pay structure or selection system.[46] To have the intended influence on performance, the HRM practices must fit well with one another and the organization as a whole[47] and be implemented in partnership with line managers who clearly translate the purpose and practical value for employees.[48] Let's take a summarizing look at how HRM practices can contribute to high performance.

Job Design

Job design can enable the organization to benefit from teamwork and employee empowerment, two of the work conditions associated with high performance. Often, a high-performance work system places employees in work teams where employees collaborate to make decisions and solve problems. Individual employees also may be empowered to serve on teams that design jobs and work processes.

Job design aimed at empowerment includes access to resources such as information technology. The Lowe's chain of home improvement stores wanted to empower its salespeople with more information they need to make sales. So it equipped the salespeople with iPhones that have apps for price scanning, locating items in the store, checking inventory, and looking up competitors' prices. Eventually, the phones also will be able to scan customers' credit cards to complete sales transactions.[49] Lowe's hopes this much access to information will enable its salespeople to initiate conversations with shoppers and walk them through the entire decision process to the closing of a sale.

Recruitment and Selection

At a high-performance organization, recruitment and selection aim to obtain the kinds of employees who can thrive in this type of setting. These employees are enthusiastic about and able to contribute to teamwork, empowerment, and knowledge sharing. Qualities such as creativity and ability to collaborate as part of a team may play a large role in selection decisions. High-performance organizations need selection methods that identify more than technical skills, like ability to perform accounting and engineering tasks. Employers may use group interviews, open-ended questions, and psychological tests to find employees who innovate, share ideas, and take initiative. For example, at Imaginet, a Winnipeg-based software application firm recognized by Queen's School of Business as "Best Small to Medium Employer in Canada," employees actively contribute to the hiring process to attract top talent.[50]

Training, Learning, and Development

When organizations base hiring decisions on qualities such as decision making and teamwork skills, training may be required to help employees learn the specific skills they need to perform the duties of their job. Extensive training and development also are part of a learning organization, described earlier in this chapter. And when organizations delegate many decisions to work teams, the members of those teams likely will benefit from participating in team development activities that prepare them for their roles as team members. In addition, high-performance organizations are developing their talent to move into positions with greater responsibility.

Performance Management

In a high-performance organization, employees know the organization's goals and what they must do to help achieve those goals. HR departments can contribute to this through

Photo courtesy of Osoyoos Indian Band.

The 540 members of the Osoyoos Indian Band, including Chief Clarence Louie, the Band's long-serving chief, live and work in one of the hottest and driest parts of Canada—the South Okanagan. The Band has developed many successful business relationships and joint ventures, including Nk'Mip Cellars.

Nk'Mip Cellars was the first Aboriginal-owned winery in North America. In 2016, it was named Intervin's Canadian Winery of the Year. More recently, Nk'Mip Cellars has gained the distinction of having the first First Nations wine-maker in North America. Osoyoos Indian Band member Justin Hall was promoted to this prestigious position in May of 2017.

Nk'Mip Cellars is one of a diverse range of businesses and initiatives that have created prosperity, full-employment and meaningful work for Band members. The Osoyoos Indian Band's strategic vision is aimed at building a future founded on its working culture and business heritage to achieve a healthy, hardworking and financially sustainable community that creates meaningful job opportunities and economically supports programs for the Band's Elders and Children.

Special thank you to Dr. Aldene Meis Mason, Indigenization Lead (Associate Professor), University of Regina.

FIGURE 11.8

Employee Performance as a Process

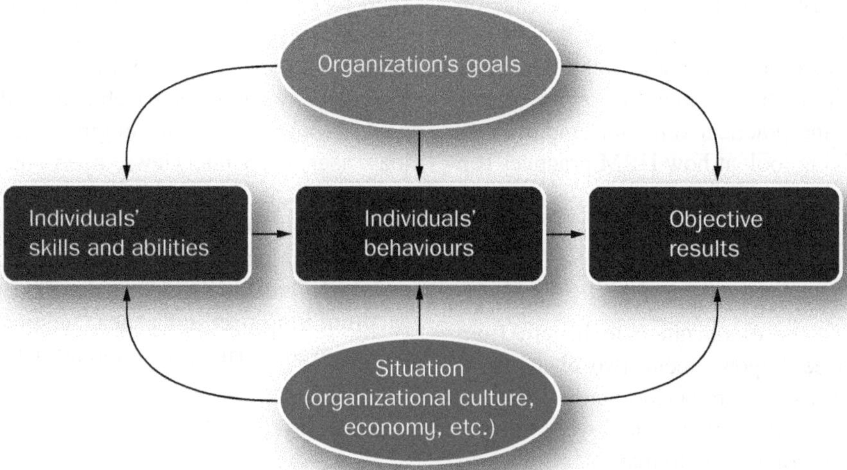

the design or redesign of the organization's performance management system. As we discussed in Chapter 7, performance management should be related to the organization's goals.

A performance management system that meets those requirements applies the process of employee performance, shown in Figure 11.8. Individuals bring a set of skills and abilities to the job and, by applying a set of behaviours, they use those skills to achieve results. The organization's goals should influence each step of the process. The situation also has an influence on every step. For example, an organization's culture might influence how hard individuals try to delight customers, and economic conditions might influence how much a salesperson sells, no matter how competent and hard working they are.

This model suggests some guidelines for performance management. First, every aspect of performance management should be related to the organization's goals. Business goals should influence the kinds of employees selected and their training, the requirements of each job, and the measures used for evaluating results. Generally, this means the organization identifies what each department needs to do to achieve the desired results, then defines how individual employees should contribute to their department's goals. More specifically, the following guidelines describe how to make the performance management system support organizational goals:[51]

- **Define and measure performance in precise terms**—Focus on outcomes that can be defined in terms of how frequently certain behaviours occur. Include criteria that describe ways employees can add value to a product or service (such as through quantity, quality, or timeliness). Include behaviours that go beyond the minimum required to perform a job (such as helping co-workers).

- **Link performance measures to meeting customer needs**—"Customers" may be the organization's external customers, or they may be internal customers (employees receiving services from a co-worker). Service goals for internal customers should be related to satisfying external customers.
- **Measure and adjust for the effect of situational constraints**—Monitor economic conditions, the organization's culture, and other influences on performance. Measures of employees' performance should take these influences into account.

This approach gives employees the information they need to behave in ways that contribute to high performance. In addition, organizations should help employees identify and obtain the abilities they need to meet their performance goals.

Compensation and Rewards

Compensation and rewards support high-performance organizations when linked in part to performance measures. A study of Canadian workers found that bonuses for new ideas were most effective when they were awarded to innovative groups rather than to individuals. This seems to inspire more creativity and teamwork and less fear of failure.[52]

Compensation also can be tied to performance-related conditions such as successful teamwork or—for a manager—employee experience or satisfaction of employees in the manager's department. Furthermore, organizations can increase empowerment and satisfaction by including employees in decisions about rewards and by communicating the basis for pay decisions.[53]

When the organization designs a pay structure, it can set up a task force that includes employees with direct experience in various types of jobs. Some organizations share financial information with their employees or have them participate in setting group goals used as the basis for paying bonuses. And, as discussed in Chapter 8, when organizations explain their reward structures to employees, the communication can enhance employees' satisfaction and belief that the system is fair.

Managing Voluntary and Involuntary Turnover

Along with surveys, more organizations are analyzing basic HR data to look for patterns in employee retention and turnover. Organizations must try to ensure that good performers want to stay with the organization and that employees whose performance is chronically low are encouraged—or forced, to leave. Both of these challenges involve *employee turnover,* that is, employees leaving the organization. When the organization initiates the turnover (often with employees who would prefer to stay), the result is **involuntary turnover**. Examples include terminating an employee for under-performance or laying off employees during a downturn. Most organizations use the word "termination" to refer only to a discharge related to a discipline problem, but some organizations call any involuntary turnover a termination. When the employees initiate the turnover (often when the organization would prefer to keep them), it is **voluntary turnover**. For example, employees may leave to go back to school, travel, take a job with a different organization, or start their own business.

involuntary turnover Turnover initiated by an employer (often with employees who would prefer to stay).

voluntary turnover Turnover initiated by employees (often when the organization would prefer to keep them).

In general, organizations try to avoid the need for involuntary turnover and to minimize voluntary turnover, especially among top performers; however, employers are not always aware of the reasons employees would change jobs. Table 11.4 identifies the five key reasons top performers in Canadian organizations would change jobs; however, these reasons contrast with the five key reasons employers *think* their top performers would leave.

TABLE 11.4

Employers Are Not Always Aware of the Reasons Top Performers Would Change Jobs

Why Would Top Performers Leave?		
Rank	**Employers Say**	**Employees Say**
1	Career development opportunities	Work-related stress
2	Promotion opportunities	Promotion opportunities
3	Relationship with supervisor	Base pay
4	Base pay	Trust/confidence in management
5	Work-related stress	Job security

Note: Rank represents the frequency the item was selected as one of the most important reasons (from a list of 23 items) top performers would leave an organization; Top performers are those whose performance was rated "far exceeds expectations" (i.e., in the top 10 percent) by their supervisors in their most recent performance review.

Source: "Leading Through Uncertain Times, The 2011/2012 Talent Management and Rewards Study: North America," Willis Towers Watson, p. 8, www.willistowerswatson.com. Reprinted with the permission of Willis Towers Watson.

Figure 11.9 shows how voluntary turnover has stabilized in recent years, at a level well below the rate for some past years (e.g., 9.7 percent for 2007–08). Voluntary turnover was much higher in the private sector (8.0 percent) than the public sector (4.4 percent) in 2016–17. Similarly, involuntary turnover was much higher in the private sector (5.3 percent) in contrast to the public sector (1.8 percent) in 2016–17.[54]

Both kinds of turnover are costly, as summarized in Table 11.5. Replacing workers is expensive, and new employees need time to learn their jobs and build teamwork skills.[55] Employees who leave voluntarily out of frustration may not be shy about generating unfavourable publicity. People who leave involuntarily are sometimes ready to take legal action against a former employer if they feel they were unfairly dismissed. The prospect of workplace violence also raises the risk associated with discharging employees. Effective human resource management can help the organization minimize both kinds of turnover,

No firm wants to lose valued high-performing employees, but often they do not know the employees are thinking about leaving until it's too late. A recent and extensive validation study across a number of different employee groups identified behaviours (that differ from the employees' usual behaviour) as signs that an employee may be thinking about leaving the organization. For example:[56]

- work productivity has decreased
- less willing to commit to long-term timeline
- expressed dissatisfaction with their current job more frequently
- expressed dissatisfaction with their supervisor more frequently
- left early from work more frequently
- shown less interest in working with customers

Effective human resource management also requires effectively supporting the departure of employee. *Employee offboarding* should be handled as carefully and positively as employee onboarding.

Despite a company's best efforts at selection, training, and compensation, some employees will fail to meet

TABLE 11.5

Costs Associated with Turnover

Involuntary Turnover	Voluntary Turnover
Recruiting, selecting, and training replacements	Recruiting, selecting, and training replacements
Lost productivity	Lost productivity
Lawsuits	Loss of talented employees
Workplace violence	

FIGURE 11.9

Voluntary Turnover Rates (average percentage of employees)

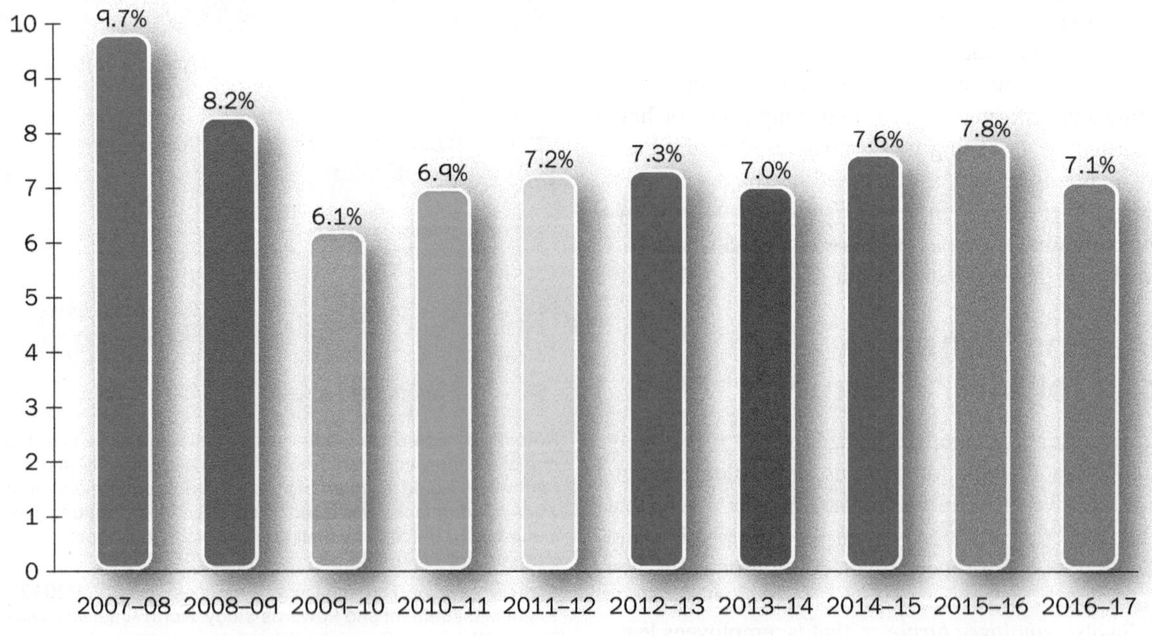

Note: Voluntary turnover applies to regular employees only, and does not include early retirements or severances.

Source: Heather McAteer, "Compensation Planning Outlook 2018," The Conference Board of Canada, October 2017, p. 27.

expectations, be uncoachable, or violate company policies. When this happens, organizations need to apply a discipline program that might ultimately lead to discharging the individual.

For a number of reasons, discharging employees can be a very difficult but potentially important way to maintain a high-performance and engaging work culture. The decision also has legal aspects that can affect the organization. Historically, if the organization and employee do not have a specific employment contract, the employer or employee may end the employment relationship at any time. This is the *employment-at-will doctrine.* This doctrine has eroded significantly, however. Employees who have been terminated sometimes sue their employers for wrongful dismissal, and in such cases the courts may award employees significant financial settlements. Publicity associated with the proceedings may also be embarrassing or harmful to the employer's reputation. Along with the financial risks of dismissing an employee, there are issues of personal safety. Distressing as it is that some former employees go to the courts, far worse are the employees who react to a termination decision with violence. Although any number of organizational actions or decisions may incite violence among employees, the "nothing else to lose" aspect of an employee's dismissal makes the situation dangerous, especially when the nature of the work adds other risk factors.[57]

Retaining top performers is not always easy either, and recent trends have made this more difficult than ever. Today's psychological contract, in which workers feel responsibility for their own careers rather than loyalty to a particular employer, makes voluntary turnover more likely. Also, competing organizations are constantly looking at each other's top performers. For high-demand positions, such as software engineers, "poaching talent" from other companies has become the norm.

Employment/labour standards laws in each of the federal, provincial, and territorial jurisdictions set out the minimum requirements employers must follow when terminating or laying off employees. For example, no notice or compensation is legally needed if the employee quit or retired, the employee had been employed for less than the required minimum (usually three months), the employee was employed on an "on-call" basis, or the employee was terminated for *just cause.* Examples of "just cause" for dismissal that are considered serious violations of the employment relationship are dishonesty, willful disobedience to a supervisor, and failure to comply with known policies or procedures or to meet performance requirements.[58]

Because of the critical financial and personal risks associated with employee dismissal, organizations must adopt a standardized, systematic approach to discipline and discharge. These decisions should not be left solely to the discretion of individual managers or supervisors. The precedent-setting Supreme Court case of *Wallace v. United Grain Growers* (1997) sent a clear message that employers must act fairly and respectfully when handling an employee termination. The *Wallace* case gave judges a legal precedent to award employees additional notice or damages if the employer treats an employee callously or unfairly during termination. In summary, policies that can lead to employee separation should be based on not only the legal requirements but also on principles of justice to ensure the system is seen as fair. Figure 11.10 summarizes these principles of justice. For example, in support

FIGURE 11.10

Principles of Justice

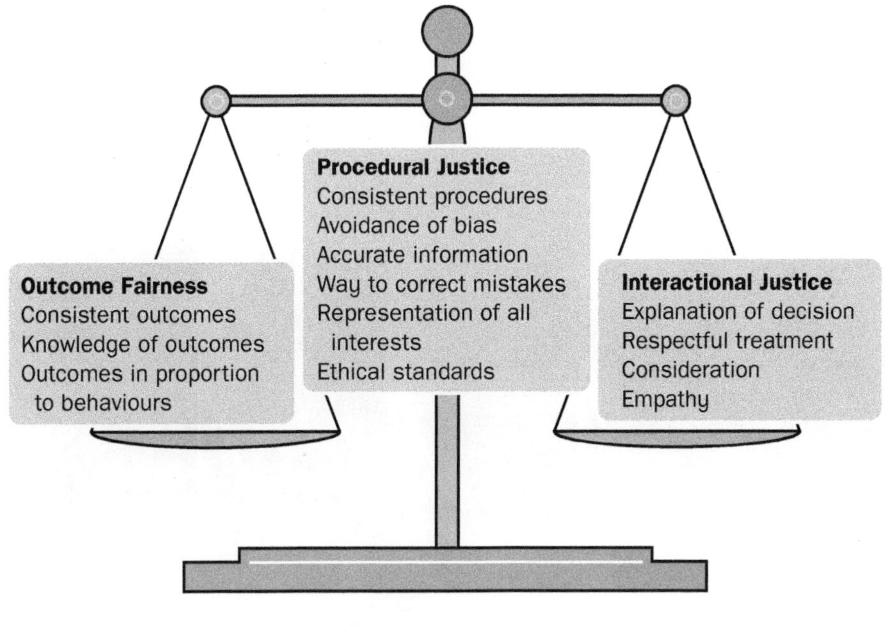

of these principles, many organizations provide **outplacement counselling**, which tries to help dismissed employees manage the transition from one job to another. Some organizations have their own staff for conducting outplacement counselling. Other organizations have contracts with outside providers to help with individual cases. Either way, the goals for outplacement programs are to help the former employee address the psychological issues associated with losing a job—grief, depression, and fear in a respectful manner—while at the same time helping the person find a new job.

outplacement counselling A service in which professionals try to help dismissed employees manage the transition from one job to another.

Handling Employee Discipline Appropriately

In order to maintain a positive, motivating, and high-performance work environment for all employees, organizations look for methods of handling inappropriate behaviour that are fair, legal, and effective.

The principles of justice suggest that the organization prepare by establishing a formal discipline process in which the consequences become more serious if the employee repeats the offence. Such a system is called **progressive discipline**. A typical progressive discipline system identifies and communicates inappropriate behaviours and responds to a series of offences with the actions shown in Figure 11.11—spoken and then written warnings, temporary suspension, and, finally, termination. This process fulfills the purpose of discipline by clarifying what is expected of employees and creating a situation in which employees must try to do what is expected. It seeks to prevent inappropriate behaviour (by publishing rules) and to correct, rather than merely punish, inappropriate behaviour.

progressive discipline A formal discipline process in which the consequences become more serious if the employee repeats the offence.

Such procedures may seem exasperatingly slow, especially when the employee's behaviour harms the team's performance. In the end, however, if an employee must be discharged, careful use of the procedure increases other employees' belief that the organization is fair and reduces the likelihood that the employee will take legal action. For situations in which inappropriate behaviour is dangerous, the organization may establish a stricter policy, even terminating an employee for the first offence. In that case, it is especially important to communicate the procedure—not only to ensure fairness, but also to prevent the inappropriate or even dangerous behaviour.

Creating a formal discipline process is a primary responsibility of the human resource department. The HR professional should consult with supervisors and managers to identify inappropriate behaviours and establish rules and consequences for violating the rules. The rules should cover disciplinary problems such as the following behaviours encountered in many organizations:

- absenteeism
- lateness
- unsafe work practices
- poor quantity or quality of work
- harassment of co-workers or customers
- theft or misuse of company property

For each infraction, the HR professional would identify a series of responses, such as those in Figure 11.11. In addition, the organization must communicate these rules and consequences to every employee. Ways of publishing rules include presenting them in an employee handbook, posting them on the company's intranet, and displaying them on a bulletin board. Supervisors should be familiar with the rules, so that they can discuss them with employees and apply them consistently.

FIGURE 11.11

Progressive Discipline Responses

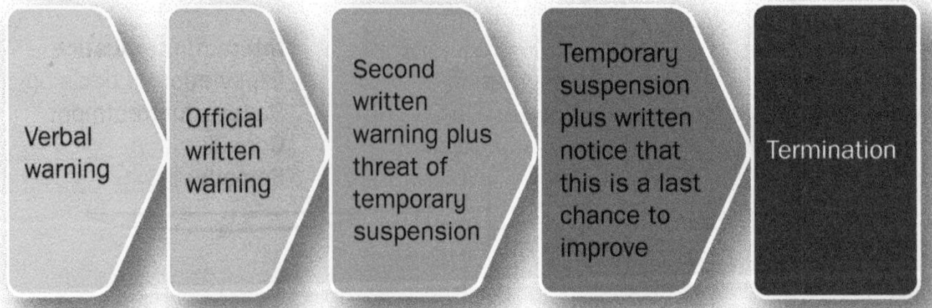

Along with rules and a progression of consequences for violating the rules, a progressive discipline system should have requirements for documenting the rules, offences, and responses. To ensure fairness, the discipline system should provide an opportunity to hear every point of view and to correct errors. Before discussing and filing records of misbehaviour, it is important for the supervisor to investigate the incident. The employee should be made aware of what they are said to have done wrong and should have an opportunity to present their version of events. A method of gathering objective performance data should be used to support the fairness and objectivity of the discipline system.

For example, a waste management company in Edmonton demonstrated the use of progressive discipline that ultimately led to dismissing an employee. The employee was disciplined four times for various infractions—he received a verbal warning for damaging a trailer during loading, a written warning for damaging a structure while backing up a loader, a one-day suspension for neglecting to perform a pre-trip inspection of his vehicle, and a three-day suspension for insubordination. Following these incidents, he was dismissed when a dashboard camera detected he was using a cellphone while driving, a violation of company policy and a violation of Alberta legislation.[59]

Besides developing these policies, HR professionals have a role in carrying out progressive discipline.[60] In meetings to communicate disciplinary actions, it is wise to have an HR representative there to support the employee's supervisor. When an employee is suspended or terminated, the organization should designate a person to escort the employee from the building to protect the organization's people and property.

Finally, the issue of off-the-job behaviour is also of concern to employers. Employers are frequently concerned if an employee's off-the-job behaviour, including social media activity, might affect the organization's business or reputation in some way.

LO3 Effectiveness and Impact of Human Resource Management

In recent years, human resource management at many organizations has been taking a customer-oriented approach. For an organization's human resource division, "customers" are the organization as a whole and its other divisions. They are customers of HRM because they depend on HRM to provide a variety of services that result in a supply of talented, motivated employees. Taking this customer-oriented approach, human resource management defines its customer groups (e.g., managers and employees), customer needs (e.g., committed and competent employees), and the HR strategies and activities required to meet those needs (e.g., training, learning, and development).

As shown in Figure 11.7, an HR measurement framework is likely to include a range of measures and metrics from *activity* (lowest level) to *impact* (highest level).

Human Resource Management Audits

HRM audit
A formal review of the outcomes of HRM functions, based on identifying key HRM functions and measures of organizational performance.

An **HRM audit** is a formal review of the outcomes of HRM functions, based on identifying key HRM functions and the measures and metrics associated with

TABLE 11.6

Four Levels of HR Measures and Metrics

Level	What is Measured?	Examples
Activity	Activities performed	• Number of new hires • Number of requests received/handled
Efficiency	Productivity of HR	• Cost per learning hour • Number of HR employees/100 employees
Effectiveness	HR activity results	• Cost per hire • Time to fill vacancies
Impact	Results of the HR activity on the organization's performance	• Profit, customer experience, quality or other overall organizational performance measure

Source: Based on: Jane Cooper and Shannon Jackson, "Talent Management Benchmarking: Human Resources Trends and Metrics, Fourth Edition," February 2017, *The Conference Board of Canada*, p. 26.

organizational performance. To conduct the audit, the HR department identifies key functions and the key measures of organizational performance adapted to the particular needs and analytical capacity of the the organization.[61]

Table 11.7 lists examples of these measures and metrics for a variety of HRM functions: staffing, rewards (compensation), benefits, training, appraisal and development, and overall effectiveness. The audit may also look at any other measure or metric associated with successful management of human resources; for instance, compliance with employment-related legislation, succession planning, maintaining a safe workplace, and positive labour relations. When HR functions are outsourced, these audits need to look at both HR functions performed internally and those that are outsourced.

TABLE 11.7

Sample Key Measures and Metrics of Success for an HRM Audit

Business Indicators	Customer Satisfaction Measures
Staffing	
Average days taken to fill open requisitions	Anticipation of human resource needs
Ratio of acceptances to offers made	Timeliness of referring qualified workers to line supervisors
Ratio of employment equity target group applicant representation in local labour market	Candidate experience feedback
Per capita requirement costs	Skill in handling terminations
Average years of experience/education of hires	Adaptability to changing labour market conditions
Compensation	
Per capita (average) merit increases	Fairness of existing job evaluation system
Ratio of recommendations for reclassification to number of employees	Competitiveness in local labour market
Percentage of overtime hours to regular time	Relationship between pay and performance
Ratio of average salary offers to average salary in community	Employee satisfaction with pay
Benefits	
Average workers' compensation payments	Promptness in handling claims
Benefit cost per payroll dollar	Fairness and consistency in the application of benefit policies
Percentage of sick leave to total pay	Communication of benefits to employees
	Assistance provided to managers in reducing potential for unnecessary claims
Training	
Percentage of employees participating in training programs	Extent to which training programs meet the needs of employees and the company
Percentage of employees receiving tuition reimbursement	Communication to employees about available training opportunities
Training dollars/days per employee	Quality of programs

Business Indicators	Customer Satisfaction Measures
Employee Appraisal and Development	
Distribution of performance appraisal ratings	Assistance in identifying management potential
Appropriate psychometric properties of appraisal forms	Organizational development activities provided by HRM department
Overall Effectiveness or Impact	
Ratio of human resources staff to employee population	Accuracy and clarity of information provided to managers and employees
Turnover rate	Competence and expertise of staff
Absenteeism rate	Working relationship between organizations and HRM department
Ratio of per capita revenues to per capita cost	
Net income per employee	

Source: Reprinted with permission. Excerpts from Chapter 15, "Evaluating Human Resource Effectiveness," pp. 187–222, by Anne S. Tsui and Luis R. Gomez-Mejia, from Human Resource Management: Evolving Roles and Responsibilities, edited by Lee Dyer. Copyright © 1988 by The Bureau of National Affairs, Inc., Washington, DC, 20037.

After identifying performance measures and metrics for the HRM audit, the staff carries out the audit by gathering information. The information for the key business indicators is usually available in the organization's documents. Sometimes the HR department has to create new documents for gathering specific types of data. The usual way to measure customer satisfaction is to conduct surveys. Employee surveys provide information about the satisfaction of these internal customers. Many organizations conduct surveys of top executives to get a better view of how HRM practices affect the organization's business success. Companies also may invite external auditing teams to audit specific HR functions. Of course, the benefits of the audit are only as great as the company's response to what it learns and applies to enhance existing processes and tools.

Analyzing the Effect and Impact of HRM Programs

Measuring HRM effectiveness and impact requires the use of a variety of HR integrated measures and metrics. This process involves measuring a program's success in terms of whether it achieved its objectives and whether it delivered value in an economic sense. For example, if the organization sets up a training program, it should set up goals for that program, such as the training's effect on learning, behaviour, and performance improvement (results). The analysis would then measure whether the training program achieved the preset goals.

The analysis can take an economic approach that measures the dollar value of the program's costs and benefits. Successful programs should deliver value that is greater than the program's cost. Costs include employees' compensation as well as the costs to deliver HR programs such as training, employee development, or satisfaction surveys. Benefits could include a reduction in the costs associated with employee absenteeism and turnover, as well as improved productivity associated with better selection and training programs. However, caution about calculating the value of human capital is needed. "Accounting deals principally with fixed assets. Once you buy them, all they do is depreciate over time," says Jac Fitz-enz, the founder of Human Capital Source Inc. "But humans are just the opposite: they appreciate over time as they grow and develop."[62]

In general, HR departments should be able to improve their performance through some combination of greater efficiency and greater impact. Greater efficiency means the HR department uses fewer and less-costly resources to perform its functions. Greater impact means that what the HR department does—for example, selecting employees or setting up a performance feedback system—has a more beneficial effect on employees' and the organization's performance. The computing power available to today's organizations, coupled with people who have skills in *people (human capital) analytics,* discussed in Chapter 1, enables companies to find more ways than ever to identify practices associated with greater efficiency and effectiveness. For example, an accounting firm improved its retention of female employees by applying analytics. The data showed not only the percentages of women in its jobs, but also that women were much likelier to leave around the point they had been with the firm for about five years.

That jump in turnover was consistent across locations and specialities. The analytics team studied patterns in employees' life events (such as getting married), as well as the association of turnover with company actions such as providing mentors or offering flexible work arrangements. By applying the analysis, the accounting firm improved retention of women and brought its workforce closer to the firm's goal of reflecting the diversity of the clients it serves.[63]

HRM's potential to affect employees' well-being and the organization's performance makes human resource management an exciting and rewarding field. As we have shown throughout the book, every HRM function calls for decisions that have the potential to help individuals and organizations achieve their goals. For HR professionals to fulfill that potential, they must ensure that their decisions are well grounded. As discussed in Chapter 1, evidence-based HRM requires leveraging credible internal and external data including the use of people (human capital) analytics, to guide leaders in developing and implementing long- and short-term strategies to address human capital challenges and opportunities. Leaders have a considerable appetite for data from HR.[64] The field of human resource management provides tremendous opportunity to future researchers and managers who want to make a difference in many people's lives and contribute to the success of organizations.

LO4 Improving HRM Effectiveness and Impact through Technology

Several current and emerging technologies can help improve the effectiveness of the HRM function. "New" technologies are current applications of knowledge, procedures, and equipment that have not been used previously. New technology usually involves automation—that is, replacing human labour with information processing or equipment, and/or artificial intelligence that simulates human thinking.

Human Resource Management Online: E-HRM

As organizations have seen the advantages of sharing information in computer networks, and the Internet has linked people around the globe, more and more organizations are engaging in *e-HRM,* providing HR-related information over the Internet. Because much human resource information is confidential, organizations may do this with an *intranet,* which uses Internet technology but allows access only to authorized users (such as the organization's employees). For HR professionals, the Internet also offers a way to research new developments, post job openings, collaborate with colleagues in other organizations, and obtain information from credible sources external to the organization. In this way, E-HRM combines company-specific information on a secure intranet with links to the resources on the broader Internet.

Since the mid-1990s, as HRM functions sought to play a more strategic role in their organizations, the first task was to eliminate transactional tasks in order to free up time to focus on traditional and transformational activities. Part of building an effective HR function requires moving much of the transactional work away from being done by HR employees so that they can have time available to work on strategic activities. Consequently, the use of technology can make HR more strategic and, by doing so, increase the value that HR adds to the business.[65]

Outsourcing some of these activities provided one mechanism for reducing this burden. However, more relevant today is the focus on the use of information technology to handle these tasks. Early on this was achieved by the development and implementation of information systems that were run by the HRM function but more recently have evolved into systems that allow employees to serve themselves. For example, employees can make their benefit enrolment, changes, or claims online. A recent survey by the Sierra-Cedar software and consulting firm found that employees reported better experience with HR when self-service was an option, and better yet when self-service was available on their mobile device.[66]

As Internet use has increasingly taken the form of social platforms, e-HRM has moved in this direction as well. For example, social platforms can be used for learning and to access job search tools. The chapter-ending HRM Social Case Study explores Google's internal platform called "Grow," which makes it easy for Googlers to find learning opportunities, jobs, one-on-one advice, and other development resources to suit their needs and interests.

HRM Information Systems

In HRM, technology has already been used for three broad functions: transaction processing; decision support systems; and expert systems.[67]

Transaction processing refers to computations and calculations used to review and document HRM decisions and practices. This includes documenting relocation, training expenses, and course enrolments and completing external reporting requirements (employment equity reports). **Decision support systems**

transaction processing
Computations and calculations used to review and document HRM decisions and practices.

decision support systems
Computer software systems designed to help solve problems by showing how results vary when the assumptions and data are altered.

HR How-To

HR Services Go Mobile

Software companies are creating apps that let employees view their pay stubs, request time off, check the amounts of their bonuses, fill out and approve timesheets, look up co-workers in company directories, and more. At the same time, a growing number of employees expect to be able to use their mobile devices for accessing work-related information. Given the possibility of and pressure for mobile HRM, here are some guidelines for making it work:

- Learn which mobile devices employees are using. Make sure applications will run properly on all devices.
- Set priorities for introducing mobile applications that support your company's strategy.
- Make sure your company has mobile-friendly version of its careers website. Many of today's job hunters are looking for leads on their mobile devices, and they expect to be able to submit an application that way.
- If your company uses online training, create versions that run well on mobile devices.
- Select vendors that not only have software for existing mobile devices but also will be flexible as hardware changes.
- Investigate the security protection built into any app you are considering.
- Test mobile HRM apps to be sure they are user-friendly. Sophisticated users of mobile devices expect to get content in small, easily digested bites.

Sources: Gary Beach, "Onboarding the Always-On Generation," *The Wall Street Journal,* January 20, 2016; http://blogs.wsj.com; Pat Galagan, "Trends and Tides in Talent Development," *TD Magazine,* October 8, 2015, https://www.td.org; Dave Zielinski, "The Mobilization of HR Tech," *HR Magazine,* February 204, Business Insights: Global, http://bi.galegroup.com; Tom Keebler, "New Considerations for HR Service Delivery Success: Where to Begin?," *Workforce Solutions Review.* December 2013, pp. 17-19.

are designed to help solve problems. They usually include a "what if" feature that allows users to see how outcomes change when assumptions or data change. These systems are useful, for example, for helping companies determine the number of new hires needed based on different turnover rates or the availability of employees with a certain skill in the labour market. **Expert systems** are computer systems incorporating the decision rules of people deemed to have expertise in a certain area. The system recommends actions that the user can take based on the information provided by the user. The recommended actions are those that a human expert would take in a similar situation. For example, an expert system could guide an interviewer during the selection process. Some organizations use expert systems to help employees decide how to allocate their benefits choices among a set of options, and help team leads schedule labour to complete projects (such as guiding a manager interviewing a job candidate). An expert system helps avoid the errors than can result from fatigue and decision-making biases, such as biases in appraising employee performance. An expert system can increase efficiency by enabling fewer or less-skilled employees to do work that otherwise would require many highly skilled employees. These technologies may be linked to employees through a network such as an intranet.

expert systems
Computer systems incorporating the decision rules of people deemed to have expertise in a certain area.

Predictive Analytics

The more recent use of technology and data has been in the area of *predictive analytics.* Predictive analytics refers to the use of data to make predictions about actions or outcomes in the future. Earlier in the chapter we discussed how HR functions can analytically evaluate their performance through either tracking certain measures and metrics or surveying internal customers. *Lagging indicators* tend to be descriptive and rely on a single source of data, which looks at the past. Although such a backward-looking approach can help the function to pinpoint areas for improvement, more recent effort has been devoted to trying to identify problems before they happen. In contrast to lagging indicators, *leading indicators* tend to rely on multiple data sources with a view to the future and predictive capability. For example, looking at data to identify indicators that an employee is about to leave would be helpful for organizations if they want to intervene. For instance, a company may find that a strong predictor of an employee's desire to leave is when the employee begins to update their LinkedIn profile. Google has developed sophisticated algorithms looking at a number of variables and uses these algorithms to identify which employees are likely to leave.

Personalization

Finally, the vast increases in technological capability and data have a number of companies looking to better customize or *personalize* an employee's experience with the organization. In the past, many companies introduced flexible benefit plans that encouraged employees to choose at least some of the benefits they most desired. However, today some firms enable employees to personalize their pay mix (e.g., take lesser or greater amounts of fixed versus variable pay, or vary the type of variable pay such as bonuses versus stock). Also, companies can proactively approach employees who may want to think about changing benefits based on changes in life events e.g, when an employee adds a child as a beneficiary, the company can suggest putting money into life insurance or into an educational savings account. In all these cases, companies are not forcing changes onto employees but rather are using the information they have about employees to help those employees better manage their work and personal lives.

LO5 The Future for HR Professionals

The future for careers in the human resource profession is bright. An increasing number of successful companies have made the top HR job a member of the senior management team, reporting directly to the chief executive officer. CEOs recognize the importance of their workforce in driving competitive success. Firms need to seek the balance between attracting, motivating, and retaining the very best talent and keeping labour and administrative costs as low as possible. Finding such a balance requires HR leaders who have a deep knowledge of the business combined with a deep knowledge of HR issues, tools, processes, and technologies.

For a reader who is just getting a first glimpse of the HRM function, to portray what a vastly different role HRM must play today compared to 20 or even 10 years ago is challenging. HRM once played a largely administrative role—simply processing paperwork as well as developing and administering hiring, training, appraisal, compensation, and benefits systems—and all of this was largely unrelated to the strategic direction of the firm. In the early 1980s, HRM took on more of a one-way linkage role, helping to implement strategy. Now strategic decision makers are realizing the importance of people issues and so are calling for HRM to become the "source of people expertise" in the firm.[68] Dr. Parbudyal Singh, professor of human resource management at York University, recently received the Distinguished Human Resources Professional Award (DHRP) from Ontario's Human Resources Professionals Association (HRPA) and summarized this transformation: "When I started, the focus was on the administrative and enforcement side of HR, but now it's become increasingly more strategic."[69]

This transformation requires that HR professionals possess and use knowledge of how people can and do play a role in competitive advantage as well as the policies, programs, and practices that can leverage the firm's people as a source of competitive advantage. This leads to an entirely new set of competencies for today's strategic HR professional.[70] HR professionals will need four basic competencies:[71]

- **Business competence**—HR professionals must know the company's business and understand its financial capacity. Because in almost all organizations the effectiveness of decisions must be evaluated in terms of dollar values, the HR professional must be able to calculate the costs and benefits of each alternative in terms of its return on investment. In addition, the non-monetary impact needs to be considered. HR professionals must be fully capable of identifying the social and ethical issues attached to HRM practices. HR professionals must often act as the conscience of the organization in all aspects; for example, promoting the perspective that "treating people well is the right thing to do even if there is cost involved."[72]
- **Professional–technical knowledge**—HR professionals must be aware of state-of-the-art HRM practices in areas such as staffing, development, performance feedback, rewards, organizational design, and communication. HR professionals must be able to critically evaluate the new techniques offered as state-of-the-art HRM programs and use only those that provide value.
- **Management of change processes**—HR professionals must be skilled in diagnosing opportunities and problems, implementing organizational changes, and evaluating results. In one survey of Fortune 500 companies, it was found that 87 percent of the companies had their organization development or change management function as part of the HR department.[73]
- **Integration competence**—HR professionals must be able to integrate the three other competencies to increase the company's value. This means that although specialist knowledge is necessary, a generalist perspective must be taken in making decisions. This entails seeing how all the functions within the HRM fit together to be effective and

recognizing that changes in any one part of the HRM are likely to require changes in other HR areas.

Google has sought to achieve this integration in its People Operations team with what it calls the "three-thirds" staffing model:

1. **One-third traditional HR people**—subject-matter experts in HR areas such as compensation and benefits, recruiting, and employment law as well as expertise in client relations. Their knowledge, pattern recognition, and emotional intelligence serve as the foundation for developing services and programs.
2. **One-third consultants**—high-end strategy experts who lack human resource experience but have a background in management consulting and thrive on solving big problems and bring a deliberate, business approach to people issues.
3. **One-third analytics professionals**—doctoral-level academics in disciplines including statistics, organizational psychology, and finance who measure, analyze, and provide insight into all that the people operations function does, and prove what really works. They have a healthy appetite for the impossible and drive experimentation to ensure that Google is as innovative on the people side as it is on the product side.[74]

The Role of the Chief Human Resources Officer

Having discussed the increasing importance of HR and the new strategic role of HR professionals, in closing we briefly examine the role of the leader of the HR function. These chief human resources officers (CHROs) have accountability for leading the HR function as well as ensuring that HR systems and processes deliver value to the company. Only recently have researchers attempted to examine what these HR leaders do and how they affect the business. Table 11.8 identifies results of a recent survey that identified seven roles that CHROs fulfill and the time spent across those roles.

The new strategic role for HRM presents both opportunities and challenges. HRM has the chance to profoundly impact the way organizations compete through people. But with this opportunity comes substantial responsibility and accountability.[75]

HRM functions of the future require individuals who view themselves as business people who happen to work in an HRM function, rather than as HRM people who happen to work in a business.

TABLE 11.8

Seven Critical Roles of the CHRO

Role	Description	Time Spent
Leader of the HR function	Working with HR team members regarding the development, design, and delivery of HR services.	22%
Strategic advisor to the executive team	Activities focused specifically on the formulation and implementation of the firm's strategy.	21%
Talent architect	Keeping the senior team focused on the talent needs of the business including identifying talent gaps and future needs.	17%
Counsellor/confidante/coach to the executive team	Activities focused on counselling or coaching team members or resolving interpersonal or political conflicts among team members.	17%
Liaison to the board of directors	Preparation for board meetings, phone calls with board members, attendance at board meetings.	10%
Workforce sensor	Activities focused on identifying workforce morale issues and opportunities.	8%
Representative of the firm	Activities with external stakeholders, such as advocating, speaking to outside groups, etc.	5%

Source: P. Wright, "Strategies and Challenges of the Chief Human Resource Officer: Results of the First Annual Cornell/CAHRS Survey of CHROs," *Technical Report* (Ithaca, NY: Cornell University), 2009.

Thinking ETHICALLY

How Should Employers Protect Their Data on Employee Devices?

One area in which business managers might consult with HR managers involves the treatment of company data on employees' electronic devices. In the past, organizations stored their data on their own hardware. But laptop computers and, more recently, tablet computers and smartphones make it possible for employees to carry around data on these mobile devices. Increasingly often, the devices are not even owned by the company, but by the employees themselves. For example, an employee's smartphone might include business as well as personal contacts in several mobile apps.

The situation is convenient for everyone until something goes wrong: a device is lost, an employee becomes upset with a manager, or the organization lays off some workers. From the standpoint of protecting data, the obvious solution is to remove the data from the devices. So far, no law forbids this. However, it has consequences for the employees. Remotely wiping data from a device will remove all of it, including the user's personal data, such as photos and addresses.

Companies are addressing concerns by crafting security policies for employees who want to use their own devices for work-related tasks such as e-mail. Typically the policy requires the employee to download a program for mobile device management. If specified conditions arise, such as loss of the device or termination of the employee, the company can use the software to send the device a message that wipes out all the data stored on the device. The company also can give the employee some notice, allowing time to save personal data, but this increases the risk to the company. Some employees have complained about their devices being unexpectedly erased after they left a company. At the same time, companies are ever more concerned about protecting their data as more and more of them experience outsiders gaining unauthorized access to their data.

Questions

1. Imagine you work in the HR department of a company considering a policy to protect its data on employees' mobile devices. In advising on this policy, what rights should you consider?
2. What advice would you give or actions would you take to ensure that the policy is administered fairly and equitably?

Sources: Scott Wooldridge, "HR Trends to Watch in 2016," *Benefits Selling,* December 2015, http://www.benefitspro.com; "Using Your Personal Phone for Work Could Cost You," *CBS Miami,* March 26, 2014, http://miami.cbslocal.com; Lauren Weber, "BYOD? Leaving a Job Can Mean Losing Pictures of Grandma," *Wall Street Journal,* January 21, 2014, http://online.wsj.com; Society for Human Resource Management, "Safety and Security Technology: Can an Employer Remotely Wipe/Brick an Employee's Personal Cell Phone?," SHRM Knowledge Center, November 5, 2013, http://www.shrm.org.

SUMMARY

LO1 Define high-performance work systems and identify the elements, outcomes, and conditions associated with such a system.

A high-performance work system is the right combination of people, technology, and organizational structure that makes full use of the organization's resources and opportunities in achieving its goals. A high-performance work system achieves the organization's goals, typically including greater productivity, higher profits, and lower turnover. Enhancing employee experience and its associated conditions contribute to high-performance work systems.

LO2 Explain how human resource management can contribute to high performance.

All areas of human resource management—for example, job analysis and design; recruitment and selection; training, learning, and development; performance management; and rewards—make specific contributions to organizational high performance. Generally, organizations try to avoid the need for involuntary turnover and minimize voluntary turnover. Organizations also need to handle employee discipline effectively in order to demonstrate fairness and meet legal requirements.

LO3 Summarize ways to measure the effectiveness and impact of human resource management.

Taking a customer-oriented approach, HRM can use an HRM audit, a formal review of the outcomes of HRM functions. The audit may look at any measure or metric associated with successful management of human resources. Audit information may come from the organization's documents and surveys of customer satisfaction. People (human capital) analytics are increasingly deployed in organizations exhibiting data curiosity and capacity.

LO4 Describe how technology can be used to improve the effectiveness and impact of human resource management.

Current and emerging technologies can be used to improve HRM effectiveness. E-HRM, outsourcing, mobile applications, and social platforms provide opportunities to reduce transactional demands on human resource professionals. HR information systems are already used for transaction processing, decision support systems, and expert systems. In addition, predictive analytics and customizing employees' experience offer significant opportunities to increase HRM effectiveness.

LO5 Discuss the future for human resources professionals and the role of the chief human resources officer (CHRO).

The future for careers in the human resource profession is bright as the nature of HRM has transformed in many organizations. HRM and the associated competencies have significantly changed to acquire strategic significance. The role of chief human resources officer (CHRO) has significant associated accountability and organizational influence. HRM requires practitioners who have a business mindset.

CRITICAL THINKING QUESTIONS

1. What is a high-performance work system? What are its elements? Which of these elements involve human resource management?
2. Is Net Promoter Score an appropriate way to assess employee experience? Why or why not?
3. Summarize how each of the following HR functions can contribute to high performance.
   a. Job design
   b. Recruitment and selection
   c. Training, learning, and development
   d. Performance management
   e. Compensation and rewards
4. Is it more important for an HR department to be efficient or effective? Discuss.
5. Why should HR departments measure their effectiveness? What are some ways they can go about measuring effectiveness?
6. How can HRM technology make a human resource department more productive? How can technology improve the quality of HRM decisions?
7. What is a real business (and human resource management) problem that could be solved with the use of predictive analytics?
8. What issues could arise when an organization frees up human resource professionals' time for strategic work by reducing their transactional work?
9. What types of specific skills (such as knowledge of financial accounting methods) do you think HR professionals will need in order to have the business, professional–technical, change management, and integrative competencies necessary in the future? How can these skills be developed?
10. Which seems more appealing—a career in HRM today or a career in HRM 20 years ago? Explain your answer.
11. Were any of "Seven Roles" of the chief human resource officer (CHRO) surprising or unexpected? Explain your answer.

EXPERIENCING HR—WHAT MAKES A COMPANY A GREAT PLACE TO WORK?

Divide into groups of about six students each. Visit the website for Canada's Top 100 Employers. Scan the complete list of companies, and then choose a company that interests your group. Click the link for the company information. Read the reasons for selecting this company as one of the best, and take notes on what you learn. Next, visit the Glassdoor website and use its search function to look up company information for the company you selected. On the company page, use the Reviews link to read the information employees have posted about what it is like to work at this company. Look for patterns, and take notes on what you learn.

As a group, discuss what these two sources tell you about the employee experience at the company you selected. What criteria does the Top 100 Employers list use for selecting organizations? What criteria do the reviewers on Glassdoor use for reporting their satisfaction or dissatisfaction? Imagine you work in HR at the company you evaluated. What would you do to build on areas of satisfaction and address any dissatisfaction you observe in the Glassdoor reviews? Be prepared to summarize your discussion in class (or, if your instructor directs, write a one-page summary of your discussion).

CASE STUDY: EVIDENCE-BASED HRM

Deere & Company (John Deere): Using Data to Accelerate HR Transformation

John Deere has worked hard to build capability in data analytics to become increasingly future oriented. For example, with the introduction of drones, HR needed to consider things like, How many people will be working with drones? Why would a candidate come to John Deere rather than another company like Amazon? What training is needed? How do we attract the best and most appropriate candidates? Using data, John Deere started hiring people in advance by creating a strategic internship program that would allow early recruits to fulfill the needed talent in such spaces. In proposing the internship program to senior management, HR applied analytics to examine how a select batch of recruits grew, how many were retained, how many became specialists, and how many became general leaders. The implications of people retiring were also considered, which led to a finding that hiring mid-career employees generally led to people retiring within 15 years of service. Based on this data, HR received immediate approval for the program.

Data analytics has also helped HR strengthen its skills in workforce planning and organizational design. Over the last six years, the company experienced a period of growth during which the business was hiring, and also a period of prolonged downturn. During this time, HR captured a large amount of data and, using analytics, was able to approach business leaders to jointly examine headcount and cost, as well as levers of control and layers of supervision. With the use of analytics, John Deere realized it had more managers than needed, with tighter spaces of control that may in turn, have a negative effect on employee engagement. These findings guided very challenging yet constructive conversations. While the numbers spoke for themselves, it was important for HR to build collaborative relationships and earn the respect of leaders through demonstrated understanding of the business.

HR has considered the extent to which practitioners need expertise in analytics and concluded that not every practitioner needs to be an expert. Practitioners do, however, need a degree of skill to tell a story to their internal customers based around analytics.

Questions

1. On the basis of the information provided in the case, is John Deere a high-performance organization? Why or why not?
2. Why is it important for HR professionals to be able to "tell a story" to their internal customers based around analytics?"

Source: Lyle Yorks, Amy Lui Abel, and Marion Devine, with April Bang and Sherlin Nair, (2017) "What's Next for 21st-Century HR? Continuous Strategic Transformation," *The Conference Board of Canada.*, pg. 36.

CASE STUDY: HRM SOCIAL

Google's "Grow" Employee Platform

In a world dominated by social media, companies such as Google are now using it for internal purposes. Google developed "Grow," an internal platform that makes it easy for Googlers to find learning opportunities, jobs, one-on-one advice, and other development resources to suit their needs and interests. Grow unifies myriad learning, development, and job search tools into a one-stop shop for Googlers to manage and act on their development. It suggests courses, opportunities, advisors, and more based on what the company knows about the Googler (e.g., role, level, location) and the data a Googler provides within the tool (e.g., skills they want to develop). Not surprisingly, given Google's search capability, this system allows employees to search for learning resources or jobs of interest.

Grow is an inherently social platform, and every Googler has a customizable profile that is visible to others. Googlers can tag skills they have (e.g., consulting, people management, and coaching) and those they want to develop (e.g., entrepreneurship and prioritization) in their profile. Skills listed in Grow help the system get to know the user and offer more personalized job recommendations. Googlers can also indicate if they would like to advise others on a particular skill. If an Google employee tags themself as a "Skill Advisor" on a topic (e.g., leadership), they will appear in Grow's search results, and other Googlers can view their skills and contact them for advice. The employee can select the option to "teach other Googlers," as well, which would connect them to Google's g2g (or "Googlers-to-Googlers") program, an internal volunteer teaching network that allows employees to teach their peers on a variety of subjects.

As mentioned earlier, Grow also allows Googlers to list skills they would like to develop. They can add up to 10 skills, and Grow will use these inputs to further customize their learning recommendations. To help Googlers get started, Grow suggests a number of skills (culled from a multi-year study of the skills that make Googlers effective in their roles). Employees' profiles also include their picture, job title, location, and a link to their internal employee page to help their fellow Googlers get to know them.

In sum, Grow profiles are a great way for Googlers to teach the tool about their skills and development areas, and get better learning and job recommendations in the process. It also helps Googlers connect with their peers as advisors, mentors, or internal teachers, in addition to providing a host of other learning and development resources.

Questions

1. On the basis of the information provided in the case, would the Grow platform enhance your employee experience if you were a Google employee? Why or why not?
2. What is your advice to enhance the value of the Grow platform to Google? To Googlers?

Source: Raymond A. Noe, John R. Hollenbeck, Barry Gerhart, and Patrick M. Wright, *Human Resource Management: Gaining a Competitive Advantage 11e* (2019), New York: McGraw-Hill Education.

Notes

CHAPTER 1

1. Shopify website, "We've Read a Lot of Cover Letters over the Years. Your Turn. We're Applying to You," June 22, 2018, http://www.shopify.ca/careers, accessed June 22, 2018.
2. Canada's Top 100 Employers (2018), http://www.canadastop100.com/national/, accessed June 11, 2018, and Craig Lord, "Shopify Ranks Third among Top Global Tech Employers: Survey, *Ottawa Business Journal,* October 27, 2017, http://www.obj.ca, accessed June 11, 2018.
3. "How Shopify Finds and Fosters Talent," *Workopolis,* January 29, 2018, https://www.hiring.workpolis.com, accessed June 22, 2018; C. Lord, "Shopify Ranks Third among Top Global Tech Employers: Survey, *Ottawa Business Journal,* October 27, 2017, http://www.obj.ca, accessed June 22, 2018; A. Bryant, "Tobi Lütke of Shopify: Powering a Team with a 'Trust Battery,'" *The New York Times,* April 22, 2016, http://www.nytimes.com, accessed June 22, 2018.
4. Janice Cooney and Allison Cowan, *Training and Development Outlook 2003: Canadian Organizations Continue to Under-Invest* (Ottawa: Conference Board of Canada, 2003), p. 1.
5. Ruth Wright, *The Strategic Value of People: Human Resource Trends and Metrics* (Ottawa: Conference Board of Canada, July 2006), p. i.
6. A. S. Tsui and L. R. Gomez-Mejia, "Evaluating Human Resource Effectiveness," in *Human Resource Management: Evolving Rules and Responsibilities,* ed. L. Dyer (Washington, DC: BNA Books, 1988), pp. 1187–227; M. A. Hitt, B. W. Keats, and S. M. DeMarie, "Navigating in the New Competitive Landscape: Building Strategic Flexibility and Competitive Advantage in the 21st Century," *Academy of Management Executive* 12, no. 4 (1998), pp. 22–42; J. T. Delaney and M. A. Huselid, "The Impact of Human Resource Management Practices on Perceptions of Organizational Performance," *Academy of Management Journal* 39 (1996), pp. 949–69.
7. Owen Parker, "It's the Journey That Matters: 2005 Strategic HR Transformation Study Tour Report 2006" (Ottawa: Conference Board of Canada, 2006), p. 1.
8. Ibid.
9. S. A. Snell and J. W. Dean, "Integrated Manufacturing and Human Resource Management: A Human Capital Perspective," *Academy of Management Journal* 35 (1992), pp. 467–504; M. A. Youndt, S. Snell, J. W. Dean Jr., and D. P. Lepak, "Human Resource Management, Manufacturing Strategy, and Firm Performance," *Academy of Management Journal* 39 (1996), pp. 836–66.
10. Charles Greer, *Strategic Human Resource Management,* 2nd ed. (New Jersey: Prentice-Hall, 2001), p. 1.
11. R. Vance, *Employee Engagement and Commitment* (Alexandria, VA: Society for Human Resource Management, 2006).
12. "2018 Trends in Global Employee Engagement," Aon, 2018, pp. 1–15.
13. Bloomberg BNA, "Bloomberg BNA Releases Annual Human Resources Benchmark Report," *PR Newswire,* October 21, 2015, http://www.prnewswire.com; Martin Berman-Gorvine, "Human Resources' 'Seat at the Table' Confined to Foot, BBNA Survey Finds," *HR Focus,* November 2015, pp. 1–4.
14. E. E. Lawler, "From Human Resource Management to Organizational Effectiveness," *Human Resource Management,* 44 (2005), pp. 165–69.
15. Lauren Wieber and Rachel Feintzeig, "Companies Say No to Having an HR Department," *The Wall Street Journal,* April 9, 2014, accessed from http://online.wsj.com.
16. "The Employee Experience Index, IBM Smarter Workforce & Globoforce," September 2016, p.3.
17. "Rewriting the Rules for the Digital Age: 2017 Deloitte Global Human Capital Trends," Deloitte University Press, 2017, p. 7; Melissa Campeau, "Emerging HR: The Biggest Trends in HR Now," *HR Professional,* December 2017, pp. 16–19.
18. W. Bunch, "The (Other) Airbnb Experience," *Human Resource Executive,* July/August 2016, pp. 14–16; J. Meister and K. Mulcahy, "The Future Workplace Experience," New York: McGraw-Hill, 2017.
19. Jane Cooper and Shannon Jackson, *Workforce Planning Practices in Canada: Human Resource Trends and Metrics Fourth Edition*, Ottawa: The Conference Board of Canada, 2017.
20. Ibid.
21. S. Greengard, "Building a Self-Service Culture That Works," *Workforce,* July 1998, pp. 60–64.
22. Joanne Sammer, "A Marriage of Necessity," *HR Magazine,* October 2011, pp. 58–62.
23. Mark Feffer, "HR Super-Heroes," *HR Magazine,* November 2015, pp. 31–37.
24. "25 Truths about Talent Management: Insights from the 2018 Talent Management Strategies Conference," The Conference Board, pp. 1–21; J. Ramirez, "The Anticipators," *Human Resource Executive,* May 2016, pp. 14–17; E. Frauenheim, "Numbers Game," *Workforce Magazine,* March 2011, pp. 20–21; P. Gallagher, "Rethinking HR," *Human Resource Executive,* September 2009, pp. 1, 13–23.
25. C. Fleck, "An Algorithm for Success," *HR Magazine,* June 2016, pp. 130–35.
26. "25 Truths about Talent Management: Insights from the 2018 Talent Management Strategies Conference," The Conference Board, pp. 1–21; J. Ramirez, "The Anticipators," *Human Resource Executive,* May 2016, pp. 14–17.
27. Wendy S. Becker, "Are You Leading a Socially Responsible and Sustainable Human Resource Function?" *People & Strategy,* March 2011, pp. 18–23.
28. "Organizational Agility: What It Is, What It Is Not, and Why It Matters," August 2013, http://faculty.weatherhead.case.edu/jxs16/docs/ORGANIZATIONAL%20AGILITY_AOM_AUGUST_2013.pdf.
29. D. Rigby, J. Sutherland and A. Noble, "Agile at Scale," *Harvard Business Review,* May/June 2018, pp. 88–96; D. Rigby, J. Sutherland and H. Taleichi, "Embracing Agility," *Harvard Business Review,* May 2016, pp. 41–50.
30. P. Capelli and A. Tavis, "HR Goes Agile," *Harvard Business Review,* March/April 2018, pp. 47–52.
31. P. Capelli and A. Tavis, "HR Goes Agile," *Harvard Business Review,* March/April 2018, pp. 47–52.; Jeff Gothelf, "How HR Can Become Agile (and Why It Needs To)," *Harvard Business Review,* June 19, 2017, pp. 2–5, https://hbr.org/2017/06/how-hr-can-become-agile-and-why-it-needs-to, accessed June 24, 2018.

32. A. Arcand and M. Lefebvre, "Canada's Lagging Productivity: What If We Had Matched the U.S. Performance?" (Ottawa: Conference Board of Canada, November 2011), p. 1.
33. "BDC Study: Productivity Matters: Benchmarking Your Company to Up Your Game," Business Development Bank of Canada, October 2016, pp. 10–11.
34. Ibid, p. 14.
35. CMO Insights and Analysis from Deloitte, "Amazon's Grocery Industry Disruption, *Wall Street Journal,* October 17, 2017, http://deloitte.wsj.com/cmo/2017/10/17/amazons-grocery-industry-disruption/, accessed June 27, 2018.
36. "Employers Opening up to Non-traditional Employment," *Benefits Canada,* April 18, 2017, http://www.benefitscanada.ca, accessed June 23, 2018.
37. A. Sussman and J. Zumbrun, "'Gig' Economy Spreads Broadly," *Wall Street Journal,* March 26, 2016, pp. A1, A2; Bloomberg BNA, "The Gig Economy: HR's Role in Navigating the On-Demand Workforce," January 2016, https:www.bna.com/gig-economy-hrs-m57982067661/.
38. J. Wald, "The Benefits or Lack Therof of the 'Gig'," *Workforce,* August 2016, pp. 22–25.
39. Nick Horney, "The Gig Economy: A Disruptor Requiring HR Agility," *People + Strategy* 39 (Summer 2016), pp. 20–27.
40. Jean-Francois Potvin, "HR Outsourcing Is Gaining Ground," *Benefits Canada,* November 23, 2012, http://www.benefitscanada.com/news/hr-outsourcing-is-gaining-ground-570, accessed January 21, 2012.
41. Yum Brands, "Yum Restaurants China," http://www.yum.com; Laurie Burkitt, "Yum Bids to Regain Consumer Confidence in China with New Menu, "*Wall Street Journal,*" March 27, 2014, http://online.wsj.com; Caitlin Bowling, "China: The Key to Yum Brands' Bounce-Back Year," *Louisville Business First,* April 24, 2014, http://www.bizjournals.com/louisville; Reuters, "Yum Brands' China Restaurant Sales Improve, Shares Rise," April 22, 2014, http://www.reuters.com.
42. "Immigration and Ethnocultural Diversity in Canada," Statistics Canada, http://www12.statcan.gc.ca/nhs-enm/2011/as-sa/99-010-x/99-010-x2011001-eng.cfm, accessed January 7, 2015.
43. Ibid.
44. http://www.statcan.gc.ca/daily-quotidien/100309/dq100309a-eng.htm, accessed March 2, 2012.
45. "Human Resources Professionals Competency Framework," Human Resources Professionals Association (HRPA), 2014, p. 26, https://www.hrpa.ca, accessed June 19, 2018.
46. "Comparing HR Designations," HRPA, https://www.hrpa.ca/hrdesignations_/Pages/default.aspx, accessed June 19, 2018.
47. Gallup, "Honesty/Ethics in Professions," Gallup Historical Trends, updated December 2–6, 2015, http://www.gallup.com; Jeffrey M. Jones, "Record 64% Rate Honesty, Ethics of Members of Congress Low," Gallup, December 12, 2011, http://www.gallup.com; Corruption Currents, "Survey Sees Less Misconduct But More Reporting and Retaliation," *The Wall Street Journal,* January 5, 2012, blogs.wsj.com.
48. "Code of Ethics and Rules of Professional Conduct," Chartered Professionals in Human Resources in Canada, 2016, https://cphr.ca/wp-content/uploads/2017/01/2016-Code-of-Ethics-CPHR-2.pdf, accessed June 19, 2018.
49. David M. Sikora and Gerald R. Ferris, "Strategic Human Resource Practice Implementation: The Critical Role of Line Management," *Human Resource Management Review* 24 (2014), pp. 271–81.
50. Andrew Fields, Sharanjit Uppal, and Sébastien LaRochelle-Côté, "The Impact of Aging on Labour Market Participation Rates," *Statistics Canada,* June 14, 2017, https://www150.statcan.gc.ca/n1/pub/75-006-x/2017001/article/14826-eng.htm, accessed June 21, 2018.
51. Rita Pyrillis, "Meeting the New Faces Who Are Shaping Employee Retirement," *Workforce,* March 6, 2018, http://www.workforce.com, accessed June 20, 2018.
52. S. Milligan, "Wisdom of the Ages," *HR Magazine,* November 2014, pp. 22–27; C. Paullin, *The Aging Workforce: Leveraging the Talent of Mature Employees* (Alexandria, VA: The SHRM Foundation, 2014); N. Lockwood, *The Aging Workforce* (Alexandria, VA: Society for Human Resource Management, 2003).
53. "Gen Z May Surprise You," Sparks and Honey, August 23, 2017, https://medium.com/sparksandhoney/gen-z-may-surprise-you-da79d1db405a, accessed June 21, 2018; "Meet Generation Z: Forget Everything You Learned about Millennials," June 17, 2014, Sparks and Honey, https://www.slideshare.net/sparksandhoney/generation-z-final-june-17, accessed June 21, 2018; "The Deloitte Millennial Survey: Big Demands and High Expectations," accessed June 21, 2018; A. Adkins "What Millennials Want from Work and Life," May 11, 2016, http://www.gallup.com, accessed February 20, 2017; S. Gale, "Forget Millennials: Are You Ready for Generation Z?," *Chief Learning Officer,* July 2015, pp. 38–48; K. Tyler, "New Kids on the Block," *HR Magazine,* October 2013, pp. 35-40; Hewlett, Sherbin, and Sumberg, "How Gen Y & Boomers Will Reshape Your Agenda,"; A. Fox, "Mixing it Up," *HR Magazine,* May 2011, pp. 22–27; K. Ball and G. Gotsill, *Surviving the Baby Boomer Exodus* (Boston, MA: Cengage, 2011). Source: Hewlett, Sherbin, and Sumberg, "How Gen Y & Boomers Will Reshape Your Agenda,"
54. J. Meriac, D. Woehr, and C. Banister, "Generational Differences in Work Ethic: An Examination of Measurement Equivalence across Three Cohorts," *Journal of Business and Psychology,* 25 (2010), pp. 315–24; K. Real, A. Mitnick, and W. Maloney, "More Similar than Different: Millennials in the U.S. Building Trades," *Journal of Business and Psychology,* 25 (2010), pp. 303–13.
55. T. Lennon, "Managing a Multi-generational Workforce: The Myths vs. the Realities," 2015, http://www.haygroup.com, accessed February 20, 2017; S. Lyons and L. Kuron, "Generational Differences in the Workplace: A Review of the Evidence and Directions for Future Research," *Journal of Organizational Behavior* 35 (2013), pp. 139–57; J. Deal, D. Altman, and S. Rogelberg, "Millennials at Work: What We Know and What We Need to Do (if Anything)," *Journal of Business and Psychology,* 25 (2010), pp. 191–99.
56. "Ethnic Origin Reference Guide, Census of Population, 2016," *Statistics Canada,* October 25, 2017, https://www12.statcan.gc.ca/census-recensement/2016/ref/guides/008/98-500-x2016008-eng.cfm, accessed June 20, 2018.
57. "Aboriginal Peoples in Canada: Key Results from the 2016 Census, *Statistics Canada,* October 25, 2016, https://www150.statcan.gc.ca/n1/daily-quotidien/171025/dq171025a-eng.htm, accessed June 20, 2018.
58. Marian Scott, "Study Shows High Workplace Diversity Encourages Tolerance," *Leader-Post,* January 21, 2012, p. B5.
59. Piali Roy, "Steam Whistle's Commitment to Hiring New Immigrants," *YongeStreet,* September 1, 2010, http://www.yongestreetmedia.ca/features/steamwhistle 0901.aspx, accessed January 24, 2012.
60. "Andini Makosinski," LinkedIn, https://www.linkedin.com/in/annmakosinski, accessed June 21, 2018; "Ann Makosinksi, 19-year-old B.C. Inventor Makes Forbes 30 Under 30," January 5, 2017, *CBC News,* http://www.cbc.news.ca, accessed June 21, 2018; Christina Nunez, "Google Science

Fair Winner Makes Flashlight Powered by Body Heat," *National Geographic,* September 24, 2013, http://www.nationalgeographic.com, accessed June 21, 2018; Reni Barlow, "Ann Makosinksi Wins at Google Science Fair 2013," *Canada Wide Science Fair,* September 23, 2013, https://cwsf.youthscience.ca/news/ann-makosinski-wins-google-science-fair-2013, accessed June 21, 2018.

61. Alison Grenier, "Inclusive Workplaces Are Better for Business," *HR Professional,* January 2018, pp. 43–44.
62. "Collective Agreement Language Responding to the Needs of Aboriginal Members," CUPE National Equality Branch," March 28, 2006.
63. "How Canada Performs: A Report Card on Canada" (Ottawa: Conference Board of Canada, June 2007), p. 82.
64. "Industry Report 2000," *Training,* October 2000, p. 48.
65. Ray Turchansky, "Proof Education Is Smart Investment," *Financial Post,* March 22, 2004, p. FP13.
66. Emily Douglas, "'Tech Has Made Us Lazy': Industry Giant Sheds Light on HR Confusion," *HRD TechNews,* June 22, 2018, http://www.hrtechnologynews.com, accessed June 24, 2018.
67. Melissa Campeau, "Emerging HR: The Biggest Trends in HR Now," *HR Professional,* December 2017, pp. 16–19.
68. Ibid.
69. C. Goodman, "Employers Wrestle with Social-Media Policies," *The Columbus Dispatch,* January 30, 2011, p. D3.
70. W. Cascio and R. Montealegre, "How Technology Is Changing Work and Organizations," *Annual Review of Organizational Psychology and Organizational Behavior,* 3 (2016), pp. 349–75; J. Bersin, "Transformative Tech: A Disruptive Year Ahead," *HR Magazine,* February 2017, pp. 29–36; G. Colvin, "In the Future, Will There Be Any Work Left for People to Do?" *Fortune,* June 2, 2014; T. Aeppel, "Jobs and the Clever Robot," *Wall Street Journal,* February 25, 2015, pp. A1, A10.
71. Jessica Vomiero, "Google's AI Assistant Must Identify Itself as a Robot During Phone Calls: Report," *Global News,* May 13, 2018, http://www.globalnews.ca, accessed June 23, 2018; Rachel Ranosa, "Man 'Fired' by Machine Shows Downside of Over-Automation," *HR TechNews,* June 29, 2018, http://www.hrtechnologynews.com, accessed July 2, 2018; S. Gale, "Ready or Not, The Future is Now," *Chief Learning Officer,* March 2017, pp. 20–21; J. Stearn, "Alexa Stop Bringing Chaos to Anyone with a Similar Name," *Wall Street Journal,* January 27, 2016, pp. A1, A8; "Are You Leaving Money on the Table? H&R Block with Watson Can Help," http://www.ibm.com, accessed February 20, 2017.
72. N. Olivarez-Giles, "Robots with Skills and Charm," *Wall Street Journal,* January 6, 2017, p. B4; A Tangel, "Latest Robots Lend an Arm," *Wall Street Journal,* November 9, 2016, pp. B1, B4.
73. Rachel Ranosa, "Man 'Fired' by Machine Shows Downside of Over-Automation," *HR TechNews,* June 29, 2018, http://www.hrtechnologynews.com, accessed July 2, 2018.
74. Mark Allinson, "BMW Shows off Its Smart Factory Technologies at Its Plants Worldwide," *Robotics and Automation,* March 4, 2017, https://roboticsandautomationnews.com/2017/03/04/bmw-shows-off-its-smart-factory-technologies-at-its-plants-worldwide/11696/, accessed June 24, 2018.
75. K. Everson, "Special Report: Learning Is All in the Wrist," *Chief Learning Officer,* http://www.clomedia.com, accessed March 18, 2015; Wearable Intelligence website, "About" and "Products," http://www.wearableintelligence.com, accessed April 21, 2015.
76. M. J. Kavanaugh, H. G. Guetal, and S. I. Tannenbau, *Human Resource Management Information System: Development and Application* (Boston: PWS-Kent, 1990).
77. A. Abbatiello, "The Digital Override," *Workforce,* May 2014, pp. 36–39.
78. Lorri Freifeld, "Training Magazine Ranks 2017 Training Top 125 Organizations," January 31, 2018, https://trainingmag.com, accessed June 24, 2018; and "Best Buy Wins Outstanding Training Initiatives Award for Gravity," *Halight/Blog,* http://www.halight.com, accessed June 24, 2018.
79. A. McAfee, "What Every CEO Needs to Know about the Cloud," *Harvard Business Review,* November 2011, pp. 124–132; B. Roberts, "The Grand Convergence," *HR Magazine,* October 2011, pp. 39–46; M. Paino, "All Generations Learn in the Cloud," *Chief Learning Officer,* September 28, 2011, http://blog.clomedia.com, accessed October 11, 2011.
80. "HR Heads to the Cloud," *Human Resource Executive,* September 2016, p. 16.
81. M. Charney, "Five Reasons Why Cloud Computing Matters for Recruitment and Hiring," http://hiring.monster.com, accessed May 17, 2015; D. Shane, "A Human Giant," *Information Age,* http://www.information-age.com, accessed May 17, 2015.
82. N. Lockwood, *Maximizing Human Capital: Demonstrating HR Value with Key Performance Indicators* (Alexandria, VA: SHRM Research Quarterly, 2006).
83. P. Choate and P. Linger, *The High-Flex Society* (New York: Knopf, 1986); P. B. Doeringer, *Turbulence in the American Workplace* (New York: Oxford University Press, 1991).
84. J. A. Neal and C L. Tronley, "From Incremental Change to Retrofit: Creating High Performance Work Systems," *Academy of Management Executive* 9 (1995), pp. 42–54.
85. K. A Miller, *Retraining the American Workforce* (Reading, MA: Addison-Wesley, 1989).
86. B. Reynolds, "Twenty-Six Companies That Thrive on Remote Work," *Flex Jobs,* http://www.flexjobs.com, accessed March 3, 2015; Company website, http://www.artandlogic.com, accessed March 3, 2015; "Working at Art & Logic," http://www.artandlogic.com/careers, accessed July 1, 2015.

CHAPTER 2

1. "Public Services and Procurement Canada," *Government of Canada,* https://www.canada.ca/en/public-services-procurement.html, accessed July 4, 2018, and "Canada's Best Diversity Employers (2018)," MediaCorp Canada Inc., http://www.canadastop100.com/diversity, accessed July 4, 2018.
2. Kristina Leung and Richard Yerema, "Public Services and Procurement Canada—Canada's Best Diversity Employers (2018)," *MediaCorp. Canada Inc.,* March 1, 2018, https://content.eluta.ca/top-employer-public-services-and-procurement-canada#diversity, accessed July 4, 2018.
3. Ibid.
4. Aliso Grenier, "Inclusive Workplaces are Better for Business," *HR Professional,* January 2018, pp. 43–44.
5. Kim Tabac, "Beyond Diversity: The Difference Between Diversity and Inclusion," *HR Professional,* January 2018, pp. 23–24.
6. Judith H. Katz and Frederick A Miller, "Inclusion: The How for the Next Organizational Breakthrough," *Practising Social Change—NTL Institute for Applied Behavioral Science,* May 2012, pp. 16–22.
7. www.ccohs.ca/oshanswers/legisl/ire.htm, retrieved February 25, 2004.
8. "HR Leaders Talk," *Canadian HR Reporter,* January 28, 2008, pp. 11–12.
9. "Business Results Through Health and Safety," Ontario Workplace Safety and Insurance Board website, http://www.wsib.on.ca/wsib/website.nsf, accessed April 19, 2004.

10. http://www.ccohs.ca/oshanswers/legisl/ire.htm, accessed February 25, 2004.
11. "Anti-Discriminatory Casebook," http://www.chrcccdp.ca/Legis&Poli/AntiDiscriminationCasebook_Recueil Decisions, accessed February 18, 2004.
12. "Teaching: Teacher Application," *Regina Catholic Schools,* http://www.rcsd.ca, accessed July 7, 2018.
13. Ran LeClair, "The Evolution of Accommodation," *Canadian HR Reporter,* February 24, 2003, p. 7.
14. "Bona Fide Occupational Requirements and Bona Fide Justifications Under the Canadian Human Rights Act," pp. 4, 5, http://www.chrc-ccdp.ca/publications/BFOR, accessed February 18, 2004.
15. "Mandatory Retirement in Canada," http://www.hrsdc.gc.ca/en/lp/spila/clli/eslc/19Mandatory_Retirement.shtml, accessed October 20, 2008; "Retiring Mandatory Retirement," February 21, 2008, http://www.cbc.ca/news/background/retirement/mandatory_retirement.html, accessed October 20, 2008.
16. Canadian Human Rights Commission, "Fact Sheet: Duty to Accommodate," January 2006, p. 2.
17. Andrew Duffy, "Steven Fletcher's Line in the Sand," *Leader-Post,* November 28, 2014, p. D8; http://www.thestevenfletcherstory.ca/about_steven.php, accessed March 23, 2012; Paul Samyn, "Tearing Down Barriers Big Job," *Winnipeg Free Press,* July 16, 2004, p. A3; Paul Egan, "He's Breaking Barriers," *Winnipeg Free Press,* July 4, 2004, pp. A1, A2; Parliament of Canada website, http://www2.parl.gc.ca, accessed April 13, 2008.
18. Liz Bernier, "Diversity Not Just About Compliance," *Canadian HR Reporter,* March 10, 2014, pp. 1, 6.
19. "Accessible Technology Program," *Government of Canada,* https://www.canada.ca/en/innovation-science-economic-development/programs/accessible-technology.html, accessed July 7, 2018, and "Announced Projects Under the Accessible Technology Program," *Government of Canada,* https://www.canada.ca/en/innovation-science-economic-development/programs/accessible-technology/announced-projects-under-accessible-technology-program.html, accessed July 7, 2018.
20. "What Is Harassment?" *Canadian Human Rights Commission* website, http://www.chrc-ccdp.ca/eng/content/what-harassment, accessed April 1, 2015.
21. "Study Reveals Slight Decline in Workplace Harassment, *OHS Canada,* July 2, 2014, http://www.ohscanada.com/health-safety/study-reveals-slight-decline-in-workplace-harassment/1003140322/, accessed April 1, 2015.
22. "Seneca Discrimination and Harassment Policy Statement," http://www.senecacollege.ca/policies/dh.html, accessed July 7, 2018.
23. Marcel Vander Wier, "Life after #MeToo," *Canadian HR Reporter,* March 14, 2018, http://www.hrreporter.com, accessed July 7, 2018.
24. Marcel Vander Wier, "Why Is Sexual Harassment Not Going Away?, *Canadian HR Reporter,* November 27, 2017, http://www.hrreporter.com, accessed July 8, 2018.
25. "Sexual Harassment," *Government of Canada,* https://www.canada.ca/en/employment-social-development/services/labour-standards/reports/sexual-harassment.html#s01, accessed July 7, 2018.
26. "Half of Working Women in Canada Have Endured Sexual Harassment, *Insights West,* December 6, 2017, https://insightswest.com/news/half-of-working-women-in-canada-have-endured-sexual-harassment/, accessed July 7, 2018.
27. "Identifying Sexual Harassment," *Ontario Human Rights Commission,* http://www.ohrc.on.ca/en/policy-preventing-sexual-and-gender-based-harassment/2-identifying-sexual-harassment, accessed March 25, 2015.
28. Reference to *Colvin v. Gillies* 2004 HRTO3 from "Identifying Sexual Harassment," *Ontario Human Rights Commission,* http://www.ohrc.on.ca/en/policy-preventing-sexual-and-gender-based-harassment/2-identifying-sexual-harassment, accessed March 25, 2015.
29. Kathleen Harris, "Mounties Offer Apology and $100M Compensation for Harassment, Sexual Abuse against Female Members," *CBC News,* October 6, 2016, http://www.cbc.ca/news/politics/rcmp-paulson-compensation-harassment-1.3793785, accessed July 9, 2018.
30. "Employment Equity Designated Groups," Government of Canada, http://jobs-emplois.gc.ca/centres/inside-ausein/ee-eng.php, accessed March 25, 2015.
31. Ibid.
32. Ibid.
33. "Summary of Privacy Laws in Canada," *Office of the Privacy Commissioner of Canada,* January 2018, http://www.priv.gc.ca, accessed July 8, 2018.
34. http://www.priv.gc.ca/fs-fi/02_05_d_15_e.cfm#contenttop, accessed March 23, 2012.
35. Ibid.
36. "A Guide for Canadians: What Is the Personal Information Protection and Electronic Documents Act?," http://www.privcom.gc.ca/information.
37. Brenda Bouw, "Ontario to freeze minimum wage, eliminate mandatory paid sick days," *The Globe and Mail,* October 23, 2018, www.theglobeandmail.com, William Watson and Susan MacMillan, "Bill 148: Key Changes and What to Do About Them," *Canadian Labour and Employment Law,* January 8, 2018, http://www.labourandemploymentlaw.com, accessed July 8, 2018; Melissa Campeau, "Bill 148: What You Need to Know," *HR Professional,* October 2017, pp. 22–26; Jason Beeho, "Bill 148—Employers Should Prepare for New Compliance Obligations," *HR Professional,* October 2017, pp. 15–17.
38. "New Family-friendly Workplace Rules in Place," *Government of Alberta,* January 2, 2018, http://www.alberta.ca, accessed July 8, 2018.
39. Zane Schwartz, "Unpaid Internships Are Just Wrong," *The Globe and Mail,* May 3, 2013, http://www.theglobeandmail.com, accessed March 26, 2015.
40. Christina Pellegrini, "Plaintiff Takes Another Swing in Long-running CIBA Lawsuit," *TheGlobe and Mail,* March 19, 2017, p. B1; Todd Humber, "Hefty Bill on Unpaid Overtime," *Canadian HR Reporter,* September 8, 2014, p. 26; Tim Kiladze, "Scotiabank Settles Class Action on Overtime Pay," *The Globe and Mail,* July 24, 2014, http://www.globeandmail.com, accessed March 29, 2015; Jacquie McNish and Tara Perkins, CIBC Overtime Lawsuit Dismissed, *The Globe and Mail,* June 19, 2009, http://www.theglobeandmail.com/report-on-business/cibc-overtime-lawsuit-dismissed/article1188529/, accessed March 24, 2012; "CN Faces $250M Class Action Lawsuit," http://www.cbc.ca/money/story/2008/03/25/en.html, accessed April 14, 2008; "CN Hit with Class-Action Lawsuit on Unpaid Overtime," *Canadian HR Reporter,* http://www.hrreporter.com, March 25, 2008; Gary Norris, "KPMG Faces Employee Class Action Lawsuit in Ontario for Overtime Pay," http://www.cbc.ca/cp/business/070904/b0904111A.html, accessed October 4, 2007; Virginia Galt and Janet McFarland, "CIBC Faces Massive Overtime Lawsuit," *The Globe and Mail,* June 5, 2007, http://www.theglobeandmail.com, accessed March 18, 2008; "CIBC Faces $600-Million Suit over Unpaid Overtime," *CanWest News Service,* June 5, 2007, http://www.canada.com/components, accessed March 18, 2008.
41. "Alberta Court Makes No Changes to Class-Action Suit against WHL," Canada Press, May 15, 2018, http://www

.sportsnet.ca, accessed July 8, 2018; “CHL Class Action,” Charney Lawyers website, http://www.charneylawyers.com/Charney/chlclassaction.php, accessed March 29, 2015, and Bob Duff, “Lawsuit Threatens to Change CHL Dynamic,” *The Leader-Post,* October 21, 2014, p. C4.

42. “Canadian Pay Equity Requirements,” *KornFerry|Hay Group,* http://www.haygroup.com, accessed July 9, 2018.
43. “How Canada Performs: Gender Income Gap,” *Conference Board of Canada,* http://www.conferenceboard.ca/hcp/details/society/gender-income-gap.aspx, accessed March 26, 2015.
44. Justin Tang, “Ottawa Working out Details of Pay Equity Legislation Announced in Budget,” *Toronto Star,* March 14, 2018, https://www.thestar.com, accessed July 9, 2018.
45. Matthew McClearn, “Mind the Gap,” *Canadian Business,* November 5, 2007, pp. 21–22.
46. Sarah Schmidt, “Report Says Male Profs Paid More Than Females,” *Winnipeg Free Press,* July 17, 2004, p. A11.
47. Ibid.
48. Liam Casey, “University of Guelph Giving Raises to Full-time Female Faculty after Review,” *Canadian HR Reporter,* June 19, 2018, http://www.hrreporter.com, accessed June 20, 2018.
49. Canadian Human Rights Commission, “2007 Annual Report,” p. 6, http://www.chrc-ccdp.ca/publication/ar_2007_ra/page6-en.asp#41, accessed April 14, 2008.
50. “Privacy Commissioner of Canada: A Guide for Canadians,” http://www.privcom.gc.ca/information, accessed March 21, 2004.
51. “Self-Help Kit: Employment Standards Self-Help: Solve Workplace Problems,” *Government of British Columbia,* https://www2.gov.bc.ca, accessed July 9, 2018.
52. “OH&S Legislation in Canada—Basic Responsibilities,” Canadian Centre for Occupational Health and Safety, http://www.ccohs.ca/oshanswers/legisl/responsi.html, accessed March 29, 2015.
53. http://www.labour.gov.on.ca/english/hs, accessed March 23, 2012.
54. http://www.ccohs.ca/oshanswers/legisl/ire.htm, accessed February 25, 2004.
55. “Workplace Health and Safety Committees—Pamphlet 6B: Information on Occupational Health and Safety,” Government of Canada website, http://www.labour.gc.ca/eng/health_safety/pubs_hs/committee.shtml, accessed March 29, 2015.
56. “OH&S Legislation in Canada—Basic Responsibilities,” *Canadian Centre for Occupational Health and Safety,* http://www.ccohs.ca/oshanswers/legisl/responsi.html, accessed March 29, 2015.
57. Monica Haberl, “Blazing the Trail: What the Legalization of Cannabis Means for Canadian Employers,” June 2018, *The Conference Board of Canada,* pp. 1–36.
58. Russel Zinn, “Driving Under Influence—of a Cellphone,” *Canadian HR Reporter,* February 25, 2008, p. 5.
59. “Distracted Driving,” The Ontario Ministry of Labour, http://www.mto.gov.on.ca/english/safety/distracted-driving.shtml, accessed April 1, 2015.
60. Mari-Len De Guzman, “Distracted Drivers to Distracted Workers: Tips for Developing Workplace Cellphone Policy,” *Canadian Occupational Safety,* April 23, 2013, http://www.cos-mag.com/safety/safety-stories/distracted-drivers-to-distracted-workers-tips-for-developing-workplace-cellphone-policy.html, accessed April 1, 2015.
61. Gail Hepburn, Charles Boyer, and Louise Chenier, “Running on Empty: Understanding Fatigue in the Workplace,” *The Conference Board of Canada,* September 14, 2016, pp. 1–42.
62. Ibid.
63. “OH&S Legislation in Canada—Basic Responsibilities,” Canadian Centre for Occupational Health and Safety, https://www.ccohs.ca/oshanswers/legisl/responsi.html, accessed March 29, 2015.
64. Ibid.
65. Ibid.
66. Andy Shaw, “Slow Evolution from WHMIS to GHS,” *Canadian HR Reporter,* March 10, 2008, p. 11.
67. “WHMIS 2015 for Workers,” Canadian Centre for Occupational Health and Safety, http://www.ccohs.ca, accessed July 9, 2018, and “Environmental and Workplace Health—WHMIS 2015,” Health Canada, http://www.hc-sc.gc.ca/ewh-semt/occup-travail/whmis-simdut/ghs-sgh/index-eng.php, accessed March 29, 2015.
68. Ann Perry, “Workplace Safety Gets a Boost,” *Toronto Star,* March 27, 2004, p. D10.
69. Kathleen Chevalier, “Metron Construction Accident Results In Criminal Conviction and $200k Fine,” Strikeman Elliott—Canadian Employment & Pension Law, September 27, 2012, https://www.canadianemploymentpensionlaw.com/employment-standards/metron-construction-accident-results-in-criminal-conviction-and-20000000-fine/, accessed March 27, 2015.
70. “OSH Answers Fact Sheets: Violence in the Workplace,” Canadian Centre for Occupational Health and Safety, http://www.ccohs.ca/oshanswers/psychosocial/violence.html, accessed March 31, 2015.
71. “OSH Answers Fact Sheets: Violence in the Workplace,” Canadian Centre for Occupational Health and Safety, http://www.ccohs.ca/oshanswers/psychosocial/violence.html, accessed March 31, 2015.
72. Sarah Dobson, “Paramedics Facing Abuse on the Job,” *Canadian HR Reporter,* January 30, 2012, p. 7.
73. L. Chénier, C. Hoganson, and K. Thorpe, “Making the Business Case for Investments in Workplace Health & Wellness,” *Conference Board of Canada,* June 2012, p. 4.
74. Gerry Bellet, “Harassed Woman Awarded $950,000,” *Leader-Post,* January 24, 2006, p. A3.
75. “Psychological Safety 2014: County of Wellington,” October 20, 2014, http://www.cos-mag.com/safety/safety-stories/4173-psychological-safety-2014-county-of-wellington.html, accessed March 27, 2015. Reprinted by permission of Canadian Occupational Safety. © Copyright Thomson Reuters Canada Ltd., October 20, 2014, Toronto, Ontario 1800-387-5164. Web: http://www.cos-mag.com
76. J. Roughton, “Managing a Safety Program through Job Hazard Analysis,” *Professional Safety* 37 (1992), pp. 28–31.
77. Ibid.
78. R. G. Hallock and D. A. Weaver, “Controlling Losses and Enhancing Management Systems with TOR Analysis,” *Professional Safety* 35 (1990), pp. 24–26.
79. Sandy Smith, “Worker Safety“ Intelligence at the Edge,” *EHS Today,* December 8, 2015, http://ehstoday.com.
80. “Young/New Workers,” Canadian Centre of Occupational Health and Safety, http://www.ccohs.ca/topics/workers/youngnew/, accessed March 30, 2015.
81. “Young Workers Zone,” Canadian Centre of Occupational Health and Safety, http://www.ccohs.ca/products/posters/youngworkers.html, accessed March 30, 2015.
82. Amanda Silliker, “Shift Workers’ Poor Diet a Health Hazard,” *Canadian HR Reporter,* February 13, 2012, p. 1, 12.
83. T. Markus, “How to Set Up a Safety Awareness Program,” *Supervision* 51 (1990), pp. 14–16.
84. J. Agnew and A. J. Saruda, “Age and Fatal Work-related Falls,” *Human Factors* 35, no. 4 (1994), pp. 731–36.
85. R. King, “Active Safety Programs, Education Can Help Prevent Back Injuries,” *Occupational Health and Safety* 60 (1991), pp. 49–52.

86. "Eye Safety at Work," *CNIB website,* http://www.cnib.ca/en/your-eyes/safety/at-work/Pages/default.aspx, accessed March 30, 2015.
87. "2014 Responsible Canadian Energy Awards," Canadian Association of Petroleum Producers website, May 21, 2014, http://www.capp.ca, accessed March 30, 2015.
88. Nikki Pavlov, "A Healthy Workplace Means Recognizing Stress Is the Enemy," *Canadian HR Reporter,* April 9, 2001, http://www.hrreporter.com, accessed September 29, 2004.
89. "Wellness Metrics in Action—Desjardins Group: Impressive Return on Investments in Wellness," *Conference Board of Canada,* August 15, 2012, p. 3.
90. "Case Study: Wellness Metrics in Action—Town of Conception Bay South: Reducing Absenteeism," *Conference Board of Canada,* August 2012, pp. 1–3.
91. "OSH Answers Fact Sheet—Employee Assistance Programs (EAP)," Canadian Centre for Occupational Health and Safety, http://www.ccohs.ca/oshanswers/hsprograms/eap.html, accessed March 31, 2015.
92. Sarah B. Hood, "Indigenous Inclusiveness," *HR Professional,* January 2018, pp. 16, 18, 20.
93. Brian Lindenberg, "Choosing the Right EAP," *Canadian HR Reporter,* March 24, 2008, pp. 22, 27.
94. M. Janssens, J. M. Brett, and E J. Smith, "Confirmatory Cross-cultural Research: Testing the Viability of a Corporation-wide Safety Policy," *Academy of Management Journal* 38 (1995), pp. 364–82.
95. Kim Tabac, "Beyond Diversity: The Difference Between Diversity and Inclusion," *HR Professional,* January 2018, pp. 23–24.
96. Based on Kirsten M. Robertson, Hayley Chase, and Arianna Castonguay, "Outfitting the Office: An Experiential Health and Safety Exercise, *Management Teaching Review,* May 23, 2018, pp. 1–24.

CHAPTER 3

1. "Exceptionally Interesting STEM Careers," *Canada2067,* https;//canada2067.ca, accessed January 17, 2018, Rebecca Kapogiannis, "What Is STEM, and How Can It Boost Your Career?", June 1, 2017, https://sciencecentre.3mcanada.ca, accessed January 24, 2018.
2. Suzanne Vranica, "Old-School Ad Execs Sweat as Data Geeks Flex Muscle," *Wall Street Journal,* August 4, 2013, http://online.wsj.com.
3. J. R. Hollenbeck, H. Moon, A. Ellis, et al., "Structural Contingency Theory and Individual Differences: Examination of External and Internal Person-Team Fit," *Journal of Applied Psychology* 87 (2002), pp. 599–606, Sam Grobart, "Hooray for Hierarchy," *Bloomberg Businessweek,* January 14, 2013, p. 74.
4. W. Cascio, *Applied Psychology in Personnel Management,* 4th ed. (Englewood Cliffs, NJ: Prentice Hall, 1991).
5. P. Wright and K. Wexley, "How to Choose the Kind of Job Analysis You Really Need," *Personnel,* May 1985, pp. 51–55.
6. Canadian Human Rights Commission website, http://www.ccrc-ccdp.ca/discrimination/barrier_free-en.asp, accessed April 3, 2004.
7. Oliver W. Cummings, "What Do Manufacturing Supervisors Really Do on the Job?" *Industry Week,* February 2010, p. 53.
8. A. O'Reilly, "Skill Requirements: Supervisor-Subordinate Conflict," *Personnel Psychology 26* (1973), pp. 75–80; J. Hazel, J. Madden, and R. Christal, "Agreement between Worker-Supervisor Descriptions of the Worker's Job," *Journal of Industrial Psychology 2* (1964), pp. 71–79; and A. K. Weyman, "Investigating the Influence of Organizational Role on Perceptions of Risk in Deep Coal Mines," *Journal of Applied Psychology 88* (2003), pp. 404–12.
9. L. E. Baranowski and L. E. Anderson, "Examining Rater Source Variation in Work Behavior to KSA Linkages," *Personnel Psychology 58* (2005), pp. 1041–54.
10. PAQ Newsletter, August 1989; and E. C. Dierdorff and M. A. Wilson, "A Meta-analysis of Job Analysis Reliability," *Journal of Applied Psychology 88* (2003), pp. 635–46.
11. E. Fleishman and M. Reilly, *Handbook of Human Abilities* (Palo Alto, CA: Consulting Psychologists Press, 1992); E. Fleishman and M. Mumford, "The Ability Requirements Scales," in *The Job Analysis Handbook for Business, Industry, and Government,* ed. S. Gael (New York: Wiley), pp. 917–35.
12. J. R. Hollenbeck, B. Beersma, and M. E. Schouten, "Beyond Team Types and Taxonomies: A Dimensional Scaling Approach for Team Description," *Academy of Management Review* 37 (2012): 82–108.
13. M. Campion, A. Fink, B. Ruggeberg, L. Carr, G. Phillips, and R. Odman, "Doing Competencies Well: Best Practices in Competency Modeling," *Personnel Psychology* 64 (2011): 225–62; R. A. Noe, *Employee Training and Development,* 5e (New York: McGraw-Hill Irwin, 2010); J. Shippmann, R. Ash, M. Battista, L. Carr, L. Eyde, B. Hesketh, J. Kehow, K. Pearlman, and J. Sanchez, "The Practice of Competency Modeling," *Personnel Psychology* 53 (2000): 703–40; A. Lucia and R. Lepsinger, *The Art and Science of Competency Models* (San Francisco: Jossey-Bass, 1999).
14. Jane Cooper and Shannon Jackson, *Talent Management Benchmarking: Human Resources Trends and Metrics,* Fourth Edition, *The Conference Board of Canada,* 2017, p. 61–62.
15. Gregory W. Stevens, "A Critical Review of the Science and Practice of Competency Modeling," *Human Resource Development Review* 12(1), pp. 86–107.
16. M. K. Lindell, C. S. Clause, C. J. Brandt, and R. S. Landis, "Relationship between Organizational Context and Job Analysis Ratings," *Journal of Applied Psychology* 83 (1998), pp. 769–76.
17. Fran Sussner Rodgers, " Who Owns Your Overtime?," *New York Times,* June 22, 2015, http://www.nytimes.com;D. S. DeRue, J. R. Hollenbeck, M. D. Johnson, D. R. Ilgen, and D. K. Jundt, "How Different Team Downsizing Approaches Influence Team-Level Adaptation and Performance," *Academy of Management Journal* 51 (2008), pp. 182–96.
18. Nick Horney, "The Gig Economy: A Disruptor Requiring HR Agility," *People + Strategy* 39 (Summer 2016), pp. 20–27.
19. R. Hackman and G. Oldham, *Work Redesign* (Boston: Addison-Wesley, 1980).
20. Joe McKendrick, "13 Jobs That Now Matter the Most, from a Digital Perspective," *Forbes,* January 30, 2016, http://www.forbes.com; "Square Root," Great Places to Work, July 6, 2015, accessed http://reviews.greatplacestowork.com.
21. M. R. Barrick, M.K. Mount, and N. Li, "The Theory of Purposeful Work Behavior: The Role of Personality, Higher-Order Goals, and Job Characteristics," Academy of Management Review 38 (2013), pp. 132–53.
22. F. W. Bond, P. E. Flaxman, and D. Bunce, "The Influence of Psychological Flexibility on Work Redesign: Mediated Moderation of a Work Reorganization Intervention," *Journal of Applied Psychology* 93 (2008), pp. 645–54.
23. M. A. Campion, G. J. Medsker, and A. C. Higgs, "Relations between Work Group Characteristics and Effectiveness: Implications for Designing Effective Work Groups," *Personnel Psychology* 46 (1993), pp. 823–50.
24. Kimberley A. Eddleston and Jay Mulki, "Toward Understanding Remote Workers' Management of Work–Family Boundaries: The Complexity of Work Embeddedness," *Group & Organization Management,* 42(3), 2017, pp. 346–87.

25. Marcel Vander Wier, "IBM Goes Against the Grain as Remote Work Gains Popularity," *Canadian HR Reporter,* 30 (8) May 1, 2017, p. 2.
26. Amanda Eisenberg, "Employers Can Save Big Bucks by Offering Telecommuting," *Employee Benefit Advisor (Online),* July 6, 2017.
27. Marcel Vander Wier, "IBM Goes Against the Grain as Remote Work Gains Popularity," *Canadian HR Reporter,* 30 (8), May 1, 2017, p. 2.
28. Ibid.
29. See, for example, S. Sonnentag and F. R. H. Zijistra, "Job Characteristics and Off-the-Job Activities as Predictors of Need for Recovery, Well-Being, and Fatigue," *Journal of Applied Psychology* 91 (2006), pp. 330–50.
30. D. May and C. Schwoerer, "Employee Health by Design: Using Employee Involvement Teams in Ergonomic Job Redesign," *Personnel Psychology* 47 (1994), pp. 861–86.
31. Franklin Tessler, "The Hidden Danger of Touchscreens," InfoWorld.com, January 11, 2012, Business & Company Resource Center, accessed from http://galenet.galegroup .com.
32. Peter Budnick and Rachel Michael, "What Is Cognitive Ergonomics?," *Ergonomics Today,* http://www.ergoweb.com/ news/detail.cfm?id=352, accessed March 25, 2008.
33. N. W. Van Yperen and M. Hagerdoom, "Do High Job Demands Increase Intrinsic Motivation or Fatigue or Both? The Role of Job Support and Social Control," *Academy of Management Journal* 46 (2003), pp. 339–348; and N. W. Van Yperen and O Janseen, "Fatigued and Dissatisfied or Fatigued but Satisfied? Goal Orientations and Responses to High Job Demands," *Academy of Management Journal* 45 (2002) pp. 1161–71.
34. Jonathan Spira, "Information Overload: None Are Immune," *Information Management,* September/October 2011, p.32.

CHAPTER 4

1. "How Lyft Plans to Woo Drivers from Uber," *Toronto City News,* November 16, 2017, http://toronto.citynews.ca; David Shum, "Lyft and Uber to battle each other for drivers and riders in Toronto," *Global News,* November 13, 2017, https:// globalnews.ca; L. Weber and R. E. Silverman, "On-Demand Workers: We Are Not Robots," *Wall Street Journal,* January 27, 2015.
2. Cameron Dow, "The Analytics Skills Gap—Canadian Edition," https://www.sas.com/en_ca/insights/articles/analytics/local/ analytics-skill-gap.html#, accessed February 8, 2018.
3. Anna Louie Sussman, "Economy Chugs on Despite Fears," Wall Street Journal, April 1, 2016, http://www.wsj.com.
4. David Gould, "Where Talent and Tech Meet," Bloomberg Businessweek, May 4, 2015, http://www.bloomberg.com
5. J. P. Guthrie, "Dumb and Dumber: The Impact of Downsizing on Firm Performance as Moderated by Industry Conditions," *Organization Science* 19 (2008), pp. 108–123; and J. McGregor, A. McConnon, and D. Kiley, "Customer Service in a Shrinking Economy," *BusinessWeek,* February 19, 2009, pp. 34–35.
6. C. D. Zatzick and R. D. Iverson, "High-Involvement Management and Workforce Reduction: Competitive Advantage or Disadvantage?" *Academy of Management Journal* 49 (2006), pp. 101–112.
7. P. P. Shaw, "Network Destruction: The Structural Implications of Downsizing," *Academy of Management Journal* 43 (2000), pp. 101–12.
8. B. Bremner, "Japan Releases a Robot Revolution," *BusinessWeek,* May 28, 2015.
9. E. Frauenheim, "Technology Forcing Firms to Shed More Light on Layoffs," *Workforce Management,* January 19, 2009, pp. 7–8.
10. Brenda Kowske, Kyle Lundby, and Rena Rasch, "Turning 'Survive' into 'Thrive': Managing Survivor Engagement in a Downsized Organization," *People & Strategy 32,* no. (4), (2009), pp. 48–56.
11. Justin Lahart, "Even in a Recovery, Some Jobs Won't Return," *Wall Street Journal,* January 12, 2010, onlinewsj.com; and Sarah E. Needleman, "Entrepreneurs Prefer to Keep Staffs Lean," *Wall Street Journal,* March 2, 2010, http://online.wsj. com.
12. CareerBuilder, "Retirement May Be a Thing of the Past, New CareerBuilder Survey Finds," news release, February 16, 2012, http://www.careerbuilder.com.
13. S. Kim and D. Feldman, "Healthy, Wealthy, or Wise: Predicting Actual Acceptances of Early Retirement Incentives at Three Points in Time," *Personnel Psychology* 51 (1998), pp. 623–42.
14. Jared Lindzon, "Freelance Work Expanding to More Sectors, Report Finds," *Special to The Globe and Mail,* August 23, 2016, http://www.globeandmail.com
15. Kristine Owram, "Uber Drivers Are Employees, not Contractors, Canadian Lawsuit Argues," *Financial Post,* January 28, 2017, http://business.financialpost.com
16. Michael Lewis, "Proposed Ontario Class-Action Claims Uber Drivers Are Employees not Contractors," *The Toronto Star,* January 24, 2018, https://www.thestar.com; and Kristine Owram, "Uber Drivers Are Employees, not Contractors, Canadian Lawsuit Argues," *Financial Post,* January 28, 2017, http://business.financialpost.com
17. P. Engardio, "Let's Offshore the Lawyers," *BusinessWeek,* September 18, 2006, pp. 42–43.
18. Steve Minter, "Moving Sourcing Closer to Home," *Industry Week,* September 2009, Business & Company Resource Center, http://galenet.galegroup.com; and Josh Hyatt, "The New Calculus of Offshoring," *CFO,* October 2009, pp. 58–62.
19. A. Tiwana, Does Firm Modularity Complement Ignorance? A Field Study of Software Outsourcing Alliances," *Strategic Management Journal* 29 (2008), pp. 1241–52.
20. Kelley Hunsberger, "The Risk of Outsourcing," PM Network, November 2011, EBSCOhost, http://web.ebscohost.com; "The Trouble with Outsourcing," The Economist, July 30, 2011, EBSCOhost, http://web.ebscohost.com.
21. P. Engardio, "The Future of Outsourcing," *BusinessWeek,* January 30, 2006, pp. 50–58.
22. "Temporary Foreign Workers," Government of Canada, http:// www.canada.ca.
23. Tara Carman and Dirk Meissner, "Tim Hortons, McDonald's Face Criticism over Foreign Worker Program," October 3, 2014, *Vancouver Sun,* http://www.vancouver.sun.com.
24. Yuqian Lu and Feng Hou, "Transition from Temporary Foreign Workers to Permanent Residents, 1990–2014," *Social Analysis and Modelling Division—Statistics Canada,* February 21, 2017, http://www.statcan.gc.ca.
25. "Limiting Hours of Work," *Front Lines: The Magazine for Nurses by the Manitoba Nurses Union,* Issue 3 (2014), pp. 4–6, https://manitobanurses.ca
26. W.J. Rothwell, *Effective Succession Planning,* 4th ed. (New York: AMACOM, 2010).
27. B. E. Dowell, "Succession Planning," in *Implementing Organizational Interventions,* ed. J. Hedge and E. D. Pulakos (San Francisco: Jossey-Bass, 2002), pp. 78–109.
28. J. Lublin and T. Francis, "Boards Often Fumble CEO Changes," *Wall Street Journal,* June 9, 2016, pp. B1–B2.
29. A. E. Barber, *Recruiting Employees* (Thousand Oaks, CA: Sage, 1998).

30. C. K. Stevens, "Antecedents of Interview Interactions, Interviewers' Ratings, and Applicants' Reactions," *Personnel Psychology 51* (1998), pp. 55–85; A. E. Barber, J. R. Hollenbeck, S. L. Tower, and J. M. Phillips, "The Effects of Interview Focus on Recruitment Effectiveness: A Field Experiment," *Journal of Applied Psychology 79* (1994), pp. 886–96; and D. S. Chapman and D. I. Zweig, "Developing a Nomological Network for Interview Structure: Antecedents and Consequences of the Structured Selection Interview," *Personnel Psychology 58* (2005), pp. 673–702.
31. J. D. Olian and S. L. Rynes, "Organizational Staffing: Integrating Practice with Strategy," *Industrial Relations* 23 (1984), pp. 170–83.
32. Patty McCord, "How to Hire: Chances Are You're Doing it All Wrong," *Harvard Business Review,* January–February 2018, pp. 90–97.
33. Kim Peters, "Employment Branding Best Way to Reach Untapped Talent," *HR Voice,* November 1, 2007, http://www.hrvoice.org/story, accessed March 18, 2008.
34. Kim Peters, "Passive Jobseekers Solution to Labour Woes," *Canadian HR Reporter,* July 16, 2007, p. 18.
35. Carolyn Brandon, "Truth in Recruitment Branding," *HR Magazine* 50, no. 11 (November 2005), pp. 89–96.
36. Patrick J. Kiger, "Burnishing Your Employment Brand," *Workforce Management,* October 22, 2007, web.eboscost.com, accessed March 18, 2008.
37. Judith MacBride-King, "Governments, Start Your Recruitment Campaigns," *Canadian HR Reporter,* October 8, 2007, p. 18.
38. "Nova Scotia: Career Home," https://jobs.novascotia.ca; and "Manitoba Government Job Opportunities," https://jobsearch.gov.mb.ca, accessed February 14, 2018.
39. M. A. Conrad and S. D. Ashworth, "Recruiting Source Effectiveness: A Meta-Analysis and Reexamination of Two Rival Hypotheses," paper presented at annual meeting of Society of Industrial/Organizational Psychology, Chicago, 1986.
40. Michael Stephan, David Brown, and Robin Erickson, "Talent Acquisition: Enter the Cognitive Recruiter: 2017 Global Human Capital Trends," *Deloitte,* https://www.2.deloitte.com.
41. Jane Cooper, and Shannon Jackson, "Talent Management Benchmarking: Human Resources Trends and Metrics, 4th ed., *The Conference Board of Canada,* 2017, p. 42.
42. J. A. Breaugh, *Recruitment: Science and Practice* (Boston: PWS-Kent, 1992).
43. Chad Rabello, "How I've Learned to Cut Back on New Hires and Make More Promotions," Fast Company, March 25, 2016, http://fastcompany.com.
44. Breaugh, *Recruitment,* pp. 113–14.
45. R. S. Schuler and S. E. Jackson, "Linking Competitive Strategies with Human Resource Management Practices," *Academy of Management Executive* 1 (1987), pp. 207–19.
46. G. Colvin, "How to Manage Your Business in a Recession," *Fortune,* January 19, 2009, pp. 88–93; M. Orey, "Hang the Recession, Let's Bulk Up," *BusinessWeek,* February 2, 2009, pp. 80–81; and J. Collin, "How Great Companies Turn Crisis into Opportunity," *Fortune,* February 2, 2009, p. 49.
47. Gerry Crispin and Mark Mehler, "Career Xroads Source of Hire Report 2014," September 2014, www.careerxroads.com.
48. C. R. Wanberg, R. Kanfer, and J. T. Banas, "Predictors and Outcomes of Networking Intensity among Job Seekers," *Journal of Applied Psychology* 85 (2000), pp. 491–503.
49. Sarah Fister Gale, "Social Media: Transforms the Recruiting Software Industry," *Workforce Management,* June 2014, p. 24.
50. "Linkedin Workforce Report|May 2017, May 2, 2017, http://www.linkedin.com and Barb Darrow, "LinkedIn Claims Half a Billion Users, Fortune, April 24, 2017, http://www.fortune.com.
51. Lauren Weber, "Help Wanted--on Writing Job Descriptions," *Wall Street Journal,* October 2, 2013, http://online.wsj.com.
52. "For Employers," accessed from https://www.hrpa.ca/forthepublic_/Pages/HR-Jobs.aspx.
53. P. Smith, "Sources Used by Employers When Hiring College Grads," *Personnel Journal,* February 1995, p. 25.
54. J. W. Boudreau and S. L. Rynes, "Role of Recruitment in Staffing Utility Analysis," *Journal of Applied Psychology* 70 (1985), pp. 354–66.
55. "Competition Partners," accessed from https://jdcwest.org.
56. B. Hundley, "On-Campus Recruiting that Resonates with Top Students," *HR Professional,* January 2015, p. 56.
57. R. Hawk, *The Recruitment Function* (New York: American Management Association, 1967).
58. Sarah Fister Gale, "Social Media: Transforms the Recruiting Software Industry," *Workforce Management,* June 2014, p. 24.
59. M. S. Taylor and T. J. Bergman, "Organizational Recruitment Activities and Applicants' Reactions at Different Stages of the Recruitment Process," *Personnel Psychology* 40 (1984), pp. 261–285; and C. D. Fisher, D. R. Ilgen, and W. D. Hoyer, "Source Credibility, Information Favorability, and Job Offer Acceptance," *Academy of Management Journal* 22 (1979), pp. 94–103.
60. L. M. Graves and G. N. Powell, "The Effect of Sex Similarity on Recruiters' Evaluation of Actual Applicants: A Test of the Similarity-Attraction Paradigm," *Personnel Psychology* 48 (1995), pp. 85–98.
61. J. M. Phillips, "The Effects of Realistic Job Previews on Multiple Organizational Outcomes: A Meta-Analysis," *Academy of Management Journal 41* (1998), pp. 673–690.
62. J.M. Phillips and S.M. Gully, "Multilevel and Strategic Recruiting: Where Have We Been and Where Can We Go From Here?, *Journal of Management* 41 (2015), pp. 1416–45;P. G. Irving and J. P. Meyer, "Reexamination of the Met-Expectations Hypothesis: A Longitudinal Analysis," *Journal of Applied Psychology* 79 (1995), pp. 937–49.
63. W.J. Becker, T. Connolly and J.E. Slaughter, "The Effect of Job Offer Timing on Offer Acceptance, Performance, and Turnover," *Personnel Psychology* 63 (2010), pp. 223–41.

CHAPTER 5

1. Ioanna Roumeliotis, "Disability in Demand: People with Autism Offer Employers a Broader Talent Pool," CBC News, October 17, 2017, http://www.cbc.ca/news/canada/autism-hiring-1.4329174, accessed March 15, 2018; Taryn Oesch, "Autism at Work: Hiring and Training Employees on the Spectrum, *Workforce Development,* April 2017, https://www.trainingindustry.com, accessed February 12, 2018; Company website, "About Us," http://www.sap.com, accessed April 6, 2016; Sharon Florentine, "How SAP Is Hiring Autistic Adults for Tech Jobs," *CIO,* December 9, 2015, http://www.cio.com;Shirley S. Wang, "How Autism Can Help You Land a Job," *Wall Street Journal,* March 27, 2014, http://online.wsj.com; Rob Preston, "SAP CEO Envisions Younger, Greener, Cloudier Company," *InformationWeek,* November 25, 2013, http://www.informationweek.com; Katie Moisse, "Tech Giant Sees 'Competitive Advantage' in Autistic Workforce," *ABC News,* May 22, 2013, http://abcnews.go.com.
2. Eva Derous and Filip De Fruyt, "Developments in Recruitment and Selection Research," *International Journal of Selection and Assessment,* Vol. 24 No. 1 (March 2016), pp. 1–3).
3. Alice Snell, "Using Technology in Sourcing Talent," *Canadian HR Reporter,* January 29, 2007, 20(3), p. 23.

4. Bill Ryan, "An Efficiency Game-Changer," *New Hampshire Business Review,"* October 2015, http://www.nhbr.com; Dave Zielinksi, "Seven Reasons to Love Your ATS," *HR Magazine,* October 2015, http://www.shrm.org; Martin Berman-Gorvine, "Analytics Said to Help Refine Recruiting Methods," *Bloomberg BNA,* March 28, 2016, http://www.bna.com.
5. Mike Roberts, "What Is Candidate Experience? How to Define, Improve and Optimize It," *Jibe,* November 30, 2016, https://www.jibe.com.
6. "2017 Talent Board North American Candidate Experience Research Report," (2018), *TalentBoard,* http://www.thetalentboard.org, pp. 1–66.
7. "A Guide to Screening and Selection in Employment," *Canadian Human Rights Commission,* March 2007, p. 4.
8. J. C. Nunnally, *Psychometric Theory* (New York: McGraw-Hill, 1978).
9. Sue Shellenbarger, "Why Likability Matters More at Work," *Wall Street Journal,* March 25, 2014, https://online.wsj.com; Logan Hill, "Only BFFs Need Apply," *Bloomberg Businessweek,* January 7–13, pp. 63–65.
10. N. Schmitt, R. Z. Gooding, R. A. Noe, and M. Kirsch, "Meta-Analysis of Validity Studies Published Between 1964 and 1982 and the Investigation of Study Characteristics," *Personnel Psychology* 37 (1984), pp. 407–22.
11. D. D. Robinson, "Content-oriented Personnel Selection in a Small Business Setting," *Personnel Psychology* 34 (1981), pp. 77–87.
12. M. V. Rafter, "Assessment Providers Scoring Well," *Workforce Management,* January 19, 2009, pp. 24–25.
13. F. L. Schmidt and J. E. Hunter, "The Future of Criterion-related Validity," *Personnel Psychology* 33 (1980), pp. 41–60; F. L. Schmidt, J. E. Hunter, and K. Pearlman, "Task Differences as Moderators of Aptitude Test Validity: A Red Herring," *Journal of Applied Psychology* 66 (1982), pp. 166–85; R. L. Gutenberg, R. D. Arvey, H. G. Osburn, and R. P. Jeanneret, "Moderating Effects of Decision-making/Information Processing Dimensions on Test Validities," *Journal of Applied Psychology* 68 (1983), pp. 600–08.
14. T. W Dougherty, D. B. Turban, and J. C. Callender, "Confirming First Impressions in the Employment Interview: A Field Study of Interviewer Behavior," *Journal of Applied Psychology* 79 (1994), pp. 659–65.
15. Edwin, Jansen, "How to Bust Interview Liars," *Canadian Business,* March 2014, p. 23.
16. Christelle Martin-Lacroux, "Without the Spelling Errors I Would Have Shortlisted Her ..: The Impact of Spelling Errors on Recruiters' Choice During the Personnel Selection Process," *International Journal of Selection and Assessment,* 25 (2017), pp. 276–83.
17. "Name-Blind Recruitment Pilot Project —Final Report, *Government of Canada,* January 25, 2018, https://www.canada.ca/en/public-service-commission/services/publications/Name-blind-recruitment-pilot-project.htmland Sarah Dobson, "Feds Try to Blank out Bias," *Canadian HR Reporter,* May 15, 2017, p. 1, 9.
18. Judy Greenwald, "Layoffs May Spark Defamation Suits," *Business Insurance,* June 1, 2009, Business & Company Resource Center, http://galenet.galegroup.com.
19. "Guide to Screening and Selection in Employment," May 2007, https://www.chrc-ccdp.gc.ca/sites/default/files/screen_1.pdf, accessed November 26, 2018.
20. A. Ryan and M. Lasek, "Negligent Hiring and Defamation: Areas of Liability Related to Preemployment Inquiries," *Personnel Psychology* 44 (1991), pp. 293–319.
21. A. Long, "Addressing the Cloud over Employee References: A Survey of Recently Enacted State Legislation," *William and Mary Law Review* 39 (October 1997), pp. 177–228.
22. Clarence Bennett, "Stop Fighting Over Reference Letters," *Canadian HR Reporter,* December 1, 2014, p. 15.
23. Lynne Van Buskirk "Can I Get a Reference?" *Canadian HR Reporter,* March 10, 2008, http://www.hrreporter.com, accessed April 3, 2008.
24. Heather R. Huhman, "What to Do When Good Talent Has Suspicious Social Media," *Entrepreneur,* March 21, 2016, http://www.entrepreneur.com
25. Marcel Vander Wier, "Dishonest References Test Recruitment," *Canadian HR Reporter,* January 2018, p. 7.
26. "Testimonials," *Sterling Talent Solutions website,* www.backcheck.net/testimonials.htm, accessed November 19, 2018.
27. Jim Middlemiss, "Didn't You Check?" *National Post,* January 31, 2007, p. WK3.
28. Shannon Klie, "Weeding Out the Fakes," *Canadian HR Reporter,* May 7, 2007, 20(9), pp. 1-2.
29. "Be Careful Who You Google," *Investment Executive,* March 1, 2012; "Pitfalls of Social Media in Background Checks," *24 Hours Toronto,* March 19, 2012; Amanda Silliker, "Tread Carefully with Social Media Checks," *Canadian HR Reporter,* January 30, 2012, p. 1, 11.
30. M I. Brown, Michael A. Grossenbacher, "Can You Test Me Now? Equivalence of GMA Tests on Mobile and Non-mobile Devices," *International Journal of Selection and Assessment,* 25 (2017), pp. 61–71 and Denise Potosky and Philip Bobko, "Selection Testing via the Internet: Practical Considerations and Exploratory Empirical Findings," *Personnel Psychology,* 57 (2004), pp. 1003–34.
31. "Office Skills Test-OST 200," Government of Canada, https://www.canada.ca/en/public-service-commission/services/staffing-assessment-tools-resources/human-resources-specialists-hiring-managers/human-resources-toolbox/personnel-psychology-centre/consultation-test-services/public-service-commission-tests/office-skills-test-ost-200.html, accessed October 21, 2018.
32. M I. Brown, Michael A. Grossenbacher, "Can You Test Me Now? Equivalence of GMA Tests on Mobile and Non-mobile Devices," *International Journal of Selection and Assessment,* 25 (2017), pp. 61–71.
33. L. C. Buffardi, E. A. Fleishman, R. A. Morath, and P. M. McCarthy, "Relationships Between Ability Requirements and Human Errors in Job Tasks," *Journal of Applied Psychology* 85 (2000), pp. 551–64; J. Hogan, "Structure of Physical Performance in Occupational Tasks," *Journal of Applied Psychology* 76 (1991), pp. 495–507.
34. "Prepare for PARE," http://www.rcmp-grc.gc.ca/en/prepare-for-pare, accessed March 16, 2018.
35. "PSC Tests by level," *Public Service Commission of Canada,* http://www.psc-cfp.gc.ca/ppc-cpp/psc-tests-cfp/index-eng.htm, accessed February 11, 2015.
36. M. J. Ree, J. A. Earles, and M. S. Teachout, "Predicting Job Performance: Not Much More Than *g,*" *Journal of Applied Psychology* 79 (1994), pp. 518–24; L. S. Gottfredson, "The *g* Factor in Employment," *Journal of Vocational Behavior* 29 (1986), pp. 293–96; J. E. Hunter and R. H. Hunter, "Validity and Utility of Alternative Predictors of Job Performance," *Psychological Bulletin* 96 (1984), pp. 72–98; Gutenberg et al., "Moderating Effects" F. L. Schmidt, J. G. Berner, and J. E. Hunter, "Racial Differences in Validity of Employment Tests: Reality or Illusion," *Journal of Applied Psychology* 58 (1974), pp. 5–6; J. A. LePine, J. A. Colquitt, and A. Erez, "Adaptability to Changing Task Contexts: Effects of General Cognitive Ability, Conscientiousness, and Openness to Experience," *Personnel Psychology* 53 (2000), pp. 563–93.
37. George Anders, "The Rare Find," *Bloomberg Businessweek,* October 17, 2011, EBSCOhost, https://www.ebsco.com.

38. "Human Resources Consultant Simulation Exercise," http://www.psc-cfp.gc.ca/ppc-cpp/psc-tests-cfp/sim-410-eng.htm, accessed April 4, 2012.
39. D. J Schleiger, V. Venkataramani, F. P. Morgeson, and M. A. Campion, "So You Didn't Get the Job . . . Now What Do You Think? Examining Opportunity to Perform Fairness Perceptions," *Personnel Psychology* 59 (2006), pp. 559–90.
40. F. L. Schmidt and J. E. Hunter, "The Validity and Utility of Selection Methods in Personnel Psychology: Practical and Theoretical Implications of 85 Years of Research Findings," *Psychological Bulletin* 124 (1998), pp. 262–74.
41. W. Arthur, E. A. Day, T. L. McNelly, and P. S. Edens, "Meta-Analysis of the Criterion-Related Validity of Assessment Center Dimensions," *Personnel Psychology* 56 (2003), pp. 125–54; C. E. Lance, T. A. Lambert, A. G. Gewin, F. Lievens, and J. M. Conway, "Revised Estimates of Dimension and Exercise Variance Components in Assessment Center Postexercise Dimension Ratings," *Journal of Applied Psychology* 89 (2004), pp. 377–85.
42. L. Winerman, "What Sets High Achievers Apart?" *Monitor on Psychology,* December 2013, pp. 28–31.
43. Kris Dunn, "The Jerk at Work Could be a Perk," *Workforce,* November 2015, http://www.workforce.com; M. Mount, M.R. Barrick, and J.P. Strauss, "Validity of Observable Ratings of the Big Five Personality Factors," *Journal of Applied Psychology* 79 (1993), pp. 272–280.
44. Eliza Gray, "Do You Understand Why Stars Twinkle? Would You Rather Read than Watch TV? Do You Trust Data More than Your Instincts?," *Time,* June 2015, pp. 41–46.
45. Pat Galahan, "Tester Beware," *TD,* September 2015, EBSCO host, https://www.ebsco.com; J.A. Shaffer and J.E. Postlewaite, "A Matter of Context: A Meta-analytic Investigation of the Relative Validity of Contextualized and Non-contextualized Personality Measures," *Personnel Psychology* 63 (2010), pp. 299–324; F.P. Morgeson, M.A. Campion, R.L. Dipboye, J.R. Hollenbeck, K.R. Murphy, and N. Schmitt, "Reconsidering the Use of Personality Tests in Personnel Selection Contexts," *Personnel Psychology* 60 (2007), pp. 683–729.
46. J.P. Hausknecht, "Candidate Persistence and Personality Test Practice Effects; Implications for Staffing System Management," *Personnel Psychology* 63 (2010), pp. 299–324; S.A. Birkland, T.M. Manson, J.L. Kisamore, M.T. Brannick, and M.A. Smith, "Faking on Personality Measures," *International Journal of Selection and Assessment* 14 (December 2014), pp. 317–55.
47. C. H. Van Iddekinge, P. H. Raymark, and P. L Rother, "Assessing Personality with a Structured Employment Interview: Construct-related Validity and Susceptibility to Response Inflation," *Journal of Applied Psychology* 90 (2005), pp. 536–52; R. Mueller-Hanson, E. D. Heggestad, and G. C. Thornton, "Faking and Selection: Considering the Use of Personality from Select-In and Select-Out Perspectives," *Journal of Applied Psychology* 88 (2003), pp. 348–55; and N. L. Vasilopoulos, J. M. Cucina, and J.M. McElreath, "Do Warnings of Response Verification Moderate the Relationship between Personality and Cognitive Ability?" *Journal of Applied Psychology* 90 (2005), pp. 306–22.
48. A. Hedger, "Employee Screening: Common Challenges, Smart Solutions," *Workforce Management,* March 17, 2008, pp. 39–46; and J. Welch and S. Welch, "Team Building: Right and Wrong," *BusinessWeek,* November 24, 2008, p. 130; S.E. Humphrey, J.R. Hollenbeck, C.J. Meyer, and D.R. Ilgen, "Trait Configurations in Self-Managed Teams: A Conceptual Examination of the Use of Seeding for Maximizing and Minimizing Trait Variance in Teams," *Journal of Applied Psychology*92 (2007), pp. 885–892.
49. D. S. One, C. Viswesvaran, and E. L. Schmidt, "Comprehensive Meta-Analysis of Integrity Test Validities: Findings and Implications for Personnel Selection and Theories of Job Performance," *Journal of Applied Psychology* 78 (1993), pp. 679–703; H. J. Bernardin and D. K. Cooke, "Validity of an Honesty Test in Predicting Theft Among Convenience Store Employees," *Academy of Management Journal* 36 (1993), pp. 1079–1106.
50. Victor M. Catano, Damian F. O'Keefe, Robbie E. Francis, and Soo M. Owens, "Construct-based Approach to Developing a Short, Personality-based Measure of Integrity," *International Journal of Selection and Assessment,* 26 (2018), pp. 75–92.
51. "Workplace Impairment Questions and Answers," *Government of Canada,* https://www.canada.ca, accessed October 21, 2018; Patrick Cain, "As Legal Pot Draws Near, Employers in Dangerous Fields Lack Clear Standards, Rules on Testing," January 12, 2018, https://globalnews.ca; "Pre-Employment Drug & Alcohol Testing," *Cann/Amm Occupational Testing,* www.cannamm.cam, accessed October 21, 2018.
52. "Canadian Human Rights Commission's Policy on Alcohol and Drug Testing," October 2009, p. 6.
53. Duncan, Marsden, "Drug and Alcohol Testing: A Divided Nation?" *Canadian HR Reporter,* October 5, 2009, pp. 5–6; Todd Humber, "Pre-employment Drug Tests Dealt Blow," *Canadian HR Reporter,* July 17, 2006, http://www.hrreporter.com, accessed April 8, 2008.
54. M. A. McDaniel, E. P. Morgeson, E. G. Finnegan, M. A. Campion, and E. P. Braverman, "Use of Situational Judgment Tests to Predict Job Performance: A Clarification of the Literature," *Journal of Applied Psychology* 86 (2001), pp. 730–40; J. Clavenger, G. M. Perreira, D. Weichmann, N. Schmitt, and V. S. Harvey, "Incremental Validity of Situational Judgment Tests," *Journal of Applied Psychology* 86 (2001), pp. 410–17.
55. M. A. Campion, J. E. Campion, and J. P. Hudson, "Structured Interviewing: A Note of Incremental Validity and Alternative Question Types," *Journal of Applied Psychology* 79 (1994), pp. 998–1002; E. D. Pulakos and N. Schmitt, "Experience-based and Situational Interview Questions: Studies of Validity," *Personnel Psychology* 48 (1995), pp. 289–308; and A. P. J. Wllis, B. J. West, A. M. Ryan, and R. P DeShon, "The Use of Impression Management Tactics in Structured Interviews: A Function of Question Type?" *Journal of Applied Psychology* 87 (2002), pp. 1200–208.
56. Todd Humber, "How BMO Financial Selects Employees," *Canadian HR Reporter,* December 6, 2004, p. G2.
57. Cris Brady, "The Neurodiversity Movement," *HR Professional,* January 2018, pp. 31–32.
58. T. Chamorro-Premuzic, D. Winsborough, R.A. Sherman, and R. Hogan, "New Talent Signals: Shiny New Objects or a Brave New World?" *Industrial and Organizational Psychology,* 9, (2016), pp. 621–40.
59. Markus Langer, Cornelius J. Konig, and Kevin Krause, "Examining Digital Interviews for Personnel Selection: Applicant Reactions and Interviewer Ratings," *International Journal of Selection and Assessment,* 25 (2017), pp. 371–82.
60. "Hilton Cuts Time to Hire Nearly 90% With HireVue Assessment," http://www.hirevue.com, accessed March 15, 2018.
61. Calin Rovinescu, "Careers Take Flight," *Enroute,* April 2018, p. 15.
62. N. Schmitt, F. L. Oswald, B. H. Kim, M. A. Gillespie, L. J. Ramsey, and T. Y Yoo, "The Impact of Elaboration on Socially Desirable Responding and the Validity of Biodata Measures," *Journal of Applied Psychology* 88 (2003), pp. 979–88; N.

Schmitt and C. Kunce, "The Effects of Required Elaboration of Answers to Biodata Questions," *Personnel Psychology* 55 (2002), pp. 569–87.

63. Hunter and Hunter, "Validity and Utility of Alternative Predictors of Job Performance."
64. R. Pingitore, B. L. Dugoni, R. S. Tindale, and B. Spring, "Bias Against Overweight Job Applicants in a Simulated Interview," *Journal of Applied Psychology* 79 (1994), pp. 184–90.
65. M. A. McDaniel, D. L. Whetzel, F. L. Schmidt, and S. D. Maurer, "The Validity of Employment Interviews: A Comprehensive Review and Meta-Analysis," *Journal of Applied Psychology* 79 (1994), pp. 599–616; A. I. Huffcutt and W. A. Arthur, "Hunter and Hunter (1984) Revisited: Interview Validity for Entry-Level Jobs," *Journal of Applied Psychology* 79 (1994), pp. 184–90.
66. Y. Ganzach, A. N. Kluger, and N. Klayman, "Making Decisions from an Interview: Expert Measurement and Mechanical Combination," *Personnel Psychology* 53(2000), pp. 1–21; G. Stasser and W. Titus, "Effects of Information Load and Percentage of Shared Information on the Dissemination of Unshared Information During Group Discussion," *Journal of Personality and Social Psychology* 53 (1987), pp. 81–93.
67. C.H. Middendorf and T.H. Macan, "Note-Taking in the Interview: Effects on Recall and Judgments," *Journal of Applied Psychology* 87 (2002), pp. 293–303; K.G. Melchers, N. Lienhardt, M. Von Aartburg, and M. Kleinmann, "Is More Structure Really Better? A Comparison of Frame of Reference and Descriptively Anchored Rating Scales to Improve Interviewers' Rating Quality," *Personnel Psychology* 64 (2011), pp. 53–87.
68. Sarah B. Hood, "Indigenous Inclusiveness Implementing Truth and Reconciliation in the Workplace," *HR Professional,* January 2018, p. 20.
69. Liz Bernier, "Hiring Managers a Thorn in HR's Side," *Canadian HR Reporter,* September 8, 2014, p. 1, 12.
70. Jane Cooper and Shannon Jackson, Talent Management Benchmarking: Human Resources Trends and Metrics, Fourth Edition, *The Conference Board of Canada,* February 2017, p. 50.

CHAPTER 6

1. "New Blanket Exercise on Indigenous History Moves RCMP cadets," *Royal Canadian Mounted Police,* December 12, 2017, http://www.rcmp-grc.gc.ca/en/news/2017/new-blanket-exercise-indigenous-history-moves-rcmp-cadets, accessed September 25, 2018; Tali Folkins, "RCMP to Use KAIROS Blanket Exercise in All Cadet Training, *KAIROS Canada,* December 12, 2017, https://www.kairoscanada.org, accessed September 25, 2018; "Media Advisory: All RCMP Cadets to Participate in Powerful Reconciliation Exercise," *KAIROS Canada,* December 5, 2017, https://www.kairoscanada.org, accessed September 25, 2018; Brad Bellegarde, "Blanket Exercise Helps Regina Public Schools Work Toward Reconciliation in the Classroom," *CBC News,* September 7, 2017, http:///www.cbc.ca, accessed September 25, 2018; Kate McGillivray, "How Blankets Can Teach 500 years of Indigenous history," *CBC News,* July 26, 2017, http://www.cbc.ca, accessed September 25, 2018; KAIROS Blanket Exercise Education Resource Kit (Edu-Kit) Planning Framework—The Blanket Exercise, *KAIROS Canada,* https://www.kairosblanketexercise.org, pp. 1–13, accessed September 25, 2018.
2. J. Roy, "Transforming Informal Learning into Competitive Advantage," *T+D,* October 2010, pp. 23–25; P. Galagan, "Unformal, the New Normal, *T+D,* September 2010, pp. 29–31.
3. S.I. Tannenbaum, R. Beard, L.A. McNall, and E. Salas, "Informal Learning and Development in Organizations," in S.W.J. Kozlowski and E. Salas (eds.), *Learning, Training, and Development in Organizations* (New York: Routledge, 2010), C.L. Morrison, M. Vickers, A. Paradise, M. Czarnowsky, M. Soyars, and K. King, *Tapping The Potential of Informal Learning, An ASTD Research Study* (Alexandria, VA: American Society of Training and Development, 2008).
4. T. Bingham and M. Conner, *The New Social Learning* (Alexandria, VA: ASTD Press, 2010).
5. "Developing Skills in the Canadian Workplace," *Canadian Workplace Gazette* 2, no. 1, p. 98, http://labour-travail.hrdc-drhc.gc.ca.
6. S. Cotsman, & C. Hall, *Learning Cultures Lead the Way: Learning and Development Outlook,* 14th Edition, Ottawa: The Conference Board of Canada, 2018, p. 60.
7. R. Noe, A. Clarke, and H. Klein, "Learning in the Twenty-First Century Workplace," *Annual Review of Organizational Psychology, Organizational Behavior* 1 (2014), pp. 245–76; U. Sessa and M. London, *Continuous Learning in Organizations* (Mahwah, NJ: Lawrence Erlbaum 2006); M. London, "Lifelong Learning: Introduction," in M. London (ed.), *The Oxford Handbook of Lifelong Learning* (New York: Oxford University Press, 2011), pp. 3–11.
8. "Training Top 125 2017 Top 100 Hall of Fame: Jiffy Lube International Inc., *Training,* January/February 2017, p. 54; L. Freifeld, "Jiffy Lube's Training Drive," *Training,* January/February 2013, pp. 34–37; M. Weinstein, "Jiffy-Lube Greases the Wheels of Success,' *Training,* January/February 2015, pp. 36–38; L. Freifeld, "Jiffy-Lube Revs Up to No. 1," *Training,* January/February 2014, pp. 30–38
9. Jon Younger, Norm Smallwood, and Dave Ulrich, "Developing Your Organization's Brand as a Talent Developer," *HR: Human Resource Planning* 30, no. 2 (2007), p. 21.
10. S. Cotsman and C. Hall, *Learning Cultures Lead the Way: Learning and Development Outlook,* 14th Edition, Ottawa: The Conference Board of Canada, 2018.
11. S. Cotsman and C. Hall, *Learning Cultures Lead the Way: Learning and Development Outlook,* 14th Edition, Ottawa: The Conference Board of Canada, 2018.
12. R. Noe, *Employee Training and Development,* 4th ed. (New York: Irwin/McGraw-Hill, 2008).
13. I. L. Goldstein, E. P. Braverman, and H. Goldstein, "Needs Assessment," in *Developing Human Resources,* ed. K. N. Wexley (Washington, DC: Bureau of National Affairs, 1991), pp. 5-35–5-75.
14. J. Z. Rouillier and I. L. Goldstein, "Determinants of the Climate for Transfer of Training" (presented at Society of Industrial/Organizational Psychology meetings, St. Louis, MO, 1991); J. S. Russell, J. R. Terborg, and M. L. Powers, "Organizational Performance and Organizational Level Training and Support," *Personnel Psychology* 38 (1985), pp. 849–63; H. Baumgartel, G. J. Sullivan, and L. E. Dunn, "How Organizational Climate and Personality Affect the Payoff from Advanced Management Training Sessions," *Kansas Business Review* 5 (1978), pp. 1–10.
15. Jull Casner-Lotto et al., *Are They Really Ready to Work?* (New York: Conference Board; Washington, DC: Corporate Voices for Working Families; Tucson, AZ: Partnership for 21st Century Skills; Alexandria, VA: Society for Human Resource Management, 2006 at http://www.infoedge.com; R. Davenport, "Eliminate the Skills Gap," *T+D,* February 2006, pp. 26–34; and M. Schoeff, "Amid Calls to Bolster U.S. Innovation, Experts Lament Paucity of Basic Math Skills," *Workforce Management,* March 2006, pp. 46–49.
16. R. A. Noe, "Trainees' Attributes and Attitudes: Neglected Influences on Training Effectiveness," *Academy of*

Management Review 11 (1986), pp. 736–49; T. T. Baldwin, R. T. Magjuka, and B. T. Loher, "The Perils of Participation: Effects of Choice on Trainee Motivation and Learning," *Personnel Psychology* 44 (1991), pp. 51–66; S. L Tannenbaum, J. E. Mathieu, E. Salas, and J. A. Cannon-Bowers, "Meeting Trainees' Expectations: The Influence of Training Fulfillment on the Development of Commitment, Self-Efficacy, and Motivation," *Journal of Applied Psychology* 76 (1991), pp. 759–69.

17. Caroline Coppel, "A Career Development Support System," *TD,* March 2018, p. 9.
18. L. H. Peters, E. J. O'Connor, and J. R. Eulberg, "Situational Constraints: Sources, Consequences, and Future Considerations," in *Research in Personnel and Human Resource Management,* ed. K. M. Rowland and G. R. Ferris (Greenwich, CT: JAI Press, 1985), vol. 3, pp. 79–114; E. J. O'Connor, L. H. Peters, A. Pooyan, J. Weekley, B. Frank, and B. Erenkranz, "Situational Constraints' Effects on Performance, Affective Reactions, and Turnover: A Field Replication and Extension," *Journal of Applied Psychology* 69 (1984), pp. 663–72; D. J. Cohen, "What Motivates Trainees?," *Training and Development Journal,* November 1990, pp. 91–93; Russell, Terborg, and Powers, "Organizational Performance."
19. Doug Stephen, "3 Ways to Rethink L&D for the Deskless Workforce," *Chief Learning Officer,* May 1, 2018, http://www.clomedia.com.
20. B. Mager, *Preparing Instructional Objectives,* 2nd ed. (Belmont, CA: Lake Publishing, 1984); B. J. Smith and B. L. Delahaye, *How to Be an Effective Trainer,* 2nd ed. (New York: Wiley, 1987).
21. S. Naraianand S. Schlessinger, "Becoming an Inclusive Educator: Agentive Maneuverings in Collaboratively Taught Classrooms," *Teaching and Teacher Education* 71 (2018), pp. 179–89.
22. S. Cotsman and C. Hall, *Learning Cultures Lead the Way: Learning and Development Outlook,* 14th Edition (Ottawa: The Conference Board of Canada, 2018), p. 42; Colin Hall, *Learning and Development Outlook, Strong Learning Organizations, Strong Leadership,* 12th Edition (Ottawa: The Conference Board of Canada, February 2014), p. 40.
23. "Putting the Distance into Distance Learning," *Training,* October 1995, pp. 111–18.
24. D. Picard, "The Future is Distance Training," *Training,* November 1996, pp. s3–s10.
25. CATSA News, April 2007, p. 6, http://www.catsa-acsta.gc.ca/english/media/bulletin/2007-04.pdf, accessed May 23, 2008.
26. Red Seal Program, Human Resources Development Canada, http://www.red-seal.ca/English/redseal_e.shtml, accessed March 21, 2004.
27. Ibid.
28. Alex Moore, "Exporting Apprenticeships," *TD,* February 2018, pp. 16–17.
29. http://www.uregina.ca/coop/students/current/handbook.shtml, accessed March 11, 2004.
30. Doug Cameron, "Dreamliner's Here: Now Learn to Fly It," *The Wall Street Journal,* November 1, 2011, online.wsj.com.
31. N. Adams, "Lessons from the Virtual World," *Training,* June 1995, pp. 245–48.
32. Ibid.
33. Ave Rio, "Virtual Reality Could Be the Answer to Sexual Harassment Training," *Chief Learning Officer,* April 2, 2018, http://www.clomedia.com.
34. Anders Gronstedt, "The Immersive Reality Revolution," TD, February 2018, pp. 32–35; Doug Stephen, "3 Ways to Rethink L&D for the Deskless Workforce," *Chief Learning Officer,* May 1, 2018, http://www.clomedia.com.
35. Julie Winkle Giulioni and Karen Voloshin, "A Case for the Mini Case Study," *TD: Talent Development,* November 2014, pp. 27–29.
36. MarkStrat, https://web.stratxsimulations.com/simulation/strategic-marketing-simulation/, accessed November 23, 2018.
37. M.T. Cardador, G.B. Northcroft; J. Whicker, "A Theory of Work Gamification: Something Old, Something New, Something Borrowed, Something Cool?" *Human Resource Management Review* 27 (2017), pp. 353–65.
38. Rachel Donley and Tara Welsh, "Put a Little Play in Your Day," *TD,* March 2018, pp. 18–19.
39. G. P. Latham and L. M. Saari, "Application of Social Learning Theory to Training Supervisors Through Behavior Modeling," *Journal of Applied Psychology* 64 (1979), pp. 239–46.
40. M. Rosenberg, *E-learning Strategies for Delivering Knowledge in the Digital Age* (New York: McGraw-Hill, 2001); "What Is Web-based Training?" from http://www.clark.net/pub/nractive/ft.html; R. Johnson and H. Gueutal, *Transforming HR through Technology* (Alexandria, VA: SHRM Foundation, 2010).
41. S. Sipek, "Learning Is Doing at PwC," *Chief Learning Officer,* June 2016, pp. 38–39.
42. American Society for Training and Development, *Learning Circuits: Glossary,* http://www.astd.org/LC/glossary.htm, accessed March 16, 2012; Katie Kuehner-Hebert, "Go Mobile?," *Chief Learning Officer,* March 2014, pp. 18–21.
43. Sarah Gale Fisher, "Cisco Reinvents Social Learning," *Chief Learning Officer,* September 2015, pp. 40–41, 49.
44. Zach Posner, "Personalizing Adaptive Learning," *TD,* January 2018, pp. 24–28 and Tony Bingham and Pat Galagan, "And Now for Something Completely Different," *TD,* May 2017, pp. 27–31.
45. "ADP, LLC: ADP National Accounts Implementation—Reduced Time to Competency," *Training,* January/February 2016, pp. 102–3.
46. "Learning Management Systems: An Executive Summary," *Training,* March 2002, p. 4; S. Castellano, "The Evolution of the LMS," *T+D,* November 2014, p. 14.
47. D. Brown and D. Harvey, *An Experiential Approach to Organizational Development* (Englewood Cliffs, NJ: Prentice Hall, 2000); and Larissa Jogi, review of *The Handbook of Experiential Learning and Management Education,* eds. Michael Reynolds and Russ Vince, *Studies in the Education of Adults* 40 no. 2 (Autumn 2008): pp. 232–34, accessed at OCLC FirstSearch, http://newfirstsearch.oclc.org.
48. J. Cannon-Bowers and C. Bowers, "Team Development and Functioning," in *A Handbook of Industrial and Organizational Psychology,* ed. S. Zedeck, 1: 597–650 (Washington, DC: American Psychological Association, 2011); L. Delise, C. Gorman, A. Brooks, J. Rentsch, and D. Steele-Johnson, "The Effects of Team Training on Team Outcomes: A Meta-analysis," *Performance Improvement Quarterly* 22 (2010): 53–80.
49. Lesley Young, "All in the Family at Toronto Hydro," *Canadian HR Reporter,* March 24, 2008, p. 16.
50. C. E. Schneier, "Training and Development Programs: What Learning Theory and Research Have to Offer," *Personnel Journal,* April 1974, pp. 288–93; M. Knowles, "Adult Learning," in *Training and Development Handbook,* 3rd ed., ed. R. L. Craig (New York: McGraw-Hill, 1987), pp. 168–79; B. J. Smith and B. L. Delahaye, *How to Be an Effective Trainer,* 2nd ed. (New York: Wiley, 1987); and Traci Sitzmann, "Self-Regulating Online Course Engagement," *T+D,* March 2010, Business & Company Resource Center, galenet.galegroup.com.
51. K. A. Smith-Jentsch, F. G. Jentsch, S. C. Payne, and E. Salas, "Can Pretraining Experiences Explain Individual Differences in Learning?," *Journal of Applied Psychology* 81 (1996), pp. 110–16.

52. W. McGehee and P. W. Thayer, *Training in Business and Industry* (New York: Wiley, 1961).
53. R. M. Gagne and K. L. Medsker, *The Condition of Learning* (Fort Worth, TX: Harcourt-Brace, 1996).
54. J. C. Naylor and G. D. Briggs, "The Effects of Task Complexity and Task Organization on the Relative Efficiency of Part and Whole Training Methods," *Journal of Experimental Psychology* 65 (1963), pp. 217–24.
55. Megan Cole, "Talent Development Pros Predict Spike in Microlearning," *TD,* May 2017, p. 9.
56. S. Cotsman and C. Hall, *Learning Cultures Lead the Way: Learning and Development Outlook,* 14th Edition, Ottawa: The Conference Board of Canada, 2018, p. 67.
57. S. Allen, "Water Cooler Wisdom," *Training,* August 2005, pp. 30–34.
58. Vince Han, "Are Chatbots the Future of Training," *TD,* September 2017, pp. 42–46.
59. Stella Lee, "Machine Learning Applications in E-Learning: Bias, Risks and Mitigation," *Chief Learning Officer,* September 12, 2018, http://www.clomedia.com.
60. Ibid.
61. Kirkpatrick, Jim D., and Wendy Kayser Kirkpatrick. *Training on Trial: How Workplace Learning Must Reinvent Itself to Remain Relevant* (New York: American Management Association, 2010).
62. S. Cotsman and C. Hall, *Learning Cultures Lead the Way: Learning and Development Outlook,* 14th Edition, Ottawa: The Conference Board of Canada, 2018, pp. 62–63.
63. S. Cotsman, & C. Hall, "Learning Cultures Lead the Way: Learning and Development Outlook - 14th Edition, Ottawa: The Conference Board of Canada, 2018, p. 64.
64. H.J. Klein, Beth Polin, and K.L. Sutton. "Specific Onboarding Practices for the Socialization of New Employees," *International Journal of Selection and Assessment* 23 (2015), pp. 263–83.
65. Keith Ferrazzi and Tim Davis, "The Employee Integration Equation," *T+D,* October 2015, pp. 57–60; Talya N. Bauer, *Onboarding New Employees: Maximizing Success, Effective Practice Guidelines* (Alexandria, VA: SHRM Foundation, 2010); T. Bauer and B. Erdogan, "Delineating and Reviewing the Role of Newcomer Capital in Organizational Socialization," *Annual Review of Organizational Psychology and Organizational Behaviour* 1, (2014), pp. 439–57.
66. Vince Han, "Are Chatbots the Future of Training," *TD,* September 2017, pp. 42–46.
67. Ibid; "Bringing New Hires Up to Speed: How Structured Onboarding Can Help," *The Conference Board of Canada,* August 2011, p. 6.
68. H. Dolezalek, "The Path to Inclusion," *Training,* May 2008, pp. 52–54.
69. F. Dobbins and A. Kalev, "Why Diversity Programs Fail," *Harvard Business Review,* July/August 2016. pp. 52–60; S.E. Jackson and Associates, *Diversity in the Workplace: Human Resource Initiatives* (New York: Guilford, 1992).
70. Anesa Diaz-Uda, Carmen Medina, and Beth Schill, "Diversity's New Frontier," Deloitte University Press, July 23, 2013, http://www2.deloitte.com, accessed April 2, 2018.
71. K. Bezrukova, C. Spell, J. Perry, and K. Jehn, "A Meta-Analytical Integration of Over 40 Years of Research on Diversity Training Evaluation," *Psychological Bulletin* 142 (2016), pp. 1227–74.
72. M. London, *Managing the Training Enterprise* (San Francisco: Jossey-Bass, 1989) and D. Day, *Developing Leadership Talent* (Alexandria, VA: SHRM Foundation, 2007).
73. R. W. Pace, P. C. Smith, and G. E. Mills, *Human Resource Development* (Englewood Cliffs, NJ: Prentice Hall, 1991); W. Fitzgerald, "Training versus Development," *Training and Development Journal,* May 1992, pp. 81–84; R. A. Noe, S. L. Wilk, E. J. Mullen, and J. E. Wanek, "Employee Development: Issues in Construct Definition and Investigation of Antecedents," in *Improving Training Effectiveness in Work Organizations,* ed. J. K. Ford (Mahwah, NJ: Lawrence Erlbaum, 1997), pp. 153–89.
74. J. H. Greenhaus and G. A. Callanan, *Career Management,* 2nd ed. (Fort Worth, TX: Dryden Press, 1994); D. Hall, *Careers in and out of Organizations* (Thousand Oaks, CA: Sage, 2002).
75. R. Noe, *Employee Training and Development,* 5th ed. (New York: McGraw-Hill Irwin, 2010).
76. A. Howard and D. W. Bray, *Managerial Lives in Transition: Advancing Age and Changing Times* (New York: Guilford, 1988); J. Bolt, *Executive Development* (New York: Harper Business, 1989); J. R. Hintichs and G. P. Hollenbeck, "Leadership Development," in *Developing Human Resources,* ed. K. N. Wexley, p. 237; and Day, *Developing Leadership Talent.*
77. Joyce Rowlands, "Soft Skills Give Hard Edge," *The Globe and Mail,* June 9, 2004, p. C8.
78. Ibid.
79. A. Thorne and H. Gough, *Portraits of Type* (Palo Alto, CA: Consulting Psychologists Press, 1993).
80. D. Druckman and R. A. Bjork, eds., *In the Mind's Eye: Enhancing Human Performance* (Washington, DC: National Academy Press, 1991); M. H. McCaulley, "The Myers-Briggs Type Indicator and Leadership," in *Measures of Leadership,* eds. K. E. Clark and M. B. Clark (West Orange, NJ: Leadership Library of America, 1990), pp. 381–418.
81. G. C. Thornton III and W. C. Byham, *Assessment Centers and Managerial Performance* (New York: Academic Press, 1982); L. F. Schoenfeldt and J. A. Steger, "Identification and Development of Management Talent," in *Research in Personnel and Human Resource Management,* eds. K. N. Rowland and G. Ferris (Greenwich, CT: JAI Press, 1989), vol. 7, pp. 151–81.
82. Thornton and Byham, *Assessment Centers and Managerial Performance.*
83. P. G. W. Jansen and B. A. M. Stoop, "The Dynamics of Assessment Center Validity: Results of a Seven-Year Study," *Journal of Applied Psychology* 86 (2001), pp. 741–53; and D. Chan, "Criterion and Construct Validation of an Assessment Centre," *Journal of Occupational and Organizational Psychology* 69 (1996), pp. 167–81.
84. R. G. Jones and M. D. Whitmore, "Evaluating Developmental Assessment Centers as Interventions," *Personnel Psychology* 48 (1995), pp. 377–88.
85. J. F. Brett and L. E. Atwater, "360-Degree Feedback: Accuracy, Reactions, and Perceptions of Usefulness," *Journal of Applied Psychology* 86 (2001), pp. 930–42; Marshall Goldsmith, "How to Increase Your Leadership Effectiveness," *BusinessWeek,* November 20, 2009, http://www.businessweek.com; and Brenda Bence, "Would You Want to Work for You?" *Supervision,* February 2010, Business & Company Resource Center, http://galenet.galegroup.com.
86. L. Atwater, P. Roush, and A. Fischthal, "The Influence of Upward Feedback on Self- and Follower Ratings of Leadership," *Personnel Psychology* 48 (1995), pp. 35–59; J. F. Hazucha, S. A. Hezlett, and R. J. Schneider, "The Impact of 360-Degree Feedback on Management Skill Development," *Human Resource Management* 32 (1193), pp. 325–51; J. W. Smither, M. London, N. Vasilopoulos, R. R. Reilly, R. E. Millsap, and N. Salvemini, "An Examination of the Effects of an Upward Feedback Program over Time," *Personnel Psychology* 48 (1995), pp. 1–34; J. Smither and A. Walker, "Are the Improvements in Multirater Feedback Ratings Over

Time?" *Journal of Applied Psychology* 89 (2004), pp. 575–81; and J. Smither, M. London, and R. Reilly, "Does Performance Improve Following Multisource Feedback? A Theoretical Model, Meta-analysis, and Review of Empirical Findings," *Personnel Psychology* 58 (2005), pp. 33–66.

87. Center for Creative Leadership, "360-Degree Feedback: Best Practices to Ensure Impact," http://www.ccl.org, accessed April 26, 2016; Jack Zenger, "How Effective Are Your 360-Degree Feedback Assessments?" *Forbes,* March 10, 2016, http://www.forbes.com; Harriet Edleson, "Do 360 Evaluations Work?" *Monitor on Psychology* 43 (November 22, 2012), accessed at http://www.apa.org.
88. M. W. McCall Jr., *High Flyers* (Boston: Harvard Business School Press, 1998).
89. R. S. Snell, "Congenial Ways of Learning: So Near yet So Far," *Journal of Management Development* 9 (1990), pp. 17–23.
90. C. D. McCauley, M. N. Ruderman, P. J. Ohlott, and J. E. Morrow, "Assessing the Developmental Components of Managerial Jobs," *Journal of Applied Psychology* 79 (1994), pp. 544–60.
91. Andrew Wahl, "Leaders Wanted," *Canadian Business,* March 1–14, 2004, pp. 33, 34.
92. M. London, *Developing Managers* (San Francisco: Jossey-Bass, 1985); M. A. Camion, L. Cheraskin, and M. J. Stevens, "Career-related Antecedents and Outcomes of Job Rotation," *Academy of Management Journal* 37 (1994), pp. 1518–42; London, *Managing the Training Enterprise.*
93. D. B. Turban and T. W. Dougherty, "Role of Protégé Personality in Receipt of Mentoring and Career Success," *Academy of Management Journal* 37 (1994), pp. 688–702; E. A. Fagenson, "Mentoring: Who Needs It? A Comparison of Protégés' and Non-Protégés' Needs for Power, Achievement, Affiliation, and Autonomy," *Journal of Vocational Behavior* 41 (1992), pp. 48–60.
94. A. H. Geiger, "Measures for Mentors," *Training and Development Journal,* February 1992, pp. 65–67; Lynnie Martin and Tyler Robinson, "Why You Should Get on Board the Mentor Ship," *Public Manager,* Winter 2011, pp. 42–45; "The Payoff," *California CPA,* October 2011, p. 12.
95. K. E. Kram, *Mentoring at Work: Developmental Relationships in Organizational Life* (Glenview, IL: Scott-Foresman, 1985); L. L. Phillips-Jones, "Establishing a Formalized Mentoring Program," *Training and Development Journal* 2 (1983), pp. 38–42; K. Kram, "Phases of the Mentoring Relationship," *Academy of Management Journal* 26 (1983), pp. 608–25; G. T. Chao, P. M. Walz, and P. D. Gardner, "Formal and Informal Mentorships: A Comparison of Mentoring Functions and Contrasts with Nonmentored Counterparts," *Personnel Psychology* 45 (1992), pp. 619–36; and C. Wanberg, E. Welsh, and S. Hezlett, "Mentoring Research: A Review and Dynamic Process Model," in *Research in Personnel and Human Resources Management,* eds. J. Martocchio and G. Ferris (New York: Elsevier Science, 2003), pp. 39–124.
96. Michele Lent Hirsch, "Mentor Makeover," *Psychology Today,* July/August 2011, EBSCOhost, https://www.ebscohost.com.
97. L. Eby, M. Butts, A. Lockwood, and A. Simon, "Protégés' Negative Mentoring Experiences: Construct Development and Nomological Validation," *Personnel Psychology* 57 (2004), pp. 411–47; R. Emelo, "Conversations with Mentoring Leaders," *T+D,* June 2011, pp. 32–37; M. Weinstein, "Please Don't Go," *Training,* May/June 2011, pp. 38–34; "Training Top 125," *Training,* January/February 2011, pp. 54–93.
98. R. A. Noe, D. B. Greenberger, and S. Wang, "Mentoring: What We Know and Where We Might Go," in *Research in Personnel and Human Resources Management,* eds. G. Ferris and J. Martocchio (New York: Elsevier Science, 2002), vol. 21, pp. 129–74; and T. D. Allen, L. T. Eby, M. L. Poteet, E. Lentz, and L. Lima, "Career Benefits Associated with Mentoring for Protégés: A Meta-Analysis," *Journal of Applied Psychology* 89 (2004), pp. 127–36.
99. Megan Cole, "Minting Your Mentors," *TD,* January 2018, p. 11.
100. D. B. Peterson and M. D. Hicks, *Leader as Coach* (Minneapolis: Personnel Decisions, 1996).
101. David Brown, "Mentoring Boosts Retention, *T&D.* But It's a Long-Term Game," *Canadian HR Reporter,* July 12, 2004, p. 7.
102. Shauna Robinson, "The Case for a Coaching Culture," *TD,* January 2018, pp. 14–15.
103. Sarah McVanel and Christine Burych, "Are You In or Out?" *HR Professional,* March/April 2015, pp. 41–42.
104. Sarah Fister Gale, "The Dawn of the Robot Coach," *Chief Learning Officer,* April 9, 2018, http://www.clomedia.com.
105. Shauna Robinson, "The Case for a Coaching Culture," *TD,* January 2018, pp. 14–15.
106. Rajiv L. Gupta and Karol M. Wasylyshyn, "Developing World Class Leaders: The Rohm and Haas Story," *People & Strategy,* December 2009, pp. 36–41; and Kathleeen Koster, "This Too Shall Pass," *Employee Benefit News,* July 1, 2009, Business & Company Resource Center, http://galenet.galegroup.com.
107. Mies De Koning, "Uncover Your Personal Methodology," *TD,* March 2018, pp. 64–66.
108. Claudine Kapel and Catherine Shepherd, "Career Ladders Create Common Language for Defining Jobs," *Canadian HR Reporter,* June 14, 2004, p. 15.
109. C.B. Derr, C. Jones, and E.L. Toomey, "Managing High-Potential Employees: Current Practices in Thirty-Three U.S. Corporations," *Human Resource Management* 27 (1988), pp. 273–90; K.M. Nowack, "The Secrets of Succession," *Training and Development* 48 (1994), pp. 49–54; W.J. Rothwell, *Effective Succession Planning,* 4th ed. (New York: AMACOM, 2010).
110. Mike Prokopeak, "ADP: Learning is the Business," *Chief Learning Officer,* June 2015, pp. 34–35.

CHAPTER 7

1. Alexia Elejalde-Ruiz, "Annual Reviews Scrapped for Real-Time Feedback," *Chicago Tribune,* April 24, 2016, http://www.chicagotribune.com; Jeff Orlando and Erica Bank, "A New Approach to Performance Management at Deloitte," *People + Strategy,* Spring 2016, pp. 42–44; Erica Bank, "Reinventing Performance Management at Deloitte," *Senior Leaders & Executive Blog(Association for Talent Development),* January 13, 2016, https://www.td.org; Marcus Buckingham and Ashley Goodall, "Reinventing Performance Management," *Harvard Business Review,* April 2015, https://hbr.org.
2. C. Allen Gorman, John P. Meriac, Sylvia G. Roch, Joshua L. Rays, and Jason S. Gamble, "An Exploratory Study of Current Performance Management Practices: Human Resource Executives' Perspectives," *International Journal of Selection and Assessment,* 25 (2017), pp. 193–202.
3. Jane Cooper and Shannon Jackson, "Talent Management Benchmarking: Human Resources Trends and Metrics, Fourth Edition," Ottawa: The Conference Board of Canada, 2017, p. 58.
4. Ibid, p. 56.
5. Ibid, p. 57.
6. Wallace Immen, "Handling the First 100 Days on the Job," *The Globe and Mail,* March 14, 2008, p. C2.
7. Angelita Becom and David Insler, "Performance Management—A Bad Process or a Broken Promise," *People & Strategy,* Volume 36, Issue 32 (2013), p. 43.
8. Chris Mason, "Patagonia's Journey into a New Regenerative Performance Approach," *People + Strategy,* Summer 2017, pp. 30–34.

9. Amy Armitage and Donna Parrey, "Reinventing Performance Management: Creating Purpose-Driven Practices," *People & Strategy,* Volume 36, Issue 32 (2013), p. 32; Christopher Collins and Bradford Bell, "The State of the Art in Performance Management," *People & Strategy,* Volume 36, Issue 32 (2013), p. 51.
10. C. Allen Gorman, John P. Meriac, Sylvia G. Roch, and Joshua L. Ray, "An Exploratory Study of Current Performance Management Practices: Human Resource Executives' Perspectives," *International Journal of Selection and Assessment* 25, 2017, pp. 193–202;A.S. DeNisi and R.D. Pritchard, (2006), "Performance Appraisal, Performance Management, and Improving Individual Performance: A Motivational Framework," *Management and Organization Review,* 2, pp. 253–77.
11. Lisa Burrell, "Co-Creating the Employee Experience," *Harvard Business Review,* March/April 2018, pp. 54–58.
12. M. Parker, "Culture Clash: Performance-managing Culture," *Financial Post,* February 20, 2012, https://business.financialpost.com, accessed May 4, 2012; "Investment in Feedback Pays Off," *National Post,* May 14, 2008, FP14; M. Parker, "It's How You Do Things, Not What You Do: Results From the 2010, Canadian Corporate Culture Study," *The Waterline*, Issue 7, July 13, 2010."
13. Melissa Campeau, "Emerging HR: The Biggest Trends in HR Now, *HR Professional,* December 2017, pp. 16–20.
14. Lori Goler, Janelle Gale, and Adam Grant, "Let's Not Kill Performance Evaluations Yet," *Harvard Business Review,* November 2016, pp. 91–94.
15. Carolyn Heinze, "Fair Appraisals," *Systems Contractor News,* July 2009, Business & Company Resource Center, http://galenet.galegroup.com.
16. Chris French, "Crowdsourcing the Performance Review," *Canadian HR Reporter,* January 27, 2014, p. 24.
17. S. Scullen, P. Bergey, and L. Aiman-Smith, "Forced Choice Distribution Systems and the Improvement of Workforce Potential: A Baseline Simulation," *Personnel Psychology* 47 (1963), pp. 149–55.
18. Heather McAteer, "Compensation Planning Outlook 2018," (Ottawa: Conference Board of Canada, October 2017), p. 33.
19. P. Smith and L. Kendall, "Retranslation of Expectations: An Approach to the Construction of Unambiguous Anchors for Rating Scales," *Journal of Applied Psychology* 47 (1963), pp. 149–55.
20. K. Murphy and J. Constans, "Behavioral Anchors as a Source of Bias in Rating," *Journal of Applied Psychology* 72 (1987), pp. 573–77; M. Piotrowski, J. Bames-Farrel, and F. Estig, "Behaviorally Anchored Bias: A Replication and Extension of Murphy and Constans," *Journal of Applied Psychology* 74 (1989), pp. 823–26; R. Harvey, "Job Analysis," in *Handbook of Industrial and Organizational Psychology,* 2nd ed. (Palo Alto, CA: Consulting Psychologist Press, 1991).
21. G. Latham and K. Wexley, *Increasing Productivity Through Performance Appraisal* (Boston: Addison-Wesley, 1981).
22. U. Wiersma and G. Latham, "The Practicality of Behavioral Observation Scales, Behavioral Expectation Scales, and Trait Scales," *Personnel Psychology 39* (1986), pp. 619–28.
23. D. C. Anderson, C. Crowell, J. Sucec, K. Gilligan, and M. Wikoff, "Behavior Management of Client Contacts in a Real Estate Brokerage: Getting Agents to Sell More," *Journal of Organizational Behavior Management* 4 (2001), pp. 580–90; F. Luthans and R. Kreitner, *Organizational Behavior Modification and Beyond* (Glenview, IL: Scott, Foresman, 1975).
24. K. L. Langeland, C. M. Jones, and T. C. Mawhinney, "Improving Staff Performance in a Community Mental Health Setting: Job Analysis, Training, Goal Setting, Feedback, and Years of Data," *Journal of Organizational Behavior Management* 18 (1998), pp. 21–43.
25. J. Komaki, R. Collins, and P. Penn, "The Role of Performance Antecedents and Consequences in Work Motivation," *Journal of Applied Psychology* 67 (1982), pp. 334–40.
26. S. Snell, "Control Theory in Strategic Human Resource Management: The Mediating Effect of Administrative Information," *Academy of Management Journal* 35 (1992), pp. 292–327.
27. Shelley Correll and Caroline Simard, "Research: Vague Feedback Is Holding Women Back," *Harvard Business Review,* April 29, 2016, https://hbr.org; Joseph Grenny and David Maxfield, "Emotional Inequality at Work," *Training,* November/December 2015, pp. 46–48; S. Snell, "Control Theory in Strategic Human Resource Management: The Mediating Effect of Administrative Information," *Academy of Management Journal* 35 (1992), pp. 292–327.
28. R. Pritchard, S. Jones, P. Roth, K. Stuebing, and S. Ekeberg, "The Evaluation of an Integrated Approach to Measuring Organizational Productivity," *Personnel Psychology* 42 (1989), pp. 69–115.
29. G. Odiorne, *MBO II: A System of Managerial Leadership for the 80's* (Belmont, CA: Pitman Publishers, 1986).
30. R. Rodgers and J. Hunter, "Impact of Management by Objectives on Organizational Productivity," *Journal of Applied Psychology* 76 (1991), pp. 322–26.
31. P. Wright, J. George, S. Farnsworth, and G. McMahan, "Productivity and Extra-Role Behavior: The Effects of Goals and Incentives on Spontaneous Helping," *Journal of Applied Psychology* 78, no. 3 (1993), pp. 374–81.
32. Christopher Collins and Bradford Bell, "The State of the Art in Performance Management," *People & Strategy,* Volume 36, Issue 2 (2013), p. 52.
33. "What Is a Balanced Scorecard?," http://www.2gc.co/UK/pdf/2GC-FAQ1.pdf, accessed July 14, 2004.
34. Cam Scholey, "Alignment—Has Your Organization Got It?," *CMA Management* 81, no. 6, pp. 16–18.
35. Mehrdad Derayeh and Stephane Brutus, "Learning from Others' 360-Degree Experiences," *Canadian HR Reporter,* February 10, 2003, http://www.hrreporter.com, accessed February 15, 2005.
36. Patty McCord, "How Netflix Reinvented HR, *Harvard Business Review,* January–February 2014, p. 74.
37. R. Heneman, K. Wexley, and M. Moore, "Performance Rating Accuracy: A Critical Review," *Journal of Business Research* 15 (1987), pp. 431–48.
38. T. Becker and R. Klimoski, "A Field Study of the Relationship Between the Organizational Feedback Environment and Performance," *Personnel Psychology* 42 (1989), pp. 343–58; H. M. Findley, W. F. Giles, K. W. Mossholder, "Performance Appraisal and Systems Facets: Relationships with Contextual Performance," *Journal of Applied Psychology* 85 (2000), pp. 634–40.
39. K. Wexley and R. Klimoski, "Performance Appraisal: An Update," in *Research in Personnel and Human Resource Management,* vol. 2, ed. K. Rowland and G. Ferris (Greenwich, CT: JAI Press, 1984).
40. F. Landy and J. Farr, *The Measurement of Work Performance: Methods, Theory, and Applications* (New York: Academic Press, 1983).
41. G. McEvoy and P. Buller, "User Acceptance of Peer Appraisals in an Industrial Setting," *Personnel Psychology* 40 (1987), pp. 785–97.
42. Joann S. Lublin, "Transparency Pays Off in 360-Degree Reviews," *The Wall Street Journal,* December 8, 2011, online.wsj.com.
43. D. Antonioni, "The Effects of Feedback Accountability on Upward Appraisal Ratings," *Personnel Psychology* 47 (1994), pp. 349–56.

44. Rachel Emma Silverman, "Performance Reviews Lose Steam," *The Wall Street Journal,* December 19, 2011, online.wsj.com.
45. H. Heidemeier and K. Moser, "Self-Other Agreement in Job Performance Rating: A Meta-Analytic Test of a Process Model," *Journal of Applied Psychology* 94 (2008), pp. 353–70.
46. J. Bernardin, C. Hagan, J. Kane, and P. Villanova, "Effective Performance Management: A Focus on Precision, Customers, and Situational Constraints," in *Performance Appraisal: State of the Art in Practice,* pp. 3–48.
47. R. Silverman, "Managers Watch Your Language," *Wall Street Journal,* September 20, 2015, p. R9; The Royal Society, "Understanding Unconscious Bias," https://wwwyoutube.com/watch?v=dPp9Z5k0dEE, accessed November 1, 2016; A. Tversky and D. Kahneman, "Availability: A Heuristic for Judging Frequency and Probability," *Cognitive Psychology* 5 (1973), pp. 207–32.
48. S. Leibowitz, "Stanford University Researchers Analyze the Language in 125 Performance Reviews from a Tech Company and Found Something Disturbing," *Business Insider,* October 1, 2015.
49. Paola Cecchi-Dimeglio, "How Gender Bias Corrupts Performance Reviews, and What to Do About It," *Harvard Business Review,* April 12, 2017, http://www.hbr.org; Tristan L. Botelho and Mabel Abraham, "Research: Objective Performance Metrics Are Not Enough to Overcome Gender Bias," *Harvard Business Review,* October 25, 2017, http://www.hbr.org.
50. K. Wexley and W. Nemeroff, "Effects of Racial Prejudice, Race of Applicant, and Biographical Similarity on Interviewer Evaluation of Job Applicants," *Journal of Social and Behavioral Science* 20 (1974), pp. 66-78.
51. G. Latham, L. Wexley, and E. Pursell, "Training Messages to Minimize Rating. Error in the Observation of Behavior," *Journal of Applied Psychology,* 60 (1995), pp. 550–55.
52. J. Bernardin and E. Pence, "Effects of Rater Training: Creating New Response Sets and Decreasing Accuracy," *Journal of Applied Psychology,* 65 (1990), pp. 60–66.
53. E. Pulakos, "A Comparison of Rater Training Programs: Error Training and Accuracy Training," *Journal of Applied Psychology* 69 (1984), pp. 581–88; E. Dierdorff, E. Surface and K. Brown, "Frame-of-Reference Training Effectiveness: Effect of Goal Orientation and Self-Efficacy on Affective, Cognitive, Skill-Based and Transfer Outcomes," *Journal of Applied Psychology* 95 (2010), pp. 1181–91.
54. H.J. Bernardin, M.R. Buckley, C.C. Tyler, and D.S. Wiese, "A Reconsideration of Strategies in Rater Training," in G.R. Ferris (ed.) *Research in Personnel and Human Resource Management,* (Greenwich, CT: JAI Press, 2000), vol. 18, pp. 221–74.
55. Silverman, "Managers Watch Your Language"; Google, "Making the Unconscious Conscious," https://www.youtube.comwatch?v=NW5s_-NI3JE, accessed November 1, 2016.
56. J. Sammer, "Calibrating Consistency," *HR Magazine,* January 2008, pp. 73–75.
57. Lori Goler, Janelle Gale, and Adam Grant, "Let's Not Kill Performance Evaluations Yet," *Harvard Business Review,* November 2016, pp. 91–94.
58. C. Allen Gorman, John P. Meriac, Sylvia G. Roch, and Joshua L. Ray, Jason S. Gamble, "An Exploratory Story of Current Performance Management Practices: Human Resource Executives' Perspectives," *International Journal of Selection and Assessment,* 25 (2017), pp. 193–202.
59. Deborah Busser, "Delivering Effective Performance Feedback, *T+D,* April 2012, pp. 323.
60. "Ceridian Canada and Harris Decima Survey Reveals Surprising Employee Attitudes Towards Performance Reviews and Corporate Training," October 24, 2011, http://www.ceridian.ca/en/news/2011/1024-pulse-of-talent.html.
61. Malcolm Gabriel and Pierre Robitaille, "Sustaining High Performance with Generation-Y Employees," *Canadian HR Reporter,* January 14, 2008, p. 13.
62. Nicole Stewart and Elyse Lamontagne, "Compensation Planning Outlook 2014" (Ottawa: Conference Board of Canada, October 2013), p. 24 and Emily Huston, "Helping Millennials Help You: Managing Your Young Workplace," *The Conference Board: Executive Action Series,* May 27, 2013, p. 4.
63. A. Adkins, What Millennials Want From Work and Life," www.gallup.com, May 11, 2016; A. Williams, "Move Over Millennials: Here Comes Generation Z," *New York Times,* September 10, 2015, p. ST1.
64. R. Feintzeig, "Everything Is Awesome! Why Can't You Tell Employees They're Doing a Bad Job?" *Wall Street Journal,* February 10, 2015, p. B1; A. Bryant, "A Boss's Challenge: Have Everyone Join the 'In' Group," *New York Times,* March 23, 2013, p. BU2.
65. Ann Pace, "Cultivating a Coaching Culture," *T+D,* February 2012, p. 16; Ann Pace, "A New Era of Performance Management," *T+D,* October 2011, p. 12.
66. James Heeney, "Personal Harassment Liability Always a Danger for Employers," *Canadian HR Reporter,* October 22, 2007, p. B15; Stuart Rudner, "Psychological Harassment Hurts Employees' Productivity," *Canadian HR Reporter,* October 22, 2007, p. 31; Christopher M. Andree Crawford, "Poor Treatment Is Constructive Dismissal," *Canadian Bar Association,* http://www.cba.org/CBA/newsletters/lab-2003/18.aspx, accessed April 27, 2008; "Bullying at Work: Another Form of Workplace Violence," http://www.emond-harnden.com/publications/feb03/bullies.shtml, accessed April 27, 2008.
67. James Heeney, "Personal Harassment Liability Always a Danger for Employers," *Canadian HR Reporter,* October 22, 2007, p. B15.
68. B. Morris, "Meet the Truck Driver of 2013," *Wall Street Journal,* November 14, 2013, pp. B1, B6; L. Katz, "Big Employer is Watching," *HR Magazine,* June 2015, pp. 67–74.
69. D. MacMillan, "Uber to Monitor Actions by Drivers in Safety Push," *Wall Street Journal,* June 30, 2016.
70. D. Lawrence, "Tracking the Enemy Within," *Bloomberg Business Week,* March 16–22, 2015, pp. 39–41.
71. C. Farr, "Fitbit at Work," *Fast Company,* May 2016, pp. 27–30.
72. L. Katz, "Big Employer is Watching," *HR Magazine,* June 2015, pp. 67–74; D. Brin, Wearable Worries, *HR Magazine,* June 2016, pp. 138–40; "Should Companies Monitor Their Employees Social Media, *Wall Street Journal,* May 12, 2014, pp. R1, R2.
73. B. Bhave, "The Invisible Eye? The Electronic Performance Monitoring and Employee Performance," *Personnel Psychology* 67 (2014), pp. 605–35.

CHAPTER 8

1. Brooke Smith, "A Week to Give Back: Cisco Creates a Formal Policy Providing Employees with up to 40 Hours for Volunteer Work," *Benefits Canada* 41.1 (2017), p. 9; "2017 Corporate Social Responsibility Report - Cisco", https://www.cisco.com/c/dam/assets/csr/pdf/CSR-Report-2017.pdf, accessed May 18, 2018; Ovais Iqbal, "How My Passions Came to Life at Cisco," *Life at Cisco,* https://blogs.cisco

.com/lifeatcisco/how-my-passions-come-to-life-at-cisco, retrieved May 18, 2018; Ovais Iqbal, https://ca.linkedin.com/pub/dir/Ovais/Iqbal, accessed May 18, 2018.
2. "World at Work Total Rewards Model," https://www.worldatwork.org, accessed October 22, 2008.
3. "Strategic Rewards in Canada: Building the Optimal Reward Plan—Watson Wyatt's 2004 Survey of Canadian Strategic Rewards and Pay Practices," in "Why Firms Develop a Total Rewards Strategy," *Canadian HR Reporter,* February 14, 2005, p. R5.
4. Heather McAteer, "Compensation Planning Outlook 2018" (Ottawa: Conference Board of Canada, October 2017), p. 19.
5. "What Is Total Rewards?," https://www.worldatwork.org, accessed November 23, 2018.
6. "Current and Forthcoming Minimum Hourly Rates for Experienced Adult Workers in Canada," Government of Canada, http://srv116.services.gc.ca/dimt-wid/sm-mw/rpt1.aspx, accessed October 22, 2018.
7. Jordan Kirkness, "Ontario Unveils Pay Transparency Legislation," *Canadian Labour and Employment Law,"* http://www.labourandemploymentlaw.com, accessed May 28, 2018, and Lisa Stam, "Bill 203: Introducing Pay Transparency," *Spring Law,* March 14, 2018, http://www.springlaw.ca, accessed May 28, 2018.
8. Gerhart and G. T. Milkovich, "Organizational Differences in Managerial Compensation and Financial Performance," *Academy of Management Journal* 33 (1990), pp. 663–91; E. L. Groshen, "Why Do Wages Vary among Employers?," *Economic Review* 24 (1988), pp. 19–38.
9. J. S. Adams, "Inequity in Social Exchange," in *Advances in Experimental Social Psychology,* ed. L. Berkowitz (New York: Academic Press, 1965); P. S. Goodman, "An Examination of Referents Used in the Evaluation of Pay," *Organizational Behavior and Human Performance* 12 (1974), pp. 170–95; J. B. Miner," *Theories of Organizational Behavior* (Hinsdale, IL: Dryden Press, 1980).
10. J. P. Pfeffer and A. Davis-Blake, "Understanding Organizational Wage Structures: A Resource Dependence Approach," *Academy of Management Journal* 30 (1987), pp. 437–55.
11. This section draws freely on B. Gerhart and R. D. Bretz, "Employee Compensation," in *Organization and Management of Advanced Manufacturing,* ed. W. Karwowski and G. Salvendy (New York: Wiley, 1994), pp. 81–101.
12. E. E. Lawler III, *Strategic Pay* (San Francisco: Jossey-Bass, 1990); G. Ledford, "3 Cases on Skill-based Pay: An Overview," *Compensation and Benefits Review,* March/April 1991, pp. 11–23; G. E. Ledford, "Paying for the Skills, Knowledge, Competencies of Knowledge Workers," *Compensation and Benefits Review,* July/August 1995, p. 55.
13. B. C. Murray and B. Gerhart, "An Empirical Analysis of a Skill-based Pay Program and Plant Performance Outcomes," *Academy of Management Journal* 41, no. 1 (1998), pp. 68–78; N. Gupta, D. Jenkins, and W. Curington, "Paying for Knowledge: Myths and Realities," *National Productivity Review,* Spring 1986, pp. 107–23.
14. Heather McAteer, *Compensation Planning Outlook 2018,* Ottawa: Conference Board of Canada, 2017, p. 10.
15. G. T. Milkovich and A. K. Wigdor, *Pay for Performance* (Washington, DC: National Academy Press, 1991); Gerhart and Bretz, "Employee Compensation"; C. Trevor, B. Gerhart, and J. W. Boudreau, "Voluntary Turnover and Job Performance: Curvilinearity and the Moderating Influences of Salary Growth and Promotions," *Journal of Applied Psychology* 82 (1997), pp. 44–61.
16. R. D. Bretz, R. A. Ash, and G. F. Dreher, "Do People Make the Place? An Examination of the Attraction-Selection-Attrition Hypothesis," *Personnel Psychology* 42 (1989), pp. 561–81; T. A. Judge and R. D. Bretz, "Effect of Values on Job Choice Decisions," *Journal of Applied Psychology* 77 (1992), pp. 261–71; D. M. Cable and T. A. Judge, "Pay Performance and Job Search Decisions: A Person–Organization Fit Perspective," *Personnel Psychology* 47 (1994), pp. 317–48."
17. Shannon Klie, "New Challenges in Pay for Performance," *Canadian HR Reporter,* April 23, 2007, p. 9.
18. R. D. Bretz, G. T. Milkovich, and W. Read, "The Current State of Performance Appraisal Research and Practice," *Journal of Management* 18 (1992), pp. 321–52; R. L. Heneman, "Merit Pay Research," *Research in Personnel and Human Resource Management* 8 (1990), pp. 203–63; Milkovich and Wigdor, *Pay for Performance.*
19. Bretz et al., "The Current State of Performance Appraisal Research and Practice."
20. T. L. Ross and R. A. Ross, "Gainsharing: Sharing Improved Performance," in *The Compensation Handbook,* 3rd ed., ed. M. L. Rock and L. A. Berger (New York: McGraw-Hill, 1991).
21. T. M. Welbourne and L. R. Gomez-Mejia, "Team Incentives in the Workplace," in *The Compensation Handbook,* 3rd ed., ed. M. L. Rock and L. A. Berger (New York: McGraw-Hill, 1991).
22. L. R. Gomez-Mejia and D. B. Balkin, *Compensation, Organizational Strategy, and Firm Performance* (Cincinnati: South-Western, 1992).
23. This idea has been referred to as the "share economy." See M. L. Weitzman, "The Simple Macroeconomics of Profit Sharing," *American Economic Review* 75 (1985), pp. 937–53. For supportive research, see the following studies: J. Chelius and R. S. Smith, "Profit Sharing and Employment Stability," *Industrial and Labor Relations Review* 43 (1990), pp. 256S–73S; B. Gerhart and L. O. Trevor, "Employment Stability Under Different Managerial Compensation Systems," working paper, Cornell University Center for Advanced Human Resource Studies, 1995; D. L. Kruse, "Profit Sharing and Employment Variability: Microeconomic Evidence on the Weitzman Theory," *Industrial and Labor Relations Review* 44 (1991), pp. 437–53.
24. James Thomson, "Rich Pickings: Four Challenges for Facebook's New Millionaires," *Business Spectator,* May 18, 2012, http://www.businessspectator.com.au/bs.nsf/Article/facebook-ipo-zuckerberg-millionires-billionaires-i-pd20120518-UE5TK?OpenDocument &src=sph&src=rot, accessedMay 18, 2012.
25. https://www.westjet.com/pdf/greatWestJetJobs.pdf, accessed May 19, 2015.
26. M. A. Conte and J. Svejnar, "The Performance Effects of Employee Ownership Plans," in *Paying for Productivity,* pp. 245–94.
27. B. Gerhart and G. T. Milkovich, "Employee Compensation: Research and Practice," in *Handbook of Industrial and Organizational Psychology,* vol. 3, 2nd ed., eds. M. D. Dunnette and L. M. Hough (Palo Alto, CA: Consulting Psychologists Press, 1992), vol. 3; and J. Swist, "Benefits Communications: Measuring Impact and Values," *Employee Benefit Plan Review,* September 2002, pp. 24–26.
28. "Canadian Employers Rate Health Plans over Cash," *The Globe and Mail,* May 12, 2004, p. C2.
29. Yaldaz Sadakova, "Employees Expect More from Their Benefits," *Benefits Canada,* June 2014, p. 9.
30. Bureau of Labor Statistics, "Employer Costs for Employee Compensation," http://data.bls.gov, accessed June 6, 2016.
31. Erik Sherman, "Four Perks Employees Love," *Inc.,* April 11, 2012, http://www.inc.com; Robert J. Grossman, "Tough Love at Netflix," *HR Magazine,* April 2010, http://www.shrm.org.

32. Kathryn M. Werntz, "Business Benefits from Facebook's Egg Freezing to Virgin Unlimited Holidays," *The Guardian,* October 21, 2014, http://www.theguardian.com/sustainable-business/2014/oct/21/facebook-apple-egg-freezing-virgin-unlimited-holidays-business-benefits, accessed May 20, 2015.
33. "Canada Pension Plan," http://www.servicecanada.gc.ca/eng/ services/pensions/cpp/index.shtml?utm_source=vanity+URL&utm_medium=print+publication, +ISPB-185, +ISPB-341&utm_term=/CPP&utm_content=Mar+2013, +eng&utm_campaign=OAS+Pension+2013,+Benefits+for+Low+Income+Seniors, accessed May 19, 2015.
34. "Employment Insurance," http://www.servicecanada.gc.ca/eng/sc/ei/index.shtml, accessed May 19, 2015.
35. Katie Fleming and Nicole Stewart, "Compensation Planning Outlook 2015" (Ottawa: Conference Board of Canada, October 2014), p. 23.
36. Sarah Beech, "Lifestyle Choices," *Benefits Canada,* March 2008, p. 45.
37. Marcel Vander Wier, "Funding Medical Marijuana," *Canadian HR Reporter,* April 2018, p. 1, 16.
38. Sara Tatelman, "CAA Honoured for Wellness Programs that Include Remote Workers," *Benefits Canada,* October 18, 2017, http://www.benefitscanada.com.
39. "The Employee Experience at Microsoft: Aligning Benefits to Our Culture," *Microsoft blog,* August 5, 2015, http://blogs.microsoft.com.
40. Brian Lindenberg, "Choosing the Right EAP," *Canadian HR Reporter,* March 24, 2008, pp. 22, 27.
41. "Phased Retirement: Aligning Employer Programs with Worker Preferences—2004 Survey Report," http://www.watsonwyatt.com/research/resrender.asp, accessed April 21, 2004.
42. Deborah McMillan, "Redefining Retirement," *Benefits Canada,* August 2007, pp. 13, 15, 17.
43. "Pension Plans in Canada, as of January 1, 2013," Statistics Canada, http://www.statcan.gc.ca/daily-quotidien/140828/dq140828d-eng.htm, accessed May 21, 2015.
44. Statistics Canada, "Table 1: Registered Pension Plan Membership, by Sector and Type of Plan," *The Daily,* July 21, 2017, CANSIM Table 280-116, http://www.statcan.gc.ca/daily-quotidien/170721/t001d.htm, accessed May 19, 2018; Statistics Canada, "Table 1: Registered Pension Plan Membership, by Sector and Type of Plan," *The Daily,* August 28, 2014, http://www.statcan.gc.ca/daily-quotidien/140828/t140828d001-eng.htm, retrieved May 21, 2015, and Statistics Canada, "Pension Plans in Canada," *The Daily,* May 9, 2011, http://www.statcan.gc.ca/daily-quotidien/110509/dq110509a-eng.htm, accessed May 17, 2012.
45. Tara Perkins, "RBC to Stop Offering Defined Benefit Plan," *Globe and Mail Update,* September 23, 2011, http://www.theglobeandmail.com/globe-investor/investment-ideas/streetwise/rbc-to-stop-offering-defined-benefit-plan/article2176656/, accessed May 17, 2012.
46. "Pension Plans in Canada, as of January 1, 2013," Statistics Canada, http://www.statcan.gc.ca/daily-quotidien/140828/dq140828d-eng.htm, accessed May 21, 2015.
47. Richard Yerema and Kristina Leung, "Canada's Top Family-Friendly Employers (2018 Winners)," November 6, 2017, *MediaCorp Canada,* http://www.canadastop100.com/family, accessed May 18, 2018.
48. Marlene Habib, "'Sandwich Generation' Has Smorgasbord of Options," *Globe and Mail Update,* November 20, 2011, http://www.theglobeandmail.com/globe-investor/personal-finance/financial-road-map/sandwich-generation-has-a-smorgasbord-of-options/article2255328/, accessed May 18, 2012, and Statistics Canada, "Study: The Sandwich Generation," *The Daily,* September 28, 2004, http://www.statcan.ca/Daily/English/040928/d040928b.htm, accessed October 22, 2008.
49. Lindsay Dodgson, "4 Companies That Give Staff Paid Time off When They Get a Puppy," *Business Insider,* March 23, 2018, http://www.businessinsider.com.
50. Government of Canada, "Part-Time Work and Family-Friendly Practices in Canadian Workplaces—June 2003," p. 1, http://www.hrsdc.gc.ca/en/cs/sp/sdc/pkrf/publications/research/2003–000183/page00.shtml, accessed October 22, 2008.
51. R. Broderick and B. Gerhart, "Nonwage Compensation," in *The Human Resource Management Handbook,* ed. D. Lewin, D.J.B. Mitchell, and M. A. Zadi (San Francisco: JAI Press, 1996).
52. Michael Fradkin, "An Ounce of Prevention Also Can Cut Disability Costs," *National Underwriter Life & Health,* April 21, 2008, Business & Company Resource Center, http://galenet.gale group.com.
53. Sarah Coles, "Package: Scratch Head at Start," *Employee Benefits,* January 14, 2008, Business & Company Resource Center, http://galenet.gale group.com.
54. Jen Wetherow, "Celebrate Canada's Best Workplaces 2018," *TheGlobe and Mail,* April 27, 2018, https://www.greatplacetowork.ca/images/article/Globe-and-Mail-Best-Workplaces-2018.pdf.
55. B. T. Beam Jr. and J. J. McFadden, *Employee Benefits,* 6th ed. (Chicago: Real Estate Education Co., 2001).
56. David Johnston, "Poorly Communicated Plans Worse Than None at All," *Canadian HR Reporter,* February 14, 2005, p. R7.
57. M. Wilson, G. B. Northcraft, and M. A. Neale, "The Perceived Value of Fringe Benefits," *Personnel Psychology* 38 (1985), pp. 309–20; H. W. Hennessey, P. L. Perrewe, and W. A. Hochwarter, "Impact of Benefit Awareness on Employee and Organizational Outcomes: A Longitudinal Field Experiment," *Benefits Quarterly* 8, no. 2 (1992), pp. 90–96.
58. Leigh Doyle, "The Growing Role of Social Media," *Benefits Canada,* April 17, 2012, http://www.benefits canada.com/pensions/cap/the-growing-role-of-social-media-27688, accessed May 16, 2012.
59. "Total Rewards Statements Help to Engage Employees," *Benefits Canada,* November 17, 2011, http://www.benefitscanada.com/benefits/health-benefits/total-rewards-statements-help-to-engage-employees-22892, accessed May 16, 2012.
60. CB Staff, "Canada's Top 100 highest-paid CEOs," Canadian Business, January 2, 2018, http://www.canadianbusiness.com.
61. David Macdonald, "Climbing Up and Kicking Down: Executive Pay in Canada," *Canadian Centre for Policy Alternatives,* January 1, 2018.
62. Ibid.
63. Sophia Harris, "Canada's Top CEOs Earn 200 Times on Average Worker's Salary: Report," *CBC News,* January 2, 2018, http://www.cbc.ca.
64. David Macdonald, "Climbing Up and Kicking Down: Executive Pay in Canada," *Canadian Centre for Policy Alternatives,* January 1, 2018, p. 10.
65. Gerhart and Milkovich, "Organizational Differences in Managerial Compensation" B. Gerhart, S. L. Rynes, and I. S. Fulmer, "Pay and Performance: Individuals, Groups, and Executives," *Academy of Management Annals* 3 (2009): 251–315.

CHAPTER 9

1. "A message to cabin crew members of CUPE 4070," November 30, 2018, *CUPE website,* https://westjet.cupe.ca, accessed December 5, 2018; Ross Marowits, "WestJet loses another unionization battle as CUPE to represent flight attendants," *Financial Post,* August 1, 2018, https://business.financialpost.com; "CUPE and WestJetters Celebrate International Flight Attendants Day!," June 1,

2018, *CUPE website,* https://westjet.cupe.ca, accessed June 1, 2018; Ross Marowits, "WestJet Union Helped by Dissatisfaction with Pay Formula, Says Flight Attendant," *The Canadian Press,* March 16, 2018, https://globalnews.ca, accessed June 1, 2018; Kyle Bakx, "WestJet Encore Pilots Unionize and Flight Attendants Could Be Next," November 1, 2017, CBC News, http://www.cbc.ca, accessed June 1, 2018; Ian Bicki, "WestJet CEO Sends Email to Employees Warning Against Unionization of Airline Staff," *The Canadian Press,* http://www.globalnews.ca, accessed June 4, 2018.

2. J.T. Dunlop, *Industrial Relations Systems* (New York: Holt, 1958); and C. Kerr, "Industrial Conflict and Its Mediation," *American Journal of Sociology* 60 (1954), pp. 230–45.
3. T. A. Kochan, *Collective Bargaining and Industrial Relations* (Homewood, IL: Richard D. Irwin, 1980), p. 25; and H. C. Katz and T. A. Kochan, *An Introduction to Collective Bargaining and Industrial Relations,* 3rd ed. (New York: McGraw-Hill, 2004).
4. "About Unifor," http://www.unifor.org/en/about-unifor, accessed April 8, 2015.
5. "About PSAC," http://psacunion.ca/about, accessed May 30, 2018.
6. "Labour Organizations in Canada 2015," Government of Canada, http://www.canada.ca/en/employment-social-development/services/collective-bargaining-data/reports/union-coverage.html, accessed May 30, 2018; "About the CLC," Canadian Labour Congress, http://www.canadianlabour.ca/about-clc, accessed May 30, 2018.
7. "Canada's unions call for better protections against workplace violence and harassment," *Canadian Labour Congress,* April 23, 2018, www.caadianlabour.ca, retrieved May 30, 2018.
8. "About the CLC," http://www.canadianlabour.ca/about-clc, accessed April 8, 2015.
9. "CUPE Local 4098-Rouge," http://www.cupe4098.ca, accessed June 6, 2018.
10. Whether the time the union steward spends on union business is paid for by the employer, the union, or a combination is a matter of negotiation between the employer and the union.
11. "Unionization of the Public Service," Canadian Museum of History, http://www.historymuseum.ca/cmc/exhibitions/hist/labour/labh37e.shtml, accessed April 8, 2015.
12. "History of Unions in Canada," http://www.mapleleafweb.com/old/education/spotlight/issue_51/history.html?q=education/spotlight/issue_51/history.html, accessed October 22, 2008.
13. Suzanne Payette, "Yesterday and Today: Union Membership," excerpt from the *Workplace Gazette* 5, no. 3 (Fall 2002).
14. "Labour Organizations in Canada 2015: Appendix 1," Government of Canada, August 2016, http://www.canada.ca/en/, accessed May 30, 2018.
15. "Labour Force Survey August 2017" *The Daily,* September 8, 2017, p. 5, *Statistics Canada,* http://www.statcan.gc.ca/daily-quotidien/170908/dq170908a-eng.pdf, accessed May 29, 2018;and "Union Coverage in Canada: Unionization Rate Stable Over Past Four Years," Human Resources and Skills Development Canada, http://www.hrsdc.gc.ca/eng/labour/labour_relations/info_analysis/overview/2010/section_6.shtml, accessed May 16, 2012.
16. "Labour Force Survey August 2017," *The Daily,* September 8, 2017, p. 5, Statistics Canada, http://www.statcan.gc.ca/daily-quotidien/170908/dq170908a-eng.pdf, accessed May 29, 2018.
17. Katz and Kochan, *An Introduction to Collective Bargaining,* building on J. Fiorito and C. L. Maranto, "The Contemporary Decline of Union Strength," *Contemporary Policy Issues* 3 (1987), pp. 12–27; G. N. Chaison and J. Rose, "The Macrodeterminants of Union Growth and Decline," in *The State of the Unions,* ed. G. Strauss et al. (Madison, WI: Industrial Relations Research Association, 1991).
18. Diane Galarneau, "Unionization Rates Falling," Chart 1 Unionization rate of employed individuals aged 17–64, 1981–2014," Statistics Canada, May 17, 2018, http://www.statcan.gc.ca/pub/11-630-x/11-630-x2015005-eng.htm#def1www.statcan.gc.ca/pub/75-006-x/2013001/article/11878-eng.pdf, accessed May 31, 2018.
19. Ibid.
20. Christopher Hallamore, *Industrial Relations Outlook 2008* (Ottawa: Conference Board of Canada, January 2008), p. 20.
21. Diane Galarneau, "Unionization Rates Falling," Chart 2 Unionization rate by sex and age, 1981–2014," Statistics Canada, May 17, 2018, http://www.statcan.gc.ca/pub/11-630-x/11-630-x2015005-eng.htm#def1www.statcan.gc.ca/pub/75-006-x/2013001/article/11878-eng.pdf, accessed May 31, 2018.
22. C. Brewster, "Levels of Analysis in Strategic HRM: Questions Raised by Comparative Research," Conference on Research and Theory in HRM, Cornell University, October 1997.
23. J. T. Addison and B. T. Hirsch, "Union Effects on Productivity, Profits, and Growth: Has the Long Run Arrived?," *Journal of Labor Economics* 7 (1989), pp. 72–105; and R. B. Freeman and J. L. Medoff, "The Two Faces of Unionism," *Public Interest* 57 (Fall 1979), pp. 69–93.
24. L. Mishel and P. Voos, *Unions and Economic Competitiveness* (Armonk, NY: M. E. Sharpe, 1991); Freeman and Medoff, "Two Faces"; and S. Slichter, J. Healy, and E. R. Livernash, *The Impact of Collective Bargaining on Management* (Washington, DC: Brookings Institution, 1960).
25. A. O. Hirschman, *Exit, Voice, and Loyalty* (Cambridge, MA: Harvard University Press, 1970); and R. Batt, A. J. S. Colvin, and J. Keefe, "Employee Voice, Human Resource Practices, and Quit Rates: Evidence from the Telecommunications Industry," *Industrial and Labor Relations Review* 55 (1970), pp. 573–94.
26. R. B. Freeman and J. L. Medoff, *What Do Unions Do?* (New York: Basic Books, 1984); Addison and Hirsch, "Union Effects on Productivity"; M. Ash and J. A. Seago, "The Effect of Registered Nurses' Unions on Heart-Attack Mortality," *Industrial and Labor Relations Review* 57 (2004), p. 422; and C. Doucouliagos and P. Laroche, "What Do Unions Do to Productivity? A Meta-Analysis," *Industrial Relations* 42 (2003), pp. 650–91.
27. B. E. Becker and C. A. Olson, "Unions and Firm Profits," *Industrial Relations* 31, no. 3 (1992), pp. 395–415; B. T. Hirsch and B. A. Morgan, "Shareholder Risks and Returns in Union and Nonunion Firms," *Industrial and Labor Relations Review* 47, no. 2 (1994), pp. 302–18; and Hristos Doucouliagos and Patrice Laroche, "Unions and Profits: A Meta-Regression Analysis," *Industrial Relations* 48, no. 1 (January 2008), p. 146.
28. "National Young Workers' Committee," http://cupe.ca/national-young-workers-committee, accessed April 8, 2015.
29. "Average Hourly Wages of Employees by Selected Characteristics and Occupation, Unadjusted Data, by Province (Monthly), Canada," Statistics Canada, May 11, 2018, http://www.statcan.gc.ca/tables-tableaux/sum-som/l01/cst01/labr69a-eng.htm, accessed May 30, 2018.
30. "Unifor Action: Featured Campaigns," Unifor website, http://www.unifor.org/en/unifor-action, accessed June 6, 2018.
31. "History and Development of Unions in Canada: The Rand Formula," http://www.law-faqs.org/nat/un-ran.htm, accessed October 22, 2008.

32. S. Webb and B. Webb, *Industrial Democracy* (London: Longmans, Green, 1987); J. R. Commons, *Institutional Economics* (New York: Macmillan, 1934).
33. Adapted from "Publication: Information Circulars No. 5," Canada Industrial Relations Board website, http://www.cirb-ccri.gc.ca/publications/info/05_eng.asp, accessed April 8, 2015.
34. R. B. Freeman and M. M. Kleiner, "Employer Behavior in the Face of Union Organizing Drives," *Industrial and Labor Relations Review* 43, no. 4 (April 1990), pp. 351–65.
35. Birch Miller and Bruce Graham, "Strengthening Union Activity in Alberta," *Canadian HR Reporter,* September 2017, p. 27.
36. Fossum, *Labor Relations,* p. 262.
37. C. M. Steven, *Strategy and Collective Bargaining Negotiations* (New York: McGraw-Hill, 1963); and Katz and Kochan, *An Introduction to Collective Bargaining.*
38. "Work Stoppages by Jurisdiction and Year," Government of Canada, May 31, 2018, https://www.canada.ca/en/employment-social-development/services/collective-bargaining-data/work-stoppages/work-stoppages-year-jurisdiction.html, accessed June 1, 2018; "Overview of Collective Bargaining in Canada, 2013," Government of Canada Labour Program, http://www.labour.gc.ca/eng/resources/info/publications/collective_bargaining/collective_bargaining.shtml, accessed April 12, 2015; Sharanjit Uppal, "Unionization 2011: Component of Statistics Canada Catalogue no. 75-001-X Perspectives on Labour and Income," Table 4, October 26, 2011, p. 11.
39. Kochan, *Collective Bargaining and Industrial Relations,* p. 272.
40. Katz and Kochan, *An Introduction to Collective Bargaining.*
41. Monica Haberl, "Industrial Relations Outlook 2018: The Changing Face of Labour," December 2017, The Conference Board of Canada, pp. 15–16.
42. "Air Canada Provides Further Details on Amendments to Long-Term Collective Agreement with Pilots," September 13, 2017, http://www.newswire.ca, accessed June 1, 2018.
43. Kochan, *Collective Bargaining and Industrial Relations,* p. 386; and John W. Budd and Alexander J.S. Colvin, "Improved Metrics for Workplace Dispute Resolution Procedures: Efficiency, Equity, and Voice," *Industrial Relations 47,* no. 3 (July 2008), p. 460.
44. T. A. Kochan, H. C. Katz, and R. B. McKersie, *The Transformation of American Industrial Relations* (New York: Basic Books, 1986), chap. 6; E. Appelbaum, T. Bailey, and P. Berg, *Manufacturing Advantage: Why High-Performance Work Systems Pay Off* (Ithaca, NY: Cornell University Press, 2000).
45. L. W. Hunter, J. P. MacDuffie, and L. Doucet, "What Makes Teams Take? Employee Reactions to Work Reforms," *Industrial and Labor Relations Review* 55 (2002), pp. 448–72.
46. Judith Lendvay-Zwicki, *The Canadian Industrial Relations System: Current Challenges and Future Options* (Ottawa: Conference Board of Canada, April 2004), http://www.conferenceboard.ca, accessed April 19, 2004.
47. J. B. Arthur, "The Link between Business Strategy and Industrial Relations Systems in American Steel Minimills," *Industrial and Labor Relations Review* 45 (1992), pp. 488–506; M. Schuster, "Union Management Cooperation," in *Employee and Labor Relations,* ed. J. A. Fossum (Washington, DC: Bureau of National Affairs, 1990); E. Cohen-Rosenthal and C. Burton, *Mutual Gains: A Guide to Union–Management Cooperation,* 2nd ed. (Ithaca, NY: ILR Press, 1993); T. A. Kochan and P. Osterman, *The Mutual Gains Enterprise* (Boston: Harvard Business School Press, 1994); and E. Applebaum and R. Batt, *The New American Workplace* (Ithaca, NY: ILR Press, 1994).
48. A. E. Eaton, "Factors Contributing to the Survival of Employee Participation Programs in Unionized Settings," *Industrial and Labor Relations Review* 47, no. 3 (1994), pp. 371–89.
49. Yaseen Hemeda, "Attracting, Engaging Young workers," *Canadian HR Reporter,* December 14, 2015, p. 19.
50. "Air Canada Concludes "Win-Win" Amendments to Long-Term Collective Agreement with Pilots," September 12, 2017, PRNewswire, http://www.benzinga.com/pressreleases/, accessed June 1, 2018; "Air Canada Provides Further Details on Amendments to Long-Term Collective Agreement with Pilots," September 13, 2017, https://finance.yahoo.com/news, accessed June 1, 2018; Kristine Owram, "Air Canada Strikes Tentative Deal with Pilots for a New 10-Year Contract as Bitter Relations Thaw," Financial Post, October 6, 2014, http://business.financialpost.com, accessed April 7, 2015.
51. "National Apprenticeship & Training Policy for the Construction Industry in Canada," p. 2, http://www.buildingtrades.ca/sites/default/files/pdf/2007_final_training_policy_document_eng.pdf, accessed April 12, 2015.
52. Monica Haberl, "Industrial Relations Outlook 2018: The Changing Face of Labour," December 2017, Conference Board of Canada, pp. 48–49.
53. "Building a Diverse and Inclusive Public Service: Final Report of the Joint/Union Management Task Force on Diversity and Inclusion," Government of Canada: Treasury Board of Canada Secretariat (2018), http://www.canada.ca, accessed February 28, 2018.

CHAPTER 10

1. Lisa Wolfson and Leslie Patton, "China's Population and Vibrant Economy Represent an Excellent Growth Opportunity for Tim Hortons in the Coming Years," *Bloomberg Business,* July 11, 2018, http://www.bloomberg.com, accessed July 19, 2018; Aleksandra Sagan, "More than 1,500 Tim Hortons Restaurants to Open in China," The Canadian Press, July 11, 2018, http://www.ctvnews.ca, accessed July 19, 2018; RBI website, "Tim Hortons to Launch in China," July 11, 2018, http://www.rbi.com, accessed July 20, 2018; "Tim Hortons' Reputation Taking a Beating as It Sinks in Another Ranking of Well-Regarded Companies," The Canadian Press, May 23, 2018, https://business.financialpost.com/news/retail-marketing/tim-hortons-falls-to-67th-in-reputation-rankings-by-reputation-institute, accessed July 19, 2018; Sylvain Charlebois, "How Tim Hortons Lost Its Connection with the Canadian Public," *Special to the Globe and Mail,* April 11, 2018, http://www.globeandmail.com, accessed July 19, 2018; Robert Benzie, "Tim Hortons Tops Menu at Kathleen Wynne Meeting in China," *Toronto Star,* October 27, 2014, http://www.thestar.com, accessed April 16, 2015.
2. Vladimir Pucik, "Human Resources in the Future: An Obstacle or a Champion of Globalization," *Tomorrow's HR Management,* ed. Dave Ulrich, Michael R. Losey, and Gerry Lake (John Wiley & Sons, Inc. New York, 1997), pp. 326–27.
3. Mark Magnier, "How China Is Changing Its Manufacturing Strategy," *Wall Street Journal,* June 7, 2016, http://www.wsj.com.
4. Bruce Einhorn, "China Tries to Perfect the Science of the Shirt," Bloomberg Businessweek, January 12, 2015, pp. 13–15.
5. **Sources:** Mary Gooderham, "Mukluks Company Steps Into Global Success," *The Canadian Trade Commissioner Service,* September 2, 2017, http://tradecommissioner.gc.ca/canadexport/0001235.aspx?lang=eng&pedisable=true; Manitobah Mukluks website, https://www.manitobah.ca, accessed July 22, 2018.

6. Tom Blackwell, "Revamped NAFTA Deal, Renamed USMCA, Will 'Rebalance' North American Trade After Canada Reaches 11th Hour agreement," *Financial Post,* October 1, 2018, https://business.financialpost.com, accessed October 1, 2018; Alex Hunt and Brian Wheeler, "Brexit: All You Need to Know about the UK Leaving the EU," http://www.bbc.com, July 12, 2018, accessed July 19, 2018; Eric Martin, "NAFTA Talks Likely to Wait Beyond July Given Full Agendas," July 11, 2018, http://www.bloomberg.com, accessed July 19, 2018; Ken Thomas, "Trump Delaying NAFTA Deal Until after Midterm Elections," *The Globe and Mail,* July 1, 2018, http://www.theglobeandmail.com, accessed July 19, 2018; "What Is the CPTPP?" Government of Canada, July 10, 2018, https://international.gc.a, accessed July 19, 2018; Dave Sherwood, "Canada, 10 Other Nations Sign Landmark TP Deal—Without U.S.," *Reuters,* March 8, 2018, https://globalnews.ca, accessed July 19, 2018.
7. "CPHR Canada, SHRM Sign Mutual Recognition Agreement," *Canadian HR Reporter,* July 17, 2018, http://www.hrreporter.com, accessed July 18, 2018.
8. Viola Beuscher, "How Lululemon Wants to Conquer Europe," *Sportswear International,* November 8, 2017, http://www.sportswear-international.com, accessed July 20, 2018.
9. Website, *Canadian Employee Relocation Council,* www.cerc.ca, accessed July 18, 2018.
10. Mike Butler, "Crossing Borders," *TD,* May 2015, https://www.td.com.
11. N. Adler and S. Bartholomew, "Managing Globally Competent People," *The Executive* 6 (1992), pp. 52–65.
12. V. Sathe, *Culture and Related Corporate Realities* (Homewood, IL: Richard D. Irwin, 1985); and M. Rokeach, *Beliefs, Attitudes, and Values* (San Francisco: Jossey-Bass, 1968).
13. N. Adler, *International Dimensions of Organizational Behavior,* 2nd ed. (Boston: PWS-Kent, 1991).
14. "Hofstede Insights," https://www.hofstede-insights.com, accessed November 7, 2018.
15. Hofstede, "Cultural Constraints in Management Theories."
16. A Ramesh and M. Gelfland, "Will They Stay or Will They Go? The Role of Job Embeddedness in Predicting Turnover in Individualistic and Collectivistic Cultures," *Journal of Applied Psychology* 95, no. 5 (2010): 807–23.
17. W. A. Randolph and M. Sashkin, "Can Organizational Empowerment Work in Multinational Settings?" *Academy of Management Executive* 16, no. 1 (2002), pp. 102–15.
18. B. Gerhart and M. Fang, "National Culture and Human Resource Management: Assumptions and Evidence," *International Journal of Human Resource Management* 16, no. 6 (June 2005); pp. 971–86.
19. Knowledge@Wharton, "Familiar Challenges, Global Scale," Human Resource Executive Online, March 21, 2016, http://www.hreonline.com.
20. Organisation for Economic Co-operation and Development, "How Much Is Spent per Student?," in *Education at a Glance: 2015 Highlights,* http://www.oecd.org; World Bank Group and International Monetary Fund, *Development Goals in an Era of Demographic Change,* Global Monitoring Report 2015/2016, http://www.worldbank.org.
21. L. Weber and R. Feintzeig, "Big Employers Are Urging Calm after U.K. Vote," *Wall Street Journal,* June 29, 2016, p. B5; L Norman, J. Gross, and V. Pop, "EU Leaders Warn U.K. of Exit Costs," *Wall Street Journal,* June 29, 2016. pp. A1, A9.
22. "Saskatchewan Looking to Lure Nurses from Philippines," February 21, 2008, https://www.cbc.ca/news/canada/saskatchewan/saskatchewan-looking-to-lure-nurses-from-philippines-1.734187, accessed November 7, 2018.
23. "Call-Centre Nation Philippines Putting up Fight as Automation Steals Jobs," *The Strait Times,* October 5, 2017, http://www.straitstimes.com; Trefor Moss, "Robots on Tract to Bump Humans from Call-Center Jobs," *Wall Street Journal,* June 21, 2016, http://www.wsj.com.
24. CERC Website, "CERP Level III—Essentials of International Relocations: CGMP Designations," http://www.cerc.ca, accessed June 22, 2018.
25. "Temporary Workers," *Government of Canada,* https://www.canada.ca, accessed July 22, 2018; "Fact Sheet—Temporary Foreign Worker Program," Government of Canada, http://www.cic.gc.ca/english/resources/publications/employers/temp-foreign-worker-program.asp, accessed April 23, 2015.
26. W. A. Arthur Jr. and W. Bennett Jr., "The International Assignee: The Relative Importance of Factors Perceived to Contribute to Success," *Personnel Psychology* 48 (1995), pp. 99–114; and G. M. Spreitzer, M. W. McCall Jr., and J. D. Mahoney, "Early Identification of International Executive Potential," *Journal of Applied Psychology* 82 (1997), pp. 6–29.
27. Delia Flanja, "Culture Shock in Intercultural Communication," *Studia Europaea* (October 2009), Business & Company Resource Center, galenet.galegroup.com.
28. J. Flynn, "E-mail, Cell Phones, and Frequent-Flier Miles Let 'Virtual' Expats Work Abroad but Live at Home," *The Wall Street Journal,* October 25, 1999, p. A26.
29. Stephanie Stephen, "What's Allowed, What's Taboo with Background Checks Outside of Canada," *Canadian HR Reporter,* pp 13, March 26, 2012.
30. E. Krell, "Evaluating Returns on Expatriates," *HRMagazine,* March 2005, downloaded from Infotract at http://web5.infotrac.galegroup.com; M. Harvey and M. M. Novicevic, "Selecting Expatriates for Increasingly Complex Global Assignments," *Career Development International* 6 no. 2 (2001), pp. 69-86.
31. M. Mendenhall and G. Oddou, "The Dimensions of Expatriate Acculturation," *Academy of Management Review* 10 (1985), pp. 39-47.
32. Arthur and Benett, "The International Assignee."
33. J. I. Sanchez, P. E. Spector, and C. L. Cooper, "Adapting to a Boundaryless World: A Developmental Expatriate Model," *Academy of Management Executive* 14, no. 2 (2000), pp. 96–106.
34. D. M. Gayeski, C. Sanchirico, and J. Anderson, "Designing Training for Global Environments: Knowing What Questions to Ask," *Performance Improvement Quarterly* 15, no. 2 (2002), pp. 15–31.
35. J. S. Black and M. Mendenhall, "A Practical but Theory-Based Framework for Selecting Cross-Cultural Training Methods," in *Readings and Cases in International Human Resource Management,* ed. M. Mendenhall and G. Oddou (Boston: PWS-Kent, 1991), pp. 177–204.
36. Abdul Nasser Kassar, Amad Rouhana, and Sophie Lythreatis, "Cross-Cultural Training: Its Effects on the Satisfaction and Turnover of Expatriate Employees," *SAM Advanced Management Journal* (Autumn 2015), pp. 4–18.
37. C. Lachnit, "Low-Cost Tips for Successful Inpatriation," *Workforce,* August 2001, pp. 42–44, 46–47.
38. Jillian Austin, "Brandon has New Foreign Workers," *Winnipeg Free Press,"* September 1, 2012, http://www.winnipegfreepress.com/local/brandon-has-new-foreign-workers-168258536.html, accessed April 19, 2015.
39. D. D. Davis, "International Performance Measurement and Management," in *Performance Appraisal: State of the Art in Practice,* ed. J. W. Smither (San Francisco: Jossey-Bass, 1998), pp. 95–131.

40. M. Gowan, S. Ibarreche, and C. Lackey, "Doing the Right Things in Mexico," *Academy of Management Executive* 10 (1996), pp. 74–81.
41. L. S. Chee, "Singapore Airlines: Strategic Human Resource Initiatives," in *International Human Resource Management: Think Globally, Act Locally,* ed. D. Torrington (Upper Saddle River, NJ: Prentice Hall, 1994), pp. 143–59.
42. "How Can a Company Manage an Expatriate Employee's Performance?" *SHRM India,* http://www.shrmindia.org, accessed May 6, 2010.
43. "Johnson & Johnson Takes World View on Compensation," *Employee Benefits,* June 2011, p. 7.
44. "Top Whack: Big Country, Big Pay Cheques," *The Economist,* January 29, 2011, https://www.economist.com/the-americas/2011/01/27/top-whack.
45. Marc Levinson, "U.S. Manufacturing in International Perspective," *Congressional Research Report R42135,* April 26, 2016, accessed from Federation of American Scientists, https://fas.org.
46. See, for example, A. E. Cobet and G. A. Wilson, "Comparing 50 Years of Labor Productivity in U.S. and Foreign Manufacturing," *Monthly Labor Review,* June 2002, pp. 51–63; Bureau of Labor Statistics, "International Comparisons of Manufacturing Productivity and Labor Cost Trends, 2008," news release, October 22, 2009, http://www.bls.gov; and Daron Acemoglu and Melissa Dell, "Productivity Differences between and within Countries," *American Economic Journal: Macroeconomics 2010* 2, no. 1 (2010): 169–88.
47. Stephen Miller, "Grasp Country Difference to Manage Global Pay," *Compensation Discipline,* March 30, 2010, http://www.shrm.org.
48. Brookfield Global Relocation Services, *Breakthrough to the Future.*
49. Lynne Molmar, "Addressing Expatriate Tax Issues," *Canadian HR Reporter,* March 13, 2006, p. 15.
50. P. J. Dowling, D. E. Welch, and R. S. Schuler, *International Human Resource Management,* 3rd ed. (Cincinnati: South-Western, 1999), pp. 235–36.
51. Ibid.; J. La Palombara and S. Blank, *Multinational Corporations and National Elites: A Study of Tensions* (New York: Conference Board, 1976); A. B. Sim, "Decentralized Subsidiaries and Their Performance: A Comparative Study of American, British and Japanese Subsidiaries in Malaysia," *Management International Review* 17 no. 2 (1977), pp. 45–51; J. Hamill, "Labor Relations Decision-Making within Multinational Corporations," *Industrial Relations Journal* 15, no 2 (1984), pp. 30–34.
52. Dowling, Welch, and Schuler, *International Human Resource Management,* p. 231.
53. Bethany Allen-Ebrahimian, "The World's Largest Union: A 'Capitalist Running Dog,'" *Foreign Policy,* April 23, 2014, http://www.foreignpolicy.com; International Trade Union Confederation."Internationally Recognised Core Labour Standards in the People's Republic of China," Report for the WTO General Council Review of the Trade Policies of the People's Republic of China (Geneva, May 10 and 12, 2010), http://www.ituc-csi.org.
54. Syed Zain Al-Mahmood and Tripti Lahri, "Bangladesh Opens Door to More Unions," *The Wall Street Journal,* May 13, 2013; Jason Burke, "Bangladesh Eases Trade Union Laws after Factory Building Collapse," *Guardian,* May 13, 2013.
55. J. K. Sebenius, "The Hidden Challenge of Cross-Border Negotiations," *Harvard Business Review,* March 2002, pp. 76–85.
56. E. Krell, "Evaluating Returns on Expatriates," *HRM Magazine,* March 2005, downloaded from Infotrac at http://web5.infotrac.galegroup.com.
57. W. "Global Mobility Policy & Practice: 2014 Survey Executive Summary Report," p. 5, http://guidance.cartusrelocation.com/rs/cartus/images/2014_Global_Mobility_Policy_Practices_Survey_Exec_Summary.pdf, accessed April 19, 2015.
58. P. Caligiuri, "The Big Five Personality Characteristics as Predictors of Expatriates' Desire to Terminate the Assignment and Supervisor-Rated Performance," *Personnel Psychology* 53 (2000), pp. 67–88.
59. Jesus F. Salgado and Maria Bastida, "Predicting Expatriate Effectiveness: The Role of Personality, Cross-cultural Adjustment, and Organizational Support," *International Journal of Selection and Assessment,* 25, no. 3 (2017), pp. 267–75.
60. P. Dowling and R. Schuler, *International Dimensions of Human Resource Management* (Boston: PWS-Kent, 1990).
61. Ibid.; M. Harvey and M. M. Novicevic, "Selecting Expatriates for Increasingly Complex Global Assignments," *Career Development International* 6, no. 2 (2001), pp. 69–86.
62. Neal Goodman, "Helping Trainees Succeed Overseas," *Training,* March 2014, EBSCOhost, http://web.b.ebscohost.com.
63. Catherine Aman, "Horses for Courses," *Corporate Counsel,* December 15, 2008, Business & Company Resource Center, http://galenet.galegroup.com.
64. Andrew L. Molinsky, "Code Switching between Cultures," *Harvard Business Review,* January–February 2012, pp. 140–41.
65. Amy Maingault, Lesa Albright, and Vicki Neal, "Policy Tips, Repatriation, Safe Harbor Rules," *HR Magazine,* March 2008, p. 34.
66. Adler, *International Dimensions of Organizational Behavior.*
67. L. G. Klaff, "The Right Way to Bring Expats Home," *Workforce,* July 2002, pp. 40–44.
68. Andy Molinsky and Melissa Hahn, "Five Tips for Managing Successful Overseas Assignments, *Harvard Business Review,* March 16, 2016.

CHAPTER 11

1. EllisDon Website, "Projects," http://www.ellisdon.com/projects/, accessed August 3, 2018.
2. Paul Gallant, "Engaging from the Very Top," *Canadian Business,* December 2015, pp. 36–39; "EllisDon Celebrated as Top Employer for 8th Consecutive Year," November 7, 2017, http://www.ellisdon.com, R. Yerema & K. Leung, "EllisDon Corporation," *Mediacorp Canada Inc.,* November 6, 2017, https://content.eluta.ca/top-employer-ellisdon.
3. J. D. Shaw, M. K. Duffy, J. L. Johnson, and D. E. Lockhart, "Turnover, Social Capital Losses, and Performance," *Academy of Management Journal* 48 (2005), pp. 594–606; R. Batt, "Managing Customer Services: Human Resources Practices, Quit Rates, and Sales Growth," *Academy of Management Journal* 45 (2002), pp. 587–97.
4. D. J. Koys, "The Effects of Employee Satisfaction, Organizational Citizenship Behavior, and Turnover on Organizational Effectiveness: A Unit-Level Longitudinal Study," *Personnel Psychology* 54 (2001), pp. 101–114; Batt, "Managing Customer Services;" T. Y. Park and J. D. Shaw, "Turnover Rates and Organizational Performance: A Meta-Analysis," *Journal of Applied Psychology* 98 (2013), pp. 268–309.
5. S. Snell and J. Dean, "Integrated Manufacturing and Human Resource Management: A Human Capital Perspective," *Academy of Management Journal* 35 (1992), pp. 467–504.
6. M. A. Huselid, "The Impact of Human Resource Management Practices on Turnover, Productivity, and Corporate

Financial Performance," *Academy of Management Journal* 38 (1995), pp. 63 http://galenet.galegroup.c 5–72; U.S. Department of Labor, *High-Performance Work Practices and Firm Performance* (Washington, DC: U.S. Government Printing Office, 1993); and J. Combs, Y. Liu, A. Hall, and D. Ketchen, "How Much Do High-Performance Work Practices Matter? A Meta-Analysis of Their Effects on Organizational Performance," *Personnel Psychology* 59 (2006), p. 501–28.

7. Jay Parkes, "EllisDon Takes Top CIPA Honours," *ITWorksCanada,* December 31, 2003, https://www.itworldcanada.com, accessed August 3, 2018.
8. J. Arthur, "The Link Between Business Strategy and Industrial Relations Systems in American Steel Mini-Mills," *Industrial and Labor Relations Review* 45 (1992), pp. 488–506.
9. For a more recent but similar perspective, see Marcus Buckingham, "Leadership and Navigation: It's All About Teams," *HR Magazine,* December 2015, https://www.shrm.org; J. A. Neal and C. L. Tromley, "From Incremental Change to Retrofit: Creating High-Performance Work Systems," *Academy of Management Executive* 9 (1995), pp. 42–54; and M. A. Huselid, "The Impact of Human Resource Management Practices on Turnover, Productivity, and Corporate Financial Performance," *Academy of Management Journal* 38 (1995), pp. 635–72.
10. Jeff Schwartz et al., "Rewriting the Rules for the Digital Age: 2017 Deloitte Global Human Capital Trends," Deloitte University Press, p. 55, http://www.deloitte.com.
11. Lyle Yorks, Amy Lui Abel, and Marion Devine, "What's Next for 21st-Century HR?," *The Conference Board,* 2017, p 16.
12. Ibid.
13. T.J. Atchison, "The Employment Relationship: Untied or Re-Tied," *Academy of Management Executive* 5 (1991), pp. 52–62.
14. Alex Adamopoulos, "'Agile' Grows Up, Readies to Take Over Your Whole Business," *VentureBeat,* February 9, 2012; Agile Alliance, "What Is Agile Software Development?" http://www.agilealliance.org.
15. D. Senge, "The Learning Organization Made Plain and Simple," *Training and Development Journal,* October 1991, pp. 37–44.
16. M. A. Gephart, V. J. Marsick, M. E. Van Buren, and M. S. Spiro, "Learning Organizations Come Alive," *Training and Development* 50 (1996), pp. 34–45.
17. T. T. Baldwin, C. Danielson, and W. Wiggenhorn, "The Evolution of Learning Strategies in Organizations: From Employee Development to Business Redefinition," *Academy of Management Executive* 11 (1997), pp. 47–58; J. J. Martocchio and T. T. Baldwin, "The Evolution of Strategic Organizational Training," in *Research in Personnel and Human Resource Management,* 15th ed., G. R. Ferris (Greenwich, CT: JAI Press, 1997), pp. 1–46; and "Leveraging HR and Knowledge Management in a Challenging Economy," *HR Magazine,* June 2009, pp. 81–89.
18. RescueTime website, http://www.rescuetime.com, accessed August 3, 2018, and H. James Wilson, "Employees, Measure Yourselves," *The Wall Street Journal,* April 2, 2012, http://online.wsj.com.
19. Martin C. Daks, "Best Large Organizations:Performance Management Standards Rule at Biggest Nonprofits," *The Non-Profit Times,* April 1, 2015, http://www.thenonprofittimes.com.
20. Government of Nova Scotia Careers website, https://jobs.novascotia.ca, accessed August 7, 2018.
21. Wayne F. Cascio and Peter Cappelli, "Lessons from the Financial Services Crisis," *HR Magazine,* January 2009, Business & Company Resource Center, http://galenet.galegroup.com; Chris Petersen, "Thou Shalt Not. . .," *Construction Today,* September 2009, p. 13; and Carolyn Hirschman, "Giving Voice to Employee Concerns," *HR Magazine,* August 2008, pp. 51–53.
22. "Corporate Social Responsibility: An Implementation Guide for Canadian Business," *Government of Canada,* 2006, p. 5.
23. "Global Firm Bans Meat at Company Events in Effort to Be Greener," The Associated Press, July 16, 2018, www.cbc.ca.
24. Paul Tsaparis, "Social Responsibility Gives Canadian Firms an Edge," *Canadian HR Reporter,* May 23, 2005, p. 18.
25. Ibid.
26. E. A. Locke, "The Nature and Causes of Job Dissatisfaction," in *The Handbook of Industrial & Organizational Psychology,* ed. M. D. Dunnette (Chicago: Rand McNally, 1976), pp. 901–61.
27. T. A. Judge, C. J. Thoresen, J. E. Bono, and G. K. Patton, "The Job Satisfaction-Job Performance Relationship: A Qualitative and Quantitative Review," *Psychological Bulletin* 127 (2001), pp. 376–407; and R. A. Katzell, D. E. Thompson, and R. A. Guzzo, "How Job Satisfaction and Job Performance Are and Are Not Linked," *Job Satisfaction,* ed. C. J. Cranny, P. C. Smith, and E. F. Stone (New York: Lexington Books, 1992), pp. 195–217.
28. "Best Employer Studies Canada: What is Employee Engagement," Aon Hewitt website, https://ceplb03.hewitt.com/bestemployers/canada/pages/driving_engagement.htm, accessed June 11, 2012.
29. For examples see M. Huselid, "The Impact of Human Resource Management Practices on Turnover, Productivity, and Corporate Financial Performance," *Academy of Management Journal* 38 (1995), pp. 635–72; S. Payne and S. Webber, "Effects of Service Provider Attitudes and Employment Status on Citizenship Behaviors and Customers' Attitudes and Loyalty Behavior," *Journal of Applied Psychology* 91 (2006), pp. 365–68; J. Hartner, F. Schmidt, and T. Hayes, "Business-Unit Level Relationship between Employee Satisfaction, Employee Engagement, and Business Outcomes: A Meta-Analysis," *Journal of Applied Psychology* 87 (2002), pp. 268–79; I. Fulmer, B. Gerhart, and K. Scott, "Are the 100 Best Better? An Empirical Investigation of the Relationship between Being a 'Great Place to Work' and Firm Performance," *Performance Psychology* 56 (2003), pp. 965–93; "Working Today: Understanding What Drives Employee Engagement," *Towers Perrin Talent Report* (2003).
30. Amy Adkins, "U.S. Employee Engagement Reaches New High in March," *Gallup,* April 13, 2016, http://www.gallup.com.
31. Aon Hewitt, *2015 Trends in Global Employee Engagement: Making Engagement Happen,* http://www.aon.com.
32. Kathleen Kindle, "Brand Alignment: Getting It Right," https://www.siegelgale.com/brand-alignment-getting-it-right/, accessed November 20, 2018; Aon Hewitt, "Trends in Global Employee Engagement," 2011, http://www.aon.com.
33. John Bersin, "Why Companies Fail to Engage Today's Workforce: The Overwhelmed Employee," March 15, 2014, http://www.forbes.com, accessed May 11, 2015.
34. Ibid.
35. Ibid.
36. D. W. Baruch, "Why They Terminate," *Journal of Consulting Psychology* 8 (1944), pp. 35–46; J. G. Rosse, "Relations among Lateness, Absence and Turnover: Is There a Progression of Withdrawal?" *Human Relations* 41 (1988), pp. 517–31; C. Hulin, "Adaptation, Persistence and Commitment in Organizations," in *Handbook of Industrial & Organizational Psychology,* 2nd ed., eds. M. D. Dunnette and

L. M. Hough (Palo Alto, CA: Consulting Psychologists Press, 1991), pp. 443–50; and E. R. Burris, J. R. Detert, and D. S. Chiaburu, "Quitting before Leaving: The Mediating Effects of Psychological Attachment and Detachment on Voice," *Journal of Applied Psychology* 93 (2008), pp. 912–22.

37. D. A. Harrison, D. A. Newman, and P. L. Roth, "How Important Are Job Attitudes? Meta-analytic Comparisons of Integrative Behavioral Outcomes and Time Sequences," *Academy of Management Journal* 49 (2006), pp. 305–25.
38. R. P. Quinn and G. L. Staines, *The 1977 Quality of Employment Survey* (Ann Arbor, MI: Survey Research Center, Institute for Social Research, University of Michigan, 1979).
39. T. Judge and T. Welbourne, "A Confirmatory Investigation of the Dimensionality of the Pay Satisfaction Questionnaire," *Journal of Applied Psychology* 79 (1994), pp. 461–66.
40. John Thackray, "Feedback for Real," March 15, 2001, http://gmj.gallup.com/conent/default.asp?ci=811, accessed November 28, 2004.
41. Ibid.
42. Terence F. Shea, "Getting the Last Word," *HR Magazine,* January 2010, Business & Company Resource Center, http://galenet.galegroup.com; and L. M. Sixel, "Keeping Top Talent Has Employers Worried," *Houston Chronicle,* March 14, 2010, Business & Company Resource Center, http://galenet.galegroup.com.
43. "Stay Interviews," www.bcjobs.ca/re/hr-centre/interview-techniques/human-resource-advice/stay-interviews, accessed June 11, 2012.
44. "What is Net Promoter Score?" http://www.netpromoter.com.
45. M. Lewis Jr., "The Heat is On," *Inside Business,* October 2007, downloaded from General Reference Center Gold, http://find.galegroup.com.
46. B. Becker and M. A. Huselid, "High-Performance Work Systems and Firm Performance: A Synthesis of Research and Managerial Implications," in *Research in Personnel and Human Resource Management* 16, ed. G. R. Ferris (Stamford, CT: JAI Press, 1998), pp. 53–101.
47. B. Becker and B. Gerhart, "The Impact of Human Resource Management on Organizational Performance: Progress and Prospects," *Academy of Management Journal* 39 (1996), pp. 779–801.
48. Lisa H. Nishii and Rebecca M. Paluch, "Leaders as HR Sensegivers: For Implementation Behaviors That Create Strong HR systems," *Human Resource Management Review* 28 (2018), pp. 319–23.
49. David Hatch, "Can Apple Polish Lowe's Reputation?" *U.S. News & World Report,* May 15, 2012, http://money.usnews.com.
50. M. Pearson, "Top-Gun Talent Make Ideal Recruiters," *The Globe and Mail,* July 21, 2011.
51. H. J. Bernardin, C. M. Hagan, J. S. Kane, and P. Villanova, "Effective Performance Management: A Focus on Precision, Customers, and Situational Constraints," in *Performance Appraisal: State of the Art in Practice,* ed. J. W. Smither (San Francisco: Jossey-Bass, 1998), p. 56.
52. Rachel Emma Silverman, "How to Pay Employees for Great Ideas," *Wall Street Journal,* December 2, 2014, http://blogs.wsj.com.
53. L. R. Gomez-Mejia and D. B. Balkin, *Compensation, Organizational Strategy, and Firm Performance* (Cincinnati: South-Western, 1992); G. D. Jenkins and E. E. Lawler III, "Impact of Employee Participation in Pay Plan Development," *Organizational Behavior and Human Performance* 28 (1981), pp. 111–28.
54. Heather McAteer, "Compensation Planning Outlook 2018," *The Conference Board of Canada,* October 2017, p. 27.
55. K. M. Kacmer, M. C. Andrews, D. L. Van Rooy, R. C. Steilberg, and S. Cerrone, "Sure Everyone Can Be Replaced . . . But at What Cost? Turnover as a Predictor of Unit-Level Performance," *Academy of Management Journal* 49 (2006), pp. 133–44; J. D. Shaw, N. Gupta, and J. E. Delery, "Alternative Conceptualizations of the Relationship between Voluntary Turnover and Organizational Performance," *Academy of Management Journal* 48 (2005), pp. 50–68; and J. Lublin, "Keeping Clients by Keeping Workers," *Wall Street Journal,* November 20, 2006, p. B1.
56. T. M. Garder, G. H. Van Iddekinge, & P. W. Horn, "If You've Got Leavin' on Your Mind: The Identification and Validation of Pre-Quitting Behaviors, *Journal of Management,* August 29, 2016.
57. M. M. Le Blanc and K. Kelloway, "Predictors and Outcomes of Workplace Violence and Aggression," *Journal of Applied Psychology,* 87, 2002, pp. 444–53.
58. "Wrongful Dismissal Law in Canada," Duhaime's Employment and Labour Law Centre, www.duhaime.orgfEmployment/ca-wd.aspx, accessed March 28, 2005.
59. Jeffrey Smith, "Truck Driver Didn't Get the Message," *Canadian HR Reporter,* April 6, 2015, p. 5.
60. K. Karl and C. Sutton, "A Review of Expert Advice on Employment Termination Practices: The Experts Don't Always Agree," in *Dysfunctional Behavior in Organizations,* eds. R. Griffin, A. O'Leary-Kelly, and J. Collins (Stanford, CT: JA1 Press, 1998).
61. Jane Cooper and Shannon Jackson, *Talent Management Benchmarking: Human Resources Trends and Metrics, Fourth Edition,* February 2017, The Conference Board of Canada, p. 26.
62. Jeff Sanford, "Value for the Money," *Canadian Business,* February 18, 2008, pp. 31–32.
63. Cindy Waxer, "Combating the Diversity Dearth with Analytics," *Computerworld,* April 2015, http://www.computerworld.com.
64. Salavatore Falletta, "In Search of HR Intelligence: Evidence-based HR Analytics Practices in High-Performing Companies," *People and Strategy* 36 (2014), pp. 28–37.
65. S. Shrivastava and T. Shaw, "Liberating HR Through Technology," *Human Resource Management* 42, no. 3 (2003), pp. 201–17.
66. Stacey Harris, "Survey Says: Mobile and HR Self-Service Make a Great Couple," *Sierra-Cedar blog,* May 27, 2015, http://www.sierra-cedar.com; Rob Bamforth, "How to Free Your Business and Staff with Self-Service" *Computer Weekly,* December 8–14, 2015, http://www.computerweekly.com.
67. R. Broderick and J. W. Boudreau, "Human Resource Management, Information Technology, and the Competitive Edge," *Academy of Management Executive* 6 (1992), pp. 7–17.
68. G. McMahan and R. Woodman, "The Current Practice of Organization Development within the Firm: A Survey of Large Industrial Corporations," *Group and Organization Studies* 17 (1992), pp. 17–134.
69. "Meet the Influencers: Dr. Parbudyal Singh, DHRP," *HR Professional,* July 2018, pp. 36–39.
70. B. Becker, M. Huselid, and D. Ulrich, *The HR Scorecard: Linking People, Strategy, and Performance* (Cambridge, MA: HBS Press, 2001).
71. D. Ulrich and A. Yeung, "A Shared Mindset," *Personnel Administrator,* March 1989, pp. 38–45.
72. G. Jones and P. Wright, "An Economic Approach to Conceptualizing the Utility of Human Resource Management Practices," *Research in Personnel/Human Resources* 10 (1992), pp. 271–99;Carol Gill, "Don't Know, Don't Care: An Explanation of Evidence-based Knowledge and Practice

in Human Resource Management," Human *Resource Management Review* 28 (2018) pp. 103–15.

73. R. Schuler and J. Walker, "Human Resources Strategy: Focusing on Issues and Actions," *Organizational Dynamics,* Summer 1990, pp. 5–19.
74. "Open Sourcing Google's HR secrets," Wharton University of Pennsylvania, February 26, 2016, https://knowledge.wharton.upenn.edu; "Google's People Operations: The Three-Thirds HR Team," *The Business Scholar,* June 19, 2014, https://the-businessscholar.blogspot.com; Dave Zielinksi, "Building a Better HR Team," *HR Magazine,* August 1, 2010, https://www.shrm.org.
75. J. Paauwe, *Human Resource Management and Performance: Unique Approaches for Achieving Long-Term Viability* (Oxford: Oxford University Press, 2004).

Glossary

360-degree performance appraisal Performance measurement that combines information from the employee's managers, peers, direct reports, self, and customers.

achievement tests Tests that measure a person's existing knowledge and skills.

action learning Training in which teams get an actual problem, work on solving it, commit to an action plan, and are accountable for carrying it out.

adventure learning A teamwork and leadership training program based on the use of challenging, structured physical activities.

applicant tracking system (ATS) A software application that streamlines the flow of information between job seekers, HR staff, and hiring managers.

appraisal politics Evaluators purposefully distorting a rating to achieve personal or company goals.

apprenticeship A work–study training method that teaches job skills through a combination of on-the-job training and classroom training.

aptitude tests Tests that assess how well a person can learn or acquire skills and abilities.

arbitration Conflict resolution procedure in which an arbitrator or arbitration board determines a binding settlement.

artificial intelligence (AI) Technology that can think like a human.

assessment centre A wide variety of specific selection programs that use multiple selection methods to rate applicants or job incumbents on their management potential.

assessment Collecting information and providing feedback to employees about their behaviour, communication style, or skills.

balanced scorecard An organizational approach to performance management that integrates strategic perspectives including financial, customer, internal business processes, and learning and growth.

behavioural interview A structured interview in which the interviewer asks the candidate to describe how they handled a type of situation in the past.

behavioural observation scale (BOS) A variation of BARS, which uses all behaviours necessary for effective performance to rate performance at a task.

behaviourally anchored rating scale (BARS) Method of performance measurement that rates behaviour in terms of a scale showing specific statements of behaviour that describe different levels of performance.

benchmarking A procedure in which an organization compares its own practices against those of successful competitors.

big data Information merged from HR databases, corporate financial statements, employee surveys, and other data sources to make evidence-based HR decisions.

Bill C-45 (Westray Bill) Amendment to the Criminal Code making organizations and anyone who directs the work of others criminally liable for safety offences.

blended learning Combining technology methods, such as e-learning, simulations, or social media, with face-to-face instruction, for delivery of learning content and instruction.

bona fide occupational requirement (BFOR) A necessary (not merely preferred) requirement for performing a job.

brand alignment The process of ensuring that HR policies, practices, and programs support or are congruent with an organization's overall culture (or brand), products, and services.

broadbanding A pay structure that consolidates pay grades into a few "broad bands."

calibration meetings Meeting at which managers discuss employee performance ratings and provide evidence supporting their ratings with the goal of eliminating the influence of rating errors.

Canada Pension Plan (CPP)/Quebec Pension Plan (QPP) A contributory, mandatory plan that provides retirement pensions, disability benefits, and survivor benefits.

Canadian Labour Congress (CLC) The umbrella organization for dozens of affiliated Canadian and international unions, as well as provincial federations of labour and regional labour councils.

candidate experience A job seeker's perception of and response to an employer's talent acquisition process.

career paths The identified pattern or progression of jobs or roles within an organization.

chatbot Automated, personalized conversation between software and human users.

checkoff provision A requirement that the employer, on behalf of the union, automatically deducts union dues from employees' paycheques.

closed shop A union security arrangement under which a person must be a union member before being hired.

cloud computing A computing system that provides information technology infrastructure over a network in a self-service, modifiable, and on-demand model

co-operative education A plan of higher education that incorporates paid work experience as an integral part of academic studies.

coach A peer or manager who works with an employee to provide a source of motivation, help him or her develop skills, and provide reinforcement and feedback.

cognitive ability tests Tests designed to measure mental abilities such as verbal skills, quantitative skills, and reasoning ability.

collective bargaining Negotiation between union representatives and management representatives to arrive at an agreement defining conditions of employment for the term of the agreement and to administer that agreement.

commissions Incentive pay calculated as a percentage of sales.

communities of practice Groups of employees who work together, learn from each other, and develop a common understanding of how to get work accomplished.

compensatory model Process of arriving at a selection decision in which a very high score on one type of assessment can make up for a low score on another.

competency An area of personal capability that enables employees to perform their work successfully.

competency-based pay systems Pay structures that set pay according to the employees' levels of skill or knowledge and what they are capable of doing.

conciliation Conflict resolution procedure in which a third party to collective bargaining reports the reasons for a dispute, the views and arguments of both sides, and possibly a recommended settlement, which the parties may decline.

concurrent validation Research that consists of administering a test to people who currently hold a job, then comparing their scores to existing measures of job performance.

construct validity Consistency between a high score on a test and a high level of a construct such as intelligence or leadership ability, as well as between mastery of this construct and successful performance on the job.

content validity Consistency between the test items or problems and the kinds of situations or problems that occur on the job.

continuous learning Each employee's and each group's ongoing efforts to gather information and apply the information to their decisions in a learning organization.

continuous learning Learning system that expects employees to acquire new skills, apply them on the job, and share what they have learned with other employees.

contributory plan All costs of the plan are funded by employees, employers, and the plan's own investments.

coordination training Team training that teaches the team how to share information and make decisions to obtain the best team performance.

core competency A set of knowledge and skills that provide a competitive advantage

criterion-related validity A measure of validity based on showing a substantial correlation between test scores and job performance scores.

critical-incident method Method of performance measurement based on managers' records of specific examples of the employee behaving in ways that are either effective or ineffective.

cross-cultural preparation Training to prepare employees and their family members for an assignment in a foreign country.

cross-training Team training in which team members understand and practise each other's skills so that they are prepared to step in and take another member's place.

culture shock Disillusionment and discomfort that occur during the process of adjusting to a new culture.

decision support systems Computer software systems designed to help solve problems by showing how results vary when the assumptions and data are altered.

defined benefit plan A pension plan that defines the benefits to be paid according to a formula stipulated in the plan.

defined contribution plan A retirement plan that specifies the contributions made by the employer as well as the employee; pension benefits are based upon the accumulated contributions and investment returns achieved.

development The acquisition of knowledge, skills, and behaviours that improve an employee's ability to meet the challenges of a variety of new or existing jobs.

differential treatment Differing treatment of individuals where the differences are based on a prohibited ground.

digital interview A technology-based interview in which interviewees digitally record their responses to interview questions that are provided digitally, without live interaction with the interviewer.

direct applicants People who apply for a vacancy without prompting from the organization.

direct compensation Financial rewards employees receive in exchange for their work.

direct discrimination Policies or practices that clearly make a distinction on the basis of a prohibited ground.

discrimination Treating someone differently, negatively, or adversely because of their race, age, religion, sex, or other prohibited ground.

diversity Having people of different backgrounds and experiences represented in the workplace.

diversity training Learning efforts designed to change employee attitudes about diversity or to develop skills needed to work with a diverse workforce.

downsizing The planned elimination of large numbers of employees with the goal of enhancing the organization's competitiveness.

downward move Assignment of an employee to a position with less responsibility and authority.

duty to accommodate An employer's duty to consider how an employee's characteristic such as disability, religion, or sex can be accommodated and to take action so the employee can perform the job.

e-learning Instruction and delivery of training by computer through the Internet or an organization's intranet.

electronic performance support system (EPSS) A technology platform that provides access to skills training, information, and expert advice.

employee assistance program (EAP) Confidential, short term, counselling service for employees with personal issues that affect their work performance.

employee benefits Compensation in forms other than cash.

employee development The combination of formal education, job experiences, relationships, and assessment of personality and abilities to help employees prepare for the future of their careers.

employee empowerment Giving employees responsibility and authority to make decisions regarding all aspects of product development or customer service.

employee engagement Degree to which employees are fully involved in their work and the strength of their commitment to their job and the organization

employee experience Set of perceptions that employees have about their experiences at work in response to their interactions with the organization.

employee health and wellness program A set of communications, activities, and facilities designed to change health-related behaviours in ways that reduce health risks.

employee stock ownership plan (ESOP) An arrangement in which the organization distributes shares of stock to all its employees by placing it in a trust.

employer branding A strategic approach of attaching a visual, emotional, or cultural brand to an organization.

Employment Insurance (EI) A federally mandated program to provide temporary financial assistance to non-working Canadians.

ergonomics The study of the interface between individuals' physiology and the characteristics of the physical work environment.

ethics The fundamental principles of right and wrong.

evidence-based HRM Collecting and using data to show that human resource practices have a positive influence on the company's bottom line or key stakeholders.

exit interview A meeting of a departing employee with the employee's supervisor and/or human resources specialist to discuss the employee's reasons for leaving.

expatriates Employees who take assignments in other countries.

experiential programs Training programs in which participants learn concepts and apply them by simulating behaviours involved and analyzing the activity, connecting it with real-life situations.

expert systems Computer systems incorporating the decision rules of people deemed to have expertise in a certain area.

external labour market Individuals who are actively seeking employment.

externship Employee development through a full-time temporary position at another organization.

feedback Information employers give employees about their skills and knowledge and where these assets fit into the organization's plans.

Fleishman Job Analysis System Job analysis technique that asks subject-matter experts to evaluate a job in terms of the abilities required to perform the job.

flexible benefits plans Benefits plans that offer employees a set of alternatives from which they can choose the types and amounts of benefits they want.

flextime A scheduling policy in which full-time employees may choose starting and ending times within guidelines specified by the organization.

forced-distribution method Method of performance measurement that assigns a certain percentage of employees to each category in a set of categories.

forecasting The attempts to determine the supply of and demand for various types of human resources to predict areas within the organization where there will be labour shortages or surpluses.

formal training Talent development programs, courses, and events that are developed and organized by the organization.

gainsharing Team incentive program that measures improvements in productivity and effectiveness and distributes a portion of each gain to employees.

gamification Applying principles of digital and computer games.

generalizable Valid in other contexts beyond the context in which the selection method was developed.

global organizations Organizations that choose to locate a facility based on the ability to effectively, efficiently, and flexibly produce a product or service, using cultural differences as an advantage.

graphic rating scale Method of performance measurement that lists attributes and provides a rating scale for each attribute; the employer uses the scale to indicate the extent to which an employee displays each attribute.

grievance procedure The process for resolving union–management conflicts over interpretation or violation of a collective agreement.

group- or team-building methods Training methods that help learners share ideas and experiences, build team identity, understand the dynamics of interpersonal relationships, and get to know their own strengths and weaknesses and those of their co-workers.

hands-on methods Training methods that require the learner to be actively involved.

harassment A form of discrimination that involves any unwanted physical or verbal behaviour that offends or humiliates you.

health and safety committees A committee jointly appointed by the employer and employees at large (or union) to address health and safety issues in a workplace.

health spending account A specific amount of money set aside per employee by the employer to cover health-related costs.

high-performance work system An organization in which technology, organizational structure, people, and processes all work together seamlessly to give an organization an advantage in the competitive environment.

high-potential employees Employees the organization believes can succeed in higher-level positions.

hiring algorithm Mathematical model that predicts which job candidates are most likely to be high performers after being hired.

home country The country in which an organization's headquarters is located.

host country A country (other than the home country) in which an organization operates a facility.

hourly wage Rate of pay per hour worked.

HR dashboard HR metrics such as productivity and absenteeism that are accessible by employers and managers through the company intranet or human resource information system

HRM audit A formal review of the outcomes of HRM functions, based on identifying key HRM functions and measures of organizational performance.

human capital An organization's employees, described in terms of their training, experience, judgment, intelligence, relationships, and insight.

human resource management (HRM) The practices, policies, and systems that influence employees' behaviours, attitudes, and performance.

incentive pay Forms of pay linked to an employee's performance as an individual, group member, or organization member.

inclusion An environment in which employees share a sense of belonging, mutual respect, and commitment from others so that they can perform their best work.

inclusion A sense of belonging: feeling respected, valued, and seen for who we are as individuals.

indirect compensation The benefits and services employees receive in exchange for their work.

indirect discrimination Policies or practices that appear to be neutral but have an adverse effect on the basis of a prohibited ground.

industrial engineering The study of jobs to find the simplest way to structure work in order to maximize efficiency.

informal learning Learning that is learner initiated, involves action and doing, is motivated by an intent to develop, and does not occur in a formal learning setting.

instructional design A process of systematically developing training to meet specified needs.

internal labour force An organization's workers (its employees and the people who work at the organization).

internal responsibility system Philosophy of occupational health and safety whereby employers and employees share responsibility for creating and maintaining safe and healthy work environments.

international organization An organization that sets up one or a few facilities in one or a few foreign countries.

internship On-the-job learning sponsored by an educational institution as a component of an academic program.

involuntary turnover Turnover initiated by an employer (often with employees who would prefer to stay).

job A set of related duties.

job analysis The process of getting detailed information about jobs.

job description A list of the tasks, duties, and responsibilities (TDRs) that a particular job entails.

job design The process of defining the way work will be performed and the tasks that a given job requires.

job enlargement Broadening the types of tasks performed in a job.

job enrichment Engaging workers by adding more decision-making authority to jobs.

job evaluation An administrative procedure for measuring the relative internal worth of the organization's jobs.

job experiences The combination of relationships, problems, demands, tasks, and other features of an employee's job.

job extension Enlarging jobs by combining several relatively simple jobs to form a job with a wider range of tasks.

job hazard analysis technique Safety promotion technique that involves breaking down a job into basic elements, then rating each element for its potential for harm or injury.

job posting The process of communicating information about a job vacancy on company bulletin boards, in employee publications, on corporate intranets, and anywhere else the organization communicates with employees.

job rotation Enlarging jobs by moving employees among several different jobs.

job sharing A work option in which two part-time employees carry out the tasks associated with a single position.

job specification A list of the knowledge, skills, abilities, and other characteristics (KSAOs) that an job holder must have to perform a particular job

job structure The relative pay for different jobs within the organization.

job withdrawal A set of behaviours with which employees try to avoid the work situation physically, mentally, or emotionally.

knowledge workers Employees whose main contribution to the company is specialized knowledge such as knowledge of customers, a process, or a profession.

labour relations A field that emphasizes skills managers and union leaders can use to minimize costly forms of conflict (such as strikes) and seek win–win solutions to disagreements.

Labour Relations Board (LRB) A specialized tribunal with authority to interpret and enforce the labour laws in its jurisdiction.

leaderless group discussion An assessment centre exercise in which a team of five to seven employees is assigned a problem and must work together to solve it within a certain time period.

leading indicators Objective measures that accurately predict future labour demand.

learning culture An organizational commitment to ongoing learning, and the processes of sharing, support, communication, and understanding that move the organization forward.

learning management system (LMS) A technology platform that can be used to automate the administration, development, and delivery of all of a company's training programs.

learning organization An organization that supports lifelong learning by enabling all employees to acquire and share knowledge.

lockout A closure of a place of employment or refusal of the employer to provide work as a way to compel employees to agree to certain demands or conditions.

long-term disability insurance Insurance that pays a percentage of a disabled employee's salary after an initial period and potentially for the rest of the employee's life.

management by objectives (MBO) A system in which people at each level of the organization set goals in a process that flows from top to bottom, so employees at all levels are contributing to the organization's overall goals; these goals become the standards for evaluating each employee's performance.

managing diversity and inclusion Creating an environment that allows all employees to contribute to organizational goals and experience personal growth.

mediation Conflict resolution procedure in which a mediator hears the views of both sides and facilitates the negotiation process but has no formal authority to impose a resolution.

mentor An experienced, productive senior employee who helps develop a less experienced employee (a protégé or mentee).

merit pay A system of linking pay increases to ratings on performance appraisals.

microlearning Small chunks of learning, less than 15 minutes in duration.

multinational company An organization that builds facilities in a number of different countries in an effort to minimize production and distribution costs.

multiple-hurdle model Process of arriving at a selection decision by eliminating some candidates at each stage of the selection process.

Myers-Briggs Type Indicator (MBTI) Psychological test that identifies individuals' preferences for source of energy, means of information gathering, way of decision making, and lifestyle, providing information for team building and leadership development.

National Occupational Classification (NOC) Tool created by the federal government to provide a standardized source of information about jobs in Canada's labour market.

needs assessment The process of evaluating the organization, individual employees, and employees' tasks to determine what kinds of training, if any, are necessary.

negligent hiring A situation where an employer may be found liable for harm an employee causes to others if references and background checks were not performed adequately at the time of hiring.

nepotism The practice of hiring relatives.

non-traditional employment Includes the use of independent contractors, freelancers, on-call workers, temporary workers, and contract company workers.

nondirective interview A selection interview in which the interviewer has great discretion in choosing questions to ask each candidate.

offshoring Moving operations from the country where a company is headquartered to a company where pay rates are lower but the necessary skills are available.

on-the-job training (OJT) Training methods in which a person with job experience and skill guides trainees in practising job skills at the workplace.

onboarding Process that focuses on transferring organizational, team, and role-specific knowledge to new employees.

organization analysis A process for determining the appropriateness of training by evaluating the characteristics of the organization.

organizational agility Ability of a firm to sense and respond to the environment by intentionally changing.

organizational behaviour modification (OBM) A plan for managing the behaviour of employees through a formal system of feedback and reinforcement.

orientation Training designed to prepare employees to perform their jobs effectively, learn about their organization, and establish work relationships.

outplacement counselling A service in which professionals try to help dismissed employees manage the transition from one job to another.

outsourcing The practice of having another company (a vendor, third-party provider, or consultant) provide services.

paired-comparison method Method of performance measurement that compares each employee with each other employee to establish rankings.

panel interview Selection interview in which several members of the organization meet to interview each candidate.

passive job seekers Individuals who are not actively seeking a job.

pay equity The concept of "equal pay for work of equal value."

pay grades Sets of jobs having similar worth or content, grouped together to establish rates of pay.

pay level The average amount (including wages, salaries, and incentives) the organization pays for a particular job.

pay policy line A graphed line showing the mathematical relationship between job evaluation points and pay rate.

pay range A set of possible pay rates defined by a minimum, maximum, and midpoint of pay for employees holding a particular job or a job within a particular pay grade or band.

pay structure The pay policy resulting from job structure and pay-level decisions.

people (human capital) analytics The use of quantitative tools and scientific methods to analyze data from human resource databases and other sources to make evidence-based decisions that support business goals.

performance improvement plan Summary of performance gaps and includes an action plan mutually agreed to by the employee and supervisor with specific dates to review progress.

performance management The process of ensuring that employees' activities and outputs match the organization's goals.

person analysis A process for determining individuals' needs and readiness for learning.

Personal Information Protection and Electronic Documents Act (PIPEDA) Sets the ground rules for how private-sector organizations collect, use, and disclose personal information in the course of for-profit commercial activities in Canada. It also applies to the personal information of employees of federally-regulated businesses

phased retirement A gradual transition into full retirement by reducing hours or job responsibility.

piecework rate Rate of pay for each unit produced.

position The set of duties (job) performed by a particular person.

Position Analysis Questionnaire (PAQ) A standardized job analysis questionnaire containing 194 questions about work behaviours, work conditions, and job characteristics that apply to a wide variety of jobs.

predictive validation Research that uses the test scores of all applicants and looks for a relationship between the scores and future performance of the applicants who were hired.

presentation methods Methods in which learners are passive recipients of information.

productivity The relationship between an organization's outputs (products, information, or services) and its inputs (e.g., people, facilities, equipment, data, and materials).

profit sharing Incentive pay in which payments are a percentage of the organization's profits and do not become part of the employees' base salary.

progressive discipline A formal discipline process in which the consequences become more serious if the employee repeats the offence.

promotion Assignment of an employee to a position with greater challenges, more responsibility, and more authority than in the previous job, usually accompanied by a pay increase.

protean career A career that frequently changes based on changes in the person's interests, abilities, and values and in the work environment.

Rand Formula A union security provision that makes payment of labour union dues mandatory even if the worker is not a member of the union.

readiness for learning A combination of employee characteristics and positive work environment that permit learning.

realistic job previews Background information about a job's positive and negative qualities.

recruiting Any activity carried on by the organization with the primary purpose of identifying and attracting potential employees.

recruitment The process through which the organization seeks applicants for potential employment.

referrals People who apply for a vacancy because someone in the organization prompted them to do so.

reliability The extent to which a measurement generates consistent results, i.e., is free from random error.

repatriation The process of preparing expatriates to return home from a foreign assignment.

sabbatical A leave of absence from an organization to renew or develop skills.

safety data sheets (SDSs) Detailed hazard information concerning a controlled (hazardous) product.

salary Rate of pay for each week, month, or year worked.

selection The process by which the organization attempts to identify applicants with the necessary knowledge, skills, abilities, and other characteristics that will help the organization achieve its goals.

self-assessment The use of information by employees to determine their career interests, values, aptitudes, behavioural tendencies, and development needs.

self-service Providing employees with online access to, or apps that provide, information about HR issues such as training, benefits, compensation, and contracts; enrolling online in programs and services; and completing online surveys.

short-term disability insurance Insurance that pays a percentage of a disabled employee's salary as benefits to the employee for six months or less.

simple ranking Method of performance measurement that requires managers to rank employees in their group from the highest to the lowest performer.

simulation A training method that represents a real-life situation, with learners' decisions resulting in outcomes that mirror what would happen if they were on the job.

situational interview A structured interview in which the interviewer describes a situation likely to arise on the job, then asks the candidate what they would do in that situation.

social performance management Social media and microblogs similar to Facebook, LinkedIn, and Yammer that allow employees to quickly exchange information, talk to each other, provide coaching, and receive feedback and recognition.

social unionism A type of unionism that attempts to influence social and economic policies of government.

stakeholders The parties with an interest in the company's success (typically, shareholders, the community, customers, and employees).

standard hour plan An incentive plan that pays workers extra for work done in less than a preset "standard time."

stay interview A meeting with an employee to explore their thoughts and feelings about the job and to uncover issues in the effort to prevent that employee from becoming disgruntled.

stock options Rights to buy a certain number of shares of stock at a specified price.

strike A collective decision by union members not to work or to slow down until certain demands or conditions are met.

structured interview A selection interview that consists of a predetermined set of questions for the interviewer to ask.

succession planning The process of identifying and tracking high-potential employees who will be able to fill top management positions or other key positions when they become vacant.

sustainability An organization's ability to profit without depleting its resources, including employees, natural resources, and the support of the surrounding community.

talent management A systematic, planned effort to train, develop, and engage the performance of highly skilled employees and managers.

task analysis The process of identifying the tasks, knowledge, skills, and behaviours that training should emphasize.

team leader training Training in the skills necessary for effectively leading the organization's teams.

teamwork The assignment of work to groups of employees with various skills who interact to assemble a product or provide a service.

technic of operations review (TOR) Method of promoting safety by determining which specific element of a job led to a past accident.

third country A country that is neither the home country nor the host country of an employer.

total compensation All types of financial rewards and tangible benefits and services employees receive as part of their employment.

total rewards A comprehensive approach to compensating and rewarding employees.

training Planned effort by an organization to facilitate employees' learning of job-related knowledge, skills, and behaviours.

training A planned effort to enable employees to learn job-related knowledge, skills, and behaviours.

transaction processing Computations and calculations used to review and document HRM decisions and practices.

transfer Assignment of an employee to a position in a different area of the company, usually in a lateral move.

Transfer of learning On-the-job use of knowledge, skills, and behaviours learned in training.

transitional matrix A chart that lists job categories held in one period and shows the proportion of employees in each of those job categories in a future period.

transnational HRM system Type of HRM system that makes decisions from a global perspective, includes managers from many countries, and is based on ideas contributed by people representing a variety of cultures.

trend analysis Constructing and applying statistical models that predict labour demand for the next year, given relatively objective statistics from the previous year.

unconscious bias A judgment outside our consciousness that affects decisions based on background, culture, and personal experience.

unfair labour practices Prohibited conduct of an employer, union, or individual under the relevant labour legislation.

union local The basic unit of union organization consisting of the unionized workers from a particular department, location, industry, or sector that are covered by a specific collective agreement.

union shop A union security arrangement that requires employees to join the union within a certain amount of time after beginning employment.

union steward An employee elected by union members to represent them in ensuring that the terms of the collective agreement are enforced.

unions Organizations formed for the purpose of representing their members' interests in dealing with employers.

utility The extent to which the selection method provides economic value greater than its cost.

validity The extent to which performance on a measure (such as a test score) is related to what the measure is designed to assess (such as job performance).

virtual expatriates Employees who manage an operation abroad without permanently locating in the country.

virtual reality A computer-based technology that provides an interactive three-dimensional (3D) learning experience.

virtual teams Teams that are separated by time, geographic distance, culture, and/or organizational boundaries and that rely almost exclusively on technology to interact and complete their projects.

voluntary turnover Turnover initiated by employees (often when the organization would prefer to keep them).

work flow design The process of analyzing the tasks necessary for the production of a product or service.

Workers' Compensation Acts Provincial programs that provide benefits to workers who suffer work-related injuries or illnesses.

workforce planning Identifying the numbers and types of employees the organization will require to meet its objectives.

workforce utilization review A comparison of the proportion of employees in protected groups with the proportion that each group represents in the relevant labour market.

yield ratios A ratio that expresses the percentage of applicants who successfully move from one stage of the recruitment and selection process to the next.

Index

Note: Page numbers followed by *f, b,* or *t* represent figures, boxed features, or tables, respectively.

T

Y